# ENGLISH GENEALOGY

# ENGLISH GENEALOGY

Sir Anthony Wagner

Phillimore

First published in 1960 by
OXFORD UNIVERSITY PRESS
Second edition 1972

This third edition published in 1983 by
PHILLIMORE & CO. LTD.
Shopwyke Hall, Chichester, Sussex

ISBN 0 85033 473 X

Printed in Great Britain by
Dotesios Printers Ltd, Trowbridge, Wiltshire

# PREFACE TO THE THIRD EDITION

I began the first edition of this book in 1960 with a half apology for my belief that an interest in family origins was widespread and tending to increase among the people of English descent throughout the world, especially perhaps outside the mother country. In the second edition in 1972 I wrote with more confidence that history on the highest plane was now more and more being seen and written in terms of individual human lives and their connections – and not least their genealogical connections. Three years later again I was able to devote a whole volume of essays* to new ways in which genealogy might, I hoped, throw light on history. And now in 1983 the general growth of interest in the subject is so evident that one no longer feels the need to draw special attention to it.

The reason for this development still seems to me essentially what I thought it was in 1960: a widespread and primitive natural impulse in whose way history has at times laid obstacles, some of which, however, it has of late years been removing. One in particular is obvious. When I first took an interest in the subject general registration of births, deaths and marriages had existed in England for less than a century and in other places for a lesser period. Since then, however, nature has added two more generations to most pedigrees, so that today's children have a much better chance than those of my day of tracing tolerably far back on one line or another.

The Addenda and corrections deal with a diversity of points to which friends and readers have drawn my attention, as well as some noticed by myself. They also refer to works recently published on different aspects of my subject matter. Of these works three deserve special mention for the importance of their contributions to the subject. *The Nobility of Later Medieval England, The Ford Lectures for 1953 and Related Studies* by the late K. B. McFarlane, appeared in 1973 and throws new light on a whole range of aspects of the subject matter of my fourth and fifth chapters. I was able to summarise these in *Pedigree and Progress* (1975, pp. 119–122) and give references here.

Between 1973 and 1981 four volumes have appeared of the *English Surnames Series*, the product of the continuing work of the Marc Fitch Fund English Surnames project at Leicester University. The first of these, *Yorkshire West Riding*, 1973, is by Dr George Redmonds and the other three, II, *Norfolk and Suffolk Surnames in the Middle Ages,* 1975, III, *The Surnames of Oxfordshire,* 1977, and IV, *The Surnames of Lancashire,* 1981, are the work of Mr Richard McKinley.

Quite a different field, but no less indicative of the growing range of genealogical scholarship, is covered by the two volumes of *Genealogical Research Methods and Sources,* published by the American Society of Genealogists, the first volume (1960) edited by Milton Rubincam assisted by Jean Stephenson and the second (1971) by Kenn Stryker-Rodda.

Recent years have also seen the appearance of certain family histories of more distinguished historical and literary character than those of former days, such as Dr A. L. Rowse on *The Early Churchills,* 1956, *The Later Churchills,* 1958, *Ralegh and the Throckmortons,* 1962, and *The Byrons and Trevanions,* 1978. What we sadly lack in these days, however, which the nineteenth and early twentieth century so amply possessed, are facilities for the extensive, annotated publication of pedigrees in periodicals, local histories or monographs. Only the Americans are largely exempt from this trouble.

* *Pedigree and Progress,* Phillimore, 1975.

# ACKNOWLEDGEMENTS

ACKNOWLEDGEMENTS are due to the authors, or their representatives, and the publishers of the following works for permission to make quotations from them.

N. G. Brett-James, *The Growth of Stuart London*, published by Messrs. George Allen & Unwin, Ltd.

Professor A. Goodwin, *The European Nobility in the 18th Century*, published by Messrs. A. & C. Black, Ltd.

The late Professor C. S. Lewis, *Mere Christianity*, published by Messrs. Geoffrey Bles, Ltd.

H. M. & Mrs. N. K. Chadwick, *The Growth of Literature*, vol. 3, and *Early Scotland*, published by The University Press, Cambridge.

Mr. G. A. Holmes, *The Estates of the Higher Nobility in 14th Century England* published by The University Press, Cambridge.

Sir John Plumb, *Studies in Social History*, published by The University Press, Cambridge.

Dr. W. G. Hoskins, *Devonshire Studies*, published by Messrs. Jonathan Cape, Ltd.

Dr. A. L. Rowse, *A Cornish Childhood*, published by Messrs. Jonathan Cape, Ltd.

Professor D. C. Douglas, *English Scholars*, published by Messrs. Jonathan Cape, Ltd.

Sir Frank Stenton, *History of National Biography 1922/1930—Biography of J. H. Round*, published by The Clarendon Press.

Archbishop David Mathew, *The Social Structure in Caroline England*, published by The Clarendon Press.

Mr. G. D. Squibb, Q.C., *The High Court of Chivalry*, published by The Clarendon Press.

The late Dr. J. H. Round, *Family Origins, Peerage and Family History*, and *Peerage and Pedigree*, published by Messrs. Constable & Co., Ltd.

Sir John Plumb, *Sir Robert Walpole, The Making of a Statesman*, published by The Cresset Press.

The late Professor T. F. O'Rahilly, *Early Irish History and Mythology*, published by The Dublin Institute for Advanced Studies.

Mr. E. D. Bebb, *Non-Conformity and Economic Life*, published by The Epworth Press.

The late Mr. R. W. Ketton-Cremer, *Norfolk Assembly*, published by Messrs. Faber & Faber, Ltd.

Mr. G. C. Homans, *English Villagers of the 13th Century*, published by The Harvard University Press.

Mr. Richard Church, *Over the Bridge*, published by Messrs. William Heinemann, Ltd.

Dr. W. G. Hoskins, *English Provincial Towns of the 16th Century*, published by the Royal Historical Society.

Mr. J. T. Adams, *The Founding of New England*, published by Messrs. Little, Brown & Co.

Dr. W. G. Hoskins, *Essays in Leicestershire History*, published by The Liverpool University Press.

The late Dr. G. M. Trevelyan, *English Social History*, published by Messrs. Longmans Green & Co., Ltd.

The late Professor A. F. Pollard, *The Evolution of Parliament in England*, published by Messrs. Longmans, Green & Co., Ltd.

The late Mr. A. L. Reade, *Johnson's Early Life*, published by Messrs. Percy Lund, Humphries & Co., Ltd.

Dr. A. L. Rowse, *The England of Elizabeth* and *The Expansion of Elizabethan England*, published by Messrs. Macmillan & Co., Ltd.

The late Sir Lewis Namier, *England in the Age of the American Revolution*, published by Messrs. Macmillan & Co., Ltd.

Dr. W. G. Hoskins, *The Midland Peasant*, published by Messrs. Macmillan & Co., Ltd.

The late Mr. A. Wadsworth and Miss J. de L. Mann, *The Cotton Trade and Industrial Lancashire*, published by The Manchester University Press.

Sir Thomas Kendrick, *A History of the Vikings*, published by Messrs. Methuen & Co., Ltd.

Mr. H. M. Colvin, *Biographical Dictionary of English Architects*, published by John Murray, Ltd.

C. Johnson, *Dialogus de Scaccario*, published by Messrs. Thomas Nelson & Sons, Ltd.

Sir Frank Stenton, *Anglo-Saxon England*, published by The Oxford University Press.

The late Mr. K. B. MacFarlane and Dr. Conway Davies, *Studies presented to Sir Hilary Jenkinson*, published by The Oxford University Press.

Miss Mildred Campbell, *The English Yeoman*, published by The Yale University Press.

A. P. Newton, *The Colonising Activities of the English Puritans*, published by The Yale University Press.

C. M. Andrews, *The Colonial Period of American History*, published by The Yale University Press.

# CONTENTS

# LIST OF TABLES

*To Gillian*

# I

## THE PURPOSE OF THIS BOOK

IT is my belief that an interest in family origins is widespread and tending to increase among the peoples of English descent throughout the world, especially perhaps outside the mother country. Some will think this claim a paradox, others a truism, according to their experience. It cannot, probably, be either proved or disproved. But I think that my opinion will in the main be shared by those who are in one way or another targets of enquiry in these matters; the professional genealogists and record searchers; the staff of genealogical institutions and societies; the custodians of records connected with the subject; and the editors of genealogical publications. Most of these, I fancy, would agree that the volume of enquiry and the variety and geographical dispersion of those from whom it comes grow year by year.

To the genealogist this is not surprising. Curiosity about one's ancestors, a wish to know who and what and where they were, seems to him an obvious and elementary form of curiosity, which no one with a reasonably active all round interest in himself and the world about him is likely to lack, unless his circumstances or upbringing have smothered it. He would support this view by reference to history. In less sophisticated times and places it has often been thought a normal part of every child's education to teach him to recite his ancestors for several generations, while the genealogies of rulers, passed down by word of mouth, with or without biographical detail, are the backbone of the oldest historical traditions.

In a tribal organization society is held together by duties, rights and prohibitions attaching to blood relationship within the family, the kindred and the tribe or nation. In the periods of such organization, therefore, the general consciousness of kinship and descent is strong. The details of descent and relationship are in the forefront of consciousness and are passed down for generations. This way of life belongs to men whose wealth is in flocks and herds or to the wanderers by land or sea who live by preying on more settled peoples. When the tribes turn to agriculture and the life of cities, legal and economic ties tend slowly to replace the bond of kinship as the main cement of society.

The feudal age of Europe stands midway between the tribal and the modern world in this.[1] The ties between lord and tenant, on which feudal society turned, were ties of law and service, not of blood. Yet the rights and duties were hereditary on both sides, so that knight and villein alike were ever conscious of their legal heritage from their ancestors and of their pedigrees so far as they might establish this. Feudal as compared with tribal society had thus a more restricted but an equally practical day to day interest in genealogy. The great political and social changes which ushered in the modern world set in motion forces which in one way or another cut off great numbers of people from their historical roots. Migration to towns from the country, or from the homeland overseas, and drastic changes of religion, occupation, or social status tended to cut families off from the recollection of their past. These things, moreover, were occurring in a world in which the ties of kindred—especially its remoter ties—were losing practical importance and political and economic ties were taking their place.

The ruling classes in the sixteenth and seventeenth centuries took a keen interest in their pedigrees. Modern scientific genealogy, indeed, originated in this period. It was a sophisticated interest, linked with family pride and a love of history, and catered for by professional genealogists. Sometimes the snobbery of the newly risen made them easy or even willing victims of genealogical fraud. During this period it came to be widely thought that pedigrees were proper only to distinguished families, to the owners of lands and titles and their progeny. This limitation in England was not a narrow one. The heralds, antiquaries and county historians were happy to include the pedigrees of minor landowners, wealthy merchants and professional men in their collections. But the assumption that a pedigree should be linked with an actual or potential stake in the country was made almost without a thought.

When democracy and the common man came into fashion, it was therefore, not unnaturally, thought by some that, as these succeeded, the interest in genealogy would fail. In fact, the opposite seems to be happening. The causes are complex but among them seem to be the following. First and most important, interest in our own and others'

[1] For the impact of feudalism on the family community and the ties of blood see Marc Bloch, *Feudal Society*, 1961, chaps. ix and x, pp. 123-5, 137-41.

kinships and origins is a fundamental and natural human interest, always ready to assert itself, where it gets a chance. There are psychological influences in the modern world which tend to suppress it and these we shall consider later. But when these are absent or can be overcome it is surprising what unlikely people find themselves becoming absorbed in one or another aspect of these matters.

Another influence is simple reaction against the confusion and rootlessness of modern life. The more the ancient landmarks are destroyed, the more many of us hunger for a firm anchorage in time and place. Through genealogy the transient flat-dweller of the cities can join himself to the peasant rooted in ancestral soil or the baron ruling from his castle. He can see himself as a leaf on a great tree growing out of the past into the future. He can by conscious effort recover the support of that sense of membership in a kindred which was once the common birthright.

History is too commonly regarded as abstract and detached rather than as continuous with ourselves, a dimension without which we cannot see our own lives in the round. To remedy this defect of our imagination some historians now turn archaeologist and make the past more real by showing us its visible relics, the buildings and the tombs, the writings and the paintings, the tools and the dresses of our ancestors. While many respond to this wholeheartedly, some reject such aids to imagination because consciously or otherwise they feel that these ghosts of the past do not belong to them. The heirs of the Industrial Revolution can feel themselves cut off from an older England almost like men of another race. Yet, when these same people perceive their derivation step by step, through their own lineage, from men of so different a world, yet of their own blood, they may see both themselves and the past in a new conjunction and perspective. This explains, at least in part, the trouble and effort with which the dispossessed of the countryside, later enriched by industry, will pursue their links with their lost past. For the imagination of surprisingly many modern Englishmen pre-industrial England has the quality of a lost home.

The most complete separation from their roots is that of settlers overseas. For a generation, or even two or three, a vivid family tradition of those roots may last, but thereafter, if not sooner, unless revived by fresh contact with the former home, it grows dim and fades, so that the descendants completely lose the sense of what they sprang from. Yet the thought that, though one's ancestor ten generations back crossed the Atlantic to settle in an American wilderness, the church and village he left might yet perhaps be located and found little altered since he left them, is surely one to stir the feeblest imagination. If the migration was more recent—to Australia, for instance, two or three generations back—the breach of tradition may seem as complete, but the clues should be better, for memories of material facts may still survive. Even in a fluid society like ours a man will often remember his grandfather's tales of his own grandfather. Memories like these are to be treasured like gold. A single name and a rough date thus given may save laborious and costly research to recover the lost clue. The historians of the new countries are now appealing for memories of their settlers to be recorded and records of them safely filed before the stream of time carries them out of sight. It is certain that in the same way an enquiry made now on the lines of the English Herald's Visitations of the sixteenth and seventeenth centuries would elicit from private papers and the memories of the aged clues to the English origins of nineteenth century settlers, which a generation hence will be sought in vain. A consciousness of this, added to the other motives, may have something to do with the wave of genealogical enquiries which have come to England of late years from the new countries.

In the past century Darwin, Mendel and Galton have started a new hare for the genealogists to hunt. As an exact science genetics rests upon experiment and observation among other species than man. Yet, as Galton and others have shown, the study of human pedigrees cannot but suggest broad inferences as to the inheritance of our own physical and mental qualities. The genealogical patterns of outstanding ability and outstanding disability alike demonstrate this. The want of scientific record of our ancestors' qualities makes it difficult, if not impossible, to do more than guess at these hereditary patterns save in some few exceptional cases, but the fascination of such guesswork is great.

Whatever their initial impulse to enquiry, those once bitten are apt to find that the fever of the chase leads them on. Their appetite for pedigree grows with eating. The detective instinct is stimulated, the collector's passion for completeness roused. To give the satisfaction they are capable of giving, however, these pursuits must be properly related to the possibilities. One must have a general idea what it is sensible to look for and reasonable to hope for. Without this one may be cast down by failure to find the unfindable or may miss the pleasure of a truly exceptional discovery.

The readers I have had in mind first of all are those bitten with a genealogical curiosity which they do not know how to satisfy; who like to know the way round a subject which interests them, but whose notions of the general background and possibilities are here so vague that they wish to orient themselves generally before they seek advice or information on specific questions.

There are very many pedigrees and guides to pedigrees in print and many more in manuscript. There are books which offer guidance —more or less elementary—to those who would try their hand at genealogical research. What does not exist, however, is any book at all which attempts a survey of English genealogy as a whole or which tries to give a general picture of what is known and might be known of the ancestry of people of English stock. The present work attempts such a survey or picture and I hope that its shortcomings may receive the indulgence accorded by custom to pioneering attempts. It would be too much to hope that errors of detail or worse have been wholly avoided in a work of this scope.

About two thirds of the book deal with the social and historical background and the subject matter of English genealogy. The rest is concerned with the study, literature and technique of the subject and the nature of the record evidence on which they rest. In my view these two approaches are complementary and necessary to each other. The nature and limitations of our knowledge of pedigrees cannot be grasped without some knowledge of the records and the work done in the past. Conversely social history helps to explain these. In the same way it is ever more widely recognized that a study of general history (of which genealogy is a part) must go hand in hand with a study of historiography, historical method and the record sources.

I know from experience that the want of such preliminary information as I have tried to give here and uncertainty how to get it are among the barriers which come between people and their potential interest in this subject. There are others which should be considered frankly here on its threshold. One is the feeling of many people that while the pedigree of a noble or ancient line may be an interest and satisfaction to its possessor, those of humble and obscure families can probably not be traced at all or if traced will be uninteresting or even mortifying.

It is, of course, true that noble pedigrees are more easily traced. Indeed, it is almost the definition of a noble family that its pedigree is known already. Furthermore such a descent has the great attraction of carrying with it a wealth of portraiture and biographical detail not often to be looked for in humbler lines. But, this having been said, it is equally true that very many humble pedigrees can be traced (though not so easily) through many generations and can fairly often be illustrated with biographical detail. The great fact to be grasped here is that Englishmen and those of English descent are fortunate in the immense bulk of the records kept and still preserved in England as compared with most other lands. This is a consequence of long continued settled government in island security under a constitution much addicted to the forms of law duly carried out and duly recorded.

Many people well established in the world are reluctant to begin enquiries which may show their origins to be even humbler than they think. Many others have no such feeling, but in the true spirit of the genealogist wish to know the facts whatever they may be. It is hardly for the genealogist to try to convert others to his way of thinking, but it may be worth pointing out that social movement, both up and down, from one class to another is much greater and more widespread than is often thought. The younger branches of gentle families are often found among the tradesmen and yeomen and it is likely, though less easily proved, that the further step down into the ranks of the labourers has frequently been taken. The exploration of these pheno-mena has been too limited for generalization, but most genealogists can point to instances.

Conversely, the ranks of the nobility and gentry have in every age been recruited from below and the rise to them has sometimes been rapid. Since the total number of the ancestors of each of us doubles in each generation we go back (save as modified by the marriage of cousins), most ancestries, if they could be carried back on all lines for eight or ten generations, would probably traverse a surprisingly wide social range. The exceptions to this would be the endogamous groups; the royal families; that minority of the high nobility and ancient gentry who have always been careful whom they married; the dwellers in the lonely valleys and the far off settlements; and the members of the straiter sects; and even these closed communities are far from being genetically watertight.

Besides those whose genealogical interest is mainly in their own ancestry I have had another class of possible readers in mind, namely those students of English history who feel the need for a clearer picture than their training has given them of the genealogical back-ground. This need may now be growing. In the recent past a kind of historical writing was favoured which aimed less at establishing what happened than at explaining why it happened; which dealt in tendencies, causes and effects, statistics and ideas, rather than particular events and persons. This kind of history has naturally less use for genealogy than the plain narratives known to our ancestors. Pedigrees might, indeed, themselves afford material for statistical analysis, if they were fully known, but much hard work would be required of the genealogists first. There is now, however, a truly modern school of historians, especially linked in England with Sir Lewis Namier, which builds up the picture of a former age round the descriptions of individuals and of their political and social relationships. To this school of historians genealogy is an essential tool and it may be that its rise will in due course lead to a higher estimation of scientific genealogy and so to a wider knowledge and better practice of its special skill and learning. It is true that these historians are generally more interested in what Dr. Peter Spufford[1] has conveniently termed 'broad genealogies' —the kinships and connections of contemporaneous persons—than in long descents. This is largely, no doubt, inevitable, but I think it also may reflect that specialization by period which now dominates so much historical study and tends sometimes to obscure the interest of the longer continuities.

Is it presumption in a genealogist to believe that his special approach to history is a necessary and fundamental one?

Human beings [wrote C. S. Lewis] look separate because you see them walking about separately. But then we are so made that we can see only the present moment. If we could see the past, then of course it would look different. For there was a time when every man was part of his mother, and (earlier still) part of his father as well: and when they were part of his grandparents. If you could see humanity spread out in time, as God sees it, it would not look like a lot of separate things dotted about. It would look like one single growing thing—rather like a very complicated tree. Every individual would appear connected with every other.[2]

It is this vision of history that the genealogist feebly seeks to realize.

I ought, I think, to indicate the nature and limits of my own experience of these matters. Genealogy was my passion from childhood and my interest was encouraged by that of my cousin Henry Wagner,

---

[1] Peter Spufford, 'Genealogy and the Historian', *The Genealogist's Magazine*, vol. 15, Nov. 1967, pp. 431–47, p. 447.
[2] C. S. Lewis, *Mere Christianity*, ed. 1952, Collins, p. 152.

F.S.A. (1840–1926), a well known student of Huguenot genealogy. For the last twenty eight years it has been my duty as a herald to trace, prove and study pedigrees for clients and enquirers of all sorts. There must, however, be a division of labour in large scale genealogical practice and in mine the greater part of the field work has been done by others, while it has been my part to coordinate and analyse material collected by them from records everywhere, but myself to carry out primary research only in a certain range of records, mainly central.

For what I have written of material known to me only at second-hand I have therefore drawn freely on the information and advice of others. I was first introduced to the world of records in my Oxford days by Mr. (now Professor) V. H. Galbraith, to whose guidance in historical fields I am greatly indebted. My conception of genealogy as an art owes more than I can say to two masters of that art who have been my friends and fellow workers; the late Alfred Butler, Windsor Herald (see p. 402), and my assistant during many years Mr. Thomas Woodard. For guidance in the special fields of Welsh and Scottish genealogy I am indebted to Major Francis Jones and Sir Iain Moncreiffe, Bt., while the former has placed me further in his debt by reading and criticizing the manuscript of this book. In American matters I have been helped and guided by the Rev. Dr. Arthur Adams and Mr. G. Andrews Moriarty. To Mr. Marc Fitch I owe most of the material on which the section dealing with his family is based. Other obligations are acknowledged in the text and on pages vii-viii. Not my least debt is to my wife but for whom this book would scarcely have been carried through and without whose constructive criticism it would be even more imperfect than it is.

# II

## THE ROOTS

To say that the barriers between classes have historically been less rigid in England than in most other countries does not mean that class distinctions were slight or unimportant—quite the contrary. With luck and effort a villein might become a freeman or a yeoman or a gentleman. There were periods of rapid change when a minority of fortunate or clever men might rise to great estate from lowly beginnings. But what made this possible was not an absence of class distinctions but a lofty structure with many shallow steps by which the skilful and persistent might climb, while some others slipped down and many more kept the framework solid by standing still. Even those who stood still might find that the ground had moved under them. A colleague now dead once told me that many years ago a small farmer of no pretensions came to enquire at the College of Arms for his pedigree, when it came to light that in the 1660's his ancestor, who had lived on and from the same land and probably in much the same style, had been entered in the Herald's Visitation book as a gentleman of coat armour.

When we come later to discuss the records we shall see that some of especial value to the genealogist start under the Tudors. It is largely for this reason that families not then of knightly rank can seldom be traced beyond the sixteenth century. There are some exceptions. Where we are lucky enough to have a full and well kept series of manorial records we can occasionally trace a line of villeins back to the fourteenth or even the thirteenth century. But this is rare and the few records of lawsuits, which trace villein lines even further back, are much rarer still.[1] Our knowledge of mediaeval pedigrees is therefore mainly confined to those of the knightly class.

This knightly class, whose members held their lands directly or indirectly of the king by feudal tenures, can in favourable cases be traced back as far as the records of the tenures go. We shall see that this means in many cases to the thirteenth century and in a fair number

[1] See p. 138.

to the twelfth. The royal or public records, which are our sole source of information in most cases, begin as a continuous series in the middle of the twelfth century (1155), so that to trace an ordinary knightly family further we depend on such rare chances as the preservation of private charters or monastic copies, which occasionally take us back to the generation of Domesday Book (1086) or the Norman Conquest (1066). The pedigrees of the greatest Norman families, the immediate counsellors of the Norman dukes and kings, the founders and earliest benefactors of religious houses in Normandy and England, can usually be traced to the Conquest or a little further. Most of the knights who served our Norman kings were their own subjects born or adventurers who left their homes to make their fortunes. But a few were scions of houses already powerful on the Continent, whose pedigrees can therefore be traced a little further back still, to the tenth or the ninth century.

When the genealogist can go no further, he is bound to ask himself the reason why. Is the obstacle accidental—a leaf which happens to be torn from the book of history—or is it something more intrinsic? Where we can answer this—and we often can—we are at least able to picture in general terms what lies beyond our precise knowledge. Behind the English knightly class there were both English and Norman blood, for the conquerors even from the first intermarried to some extent with the conquered and as time went on their blood became ever more commingled. Behind the Norman invaders themselves lay both the blood of the Vikings who came to Normandy with Rollo about 911 and the mingled Frankish and Gallo-Roman strains they found there. When the Normans pressed on from England as conquerors into Wales and Ireland and by invitation into Scotland, their blood was mingled again with that of earlier dwellers in these lands.

This horizon then our lighthouse beam may circle, France, the rovers of the north, the Celtic west and our Anglo-Saxon roots. Without too much oversimplifying their differences may be seen in terms of their distance from the wandering tribal life.

## I. THE ANGLO-SAXONS AND THE VIKINGS

The German tribes who broke the barriers of the Roman Empire in the fourth and following centuries were whole nations on the move, some of them driven from behind by others, as the Franks were driven by the Saxons and the Ostrogoths by the Huns. In the second century A.D. the Burgundians lived in eastern Germany, but by the fifth

century they had moved or been driven westward to the borders of
France leaving no trace behind save in the name of the Danish island
of Bornholm (Burgundarholm). The Angles, Jutes and Saxons who
invaded Britain in the fifth and sixth centuries were less complete in
their migrations, as a vestigial Angel in Schleswig, a Jutland in Denmark and a Saxony still the home of Saxons, witness. The Northmen
or Vikings of the eighth and following centuries were no longer
wandering nations but smaller groups of adventurers, leaving the
fiords and forests of Scandinavia to raid or conquer the settled lands,
or to colonize the wilderness. Yet the society they came from was still
tribal; still lived in a heroic age such as Homer tells of, where power
and honour belonged to the doughty fighter and the chieftain sprung
from the gods. Some of the sagas, in which the Vikings still live,
record their genealogies, which must have passed from generation to
generation by word of mouth long before they were committed to
writing.

Among the small and numerous tribes of this heroic age royal
families were plentiful and it seems from the sagas that the leaders of
the earlier raids and expeditions generally belonged to them. Often
these were princes who had to flee their homes because of blood feuds,
murders of kindred, or the like. Among those who established kingdoms in Britain were members of at least eight distinct families, which
claimed royal or divine ancestry. Sir Frank Stenton suggests that the
claim of these families to rule rested on their supposed divine descent.[1]
Where these succeeded in their conquests one may guess that there
were many more who failed. It is not till the latter part of the ninth
century, says Chadwick, that we find men of humbler origin leading
powerful expeditions and forming settlements on their own account.[2]
By the end of the eighth century, however, Alcuin (d. 804)[3] could write
that scarce one of the ancient royal kindreds still survived and he
attributed the chaos into which the kingly power had fallen to this fact
and to the uncertainty of the lineage of those who claimed it. Earlier
in the century (c. 720) Daniel, Bishop of Winchester had instructed
Boniface that in his mission to the Frisians he must undermine their
belief in their gods, even though in so doing he undermined their

[1] F. M. Stenton, *Anglo-Saxon England*, 1943, p. 47.
[2] H. M. Chadwick, *The Origin of the English Nation*, Cambridge, 1924, pp. 161, 165.
[3] A. W. Haddan and W. Stubbs, *Councils and Ecclesiastical Documents relating to Great Britain and Ireland*, 1871, vol. iii, p. 510, quoting Alcuin's letter of A.D. 797 to the Clergy and Nobles of Kent, from Alcuin, Epist., ed. Froben, No. 59.

belief in the legitimacy of the rule which their kings exercised by virtue of the descent they claimed from those gods.[1]

A heathen king who became Christian had to face the fact that he thereby threw away his title to rule as a descendant of the gods. The Frankish Clovis, whose conversion in 506 gave France her special continuity with Roman civilization, was congratulated by Saint Avitus upon daring to begin his genealogy with himself, and an actual consequence was that the details of his claim to divine descent were not remembered.[2]

Rollo, the invader and first Duke of Normandy (911–31), belonged to this ruling class if his identification in the Heimskringla with Ganger-Rolf the exiled son of Ragnvald, Jarl of Möre in Norway, is right.[3] Many Vikings fled from Norway to escape subjection to Harald Fairhair (d. 936) who made himself its first king by conquering his fellow chieftains. Some fled to Iceland, some to the Faroes and some to the Western Isles. In pursuit of some of them Harald about 874 conquered Orkney and Shetland, of which he made Ragnvald of Möre jarl. Ragnvald's male line held Orkney till 1156 and female lines thereafter carried his blood into the Scottish nobility.[4] Rurik of Novgorod (d. 879), the founder of the dynasty which made Russia, was a Viking from across the Baltic and may have been the same as Rorik of Friesia, descended from a princely line in Sweden.[5] Almost all the dynasties of mediaeval Russia were or claimed to be of his blood, most notably the Tsars of Muscovy down to 1605, when their male line ended with Boris Godunov. Among the families still claiming male descent from Rurik are those of Bariatinsky, Obolensky, Dolgorouky and Lvov.

Sir Thomas Kendrick has an interesting comment on the motives of those who fled from Norway under Harald Fairhair, rather, it is said, than to submit to him.

Not mere hostility to Harald [he says] but some greater impulse was the cause of this notable emigration of the vikings. This was, in its practical expression for the Norse emigrants to Iceland, the wellnigh irresistible appeal of large estates, easily to be taken and free from all complications and restric-

---

[1] Haddan and Stubbs, op. cit. iii, pp. 304–6.

[2] Godefroid Kurth, *Clovis*, 2nd ed. 1901, tome i, pp. 163–4.

[3] For criticisms see T. D. Kendrick, *A History of the Vikings*, 1930, p. 220.

[4] *Complete Peerage*, vol. x, app. A.

[5] Col. N. J. Belaiew, C.B., 'Rorik of Jutland and Rurik of the Russian Chronicles', *Saga-Book of the Viking Society*, x. 267–97, presents in careful and plausible form the arguments for this identification first suggested in 1838 by Kruse.

tions of inherited tenures, in a land where each man was as good as his neigh-bour and none was lord.[1]

The imputation of motives is risky and the motives may be mixed, but the same thing has been said of other emigrants in search of civil or religious liberty. 'Why', said an American friend to me, gazing upon a Cotswold landscape, 'did my ancestors leave this beautiful country for that barren, harsh New England? They said it was for liberty, but I think it was for land.' When all is said the difference may not be so great, for opportunity and the sense of freedom go together.

The tribes and sea rovers of the north stand to us as a type of free society. Settlement, agriculture and organization into larger units necessarily limit freedom. However the land is held, the problem is there. In the pre-Christian society described in the old English epic *Beowulf* a lord's followers held their land of him for life only and he was expected to provide for their sons when they came of age. But there would be a tendency to grant a father's lands to his son and thus in three generations to make them a hereditary possession.[2] In just this way the Anglo-Saxon kings provided for the sons of their nobles who entered their personal service.

We know that this society had three ranks, the nobles, the churls or common free men and the slaves. The chief source of slaves was doubtless capture in war and in England they might be either Romano-Britons or the victims of tribal warfare among the invaders. But en-slavement could also be inflicted as a legal penalty, or could result from a voluntary surrender of freedom in return for protection. The stages by which such slavery passed at length into a villeinage, which merely imposed certain legal disqualifications, which themselves were by degrees thrown off, must be touched on later.[3] In some tribal societies the proportion of those of higher rank to the rest was surprisingly high, as it was in Wales, but for Anglo-Saxon England we lack the evidence.

The royalty and nobility of these early Anglo-Saxon and Viking kings, princes and noblemen seem to be primitive and aboriginal— without traceable beginning. Adventurers may win for themselves

[1] *A History of the Vikings*, p. 340.

[2] H. M. Chadwick, *The Origin of the English Nation*, pp. 159–60.

[3] p. 121. Of 1,002 identifiable first settlers of Iceland c. 900 Professor Gudmundr Hannesson noted 38 per cent as of noble birth and 5·8 per cent as slaves, *Korpermasze und Korperproportionen der Isländer . . . Beilage zum Jahrbuch des Universität Islands*, Reykjavik, 1925, quoted by Halldor Hermansson, *The Book of the Icelanders (Islandingabók)*, by Ari Thorgilsson, Cornell Univ. Library, 1930, p. 8.

kingdoms and lordships, but they seem always to be adventurers of
noble blood. We appear to have no record of this epoch of a slave or
churl raised to nobility, though the converse could occur. Such pedigrees of them as we have come from two main types of source, traditional pedigrees passed down for generations by word of mouth and
put into writing only at some relatively late date, and the contemporary
evidence of documents, at this period usually chronicles and the lives
of saints, but occasionally charters and inscriptions. The value of
traditional pedigrees generally will be considered later.[1] Here it is
enough to note that the attitude of historians to them has changed
greatly in the last half century. Fifty years ago they were treated as
figments of monkish or bardic imagination, while today some of them
at least are regarded as embodiments of genuine, though possibly
distorted, tradition and among the most important evidences for dark
age history.

Bede's *Ecclesiastical History*, finished in 731, gives certain Anglo-
Saxon royal lines of descent and the rest appear in sources of ninth
and tenth century date. Sir Kenneth Sisam, who has studied and
compared them minutely, concludes that many of these probably rest on
a systematic collection of pedigrees made and written down for Offa,
King of Mercia (d. 796). For later additions and backward extensions
probable dates can likewise be inferred.[2]

From some of these early chieftains descents can be traced through
later royal and noble lines to the present day and, as we shall see,[3]
where such descents can be traced at all, they are now shared by very
many. Among the royal families of the so called Heptarchy or seven
kingdoms, which the Anglo-Saxon invaders set up in Britain, one,
that of the Kings of Mercia, appears to have possessed the unique
distinction of a descent from the kings who ruled over all the Angles
in their continental home of Angel in Schleswig before they invaded
England. Professor Chadwick[4] has shown that a date about A.D. 350
for Wermund, King of Angel, fits all the evidence and that there is
reason to think that Icel, the great-great-grandson of Wermund, came
to England about a century later. Penda, the powerful heathen King of
Mercia, who died in 654, was fifth in descent from Icel. It is thought

[1] pp. 16–22.
[2] Kenneth Sisam, 'Anglo-Saxon Royal Genealogies', *Proc. of the British Academy*,
xxxix, 1953, pp. 287–348.
[3] p. 235.
[4] H. M. Chadwick, *The Origin of the English Nation*, 1924, pp. 15–16 and chap. vi.

that the name *pending* the earliest form of 'penny' was first given to coins struck by his authority.[1]

There are two lines by which descents from the Kings of Mercia may perhaps be traced to the present day. Cadwallon, Prince of Gwynedd (d. 634), allied himself with Penda and the statement of some Welsh genealogies that the mother of his son Cadwallader was the daughter of Pyt and the sister of Banna probably means that she was the daughter of Pybba and sister of Penda and is considered by good authorities likely to be authentic.[2] Rhodri Mawr (d. 878), the ancestor of the later Welsh princes, from whom many lines are traceable, was sixth in descent from Cadwallader, son of Cadwallon, through his father's mother,[3] so that if Cadwallader was indeed the son of a Mercian princess descents from an Anglian king of the mid fourth century are known.

The other line is through the mother in law of King Alfred (d. 901), by name Eadburh, who, Asser tells us, was of the Mercian royal family. Unfortunately, however, we have no details of her ancestry.

The ancestral line of Alfred himself—that of the Kings of Wessex—is taken back to Cerdic who traditionally conquered that part of Britain which became Wessex about the year 500. Contradictions in the evidence regarding his invasion[4] need not destroy belief in Cerdic's historical reality, though this has been impugned.[5] Mr. Sisam decides that the whole of the pedigree before Cerdic is either fiction or error. From Cerdic down to Ine (d. 726) he thinks it defensible, though there is a question in regard to Creoda, whom one version makes the son of Cerdic and the father of Cynric (d. 560), while the other makes Cynric Cerdic's son. From Ingild, Ine's brother, downward, Mr. Sisam thinks the pedigree 'may reasonably be trusted'.[6]

Of the Viking royal lines the two with the best apparent claims to the greatest antiquity are the Ynglings and the Scyldings. The Yngling line reigned in Sweden. At what point the saga pedigree becomes historical may not be known with certainty, but Kendrick[7] seems to

[1] F. M. Stenton, *Anglo-Saxon England*, 1943, p. 221.

[2] It occurs in *Hanesyn Hen* (Cardiff Public Library, Breeze MS. 25), fo. 65, an important seventeenth century copy of eleventh to thirteenth century material (F. Jones, *Approach to Welsh Genealogy*, p. 345). Major Francis Jones points out (in a letter to the writer) that the absence of further detail, the Anglophobia of the early Welsh genealogists and the actual corruption of the names support the authenticity of the statement. Cf. J. E. Lloyd, *A History of Wales*, 1911, i. 185 n.          [3] p. 29.

[4] Stenton, op. cit., pp. 19–28.          [5] Chadwick, op. cit., chap. ii.

[6] Op. cit., pp. 321–2.          [7] *History of the Vikings*, p. 78.

think it so from Ottar living perhaps in the sixth century. Ingjald Illradi, fourth from Ottar, in the seventh century, suffered loss if not overthrow at the hands of Ivar Vidfadmi of Denmark. His grandson Halfdan Hvitbein, at all events, moved into Norway and conquered Vestfold there. His great-grandson was Harald Fairhair, who made himself King of all Norway about 875,[1] and from him many lines are traceable to the present day.

The Scylding pedigree likewise starts with myth but reaches history with Halfdan, King of Denmark, early in the seventh century.[2] Ivar Vidfadmi is said to have been his fifth descendant and to have made himself king both of Denmark and Sweden in the seventh century. But his conquests were ephemeral and though his grandson Harald Hilditonn repeated them they did not last. It is Harald's grandson Rorik of Friesia (d. 876) who has been identified with Rurik the founder of Russia.[3] If this be accepted, Scylding descents are traceable through him.

It is one of the curiosities of genealogy—and at the same time a reminder of the unity of mediaeval Europe—that the blood of Harold Godwinson, the last Saxon King of England, who lost his life at Hastings in 1066, should at length have returned to the English throne, ten generations and two and a half centuries later, in the person of Edward III, who descended from Harold by a line passing through ruling houses in Russia, Hungary, Arragon and France.[4]

## 2. THE CELTIC WEST

Our view of the early Celtic royal and princely pedigrees, more than of any others, will be governed by our attitude to traditional genealogy as such. The time has therefore come to consider this. Fifty years ago critical genealogists were inclined to lump together as the inventions of pedigree-making imagination all genealogies which could not be proved by the independent evidence of contemporary documents. This attitude was a natural consequence of the critical campaign[5]

---

[1] Kendrick, *History of the Vikings*, p. 108.
[2] Ibid., p. 82.      [3] Ibid., p. 206, and *supra*, p. 12.
[4] E. A. Freeman, *The History of the Norman Conquest of England*, 1871, iv. 654. n. R. 'The Children of Harold' sets out the evidence of Snorri and Saxo for the marriage of Harold's (probably illegitimate) daughter Gytha to Waldemar (i.e. Vladimir), King of Holmgard (i.e. Novgorod). Harold's children took refuge after 1066 with their cousin Svein Estridsson, King of Denmark, and it was he who arranged the marriage. The identification of King Waldemar with Vladimir Monomach (d. 1125) appears to be accepted by continental genealogists.      [5] See pp. 389-3.

which had been needed to dislodge Elizabethan and later concoctions from general acceptance, but it had the effect of throwing out the baby with the bath water and left those who knew something, but not quite enough, with the conviction that there was no such thing as a genuine traditional pedigree.

It was left to such scholars as the late Professor H. Munro Chadwick to restore the balance by demonstrating the historicity of important and largely distinguishable elements in the stories and genealogies handed down from so called 'Heroic Ages' of widely separated times and peoples, and by establishing, through close analysis and comparison, the general influences to which the oral transmission of pedigrees is subject.[1] Chadwick's general conclusion may be given in his own words.

Genealogies, especially of royal families, but often also of priestly or mantic families, were preserved among all the ancient peoples whose literatures we have discussed. . . . The family genealogies, especially those of royal lines, seem as a rule to be trustworthy for a certain number of generations before the time when they were first committed to writing, though occasionally they may be confused with lists of kings. Beyond a certain point suspicious names usually appear, and the genealogies are extended into mythical elements. . . . Genealogies have a practical as well as an antiquarian interest, as may be seen from the story of the Maori who occupied the attention of a court for three days by his recitation of genealogies. Parallel instances, though not on such an ambitious scale, might be cited from the sagas of the Icelanders. . . . In the time before oral tradition had been displaced by documents every man of position must know his genealogy. But the long genealogies of the Irish, the Indians, the Hebrews and the Polynesians are, usually if not always, products of mantic learning or revelation. In Ireland it is the filid, in Polynesia the tohungas, who are responsible. The genealogies of the Mahabharata and the Puranas are ascribed to Vyasa and other famous seers.[2]

Modern examples teach us that the memorizing of their genealogies is normal and not uncommon among illiterate peoples, whose social customs or organization makes knowledge of a man's ancestry important. According to Vambèry (in the last century): 'When two Kirghiz meet, the first question asked is: "Who are thy seven fathers—ancestors?" The person addressed, even if a child in his seventh year

[1] H. Munro Chadwick and N. Kershaw Chadwick, *The Growth of Literature*, Cambridge, 1932. See especially i, chap. vii, pp. 270–6 and 304–17; ii. 541–3 and 687; iii. 10, 140, 235–8 and 803–4. On folk memory in Western Europe, see Marc Bloch, *Feudal Society*, 1961, chap. vi.

[2] H. Munro Chadwick and N. Kershaw Chadwick, op. cit. iii. 803–4.

has always his answer ready, for otherwise he would be considered as very ill-bred.'[1] Other equally striking instances are given of the importance attached to lineage by the nomad Tartars and their consequent care in committing to memory the details of their ancestry.

The settlement of Iceland from Norway, between 870 and 930, is recorded in more detail than any other early settlement in the *Land-namabók*, written down in the thirteenth century from oral tradition. It names some 400 chieftains among the first settlers and over 2,500 others and carries the pedigrees of their descendants down six or more generations.[2]

Skene stresses the practical importance of pedigrees in Celtic Scotland.

In considering the genealogies of the Highland clans [he says] we must bear in mind that in the early state of the tribal organisation the pedigree of the sept or clan, and of each member of the tribe, had a very important meaning. Their rights were derived through the common ancestor, and their relation to him, and through him to each other, indicated their position in the succession, as well as their place in the allocation of the tribe land. In such a state of society the pedigree occupied the same position as the title-deed in the feudal system, and the Sennachies were as much the custodiers of the rights of families as the mere panegyrists of the clan.[3]

Major Francis Jones makes the same point in relation to Welsh pedigrees and their legal importance, or rather necessity.[4]

The Irish *filid* or hereditary historians handed down a great body of genealogical knowledge till the troubles of the seventeenth century destroyed their order. But even into the nineteenth century

senchaidhes or professional genealogists flourished in the South of Ireland. One of these in the barony of Barrymore was a Mrs Bridget Fitzgerald, called in Gaelic Brighid na Senchas, 'Bridget of the Histories', who died, aged ninety years, in A.D. 1808. On the 16th of August, 1896, and again in December, 1898, Philip W. Creagh, Esq. J.P., told the Rev. E. Barry, that

[1] H. Munro Chadwick and N. Kershaw Chadwick, op. cit., p. 10.

[2] H. Hermannson, op. cit., inclines to the view that Ari (1067–1148) and his contemporary Kolskegg the Wise collected in written form much of the source material of the Landnama. He points out that the Icelanders' early interest in history and genealogy and the fact that, when they settled Iceland in the ninth century, they found no aborigines, gives them a knowledge of their origin such as no other nation of the Old World has. He adds that many at the present day can trace their descent from the first settlers. 'Early Genealogies from the Sagas' besides those in the *Landnamabók* are printed in *Origines Islandicae A Collection of the more important Sagas and other native writings relating to the settlement and early history of Iceland*, ed. and tr. by Gudbrand Vigfusson and F. York Powell, Oxford, 1905.

[3] *Celtic Scotland*, iii. 334–5.     [4] *Cymmrodorion Soc. Trans.*, 1948, pp. 315–21.

Mr Creagh's mother, 'who was not married until A.D. 1818, remembered Brighid ne Senchas, who had a gold-headed walking stick, and used to go about to the houses of the gentry'. According to David Cotter and others, an Earl of Barrymore once entered Bridget's house at Loughaphreaghaun, between Castlelyons and Rathcormac, to ascertain from her own lips that she held his descent less honourable than that of some others of the Barries. When leaving, the Earl said: 'have the honour, but I'll have the land', and forthwith he deprived her of her farm. David Cotter alleged Brighid na Senchas as an authority for his father's version of the co-origin of the Earls of Barrymore and the Barries of Dundullerick. For two generations or more Bridget's descendants were genealogists, and professed, no doubt truly, to possess genealogies taken down from the lips of Bridget during her last illness. Her genealogical knowledge of the leading families in the neighbourhood was immense, but being wholly traditional, it was inaccurate regarding remote events, in some proportion perhaps to their remoteness.[1]

The slur cast upon Lord Barrymore's descent by Bridget in the eighteenth century was in respect of the bigamy of James Barryroe of Ibawne in the fifteenth.[2]

In certain secluded Yorkshire valleys the oral tradition of genealogy lasted into the mid twentieth century. On 30 September 1964 the former Mr. Hervey Rhodes, Labour Member of Parliament for Ashton-under-Lyne, 1945–64, came to see me in connection with his creation to be a Life Peer as Lord Rhodes.[3] He told me that his family, of yeomen and clothiers turned into factory hands by the industrial revolution,[4] but always living in the valleys of Saddleworth in Yorkshire on the Lancashire border, had preserved its pedigree orally; he himself being taught as a child that he was 'Hervey of Jack's of Bill's of Jack's of Joe's of John's of Thomas's of Dean Head'. Soon after election to Parliament he introduced himself at a meeting at the far end of his constituency by reciting this; when an old, white bearded man in the audience rose and corrected him, saying that Thomas was not of Dean Head but of Dean Head Clough—the smaller of two neighbouring houses or mills built and lived in by the family. I confess that this late survival in industrial England of a seven generation genealogical oral tradition astonished me.

The longest and most valued genealogical oral traditions of modern times are probably those of the Polynesians. The Maori referred to above was the chief Tamarau. When he appeared before the New Zealand Land Commission at Ruatoki,

---

[1] Rev. E. Barry, 'Records of the Barrys', *Journ. of the Cork Hist. and Arch. Soc.*, viii, 2nd ser. 1902, pp. 3–4.   [2] *Complete Peerage*, i. 441, 452.   [3] Lord Rhodes was made a Knight of the Garter in 1972.   [4] See p. 177 *infra*.

in order to explain the claim of his clan to certain lands, he traced the descent of his people from an ancestor who flourished thirty-four generations ago. The result was a long table of innumerable branch lines, of a multitude of affinitive ramifications. This marvellous recital occupied the attention of the Commission for three days. The old man gave much evidence as to occupation, extra-tribal marriages, etc. . . . and the genealogical table contained well over fourteen hundred names of persons.[1]

Examples of this kind do not, of course, establish the authenticity of the material so preserved, but they illustrate the determination at certain times and places to pass on genealogies by word of mouth and they show that the weakness of the human memory is in favouring circumstances no bar to their oral transmission in great quantity and detail. Chadwick classifies under five heads[2] the evidence by which historical elements in heroic stories may be tested, and the same tests apply to genealogies. These are (a) contemporary native historical records, (b) foreign historical records, (c) the existence of independent traditions in different regions, (d) the existence of independent traditions in the same region and (e) the consistency of heroic tradition.

Polynesia provides a striking application of test (d). A comparison of pedigrees preserved orally and collected in modern times from different islands of the same group or from different island groups has shown striking agreements in the remoter generations of the pedigrees of lines of chieftains, believed to have lost contact with each other for something like five centuries, with thousands of miles of sea between them. From the different branches of the Polynesian race, the Hawaians, the Tahitians, the Rarotongans, the Maori of New Zealand, and others come these pedigrees which, it is claimed, converge as they go back. And on a reckoning of three generations to a century has been based a chronology regarded as fairly close back to the fifteenth century and as approximate back to 1300 or earlier.[3]

Among many applications of text (a) noticed by Chadwick[4] are the confirmation of ninth century Welsh genealogies by the surviving monumental stones of the sixth century British King Voteporix of Dyfed[5] and the seventh century Cadfan King of Gwynedd[6] and by the

---

[1] Chadwick, op. cit. iii. 235, quoting Elsdon Best, *The Maori School of Learning*, Dominion Museum Monographs No. 6, Wellington, 1923, p. 5.

[2] Ibid. i. 133.          [3] Ibid. iii. 236–8.          [4] Ibid. i. 143 ff.

[5] J. E. Lloyd, *A History of Wales*, 1911, i. 115, 132. The stone, inscribed MEMORIA VOTEPORIGIS PROTICTORIS, was previously in the churchyard of Castell Dwyran.

[6] Ibid., pp. 116, 182. The stone, inscribed CATAMANUS REX SAPIENTISIMUS OPINATISIMUS OMNIUM REGUM, was long the lintel of the south door of the church of Llangadwaladr, Anglesey.

mention by the sixth century writer Gildas of the same Voteporix (as Vortiporius) and of the more famous Maelgwn of Gwynedd (as Maglocunus).[1] Similarly Welsh traditional pedigrees committed to writing in the sixteenth and seventeenth centuries have been confirmed by the contemporary evidence of thirteenth and fourteenth century documents.[2] When H. J. T. Wood tried to assert the possibility of this in 1903[3] he was severely criticized by Horace Round,[4] who quoted with approval an assertion of Gwenogvryn Evans that 'when a pedigree reaches back beyond the third generation of the time in which it was originally drawn up, *unless supported by independent documentary evidence*, the work of even the most honest men cannot be trusted'.

Undoubtedly great caution and judgement as well as great learning are needed if traditional materials are to be made the basis of historical or genealogical conclusions. A little learning, here, is a dangerous thing indeed, and there is a risk, not to be ignored, that the cautious pronouncements of the learned might be turned into a pedigree-makers' charter. Chadwick's own conclusions have not all gone unquestioned,[5] and it would be a bold man who ventured without his learning to carry acceptance of such material further than he did, unless on the strength of fresh evidence.

The criticism of traditional genealogies has to take account of the special forms of corruption of text and content to which they are liable. Names can creep in or drop out, especially where the same or similar names recur, and this may sometimes explain a chronological dislocation. But more often such a dislocation may be a warning that a genuine traditional descent has been joined by a later genealogical theorist onto a line to which it does not belong. The extensions of the Irish royal lines backwards to link with the sons of Noah are an instance, though here great care was taken to fit the supposed chronology. The genealogies which trace the origins of the Scottish clans are less successful for they prove on analysis to fall short by two or more centuries of the number of generations needed to link up their later portions with their beginnings. Chadwick concludes that 'the long genealogy of Kenneth MacAlpin's family doubtless stimulated the desire for

[1] Ibid., pp. 128–33.
[2] Op. cit., p. 18, n. 2.
[3] *The Ancestor*, iv. 47–60; vi. 62–5. The example Wood chose was unluckily not a traditional pedigree at all but a piece of late pedigree making, which Round of course easily demolished.
[4] Ibid. v. 47–51.
[5] Chadwick, *Early Scotland*, p. 134, n. 2.

similar pedigrees among the Pictish nobility', which was fulfilled by attaching their known ancestries to Kenneth's or other early Irish lines.[1]

In the same way the life of Griffith ap Cynan (d. 1137) of North Wales, written within a generation after his death, gives his pedigree for many generations back on several lines, but makes a mistake within four generations back on one line and within six on another.[2]

## (i) *Ireland*

It was Chadwick's view

that all peoples which preserve a native learning, not introduced from abroad, possess also an intellectual class which is largely occupied with such studies. The activities of this class are devoted partly to the preservation and interpretation of traditions, and partly to attempts to reconstruct the unknown past by means of revelation or imagination. In Ireland these activities were carried by the native scholars, the *filid* (lit. 'seers') to a degree of perfection unsurpassed elsewhere in ancient Europe, except perhaps in Greece. But when Biblical and Classical chronology became known in Ireland, through the Chronicle of Eusebius, probably in the sixth century, a great opportunity was opened up for the imaginative element. For it was thought necessary to carry Irish history back, far beyond the limits of native tradition, so as to link up with the descendants of Noah mentioned in the Book of Genesis. One cannot fail to admire the ingenuity shown in filling up the gap. Eremon, son of Mil, who is represented as leading the Gaedil to Ireland, is placed more than fifty generations before St. Patrick's time, and about thirty generations below Noah.[3]

A parallel to the derivation of the Welsh and Irish kings from biblical ancestors is to be found in the derivation of the Bagratid kings of Armenia and Georgia from the House of David and of the Artsruni of Armenia from Sennacherib of Assyria. Professor Prince Cyril Toumanoff assigns these 'new fashions in genealogy' to the Christian phase of Armenian history which succeeded the Parthian phase in the fifth century A.D. and sees it as a substitution for a previous derivation from pagan gods.[4]

Existing Irish annals are thought to derive from chronicles composed in the eighth (or perhaps the seventh) century and later.[5] Back

---

[1] *Early Scotland*, pp. 95–96; Skene, *Celtic Scotland*, iii. 334–65 and 458–90.

[2] *The History of Gruffydd ap Cynan*, ed. Arthur Jones, 1910, pp. 38–46.

[3] *Early Scotland*, p. 88.

[4] Cyril Toumanoff, *Studies in Christian Caucasian History*, Georgetown University Press, 1963, pp. 297–305, 326–9.

[5] E. MacNeill's theories of an Irish version of Eusebius and of the nature and date of the oldest annals have been controverted by T. F. O'Rahilly, *Early Irish History and*

to the fifth century, however, when Latin culture came to Ireland in the wake of St. Patrick and Christianity, they probably rest partly upon written records, now lost except in so far as the Annals incorporate them. Their record of events before the fifth century must rest on orally transmitted material pieced together and supplemented by imagination. Besides the Annals we have heroic tales separately preserved in oral tradition and surviving in texts of the twelfth and later centuries but probably first committed to writing in the eighth and ninth centuries,[1] while genealogies actually survive in an eighth century text.[2]

The history given us by these sources is detailed and coherent back to the seventh century and though before that less detailed, seems to contain a clearly factual element back to the fifth century. Niall Noigiallach (Niall of the Nine Hostages), king in[3] Ireland in the generation before St. Patrick is accepted as historical and as ancestor of succeeding high kings chosen from one or other of two lines of his descendants, the Ui Ne'ill of the north and the Ui Ne'ill of the south, until 1002 when Brian Boru, ruler of the little state of Dal Chais made himself high king. Niall's death is placed by the Annals in 405, but Chadwick argues for a date a generation later.[4] O'Rahilly, who places Niall's death about 427, is for once in a way nearly in agreement and is furthermore prepared to regard Eochu, Niall's father, as historical.[5]

Of the historicity of the kings before Niall there is great doubt, but a fairly clear distinction can at any rate be made between those later portions of the genealogies containing names known in story and the earlier portions composed of shadowy names which show every sign of invention to fill the gap between Biblical and Irish history according to the chronological scheme of Eusebius. With Conchobor King of Ulster, whom a reckoning of generations would place about the Christian Era, we are definitely in the region of ancient story.[6] Chadwick saw 'no adequate reason for doubting that the genuine native portions' of the genealogies 'may go back—I will not say

*Mythology*, Dublin, 1946, p. 252 and app. ix. The study of these questions entered a new phase with the publication of M. A. O'Brien, *Corpus Genealogiarum Hiberniae*, the Dublin Institute for Advanced Studies, vol. i, 1962. For other references see M. D. Falley, *Irish and Scotch–Irish Ancestral Research*, Evanston, Illinois, 1962, vol. i, pp. 440–64.

[1] *The Growth of Literature*, i. 47.  [2] Ibid. i. 272.

[3] For a demonstration that Niall should not be called 'high king of Ireland', since the high kingship did not exist at this early date, see R. P. C. Hanson, *Saint Patrick*, 1968, app. 2.  [4] *Early Scotland*, pp. 135–6.

[5] *Early Irish History and Mythology*, pp. 215, 220, 234.

[6] *The Growth of Literature*, i. 168.

without change—to about the beginning of our era, or even one or two centuries earlier'.[1] O'Rahilly, on the contrary, holds 'that no trust can be placed in the pedigrees of pre-Christian times'. The object of the compilers of the Irish pre-history and its genealogies was, he argues,

> to invest the Goidelic occupation of Ireland [which really took place, he thinks, about 50 B.C.[2]] with an antiquity to which it was entitled neither in fact nor in tradition: for only in this way would it be feasible to provide a Goidelic descent for tribes of non-Goidelic origin, and to unify the divergent elements in the country by tracing them back to a common ancestor.[3] . . . It is sometimes argued [he says] that, because people have been known who could repeat their pedigree back for seven generations, the pedigree of King Loegaire (+463) must be trustworthy for at least a couple of centuries previous to his time. Unfortunately the cases are not parallel. The record that we possess of the ancestors of Loegaire was not derived from Loegaire himself or from any contemporary of his, but form part of a lengthy pedigree, invented several centuries after his death, in which his descent is traced back to the fabulous Mil.[4]

Nevertheless, O'Rahilly is prepared to regard Tuathal, who figures in this pedigree, as an historical person and the leader of the Goidelic invasion of Ireland,[5] which he dates between 150 and 50 B.C. and probably nearer the latter.[2] In any case, as we have seen, he agrees that we reach history about A.D. 400.

The Irish thus have grounds for claiming that their pedigrees are the longest in western Europe, though few male lines can probably be traced from the high kings to the present day. The *filid* and their genealogical traditions lasted down to the seventeenth century, when the wars and social changes destroyed them. The oldest of their genealogies which we have date, perhaps, from the seventh or eighth centuries.[6] Before they vanished the latest forms of their genealogies were codified and recorded for posterity by such scholars as Duald MacFirbis, the O'Clerys, Geoffrey Keating and Roderic O'Flaherty. In spite of the deficiencies of later Irish records a number of pedigrees can be carried back to connect with the traditional lines, but the criticism

---

[1] *Early Scotland*, p. 93.
[2] *Early Irish History and Mythology*, p. 208.
[3] Ibid., p. 162.    [4] Ibid., p. 267.    [5] Ibid., p. 169.
[6] *The Growth of Literature*, i. 272, but cf. *Early Irish History and Mythology*, app. viii. On the *filid* see *Irish Men of Learning. Studies by Father Paul Walsh edited by Colin O'Lochlainn*, Dublin, 1947.

of these lines themselves presents difficult problems. Few independent contemporary records, such as those by which many Welsh pedigrees can be checked, exist in Ireland. The descents of the principal ruling families, however, are proved by the Annals, so that one may be confident of the descent of Lord Inchiquin from Brian Boru (d. 1014) through the Princes of Thomond,[1] and of that of O'Conor Don from the Kings of Connaught,[2] whose ancestry is traced back to King Daui Galach (d. 502) the son of Brion, who is regarded as historical, though the descent is disputable in the earlier generations.[3] To prove the male line of the Ui Ne'ill to the present day is harder, for they wholly lost their inheritance, but Irish genealogists have accepted the descent of the present O'Neills of Lisbon from the Kings of Ulster and the Princes of Tyrone.[4] Their pedigree, now in the fiftieth generation of the male line of Niall of the Nine Hostages, will not easily be surpassed in western Europe. In the female line many descents from the Irish kings can be traced to the present time.

One highly probable, though imperfectly recorded, male line from Niall is traceable outside Ireland. St. Columba (d. 597), the apostle of Scotland and founder of the abbey of Iona, was his great-grandson. Now the Celtic abbots were drawn from the kin of the founders of the abbeys[5] and extensive pedigrees are preserved of the kindred of Columba down to the tenth century.[6] In the ninth century Dunkeld, to which the saint's relics had been brought, became the chief Columban

---

[1] John O'Donoghue, *Historical Memoir of the O'Briens*, 1860; Hon. D. O'Brien, *A History of the O'Briens from Brian Boroimhe, A.D. 1000 to 1945*, 1949.

[2] R. O'Connor, *A Historical and Genealogical Memoir of the O'Conors Kings of Connaught*, 1861.

[3] Rev. Dr. Paul Walsh, 'Christian Kings of Connacht', *Journ. Galway Arch. and Hist. Soc.* xvii, 1939, pp. 124 ff.; O'Rahilly, op. cit., pp. 221, 395–404. The genealogies make Brion a brother of Niall of the Nine Hostages, but O'Rahilly rejects this.

[4] T. Mathews, *The O'Neills of Ulster; Their History and Genealogy*, 1907, iii. 323–56. *Complete Peerage*, vol. xii, pt. ii, app. C, p. 13, n. 1, dismisses the pedigree of O'Neill of Martinique but accepts the probable existence of male lines of O'Neill of Tyrone, citing O'Donovan's note in his edition of the *Annals of the Four Masters*, 1851, vol. vi, pp. 2422–4. These lines are brought down to the present day by Sir Iain Moncreiffe in *Burke's Peerage*, 1963 and 1967, s.v. O'Neill. For the Spanish O'Neills see Micheline Walsh, 'The O'Neills in Spain', O'Donnell lecture, Nat. Univ. of Ireland, Apr. 1957, and 'Spanish Knights of Irish Origin', Dublin, 1960.

Hogan, 'The Irish Law of Kingship', *Royal Irish Academy, Proceedings*, vol. 40, 1932, section C, pp. 186–254, gives the male descent from Niall of O'Donell of Tyrconnel, for which see also Irish MSS. Comm. *Analecta Hibernica*, no. viii, pp. 391–5; *Complete Peerage*, xii, pt. ii, pp. 110–15; *Annals of the Four Masters*, vol. vi, App., pp. 2377–2420.

[5] Skene, *Celtic Scotland*, ii. 67–9.

[6] Adamnan, *Life of St. Columba*, ed. W. Reeves, Historians of Scotland, vi, 1874, p. clxxxv.

abbey in Scotland. Crinan the thane (d. 1045) was hereditary abbot of Dunkeld[1] and is thus reasonably inferred by Scottish genealogists to have been of the kin of St. Columba and of the line of Niall of the Nine Hostages.[2] Crinan married about 1005 the daughter of Malcolm II, King of Scots, and their eldest son was Duncan, King of Scots, whom Macbeth murdered in 1040. Duncan's known male line expired in 1286, but that of his brother Maldred continues to this day.

Maldred married Edith, daughter of Uhtred, Earl of Northumberland, by Elgiva, daughter of Ethelred II, King of England. Gospatric (d. c. 1075), the son of this marriage, paid a large sum of money to William the Conqueror for the earldom of Northumberland, to which he had through his mother some hereditary claim. He took part in the conspiracy against the Conqueror on behalf of his cousin, Edgar the Atheling, the heir of the English kings. When this failed, he fled to Scotland, but later returned and made his peace with the Conqueror. In 1072, however, William turned against him and he fled again to Scotland, where his cousin King Malcolm III gave him Dunbar with the adjacent lands in Lothian.

From Gospatric sprang a line which held the earldom of Dunbar or March down to its forfeiture by George, the 10th (or 11th) earl (d. c. 1455) in 1435.

His senior male line expired in 1564.[3] John de Dunbar (d. c. 1391), younger brother of the last Earl of Dunbar but one, was created Earl of Moray in 1372. His grandson James, Earl of Moray (d. 1429), left an illegitimate son Sir Alexander Dunbar of Westfield, from whom descend in the male line the Dunbars, Baronets of Mochrum, and other branches still extant.

It has been believed since the early sixteenth century at least[4] that the great English house of Neville of Raby was descended in the male line from the house of Gospatric, though the attempts to establish the line have been at variance and have lacked clear proof. Robert Fitz-Maldred (d. 1242–8), who married the heiress of the Norman Nevilles, whose name his descendants took, was the grandson of Dolfin fitz Uchtred, who in 1131 had a grant of Staindrop and Staindropshire from the prior of Durham, reserving his homage to the Kings of England and Scotland and the Bishop of Durham. Round points out

---

[1] A. O. Anderson, *Early Sources of Scottish History*, 1922, i. 576–7.

[2] *Scots Peerage*, iii. 239, and information from Sir Iain Moncreiffe of Moncreiffe, Bt.

[3] Ibid. 278; *Complete Peerage*, iv. 510.

[4] MS. of Sir Thomas Wriothesley, Garter (d. 1534), in my possession, 'A booke of petegrewes of the north parties', fo. 6 b. Dugdale, *Baronage*, i. 291.

that this shows him to have been of high Northumbrian birth.[1] Canon William Greenwell suggested[2] that Uchtred the father of this Dolfin was Uchtred the son of Maldred who, with his brother Robert, and Edgar, a bastard of Earl Gospatric II (d. 1139), raided the lands of the monks of Durham from the Northumberland side in 1138.[3] Greenwell's suggestion is that this Maldred (Uchtred's father) was the brother of Gospatric I (d. *c.* 1075) and son of Maldred the brother of King Duncan. This theory lacks proof and is not free from difficulty, though a fresh argument for the existence of a descent was later adduced by G. A. Moriarty.[4] The repetition of names makes some close relationship likely, but it may have been through a female line and, as Round points out, 'one cannot ... be too careful ... in identifying two individuals of the same Christian names, when, in these northern districts the names in question were so widely borne'. The problem may yet be solved and a pedigree which gives the king-maker, Richard Neville, Earl of Warwick and Salisbury (d. 1471), and the extant line of the Marquess of Abergavenny a male descent from Niall of the Nine Hostages would indeed be a genealogical phenomenon.[5] In 1964 Mr. George S. H. L. Washington put forward evidence and powerful arguments for deriving the male line of the first President of the United States of America from a younger branch of the Earls of Dunbar and thus from Crinan and perhaps from Niall.[6] He identifies Robert de Washington (d. 1324) of Carnforth in Warton, Lancashire, ancestor of the Washingtons of Sulgrave, Northamptonshire, and of Virginia, as a younger son of Sir William de Washington of Washington, Co. Durham. This Sir William was the great-grandson of Sir William de Washington or de Hertburn, living in 1184, whom Mr. Washington identifies as William son of Patric of Offerton, Co. Durham (adjoining Washington) and this last as Patric of the Hirsel, younger son of Gospatric III (d. 1166), Earl of Dunbar, great-grandson

---

[1] J. H. Round, *Feudal England*, 1909, p. 490; *Complete Peerage*, ix. 494.

[2] *History of Northumberland*, vii. 1904, pedigree facing p. 104. A variant theory is referred to by W. A. Littledale, *Antiq. Journ.* ii, 1922, p. 211.

[3] *The Priory of Hexham*, Surtees Soc. xliv, 1863, p. 95.

[4] *New England Hist. and Gen. Reg.* cvi, 1952, pp. 186–90.

[5] As this goes to press Mr. George S. H. L. Washington has contributed to *The American Genealogist*, vol. 46, no. 3 (July 1970), pp. 164–8, an article on 'The Origin of the Nevilles' in which he identifies Uctred the father of Dolfin with an Uctred (living 1116) son of a Maldred, younger son of Maldred (brother of King Duncan I of Scotland) by Edith of Northumberland.

[6] Washington, *The Earliest Washingtons and their Anglo-Scottish Connexions*, privately printed for the author, Cambridge, 1964.

of Maldred son of Crinan. Sir Charles Clay has told me that he regards
the evidence as acceptable. The author also (p. 17) cites 'heraldic and
tenurial affinities' between the Washington and Neville ancestors in
support of the view that the latter also were of Gospatric's race.

### (ii) *Scotland*

The origin of the kingdom of Scotland is usually dated from the
union of the kingdom of the Picts, in central Scotland, with that of
the Scots of Dalriada in Argyll in 848–9 under Kenneth MacAlpin, the
King of Dalriada, who perhaps enforced by arms an hereditary claim
to the Pictish throne.[1] The home of the Scots was Ireland and they
came to Argyll, which they called Dalriada, across the sea from an
older, smaller Dalriada in County Antrim, late in the fifth century
under their king, Fergus Mor MacEirc, said to have died in 501.[2]
Kenneth MacAlpin was twelfth in descent from Fergus Mor according
to what Chadwick thought 'one of the safest genealogies which have
come down to us',[3] Fergus Mor himself is made fifteenth in descent
from an Irish king Conaire Mor, whose death forms the subject
of a saga and who was regarded as the ancestor of the royal line as late
as the twelfth century.[4] Fergus Mor and his brothers and doubtless
Eirc their father are accepted as historical, whatever view be taken of
their alleged ancestry.

The male line of Fergus Mor ended with the death of King Malcolm
II in 1034, from the marriage of whose daughter Bethoc with Crinan[5]
succeeding kings sprang. Crinan, we have seen, was probably himself
sprung from an Irish kingly line. His last male descendant on the throne
of Scotland was Alexander III (d. 1286), though the family of Dunbar
can show male descent from him to this day. The succeeding Scottish
dynasties, Balliol, Bruce and Stewart were by paternal origin Picard,
Norman and Breton respectively, though their claim to the throne
came by descent from Fergus Mor.

Very many English families descend from Fergus Mor and Crinan
through the marriage of Henry I of England (d. 1135) to Maud
(d. 1118), daughter of Malcolm III of Scotland (d. 1093), in 1100.
Malcolm's son David I (d. 1153), who had spent his youth at Henry's
court, introduced Norman knights and feudal organization into Scotland and between his day and the renunciation of English claims over

[1] Chadwick, *Early Scotland*, pp. xxii, 133.      [2] Ibid., p. 121.      [3] Ibid., p. 132.
[4] Ibid., p. 121; Skene, *Chronicles of the Picts and Scots*, 1867, pp. 130, 137.
[5] p. 26.

Scotland in 1328 a number of marriages between families of the English and Scottish baronage took place.

The seven original earldoms or mormaerships of Scotland represented, more or less, the seven provinces which made up the Pictish kingdom of Alban. The heirship of the Celtic Mormaers of Buchan passed by marriage to the Norman Comyns and from them to the English Lords Beaumont. In 1243 Maud, Countess of Angus, married a Northumbrian baron Gilbert de Umfreville, whose descendants were English and after 1381 did not even claim their Scottish earldom. She married secondly (*c.* 1247) Richard of Dover, son of Richard FitzRoy, a bastard of John, King of England, and Isabel her daughter by this marriage married David, Earl of Atholl (d. 1270), whose descendants thus acquired English interests which led to their final settlement in England.[1]

All the three daughters and coheirs of Alan, Lord of Galloway (d. 1234), married Anglo-Norman lords. Elena was married to Roger de Quincy, Earl of Winchester (d. 1264), Christina to William de Forz, Earl of Aumale (d. 1260) and Dervorgilla (d. 1290) to John de Balliol of Barnard Castle (d. 1269). The English descendants of Elena are very numerous.

## (iii) *Wales*

The oldest surviving Welsh royal genealogies[2] appear from internal evidence to have been drawn up in the time of Rhodri Mawr (d. 877),[3] King of North Wales, and trace his ancestry on several lines and the ancestry of princes contemporary with him. The oldest and historically the most important line is that of the older dynasty of Gwynedd from which Rhodri was descended through his grandmother. Its founder was Cunedda who came to Gwynedd (North Wales) from Manaw Gododdin, near the Firth of Forth, about A.D. 450, with his sons, and with great slaughter drove out the Scots (i.e. Irish) from Gwynedd, so that they never returned. The names of the father, grandfather and great-grandfather, of Cunedda in the genealogy, Edeyrn, Padarn Beisrudd (of the Red Robe) and Tegid, are thought to be historical names of Romanized Britons or Picts, Eternus, Paternus and Tacitus.[4]

---

[1] *Complete Peerage*, i. 308–9.

[2] The texts will be found in *Early Welsh Genealogical Tracts*, ed. P. C. Bartrum, Univ. of Wales Press, 1966.      [3] Chadwick, *Growth of Literature*, i. 150.

[4] J. E. Lloyd, *History of Wales*, i. 118; Chadwick, *Early Scotland*, p. 149; *The Dictionary of Welsh Biography down to 1940 under the auspices of the Honourable Society of Cymmrodorion*, 1959, pp. 87–8.

Among the sons of Cunedda were three with Roman names, Romanus (Rhufon), Donatus (Dunod) and Eternus (Edeyrn). His grandson Marianus (Meirion) gave his name to Merioneth. His great-grandsons Cynlas (Cuneglasus) and Maelgwn (Maglocunus) were among the British princes against whom Gildas inveighs about 540.[1] Maelgwn (d. *c.* 548) was the ancestor of Rhodri Mawr. Coel Hen Godebog, whose daughter Cunedda is said to have married[2] and from whom are traced most of the lines of British princes ruling in the Scottish border counties in the sixth century, is also regarded as historical.[3]

Wales, like Ireland, had its pedigree-makers, whose aim was to glorify their nation by linking its royal ancestry with biblical and classical antiquity. Britain was derived from Troy through Brutus, a grandson of Aeneas, who came here by way of Spain and gave Britain its name. Above Brutus the line is traced through the Kings of Troy, Jupiter, Saturn, and four less familiar figures to Javan, son of Japhet, son of Noah. A long line of kings derived from him comes down to Roman times. The story, appearing to derive in some way from the Old Irish Chronicle,[4] was already current in the ninth century, when Nennius wrote the *Historia Brittonum*, and may well be older. But its elaboration into a detailed and absorbing history was the work of Geoffrey of Monmouth about 1135. Sir Thomas Kendrick in his *British Antiquity* (1950) has set this notable work in its historical perspective and has recounted its acceptance for four centuries and the stages by which historical criticism then gradually undermined belief in it in the sixteenth and seventeenth centuries.[5]

Rhodri Mawr's male ancestry is traced to Coel Hen Godebog in the fifth century and a male descent from him is claimed at the present day among others by the families of Anwyl of Lligwy, Co. Merioneth, and its illegitimate branch Williams-Ellis of Glasfryn, Co. Carnarvon, now in the forty sixth generation from Coel.[6] In the twelfth and thirteenth

[1] Lloyd, op. cit., pp. 128–33.                    [2] *Early Scotland*, p. 149.
[3] Ibid., pp. 143 ff., and W. F. Skene, *Four Ancient Books of Wales*, i. 168 ff.
[4] James Carney, *Studies in Irish Literature and History*, p. 349.
[5] For a list of fifteenth and early sixteenth century genealogies of the Kings of England with and without the British descent see Sydney Anglo, 'The *British History* in early Tudor propaganda with an appendix of manuscript pedigrees of the Kings of England Henry VI to Henry VIII', *Bulletins of the John Rylands Library*, vol. 44, 1961, pp. 17–48.
[6] *Heraldic Visitations by Lewis Dwnn*, ed. Sir Samuel Rush Meyrick, 1846, ii. 70; J. E. Griffith, *Pedigrees of Anglesey and Carnarvonshire Families*, 1914, pp. 210, 242. *Dict. of Welsh Biog.*, p. 12. Thomas Ellis (d. 1703) of Porthdinllaen, Co. Caernarvon, was a natural son of Ellis Anwyl, *Burke's Landed Gentry*, ed. 1965, p. 227.

centuries several daughters of his house married Normans from whom numberless English families trace descent.[1] Thus Osbern fitzRichard, the Norman lord of Richard's Castle, Herefordshire, married Nest, daughter of the Welsh Prince Gruffydd ap Llewelyn (d. 1063).[2] Their daughter married Bernard of Neufmarché and from their daughter's marriage to Miles of Gloucester (d. 1143) an extensive progeny springs.[3] In the same phase of the Norman invasion of South Wales, Nest, daughter of the Welsh Prince Rhys ap Tudor Mawr (d. 1093), married Gerald of Windsor and became ancestress of the Fitzgeralds.[4] Llewelyn ap Iorwerth (d. 1240), Prince of North Wales, married a bastard daughter of King John of England and four of her daughters married Englishmen. One of them, Gladys Dhu (d. 1251), left many descendants by her second husband Ralph de Mortimer (d. 1276).[5] Gwenllian, daughter of Rhys Mechyll (d. 1244), Lord of Dynevor, a cadet of Rhodri's house, married Gilbert Talbot (d. 1274) and was ancestress of the great house of Talbot.[6]

From another daughter, Angharad, wife of Maelgwn Fychan (d. 1257), Prince of Uwch Aeron, Owen Glendower (d. 1416), the great Welsh patriot, was sixth in descent.[7] He has many descendants, all, ironically, through English lines.

The Welsh principality of Powis, ruled by its own dynasty, appears to have become an English barony about 1290 under its former Prince Owen ap Griffith ap Gwenwynwyn. His male ancestry is known from *c.* 1000 and he descended from Rhodri in the female line. His male heirs held the barony till 1317 and his descendants by female lines are many.[8]

### 3. FRANCE

As we have seen, the oldest Anglo-Saxon, Viking and Celtic pedigrees known to us are almost without exception those of families whose royalty or nobility was primitive, without known beginning, and often traced back to tribal gods. Each of these peoples has such a nobility when it comes into our ken and long retains it. So had most or all of the Germanic peoples who invaded the Roman Empire, but there

---

[1] p. 77.

[2] J. E. Lloyd, *A History of Wales*, 1911, ii. 397 n. and 767, and see p. 77 *infra*.

[3] *Complete Peerage*, vi. 453.      [4] p. 82; Lloyd, op. cit. ii. 416–18, 767.

[5] *Complete Peerage*, ix. 276; Lloyd, op. cit. ii. 766.

[6] *Complete Peerage*, xii, pt. i, p. 609.

[7] Information from Major Francis Jones.

[8] *Complete Peerage*, x. 641; Conway Davies, 'Lordships and Manors in the County of Montgomery', *Montgomeryshire Collections*, xlix, 1946, esp. pp. 92–101.

was one which soon lost it, namely the Franks.[1] This was the direct
result of the circumstances of their conquest of Gaul, where the provincial Roman society retained a greater strength and vigour than in
other provinces of the Western Empire, which the barbarian but
baptized conqueror Clovis (d. 511) preferred to use rather than destroy.
Of his fellow Frankish chieftains he destroyed many as potential
rivals. The new aristocracy which grew out of the acquisition and
inheritance of wealth and office under him and his successors was built
up largely from the able and wealthy members of Gallo-Roman
families, partly no doubt from Franks of noble birth and partly from
bold and able men of the meanest birth, both Frankish and Gallo-
Roman.

The principal offices, both inherited from Rome, were count (*comes*)
and duke (*dux*). Both were court offices, and some of the counts and
dukes never left the court precincts. For the most part, however, they
were employed in the administration of provincial districts, civil and
military respectively. Such local office, though not hereditary in
theory, often tended to become so in fact, especially when conferred
in a district where its recipient already held great estates.[2]

Among the greatest Gallo-Roman houses was that of the Syagrii,
whose estates were in Burgundy and about Soissons. Afranius Syagrius
had been consul in 382. In the break-up of the Roman power in the
next century his descendant Aegidius (d. 464), cut off from Rome
between three powerful German tribes, maintained what became in
effect an independent kingdom in the valley of the Seine and central
Gaul. His son Syagrius was overthrown by Clovis in 486, but descendants of the Syagrii were prominent under the Frankish kings in the
next century and perhaps, as we shall see, still later.

It is clear from the *History of the Franks* of Gregory of Tours
(d. 593–4) that great Gallo-Roman families still retained power and
wealth in the sixth century and were welcomed at the courts of the
Frankish kings. Many of their members were appointed to bishoprics
with those kings' sanction, but this very fact helped these families
towards extinction, and it has been noticed that Gregory mentions
many of their members in the first half of the sixth century, but very
few in the second—that is in his own day. Marriages between their

[1] Sir Samuel Dill, *Roman Society in Gaul in the Merovingian Age*, 1926, bk. ii, chap. i.
See also Marc Bloch, *Feudal Society*, 1961, p. 101, on the loss of folk memory by the
Franks and pp. 283–4 on the disappearance of Frankish and other barbarian nobility.

[2] Bloch, op. cit., pp. 194–9, traces the stages by which honours and fiefs became
hereditary in France and Germany.

members and powerful Franks became frequent, so that it is thought a complete fusion was effected and a Gallo-Frankish aristocracy formed in the course of the seventh century, which at length destroyed the monarchy of the house of Clovis (the Merovingians).[1] From the weakness of King Chlotar II they exacted in 614 an edict which established their position, not least by the king's promise to appoint no local administrators foreign to the districts which they had to administer. They found a leader in the Mayor of the Palace and it was from a family of Mayors of the Palace that the new Carolingian dynasty sprang.

But though it seems likely that there was at least some continuity of descent in the Frankish aristocracy from Roman times to Carolingian, genealogies to prove it are wholly, or almost wholly, lacking. The society which preserved genealogies orally had gone, but the society which produces documents from which they may be constructed had not yet come. The Merovingian royal line indeed is chronicled, but it expired and the descents claimed from its daughters are open to doubt.[2] Apart from this our scraps of seventh and eighth century Gallic genealogy come from a few monastic charters and from lives of saints—who were numerous among the Gallo-Roman prelates.

There is one genealogy so constructed which with a fair approach to certainty connects the Roman Empire with the modern world— that of Charlemagne himself. His father Pepin (d. 768) deposed the last Merovingian king, whose Mayor of the Palace he had been, and so became king himself. Pepin's father Charles Martel (d. 741), his father Pepin of Heristal (d. 714), and his father Duke Ansgise (d. 685), had been Mayors of the Palace also. The father of Ansgise was St. Arnulf, Bishop of Metz (d. 640), whose life tells us that he was born about 582 and links him (though not genealogically) with a court official Gundulf, who seems to be the same as St. Gundulf (d. 607), another Mayor of the Palace, who as an old man became Bishop of Tongres. The life of St. Gundulf refers to an Arnulf—apparently St. Arnulf—as son of a *dux* Bodegisel and this Arnulf is called *nepos mei* by St. Gundulf. Professor David Kelley argues that the word *nepos* is here used in its basic sense of grandson, making St. Arnulf grandson of St. Gundulf. The latter's life further tells us that he was son of Munderic, a member, as Gregory of Tours tells us, of the Merovingian house and a kinsman

---

[1] Ferdinand Lot, *The End of the Ancient World*, 1931, p. 358.

[2] The *Chronicon Episcoporum Tungrensium* says that St. Gundulf's mother was a daughter of King Chlotar.

of Clovis. Munderic's father Cloderic was the son of Siegbert, King of Cologne. In 509 Clovis instigated Cloderic to murder his father Siegbert, and thereupon had him murdered and absorbed his kingdom. Siegbert's father was Childebert, King of Cologne, probably the son of another Clovis, king there early in the fifth century.[1]

A pedigree of Charlemagne current in the ninth century, but rejected by modern critics, made St. Arnulf grandson of the Gallo-Roman senator Ansbert, by Blithilde, daughter of the Merovingian King Chlotar I (d. 561), and makes Ansbert a grandson of Tonantius Ferreolus, consul in 453 and son of a daughter of Afranius Syagrius, consul in 382.[2] Professor David Kelley's view is that there is nothing in this pedigree which was not a reasonable interpretation of documents existing at the time of its composition, though we now know that one section of it is erroneous and it is clearly a composite based on several earlier documents. His conclusion is that it is really the pedigree, not of St. Arnulf but of Arnoald, Bishop of Metz, whose granddaughter, he suggests, married Arnulf's son.[3] If this could be established it would give Charlemagne a Gallo-Roman ancestry of the utmost distinction. Hodgkin, however, argues from the silence of Paul the deacon, the friend and courtier of Charlemagne, that the latter can have known nothing of his ancestry beyond St. Arnulf.[4]

It is possible that descent from the Merovingians can be traced through Charlemagne's mother Bertha (d. 783) the daughter of Caribert, Count of Laon (d. 747), whose own mother Bertha, Chaume[5] thinks, was a sister of the Merovingian King Chlotar IV (d. 719). This would make her seventh in descent from Clovis (d. 511), whose, father Childeric (d. 481) is said to have been the son of Merovech, the eponymous ancestor of the dynasty.

Doubtless the Carolingians raised up new men to office and their families consequently to eminence, but it is likely that among their magnates were many members of old established families also. Our evidence, however, does not take the genealogies far enough back to prove the point. By the year 1000 many dynasties of dukes, counts

---

[1] J. Depoin, 'Les grandes figures monacales au temps mérovingiens', *Revue Mabillon*, xi, 1921, pp. 245–58, and xii, 1922, pp. 13–25, 105–18; David H. Kelley, 'A New Consideration of the Carolingians', *New England Hist. and Gen. Reg.*, ci, 1947, pp. 109–12. Letter from Professor Kelley, 28 Nov. 1968.

[2] p. 32.

[3] *New England Hist. and Gen. Reg.*, loc. cit., and letter from Professor Kelley, 28 Nov. 1968.

[4] Thomas Hodgkin, *Italy and her invaders*, vol. vii, 1899, p. 28 n.

[5] Chaume, *Les Origines du duché de Bourgogne*, i. 546–7.

and lesser lords were holding and ruling lands by inheritance under the kings who had succeeded to the realm of Charlemagne in what are now France, Germany and the adjoining countries. From many of these descents can be traced at the present day—from a few in the male line. To trace these comital houses much before 1000 is difficult, though in many cases the genealogists of less critical ages have provided them with mythical pedigrees going back to a remote antiquity. The evidence, where there is any, consists of brief and scanty references in chronicles and copies of charters recording gifts to monasteries.

Evidence of this kind may include a definite statement that a Count Theobald was the son of a Count Herbert, but it may merely give us unconnected references to a Count Herbert and a Count Theobald in the same place and in successive generations, in which case we can guess but shall not know for certain that they were father and son. We have seen that such offices as that of count were at first royal appointments and not hereditary, though they tended to become so in locally powerful families. It cannot, therefore, be assumed in the earliest times that successive counts in the same region were members of the same family. It has, however, been observed that in late Merovingian and Carolingian France, though there were of course no family surnames, the repetition of characteristic Christian names in a family was very common. Thus the names Renier and Giselbert recur in the family of the Counts of Hainault, the names of Ralph and Walter in that of the Counts of Valois. With such name patterns as additional guides the Abbé Chaume[1] worked out a series of tentative pedigrees linking together many shadowy figures of the eighth, ninth and tenth centuries in plausible and interesting ways. He is scrupulous in his tables to join only by dotted lines the names of persons whose relationship is merely inferred from evidence of this sort. Such tables, we must remember, embody plausible theories of the origins and links of the families in question rather than proved pedigrees. In a case where other evidence has taken us most of the way, the evidence of a name pattern—as we shall see when we come to discuss modern genealogy—may sometimes drive the nail home. However, we may agree with Bloch that, once the crucial turning point of the year 800 is reached, obscurity prevails and that hardly any, even of the greatest dynasties, can be carried back so far.[2]

One of the most vexed questions in continental genealogy is that

[1] *Les Origines du duché de Bourgogne*, Dijon, 1923, app., pp. 505–53.
[2] *Feudal Society*, pp. 284–5.

of the origin of the house of France, the so called Capetians, the family whose male line gave France all her kings from the election of Hugh Capet in 987 to the abdication of Louis Philippe in 1848 and which still exists in the Spanish and French Bourbons as well as in illegitimate lines. The great-grandfather of Hugh Capet was Robert the Strong, Count of Paris (d. 866), whose origin has long been disputed. Chaume by a series of ingenious inferences would make him sixth in descent from a certain Warin (d. 677) who was grandfather of Charlemagne's mother and brother of St. Leger (d. 677), Mayor of the Palace and Bishop of Autun[1] but Bloch did not accept this.[2]

In a still more tentative way Chaume seeks to establish the male descent of our own so called Plantagenet kings (from Henry II, 1154, to Richard III, d. 1485) from the same ancestor. The ancestry of Geoffrey Plantagenet, Count of Anjou, the father of King Henry II, is known back to Aubri, Count in the Gatinais, living in 990. Chaume plausibly derives him from a succession of Aubris and Geoffreys, Vicomtes of Orleans, beginning with an Aubri who witnesses a charter in 886. Before him the pedigree becomes very speculative but is taken back to Guérin, Count in Thurgovia (d. 772), conjectured to be brother of Mille, the supposed ancestor of the Capetians, and great-grandson of Warin (d. 677) above mentioned.[3] This theory is put forward only in a most tentative way, but one is struck even by the bare possibility that the Kings of France and England, who fought each other so long, might have been of one paternal race.

The legitimate Plantagenet male line became extinct on the death of Edward, Earl of Warwick, in 1499, but certainly one and possibly three illegitimate male lines still exist. The first and certain one is the family of Somerset, Dukes of Beaufort, descended from Charles Somerset, Earl of Worcester (d. 1526), bastard son of Henry Beaufort, Duke of Somerset (d. 1463), grandson of John Beaufort, Earl of Somerset (d. 1410), legitimated bastard son of John of Gaunt. The Duke of Beaufort is thirty first in descent from Count Aubri (d. 990).

The second line is the family of Cornewall, Barons of Burford in Shropshire, and of Berrington, Delbury and Moccas, Herefordshire, descended from Richard of Cornwall, natural son of Richard, King of the Romans and Earl of Cornwall (d. 1272), younger son of King

---

[1] L'Abbé M. Chaume, 'Robert le Fort', in *Recherches d'histoire chrétienne et médiévale*, Dijon, 1947, pp. 195–216, and *Les Origines du duché de Bourgogne*, i, 1925, pp. 536–7.
[2] Op. cit., p. 285.
[3] *Les Origines du duché de Bourgogne*, i. 531–3, 549.

John. An heir male of the Delbury line, Henry Hamilton Cornewall (b. 1901) was living in 1908,[1] but I have not ascertained whether he is living still or has left male issue. There may be other male branches of the family extant also.

The third line descends from Hamelin (d. 1202), bastard of Geoffrey Plantagenet, who became Earl of Surrey by marriage with Isabel de Warenne in 1164. Their great-great-grandson John de Warenne, Earl of Surrey, died in 1347 without legitimate male issue, but left by Maud de Nerford a bastard son Edward Warren, ancestor of the Warrens of Poynton and Stockport, Cheshire, who continued at Poynton until the death of Sir George Warren, K.B., without issue in 1801.[2] Male descendants of this family may still exist, though no claim has been proved and some made have been disproved.

Scions of a handful of such early ruling houses founded families in England at different dates. So small is their number and so splendid are their pedigrees that they deserve separate, if brief, discussion.

## (i) *Tracy*

Dreux, Count of the French Vexin (d. 1035), married Godgifu, sister of King Edward the Confessor, and their younger son Ralph (d. 1057) was given English lands and perhaps an earldom by his uncle King Edward.[3] Dreux (said by Orderic to have been of the race of Charlemagne) was the grandson of Walter I, Count of Amiens, and probably also of Vexin and Valois (d. 992–8). Walter's father Count Ralph, probably of Valois, may have been the one so named who died in 943, or that Ralph's father, Ralph de Gouy, Count of Amiens, who died in 926 and whose mother was named Heiliwich.

There are three theories of the ancestry of Ralph de Gouy. Chaume[4] believed that he was son of Walter, Count of Laon, whose ancestry he takes back to the same Warin (d. 677) from whom he deduced the Capetians and Plantagenets. Mr. Philip Grierson[5] argues against this and suggests that the father of Ralph de Gouy was Hucbold, Count of Ostrevant (d. after 895). If so, Heiliwich would be the daughter of Eberhard of Friuli (d. 864–6) by Gisela, daughter of the Emperor

---

[1] *The House of Cornewall*, by the Earl of Liverpool and Compton Reade, 1908, p. 140.

[2] *Complete Peerage*, xii, pt. 1, pp. 499–512; Ormerod's *History of Cheshire*, ed. Helsby, iii. 685.

[3] *Complete Peerage*, xii, pt. i, pp. 411–12.

[4] *Les Origines du duché de Bourgogne*, i. 537; J. Depoin, 'Études préparatoires à l'histoire des familles palatines', *Revue des Études historiques*, 1908.

[5] *Le Moyen Âge*, xlix, 1939, pp. 81–125.

Lewis the Pious, the son of Charlemagne. Professor David Kelley, however, suggests that Ralph de Gouy was the son of a Count Thuederic (living 888) of the Nibelungen family, son of Nibelung, Count of Vexin in 864, who is inferred by the descent in the family of the lordships of Perrecy and Jully to have been descended from Count Childebrand I, lord of Perrecy (d. 752), half-brother of King Charles Martel (the grandfather of Charlemagne). The details of the descent are uncertain, but Count Childebrand was father of Nibelung, lord of Perrecy (living in 768), who was grandfather of Nibelung, Count of Vexin in 805. He in turn was probably grandfather of the Nibelung, Count in 864, mentioned above. If this were accepted the Tracys would share the Carolingian male ancestry.[1]

After the death of Count Dreux (d. 1035) his widow married Eustace, Count of Boulogne, one of William the Conqueror's chief supporters, and this connection and his French origin no doubt led the Normans to regard Ralph's son Harold de Sudeley as one of themselves rather than as one of the conquered. At all events he still held his father's lands at Sudeley and Toddington in Gloucestershire and Chilvers Coton in Warwickshire at the time of the Domesday survey in 1086 and they long remained with his descendants. Harold's son John married Grace, daughter of William de Tracy, a bastard son of King Henry I. Their elder son Ralph continued the line of Sudeley while their younger son William bore his mother's name of Tracy and was accepted by Freeman and Round as the ancestor of the Tracys of Toddington, on the strength of inheritance of the fee, though the exact line is not yet clearly established between the late twelfth and the late thirteenth century. The Tracys held Toddington down to 1797 when Henry, 8th Viscount Tracy of Rathcoole, died without male issue.[2] His daughter conveyed Toddington to her husband Charles Hanbury, who took the name of Hanbury-Tracy and in 1838 was created Lord Sudeley. It was owned by their descendants until the late nineteenth century and I know of no other land in England which passed so long by inheritance from a date before the Conquest.

Though the senior male line of Tracy expired in 1797 it is possible that heirs male of a junior line or lines may exist. Richard Tracy of Stanway (d. 1569), a younger son of William of Toddington, was

---

[1] p. 33 *supra*.

[2] *Complete Peerage*, xi, app. D, p. 109. A short account of the Tracy family, contributed by the writer, is in *Burke's Peerage*, 1967. This is amplified in 'Toddington and the Tracys' by the Lord Sudeley, *Bristol & Gloucestershire Arch. Soc.*, vol. 88, 1969, pp. 121–172.

father of Sir Paul Tracy, created a baronet in 1611. His male issue and
baronetcy are said to have expired on the death of Sir John, the fifth
baronet, in 1678. Yet his cousin Paul Tracy conveyed land in Banstead
in 1668[1] and a Mr. Paul Tracy was buried there in 1746. Furthermore,
Sir Paul, the first baronet, had a younger brother, Samuel Tracy of
Clifford Priory, Herefordshire, whose great-grandson Samuel was
living unmarried aged 29 in 1683 and may have married thereafter.[2]
I have not so far been able to justify Round's assertion that the male
line of this family still exists,[3] but it well may.[4]

## (ii) *Louvain—Percy—Mountbatten*

The old Counts of Hainault, the Counts of Louvain, the Dukes of
Brabant and the Landgraves, Dukes and Grand Dukes of Hesse are
one family and one male line, from which three distinct lines have
branched into the nobility of England. Their origin is traced to Giselbert, Count in the Maasgau, who was living in 840 and died after 870
and was father of Rainier I, Count of Hainault (d. 915–16). According
to one theory Giselbert was grandson of another Giselbert, mentioned
in 772.[5] Chaume, on the other hand, sought to derive him from Mainier,
Count of Sens (d. 800),[6] and possibly from Ragnacharius, King of
Cambrai, mentioned by Gregory of Tours as a kinsman of Clovis.[7]

Godfrey the bearded, Duke of Lower Lorraine (d. 1139), was
seventh in descent from Count Giselbert. His eldest son Godfrey was
ancestor of the Dukes of Brabant and Hesse while his daughter Adeliz
(d. 1151) married, as his second wife, King Henry I of England (d.1135).
Her brother Jocelin of Louvain (d. c. 1180) came to England also and
was given the honour of Petworth in Sussex (still the home of his
descendant Lord Leconfield), by his sister and her second husband
William d'Aubigny, Earl of Arundel, before her death in 1151. He

---

[1] *Victoria County History, Surrey*, iv. 258.

[2] Visitation of Herefordshire, 1683.

[3] J. H. Round, *Peerage Studies*, 1901, p. 149. *A Short Memoir, critically illustrating
the Histories of the Noble Families of Tracy and Courtenay . . .*, by John Tracy, 1796,
traces a thirteenth century cadet branch of the Toddington line for a short distance rather
sketchily.

[4] A suggestion by Dr. Dwight Tracy in the *Journ. of American History*, i. 1907,
pp. 517–44, that Thomas Tracy who settled at Salem, Massachusetts in 1636, was a
grandson of Sir John of Toddington (d. 1591) has been disproved, John G. Hunt,
'Thomas Tracy in England', *American Genealogist*, vol. 41, Oct. 1965, pp. 250–1.

[5] *American Genealogist*, xxv. 224–32, quoting Knecht, *Das Haus Brabant*, 1931.

[6] *Les Origines du duché de Bourgogne*, 1923, tome i, p. 548.

[7] *Historia Francorum*, ii. 27.

married an Anglo-Norman heiress, Agnes de Percy, and their descendants were the great house of Percy, Earls of Northumberland from 1377, to which Harry Hotspur belonged. It is uncertain whether Jocelin was a bastard of Duke Godfrey or a legitimate son of his second marriage.[1]

The senior male line of Jocelin's descendants became extinct on the death of Joceline, Earl of Northumberland, in 1670. His great estates passed to his only daughter and heiress Elizabeth (d. 1722), who after being twice married and twice widowed before she was fifteen married as her third husband Charles Seymour, Duke of Somerset (d. 1748). Their son Algernon, Duke of Somerset (d. 1750), left only a daughter, Elizabeth (d. 1776), who conveyed the Percy estates to her husband Sir Hugh Smithson (d. 1786). He in 1750 took the name of Percy by Act of Parliament and in 1766 was created Duke of Northumberland. The present Duke of Northumberland is his descendant and so by male ancestry a Smithson.

When Earl Joceline died in 1670 the earldom of Northumberland was claimed by James Percy, trunkmaker of Dublin, who first put forward a pedigree deducing himself from a son of the 12th earl and later another deriving himself from a son of the 9th earl. Both were clearly false and in 1689 his pretensions were dismissed as 'groundless, false and scandalous' and he was sentenced to be brought before the courts in Westminster Hall, wearing a paper on his breast with the words, 'The false and impudent pretender to the Earldom of Northumberland.'[2] His son Sir Anthony Percy (d. 1704) was Lord Mayor of Dublin in 1699 and left descendants, but the male line seems to be extinct.[3]

Though the pedigrees he propounded were incorrect and he certainly had no claim to the earldom it is still possible that the trunkmaker may have had a male descent from the Northumberland family. There were certainly heirs male of the house extant down to 1755 in the Percys of Cambridge descended from Joscelyn Percy (d. 1532) a younger son of the 4th earl. The last known male of this line was the Rev. Joscelyn Percy (1698–1755) of Castor, Northamptonshire.[4] From Sir Ralph Percy (d. 1464), seventh son of the 2nd earl, Thomas

---

[1] *Complete Peerage*, x. 446.

[2] *Collectanea Topographica et Genealogica*, vi, 1840, p. 271.

[3] Ibid., p. 283. Another Irish family of Percy, that of Ballintemple, King's County, seems wrongly to have claimed descent from him. Its ancestor Richard Percy came to Ireland in the seventeenth century. Their male line existed in 1815 and may exist still. Sir Arthur Conan Doyle had a female descent from this family.

[4] *Coll. Top. et Gen.* ii. 62.

Percy (1729–1811), Bishop of Dromore, the editor of the *Reliques of Ancient English Poetry*, claimed descent,[1] but the evidence he adduces does not amount to proof.

Another branch of the house of Brabant settled in England with Godfrey de Lovaine (d. before 1226), younger son of Godfrey III, Duke of Brabant, and great-nephew of Queen Adeliz. His male line expired, however, at the death in 1347 of his great-great-grandson John de Lovaine.

The male line of the Dukes of Brabant ended in 1355, but Henry, younger son of Duke Henry II (d. 1248), became Landgrave of Hesse and his male line has continued to the present day. Sixteenth in descent from him was Ludwig II, Grand Duke of Hesse (d. 1848),[2] whose younger son Prince Alexander left two sons who settled in England. The elder of these, Prince Louis of Battenberg (d. 1921), was naturalized a British subject in 1864 and in 1884 married a granddaughter of Queen Victoria. In 1917 he took the surname of Mountbatten and was created Marquess of Milford Haven. Earl Mountbatten of Burma is his younger son. His younger brother, Prince Henry of Battenberg (d. 1896), married the youngest daughter of Queen Victoria, Princess Beatrice, and their son is the Marquess of Carisbrooke. There are thus at the present time three members of this family in the peerage of the United Kingdom.

### (iii) *Courtenay*

The English Courtenays descend from Renaud de Courtenay, who appears in 1150–1 as a witness at Rouen to a charter of Henry Duke of Normandy (later King Henry II). In 1160 Henry II gave him Sutton in Berkshire (Sutton Courtenay) and from that time till his death in 1190 he was in constant attendance on the king.

Ezra Cleaveland (d. 1740), Rector of Honiton, published in 1735 *A Genealogical History of the Noble and Illustrious Family of Courtenay*, in which he identified[3] this Renaud with Renaud de Courtenay, lord of Courtenay in the Gatinais and of Chateau Renard, to whose daughter Elizabeth King Louis VII of France married his own son Peter, endowing him with the great Courtenay heritage. This

[1] Nash's *History of Worcestershire*, ii. 318.
[2] Dr. Wilhelm Karl Prinz von Isenburg, *Stammtafeln zur Geschicte der europäischen Staaten*, Berlin, 1936, i. 8; ii. 97–105. See also *The Mountbatten Lineage*, prepared for private circulation by Admiral of the Fleet the Earl Mountbatten of Burma, K.G., 1958; *Burke's Peerage*, 1963, 1967, s.v. Milford Haven.
[3] pp. 114–15.

identification has been widely accepted[1] but in 1958 was challenged by Mr. H. F. Seversmith[2] on grounds of lack of evidence and indeed discrepancy of chronology, character and status between the two men. He concluded that the parentage of Renaud of Sutton Courtenay has not been established and this was indeed the view of G. E. Cokayne.[3] The two men, if distinct, may, of course, have been related.

The pedigree of the French Courtenays goes back to Athon, Lord of Courtenay in the Gatinais and of Chateau Renard, living early in the eleventh century.[4]

His grandson Joscelin (d. 1131), in Gibbon's words,

is enrolled among the heroes of the first crusade. A domestic alliance (their mothers were sisters) attached him to the standard of Baldwin of Bruges, the second count of Edessa: a princely fief, which he was worthy to receive, and able to maintain, announces the number of his martial followers; and after the departure of his cousin, Joscelin himself was invested with the county of Edessa on both sides of the Euphrates. By economy in peace his territories were replenished with Latin and Syrian subjects: his magazines with corn, wine and oil: his castles with gold and silver, with arms and horses. In a holy warfare of thirty years he was alternately a conqueror and a captive; but he died like a soldier, in an horse-litter at the head of his troops; and his last glance beheld the flight of the Turkish invaders who had presumed on his age and infirmities.[5]

His son and grandson held Edessa till the Turks expelled them in 1165.

Joscelin's elder brother Miles remained at Courtenay and was succeeded by his son Renaud, whose daughter King Louis VII of France married, as mentioned above, to his own son Peter. Their son Peter of Courtenay (d. 1218) was elected Latin Emperor of Constantinople in 1216 and his sons Robert (d. 1228) and Baldwin (deposed 1261, d. 1273) followed him. 'The purple of three emperors who have reigned at Constantinople', says Gibbon, 'will authorise or excuse a digression on the origin and singular fortunes of the house of COURTENAY.' We need not here, however, follow the fate of the second

---

[1] *Complete Peerage*, iv. 317; *Victoria County History, Berkshire*, iv. 372.

[2] H. F. Seversmith, *The Ancestry of Roger Ludlow*, bk. i (Colonial Families of Long Island, New York and Connecticut, vol. v), 1958, pp. 2422–4.

[3] *Complete Peerage*, 1st edn., iii. 102 n.

[4] Du Bouchet, *Maison de Courtenay*, 1661; Anselme, *Histoire généalogique de la maison de France*, tome i, p. 527.

[5] Edward Gibbon, *The Decline and Fall of the Roman Empire*, ed. J. B. Bury, vi. 447. For the pedigree of Courtenay of Edessa see Steven Runciman, *A History of the Crusades*, ii, 1952, app. iii.

house of Courtenay, sprung paternally from the Kings of France, for the English Courtenays, contrary to what was once believed, descend not from them but, if from the French line at all, from the first house.

Renaud (d. 1190), the grantee of Sutton, left a son Renaud (d. 1194) who acquired broad lands in Devon by a marriage with Hawise, lady of Okehampton, and their son Robert de Courtenay of Okehampton (d. 1242) married the daughter of William de Vernon, Earl of Devon, which at length brought that earldom to their great-grandson Hugh de Courtenay (d. 1340). The earldom of Devon, more than once forfeited and restored, is held at the present time by his heir male.[1] Gibbon, though opining that 'The Rector of Honiton had more gratitude than industry, and more industry than criticism', accepted his identification of Renaud and ends with a reference to

the plaintive motto [*Ubi lapsus! Quid feci*] which asserts the innocence, and deplores the fall of their ancient house. While they sigh for past greatness, they are doubtless sensible of present blessings; in the long series of the Courtenay annals, the most splendid era is likewise the most unfortunate; nor can an opulent peer of Britain be inclined to envy the emperors of Constantinople, who wandered over Europe to solicit alms for the support of their dignity and the defence of their capital.

### (iv) *Beaumont*

The Courtenay and Beaumont pedigrees are in some ways parallel. Both are traceable in France from about the same epoch (Beaumont from rather earlier), both produced Latin Emperors, and both are represented to this day by English branches. To both, moreover, male descents from the house of France have been attributed in error. Engelbert I, Count of Brienne, is mentioned in the year 950.[2] Seventh in descent from him was Count Erard II, whose younger son was John de Brienne (1148–1237).

It was only in the age of chivalry [says Gibbon] that valour could ascend from a private station to the thrones of Jerusalem and Constantinople. The titular kingdom of Jerusalem had devolved to Mary, daughter of Isabella, and Conrad of Montferrat, and the grand-daughter of Almeric or Amaury [King of Jerusalem]. She was given to John of Brienne, of a noble family in Champagne, by the public voice, and the judgment of Philip Augustus, who named him as the most worthy champion of the Holy Land. In the fifth crusade he

[1] *Complete Peerage*, iii. 465, and v. 317, 323, 335.
[2] Chaume, *Recherches d'histoire chrétienne et médiévale*, Dijon, 1947, pp. 281–3; Anselme, *Hist. gén. de la maison de France*, vi. 127–9.

led an hundred thousand Latins to the conquest of Egypt; by him the siege of Damietta was achieved.[1]

His kingdom in Palestine never in fact extended far beyond the walls of Acre and Tyre and in 1223 he left it. He then became commander in chief of the papal army but in 1229 was elected Latin Emperor of Constantinople for life.

The elder line of the house of Brienne had further links with the Latin East through John's nephew Walter, Count of Jaffa, and his grandson Walter, Duke of Athens, killed at the battle of the Cephissus in 1311. John himself by Berengaria daughter of Alfonso IX King of Leon and aunt of Edward I's Queen Eleanor of Castile had a younger son Louis, who became Vicomte of Beaumont in Maine in right of his wife Agnes de Beaumont. Their younger son Henry de Beaumont (d. 1340) came to England and served with distinction in the wars of the first three Edwards. He obtained the Scottish earldom of Buchan by marriage with its heiress and at different times was Lord of the Isle of Man, Constable of England, and Justiciar of Scotland. His brother, Louis de Beaumont (d. 1333), became Bishop of Durham.

Henry's descendants lost his Scottish earldom but were Lords Beaumont in England till their senior male line ended in 1507. John, 4th Lord Beaumont (d. 1396), Henry's great-grandson, had, however, a younger son Thomas whose line, long seated at Cole Orton in Leicestershire, has continued to this day. Sir George Howland Beaumont, 7th baronet (d. 1827) was known as the friend and patron of painters and poets, among them Wordsworth and Coleridge. From a younger branch sprang Francis Beaumont (d. 1616) the Jacobean dramatist and collaborator with John Fletcher. The present Sir George Beaumont is thirty first in descent from Count Engelbert I.

## (v) *FitzRandolph*

Count Alan the Red (d. 1089), of the family of the Dukes of Brittany, was probably with the Conqueror at the battle of Hastings and was granted by him lands in Yorkshire within which he built the castle of Richmond.[2] His nephew, Count Alan the Black, was given in 1136 the earldom of Richmond which his descendants the Dukes of Brittany long held. Alan the Red was son of Count Eudon (d. 1079), the son of Geoffrey, Duke of Brittany (d. 1008), grandson of Juhel, Count of

[1] *Decline and Fall of the Roman Empire*, ed. Bury, vi. 432.
[2] *Complete Peerage*, x. 779–88.

Rennes (d. 952), who was probably grandson of Gurvand, Count of Rennes (d. 877).

Count Eudon (d. 1079) had, besides Alan the Red and other sons, a bastard son Ribald (d. *c.* 1120–30) who became his brother Alan's tenant at Middleham in Yorkshire and in Norfolk.[1] Ribald's grandson Robert (d. 1184–5) married Helewise, a daughter of Henry II's great justiciar Ranulf de Glanville, and so brought the name Ranulf or Randolph into the family. Robert had a son Ranulf (d. 1252) whose elder son Ralph (d. 1270) left only daughters of whom the eldest, Mary, married Robert de Neville of Raby and conveyed her father's lands to the Nevilles. But the younger son of Ranulf (d. 1252), another Ranulf, of Spennithorne, left male issue who continued there for seven more generations down to Sir Ralph FitzRandall or FitzRandolf, who died in 1517,[2] leaving five daughters his coheirs of whom Elizabeth, the eldest, was married to Sir Nicholas Strelley of Linby, Nottinghamshire.

Now in 1514–15 a certain Christopher FitzRandolf acquired lands in Nottinghamshire and Derbyshire by a settlement executed by Cuthbert Langton on the marriage of his daughter Joan to the said Christopher. Of this settlement Nicholas Strelley, above mentioned, was a trustee and I have pointed out elsewhere[3] the strong probability (which should be convertible into certainty by research) from this and other evidence that Christopher was a member of the Spennithorne family. There is also good reason to believe that one of his descendants (possibly his great-grandson) was Edward FitzRandolph baptized at Sutton-in-Ashfield, Nottinghamshire, in 1607, and that this Edward was the same who sailed to New England in the Winthrop Fleet in 1630 and settled at Scituate, Massachusetts.[4] His descendants on several male lines exist to the present day in the United States.[5]

[1] C. T. Clay, *Early Yorkshire Charters*, v. 298–306.
[2] *Victoria County History, North Riding of Yorkshire*, i. 258–9.
[3] *New England Hist. and Gen. Reg.* xcix, 1945, pp. 335–6.
[4] Ibid. xcvii. 275, 295–8.
[5] Ibid. xcvii–xcix.

# III

## ENGLISH AND NORMAN

### I. NOBILITY, KNIGHTHOOD AND FEUDALISM

THE Normans, coming as conquerors, for a time formed a governing class superimposed on the English, though as time went on more and more Englishmen were admitted to it. To follow this development we have to look at that of the governing class in general, at the concept of it which the Normans brought with them and the special form which it took in England.

French historians have drawn a distinction between a nobility, in the sense of a social class possessing a legal existence and hereditary legal privilege, and an aristocracy, in the sense of a class possessing hereditary social standing and influence, but without privilege guaranteed to it as such by law. In its context this distinction is convenient but runs counter to etymology, for the root meaning of aristocracy is political (Greek, government by the best) while that of noble (Latin, knowable, notable, illustrious) is rather social or moral.

The legal privilege of nobility as understood on the continent of Europe has had slight importance or even existence in England. One has only to compare the nobility abolished at the French Revolution (1789–90), numbering at least 100,000 persons, exempt from most forms of taxation and possessing a monopoly of the higher ranks in the army and the higher civil posts, with the contemporary British peerage of some 300, whose sole exclusive legal privilege was that of trial by their peers. It was part of the continental conception of nobility that all the sons of a nobleman and their descendants forever should be noble unless they lost their nobility by being convicted of certain crimes, or by *dérogeance*—engaging in an occupation unworthy of a nobleman, such as most forms of industry and trade. It can easily be seen how these principles must bring into existence alongside the great nobility a vast number of impoverished noblemen, with an outlook and manners conditioned at once by privilege and limitation, for whom the State must provide employment since they could not do so for themselves.[1]

[1] For a short account of the nobilities of the different countries of Europe see the article on 'Nobility' by Professor F. L. Ganshof in *Chambers's Encyclopaedia*, ed. 1950,

This divergence between England and the Continent is of great historical interest. Its different aspects and phases have been the subject of much learned research but many of the conclusions drawn are still provisional and much remains to be done before even a provisional conspectus of the whole subject which is its background becomes possible. Such a conspectus would compare and classify social systems and patterns throughout the world and would try to distinguish racial, cultural, political, religious and economic factors which have influenced and differentiated these. Among the theories put forward to account for the unique caste system, which governs every aspect of Hindu life, is the view that it is a response to a unique problem, the demand for stabilization among the extraordinary diversity of human types poured into India by successive settlements and invasions yet kept from merging into one race by geographical factors.[1] Such an extreme of racial and social complexity may help to clarify racial factors in social structure present but less conspicuous elsewhere, though the present Apartheid movement in South Africa may show us a similar response to a comparable problem in action. Probably, however, the effect of legal institutions, such as those affecting property and the family, upon social structure, can be better seen, at least in relation to European society, by study of that society itself in its classical, mediaeval and modern phases.

The unlearned tend to put all learning and all the learned too much upon a level. There are some subjects of which so much is known that the questions of general principle most often asked about them can be answered with confidence. The subject we are here discussing is far indeed from this condition. Men of great ability and industry have given their lives to some of its aspects and working on the same material have differed totally in their conclusions. Where mankind is the subject of its own study detachment is difficult, if not impossible, and those who dogmatize most are most to be suspected of bias. Furthermore, much essential evidence is undiscoverable. The generalizations which follow are offered subject to this caution.

It is thought, as we have seen,[2] that the Franks, after their conquest of Roman Gaul, lost the primitive tribal nobility, which they like the other Germanic peoples had had. The new aristocracy of wealth and office which grew up among them under the Merovingian

x. 51–54, and for details of its period see *The European Nobility of the Eighteenth Century*, ed. A. Goodwin, 1953.

[1] J. H. Hutton, *Caste in India*, 1946, chap. xii.                    [2] p. 32.

kings does not seem to have had the fixity and legal privilege of the later nobility which developed in the eleventh century out of knighthood.

In spite of this and of the obscurity which veils the subject we may reasonably guess that there was at no point a complete replacement of old families by new ones in the seats of power. 'It is hard', as Marc Bloch wrote, 'not to believe that, in spite of repeated remodellings, of social rise and fall and the luck of all sorts of adventurers, the old core of the noble class was formed by the descendants of . . . rustic chieftains, among whom were recruited—for they had to be recruited somewhere —most of the vassals and most of the knights.' The origin of these 'rustic chieftains' he tentatively traces to 'that ancient cleavage which had occurred in the dawn of history between "client" peasants and the local chief who was fed in part by what they gave him; between the people of Brennacum and that Brennos who gave his name to the village.' He points out that

the existence of these village chiefdoms is clearly attested in Gaul before Caesar and in Germany before the invasions; it may be traced in the society of Armorica; it appears more distinctly in that of Wales. We may assume something of the sort in ancient Europe more or less everywhere. Evidently we are here in touch with one of the oldest lines of cleavage in our civilisation. Medieval and modern nobilities grew up much later and in a very different environment. The medieval nobility, as defined by the custom and law of the twelfth and thirteenth centuries, was distinguished by its hereditary calling to knighthood. The noble man was normally also a military vassal; and it was from the customs of vassalage that the noble class, once it had been consolidated, borrowed its way of life, its class cohesion, and the fundamental rules of its law.[1]

The professional warriors who fought on horseback and possessed a full equipment of armour attained a high social status between the eighth and the tenth centuries under the house of Charlemagne.[2] But it was the decay of the Carolingian monarchy which enabled this knightly class, especially in France, to establish for itself hereditary legal privilege, and to close its ranks and make itself a caste by denying admission to outsiders. The essentials of this development seem to have

---

[1] *The Cambridge Economic History of Europe from the Decline of the Roman Empire*, ed. J. H. Clapham and Eileen Power, i, 1941, chap. VI: 'The Rise of Dependent Cultivation and Seigniorial Institutions', by Marc Bloch, pp. 271–2. See also Bloch, *Feudal Society*, 1961, pp. 288–9.

[2] For an explanation of the eighth century origin of the knightly class see Lynn White, Jr., *Medieval Technology and Social Change*, 1962, chap. i.

been achieved in the eleventh century, though later modified in various ways, especially through the creation of nobles directly or indirectly by sovereigns. We are not concerned with the marked divergences of development between France and Germany, but only with the much greater difference of England from them both.[1]

Feudalism is a term invented by historians and used by them in differing senses, but the developments which it connotes centre on the personal relationship of vassal to lord by which homage was performed and fealty promised and on the grant by the lord to each vassal of land to be held as an hereditary fee or fief (Latin, *feudum, feodum*) in return for the performance of service to him—in the normal case, though not in all, military service as his knight. The baron who owed a service of so many knights to his lord the king, might perform this by in his turn enfeoffing knights as his feudal tenants, and if they in turn enfeoffed subtenants a complex pyramid of feudal obligations was built up. Upon this framework of personal allegiance and land held on tenures of military service, cumbersome as it may now seem, the nation states of western Europe grew and erected systems of order and government in which civilization could once more lift its head above the barbarism which had engulfed the Roman Empire.[2]

In this growth of the feudal system the great difference between England and the Continent was that feudalism was established in England by one man—William the Conqueror—who had both the personal force and the opportunity, from the circumstances of his conquest, to establish his own clear supremacy at the summit of the feudal pyramid;[3] and this his successors confirmed by forcing all free tenants of land to swear fealty to the king instead of merely to their immediate feudal lords. Therefore, periods of rebellion and civil strife notwithstanding, the great English lords never became independent or even half-independent princes, whereas the great dukes and counts of France and Germany were able to do just this, so that the King of France had long to struggle with his great feudatories, while in Germany the sovereignty of feudal principalities overcame that of the Empire. Because in England the king's power held that of the knights in check, they were never able to make themselves a caste or prevent the entry of outsiders into their ranks. The social consequences of this we shall consider further.

[1] Bloch, op. cit., pp. 320–31, traces the steps in the consolidation of the knighthood into an hereditary nobility with legal privilege, contrasting 'the exceptional case' of England with the rest.

[2] F. L. Ganshof, *Qu'est-ce que la féodalité*, 2nd ed. 1947.          [3] p. 98.

## 2. THE ENGLISH

Sir Frank Stenton has brought together from widely scattered sources surviving evidence for the fate of English families at and after the Conquest.[1] Their ranks had probably already been thinned by the death of heirs in battle. Many more seem to have emigrated, some to Denmark, some to Scotland and some to join the imperial Varangian guard at Constantinople. The Conqueror does not, however, seem to have expropriated Englishmen as such. He wished to rule as the legitimate successor of Edward the Confessor and the house of Wessex and at first, accordingly, left in possession those English earls who had not opposed him and doubtless many English landowners. But the English would not thus accept him. Rebellion in 1069 was followed by confiscations and by 1086, the date of Domesday Book, only two Englishmen were left south of the Tees 'holding estates of baronial dimensions directly of the king'. One of these two, Colswein of Lincoln, left only female issue. His daughter Muriel appears to have married Robert de la Haye, a Norman, and left descendants.[2] The other, Thurkill of Arden, was son of Aelfwine who had been Sheriff of Warwickshire under Edward the Confessor. The unique pedigree of his male descendants, the Ardens, is discussed below.

There are also a few instances in which it seems likely that barons of the Conqueror acquired their lands by marrying English heiresses, as Robert d'Oillé, the castellan of Oxford, is said to have married a daughter of the Confessor's kinsman Wigot of Wallingford, and as Geoffrey de Wirce married Alveva the heiress of a Warwickshire thegn, Leofwine.[3]

The thegns in general seem, however, to have fallen upon evil days, sometimes losing their lands, sometimes still holding as villein tenants what they had once held freely. The lowest point of their fortunes was probably reached between 1080 and 1120, after which opportunities to qualify and serve the king as knights began once more to open to them. The families in this class mentioned below and the very few others known belong mainly to the wilder parts of the north country, to which the Norman settlers were little attracted, so that English landowners there had a better chance than in the fertile south to hang on till times grew better for them.

¹ F. M. Stenton, 'English Families and the Norman Conquest', *Trans. Royal Hist. Soc.* 4th ser., xxvi, 1944, pp. 1–12, and *Anglo-Saxon England*, 1943, p. 618.

² Round, *Calendar of Documents in France*, p. xlviii; A. R. Wagner, 'The Origin of the Hays of Erroll', *The Genealogists' Magazine*, xii. 1.

³ Stenton, op. cit. ('English Families'), pp. 5–6.

So far as I know, the ancestry of two extant English families only, Arden and Berkeley, can be carried back to pre-Conquest Englishmen. After these we shall consider some examples of the small but larger class of those whose ancestry, though not traceable so far, must, from the evidence of names, have been English.

## (i) *Arden*

The great genealogist Horace Round referred to Arden as 'a house enjoying a distinction perhaps unique. For it had not only a clear descent from Aelfwine, sheriff of Warwickshire in days before the Conquest, but even held, of the great possessions of which Domesday shows us its ancestor as lord, some manors which had been his before the Normans landed, at least as late as the days of Queen Elizabeth.'[1] Freeman comments that 'his son Turchil stands out more conspicuously in Domesday than any other Englishman, his lands filling more than four columns',[2] and Dugdale notes that 'he was one of the first here in *England*, that in Imitation of the Normans, assumed a Sirname; for so it appears that he did and wrote himself *Turchillus de Eardene*, in the Days of K. *Will. Rufus*'.[3] William Rufus did not allow Turchil's son Siward of Arden to keep the great inheritance which his father had held as a tenant in chief of the Conqueror. Most of it was given to the Norman Henry, Earl of Warwick, for augmentation of his earldom, but the Ardens continued in possession of substantial lands as tenants of the earls.

The legend recorded by John Rous in the fifteenth century tried to make the Norman Earl Henry appear the legitimate heir of his English predecessors by marrying him to an imaginary Margaret, daughter of Turchil.[4] It is interesting and probably significant that the Roll compiled by Rous (now in the College of Arms) belonged in 1636 to Robert Arden of Park Hall.[5]

The only documented pedigree of the Ardens is that printed by Dugdale in 1656.[6] Dugdale was the prince of English genealogists but several of the sources he refers to here are unedited and the Arden pedigree is so interesting that a modern study of it is much to be

---

[1] *Peerage and Pedigree*, ii. 127.
[2] E. A. Freeman, *The History of the Norman Conquest of England*, iv. 780.
[3] *Antiquities of Warwickshire*, ed. 1765, p. 650.
[4] *Rous Roll*, ed. Courthope, 1859, No. 30.
[5] Wagner, *Catalogue of English Mediaeval Rolls of Arms*, p. 117.
[6] Op. cit., pp. 650–6. The descent of Curdworth, as given in *V.C.H. Warwick*, iv. 1947, ed. L. F. Salzman, pp. 61–62, goes far to establish the details.

desired. For the period between Domesday Book (1086) and the beginning of a continuous series of public records (1155), which often presents
insuperable difficulties to the genealogist, we have in this case both
evidence of monastic charters and the record of a lawsuit of 1208[1] which
recites the pedigree.

The senior line of Park Hall in Curdworth, Warwickshire, continued
till 1643 when Robert Arden 'being much accomplisht with Learning,
and other excellent Parts, died in the Flower of his Youth, whereby the
Inheritance of this antient Family resorted to his Sisters'. But the male
line was continued by the progeny of his great-great-grandfather's
younger brother Simon Arden of Longcroft in Yoxall, Staffordshire,
who still exist,[2] Dr. George Arden being twenty seventh in descent
from Aelfwine the sheriff.

There is yet another great distinction to which this Arden family has
a likely but not a clearly proved claim, that of having produced the
mother of William Shakespeare, Mary Arden, who married John Shakespeare about 1557, was the granddaughter of Thomas Arden of Wilmcote in Aston Cantlow, Warwickshire, and it has been suggested that
he was the same as a Thomas, younger brother of Sir John Arden
(d. 1536) of Park Hall. However, the fact that Ardens occur near
Stratford on Avon some time before this suggests that, though probably
derived ultimately from the Park Hall line, the Wilmcote Ardens
branched off earlier.[3]

### (ii) *Berkeley*

One other English family can show a probable descent from a pre-
Conquest Englishman, though one link in the chain is open to doubt
and the suggested identification of the first ancestor is no more than a
conjecture. Berkeley Castle in Gloucestershire, the scene of the murder
of King Edward II, both for historical and architectural interest stands
in the first rank of English houses, but its unique distinction is that the
Berkeley family has held it for eight centuries, since Henry of Anjou
(afterwards King Henry II) gave it to their ancestor Robert Fitz-
Harding in 1153 or 1154. This Robert was a rich merchant of Bristol
and the identity of Harding his father has long been a subject of conjecture and dispute. He is now, however, generally held to have been
the same as Harding, son of Eadnoth, who held Merriott in Somerset

---

[1] Dugdale, op. cit., p. 746; Wrottesley, *Pedigrees from the Plea Rolls*, p. 475.
[2] *Burke's Landed Gentry*, 1952. There is an Australian branch also.
[3] E. K. Chambers, *William Shakespeare*, 1930, ii. 28–32.

in 1086 and was ancestor through his elder son Nicholas FitzHarding of the Family of Meriet, which held and took its name from that place.

Eadnoth, the father of this Harding, was certainly a pre-Conquest Englishman, but a further theory has been put forward identifying him with a well known Eadnoth, a 'staller' or household officer of Edward the Confessor, who was given a command by William the Conqueror and was killed in 1068 leading the men of Somerset against a raid by the sons of King Harold. The name Eadnoth is too common to let us regard this identification as more than an interesting possibility, but on any showing Mr. Robert Berkeley, now of Berkeley, is twenty fourth in descent from Harding, whose father was probably a thane Eadnoth living before the Conquest.[1]

The later history of the Berkeleys cannot even be summarized here, but their long continued eminence in the mediaeval baronage and the modern peerage coupled with their romantic vicissitudes give it unique interest.[2]

### (iii) *Ingoldsby*

In 1086 one Colegrim, whose name proclaims him an Englishman, was a tenant of Count Alan of Brittany in Fulbeck and elsewhere in Lincolnshire and as a king's thegn held in Ingoldsby and elsewhere in the same county. His son and successor Osbert occurs in 1130 and from him Sir Charles Clay has proved the line through five generations to Sir Roger de Ingoldsby living in 1286.[3] An eighteenth century pedigree, which there is no reason to distrust, carries the descent from Sir Roger down to Ralph Ingoldsby who acquired the manor of Lenborough in Buckingham by marriage in the fifteenth century.[4] His last proved male descendant was Thomas Ingoldsby of Waldridge in Dinton, Buckinghamshire, who died in 1760, apparently the twentieth in descent from Colegrim. But this Thomas's uncle Francis, a spendthrift, who had been forced to sell Lenborough to his own steward and had died a pensioner in the Charterhouse in 1681, had had male issue and I have seen no proof of its extinction.[5]

Mr. D. L. Jacobus has suggested a possible connection between this

---

[1] *Complete Peerage*, ii. 124–5; *Ancestor*, viii. 73; Greenfield, *Pedigree of Meriet*; Freeman, *Norman Conquest*, iv. 760.

[2] See H. P. R. Finberg, *Gloucestershire Studies*, 1957, pp. 145–59.

[3] C. T. Clay, *Early Yorkshire Charters*, v. 255–8.

[4] *The Genealogist*, new ser., iii. 136–9; *Victoria County History, Buckinghamshire*, iii. 483.

[5] Lipscombe's *History of the County of Buckingham*, ii. 169; *V.C.H. Bucks.*, iii. 484.

line and a family of Ingoldsby of Fishtoft and Frieston, Lincolnshire, but he does not trace it after 1638.[1] However, a record of the apprenticeship of a Samuel Ingoldsby in 1754 to a blacksmith of Frieston suggests that the family was then still extant there.[2]

### (iv) *Stanley and Others*

Those English families which kept or achieved knightly rank in the two centuries which followed the Norman Conquest became assimilated to the Normans and sooner or later gave their children Norman Christian names. Therefore, when one traces back through men with Norman names to a first ancestor with an English name, there is a strong presumption that he was of English descent even though his ancestry may not be traceable back to the Conquest. Dr. Reaney shows from villein pedigrees recited in cases in the King's Court that about 1200 French personal names were replacing English, though some families were more conservative than others. The repetition of the first or the second element in the names of different members of a family was an old habit which did not die quickly.[3] The converse proposition does not apply, for a man with a Norman name in 1200 might well be of English descent, though a French Christian name in 1086 may be taken to indicate a French origin.

No other extant family but Arden and Berkeley has proved an actual pedigree from a pre-Conquest Englishman, but other families can establish a strong probability of English ancestry by showing descent from a twelfth century ancestor with an English (or Danish) name. Such a family was Okeover of Okeover in Staffordshire, whose male line expired in 1955 and whose first known ancestor, Orm, was enfeoffed in Okeover before 1113.[4]

In the view of Sir Frank Stenton

The number of thirteenth-century landed families which can be traced backwards to an ancestor bearing an English or a Danish name is by no means inconsiderable. It includes some families of baronial rank, such as Berkeley, Cromwell, Neville, Lumley, Greystoke, Audley, Fitzwilliam of Hinderskelfe and Fitzwilliam of Sprotborough, and many others of less

---

[1] *The American Genealogist*, xi. 1934, pp. 143–5, 208–16.

[2] P.R.O. Inland Revenue Books, xix. 210.

[3] P. H. Reaney, *The Origin of English Surnames*, 1967, pp. 103–5, and 'Pedigrees of Villeins and Freemen', *Notes and Queries*, vol. 197 (1952), pp. 222–5. On the relation of Anglo-Saxon to other Germanic naming customs see Henry Bosley Woolf, *The Old Germanic Principles of Name-giving*, Baltimore, The Johns Hopkins Press, 1939.

[4] *The Ancestor*, v. 191; leading article in *The Times*, Jan. 1955.

prominence which were influential in their own districts. Isolated families of position with such an ancestry can be found in most parts of England, but they were especially numerous in the far north, where they were indistinguishable from the English aristocracy of southern Scotland, in Yorkshire and Lancashire, and in the northern midlands. A few families of this type are known to have been descended from English landowners of 1086, and a small minority of these families are carried back by Domesday Book to the time of King Edward. But there are many which cannot be traced before the first half of the twelfth century, and of which the origin must be left an open question. Their distribution suggests that some at least of them were founded by Englishmen who had been planted by the king or by some Norman lord on lands devastated in the wars of the Conquest. It may be hoped that more descents of this kind will be worked out in the future, for every established case helps to reduce the abruptness of the transition from the English to the Norman order.[1]

One of the most notable families in this class is that of the Stanleys, Earls of Derby. Adam de Stanley of Stanley in Staffordshire, living about 1150, was probably the brother of Liulf de Audley, whose son refers to Adam as his uncle in a charter of *c.* 1170–90.[2] Liulf is an English name and he and Adam may have been descendants of Gamel (another English name) who in 1086 held lands which were later theirs. The greatness of the Stanleys began only in the fifteenth century, but the present Earl of Derby is probably twenty sixth in descent from Adam de Stanley.

Among other extant families whose English origin may be assumed, though the proved or highly probable descent goes back only to the twelfth century are Lumley, Fitzwilliam and Assheton. Twenty four generations of Lumleys, from Uchtred in the middle of the twelfth century to the present Earl of Scarbrough, have held lands in Lumley, Co. Durham.[3] Though a link in the fifteenth century is uncertain, Earl Fitzwilliam probably descends from Ketelborn who held land in Hopton, Yorkshire, in 1135[4] while Orm, who was granted Ashton under Lyne before 1189, was probably ancestor of the Asshetons and grandson of Orm, son of Ailward, who likewise held land there.[5] Evidence cited later (p. 215) suggests that the Weedons of Weedon

[1] F. M. Stenton, *Anglo-Saxon England*, 1943, pp. 675–6.

[2] *Complete Peerage*, xii, pt. i, pp. 243–6; Round, *Peerage and Pedigree*, ii. 22–30.

[3] *Complete Peerage*, viii. 266.

[4] Ibid., v. 518–20; J. W. Clay, *The Extinct and Dormant Peerages of the Northern Counties of England*, 1913, pp. 76–80; A. R. Maddison, *Lincolnshire Pedigrees* (Harleian Soc. l), i. 355–6; *The Ancestor*, xii. 110–17.

[5] *Victoria County History, Lancashire*, i. 327 n.; iv. 341; viii. 392–6.

Hill in Chesham, Buckinghamshire, may derive from Almar, tenant there before the Conquest.

### 3. THE NORMANS

By comparison with the families of proved English descent those whose Norman origin can be shown are numerous. Lewis Loyd,[1] whose critical standard was very high, accepted some three hundred such origins as proved in the sense that the actual place in Normandy from which families (not necessarily now extant) came could be established; and besides these there are instances where Norman or at least French origin is a virtual certainty though the precise place from which the family came remains uncertain. Loyd's work is an object lesson both in the treatment of the special problems of Anglo-Norman genealogy and in genealogical method generally. The cases where success has been achieved are a small proportion of the total number and its achievement even so has called for very great skill and knowledge. As Round put it, 'the fact is that it is no less difficult to trace the minor companions of the Conqueror—those who became in England under-tenants—to their homes in Normandy than it is in the seventeenth century to affiliate with certainty Englishmen who settled in Ireland or in New England'.[2]

The majority of the knights who came with William to conquer England in 1066 were doubtless his own Norman subjects, but they included also a large Breton contingent and smaller groups from the county of Boulogne, Picardy and Flanders.[3] The Breton element is found in most parts of England, but especially on the lands of the Earl of Richmond, a cadet of the Breton ducal house, in Lincolnshire, the North Riding of Yorkshire, Suffolk, Cambridgeshire and Essex.[4] Hervey de Ispania, a Domesday tenant of the Honour of Richmond in Essex, probably derived his name from Espinay and gave it to Willingale Spain, Spains Hall in Finchingfield and Spaynes Hall in Great Yeldham. Surnames presumably derived from Breton personal names, such as Jekyll from Judicael, are found in these parts.[5] A charter of about 1200, addressed by a Norman lord in Cambridgeshire to all his men *Francis et Anglis et Flandrensibus* surprisingly shows the

---

[1] *The Origins of Some Anglo-Norman Families*, by the late Lewis C. Loyd, ed. C. T. Clay and D. C. Douglas, 1951, Harleian Soc. ciii; P. H. Reaney, *The Origin of English Surnames*, 1967, p. 69, has a map showing the distribution of French place names surviving as English surnames and discusses and lists these on pp. 68–73.

[2] *Family Origins*, p. 133.     [3] F. M. Stenton, *Anglo-Saxon England*, 1943, p. 621.

[4] F. M. Stenton, *The First Century of English Feudalism 1066–1166*, 1932, pp. 24–26; p. 44 *supra*.     [5] P. H. Reaney, *The Origin of English Surnames*, 1967, pp. 147–9.

distinction between them still existing.[1] This may, however, mean no more than conservatism of legal formula. The *Dialogus de Scaccario* of 1179 tells us that 'nowadays, when English and Normans live close together and marry and give in marriage to each other, the nations are so mixed that it can scarcely be decided (I mean in the case of freemen) who is of English birth and who Norman; except of course the villeins, who cannot alter their condition without the leave of their masters'.[2]

Bloch sees a direct connection between the appearance of surnames and the disintegration or contraction into smaller families, of the great kindreds of early times from about the thirteenth century. In England this dissolution of the ties of kindred began earlier than elsewhere because of Scandinavian inroads followed by the Norman Conquest.[3]

It is with the Normans that family surnames come into the English picture. They must be distinguished from personal surnames such as are found among the Vikings, whether patronymics (Godred Olafsson, Egil Skallagrimsson) or descriptive nicknames (Harald Fairhair, Thorstein the Red, Ivar the Boneless, Eric Bloodaxe) which did not pass from father to son. Such names become family names only when the son of a Richard Basset (short) or Grimbald Pauncefote (round belly) uses his father's nickname as his own surname merely because it was his father's; or when the son of William FitzAlan (son of Alan) is himself known as William FitzAlan (instead of William FitzWilliam).

By far the greatest number of Norman surnames, however, are local, deriving from the family's place of origin or its chief lordship. These in the course of centuries suffered varying degrees of Anglicization and corruption. Bohun became Boone, Craon Crowne, Glanville Glanfield, Estouteville Stutfield, Turville Tuffill and Tuffield, Helion (from Helléan) Hellings and Hilling,[4] Normanville Nornable and so on. A certain number of Norman families (Stafford, Marston, Clare, Shirley, Wrottesley, Windsor, Gresley, Clifford and perhaps Clinton and Montagu) took their surnames from English lordships or homes acquired after the Conquest, but the majority, at least of those whose Norman origin can be proved, derive their names from places in France.

[1] F. M. Stenton, op. cit., p. 28.
[2] *Dialogus de Scaccario*, tr. and ed. Charles Johnson, 1950, p. 53.
[3] Marc Bloch, *Feudal Society*, 1961, chaps. ix, x, pp. 123–5, 137–41.
[4] P. H. Reaney, *The Origin of English Surnames*, 1967, pp. 63–64.

Older genealogists have been inclined to accept the derivation of such families from places bearing their names in France without requiring much further proof. Thus the derivation of the name of Robert de Brus, the ancestor of the de Brus Lords of Skelton in Yorkshire as well as the Bruces of Annandale, later Kings of Scotland, from Brix in the *arrondissement* of Valognes has been accepted.[1] Loyd, however, thought the evidence insufficient.[2] Another Norman family which acquired the kingdom of Scotland shows the traps which await incautious genealogists. It was long supposed that Guy de Balliol, the ancestor of the Balliols of Barnard Castle, Co. Durham, of whom were the founder of Balliol College, Oxford, and his son the King of Scotland, came from Bailleul-Neuville near Rouen.[3] Round, however, showed that he came not from Normandy at all but from Bailleul-en-Vimeu in Picardy.[4] But the depth of the pitfall was only seen when Loyd identified two other distinct families of Balliol, both from Normandy, one as really coming from Bailleul-Neuville and the other from Bailleul-en-Gouffern, in the department of Orne.[5]

Even when there is only one place of a name it is possible for more than one family to derive a surname from it, if its ancestor's description as 'of such and such a place' merely means that he lived or was born there.[6] At the date we are considering, however, such a description is likely to signify lordship of the place, and though conceivable, it is unlikely that distinct families should derive the same surname from lordship of or in the same place. Where, however, there are more places of a name than one, we should not be surprised to find distinct families of the same name derived from each of them. Round puts the point with his usual force in the course of his demonstration of the distinct origins of the Grenvilles ultimately Dukes of Buckingham and the Grenvilles or Granvilles of the West Country.[7] Loyd distinguishes three families or Mandeville, derived respectively from Manneville, Magneville and Manneville-sur-Risle,[8] and two families of Aubigny (Daubeney, de Albini) from Saint-Martin d'Aubigny and Saint-Aubin d'Aubigné.[9] In modern genealogy one has in the same way always to

---

[1] *Complete Peerage*, ii. 358.                  [2] *Anglo-Norman Families*, viii. 43.

[3] *Complete Peerage*, i. 385.

[4] J. H. Round, *Calendar of Documents in France*, p. 513, and see *Northumberland County History*, vi. 72.                  [5] *Anglo-Norman Families*, p. 11.

[6] C. L'Estrange Ewen, *A History of Surnames of the British Isles*, 1931, p. 229, quotes early instances of this from 'des Rôles de Taille Parisiens, 1292–1313'.

[7] J. H. Round, *Family Origins*, 1930, pp. 130–3.

[8] Op. cit., pp. 57–59.                  [9] Ibid., p. 7. See p. 72.

remember that the frequency of such place names as Hill and Wood, Lee and Mill, Burton, Hampton and Ford is reflected in the occurrence of totally distinct families of these names.

Direct proof that a Norman of the generation of the Conquest derived a surname from a particular place is surprisingly rare. There are, of course, well known instances. The family of Ralph de Tony, who was at Hastings with the Conqueror, had held Tony since the tenth century,[1] the great house of Warenne, Earls of Surrey, held Varenne near Arques before the Conquest,[2] and their Mortimer kinsmen held Mortemer-sur-Eaulne before 1054.[3] In most cases, however, the link with the Norman place of origin has to be established from evidence of a date well after the Conquest and often by inference. The scantiness of direct evidence about most of those who took part in the Conquest is shown by the shortness of the list of those who can be proved to have fought at Hastings with the Conqueror in 1066. In the opinion of Mr. Geoffrey White only fifteen can be proved to have taken part in the battle, though a further five can be shown to have been in William's army and almost certainly at Hastings.[4] From only one of these, William Malet, can a probable male line descent to the present day be shown,[5] though female line descents can be proved from several.

Where an Anglo-Norman family kept the lands in Normandy from which its name was taken as late as the twelfth century, as Richard de Glanville held Glanville in Calvados down to the loss of Normandy by the Kings of England in 1205,[6] the proof of its origin is easy. But usually the inference is more complicated. Loyd concludes that the Gamage family of Mansell Gamage, Herefordshire, must have come from Gamaches near Les Andelys and not from the better known Gamaches near Abbeville, from the fact that Matthew de Gamaches, whose relationship to the Herefordshire line is proved, about 1184 gave the abbey of Lyre in Normandy a grange in Flipou which is near the first named Gamaches.[7]

In other cases the feudal groupings give the clue. Ferrers, Earl of Derby, must be derived from Ferrières-Saint-Hilaire, but Ferrers of Devonshire from Ferrières near Mortain, because feudal tenants of the

---

[1] *Complete Peerage*, xii, pt. i, p. 753; p. 71.

[2] Loyd, 'The Origin of the Family of Warenne', *Yorkshire Arch. Journ.* xxxi. 97–113.

[3] *Complete Peerage*, ix. 266.

[4] *The Genealogists' Magazine*, vi. 51–53; ix. 417–24; *Complete Peerage*, xii, pt. i, app. L, pp. 47–48; see also Professor D. C. Douglas in *History*, xxviii. 129–47.

[5] p. 66.                                                    [6] Loyd, op. cit., p. 46.

[7] Op. cit., p. 45.

Derby family are linked with the neighbourhood of the former and the feudal overlords of the Devon family with that of the latter.[1] Group settlement in the nature of the case reproduces old patterns in the new setting and the genealogist must not neglect the clues this offers him whether it be a Pilgrim Father[2] or a Norman knight whose origin he seeks. For the tracing of knightly pedigrees, from the eleventh century to the fourteenth, it is the analysis of feudal or tenurial links and patterns that must guide us most of the time.

Where a Norman place name seemed rare or unique Loyd rightly required less corroboration of a surname's derivation from it. The derivation of the ancestor of the Oglander family of the Isle of Wight from Orglandes is, as it happens, well evidenced, but even had it not been the rare name would have afforded a strong presumption. The evidence linking the English Umfrevilles with Offranville near Dieppe might have seemed too weak had the place name been commoner.

Descents can be traced by female lines to the present day from many of Loyd's three hundred or so ascertained Norman families, but when one looks for existing male line descendants the picture is different. Fiefs in England were descendible to heirs general so that, if the lord of a manor left a daughter but no son, she would succeed in preference to her father's younger brothers or heirs male and if she married and left issue would carry the inheritance to another name. Younger sons might acquire fiefs for themselves by marriage to an heiress or service to a lord, but in such a case evidence of their own origin, being irrelevant to their new position, may be hard or impossible to find. Name, heraldry and tradition make it likely that the St. Johns of Bletsoe and the Lords Bolingbroke are cadets of St. John of Basing, whose male line ancestor, Hugh de Port, was a tenant in chief in 1086 and witnessed a charter of the Conqueror before the Conquest. But in fact their ancestry has not been proved beyond Alexander de St. John of Instow, Devonshire, living in 1340.[3]

The surviving line of the great house of Basset, which possessed Tehidy, Cornwall, from soon after 1205 to 1915, can show a clear descent from Osmund Basset of Ipsden, Oxfordshire, in the reign of Henry I (1100–35) and is linked by strong heraldic and other presumptive evidence with the baronial lines of Basset of Weldon, Drayton, Sapcote and Wycombe. Yet the actual link has not been found or

[1] Op. cit., p. 42.                                                                    [2] p. 296.
[3] *Complete Peerage*, xi. 316, 333–4; J. Brownbill in *The Genealogists' Magazine*, v. 355–9.

proved.[1] There is a similar difficulty in linking different lines of Giffard which are yet in all probability of one stock.[2] So late as 1300 we should be unable to show the exact relationship of Sir Hugh Wake (d. 1315) of Blisworth, Northamptonshire, ancestor of the existing Wakes of Courteenhall, to the old line of Wake of Liddell, were it not for a chance reference to him in a roll of arms as *Sire Huge Wake, le oncle*, which makes it clear that he was uncle to the then head of the family.[3] It was only in the fourteenth century that the decay of feudal tenures and changes in legal practice began to make it easier for landowners to endow their younger sons by dividing their property.[4]

If cadet lines which retained knightly status are hard to link to the main stem, how much harder are those which came down in the world, as many may well have done though the evidence so far brought to light is very scanty. An instance, discussed later,[5] is that of Giffard of Dry Drayton, Cambridgeshire, where it looks as if younger branches of a knightly house, for whom knightly fiefs could not be found, had sunk into the position of free tenants or franklins (later called yeomen) on lands of which the head of their house had once been lord. A man named Robert Pomerai in 1285 could scarcely be of other than Norman descent, yet he is recorded as a villein, a customary tenant of the widow of John de Meriet, a Somersetshire knight.[6] Perhaps an explanation may be found in the fact that Terry de la Pomerai, lodging at Merriott (Meriet) in 1265, was a landless malefactor, who took part with the rebels against Henry III.[7] In 1355 John Pomerai held a free tenement in Buckerell, Devonshire, where the Pomerais of Berry Pomeroy were lords of the manor, while of Margaret, the widow of John Beauchamp of Ryme Intrinseca, he held as a villein and Bartholomew Pomeray likewise was her villein.[8] A Yorkshire knight wrote to a cousin in 1486 that he was 'a poore gentilman borne thof he never werr taken heir bot for a yoman'.[9] Other apparent examples of family decline are mentioned in a later chapter (pp. 214–22).

The explanation of a fifteenth century yeoman's Norman name might sometimes be female descent from a knightly house through a

[1] *The Ancestor*, xi. 55–56; Dugdale, *Baronage*, i. 378–85; *Burke's Landed Gentry*, 1952.
[2] pp. 67–71.     [3] *The Ancestor*, ii. 112–13.
[4] May McKisack, *The Fourteenth Century*, Oxford, 1959, pp. 260–1, citing K. B. McFarlane's unpublished Ford Lectures, 1953, 'The English Nobility 1290–1536'.
[5] p. 69.
[6] Edward B. Powley, *The House of De la Pomerai*, 1944, p. 50.
[7] Ibid., p. 49.     [8] Ibid., p. 73.
[9] S. Thrupp, *The Merchant Class of Medieval London*, p. 238, citing *York Civic Records*, Yorks Arch. Soc., Rec. Ser., 103, 1941, pt. i, 169.

coheir. The Montagus of Boughton, Northamptonshire, who acquired a barony in 1621, an earldom in 1689, the dukedom of Montagu in 1705, and in their younger branches the earldom of Manchester in 1626, the dukedom of Manchester in 1719, and the earldom of Sandwich in 1660, descend from Richard Montagu alias Ladde, a yeoman or husbandman, living in 1471 at Hanging Houghton, Northamptonshire, where the Laddes had been tenants since the fourteenth century. Alias names, in some respects the forerunners of the modern compound (or double-barrelled) name, were common in the Middle Ages. In the earliest times, when surnames were new, an alias may just mean indecision between equally attractive alternatives. Later they sometimes indicate bastardy (one name perhaps being the father's and one the mother's), but in most cases probably mark inheritance through an heiress whose name was thus perpetuated.[1] A good case has been made out for the possibility that the Ladde alias came from a division among coheirs about 1420 of the remaining small inheritance of a line of Montagus at Spratton and Little Creton, also in Northamptonshire.[2] This line was of knightly origin and probably a branch of the baronial Montagus (Earls of Salisbury from 1337), whose almost certain ancestor Dru de Montagud was a tenant-in-chief in 1086.[3] Other yeoman Montagus are found in Buckinghamshire from 1354 when Roger Montagu appears as a witness to a quitclaim of land in Great Kimble,[4] notably in Halton where a family of Montagu alias Elot held land from about 1440 to 1610. A line of Montagus found in Waddesdon from about 1540 may have branched from these. These in the eighteenth century were shepherds and drovers and one set up in Aylesbury as a wheelwright and another as a tailor.[5] Another line, also possibly branched from Halton, is found at Boveney and Dorney in the sixteenth and seventeenth centuries. This produced Richard Montagu, Bishop of Chichester (1628–38) and Norwich (1638–41), and Peter Montagu, who settled in Virginia.[6] It should be made quite clear, however, that the suggested links between these several families, though not unlikely, are but guesswork. Other cases of the kind are mentioned hereafter.[7]

Such instances may help to show why, rare as is a proved male descent from a thirteenth century knight with a Norman name, a male descent from an actual proved Norman invader is much rarer still.

[1] P. H. Reaney, *The Origin of English Surnames*, 1967, p. 85.
[2] *Complete Peerage*, ix, app. D.                                              [3] Ibid., p. 75.
[4] De Banco Rolls, charters 377, mem. 1, ex. inf. A. Vere Woodman, F.S.A.
[5] An ancestor of the writer.                              [6] Harleian Soc. lviii. 93.
[7] See p. 214, n. 4.

Such a genealogy can only be looked for among lords of manors—
not merely in the knightly class. And even among these the lack of
record in the first two centuries after the Conquest usually makes an
insurmountable barrier. Most of the cases where this can be surmounted
are in the great baronial families whose descents are noticed by the
chroniclers or preserved by the record of their benefactions to religious
houses. But with these baronial lines one has the contrary difficulty that
they do not last down to the present day, but succumb to civil strife,
royal jealousy, their own imprudence, or the failure of heirs male.
Where descents from such families can be proved they are usually
those of younger branches.

The barons of the Conqueror were a close knit group, much linked
by cousinship and marriage with him and with each other. Most of
those who became barons in England seem to have been barons in
Normandy, though the fortunes of a few, such as Roger Bigod and
Hugh de Port, were made by the Conquest.[1] Professor D. C. Douglas
concludes that a new Norman aristocracy took its rise from the early
eleventh century and cites the families of Tony,[2] Beaumont, Vernon
and Montfort-sur-Risle.[3] Robert of Torigny's pedigrees, he points
out, suggest that the advancement of the kin of the Duchess Gunnor,
widow of Duke Richard I, some of whom certainly acquired former
ducal lands, may have been a factor in the rise of many houses in the
reign of Richard's son Richard II (996–1026).[4] On the whole the
great families of the Conquest kept their eminence for some generations
thereafter, though newcomers joined them, rising by several routes—
marriage, military prowess and the favour of their lords—but chiefly
by household and administrative service to the king. The great house,
whose principal English branch took its name from Clare in Suffolk and
acquired the earldoms of Hertford, Pembroke and Gloucester, was a
bastard branch of the house of the Dukes of Normandy (they were
Counts of Brionne before the Conquest) and endured in the senior
male line to 1314 and in its younger branch, that of the Lords Fitz-
Walter, to 1471. It is possible, though not proved, that the Lords
Moels (1299–1337), whose name came from Meulles in Calvados, were
male descendants of Baldwin the sheriff a son of Count Gilbert of

[1] F. M. Stenton, *Anglo-Saxon England*, p. 623; Loyd, op. cit. vii. D. C. Douglas,
*William the Conqueror*, 1964, pp. 84–85, utters a caution, however, against acceptance
without corroboration of the famous Norman genealogies added by Robert of Torigny
in the late twelfth century to the chronicle of William of Jumièges (ed. Marx, pp. 320–9).
[2] p. 71.                                                          [3] pp. 43, 65.
[4] Douglas op. cit., 1964, pp. 85–89.

Brionne, ancestor of the Clares,[1] and it is also possible, though quite unproved, that the family of Mules of Ernsborough and Halmeston, Devon, of which descendants probably exist, sprang from a Moels cadet.[2] Henry de Ferrers, a prominent counsellor of the Conqueror, was the son of Walkelin, Lord of Ferrières, who was killed in the civil wars which divided Normandy in the Conqueror's minority. He founded a house in England which acquired the earldom of Derby in 1138 but lost it in 1266 through the confiscation of the lands of his earldom following rebellion. This, presumably, would not affect his peerage dignity of earl in modern peerage law and a claim to it by his heir would raise interesting questions. Male descendants of the last earl held the baronies of Ferrers of Chartley (1299–1450) and Ferrers of Groby (1299–1445). The Ferrers of Tamworth, cadets of the Groby line, lasted till 1680, while male descendants of their cadets, the Ferrers of Baddesley Clinton, Warwickshire, still exist.[3]

Roger Bigod, an important counsellor of the Conqueror, is placed by Loyd at the head of those men, of no particular importance in Normandy, whose fortunes were made by the Conquest, probably through the patronage of his lord Odo, Bishop of Bayeux, the Conqueror's half-brother.[4] His grandson Hugh Bigod was made Earl of Norfolk in 1140–1, and the family held this earldom until Earl Roger Bigod (d. 1306) surrendered this and his office of Marshal of England to King Edward I. The validity of his surrender of the earldom was not questioned until recent times, but in 1906 the House of Lords decided that it was invalid and thus avoided the need for a decision on Lord Mowbray's claim to the earldom of Norfolk conferred by Edward II on his younger brother Thomas of Brotherton in 1312. By the 1906 decision Edward II's creation of 1312 was ruled invalid, so that there was no earldom for Lord Mowbray to claim. The editor of the *Complete Peerage* criticizes the 1906 decision in severe terms, but the essence of the matter is summed up in his last words, that 'this judgment affords a very good example of the different point of view from which lawyers and genealogists regard a question of peerage law'.[5]

According to a contemporary chronicler, Walter of Guisborough, the reason for Roger Bigod's surrender of his earldom and office—which was not to and did not take effect till his death—was that he had

---

[1] *Complete Peerage*, ix, p. i.

[2] Lysons, *Devonshire*, p. ci; *Burke's Landed Gentry*, 1853 supp., p. 238.

[3] *Complete Peerage*, iv. 190–203; v. 305–21, 333, 340–58; *Burke's Landed Gentry*, 1937, 1952.

[4] *Anglo-Norman Families*, vii. 14–15.　　　　　　　[5] *Complete Peerage*, vi. app. E.

borrowed money from his brother John (d. 1305) a very wealthy man. When John asked to be repaid the earl pointed out that as he had no son John would inherit all he had. John answered that he did not care about the inheritance but wanted his money. Roger thereupon in a huff went to the king and made an agreement to surrender to him his earldom, the marshalcy and all his lands in return for a regrant of them to him for life only with additional lands worth £1,000 a year. The 1906 decision, however, invalidating this agreement so far as it relates to the earldom, seems to leave the way open for John's heirs, if they could prove themselves such, to claim it. To trace them, however, is not easy. Sir John Bigod had three sons. The male line, and probably the whole issue, of the eldest became extinct in 1416, but male heirs of the second continued at Settrington in Yorkshire down to 1569.[1] Dorothy, the sister and heir of the last Ralph Bigott of Settrington, who died in that year, left issue by her husband Roger Radclyffe of Mulgrave Castle, but her grandson, another Roger Radclyffe, parted with his property and the fate of his progeny is obscure.[2] A cadet male branch of the Settrington Bigods continued near by at Scagglethorpe down to about 1630 and it is possible that a yeoman family of the name, resident at Barton on Humber from 1664 till recently, descends from them.[3] It is not improbable that Bygod Eggleston, who was baptized at Settrington in 1586 and settled about 1630 at Windsor, Connecticut,[4] where he left issue of which many descendants now exist, had some female Bygod descent.

The best hope of adding to the very small number of proved male descents from Norman subjects of the Conqueror lies in tracing such unknown cadet lines of the great baronial families, whose early generations are already proved or at least strongly indicated by presumptive evidence. It is very likely, for example, that the Montforts of Beaudesert, Warwickshire, were cadets of the pre-Conquest house of Montfort-sur-Risle of whom Hugh de Montfort was at Hastings.[5] The last Lord Montfort of Beaudesert died in 1369–70, but left a bastard, Richard de Montfort of Kingshurst, Warwickshire, whose male descendants

[1] Rev. Charles Moor, 'The Bygods, Earls of Norfolk', *Yorkshire Arch. Soc. Journ.* xxxii, 1935, pp. 172–213.

[2] Surtees, *Durham*, iii. 129; Francis, son of Roger Radcliff, entered University College, Oxford, in 1638 and Gray's Inn in 1642. His father is described as of Mulgrave Castle.

[3] Moor, op. cit.

[4] C. A. Torrey, 'English Origin of Bygod Eggleston', *The American Genealogist*, x. 1933, p. 197.

[5] *Complete Peerage*, ix. 120–30; Loyd, op. cit., p. 68; D. C. Douglas, *The Domesday Monachorum of Christ Church, Canterbury*, pp. 65–70.

continued to the eighteenth century[1] and probably exist still. If Robert de Neufbourg, who held Winfrith Newburgh, Dorset, about 1130 could have been identified, as Hutchins thought he could, with his namesake the son of Henry Earl of Warwick, a family of Newbery, Newberry or Newbury, widespread today on the Devon and Dorset border, perhaps with a branch in New England, might possibly be derived from Thorold, lord of Pont-Audemer, a follower of Duke Richard I of Normandy (d. 996). This identification has, however, been disproved. From Robert of Winfrith to the seventeenth century the line appears clear and Dorset wills and modern directories show the name continuing in the same places. The derivation from this line of Thomas Newberry (1594–1635) the 1634 settler at Dorchester, Massachusetts, which has been suggested seems incorrect, yet he may descend from it somehow.[2]

It is generally accepted that the Malets of Curry Malet, Somerset, the last of whom was a surety of Magna Carta, were descended from William Malet who was at Hastings in 1066, though the line of descent in the early twelfth century is not clearly proved.[3] A plausible theory of the derivation of the Malets of Enmore (c. 1166–1656) from those of Curry Malet was put forward by Lt. Col. G. E. G. Malet[4] and male cadet branches of the Enmore line are extant.[5] Through female lines its senior coheir was the great genealogist John Horace Round (1854–1928).[6] Could the early links but be made clear beyond all doubt the Malets would have the unique distinction of a proved male descent from a man who fought at Hastings. An example of a non-baronial male descent from the Conqueror's day is that of Nevile of Thorney, Nottinghamshire, and Aubourn, Lincolnshire. Sir Charles Clay has given reasons for believing that Jollan de Neville (dead 1208) of

[1] Dugdale, *Warwickshire*, 1765, ed. p. 715; Harleian Soc. xii (*Visitation of Warwick, 1619*), p. 56; Wm. Salt Soc. v, pt. ii (*Visitation of Stafford, 1663*), pp. 219–20, 'The entries in the Walsall registers from this date [1701] are numerous, and it is pretty evident that the ancient family of Mountfort is not yet extinct.' T. C. Willmore, *History of Walsall*, p. 282. Harleian Soc. li (Lincs. Peds.), pp. 696–7. Mr. E. J. Homeshaw informs me that this line was represented by Mr. Charles Mountfort, saddler's ironmonger of Walsall, who died in March 1960.

[2] William Farrer, *Honors and Knights' Fees*, vol. i, p. 39; J. H. Round, *The King's Serjeants*, p. 123; I. J. Sanders, *English Baronies*, 1960, pp. 72–73; *Sir Christopher Hatton's Book of Seals*, ed. L. C. Loyd and D. M. Stenton, 1950, pp. 240–1; Hutchins, *History of Dorset*, 3rd ed., 1868, vol. i, pp. 366–8, 429, 436–7, 708–12; *Complete Peerage*, vii. 520–1, xii. ii, 357 and app. A; J. Gardner Bartlett, *Newberry Genealogy The Ancestors and Descendants of Thomas Newberry of Dorchester, Mass., 1934*, Boston, 1914.

[3] Dugdale, *Baronage*, i. 110–11.    [4] *The Genealogists' Magazine*, viii. 316–24.
[5] *Burke's Peerage* and *Landed Gentry*.    [6] *Complete Peerage*, xi. 49 n.

Pickhill, Yorkshire, Rigsby, Lincolnshire and Rolleston, Nottingham-shire, the ancestor of this family, was third in descent from Losoard, probably a Breton, the Domesday tenant of Rigsby. Mr. H. R. Nevile of Thorney is probably twenty fifth in descent from Losoard. Clay suggests that the surname Nevile came in through the marriage of Rocelin, father of Jollan, to a daughter of Gilbert de Neville (dead 1169), ancestor by another female line of the Nevilles of Raby.[1]

## (i) *Giffard*

The Giffards were of the inner circle of the Conqueror's barons, related to him by the marriage of their first known ancestor Osbern de Bolebec to Wevie, sister of Gunnor, wife or concubine of Richard I, Duke of Normandy (d. 996), and great-grandmother of the Conqueror. Robert of Torigny says that Walter Giffard, Lord of Bolebec and Longueville, who was with the Conqueror at Hastings in 1066, was son of Osbern and Wevie, but Mr. G. A. Moriarty argues on chrono-logical grounds that he was their grandson, the son of another Walter their son.[2]

Walter Giffard who was at Hastings had (with a younger son William Giffard, d. 1129, Chancellor of England and Bishop of Winchester) a son and namesake, who seems to have been made Earl of Buckingham and died in 1102 leaving a son Walter Giffard, Earl of Buckingham, who died childless in 1164.[3] At his death there remained, however, two lesser but still baronial lines of Giffard, that of Brimpsfield in Glou-cestershire and that of Fonthill in Wiltshire, whose feudal connections with the Earls of Buckingham and with each other show that they must have been related, though the precise relationship has not been proved.[4]

The ancestor of the Brimpsfield line was Osbern Giffard, who 'came to the Conquest' and was tenant in chief of Brimpsfield and many other manors in 1086. Mr. Moriarty suggests that he was a younger brother of Walter, who was at Hastings, but proof is lacking.

His descendants continued as barons at Brimpsfield till 1322, when John, Lord Giffard, having fought against the king was captured after the battle of Boroughbridge and hanged at Gloucester.[5] He left no

---

[1] C. T. Clay, *Early Yorkshire Charters*, vol. v., *The Honour of Richmond Part II*, 1936, pp. 154–6; Drummond, *Noble British Families*, ii, Nevile, Tab. VII; *Burke's Landed Gentry*: *Complete Peerage*, ix. 492.

[2] *New England Hist. and Gen. Reg.* cv. 292–4.      [3] *Complete Peerage*, ii. 386–7.

[4] 'The Giffards', by Major General the Hon. George Wrottesley, *William Salt Society Collections*, new ser. v, 1902; *The Ancestor*, iii. 223–8.

[5] *Complete Peerage*, v. 639–49.

sons but the male line was continued by the descendants of his grandfather's younger brother Sir Osbern Giffard (d. 1237) of Winterborne
Houghton, Dorset.[1] From Sir Osbern's younger son Sir John Giffard
of Twyford, Buckinghamshire, called 'le Boef',[2] descended a line which
continued there till 1550.[3] A cadet of this line, Roger Giffard (d. 1543),
leased the manor of Middle Claydon, Buckinghamshire, from the
Verney family in 1495, and his younger son Nicholas (d. 1546),[4] who
was active in the work of dissolving the monasteries under Thomas
Cromwell, obtained in 1545 a grant of the house and lands of the former
St. James Abbey, Northampton, which his grandson, however, sold
in 1637.

Another grandson, a clergyman, continued the line and the next two
generations of the family included six parsons, besides London tradesmen, both often found at this date in the younger lines of prolific gentle
families.

In 1780 John Giffard (1766–1855), the son of a London skinner of
this branch, entered the Navy and after long and distinguished service
became an admiral in 1841. Many of his descendants have served in the
forces, among them the late General Sir George Giffard, who was
twenty fourth in descent from Osbern the Domesday tenant.[5]

Other male branches of the Giffards of Brimpsfield probably exist
and one at least has been traced down to the present century, though
branching off so far back as the twelfth. This line descends from Walter
Giffard of Boyton, Wiltshire, younger brother of the third Elis
Giffard of Brimpsfield.[6] His son Sir Hugh Giffard (d. 1246), who raised
himself in the royal service and by a wealthy marriage, was father of
Walter Giffard (d. 1279), Archbishop of York and Godfrey Giffard
(d. 1301), Bishop of Worcester, both Chancellors of England. They
had a brother Sir William Giffard, who inherited from them lands at
Itchell in Hampshire and Weston under Edge in Gloucestershire, which
his descendants kept down to the sixteenth century.[7] If a modern

---

[1] *Complete Peerage*, v. 650.

[2] G. A. Moriarty proved his parentage in *The Genealogist*, new ser. xxxviii.
91–98.

[3] G. A. Moriarty in *New England Hist. and Gen. Reg.*, pp. 74, 75.

[4] Nicholas's daughter Margaret married Hugh Sargent of Courteenhall and their
grandson William Sargent, who settled at Charlestown, Massachusetts, about 1638, has
many American descendants. Hence the interest of the well known American genealogist
Mr. Moriarty in the Giffards.

[5] *Burke's Landed Gentry*, 1937, 1952.

[6] *The Genealogists' Magazine*, vii. 250.

[7] Wrottesley, op. cit., pp. 53–59; *Victoria County History, Hampshire*, iv. 7.

pedigree may be trusted[1] cadets of this line settled in Ireland and have survived there to the present century.

The other baronial line of Giffard, that of Fonthill, Wiltshire, which Berenger Giffard held in 1086, is linked with the Brimpsfield line by the fact that Gerard Giffard of Fonthill held a knight's fee under Elis Giffard of Brimpsfield in 1166, while both families obtained large feoffments of land from William Giffard (d. 1129), Bishop of Winchester, who was certainly a brother of Walter, Earl of Buckingham.[2] The Fonthill main line expired in 1220 but it is almost certain that Peter Giffard, who was granted Chillington, Staffordshire, about 1178, belonged to it, though his exact descent cannot be ascertained.[3] From that day to this Chillington has remained in the male line of Giffard and the present Mr. T. A. W. Giffard of Chillington is nineteenth in descent from Peter.

The group of knightly Devonshire families of Giffard,[4] from one of which the Earl of Halsbury descends, were doubtless one family, but there is so far no demonstration that their probable common ancestor Walter Giffard, who held Aveton Giffard in the first half of the twelfth century, was akin to the Earls of Buckingham, though his Christian name suggests it and General Wrottesley has conjectured that he may have been of the Fonthill branch.[5]

There is another family of Giffard of which I wrote some years ago that it could be shown with certainty to have no connection with the rest.[6] That may have been too positive, but certainly there is so far no indication of a link and the surname of this family seems to begin with a Robert, son of Giffard, living in 1130 whose father Giffard apparently bore this as a *Christian* name, whereas the Giffards of Bolebec and Buckingham bore it as a surname before 1066. Robert's father was probably the Giffard of Drayton who was a juror for the hundred of Chesterton in Cambridgeshire for the great survey of 1086 which Domesday Book records. There is reason to think[7] that this Giffard was the brother of a certain Robert, an Usher of the King's Court, who held land in Westwick, the parish adjoining Dry Drayton and also (assuming that it was the same Robert the Usher) in Howes and Long Clawson, Leicestershire. The odd chance of a duplicate entry of the relevant section of Domesday Book in that case takes us back another

---

[1] *Burke's Landed Gentry of Ireland*, 1912, p. 265.
[2] Wrottesley, op. cit., p. 12.   [3] Ibid., p. 85; *The Ancestor*, iii. 225; vi. 143–5.
[4] Wrottesley, op. cit., pp. 19–44.   [5] Op. cit., p. 17.
[6] *New England Hist. and Gen. Reg.* xcv. 240.
[7] I have discussed the evidence more fully in *New England Hist. and Gen. Reg.* xcv. 241.

generation, for Robert is entered once as 'the Usher' and the second time as 'son of William the Usher'.[1] William the Usher (if all the entries relate to the same man) is more prominent in Domesday Book than his son, holding land of the king in two places in Nottinghamshire and ten places in Devon.

In the Pipe Roll of 1130 the Cambridgeshire return records that Robert the Usher, son of Giffard, paid one gold mark and seven ounces for his father's office, and there is reason to think that this was the Robert Giffard who was party to a division of lands in Dry Drayton in that county with Edward, abbot of Crowland (1143–73), and other lords of manors there. The next three generations in Dry Drayton were still of knightly status but like many knights before the enactment of the Statute of Mortmain in 1279 they reduced their patrimony by gifts to religious houses, in this case Crowland Abbey and Barnwell Priory. Roger Giffard of Oakington was among the tenants of the Abbot of Crowland 'who was in the Isle of Ely against the Lord King' and among those condemned to confiscation of lands by the Parliament of 1265. Though redemption of forfeited property was allowed in 1266 by the Mise of Kenilworth, it seems likely that this may explain the decline of the knightly Giffards.[2] In the middle of the thirteenth century a Barnwell record makes mention of several lesser Giffards holding small acreages as tenants of Roger Giffard, the then head of the house, and in the next century, when the senior line seems to vanish, Giffards who must descend from such poor relations are still found in Dry Drayton and adjoining Oakington as free tenants of the abbots of Crowland. From 1290 to 1528 the splendid manorial rolls kept for the monks preserve for us a continuous series if not actually a pedigree of Giffard names until with Henry Giffard, who made a will in 1496, we reach a connected line of substantial yeomen, whose progeny is traced to the present day. Between 1564 and 1664 the Dry Drayton parish register records no fewer than 193 Giffard baptisms, a large proportion of which can be fitted into their places in the pedigree.

George (d. 1600), son of Boniface Giffard of Dry Drayton, entered Christ's College, Cambridge, in 1570 and became vicar of Maldon, Essex, and a puritan divine of enough distinction to find a place in the

[1] J. H. Round, *Feudal England*, pp. 26–27.
[2] Frances M. Page, *The Estates of Crowland Abbey, A Study in Manorial Organisation*, 1934, p. 64; *Retuli Selecti ex Archivis in domo Capitulari Westmonasteriensi*, Pipe Roll Soc., p. 236.

*Dictionary of National Biography.* His son John Giffard, rector of Hoxton, obtained a grant of arms in 1626. The design is amusing for it combines elements from the arms of both the Brimpsfield and the Chillington Giffards, who had at most only a remote connection with each other and possibly none at all with this family.

James Giffard, born at Dry Drayton in 1686, was in all probability fourth in descent from a brother of the vicar of Maldon. His son James (1714–74) was apprenticed in Cambridge and prospering there as a wine merchant at length became alderman and mayor. His son 'designed to succeed to his father's business', 'disliking trade' retired from it and lived on his fortune at Quy Hall near Cambridge, which his son (James Giffard, 1775–1849), finding most of the fortune gone, sold and entered the Church. Two generations of clergymen followed him and the late representative was Major W. L. Giffard of Epsom.

Though a continuous pedigree cannot be proved, the identity of the family from Giffard of Drayton in 1086 to the present day descendants of James Giffard, who was baptized at Drayton in 1686, can hardly be doubted, and what makes this so exceptional is that after about 1300 the Giffards of Drayton were no more than franklins or yeomen.

### (ii) *Tony and Gresley*

In the year 942 William Longsword, Duke of Normandy, invited to Normandy one Hugh (d. 989–90), a Frenchman and a monk of St. Denis and made him Archbishop of Rouen. This Hugh was of noble birth, the son of one Hugh de Calvacamp. He handed over to his brother Ralph the domain of Tosni, which formed part of the estates of the archbishopric, and Ralph's descendants thus became leading barons of the Dukes of Normandy, with whose family they intermarried. This Ralph's great-grandson, another Ralph de Tony (d. *c.* 1102), was at the battle of Hastings with William the Conqueror by whom he was given lands in seven English counties. His descendants in the male line held a high place in the English baronage down to their extinction in 1309.[1] His younger brother Robert de Stafford (d. *c.* 1088) likewise received lands in several counties from the Conqueror, notably in the county of Stafford. Millicent his great-granddaughter and her brother's heir, conveyed these to her husband Hervey Bagot, who thereupon assumed the name of de Stafford, and from them sprang the great house of Stafford, Barons and later Earls of Stafford.[2]

It was Dugdale's opinion that Nigel de Stafford who in 1086 held

---

[1] *Complete Peerage*, xii, pt. i, pp. 753–75.  [2] Ibid., pp. 168–88.

Drakelowe and other Derbyshire manors directly of the king and other manors as a tenant of Henry de Ferrers, was a brother of Robert de Stafford.[1] This would make him a son of Roger de Tony (d. c. 1039) and great-grandson of Hugh de Calvacamp and would give the extant family of Gresley of Drakelowe, which descends from him, a Norman baronial pedigree difficult or impossible to parallel. Unfortunately this identification, though not unlikely, cannot be proved.[2] Even without it the descent of the Gresleys from a Domesday tenant in chief[3] is uncommon in the highest degree. Drakelowe, which their ancestor held in 1086, remained in the family down to the present century, but Round was driven to the conclusion that the family lost Drakelowe, probably by exchanging it for another manor, soon after 1086 and only regained it by a grant in 1170–1.[4]

Throughout the Middle Ages the Gresleys remained a prominent knightly house but no more, their estate varying little up or down. In 1611 Sir George Gresley received a baronetcy among the first creations of that honour, 'an interesting testimony to the character of the class from which it was originally recruited'. The present baronet is twenty eighth in descent from the Domesday tenant.

An ancient confusion has made another notable line into a branch of the Tonys by making Robert de Tony, the Lord of Belvoir in 1086 (who probably was of this Tony family, though the link has not been ascertained),[5] into the father of William d'Aubigny, called 'the Breton' (William de Albini Brito) to distinguish him from a namesake, William d'Aubigny, the Master Butler (Pincerna). William d'Aubigny the Breton did indeed succeed a son of Robert de Tony at Belvoir, but it was, as Round showed, in virtue of his marriage to Robert's grand-daughter Cicely.[6] As if to increase the scope for confusion, Cicely's sister Maud married the other William d'Aubigny, the Butler.[7] From Ralph, a younger son of William d'Aubigny the Breton, sprang the Daubeneys of South Petherton, Somerset, Lords Daubeney (1486) and Earls of Bridgwater (1538–48), of whom cadet lines are still extant.[8]

---

[1] *Baronage*, i. 156.　　　　　　[2] Cf. J. H. Round in *The Ancestor*, i. 195–6.

[3] Falconer Madan, *The Gresleys of Drakelowe*, 1899.

[4] Ibid., p. 197.

[5] Loyd, *Anglo-Norman Families*, p. 104; *Complete Peerage*, xii, pt. i, p. 755 n.

[6] *Hist. MSS. Comm. MSS. of the Duke of Rutland*, iv. 106; *Complete Peerage*, ix. 577.

[7] *Complete Peerage*, ix. 367.

[8] *Burke's Landed Gentry*, 1937 and 1952, where, however, the beginning of the pedigree is involved in confusion.

Though the Conqueror's knights were many and his great barons and close counsellors few, proved descents from the families of the latter are, for reasons which we have discussed, relatively much more common than from those of the former. The descent even of such a family as Talbot (now Earls of Shrewsbury), which had acquired much importance by 1300, has not been proved further back than 1156 though there were Talbots in the Conqueror's time prominent both in England and Normandy whose connection with the later family Loyd thought in the highest degree probable.[1]

The pedigree of a lesser knightly house may be far more obscure, even where the Norman beginning is reasonably clear and the fact of descent from that beginning open to little doubt. Mynors of Herefordshire is an instance. Four generations are clear from Gilbert de Miners about 1100 to Henry who died in 1217 and Loyd sets out the reasons for the conjecture that Gilbert took his name and origin from Les Minières near Breteuil.[2] Between 1226 and 1394 there are references to successive Miners at Burghill (of which the older line had held the manor) and these are linked with the later Treago line by the fact that their charters came to Treago and that Richard Mynors of Treago, who died in 1528, likewise held land in Burghill. Above this Richard's father Philip, however, there is only a traditional pedigree, found in two inconsistent versions, neither linking up with the earlier data and so far unconfirmed by record evidence. The explanation is a local defect of record. But that lack of record did not here mean unimportance is shown by the character of the surviving fifteenth century structure of Treago and the standing of its lords when they begin to be recorded. The male line continued to 1765 and descendants of a daughter who took the name and arms of Mynors have continued to hold Treago down to the present day.

The early pedigree of another Herefordshire family with a Norman name, which later attained great distinction, that of Devereux, is most obscure, as are those of many such families throughout the country. In this case as in many others a sixteenth or seventeenth century genealogist, finding successive occurrences of the name, has unwarrantably strung them into a pedigree. In some such instances proof of the true descent may yet be brought to light by research, but in many more it almost certainly does not exist. There are other cases where a pedigree

---

[1] *Anglo-Norman Families*, p. 100; *Complete Peerage*, xii, pt. i, p. 606.

[2] *Mynors of Treago Co. Hereford*. A Genealogy [by H. C. B. Mynors], printed privately, 1954; *Anglo-Norman Families*, pp. 64–65.

worked out in the seventeeth century may well be right in the main, if not in every detail, yet a fresh critical study of the evidence is needed before one can reach a definite conclusion. Notable among pedigrees awaiting such reassessment are those of Curzon and Villiers.

### (iii) *Clifford and Poyntz*

The sons of Ponz or Poinz, the ancestor of the Cliffords, were by no means magnates of the realm or members of the king's inner circle, though two of them were tenants in chief in 1086. It was from neither of these, but from their brother Richard who made his way by his part in the Norman invasion of South Wales that the Cliffords sprang. His son acquired Clifford Castle on the Welsh border, which gave the family their name.[1] His granddaughter was Fair Rosamund, the mistress of King Henry II, and for four generations the Cliffords were great men on the Welsh border. About 1270 the marriage of Roger de Clifford with the heiress of the Viponts, hereditary sheriffs of Westmorland, transferred their power to the north. In 1525 Henry, Lord Clifford, was created Earl of Cumberland, but his male line expired in 1644. Through a famous lady, Anne Clifford (1590–1676), Countess of Dorset, Pembroke and Montgomery, the vast northern estates of the Cliffords passed through the Tuftons, Earls of Thanet, to the Lords Hothfield.[2]

Sir Lewis Clifford, K.G. (d. 1404), is said by Dugdale to have been a younger son of Roger the 5th Lord Clifford of this line,[3] and from him the Cliffords of Bobbing in Kent claimed descent in the sixteenth century. From a cadet of this house seventeenth century genealogists derived the Cliffords of Borscombe, Wiltshire, ancestors of the existing Lords Clifford of Chudleigh. None of this, however, is as clearly proved as one would wish.

The ancestor of the Poyntz family, Simon, son of Ponz, was in all probability a brother of Richard FitzPonz, the ancestor of the Cliffords. The senior, baronial line of Poyntz expired in 1376, but the cadet line of Iron Acton, Gloucestershire, maintained its importance down to the

---

[1] J. E. Lloyd, *History of Wales*, ii. 429, &c.

[2] Dugdale, *Baronage*, i. 335–46; J. W. Clay, *The Extinct and Dormant Peerages of the Northern Counties*, pp. 21–27.

[3] Sir Iain Moncreiffe, Bt., refers to the useful discussion of Sir Lewis Clifford's parentage and descendants by Sir N. Harris Nicolas, *The Scrope and Grosvenor Roll*, vol. ii, 1832, pp. 427–8, 432–3, where it is shown that Dugdale must be wrong and that Sir Lewis was probably a younger brother of Roger 5th Lord Clifford.

seventeenth century and substantial and clearly proved younger branches have continued to the present day.[1]

## (iv) *Shirley*

It used to be thought that Sewal, the ancestor of the Shirleys, was an Englishman, but the fact that he was in 1086 an undertenant of the Ferrers, while the name Sewal is found on the Continent, suggests that he came with the Normans[2] though no Norman place of origin can be proved for him and his descendants took their surname from Shirley in Derbyshire, where they were granted land before 1165 and own land still. The senior male line from Sewal held Little Ireton in Kedleston, Derbyshire, from the twelfth to the sixteenth century and took from it the surname of Ireton. Of this family was Henry Ireton (1611–51), the regicide, Cromwell's son-in-law and Deputy Governor of Ireland. At the same epoch his remote kinsman, Sir Robert Shirley (d. 1656), the ancestor of the Earls Ferrers, suffered for his loyalty to his king. The inscription over the door of the famous church which he built at Staunton Harold in Leicestershire records that 'In the yeare 1653 when all things Sacred were throughout the nation either demollisht or profaned Sir Robert Shirley, Barronet, Founded this church; Whose singular praise it is, to have done the best things in the worst times, And hoped them in the most callamitous.'[3] The cadet line of Shirley of Ettington enjoys a distinction, which seems to be unique, in possessing still a lordship which its male line ancestor held in 1086—for Sewal held Ettington of Henry de Ferrers at the Domesday survey.

### 4. LONG TENURES

There are indeed other lands which have come down by continuous succession from the same epoch, but in every other case known to me they have passed once or more through females. Thus East Quantockshead in Somerset, which Ralph Paynel held in 1086, passed by the marriage of Frethesant Paynel to Geoffrey Luterel about 1200 and the Luttrells hold it still.[4] Belvoir in Rutland has come down to the Duke of Rutland from Robert de Todeni, who held it in 1086, through the

---

[1] *Complete Peerage*, x. 559–60; Sir John Maclean, *An Historical and Genealogical Memoir of the Family of Poyntz*, 1886. The account in *Burke's Landed Gentry*, 1952, contributed by the present writer, brings Maclean's account up to date.

[2] Cf. *The Ancestor*, iii. p. 215. Professor Eilert Ekwall, however, equates Sewal with a supposed Old English Saewald in *Early London Personal Names*, Lund, 1947, pp. 59–60.

[3] E. P. Shirley, *Stemmata Shirleiana*, 1841 and 1873; *The Ancestor*, iii. 219.

[4] C. T. Clay, *Early Yorkshire Charters*, vi, p. vii.

families of Bigot, d'Aubigny and Ros.[1] Bletsoe in Bedfordshire was held in 1086 by Osbert de Broilg and from him passed by succession through the Pateshull and Beauchamp families to the St. Johns, now Lords St. John of Bletsoe, who hold or recently held it.[2] Bramber Castle in Sussex was held by William de Briouze before 1080 and passed through the Mowbrays to the Howards, Dukes of Norfolk. Scrivelsby in Lincolnshire was held in 1086 by Robert Dispensator to whom succeeded his brother Urse d'Abitot. Roger Marmion held it *c.* 1115–18, having perhaps acquired it by marriage with a daughter of Urse. From the Marmions it passed through the Ludlows to the Dymokes, who hold it to this day by the tenure of performing service as Champion on the day of the King's (or Queen's) Coronation.

Kirklington in Yorkshire is, or was lately, held by the Wandesfordes, who acquired it about 1370 by marriage with the heiress of the Musters family, whose ancestor Robert held it in 1086. In 1937 it had passed through thirty generations.[3] Basing, Hampshire, was the *caput* of the barony of Hugh de Port in 1086. From soon after 1200 his male heirs were named St. John from inheritance through a marriage. This line expired in 1348. Basing then came by marriage to the Poynings family and after 1429 to their heirs the Paulet or Powlett family, with whom it remained until the death of the last Duke of Bolton in 1794. He left this and other estates to his natural daughter, who married Thomas Orde, created Baron Bolton in 1797. With their Orde–Powlett progeny it remains.[4]

Richard Estormit, a servant of the king, held lands adjacent to Savernake Forest in Wiltshire in 1083, and the Esturmys his successors were hereditary Wardens of the Forest and landowners beside it till their male line ended in 1427. Through their heiress office and lands then passed to the Seymours, in due course Dukes of Somerset, and from them by marriage in 1675 to the Bruces, Earls of Ailesbury, and thence in 1747 to the Brudenells, Earls and Marquesses of Ailesbury. The present marquess is probably twenty seventh in descent from Richard Estormit.[5]

[1] *Hist. MSS. Comm. MSS. of the Duke of Rutland,* iv. 106–7; *Complete Peerage,* xi. 95–108.

[2] *Victoria County History, Bedfordshire,* iii. 40–41.

[3] C. T. Clay, *Early Yorkshire Charters,* v. 242–6.

[4] *Complete Peerage,* xi. 316–31: xii. ii, 757–70: ii. 210–17; *Victoria County History, Hampshire,* iv. 116. In 1970 the property was put on the market, but a suggestion made to the family that continuity should be kept by the retention of some minute portion of it has been favourably received.

[5] The Earl of Cardigan, *The Wardens of Savernake Forest,* 1949.

There are other cases of continuity since 1086 and continuity since the twelfth century can be proved in an appreciable number of instances. These include Greystoke, Egremont, Cockermouth, Arundel, Petworth and the manor of Arches in East Hendred in Berkshire. But the longest tenures of all are to be found among church properties such as Tillingham in Essex, which was given to St. Paul's Cathedral by Ethelbert, King of Kent (d. 616) and belongs to the Church still.

## 5. THE NORMANS BEYOND ENGLAND

### (i) *Wales*

In the century and more which followed 1066 many Norman knights, unsatisfied in England, journeyed on to further conquest or fortune in Wales, Ireland and Scotland, and in all these lands their names and progeny are still to be found. Roger, Lord of Montgomery in Calvados, was made Earl of Shrewsbury by the Conqueror in 1074. The new castle of Montgomery which he built in 1086 on the Welsh border was a starting point of attacks on Welsh territory. In 1093 he occupied Cardigan, whence his followers advanced into what is now Pembrokeshire, which the king conferred on Roger's son Arnulf.[1] Normans were established even before 1066 in Shropshire and Herefordshire, where Richard fitzScrob, a Norman favourite of Edward the Confessor, had given his name to Richard's Castle.[2] His son Osbern fitzRichard had married Nest, a daughter of the Welsh prince Gruffydd ap Llewelyn (d. 1063), but this did not prevent their son-in-law Bernard of Neufmarché (near Gournay in eastern Normandy), invading and conquering Brecknock in 1093.[3] About the same time Robert fitzHamon conquered Glamorgan.

In the great seventeenth century collections of Welsh genealogies those of the *Advenae* or *Adventurers* of the several counties of South Wales are separated from those of the native stocks. It is likely that by no means all these families were descended from the first invaders. In some cases this can be shown. J. E. Lloyd[4] concluded that 'the Flemings, the St. Johns and the Stradlings were undoubtedly later arrivals' in Glamorgan, 'notwithstanding the attempts . . . to connect them with the conquest'. Sir Peter de Stradling was connected with Glamorgan by 1298, when he married the heiress of the family of Hawey (de

[1] J. E. Lloyd, *A History of Wales*, ii. 401.    [2] Eyton, *Shropshire*, iv. 302–12.
[3] Lloyd, ii. 397.
[4] *History of Wales*, ii. 441 n.; Lewis D. Nicholl, *The Normans in Glamorgan, Gower and Kidweli*, 1936.

Halweia), who were in Glamorgan by about 1150 but also held land in Devon. The Stradlings held lands which came to them from the Haweys down to the eighteenth century. Sir Peter was probably son of Sir John de Stratelinges, a nephew of Sir Otes de Grandison, the King's Justiciary in Wales in 1284. The Grandisons came from Granson on the lake of Neuchatel in Switzerland[1] and C. J. O. Evans made the plausible suggestion that the Stratelinges or Stradling family came from Strättligen near Thun, not far away.[2] In later days to have come to Glamorgan with FitzHamon or to Brecknock with Bernard of New-march (as he was called) was the equivalent among the Advenae of coming to England with the Conqueror. Little attempt has yet been made to document the traditional pedigrees, but it may be noted that, though most purport to start with the invasion, some seem to lack the requisite number of generations.

Some of the Advenae, however, appear in the first or second genera-tion of settlement as witnesses to charters or as benefactors of monas-teries. In Glamorgan Herbert de St. Quintin, Robert le Sor, William de Londres, Payn de Turbeville, Robert de Sumeri, Richard de Gran-ville and Robert de Umfreville[3] appear in or before 1130; while the Cartulary of Brecon[4] shows that Picards, Turbevilles, Burghills, Walde-boefs, Havards and Baskervilles were among the first settlers in Breck-nock. Theophilus Jones remarked in 1809[5] that the Havards 'have multiplied their species, and their name is more frequently heard in Breconshire at this day, than any other of the followers of Bernard Newmarch'. It exists in South Wales still, though I do not know how far those who bear it can prove their descent. There were Turbervilles both in Brecknock and Glamorgan down to the eighteenth century.[6] The early pedigree, as with all these families, is shaky, but the exis-tence of a descent is hardly doubtful and a common origin with the Turbervilles of Dorset, whom Thomas Hardy transmuted into the D'Urberville ancestors of Tess, is probable.[7]

[1] p. 246.

[2] Nicholl, op. cit., pp. 67 n., 68; *Calendar of Patent Rolls*, 1281–92, p. 373; *The Dictionary of Welsh Biography down to 1940 under the Auspices of the Honourable Society of Cymmrodorion*, 1959, pp. 925–7.

[3] Lloyd, op. cit., ii. 440–1.

[4] *Archaeologia Cambrensis*, iv. xiii, 1882, pp. 275–308; xiv, 1883, pp. 18–49, 137–68, 221–36, 274–311.

[5] *History of Brecknockshire* (1898 ed.), p. 229.

[6] G. T. Clark, *Limbus patrum Morganiae et Glamorganiae*, 1886, pp. 447–62.

[7] G. A. Moriarty wrote to me of a Turbeyfile family of small farmers, mechanics and tradesmen in the back mountains of North Carolina, descended from a settler in Virginia.

That the Normans who came to Wales did not quickly lose the habit of adventure will appear when we come to speak of the invasion of Ireland in which Normans from Pembrokeshire were conspicuous. In one of the Waldeboef (later Walbieffe or Walbeoffe) family of Llanhamlach in Brecknockshire some have discerned an adventurer, who wandered far but came home again, leaving his heirs a claim to a kingdom, though one so ineffectual that they all but forgot it.

The Kingdom of Man and the Isles was ruled by a Norse dynasty till the death of King Magnus in 1265. Alexander II of Scotland then occupied the island and on his death in 1290 Edward I of England claimed it as suzerain. About 1293 two ladies petitioned him to recognize them as heirs of the Norse kings. They were Aufrica de Connoght, kinswoman and heiress of King Magnus (who in 1304 made over her claim to Sir Simon Montagu),[1] and Mary, wife of John Waldboef, daughter of Reginald (d. 1249),[2] later King of Man, brother and predecessor of King Magnus. Mary's claim was renewed in 1305 by her grandson John de Waldboef, son of her son William,[3] but equally without success. Were these Waldboefs of the Brecknock line or of some other such as that of Bedfordshire?[4] Two fragments of evidence, though inconclusive, favour the Brecknock family. The names of a Robert and a William de Waldebeuf occur among those campaigning in Ulster in 1210 in association with names certainly from South Wales, including actually that of a Stephen de Lanhamelach.[5] About the end of the sixteenth century Lewis Dwnn at his Visitation of Wales, set down the traditional descent of the then William Walbeoffe of Llanhamlach and in the tenth generation back showed a Philip Walbyf married to 'Jane doughter to Sir Humphrey Stanley earle of Derby and Lord of the yle of Man'.[6] There is complicated confusion here, for there was no Humphrey, Earl of Derby; the Stanleys were not Lords of Man till

[1] *Complete Peerage*, ix. 79. No evidence has been found for Sir Simon's alleged marriage to her.

[2] Reginald was son of Olaf II (d. 1237), son of Godred II (d. 1187) by Fingola, daughter of Melaghlin O'Loughlin, son of Murtough O'Loughlin (d. 1166), King of Ireland, a descendant of Niall of the Nine Hostages; cf. G. H. Orpen, *Ireland under the Normans*, ii. 11.

[3] *Manx Soc.* vii. 135–6, quoting Roll of Parliament, 33 Edward I. I owe these references to Mr. B. Megaw, Director of the Manx Museum, Douglas.

[4] *Miscellanea Genealogica et Heraldica*, 5th ser. ix. 83.

[5] *Ulster Journ. of Arch.* 3rd ser. iii, 1940; H. C. Lawlor, 'The Vassals of the Earl of Ulster', pp. 20, 22. I owe these references to Mr Megaw. Llanhamlach was the home of the Walbeoffes in Brecknock.

[6] *Heraldic Visitations of Wales*, by Lewis Dwnn, ed. Sir Samuel Rush Meyrick, 1846, ii. 58.

1405 nor Earls of Derby till 1485; and Theophilus Jones thought that Humphrey Stanley was a misreading of the name of Humphry Sollers on a tombstone.[1] All this, however, might be compatible with a faint tradition, surviving in Dwnn's time, of descent from the daughter of a Lord of Man.

John Walbeoffe, in the late seventeenth century,

being [says Jones] of a gay and extravagant turn, left the estate very much incumbered to his son Charles and soon after his death it was foreclosed and sold. . . . The last named John Walbeoffe, besides the children named in the pedigree had several other *by his wife*;[2] it is very singular that at so short a distance of time it is not known what became of the greatest part of them or their descendants. Thomas Walbeoffe of Pen y lan in Glasbury, master and commander in his majesty's navy, great grandson of John, died in 1805 unmarried; he was of opinion that many of them went to America, where the name was well known.

'It remains lingering', says Jones, 'in the hundred of Crickhowell', adding that Charles Walbeoffe, one of the grandsons of John, was an innkeeper and kept the Old Bear in Brecon in 1709, and that he or his brother had left descendants living in his own day, 'though all of them are poor and some have even received parochial relief'.[3] Mr. John William George Walbeoff, meat purveyor, of Phillips Town, Monmouthshire (b. 1902), is fifth in descent from Lewis Walbeoff of Llangenny, Brecknockshire, who married before 1752 and may have sprung from this branch.[4] If any other of this ancient name survives in America or elsewhere, there lies before him an uncommonly exciting prospect of ancestral exploration, for in South Wales there are possibilities, as yet too little used, of checking tradition by documents.

According to G. T. Clark[5] 'All the older and most of the later Advenae were connected with the Honour of Gloucester and followed in the train of their liege lords. They were either the heads or cadets of families in the shires of Gloucester, Somerset, Devon and Cornwall, and what little is known of them is derived mainly from the records of those counties.' However this may be it is certain that some of them in succeeding centuries maintained or established links with the English counties on the border and across the Bristol Channel, though others,

[1] Op. cit., p. 451.
[2] The italics no doubt allude to the frequency in Welsh pedigrees of secondary families by concubines.
[3] *History of Brecknockshire*, pp. 454, 384.
[4] Papers of the late A. T. Butler, Windsor Herald, in my possession.
[5] Op. cit., p. 336.

who intermarried with the Welsh and adopted their language, became indistinguishable from them. Others again came back to England among the many Welsh who settled in England under the Tudors. Thus the Aubreys of Brecon and Glamorgan sent cadets into Wiltshire of whom was John Aubrey the antiquary (d. 1697), and the Kemeys of Glamorgan had cadets in Gloucestershire. The ancestors of John Harvard (d. 1638), the founder of Harvard College, may have been Havards from Wales, though his father lived in Southwark and married in Stratford on Avon.

Into what became Pembrokeshire Henry I transported large numbers of Flemings, who had come into England not long before, and their descendants seem to have played some part in the anglicization of a portion of that county.[1] We shall see that the twelfth century invaders of Ireland were drawn largely from the Norman and Flemish knights of Pembrokeshire.

### (ii) *Ireland*

The Norman invasion of Ireland began with an invitation from an exiled Irish king, Dermot MacMurrough, King of Leinster, driven from his kingdom by Rory O'Connor of Connaught, who had made himself King of Ireland. He travelled to Aquitaine and doing homage there to Henry II of England was promised help to regain his kingdom. Accordingly in 1167 he returned to Ireland with a band of Norman adventurers, whom others soon followed. Dermot gave his daughter Eve in marriage to Richard FitzGilbert, Earl of Pembroke (d. 1176; called Strongbow), and promised him the succession to his kingdom, which, however, Richard offered to hold as a lordship from his own King Henry. Henry came to Ireland and in 1171–2 was accepted as lord by the Irish kings of the centre and south. He granted lordships in Leinster and Meath to the leading Norman invaders and they in turn enfeoffed their followers and pressed on further into the country by infiltration or conquest.

The Norman invasion of Ireland stopped far short of complete conquest and when its impetus was spent the invaders' heirs became Irish in life and language in different degrees, according to their geographical situation; those of Meath, Louth, Dublin, Kildare, and Wexford remaining more English than their remoter cousins. Orpen thought that the descendants of those Norman invaders who had taken Welsh wives in and about Pembrokeshire were readier than

1 Lloyd, op. cit., p. 424.

the rest to intermarry with Irish noble families and to conform to Irish modes of life. A number of the Norman families developed into clans or septs like those of the native Irish. In such cases the clan sur-name was probably at times taken by families not originally of its blood who joined it and gave allegiance to its chieftain. Some of these indeed might be descendants of the previous inhabitants of the clan territory. Thus Burke, originally de Burgh, a purely English name in origin, is now the fourteenth commonest surname in Ireland and its bearers there alone are reckoned to number some 19,000. It is thus questionable whether all are true de Burghs by male descent. On the other hand, we have to credit with a possible Norman origin those bearers of such purely Irish surnames as were assumed by some hibernicized branches or septs of Norman families. Thus descendants of the Norman Fitz-Simons are said to have become MacRuddery, of the Berminghams MacCorish, of the Archdeacons MacOda or Coady, and so on.[1]

For the Norman invasion of Ireland we have the first hand and first rate account of Gerald de Barry (d. *c.* 1223) called Giraldus Cambrensis (the Welshman) who tells us that his family took their name from Barry Island. Gerald, who was in fact three quarters Norman and a quarter Welsh, was son of William de Barry of Manorbier Castle, Pembroke-shire, by Angharad, daughter of Gerald of Windsor[2] by Nest, daughter of Rhys ap Tudor Mawr, Prince of South Wales. Philip de Barry, Gerald's brother, was among the invaders and was granted Olethan and other lands in County Cork about 1180. From him descended the Lords Barrymore and Buttevant extinct in 1823 though an extant illegitimate branch from them and in all probability cadet lines still exist.[3] During the fifteenth century 'The Lord Barry, was well as the Lords Athenry, Lords Kingsale and Lords Kerry became', as the *Complete Peerage*[4] puts it, 'mere Irish Chieftains, many of them assuming Irish names, and being entirely hostile to the English Government.' They formed septs or branches with such names as Barry Mor, Barry Óg and Barry Roe, while one line took from its founder Adam Barry the surname MacAdam.[5]

Giraldus stressed the part of Pembrokeshire knights in the invasion and in fact more than one of those who founded powerful lines in Ireland took his name from a Pembrokeshire place. Maurice de Pren-

---

[1] Edward MacLysaght, *Irish Families*, 1957, pp. 10–11, 17, 66, 292, 161.

[2] See pp. 84–6.

[3] *Complete Peerage*, i. 436–47, 451; *Journ. of the Cork Hist. and Arch. Soc.* 2nd ser. v–viii. See also p. 19 *supra. Burke's Landed Gentry*, 1937, pp. 2536–8.

[4] i. 438 n.                                        [5] MacLysaght, op. cit., p. 52.

dergast from Prendergast near Haverfordwest, whose male line seems to be traceable to 1817 and may still exist,[1] was possibly not a Norman but a Fleming,[2] and so too were the sons of Godibert the Fleming, of Roche Castle, Pembrokeshire, the ancestors of the Lords Roche.[3] Jocelin de Nangle came from Angle, Pembrokeshire, and the barony of Navan, County Meath, granted him by Hugh de Lacy (d. 1186), was still held by Nangles in the seventeenth century. The name still exists as Nagle or Neagle. At an early date some of this family are said to have become hibernicized as MacOisdealbh (sons of Jocelin), later MacCostello and Costello and to have formed a numerous sept in Mayo and the adjoining counties.[4] The Carews,[5] who took their name from Carew Castle, Pembrokeshire, held lands in Ireland as well as England down to the fourteenth century when they disposed of them.[6] Miles de Cogan, from Cogan in Glamorgan, left descendants both in England and Ireland.[7]

Among the invaders with French surnames the most conspicuous were the great leaders Hugh de Lacy (d. 1186) and John de Courcy (d. c. 1219).[8] Patrick de Courcy (*fl.* 1221–51), ancestor of the Lords Kingsale, may have been the latter's bastard or otherwise related to him.[9] Gilbert de Nugent was granted the barony of Delvin, Co. Westmeath, by Hugh de Lacy (d. 1186). Its descent between the twelfth and the late fourteenth century is obscure, but it is not unlikely that William Nugent (d. c. 1422), who acquired it by marriage with the sister and heir of John fitzJohn (d. 1382) was of the blood of Gilbert de Nugent.[10] From him descend the Earls of Westmeath.

Theobald Walter or FitzWalter (d. 1205), the son of Hervey Walter of West Dereham, Norfolk, the grandson of another Hervey Walter and the elder brother of Hubert Walter the Archbishop of Canterbury

---

[1] *Burke's Landed Gentry*, 1937, p. 2664; (4th) Viscount Gort, *The Prendergasts of Newcastle, County Tipperary, 1069–1870*, 1879. Mrs. Jeffry J. (Dr. Caroline M.) Prendergast of Redlands, California, wrote that in 1965 there were in California thirty-four descendants of Francis Ensor Prendergast (d. 1897), who emigrated in 1866 and claimed headship of the family, being son of John Patrick Prendergast, B.A. of Trin. Coll. Dublin (d. 1897).

[2] Orpen, op. cit., i. 148.

[3] *Complete Peerage*, xi. 41; Henry Owen, *Old Pembroke Families*, 1902, pp. 68–69.

[4] Orpen, ii. 84; MacLysaght, op. cit., pp. 95–96.          [5] p. 85.

[6] Orpen, ii. 48; iii. 147–55.          [7] *Complete Peerage*, iii. 356–9; Orpen, iii. 119, &c.

[8] For the ancestors of John de Courcy in Normandy and England see Farrer, *Honors and Knights' Fees*, i. 103–8, Maxwell-Lyte in *Somerset Arch. Soc. Proc.* lxvi. 98–126.

[9] *Complete Peerage*, vii. 280.

[10] Ibid. iv. 170–1; *The Peerage of Ireland*, by John Lodge, ed. Mervyn Archdall, 1789, i. 215–50; and C. T. Clay, *Early Yorkshire Charters*, vii. 36–37.

(d. 1205), came to Ireland in 1185 with the future King John and was granted vast estates there and the great office of Butler which gave his descendants their surname. The fortunes of the family had been advanced in England by the marriage of Theobald's father with the sister of the wife of Henry II's great justiciar, Ranulf de Glanville (d. 1190). The greatness of the Butlers among the Anglo-Norman nobility of Ireland grew till it was second only to that of the Fitzgeralds. Edmund Butler was created Earl of Carrick in 1315 and his son James Earl of Ormonde in 1328. Among the titles of his descendants were Earl of Ossory, Viscount Thurles, Marquess and Duke of Ormonde.[1]

William de Burgh, the ancestor of that other great Irish house of Burgh or Bourke or Burke, Earls of Ulster (from before 1265), and, in its younger branches called MacWilliam Eighter and MacWilliam Oughter, respectively Earls of Clanricarde (1543) and Viscounts Mayo (1627), was brother of the great Hubert de Burgh, Earl of Kent (d. 1243), but their parentage is uncertain.[2] The Burkes became more completely hibernicized than any other Norman family, formed septs and minor branches such as MacSeoinin, now Jennings, and Mac-Gibbon, now Gibbons, and are so numerous that in Dr. MacLysaght's view 'it is hardly possible that they all stem from the one ancestor'.[3] The pedigrees of the main lines are, however, well authenticated. Robert de Bermingham, an invader in or before 1175, probably took his name from Birmingham in Warwickshire. His descendants, who became Lords Athenry, were extant in the last century and may be still. They are also said to survive under the name MacCorrish or Corrish.[4]

## Windsor, Carew, Fitzgerald and Fitzmaurice

The most famous of all Norman-Irish families is that of the Geraldines. Its patriarch Walter FitzOther was in 1086 a tenant in chief in five counties, though not one of the greatest, and was castellan of the king's castle of Windsor, dying after 1100. His eldest son William of Windsor was ancestor of the Windsors of Stanwell, Middlesex, Lords Windsor from 1529 to 1641, when the male line expired. The Windsor-Clives, Earls of Plymouth, represent them through the female line. As often among the Normans, service to magnates in office of a certain

---

[1] Oswald Barron in the *Encyclopædia Britannica*, 1910, iv. 879–81; *Complete Peerage*.
[2] J. H. Round in the *Encyclopædia Britannica*, 1910, iv. 814–15; *Complete Peerage*.
[3] Op. cit., p. 66. There are some 19,000 in Ireland and far more in America and elsewhere. Clan recruitment may have taken place through sons of Burke daughters taking the name.                                                     [4] Ibid., p. 17.

type ran in the family of Walter the castellan, himself a royal officer. His son Maurice of Windsor was made steward of the great abbey of Bury St. Edmunds before 1119. Another son Reinald was steward to Adeliza, Queen of Henry I, while a third son, Gerald of Windsor, was a steward also and became the constable and captain of Arnulf de Montgomery, when he invaded Wales and built Pembroke Castle. Arnulf's brother Robert, Earl of Shrewsbury, got himself into trouble with Henry I and he and his family lost their Welsh and English lands in 1102 and retired to Normandy. Gerald of Windsor, who meantime had strengthened his position by marrying Nest, daughter of Rhys ap Tudor Mawr, Prince of South Wales, stepped into his master's shoes and was granted the custody of Pembroke Castle.

Gerald's eldest son William (d. 1173–4) had himself, as Round proved, a son Odo (d. *c.* 1204), called of Carew from his castle of Carew in Pembrokeshire. He also held Moulsford, Berkshire, and the succession to his lands of Nicholas Carew at the end of the thirteenth century was accepted by Round as clear evidence of descent from him, though intervening links are uncertain. From Nicholas descend the Carews of Devon and Cornwall still represented in the male line by the Baronets of Haccombe.[1]

Besides William, the Carews' ancestor, Gerald of Windsor and Nest of South Wales had a daughter Angharat, the mother of the historian Giraldus Cambrensis (from whose voluminous writings much of our knowledge of his mother's family comes), and two more sons, David fitzGerald, Bishop of St. David's (d. 1176), and Maurice fitzGerald (d. 1176), the ancestor of the Irish Geraldines. By invitation of Dermot MacMurrough, the dispossessed King of Leinster, who promised to give Wexford to him and his half-brother if they helped him to regain his kingdom, Maurice landed there with two shiploads of followers in 1169 and both began the Norman Conquest of Ireland and founded the fortunes of his family there. Their history is inseparable from that of Ireland between the twelfth and the seventeenth centuries. The senior extant line of his descendants is that of FitzGerald, Barons of Offaly from *c.* 1180, Earls of Kildare from 1316, and Dukes of Leinster from 1766.[2] The present duke is twenty fifth in descent from Other. At the present day, according to Dr. MacLysaght, there are some thirteen

---

[1] J. H. Round, 'The Origin of the Carews', *The Ancestor*, v. 19–53; J. L. Vivian, *The Visitations of the County of Devon*, pp. 133–45.

[2] J. H. Round, 'The Origin of the Fitzgeralds', *The Ancestor*, i. 119–26; ii. 91–97; *Complete Peerage*, x. 10–17; vii. 200, 218–45 and 573–8; *Encyclopædia Britannica*, art. 'Fitzgerald', by J. H. Round.

thousand Fitzgeralds in Ireland, principally in Munster, in all classes of life.[1]

From Thomas fitzMaurice (d. 1213), youngest son of Maurice Fitz-Gerald (d. 1176), sprang the FitzGerald Earls of Desmond (1329–1601), while from younger sons of his son John fitzThomas (d. 1261) are said to descend the FitzGerald lines of the White Knights, the Knights of Glin (or Black Knights), and the Knights of Kerry (or Green Knights), feudal dignities said to have been conferred by their ancestor the Lord of Decies and Desmond.[2]

The exact descent of the FitzMaurices, Barons of Kerry and Lixnaw, from c. 1295, Earls of Kerry from 1723 and Marquesses of Lansdowne from 1784, was uncertain until Dr. Goddard H. Orpen showed that their ancestor Thomas FitzMaurice (d. 1280) was a son of Maurice Fitz-Thomas, a younger brother of John fitzThomas (d. 1261), ancestor of the Earls of Desmond.[3] The present Marquess of Lansdowne is thirtieth in descent from Other.

## (iii) *Scotland*

The Normans came to Scotland not as conquerors or invaders but by invitation. Norman influence in these islands began with the marriage of Ethelred (d. 1016) of England in 1002 to Emma (d. 1052), daughter of the Duke of Normandy, who brought Normans with her, so that her son King Edward the Confessor (d. 1066) grew up with a fondness and admiration for the Normans and their ways and further introduced both into England. Malcolm Canmore (d. 1093), King of Scotland, became acquainted with Norman influence in his childhood as an exile in England under Edward's protection and at his court. When in 1069 he married Edward's great-niece Margaret, whose brother Edgar the Atheling submitted to William the Conqueror and lived at his court, Norman influence at the Scottish court increased and was reinforced by further intermarriages. The most important was that of David (d. 1153), the youngest son of Malcolm and Margaret in 1113 to Maud (d. 1130–1), daughter of Waltheof, Earl of Huntingdon and Northampton (d. 1076), by Judith, niece of William the Conqueror. By this marriage David of Scotland himself became Earl of Huntingdon, the greatest baron of the King of England and a lord of many Norman knights. Both before and after 1124 when he succeeded his elder brother as king, he brought into Scotland many Norman knights, gave them

[1] Op. cit., p. 142.        [2] *Complete Peerage*, iv. 233–57.        [3] Ibid., vii. 201–16.

Scottish lands and through them introduced to Scotland the Norman or Anglo-Norman system of government.[1] In so doing he set on Scotland a mark comparable with that set upon England by William the Conqueror.

Among the Normans brought in by David, knights from his own English lands in Northamptonshire, Huntingdonshire and elsewhere may well have formed a majority, but the record is too scanty to afford proof. The family of Hugh de Moreville (d. 1162), whom David made Constable of Scotland, and who founded Dryburgh Abbey, held lands of the honor of Huntingdon in Northamptonshire, Huntingdonshire and Rutland. They came from Morville near Valognes in Normandy and others of the name are found in Dorset and Somerset.[2] The Haigs, ancestors of Earl Haig, held Bemersyde, on the Tweed close to Dryburgh, as early as the twelfth century and their ancestor Peter de la Haga witnessed charters of Richard de Moreville (d. 1189) from 1162. Loyd[3] was satisfied that he must have come from the district of La Hague near Cherbourg, not far from Morville. Professor G. W. S. Barrow[4] places also among the families which came with the Morevilles those of Néhou, Sinclair (St. Clair), Clephane and Gundeville. Loyd[5] establishes the link between the St. Clairs of Hamerton, Huntingdonshire, and Saint-Clair-sur-Elle near St. Lô in Normandy, both places close to Moreville lordships. St. Clairs in the twelfth century were vassals of the Morevilles at Lauder, Berwickshire, and Cunningham, Ayrshire, and from these probably sprang the Sinclairs of Roslin, the Earls of Orkney and Caithness and the Lords Sinclair.

David Olifard was King David's godson and saved him from being made prisoner in battle in 1141. From 1144 to 1170 he is conspicuous in Scotland and was almost certainly ancestor of Laurence Oliphant (d. 1499), created Lord Oliphant about 1460, though the precise relationships of the intervening heads of the family remain unproved. He was doubtless of the family which held Lilford, Northamptonshire, and other lands of the honor of Huntingdon, from the time of Roger Olifard, who witnessed a charter of Simon, Earl of Huntingdon, not

---

[1] Cf. R. L. G. Ritchie, *The Normans in Scotland*, 1954.

[2] Loyd, *Anglo-Norman Families*, pp. 49–50, 70; Farrer, *Honors and Knights' Fees*, ii. 356–8. See also Ritchie, op. cit., p. 154, who unfortunately, however, appears to be unaware of Loyd's work.

[3] Op. cit., pp. 49–50.

[4] 'Les familles "normandes" d'Ecosse', *Annales de Normandie*, 15ᵉ Année, No. 4. Dec. 1965, pp. 493–575.

[5] *Anglo-Norman families*, pp. 88–89. For the Huntingdonshire St. Clairs see Farrer, *Honors and Knights' Fees*, ii. 287–91.

later than 1108. The Oliphants of Gask, male descendants of the Lords Oliphant, continued down to 1847 and the Oliphants of Condie, still extant, claim descent from the same line.[1]

Robert de Brus (d. 1141, possibly from Brix in Normandy),[2] the ancestor of the Bruce Kings of Scotland, was a great Yorkshire baron, who was granted Annandale by David about 1124 (for what reason we know not) as a mere addition to his greater English lands. But the English lands passed to his elder son and those in Scotland to his younger son Robert (d. 1194), who thus became established there. This Robert's grandson made the marriage with a great-granddaughter of King David, which gave his heirs their claim to the Scottish throne.[3] The Bruces of Clackmannan, from whom the extant families of Bruce descend, are traceable from 1348 and are supposed to be an illegitimate branch of the Bruces of Annandale.[4]

The connection of the family of John Balliol (d. 1313), the rival of Robert Bruce for the throne of Scotland, with that country was slight until his father's marriage with a great-great-granddaughter of King David in 1223. They came from Picardy and their lands were in the north of England.[5]

The Somervilles, extant in the male line down to 1870 and perhaps so still, probably descend from William de Somerville who witnesses charters of King David. But attempts to link him with Sémerville in Normandy and the Somervilles of Wichnor, Staffordshire, are but guesswork.[6]

William de la Haye, the ancestor of the Earls of Erroll and Kinnoull, appears in Scotland in the reign of David's successor Malcolm IV (d. 1165), but his uncle Ranulf de Soules (d. *c.* 1170), Butler of Scotland, was there by 1125[7] and Professor Barrow thinks that William probably came with him.[8] La Haye (the hedge or stockade) is too common a Norman place name and surname for any theory of origin to be based on this alone, but I have set out fully elsewhere evidence

---

[1] *Complete Peerage*, x. 48–61; *Scots Peerage*, vi. 521–63; Ritchie, op. cit., 279–80; J. H. Round, *Feudal England*, pp. 223–4; Farrer, *Honors and Knights' Fees*, ii. 354–5; Joseph Anderson, *The Oliphants in Scotland*, 1879.

[2] p. 25 *supra*; Barrow, op. cit., pp. 500–2.

[3] Dugdale, *Baronage*, i. 447, 451; *Scots Peerage*, ii. 428–37.

[4] *Scots Peerage*, iii. 466–7.

[5] p. 28 *supra*; *Northumberland County History*, vi. 72.

[6] *Scots Peerage*, viii. 1–45; *Complete Peerage*, xii. i. 92–108; Ritchie, op. cit., p. 18.

[7] Ritchie, op. cit., pp. 187–8.

[8] *Regesta Regum Scottorum. Vol. I. The Acts of Malcolm IV King of Scots 1153–65* ed. G. W. S. Barrow, 1960, p. 34, n. 6.

which points to the conclusion that William de la Haye came from what is now La Haye-Bellefond near Saint Lô.[1] The chief reasons are that La Haye-Bellefond adjoins Soulles, the probable place of origin of the Soules family, and that in the fourteenth century the French De la Hayes who lived there bore the same arms as the Hays of Erroll.

The ancestors of two of the greatest Scottish families came in with David and bore French Christian names, but their surnames seem to be taken from their homes in England. Walter de Lindsey, who was in Scotland by 1120, possessed Fordington in the district of Lindsey in Lincolnshire, whence probably he took his name. From him sprang the great house of the Lindsays, Earls of Crawford.[2] Similarly William de Graham, who witnessed a charter of King David in 1127, almost certainly took his name from Grantham in Lincolnshire, of which Graham is an old form.[3] As in most of these Scottish pedigrees the precise links in the earliest generations are uncertain, but it is clear that William de Graham was the ancestor of the Dukes of Montrose and the other branches of the great house of Graham.[4] Among other families believed by Professor Barrow to have come to Scotland in David's time are those of Corbet, Burneville, Avenel, Ridel and Giffard of Yester, brought in by Ada de Warenne, wife of David's son Henry, and perhaps a branch of Giffard of Longueville (p. 67).

There was a second influx of Normans under Malcolm IV and William the Lion, between about 1160 and 1200. Among the families whose entry Professor Barrow assigns to this phase are Moubray, Ramsay, Laundells, Valognes, Boys, Fraser, Bisset, Barclay and Menzies. A list made by Sir Thomas Gray in the middle of the fourteenth century of families, whose ancestors, he says, were brought into Scotland by King William the Lion in 1175, includes, with some of the above and others known to have come earlier, those of Montgomery and Colville.[5]

### Stewart

Walter FitzAlan (d. 1177), the ancestor of the Stewart Kings of Scotland and England, was brought into Scotland by David in 1141

---

[1] A. R. Wagner, 'The Origin of the Hays of Erroll', *The Genealogists' Magazine*, xi. 535–40; xii. 1–6.

[2] Ritchie, op. cit., pp. 157–8; *Scots Peerage*, iii. 1–51; *Complete Peerage*, iii. 507–26; *The Genealogist*, N.S. xii. 1, 75.

[3] *Complete Peerage*, vi. 51; Ritchie, op. cit., p. 189.      [4] *Scots Peerage*, vi. 191–274.

[5] *Scalachronica*, Maitland Club edition, 1836, p. 41; also printed by Ritchie, op. cit., p. 378, and referred to by G. F. Black, *The Surnames of Scotland*, 1946, p. xiv.

and made steward of his realm. In 1158 this office was made hereditary and gave the family its surname.[1] The old Scottish tale immortalized in *Macbeth* made Walter son of Fleance, son of Banquo, thane of Lochaber, but in 1807 George Chalmers showed that he was in fact the son of Alan FitzFlaald, Sheriff of Shropshire and brother of William FitzAlan, ancestor of the FitzAlans, Lords of Clun and Oswestry in Shropshire and Earls of Arundel from about 1290 down to 1580. It was left for Horace Round to prove that Flaald, the father of Alan and grandfather of William and Walter Fitzalan, was himself the son of another Alan, *dapifer* (seneschal or steward) of the Lord of Dol in Britanny.[2] The eldest son of this Alan occurs in Britanny before 1080 and was a leader on the first Crusade in 1097. Flaald is found in Monmouth in 1101–2 as a follower of its lord William, son of Baderon, another Breton. The rise of Alan fitzFlaald under Henry I is linked by Round with the support given to Henry by the Bretons before his accession, when he was Lord of the Cotentin.

Besides William of Shropshire and Walter of Scotland, Alan Fitz-Flaald had a third son Jordan, who succeeded him in Brittany as *dapifer* of Dol and left a son and successor, who still lived there in 1167.

The marriage of Walter, High Steward of Scotland (d. 1327) and fifth in descent from Walter FitzAlan, to Marjory, daughter of King Robert Bruce, in 1315, brought the throne of Scotland to his son King Robert II in 1371. His last heir male on that throne was James V who died in 1541, but James V's daughter Mary Queen of Scots (d. 1587), married Henry Stewart, Lord Darnley (d. 1567), the descendant of an uncle of Walter the High Steward (d. 1327), so that their son James VI of Scotland and I of England (d. 1625) had still the Stewart blood. This male line expired at the death of Henry, Cardinal York, in 1807, but many illegitimate Stewart male lines exist and probably some lègitimate lines also, though these are less easily proved.

[1] Ritchie, op. cit., pp. 279–81, 364–5.
[2] J. H. Round, *Studies in Peerage and Family History*, 1901, pp. 115–46, 'The Origin of the Stewarts'.

# IV

## THE SOCIAL FRAMEWORK

A GENERAL picture of the framework or class structure of English society through the centuries is necessary to the genealogist as a guide to what to look for and what to believe. He needs a mental picture both of the social classes which have existed at different dates, with their distinctions and dividing lines, and of the nature and extent of movement up and down and sideways, from one to another, by families and individuals. The study of this framework, structure and movement falls, however, between several studies, none of whose specialists have yet treated it comprehensively. The economic historians, the social historians, the legal historians, the local historians and the genealogists themselves all have elements to contribute, without any of which the picture will be incomplete. I have looked in vain for an attempt at a general synthesis, the nearest to this being those general pictures of the state of England at different epochs in the painting of which several of our best historians from Macaulay onward have displayed their highest skill. I have thus been forced to make my own brief abstract of some few essential points for my special purpose and in doing so I have not wished to disguise the grave and numerous gaps in knowledge—or at least in my knowledge—waiting to be filled by research and study.

There is a perennial tension in human society and in the soul of man between the claims of community and individuality; the demands of fellowship and the demands of excellence. The voice of fellowship calls for equality. 'Man is born free and everywhere he is in chains', and is it not his fellow man who has chained him? The voice of excellence demands fulfilment of man's powers and destiny through the leadership of the gifted and the full development of their talents. To shackle strength and genius, says this voice, is an envious denial of the spirit of man: 'One law for the Lion and Ox is oppression.'[1]

The reconciler of this conflict, said our forefathers, is the principle of order or degree. Society, like man's body, has its head, its heart, its

---

[1] William Blake, *The Marriage of Heaven and Hell.*

hands, its belly, its feet, each appointed to its own work, to rule, to warm, to defend, to feed, to support.

> The heavens themselves, the planets, and this centre
> Observe degree, priority and place,
>
>       .    .    .    .    .    .    .
>
>              O! when degree is shak'd,
> Which is the ladder to all high designs,
> The enterprise is sick. How could communities,
> Degrees in schools, and brotherhoods in cities,
> Peaceful commerce from dividable shores,
> The primogenitive and due of birth,
> Prerogative of age, crowns, sceptres, laurels,
> But by degree, stand in authentic place?[1]

The sentiments which Shakespeare puts in Ulysses' mouth express the orthodox Elizabethan view derived from the Middle Ages.[2] Indeed its ancestry goes back much further for Plato held that the same tensions which divide classes in the state are found also within each soul, and that reconciliation and justice are to be sought in due order.

The European hierarchical concept had a special English inflexion. 'Like their descendants in every age', says Sir Frank Stenton, 'the English peasants of the earliest time were very sensitive to diversities in rank, and in particular to the distinction between themselves and those whose birth entitled them to a place among the retainers of the king.' The laws of King Ine (d. 726) picture the social order of Wessex about 694. 'Its pattern', says Stenton, 'implies that it arose from mass migrations of free peasants, familiar with life in communities, accustomed to discussion in popular assemblies, and deferential to kingship as part of the natural order of the world.'[3]

The social development of England between the Saxon invasions and the Norman Conquest was in Sir Frank Stenton's opinion from a mainly free peasantry to a stratified society in which *thegns* or noblemen, who themselves differed in rank, were divided by a deep gulf from the free peasants, below whom again were several grades of serfs and

---

[1] Shakespeare, *Troilus and Cressida*, Act I, scene iii. For examples of Elizabethan insistence on degree see Mildred Campbell, *The English Yeoman Under Elizabeth and the Early Stuarts*, 1942, pp. 21–22. For mediaeval attitudes to social stratification and mobility see Sylvia L. Thrupp, *The Merchant Class of Medieval London*, Univ. of Chicago, 1948, pp. 288–319, and on those of the sixteenth century Lawrence Stone, *The Crisis of the Aristocracy 1558–1641*, 1965, chaps. ii and iii.

[2] For a modern exposition of the view that 'any organized social group is always a stratified social body', see Pitirim Sorokin, *Social Mobility*, 1927, chap. ii.

[3] *Anglo-Saxon England*, p. 310.

slaves.[1] He suggests that this came about because poverty and the dangers of Viking raids led freemen to submit themselves to lords for the sake of protection. Marc Bloch[2] pointed to evidence which he thought showed that the greater fluidity which distinguished English from French society after the Norman Conquest already existed in Anglo-Saxon times. Alcuin in 801 describes an armed band attached to the household of the Archbishop of York as including both noble and non-noble warriors. The meanings of class names appear to shift; and, whereas in Frankish Gaul the distinction between vassalage and lower forms of service is reflected in consistent differences in the acts of submission, in England the ceremony of joined hands was used or not used at will, irrespective of the social ranks involved.

The Norman Conquest, besides probably reducing some English thegns to the level of serfs, placed over them a Norman feudal hierarchy of lords and knights and as time went on carried further in some directions and modified in others the pre-Conquest stratification in the countryside. As towns, and especially London, grew in size and wealth the stratification of their inhabitants likewise developed. Whether there is any social or economic law by which growing wealth and a developing division of labour necessarily produce a finer class stratification, I do not know, but there is no doubt that the two things have often gone together.

Legislators and lawyers in the Middle Ages liked tidiness and took much trouble to reduce facts, which were too often inconveniently recalcitrant or in course of change, to at least an appearance of system. Therefore, in interpreting their accounts of social classes and the legal obligations attaching to them we must not forget that the order of things they were seeking to impose may have differed materially from what actually existed. 'The most striking feature', says Pollard,[3] 'of English Society in the early middle ages is the confusion of classes.' Thus the distinction between freeman and villein, to which the lawyers attached so much importance and gave so much thought, seems often, as we shall see,[4] to have been much less well defined than they would have wished. Common interests and common antipathies have at times linked and united classes which at other times were divided and opposed. Country landowners great and small have at times had more in common with each other than either with the townsmen. At other times, on the contrary, for example in the fourteenth century, political circumstances

[1] Ibid., pp. 463–84.　　　　　　　　　　　　[2] *Feudal Society*, 1961, p. 183.
[3] A. F. Pollard, *The Evolution of Parliament*, 2nd ed. 1926, p. 63.　　　[4] pp. 138–41.

linked the smaller landowners more closely to the citizens than to the great lords.[1] Such shifts of pattern, which themselves owed much to the strength of the Crown, helped to keep class barriers from crystallizing.

In the constantly changing structure of English society there have often been discrepancies between legal, economic and social class divisions. All are important to the genealogist, though for different reasons. A social class for him means an endogamous class, one, that is, whose members normally marry within it. To ascertain those social frontiers across which marriage was rare is a work in which the genealogist himself must share. Its value to him, if accomplished, is evident. Endogamous social classes share with families on the one hand and nations on the other a feeling that their members belong together against the world outside. This sense of belonging is reflected in, fostered and even formed by community of speech, manners, outlook and education. To complete the picture, therefore, all these class attributes need separate study. But this is for others than genealogists and in what follows can barely be glanced at. The attributes of other cross sections of the community, where they can be learned, may help the genealogist no less; for example the recruitment, geographical and social movements, marriages, standing and way of life of the members of different trades and occupations.

From the survey which follows it will be seen how the history of occupational classes illustrates that of social classes and conversely. The clergy, for instance, have never been a homogeneous class but a cross section of society, deriving members from all classes and mingling with all, yet providing at times a ladder of social ascent and contributing essential elements to class character. Long ago, just as today, a man might raise himself into a higher economic class while remaining socially and perhaps legally in the class where he started—and conversely. No one principle of classification, therefore, will meet our need and the classes we shall describe to some extent overlap each other.[2] Thus a merchant may or may not be a gentleman. A fifteenth century example shows how distinct and even, at first sight, incompatible characters could be combined in one man. In 1459 a general pardon was issued to John Thame of Fairford, junior, husbandman, alias merchant, alias gentleman, alias woolman, alias yeoman.[3] Nor is this a solitary

---

[1] Stubbs, *Constitutional History of England*, ii, 4th ed. 1906, pp. 193, 196–7.
[2] The subtlety of English class distinctions at the present day is well brought out in *The Sociology of an English Village: Gosforth*, by W. M. Williams, 1956, chap. v.
[3] K. R. Memoranda Roll, Mich. 38 Henry VI, m. 32 d, quoted in Eileen Power and

instance. The difficulties of classification appear again in a lawsuit which arose in 1575 out of the practice whereby the churchwardens of St. Martin's, Leicester, 'did place every man and woman according as they grew in substance and credit within the parish into their seats in the church'.[1]

In the Middle Ages it was thought proper that dress should indicate calling and station and from time to time laws were made to control 'the outrageous and excessive apparel of divers people against their estate and degree to the great destruction and impoverishment of all the land'. A statute of this kind made in 1363[2] shows us the legislature seeking a common measure of the status of knights, esquires and gentlemen on one hand, merchants, citizens and craftsmen on another, and the clergy over against both. A points system is applied in which rank and wealth both count for something. The knights are divided into two classes according to wealth. Below the poorer knights come esquires with land or rents worth £200 a year, who are put on a level with merchants, citizens, burgesses, artificers and people of handicraft possessing goods worth £1,000. Below them again come esquires and gentlemen under the rank of knight, worth under £100 a year, on a level with merchants, citizens, burgesses, artificers and people of handicraft possessing goods worth £500. Below these come craftsmen and holders of office of yeoman rank;[3] yeomen in lord's households and, on the same level, the grooms, yeomen and servants of merchants; the grooms of lords and of artificers; and, on the lowest rung, carters, ploughmen, drivers of the plough, oxherds, cowherds, shepherds, swineherds, keepers of beasts, threshers of corn and all manner of people of the estate of groom serving husbandry and others not possessing goods worth forty shillings. The clergy are grouped into those of degree in churches, cathedrals, colleges, or schools, and those with property worth under £100 a year.

---

M. M. Postan, *Studies in English Trade in the Fifteenth Century*, 1933, p. 53. On alias descriptions see S. Thrupp, *The Merchant Class of Medieval London*, pp. 269–71.

[1] *Studies in Social History*, ed. J. H. Plumb, 1955, W. G. Hoskins, 'An Elizabethan Provincial Town; Leicester', p. 60. On the hierarchical conception of society and the forces of Calvinism and the Enlightenment, which attacked it in the seventeenth and eighteenth centuries, see J. H. Hexter, *Reappraisals in History*, 1961, pp. 114–16, and Stone, *The Crisis of the Aristocracy*, *passim*.

[2] *The Statutes of the Realm*, i, 1810, pp. 380–1. On fourteenth century social stratification see May McKisack, *The Fourteenth Century, 1307–1399*, Oxford, 1959, p. 346.

[3] Mildred Campbell, *The English Yeoman under Elizabeth and the Early Stuarts*, 1942, p. 8, defines a yeoman in this sense as 'a retainer or attendant or servitor, a person giving not menial but honourable service'. See p. 143 *infra*.

A similar statute of 1463,[1] a century later, adopts a rather different classification, which exhibits further interesting equations, placing for example on the same level aldermen and recorders of London, mayors and sheriffs of such cities, towns and boroughs as be counties corporate, mayors and bailiffs of other cities, serjeants and officers of the king's household, yeomen of the crown, yeomen of the king's chamber, and esquires and gentlemen worth £40 a year.

The details are less important than the approach, so expressive, to adopt Sir Lewis Namier's phrase 'of the peculiar character of English society, civilian and plutocratic, though imbued with feudal habits and traditions'.[2] A Swiss artist, who had lived many years in England, thus summed up the position in 1755.

The English have still kept up the distinction of rank and family: this is the first as it ought in reason to be: the second is that of wealth; and any other is hardly perceptible.

Every Englishman constantly holds a pair of scales, wherein he exactly weighs the birth, the rank and especially the fortune of those he is in company with, in order to regulate his behaviour and discourse accordingly; and on this occasion the rich tradesman is always sure to outweigh the poor artist. And here let us observe by the way, that nothing can be more ridiculous than the extreme nicety of most of the English women in respect to the notion of precedency, from those who may have some reason for their pretension, down to those who have no right to any such pretension at all.[3]

In the analysis which follows it will be seen how differences of rank, wealth and education have reacted on one another, each in turn modifying and contributing elements to the whole pattern, while the passionate English interest in social niceties has luxuriated in the consequent complication.

An assessment of the effect of recent political and economic changes on the relative position of classes refers to 'the really astonishing carry-over, from the days of the Two Nations', to the present day 'of distinctions which are distinctions of *class* and not merely of money'. But the author's understanding of the fact that, 'this snobbery, complex, subtle, guilty and enjoyable, is part of the English heritage',[4] suggests

---

[1] *The Statutes of the Realm*, ii. 399.

[2] L. B. Namier, *England in the Age of the American Revolution*, 1930, p. 6.

[3] *The Present State of the Arts in England*. By M. [Jean] Rouquet, Member of the Royal Academy of Painting and Sculpture; Who resided Thirty Years in this Kingdom. London. Printed for J. Nourse at the Lamb opposite Katherine Street in the Strand. MDCCLV.

[4] J. D. Scott, *Life in Britain*, 1956, p. 12.

that he does not himself find this as astonishing as he thinks his readers will.

Naturam expellas furca tamen usque recurret.[1]

### I. BARONS AND PEERS

Though the modern peerage was formed out of the mediaeval baron-age, confusion has been caused by attempts to equate the two, while to think of either as a nobility in the continental sense is misleading. Socially, though not legally, our nearest equivalent to a nobility in this sense is the class which we shall deal with next, that of the gentry, which arose out of the general class of knights, while the barons formed a small and dominant group within that class.

Baron, etymologically, means a man. The king's baron was his own man, one who held a lordship of him directly and owed him service for it, that is a tenant in chief. Sir Frank Stenton puts the number of the Conqueror's barons at about 180,[2] including the whole range from the great earls to those minor barons whose 'honors', as the lands of their endowment were called, were relatively small. The word earl was the Scandinavian equivalent of the English word ealdorman, which it superseded in the reign of Canute (1016–35). The earldorman was the king's governor of a province or of one or two shires, and his office was not hereditary. But from the Conqueror's time earldoms were limited to single counties (though two were sometimes joined into one earl-dom, as Norfolk and Suffolk for some time were), and soon became hereditary, while earls lost to the sheriffs their official function as king's representatives in the shires. Nevertheless, till long after the Conquest earldom meant an office and barony meant a tenure, while neither had its modern sense of a title of honour.

Each baron's honour was assessed at so many knights, whom he must bring to the king's service. The total number of knights so demanded by the Conqueror of his barons was not less than 4,000 and may have been much more.[2] The barons might raise these contingents in more than one way, but in the century which followed the Conquest they in fact by degrees granted from their lands holdings of differing size to sub-tenants who held of them by knight service. The total obligations of such sub-tenants' service exceeded those imposed on their lord by the king. Among the sub-tenants of the greatest barons were some whose holdings equalled those of the king's lesser barons. These great

---

[1] Horace, *Epistles*, bk. i, ep. x, l. 24.          [2] *Anglo-Saxon England*, p. 626.

sub-tenants, though not the king's barons, were social equals of those who were and were known as barons. Sir Frank Stenton has conveniently named them honorial barons.[1] We have seen already[2] that most of those who became barons in England seem to have been barons in Normandy before the Conquest, though the Conquest itself made the fortunes of a few.

It was the Conqueror's custom to meet the great lords of England in council at Christmas, Easter and Whitsuntide. In August 1086, however, he held at Salisbury a council of unusual character, for to it, the *Anglo-Saxon Chronicle* tells us, came all the landowners of any account in England, whose men soever they might be, and became his men and did him homage and swore him fealty, that they would be faithful to him against all others. Mr. Enoch Powell points out that the Conqueror was here making skilful use of English tradition to overcome the centrifugal tendencies of feudalism, for the practice of swearing fealty to the king (though not in connection with tenure of land) went back at least to the reign of Edward the Elder (899–924).[3] Stenton thinks it probable that ordinary knights would not at this date be thought landowners of any account and that those who then did fealty, apart from the king's own tenants in chief, were the honorial barons above mentioned.[4] The Conqueror's success in thus imposing direct allegiance to himself upon the undertenants of his barons may be looked on as the root of that royal dominance, which prevented the consolidation of an English nobility like those of the Continent, gave the English peerage part of its special character, and made possible a general social fluidity.[5]

In the thirteenth century a system developed of summoning to the Council, or Parliament as it came to be called, not only the magnates of the realm but locally chosen representatives of the shires and boroughs. The magnates thus summoned by writs addressed to them individually were the forerunners of the House of Lords. The knights of the shire and burgesses, who came in pursuance of general writs directing the shires and boroughs to choose and send them, were the forerunners of the House of Commons. As early as 1215 King John had assented in Magna Carta to the proposition that archbishops, bishops, abbots,

---

[1] F. M. Stenton, *English Feudalism*, pp. 83–111; *Anglo-Saxon England*, p. 628; A. L. Poole, *Domesday Book to Magna Carta*, p. 11. For the legal tests and meaning of Barony see the Preface to *English Baronies. A Study of their Origin and Descent 1086–1327*, by I. J. Sanders, Oxford, 1960, and J. Enoch Powell and Keith Wallis, *The House of Lords in the Middle Ages*, 1968, pp. 223–4.

[2] p. 631.          [3] Powell and Wallis, op. cit., p. 44.
[4] *Anglo-Saxon England*, p. 610.          [5] pp. 9, 49, 73.

earls and greater barons should receive individual summonses.[1] But where the line should be drawn between greater and lesser barons took long to settle. Both the numbers and selection of those summoned varied, to a startling and till recently unexplained extent, between the beginning of continuous record of summonses in 1295 and the middle years of the following century. The nature of these variations has for the first time been fully discussed and convincingly explained by Mr. J. Enoch Powell and Mr. Keith Wallis in their book *The House of Lords in the Middle Ages. A History of the English House of Lords to 1540*, which appeared in 1968; a result which would not have been achieved without what the authors themselves call 'a determined and almost pedantically chronological arrangement of the evidence'.[2]

Their conclusion is that for a strong king like Edward I it sufficed to summon to a parliament 'a chance selection of fifty to a hundred of the sort of substantial people who were regularly called on for service'.[3] Under Edward II what the magnates who dominated their king wanted was a fixed list and a relatively short one.[4] This restriction of the list may have stimulated research, designed to secure a place on it by proving succession to lands, formerly held by one summoned to Parliament.[5]

By the 1340's Edward III had reversed the balance of power and wished to bring into Parliament members of the circle he had created and endowed of new men distinguished by their service to him in his wars and administration. His right so to summon them was not questioned, but the propriety of calling them barons was, since the name of baron was now attached to those who claimed summons by hereditary right from ancestors summoned by Edward I.[6] Thus in 1344 we find these new men summoned as *bannerets*, a name first used in England in the 1270's to denote a higher military command, but by this time a social or financial grade.[7] By Richard II's time the barons in Parliament were called *le sire de* and the bannerets (with the judges) *monseigneur*.[8]

In the 1380's Richard II wished to bring new men into Parliament,

---

[1] William Sharp McKechnie, *Magna Carta*, 1905, p. 291.
[2] Powell and Wallis, op. cit., p. xii.     [3] Ibid., p. 231.
[4] Ibid., pp. xvi, 309.     [5] Ibid., pp. 312–14.     [6] Ibid., p. 337.
[7] Ibid., pp. 288, 353.
[8] p. 390. Sir Iain Moncreiffe deduces from the Scots Act of 1428 that by this date the Scots Parliament, following the rather earlier English practice, comprised, in addition to the hereditary peers, a category of bannerets, whom the king might summon in the same way.

as his grandfather had done, but, lacking his grandfather's resources of lands to endow them or the acquiescence of existing lords, had recourse to a new expedient, the creation of a baron by letters patent. Earldoms since the twelfth century had been conferred by royal charters which made them hereditary. In 1322 Sir Andrew Harcla had been created Earl of Carlisle with a remainder limited to the heirs *male* of his body, instead of as previously the heirs general—perhaps (Powell and Wallis suggest) to avoid the difficulties which could arise when an earl had no sons, but daughters who became his coheirs. Certainly (as they point out) it marks a step towards the conception of an earldom as a dignity capable of existence independently of lands.[1]

This limitation to heirs male of the body, applied in the interval to four dukedoms and three earldoms, was applied for the first time to a barony when in 1387 John de Beauchamp was created Lord de Beauchamp and Baron of Kidderminster.[2] No further such creation—of a barony, by letters patent, with a limitation to heirs male—was made till 1441, when Sir Ralph Boteler was made Lord Sudeley, but from that time on this became the normal, though not invariable, form.[3] It was a logical, if not inevitable development and parliamentary baronage thus became firmly established as an hereditary dignity, so that in the next century those who had been merely accustomed to receive writs began to claim that they, like the heirs of the new barons created by patent, had an absolute hereditary right to sit among the Lords in Parliament.[4]

These and subsequent slow developments were long obscured by the lawyers' requirement that what historically had been indefinite should in retrospect be given sharp and logical definition. Thus in 1674 upon a claim by the heir general to the barony of Clifton it was decided by the judges, to whom the Lords had referred the question, that a writ of summons to Parliament creates a barony descendible to heirs general.[5] It had been asserted by Sir Edward Coke in 1610[6] that such a summons, to create a barony, must have been followed by a sitting in Parliament, and this rule also was in time accepted as a part of the law. It was further necessary to decide which thirteenth century Parliaments were, for this purpose, to be regarded as valid Parliaments—whether, for

[1] Powell and Wallis, op. cit., p. 296.
[2] *Complete Peerage*, viii, app. E. and F., pp. 724–5; Powell and Wallis, op. cit., pp. xviii, 402.
[3] Ibid., p. 470.      [4] *Complete Peerage,* iv, app. H.
[5] *Complete Peerage*, iv, app. H., p. 706; *Lords' Journals*, xii. 630 a.
[6] J. H. Round, *Peerage and Pedigree*, i. 166–201.

example, the rebel Parliament held by Simon de Montfort in 1265 and the meeting held by Edward I at Shrewsbury in 1283 should qualify or not.[1] These points arose on claims made in the nineteenth century and the decisions were not all consistent in their implications. If the lawyers had been content to make it clear that they were not discussing mediaeval history but merely settling modern law, the historians would have had little ground for complaint.[2] But for judges to admit this would be to admit themselves to be legislators and not merely interpreters of law, and this fact is among the *arcana imperii*. The writing of history to suit contemporary modes in law or politics is and has always been too important an activity to be surrendered wholly to scholars.[3]

By a series of decisions in individual cases between the sixteenth and the twentieth centuries a set of rules of qualification and succession was built up with retrospective application to the interpretation of thirteenth and fourteenth century events for modern purposes. In consequence of this, historical persons are shown as barons in the modern peerage books who did not, historically, enjoy baronial style or privilege. Such were the Lords Hastings, from the so called sixth lord who died in 1393 to the so called fifteenth lord who died in 1542.[4] By a similar posthumous application of modern logic to history the doctrine of abeyance was evolved, though a time came when it was felt to have got out of hand and by administrative action a halt was called.[5]

The social history of the mediaeval baronage is not greatly concerned with these ghost barons of modern peerage law, who were not in their lifetimes looked upon as such by themselves or anyone else. But we must, as a corollary, recognize that the baronage, like other English social classes, had no sharply defined frontiers but shaded off imperceptibly into the wider class of knights. The tests used to distinguish barons were approximate only. The line drawn in the thirteenth century between the greater barons, who were summoned individually to Parliament, and the lesser barons and knights, who escaped this but conversely bore the greater burden of local duties, was as we have seen a shifting and uncertain one, though by degrees the very drawing of

[1] *Complete Peerage*, vi, app. G.

[2] A. F. Pollard, *The Evolution of Parliament*, ed. 1926, pp. 82–85.

[3] Cf. Herbert Butterfield, *The Englishman and His History*, 1944, and J. G. A. Pocock in the *Cambridge Hist. Journ.* x, 1951, pp. 189–96.

[4] *Complete Peerage*, vi. 354–65. It can, however, be argued that Sir Edward Hastings (d. 1438), now regarded as *de jure* 9th Lord Hastings, was by his famous suit in the Court of Chivalry against Lord Grey, for the undifferenced arms of Hastings, in effect claiming a baronial status which was denied him.

[5] *Report from the Select Committee on Peerage in Abeyance*, H.M. Stationery Office, 1926.

this line tended to create a class distinction at its point of incidence.[1] Sometimes, at least, the bannerets—military commanders entitled to display their arms on banners, and not only on shields like the ordinary knights, or bachelors—were regarded as peers or equals of the barons.[2] By the middle of the fourteenth century a rule had been arrived at that the holder of $33\frac{1}{3}$ knights' fees should be regarded as a baron.[3] This underlines the point that his standing depended far less on his position as a counsellor of the Crown than on his weight in his own locality. When the Crown was weak this was more marked. The ambition of Henry VI's great lords

was not to sit as lords of council or of parliament at Westminster, but to rule as princes in the provinces; a special writ of summons to parliament added nothing to the prestige of a Neville or a Percy, and threatened an irksome distraction from more local and more congenial occupations. It was not for the writs of summons attached thereunto that these lords of misrule sought dukedoms, marquisates, earldoms, viscounties and baronies, but for the lands, pensions, and other grants which accompanied the conferment of these dignities.[4]

Though this was true of the very great, it seems to have been just at this time that the lesser men began to value the summons to Parliament, as adding to their dignity, instead of seeking to avoid it as a burden. A petition made by Reynold Lord la Warre in 1427 for the precedence which he said his ancestors had enjoyed in Parliament is an early symptom of the new attitude.[5]

Much remains to be learned of the slowly changing pattern of the mediaeval baronage. 'It has been suggested', says Dr. G. A. Holmes, of some periods in English history . . . that there was a tendency for the reigning aristocracy to be superseded as its lands passed to new families.' His researches into the history of the estates of the great earls have, however, shown that 'whatever may be the case in other periods, . . . no social movement of this kind was happening in the fourteenth century. As long as the family did not die out, a great inheritance tended to expand, for there was always a willingness to acquire new land, and there

---

[1] Stubbs, *Constitutional History of England*, ii, 4th ed. 1906, p. 194.

[2] Pollard, op. cit., pp. 69, 95; Stubbs, op. cit., iii, 5th ed., p. 456.

[3] *Modus tenendi Parliamentum*, quoted by Stubbs, *Select Charters*, 1905 ed., p. 503. S. Thrupp, *The Merchant Class of Medieval London*, pp. 236–7, quotes fourteenth and fifteenth century evidence of leading knights, esquires and 'gentils', grouped with the baronage as against the generality of landowning esquires and gentlemen.

[4] Pollard, op. cit., p. 102.

[5] *Complete Peerage*, iv, app. H, pp. 697–9; Powell and Wallis, op. cit., pp. 456–7.

does not seem to have been, at any time in this period, a need to sell', despite the fact that the magnates

endured in the Black Death and the Peasants' Revolt two of the most violent crises in the history of landowning in England. . . . They were threatened with revolution but not with peaceful dispossession. New inheritances were the creatures of politics, built up by royal favours and power at court. Some men like Roger Mortimer, the tyrant of the court from 1327 to 1330, Montague, Ufford and Clinton, the favourites of the young Edward III, Thomas Percy, Despenser and Scrope, Richard II's appellants, had simple grants of land. Others like Hugh le Despenser the younger and Edward III's sons, were served with the marriages of well-endowed heiresses. The effect was the same. When a family died out in the main line, and in spite of many revolts and forfeitures no family was permanently separated from the bulk of its estates except by failure of heirs, the inheritance passed either by previous marriage treaty into the hand of another family . . . or into the king's hands to be regranted to his friends or relations.[1]

For the greatest estates and for the fourteenth century Dr. Holmes here paints a picture which the rest of his book limns at large. Stubbs long since drew a larger picture which still awaits much filling in of detail. The greatest landowners, as he points out, were by no means always those of highest rank.

The fortunes of the Nevilles and Percies were the result of a long series of well-chosen marriages, and were in no way inferior to those of the dukes and marquesses. . . . The kingmaker Warwick was content to remain an earl. . . . There was a marked difference between the stronger earldoms like those of the Bohuns, the Clares and the Bigods, on which the dukedoms were founded, and the smaller accumulations of the Veres and Montacutes of Oxford and Salisbury.

The greatest lordships on the whole were found in the north, while 'the southern counties were thickly sown with smaller lordships' and in the midlands the baronage was less strong and the Crown and Duchy of Lancaster very powerful. Political attitudes ran in families and could be illustrated in their marriage connections.[2] Professor McKisack makes the point[3] that the greatest threat to the continuance of great families was failure of heirs and those which, like Mortimer and Beauchamp,

[1] G. A. Holmes, *The Estates of the Higher Nobility in Fourteenth-Century England*, 1957, pp. 8–9.

[2] Stubbs, *Constitutional History of England*, iii, 5th ed. 1903, pp. 545–8.

[3] May McKisack, *The Fourteenth Century*, Oxford, 1959, pp. 259–60, citing the unpublished MS. of K. B. McFarlane's Ford Lectures (1953), 'The English Nobility 1290–1536'.

continued in unbroken male line from the thirteenth century to the fifteenth were rare exceptions. A great lord whose heir was his daughter could take his pick of suitors and the union of great estates by heiress marriages meant a growing concentration in fewer hands. As Professor Jacob points out, the immense wealth and power accumulated by the Nevilles well exemplifies a marked tendency in the fifteenth century baronage for the rich to grow richer but fewer and for larger units to absorb smaller.[1] To those with property and children fourteenth century legal developments gave greater freedom than heretofore to disperse the former among the latter, so that younger children could be better provided for and land disposed of by will.

Pollard thinks that 'the development or perversion of the king's council in parliament into an hereditary house of lords is mysteriously connected with the growth of heraldry, which characterized the decline of the middle ages' and refers to the incorporation of the heralds in 1484, the sixteenth century Heralds' Visitations and the prominent ceremonial place assigned to Garter King of Arms by Henry VIII.[2] I venture to suggest, however, that the first and most significant move in this direction was Henry V's foundation of the office of Garter King of Arms in 1415. Evidence exists to support Doubleday's suggestion that the claims of barons under Henry VI 'must have given a great opportunity for the activities of the heralds'.[3]

Down to about the reign of Richard II or a little later the baronial families were predominantly Norman by male descent, though, as we have seen,[4] a certain number of English families entered their ranks at quite an early date. The proportion of knightly houses of English origin was, however, much larger;[5] and as baronial and knightly houses intermarried extensively the proportion of English blood in the baronage through female descents slowly but steadily increased. As by Norman custom a daughter succeeded her father if he had no son, baronies and other fiefs from time to time passed by descent from old families to new ones. As no woman could be lawfully married without her lord's consent, the king frequently gave his barons' heiresses in marriage to his friends or to the highest bidder.[6] Promotion into or

[1] E. F. Jacob, *The Fifteenth Century, 1399–1485*, Oxford, 1961, pp. 319–26, 329–30.

[2] Op. cit., p. 104.

[3] See p. 355. *Complete Peerage*, app. H, pp. 697–9; Wagner, *Heralds of England*, 1967, pp. 132–3.

[4] p. 54.                                                    [5] pp. 54–55, 114.

[6] See J. H. Round's introduction to the *Rotuli de Dominabus*, Pipe Roll Soc. xxxv; C. Moor, 'The Mediaeval Marriage Market', *The Genealogists' Magazine*, xii. 221–4, 298–301, 257–64.

within the baronage came mainly by royal favour, whether moved by friendship, service, or payment, and the grant of a rich heiress in marriage was one of the vehicles of such favour.[1] Among newcomers to the baronage Professor McKisack draws attention[2] to two sons of successful lawyers, Henry de Cobham, a Baron of the Exchequer, and Richard le Scrope, summoned as a baron in 1371, son of Henry Scrope, chief justice 1329; to a kinsman of an influential bishop, Edward Burnell, summoned in 1311, great-nephew of Bishop Robert Burnell, Edward I's Chancellor; and to the unique case of Michael de la Pole, the son of a great merchant, created Earl of Suffolk in 1385.

Forfeiture for treason or other offences from time to time put lands at the disposal of the Crown and these, with the great estates which came to it by inheritance might be used to set up new families. The centuries between the twelfth and the fifteenth saw many changes and most of the great names of the twelfth century baronage had by the fifteenth given place to others. The latter were, however, predominantly the heirs and descendants of the former both in blood and lands. While this is generally understood, it is often thought that the Wars of the Roses and the measures of Henry VII made such inroads in the ranks of the peers that the Tudors and their successors had in effect to raise up a new nobility.

This is a considerable exaggeration. The peerage was, in the words of Stubbs, 'attenuated in power and prestige rather than in numbers. Even the bloodshed and attainder fall within a narrow circle: generation after generation perishes out of a few great houses; the majority continue in succession and either escape ruin or soon recover'.[3] But though the numbers had not been greatly diminished, 'all the tallest heads' as Pollard points out, 'were gone. Before 1509 the dukedoms of Norfolk, Suffolk, Somerset, Exeter, York, Gloucester, and the earldoms of Salisbury, Warwick, Lincoln, Nottingham, Rivers, March, Rutland and Worcester had all disappeared; and there was but one duke (Buckingham) and one marquis (Dorset) left in all England.'[4]

All the Tudors were sparing in their creations of peers, Elizabeth I especially so. Most of their new peers were men of outstanding ability who in one way or another had served their sovereigns conspicuously.

---

[1] See E. F. Jacob, *The Fifteenth Century*, pp. 326–8, 331, 333.

[2] *The Fourteenth Century*, p. 264.

[3] William Stubbs, Bishop of Chester, *Seventeen Lectures on the Study of Mediaeval and Modern History*, 1886, p. 355.

[4] A. F. Pollard, *The Reign of Henry VII*, iii, 1914, p. 319.

Some were of distinguished ancestry or of ancient if minor stock,[1] but a few sprang from wealthy merchant families[2] and a few were of obscure origin and wholly self made.[3] Most of these new peers—or, if not they, their sons or grandsons—took wives from older baronial or at least knightly families, so that there was no breach of genealogical continuity between the mediaeval and the modern nobility. It would be of interest to give this generalization statistical form by working out the sixteen great-great-grandparents of every peer of Elizabeth I and the two following generations.

In succession to lands the forfeitures of the fifteenth century made a greater breach, while Henry VIII's dissolution of the monasteries made available a vast additional acreage for the endowment of new families. Though many monastic estates passed quickly from hand to hand, some have come down in the same families from the sixteenth century to our own times, notable among the greatest being those of the Russells, Dukes of Bedford, the Cavendishes, Dukes of Devonshire, the Cavendish-Bentincks, Dukes of Portland, and the Thynnes, Marquesses of Bath. It is sometimes said that the greatest landowners in England owe their possessions to monastic spoils. The truth is less simple and it is at least interesting to reflect that two of the greatest estates in England, those of the Dukes of Northumberland and Norfolk are founded on mediaeval aggregations.

Professor Trevor-Roper[4] has effectively attacked the thesis that the Elizabethan aristocracy was on the verge of bankruptcy, while the gentry rose at its expense. As Dr. Rowse briefly puts it, 'it is obviously absurd to talk as if the Elizabethan aristocracy were on its last legs; if that were so, how is it that Howards and Percys, Berkeleys and Courtenays, Cecils, Cavendishes, Russells, Pagets, Paulets and others who were important in those days continued to decorate the landscape right up to ours?'[5] Professor Trevor-Roper's argument illustrates the point already made—and to be made again—that the peerage is not a nobility and does not constitute a sharply defined class clearly separable from the gentry. This follows from the personal character of a peer's

---

[1] Conyers, Manners, Windsor, Seymour, Darcy of Chiche, St. John, Compton, Norreys, Marny, Mordaunt, Wentworth, Paulet, Parr, Eure, Brydges, Sackville, Cary.

[2] Bullen, Rich, North.

[3] Cromwell, Audley of Walden, Paget.

[4] H. R. Trevor-Roper, 'The Gentry 1540–1640' (Econ. Hist. Rev. Supplement, n.d.).

[5] *The England of Elizabeth*, p. 224. On money-making aristocrats from the fourteenth to the seventeenth century, see J. H. Hexter, *Reappraisals in History*, 1961, pp. 85–92.

position, hereditary indeed, but not shared with other members of his family. The custom of primogeniture secured to the eldest son and heir substantially the whole ancestral estate and the legal privileges of peerage were equally confined to him. The cadets of a peer's house thus had little but reflected glory and somewhat better opportunities to distinguish them from other gentlemen.

When we reach the reign of Charles I

it can hardly be said that the greater gentry were . . . in any serious respect distinct from the country peers who shared their outlook and their economic interests. It is true that the peers possessed a seat in the House of Lords, but attendance registers would reveal that this was seldom occupied by those who lived in the distant counties. The new[1] possibility of a town house seems to have been confined to those who held office in court and government and to a very restricted number of rich men dwelling in the south of England. . . . The difference in life and in approach came rather between the lesser peers, who ranked with the gentry, and the heads of those great houses which possessed an inevitable political significance. This division was in the last resort based upon economic factors and on a certain breadth of political and financial operation. The head of a newly ennobled stock, like that of the Earls of Clare, would thus take his place by virtue of his wealth alongside the inheritors of the great Elizabethan fortunes. Intermarriage still linked even the richest peers with the body of the established gentry. The suggestion made apparently by Lord and Lady Leicester that Edmund Waller was not a sufficient match for *Saccharissa* implies an approach that belonged essentially to the next century.[2]

Queen Elizabeth's example of parsimony in creating peers was not followed by her successor. In the twenty two years of his reign (1603–25) James I raised forty six commoners to the English peerage and Charles I in his first four years raised twenty six. Thus between 1603 and 1629 the numbers of the peerage were doubled. The reasons for this were partly political and partly financial. 'After the Entrance of King James, the Sale of Honours was become a Trade at Court' and sums of about £10,000 apiece were paid for the baronies of Teynham, Houghton, Robartes of Truro, and others.[3] The payments in the three cases mentioned were made to George Villiers, Duke of Buckingham, the king's favourite. James's institution of the Order of Baronets in

[1] Not entirely new; cf. p. 154.
[2] David Mathew, *The Social Structure in Caroline England*, 1948, pp. 39–40.
[3] Trevor-Roper, op. cit., pp. 10–12; *Complete Peerage*, xii, pt. i, p. 680; iii. 247; xi. 36. Of such payments and 'the inflation of honours' in general Professor Lawrence Stone in *The Crisis of the Aristocracy 1558–1641*, pp. 65–128, has superseded all previous accounts.

1611 was a means of raising funds for the settlement of Ulster.[1] Charles I was reluctant to make 'merchandise of honour', but in the time of his great necessity in 1642 he consented to accept £6,000 from Sir Richard Newport to create his father Baron Newport of High Ercall.[2] Sir Edward Walker, Garter King of Arms, wrote in 1653 of 'the frequent Promotions to Titles of Honour and Dignity, since King *James* I came to the Crown of England' that 'it took off from the Respect due to Nobility, and introduced a parity in Conversation, which considering *English* Dispositions proved of ill Consequences, Familiarity (which such Persons were obliged to use) begetting Contempt, and the Curtain being drawn they were discovered to be Men that heretofore were reverenced as Angels'.[3]

City fortunes such as that of Lionel Cranfield, the London mercer's son, whom James I made Earl of Middlesex in 1622,[4] were conspicuous at this time, though a rarer foundation than public office for the fortunes which led to peerage.[5] Comedies of the day exploit 'the theme of intermarriage between the children of the self-made and the decaying nobility and gentry'.[6]

Individual peers suffered in the troubles of the Civil War and Commonwealth, but the peerage continued in existence, if somewhat blown upon. Cromwell deprived it of its legislative function and at length in 1657 set up a shortlived, non-hereditary Upper House of his own, which he hoped would prove 'a great security and bulwark to the honest interest' and would not be 'so uncertain as the House of Commons which depends upon the election of the people'.[7]

Charles II added largely to the peerage, notably by the creation of dukes, five of them his bastard sons.[8] The profuse creation of dukes continued under William and Mary, Anne and George I, but thereafter ceased. The Revolution of 1689 established the basis for the gradual transference of the initiative for creating peers from the sovereign to his ministers. Peerages in the eighteenth century were given mainly for political reasons—to secure or reward political services to the government of the day.

[1] On the Baronets see Stone, op. cit., pp. 83–97.

[2] *Complete Peerage*, ix. 554.

[3] *Historical Discourses upon Several Occasions*, 1705, p. 303.

[4] *Complete Peerage*, viii. 688.                    [5] Trevor-Roper, op. cit., p. 12.

[6] C. V. Wedgwood, 'Comedy in the Reign of Charles I', in *Studies in Social History. A Tribute to G. M. Trevelyan*, ed. J. H. Plumb, 1955, pp. 120–2.

[7] *Complete Peerage*, iv, app. G.

[8] Oxford Historical and Literary Studies, iii, A. S. Turberville, *The House of Lords in the Reign of William III*, 1913, pp. 2–5; *Complete Peerage*, vi, app. F.

The latter part of the seventeenth century and the first part of the eighteenth saw a powerful and continued movement by the great land-owners to add to their estates by marriage and purchase at the expense of lesser gentry and freeholders.[1] The legal device of the strict settlement, perfected in the seventeenth century, mainly, it is said, by Sir Orlando Bridgeman (d. 1674), helped them to make sure that their progeny did not disperse them.[2] The great Whig oligarchs of the eighteenth century set a greater distance in power, wealth and social station between themselves and others than most of their predecessors or successors. The example of France, first strongly felt through the French associations of Charles II and the contemporary prestige of the court of Louis XIV, had a powerful influence on this trend, which the habit of the Grand Tour and the fashion for continental culture continued to fortify until 1789, when the French Revolution and the ensuing war and economic movements drove England once more in upon herself and strengthened a contrary movement already in being.

The great houses of the Whig oligarchy, Houghton, Holkham, Castle Howard, Wentworth Woodhouse and the rest are its enduring monument.[3]

There were very few aristocrats—perhaps never more than a hundred and fifty really active ones. . . . They were rich, and getting in general richer; they dominated the Court and the social life of London. They were educated to consider themselves a separate order of society. . . . It was natural that pride should breed a competitive spirit and that the nobility's growing wealth should lead to an exuberant display. Houses became ever larger; decoration richer and more ornate; furniture more expensive; pictures more costly. . . . Such grandiose palaces demanded a style of living which the sovereign princes of Germany and Italy might have envied. Europe was ransacked for pictures and statuary; manuscripts, books, medals, exotic plants and birds, all that could give distinction or singularity were collected assiduously and regardless of expense. . . . Younger sons could be fobbed off with a career in the Army, the Church or even in trade, but daughters had to be married high. This could not be done cheaply. His daughters' portions cost Daniel Notting-ham £52,000. . . . The effect of course was to bind aristocratic families in a close union of blood relationship which gave rise to a heightened sense of

[1] H. J. Habakkuk, 'English Landownership, 1680–1740', *Econ. Hist. Rev.* x, 1939–40, pp. 1–17.

[2] Frederick Pollock, *The Land Laws*, 1883, pp. 106–12; *The European Nobility in the Eighteenth Century*, ed. A. Goodwin, 1953, chap. 1, England, by H. J. Habakkuk, pp. 2–3.

[3] The relation of the great houses of *c.* 1710–60 to the social standing and aims of their builders is discussed by Sir John Summerson in his Cantor Lectures, 'The Classical Country House in 18th Century England', *Journ. Roy. Soc. of Arts*, vol. cvii, where a similar socio-architectural study of the ensuing epoch is desiderated.

caste and privilege. . . . George I and George II were so determined to protect the peerage from dilution that they ennobled very few men and the aristocracy hardly increased at all during their reigns.[1]

It was noted by foreign observers that the eminence of the oligarchs did not extend to their families. Voltaire wrote, 'A peer's brother does not think trade beneath him. When the Lord Townshend was Minister of State, a brother of his was content to be a City Merchant; and at the time that the Earl of Oxford governed Great Britain, a younger brother was no more than a factor in Aleppo, where he chose to live, and where he died.'[2] On the other hand, the use of their patronage to reward those who served them and the maintenance of their influence through kinsmen and friends in the House of Commons were essential elements in the system of the Whig oligarchs. Out of 5,034 Members of Parliament in the years between 1734 and 1832, 883 were sons of peers, 451 were baronets and 64 were Irish peers, when first elected—more than a quarter of the total; while 1,715, over a third, ended their time as members with such status. Many more were related to peers or baronets by birth or marriage.[3] This situation had developed by degrees since Tudor times, when membership of the House had begun to attract men of a higher class, including peers' sons.[4]

Within this representation of the aristocracy in the eighteenth century House of Commons a special representation of a limited number of families has been noted. Of the 5,034 Members mentioned above 3,045 belonged to 922 agnatic families, but 1,527 to only 247, while a small group of only 31 families provided 382 Members—one in every 13.[5] Some significance attaches also to the fact that 13 peers' bastards were in this period Members of Parliament of whom 5 were created baronets and and 1 an Irish peer.[3]

Of the new creations in this period, says Professor Habakkuk,

the largest single group consisted of men ennobled for service to the state; statesmen like Walpole [1742] and Pitt [1766], politicians of second rank like

---

[1] J. H. Plumb, *Sir Robert Walpole, The Making of a Statesman*, 1956, pp. 8–11.

[2] *Letters Concerning the English*, x. 1733, trans. D. Flower, *Voltaire's England* (Folio Society), 1951, pp. 50–51.

[3] Gerrit P. Judd, IV, *Members of Parliament 1734–1832*, Yale U.P., 1955, pp. 31, 33.

[4] Wallace Notestein, *The Winning of the Initiative by the House of Commons*, 1924, pp. 48–49; Neale, *The Elizabethan House of Commons*, pp. 146–7, 301.

[5] These were Manners 21; Townshend 17; Buller, Finch and Fitzroy 15 each; Cavendish, Fane, Stuart (Bute), 15 each; Grenville, Spencer, 13 each; Bouverie, Ponsonby, Stuart (Galloway), Yorke, 12 each; Cavendish-Bentinck, Clive, Dundas, Foley, Heathcote, Herbert, Hope, Leveson-Gower, Paget, Pitt, Seymour, Smith (Carrington), Walpole, 11 each; Lowther, Onslow, Percy, Williams-Wynn, 10 each.

Speaker Onslow [1716] and George Lyttelton [1756], lawyers like Cowper [1706], Harcourt [1711] and Macclesfield [1716], soldiers like Cadogan [1716] and Cobham [1714], sailors like Hawke [1776] and Rodney [1782]; of these only the lawyers can properly be said to represent new men. Another group, not entirely exclusive of the first, consisted of the sons of peers, men who had acquired a claim to titles by marrying into the families which had borne them in some previous period, Irish peers and baronets of old landed families. All these were men to whom a peerage was only one step in promotion. The peer of obscure social origin was rare, and there were none who had been actively engaged in trade, nor until Smith was made Lord Carington [1796], was there any financier. The great merchants and financiers were rewarded less lavishly, by baronetcies or by Irish peerages.[1]

George III at first maintained this policy but William Pitt became Prime Minister in 1783 and in 1784 a new phase of lavish creations for political purposes began. In five years nearly fifty additions were made to a peerage of under 200 and throughout the rest of George III's reign the number of the peers was steadily increased. Wraxall[2] blames for this 'Burke's eagerness to diminish the supposed overgrown influence of the Crown, arising from the distribution of offices among the members of the House of Commons' to which the Economical Reforms of 1780 gave some effect. In consequence of this, says Wraxall, 'The Minister, deprived of the means of procuring parliamentary attendance and support, by conferring places on his adherents, has in many instances been compelled to substitute a far higher remuneration; namely Peerages.——Mr. Pitt had in fact little left him to bestow, in proportion to the crowd of claimants, except dignities; and he was not parsimonious in their distribution.' He adds that Burke himself lived to express regret for his part in this. Other factors may, however, have contributed to Pitt's policy. Sir Egerton Brydges[3] writes of 'the deterioration and proximate annihilation' of the higher classes of landed gentry by Pitt's 'ill-selected profusion of honours; by his palpable preference of mercantile wealth, and by his inborn hatred of the old aristocracy', which Brydges says he inherited from his father, 'but he had not the same excuse for it as his father had'.[4]

Though the purpose of these creations was in general immediate

---

[1] *The European Nobility in the Eighteenth Century*, ed. A. Goodwin, 1953, pp. 17–18.
[2] *Historical Memoirs of my Own Time by Sir N. William Wraxall, Bart.* (1904 ed. Kegan Paul p. 446).
[3] *The Autobiography . . . of Sir Egerton Brydges, Bart.*, 1834, vol. i. p. 196.
[4] Ibid., p. 335.

political advantage, the willingness to use such an expedient showed that the more exalted notions of a Peer's inherent superiority to those below him were in process of dilution.

> The exclusive . . . character of the English peerage was destroyed [says George W. E. Russell] finally and of set purpose, by Pitt when he declared that every man who had an estate of ten thousand a year had a right to be a peer. In Lord Beaconsfield's words, 'He created a plebeian aristocracy and blended it with the patrician oligarchy. He made peers of second-rate squires and fat graziers. He caught them in the alleys of Lombard Street, and clutched them from the counting-houses of Cornhill'.[1] This democratization of the peerage was accompanied by great modifications of pomp and stateliness in the daily life of the peers. . . . Horace Walpole describes how, when a guest playing cards at Woburn Abbey dropped a silver piece on the floor, and said, 'Oh, never mind; let the Groom of the Chambers have it,' the Duchess replied, 'Let the carpet-sweeper have it; the Groom of the Chambers never takes anything but gold'. These grotesque splendours of domestic living went out with the eighteenth century. Dr Johnson, who died in 1784, had already noted their decline. There was a general approach towards external equalization of ranks, and that approach was accompanied by a general diffusion of material enjoyment.[2]

The French Revolution hastened what Pitt had begun, but the special superiority of the great Whig families survived, not only this but the Reform Bill of 1832, and only began to vanish after the middle of the nineteenth century.

> Whiggery, rightly understood [says G. W. E. Russell] is not a political creed but a social caste. The Whig, like the poet, is born, not made. It is as difficult to become a Whig as to become a Jew. Macaulay was probably the only man who, being born outside the privileged enclosure, ever penetrated to its heart and assimilated its spirit. . . . When Lord John Russell formed his first Administration [in 1846] his opponents alleged that it was mainly composed of his cousins, and one of his younger brothers was charged with the impossible task of rebutting the accusation in a public speech.

From John, Earl Gower (d. 1754), were said to be descended 'all the Levesons, Gowers, Howards, Cavendishes, Grosvenors, Russells, and

---

[1] Professor Habakkuk, *The European Nobility in the Eighteenth Century*, p. 18, points out that *pace* Disraeli the new peers were drawn predominantly from among the older and more substantial families of squires.

[2] George W. E. Russell, *Collections and Recollections*, 1903, pp. 75–76. In his Cantor Lectures, 'The Classical Country House in 18th Century England', *Journ. Roy. Soc. of Arts*, vol. cvii, Sir John Summerson traces the reflection in architectural trends of the change from the overweening greatness of the Whig Oligarchs of *c.* 1710–60 to the more widely diffused luxury of the ensuing years.

Harcourts, who walk upon the face of the earth'.[1] The exclusiveness of these families loosened, however, as their political power weakened. The agricultural depression of the 1880's by undermining the land-owning interest played a part also in undermining the prestige and power of aristocracy. Mr. W. L. Guttsman holds that in the past century we have exchanged a traditional for a capitalist aristocracy, though he gives pedigrees which show politico-aristocratic groups persisting into the 1950's.[2]

Just as the holders of public office and the great merchants of London had in the seventeenth century with wealth and power gained an importance which brought some of their number into the House of Lords, so in the late nineteenth and the twentieth centuries importance which arose from the new industrial sources of wealth began to be represented there. In 1896 167 peers were directors of companies and by 1920 232 (including courtesy peers and peeresses), the increase, according to Vicary Gibbs, coming about 'not so much by more peers in search of commercial enterprises of which they have no special knowledge, ... as by the fact that many magnates in coal, shipping, and other industries have of late been raised to the Peerage'.[3] A still more recent commentator has observed 'company directors yielding in turn to high-salaried executives, often in official or quasi-official appointments'.[4]

## 2. KNIGHTS, ESQUIRES AND GENTLEMEN[5]

The origin of knighthood and its introduction into England have already been discussed[6] with the brevity necessary in a book of this kind. The Conqueror's knights were his fighting men, the possessors of full military equipment, and his barons were their commanders. The barons were granted lands upon condition of producing prescribed numbers of knights for the king's service. Some of the barons continued for some time to keep their knights constantly about them in

---

[1] Russell, op. cit., p. 146.

[2] *The British Political Elite*, 1963, pp. 78, 127, 134, 216–24.

[3] *Complete Peerage*, v, 1926, app. C.

[4] *Times Literary Supplement*, 13 May 1949. Review of *Burke's Peerage*. For family links between the peerage and others eminent in politics and affairs today see Anthony Sampson, *Anatomy of Britain*, 1962, pp. 19–20, and pedigree at p. 34 abridged from diagrams published by Lupton and Wilson in the *Manchester School* in 1960, commenting on the Bank Rate Tribunal.

[5] On the subject matter of sections 2, 4 and 8, see Sylvia L. Thrupp, *The Merchant Class of Medieval London* [*1300–1500*], University of Chicago Press, 1948, Chapters v and vi, and Appendices A and C, where important references are given.

[6] pp. 48–49.

their households. But some soon and all in time found it more convenient to deal with their knights as they themselves had been dealt with by the king. They planted them on their lands and granted them manors in return for the performance of specified service when called upon. Many of these knights in turn enfeoffed others on their lands, so that fractional services came to be owed. Such subinfeudation produced holdings of a half, a quarter, a tenth and even a hundredth of a knight's fee,[1] and chains of as many as five sub-tenants holding one from another below the king.

This was one of the difficulties which progressively led to the commutation of the military service due to the lord for a money payment called scutage or shield money. Scutage appears in England soon after knight service and before the accession of Henry I.[2] The knights hired by the king or barons with the money paid were still actual knights, but the tenants by knight service who paid scutage need no longer be knights at all. By 1205, when some 4,000 knights secured exemption from knight service by payment of scutage or fine, the feudal levy as a fighting force had been replaced by a paid army.[3] This did not, of course, mean that knights no longer fought, merely that they did not do so in virtue of their feudal obligation, and that the tenure of lands by knight service and actual service as a knight became dissociated. By the statute *Quia Emptores* in 1295 subinfeudation was forbidden.

The origins of the knightly class have been far less fully studied than those of the barons. Dr. Charles Moor's great index to the *Knights of Edward I* would provide a starting-point.[4] Pending this we can perhaps do no better than quote the view of Stubbs.

So wide a class [he says] contained, of course, families that had reached their permanent position by different roads. Some were the representatives of old land-owning families, probably of pure English origin, which had never been dispossessed, which owned but one manor, and restricted themselves to local work. Others had risen, by the protection of the barons or by fortunate marriages, from this class, or from the service of the great lords or of the king himself, and, without being very wealthy, possessed estates in more than one county, and went occasionally to court. A third class would consist of those . . . of semi-baronial rank. The two latter classes in all cases, and the first in later times, would have heraldic honours. From the second came generally the men who undertook the offices of sheriff and justice. All three

---

[1] A. L. Poole, *Domesday Book to Magna Carta*, p. 17; A. L. Poole, *Obligations of Society in the XII and XIII Centuries*, 1946, pp. 5, 45.    [2] Ibid., p. 41.
[3] Ibid., p. 52.    [4] Harleian Soc. lxx–lxxiv, 1929–32.

occasionally contributed to the parliament knights of the shire: the humbler lords of manors being forced to serve when the office was more burdensome than honourable, the second class being put forward when political quarrels were increasing the importance of the office, and the highest class undertaking the work only when political considerations became supreme . . . from the beginning of the fourteenth century the parliaments are filled with men of pure English names, small local proprietors.[1]

The inheritor or grantee of a knight's fee was not a knight till he had come of age and had been formally knighted. Under Henry III a reluctance among those qualified for it to be knighted and thus to incur the burdens, administrative as well as military, which were placed upon knights, became marked. In 1224 Henry III first introduced distraint of knighthood, a summons to those qualified to receive knighthood, with a fine as penalty for whose who declined. Whether on this and subsequent occasions of distraint the Crown was more anxious to secure knights or funds is a nice question, not admitting of a simple answer.[2]

Mr. Denholm-Young has reckoned the numbers of actual and potential English knights at this time. The contracts made by the Conqueror with his tenants in chief required them to provide him with about 5,000 knights and the services of a smiliar number were due in 1166. By the thirteenth century this figure had risen to 6,500. These, however, are not figures of the actual number of knights available. Before the thirteenth century those actual figures are unknown to us, but from the records, which then become fuller, Dr. Denholm-Young[3] estimates that under Edward I the total number of men qualified to take up knighthood was about 3,000 and the number of those who had done so about 1,250, of whom some 500 would be actually available for fighting. By the reign of Edward II, when we first know the names of the knights of the shire sent by the shires to Parliament, nearly half of them turn out not to be knights at all.[4] The so-called Parliamentary

---

[1] *Constitutional History of England*, iii, 5th ed. 1903, p. 565.

[2] N. Denholm-Young, *Collected Papers on Mediaeval Subjects*, 1946, p. 64; Powicke, *The Thirteenth Century*, pp. 546–8.

[3] Op. cit., pp. 56–61, 67.

[4] Ibid., quoting G. Lapsley, 'Knights of the Shire in the Parliaments of Edward II', *English Hist. Rev.*, 1919. For a sheriff's apology in 1360 that knights of the shire were not knights see Arch. Aeliana, 4th Series, 1934, xi. 22: for reluctance to take up knighthood and merchants who did so in the fourteenth and fifteenth centuries see S. Thrupp, *The Merchant Class of Medieval London*, pp. 375–8. On Knights of the Shire, who were not knights, see also N. Denholm-Young, *The Country Gentry in the Fourteenth Century*, Oxford, 1969, pp. 56–59.

Roll of Arms of *c.* 1310 is regarded as not far from a complete census of the knights then existing.[1]

The diminution in the numbers of the knights continued until the middle of the fourteenth century, when the development of courtly chivalry restored some of the older character of knighthood and made it once again a military rank. 'But the class of squires had then for all practical purposes attained equality with that of knights, and all the functions which had once belonged exclusively to the knights were discharged by the squires.' Certain families, such as those descended from the old minor barons and the great legal families, continued to take up their knighthood when many others had ceased to do so.[2]

The ceremony of dubbing a man knight was in early times performed by the new knight's father or his lord or by another knight. In the twelfth century the knight's son would enter on his training in arms and chivalry at an early age as a valet (*vassaletus*); would become an esquire (Latin *armiger, scutifer*) at about fourteen and would be knighted when he came of age. Dr. Denholm-Young shows that in 1300 *vallettus* and *scutifer* could be interchangeable terms[3] and that in the fourteenth century these terms were at times applicable to franklins.[4] In the course of the thirteenth century, as knighthood came to be looked on as a burden, ceremonial dubbing came to be restricted to special occasions and ultimately was performed only by the king. The man of knightly birth and training who had not been knighted remained simply an esquire or valet.

The evolution by which the word esquire or squire came, from meaning an apprentice knight, to mean the lord of a manor, and, still later, merely to indicate an ill defined and ever declining social position, is an index of the development of the knightly class into the gentry. From the fifteenth century to the nineteenth the esquires were the top layer of the gentry, but the difficulty of defining just where that layer ended grew ever greater. Miss Thrupp points out that senior rank in a great household carried with it recognition of gentility. John

---

[1] N. Denholm-Young, *Collected Papers on Mediaeval Subjects*, 1946, p. 62. See also Powicke, op. cit., p. 552, and for an account of this Roll, A. R. Wagner, *Catalogue of English Mediaeval Rolls of Arms*, pp. 42–50.

[2] Stubbs, *Constitutional History of England*, iii, 5th ed. 1903, pp. 564–5. On reluctance to take up knighthood and merchants who did so in the fourteenth and fifteenth centuries see Thrupp, op. cit., pp. 375–8.

[3] *Heraldry and History 1254 to 1310*, 1965, p. 21, citing *Liber Quotidianus Contrarotulatoris Garderobae* of 28 Edward I (Soc. Ant. 1787), p. 232, where *Scutiferi* in the text are called *Valetti* in the margin.

[4] *The Country Gentry in the Fourteenth Century*, 1969, pp. 19, 20, 23, 26.

of Gaunt's butler, master cook, master carpenter, steward, seneschal, under-seneschal and some of his porters, constables and wardens of fees were styled esquire.[1] Robert Glover, Somerset Herald, noted in 1580[2] that 'at this day that vocation is growen to be the first degree of gentry'. He set out specific qualifications for the title which must have found favour, for other heralds repeat them and as late as 1681 heralds making a Visitation were instructed to

allow the Title of Esquire to these and no other. 1. The heir Male of the Younger Son of a Nobleman. 2. The heir Male of a Knight. 3. Officiary Esquires. Vizt. Such who are made so by the King by putting on the Collar of S.S. or such who are so Virtue Officii without that Ceremony as the high-Sheriff of a County, and a Justice of Peace, during their being in Office or Commission, . . . Barristers at Law, you shall Enter by that Title, but you shall accept them as Gentlemen only, unless otherwise qualified to bear the Title of Esquire.[3]

These in substance were Glover's categories of 1580. In the reign of James I Sir Robert Knollys put forward a plan for the regulation of the title of Esquire by letters patent on payment of fees, but this was not adopted.[4]

A case of argument on the borderline between esquires and gentlemen is quoted by Mr. G. D. Squibb from the records of the Court of Chivalry. In 1640 John Pincombe of Poughill, Devonshire, called a witness to depose that he 'was and is commonly accounted, reputed and taken to be an Utter Barrister, having studied in the Middle Temple, London, and therefore an Esquire as he believeth, for he is commonly called by the name of Esquire'.[5]

Gregory King in 1695 reckoned the number of esquires at 3,000 as against 600 knights and 12,000 gentlemen. In 1322 *valletti* seem to be esquires,[6] but by 1400 *valettus* was translated yeoman and was being used to signify the class next below the knightly class,[7] and later its meaning declined still further to the sixteenth century varlet and the modern valet.

The derivation of gentle (Latin *gentilis*, French *gentil*), in the medi-aeval sense of well born, from the classical *gentilis*, member of a *gens*,

---

[1] Op. cit., pp. 240–1.                    [2] Coll. Arm. MS. MjD. 14, p. 95.

[3] Wagner, *Heralds and Heraldry in the Middle Ages*, 2nd ed. 1956, p. 147.

[4] Lawrence Stone, *The Crisis of the Aristocracy 1558–1641*, p. 70.

[5] George Drewry Squibb, Q.C., *The High Court of Chivalry*, pp. 175–6, citing College of Arms, Cur. Mil. Boxes, 16/4c. *Pincombe* v. *Prust*, 1640.

[6] Stubbs, op. cit. iii. 574–5.

[7] Sir George Sitwell, Bt., F.S.A., 'The English Gentleman', *The Ancestor*, i, 1902, pp. 58–103, 68.

or the late Latin *gentilis*, a gentile (non-Jew, non-Christian or barbarian) is somewhat obscure,[1] but this usage was established by the twelfth century. Down to the fifteenth century noble and gentle, in their social sense, were interchangeable and in the conservative official language of the heralds so continued far into the sixteenth. Until after 1400, therefore, *gentil homme* or gentleman includes barons and knights as well as men of the knightly class who had not been knighted. Its use to distinguish these last named, the *mere* gentlemen, from their baronial and knightly superiors seems to begin in the fifteenth century and Sir George Sitwell put forward a theory that it dated from a statute of 1413, which laid down that in legal actions of certain kinds the 'estate, degree or mystery' of the defendant must be stated.[2]

However that may be, a name for the class in question was beginning to be needed. Nicholas Upton, who wrote of heraldry and the customs of war about 1440, noted that 'in these days we see openly how many poor men through their service in the French wars have become noble, some by their prudence, some by their energy, some by their valour, and some by other virtues which . . . ennoble men. And many of these have upon their own authority taken arms to be borne by themselves and their heirs.'[3]

The connection between armorial bearings and nobility derives from the fact that heraldry as a system was developed for and by the knights in the twelfth century to distinguish one from another when armed in war and tournament.[4] Examples brought together by Dr. Paul Adam-Even suggest that in thirteenth century France the use of a seal was at first a privilege of knights so closely guarded that even a knight's son, if only an esquire and not yet knighted, might not use one. The next stage would be for esquires to use non-heraldic seals, bearing only non-armorial devices not charged on shields. It thus seems likely that at this

[1] Sir George Sitwell, Bt., F.S.A 'The English Gentleman', *The Ancestor*, i, 1902, pp. 97–102.

[2] Ibid., p. 73. For a criticism of Sir George Sitwell's views see S. Thrupp, *The Merchant Class of Medieval London*, pp. 235–6. See also N. Denholm-Young, *The Country Gentry in the Fourteenth Century*, Oxford, 1969, pp. 1–2 and *passim*. Legal opinion of 1448 and 1450 that gentility could be lost on dismissal from office is quoted in Thrupp, op. cit., p. 245, from Sir John Doderidge, *The Magazine of Honour*, 1642, pp. 1145–6.

[3] *Nicolai Uptoni de Studio Militari Libri Quatuor*, ed. Edward Bysshe, London, 1654, pp. 257–8.

[4] Some account of the origin of heraldry is given in my chapter (xi) on heraldry in *Medieval England*, new ed., ed. A. L. Poole, Oxford, 1958, and a fuller discussion of arms and nobility in my *Heralds of England*, 1967, pp. 25–38.

early date in France armorial bearings were a sign and index of knightly status or nobility. At the same date great lords used large equestrian seals, and their sons who were not yet knighted used simple armorial seals with shields of arms only.[1]

From this early theory practice soon departed, but differently in different regions. In France, as we shall see, a hereditary nobility crystallized in a way which largely deprived heraldry of this kind of significance. In England this did not happen but heraldry nevertheless was soon adapted for civilian use on seals and in other ways and heraldic devices began to be adopted for these purposes by others than knights; first in the twelfth century by ladies; then, occasionally, in the thirteenth by merchants and artisans; and in the fourteenth by bishops, abbeys, cities and boroughs. By the thirteenth century in several parts of Europe, but especially in the free cities, merchants, craftsmen and others not of knightly class or status were engaged in purchases of land and other transactions which required them to use personal seals and so to adopt seal devices. These were commonly non-heraldic in character, but the shield of arms had an attractiveness and perhaps a prestige which led to its occasional use in this non-chivalric context.[2] The evidence is all too scanty but it is clear that by the fourteenth century there were two well defined schools of thought. One held that arms were ensigns of nobility, which would be granted on enoblement, but might not be adopted at will. The other argued that any man might adopt arms provided that the device in question was not already borne by another.

It is only in recent years that the obscure and scattered evidence on this subject has begun to be brought together and on many points it is still too soon to form conclusions. One difficulty is the variation in law and practice between one region and another. We cannot argue from France to England or from Savoy to Flanders. On the other hand, regional differences in the law and practice of the use of arms would, if one could but ascertain them clearly, throw an interesting light on the corresponding social and political variations. Another problem is to

---

[1] P. Adam-Even, *Les Sceaux d'écuyers au XIIIᵉ siècle*, offprint from *Archives héraldiques suisses*, 1951. N. Denholm-Young, *The Country Gentry in the Fourteenth Century*, Oxford, 1969, pp. 4, 5, 23, dates the recognition as armigerous of knights' sons, who were not knights, to the middle of the fourteenth century.

[2] Thrupp, op. cit., pp. 249–56, discusses the use of arms by merchants in the middle ages, mentioning (p. 251) eighty merchants, besides aldermen, who sealed with arms in the fourteenth century and the conversion of merchants' marks into false arms by fifteenth century merchants (p. 253).

distinguish the theories of heralds and jurists from actual practice and
from the law as laid down by statute or decided in the courts. The con-
fusions and cross purposes which may arise from a neglect of these
distinctions are exemplified in the controversial exchanges of 1900–4
between Oswald Barron, A. C. Fox-Davies, W. P. W. Phillimore and
others on the subject of the Right to Bear Arms, in the course of which
the argument oscillated unobserved between such different questions
as, 'What is the law of arms now?', 'What ought it to be?', 'What was
it in the middle ages?' and 'What was then the practice?'[1]

In seventeenth century France arms were freely used by noble and
roturier alike, until in 1696 Louis XIV made their use subject to payment of a tax. Heraldic writers of that century looked back, however,
to a time when only noblemen bore them and believed that merchants
and artisans had but aped the nobility in doing so.[2] In France, where the
privileges of nobility were defined by law, an exclusive right to bear
arms was not among them. In England, where the tests of nobility (in
this context synonymous with gentility) were vague and elastic, the
status of arms as ensigns of gentility and indeed as the surest evidence
of its existence, was officially insisted on.[3] This is not the paradox it may
at first seem. The very fact that the English gentleman's status was less
well defined that that of the French noble made necessary this insistence
on its outward marks, and a right to arms had come by the sixteenth
century to be looked on as decisive evidence of gentility.

The development of this position presents analogies to that of the
peerage. Enactments or assumptions by the Crown are followed at
some distance by judgements of the relevant court of law, in this case
the Court of Chivalry. Mr. G. D. Squibb, whose researches have placed
our knowledge of this court's history on a new footing, has recently
refuted the view previously accepted that it was in our sense a military
court, the predecessor of the modern court martial. Its Latin name
*Curia militaris* in fact means the court of the knighthood or chivalry,
the court, that is, in which offences against the English form of the
international code of knightly or chivalric conduct were tried. Mr.
Squibb dates the court's origin between 1347 and 1348, which
would connect it with the exigencies of Edward III's warfare in France.

---

[1] X (i.e. A. C. Fox-Davies), *The Right to Bear Arms*, 1900; W. P. W. Phillimore,
*Heralds' College and Coats of Arms*, 1903 and 1904; *The Ancestor*, i. 77–88 (Sir G. Sitwell);
ii. 40–47, 222–3 (W. P. W. Phillimore); vi. 155–74 (Oswald Barron); vii. 267 (Phillimore); viii. 113–44; and ix. 214–24 and x. 52–69 (W. Paley Baildon).

[2] Rémi Mathieu, *Le Système héraldique français*, 1946, p. 44.

[3] A. R. Wagner, *Heralds and Heraldry in the Middle Ages*, passim.

He infers also that before this date jurisdiction in armorial disputes was exercised by commissioners specially appointed by the Crown. The Court of Admiralty, which was likewise governed by the civil law and had international connections, came into existence about the same time (between 1340 and 1357) by delegation of a jurisdiction previously exercised by the King's Council. The Court of Chivalry may well therefore have originated in the same way.[1]

The oldest heraldic causes in the court of which we have record date (with one doubtful exception) from the reign of Richard II. It was he who, as we have seen, first created hereditary peerages by letters patent.[2] In 1389 he granted nobility and arms to one John de Kyngeston to enable him to accept the challenge of a French knight to perform certain deeds of arms with him.[3] Henry V promised before Agincourt to ennoble all who fought with him there and gave them leave to wear his livery collar of SS.[4] Shakespeare refers to this:

> For he, to-day that sheds his blood with me,
> Shall be my brother; be he ne'er so vile,
> This day shall gentle his condition.[5]

But of what use was a privilege which others could usurp? And so we find two years later in 1417 Henry remarking that in recent campaigns abroad many had taken to themselves arms and tunics of arms called *cote armures*, when neither they nor their ancestors had used such in times past, and forbidding such use to all—except those who had borne arms with him at Agincourt—unless they possessed arms by ancestral right or by the grant of some person having authority sufficient thereunto.[6] At least one continental parallel can be cited. By a statute of 1430 Amadeus VIII of Savoy forbade the bearing of arms to all not noble or ennobled on pain of having them ignominiously torn down.[7]

It was in this century that grants of arms began to be made by the

---

[1] George Drewry Squibb, Q.C., *The High Court of Chivalry*, 1959, pp. 13–15.
[2] p. 100 *supra*.                    [3] Rymer's *Foedera*, vii. 630.
[4] Jean Juvenal des Ursins, *Histoire de Charles VI Roy de France*, ed. Michaud et Poujoulat, 1850, tome 2, p. 521. For another view of this see Nicolas, *History of the Battle of Agincourt*, 1833, p. 98, and Squibb, op. cit., p. 182, n. 1.
[5] *Henry V*, Act IV, scene iii, ll. 61–63.
[6] Rymer's *Foedera*, ix. 457–8; *Heralds and Heraldry*, p. 63.
[7] Robert Chabanne, *Le Régime juridique des armoiries*, p. 43, quoting J. Nevizanus, *Decreta seu statuta vetera*, cap. xliv, p. 106, and a reference of Bonus de Curtili, a fifteenth century jurist, to this statute as a prohibition of the assumption of new arms save by licence of the prince.

English kings of arms under delegated authority from the king. In 1492 Henry VII expressly confirmed the validity of a grant of arms by Garter as establishing the gentility of its recipient, when this had been questioned by noblemen who would not have him joust with them. The grantee in question was one of the king's Welsh protégés, Hugh Vaughan. Garter Wriothesley stated in 1530 that those 'not vile born or rebels might be admitted to be ennobled to have arms having lands and possession of free tenure to the yearly value of ten pounds sterling or in moveable goods £300 sterling': and about this date the Earl Marshal laid down fees payable on grants of arms upon a scale varying them with the grantee's wealth.[1]

In 1498–9 Henry gave a 'placard' or licence (probably a warrant under the privy seal or signet) to Garter and Clarenceux Kings of Arms 'to visit the arms and cognizances of gentry and to reform the same if it were necessary, according to their oath and bond made at their creations'.[2] Much fuller powers for the Visitation of gentry and correction of their arms, with the reformation and defacement of 'all false armory and arms devised without authority', were, however, conferred by Henry VIII's letters patent of 1530 which inaugurated the series of Heralds' Visitations proper. These were made county by county at intervals of a generation down to the 1680's. Authorized arms with their owners' pedigrees were entered in the Visitation books, while usurpers of arms were forced to disclaim all pretence to them and to the title of gentlemen. The Visitation books are preserved at the College of Arms.[3]

As Dr. A. L. Rowse[4] has pointed out, heraldic visitation served a social and political purpose. 'It was a way of keeping the class distinctions of an hierarchical society in some sort of order amid so much economic flux, and—perhaps of most importance—of regulating, though not obstructing, entry to the governing class.' Mr. Rowse adds that the rise of the gentry, although 'the dominant feature of Elizabethan society', was far from being a new phenomenon at that date, having been in progress all through the fifteenth century, to a lesser extent in the fourteenth, and even in a small measure in the thirteenth.[5] There is room for misunderstanding here. 'The rise of the gentry' may mean the rise of men or families into or within or out of the class of

---

[1] Wagner, *Heralds and Heraldry*, pp. 79–80.          [2] Ibid., pp. 92–93.
[3] pp. 341, 371–4 and A. R. Wagner, *The Records and Collections of the College of Arms*, 1951, pp. 55–84.
[4] *The England of Elizabeth*, p. 248.          [5] Ibid., pp. 234–5.

gentry, or it may mean the rise of the gentry as a class relative to other classes. The rise and fall of families is an immemorial process which must be considered later,[1] so that here only the second sense concerns us. In what sense, if any, can it justly be said that the gentry as a class appeared in the thirteenth century, emerged in the fourteenth, and became prominent in the fifteenth?

Whether anything very definite can be said on this subject until research has gone further seems to me doubtful. The work now in progress on the Society of Antiquaries' new Dictionary of Arms might provide a starting point. In the fifteenth century, indeed, the existence of the gentry as a class is clear. The name gentleman is in distinctive use and armorials of this date give coats for many families not named in earlier rolls of arms but prominent as gentry thereafter. The ancestors of these were in many, perhaps most, cases franklins,[2] probably in general of English origin. But the same class comprehended men of old knightly descent and others whose names and arms suggest descent from younger branches of knightly houses while some derived from city merchants who bought country manors.[3]

In status and function it is hard to see the gentry of the fifteenth and sixteenth centuries as anything but direct successors of the knights, who 'by the end of the twelfth century were training themselves in the arts of local government which in the following centuries they were so largely to control'. Many of them in the next century, as hired armies succeeded the feudal levy, 'laid aside their arms and armour and took to the life of country gentlemen'.[4] A familiar piece of evidence for this is the incorporation of so much of chivalry, the code of knightly conduct, in the concept of gentlemanly behaviour. We have seen that heraldic causes were tried in the Court of Chivalry—the court of the knights or the knighthood[5]—yet before 1400 others than knights were parties to such causes, while in the seventeenth century claims to the court's protection in cases of 'scandalous words provocative of a duel' depended on proof that the plaintiff was *a gentleman*.[6] That the knights' families had by the fifteenth or the sixteenth century been joined or

---

[1] pp. 205–45.

[2] p. 142. J. H. Hexter, *Reappraisals in History*, 1961, pp. 88–89, cites Henry de Bray, who in a lifetime of acquisition *c.* 1300 built up a large estate, from some 500 acres, as the founder of such a family, cf. *The Estate Book of Henry de Bray*, ed. D. Willis, Camden Soc., 3rd Ser. 27 (1916).

[3] Thrupp, op. cit., pp. 279–87.

[4] A. L. Poole, *Obligations of Society in the XII and XIII Centuries*, 1946, p. 56.

[5] p. 121.

[6] e.g. *John Massey of Tatton* v. *John Massey of Potington, Cheshire*, 1378 (*The Ancestor*,

succeeded by others, who arrived at gentility by various routes is in no way distinctive of this particular class or epoch.

The difference between the gentry and the class below them, that of the franklins or yeomen, whom I deal with later,[1] was one of status and way of life rather than of wealth. A yeoman in the sixteenth century might be richer than many gentlemen his neighbours, and the more so since his simpler ways of life saved him what they must spend on elegance or show. Thomas Bradgate of Peatling Parva, Leicestershire, was not merely the richest yeoman in the county in 1524 but had the second highest tax assessment there in any class. His son Richard in 1567 bought the manor on which he lived but was still described as yeoman at his death in 1572 and it is not till near the end of the century that his son begins to be called gentleman.[2] A father might remain a yeoman to his dying day, while his son, who had perhaps learned more polished manners, moved even in his father's lifetime into the ranks of the gentry.[3] In other cases the son who had made his way might arrange for a grant of arms to be made to his father, as it seems likely that Shakespeare did, thus making himself a gentleman of the second generation.[4]

Intermarriage between the families of the poorer gentry and the richer yeomen was common and no doubt they often lived on terms of social equality. But in other cases pride or difference of wealth might lead to insistence on the difference of rank.[5] The kings of arms, who had it in their power, by making or refusing grants of arms, to further or reject aspirations to gentility, were inevitably at times the target of criticism. Garter Wriothesley was accused in 1530 of granting arms to bondmen and vile persons not able to uphold the honour of nobless.[6] Clarenceux Cooke (d. 1592) was said to have confirmed and given arms and crests without number to base and unworthy persons for his private gain.[7] In 1602 Garter Dethick was accused of granting arms to base

---

ix, 1904, p. 217); *Thomas Baude* v. *Nicholas de Singleton*, 1393 (*Cal. Pat. Rolls, 1391–6,* pp. 352, 576 and *1396–9*, p. 89); and *Alice, widow of Roger Wight* v. *William Tanner,* 1394 (*Cal. Pat. Rolls, 1391–6,* p. 380).

[1] p. 141 *infra.* For the distinction between gentlemen and yeomen in the fifteenth century see Thrupp, op. cit., pp. 238–47.

[2] W. G. Hoskins, *Essays in Leicestershire History*, 1950, pp. 128, 157–8.

[3] Mildred Campbell, *The English Yeoman under Elizabeth and the Early Stuarts*, 1942, pp. 38–42 gives examples of the transition.

[4] E. K. Chambers, *William Shakespeare*, ii. 18–32.

[5] Campbell, op. cit., pp. 40–50.

[6] Wagner, *Heralds and Heraldry*, p. 90, and *Heralds of England*, pp. 164–7.

[7] Coll. Arm. Arundel MS. 40, Lant's Observations, fo. 29/123.

persons.[1] It was a question of what one thought the standard ought to be. The judicious Sir Thomas Smith (d. 1577) argued in favour of social elasticity. 'The prince lost nothing by it as he would in France: here the yeoman or husbandman was not taxed as such, the gentleman bore greater charges, which he accepted for the sake of honour and reputation.'[2] Though some criticized or made fun others 'considered rapid gain in numbers among new-made gentlemen a sign "whereby it should appeare that virtue flourisheth among us", and, Thomas Fuller made it one of England's chief claims to superiority over other nations, boasting that here the *Temple of Honour* was bolted against none'.[3]

Serjeant Doderidge in the Abergavenny case of 1588, paraphrasing Smith and others, put the matter in a nutshell.

In these days [he said] he is a Gentleman, who is so commonly taken, and reputed. . . . And whosoever studieth in the Universities, who professeth the liberall sciences, and to be short, who can live idly, and without manuall labour and will beare the Port charge, and countenance of a Gentleman, he shall be called Master: For that is the title that men give to Esquires, and other Gentlemen: For true it is with us, as one said; *Tanti eris aliis quanti tibi fueris*: and if need be, a King of Heralds shall give him for money armes newly made, and invented with the Creast and all: the title whereof shall pretend to have bin found by the said Herauld, in the perusing and viewing of old Registers, where his ancestors in time past had beene recorded to beare the same: or if he will do it more truly, and of better faith, hee will write, that for the merits of, and certaine qualities that he doth see in him, and for sundry noble acts which he hath performed, hee by the authority which he hath asking of Heralds in his Province, and of armes, giveth unto him and his heires, these and these heroicall bearings in arms.[4]

Cases quoted by Mr. Squibb from the records of the Court of Chivalry help to show where the disputable borderline of gentility lay a generation later. The cases in question were not armorial causes but cases of 'scandalous words provocative of a duel', where the plaintiff must establish that he was a gentleman in order to claim the court's protection and might damage the defendant by showing that he was none. In these cases the simple proof by establishing a right to arms is rare. Though only a gentleman could bear arms by right, a man with

[1] *Heralds of England*, pp. 203–4.
[2] Rowse, op. cit., p. 244, citing Sir Thomas Smith, *De Republica Anglorum*, ed. L. Alston, pp. 39–41.
[3] Mildred Campbell, op. cit., pp. 45–46, citing *The Institution of a Gentleman*, 1586, bk. iv and *The Holy State*, p. 106.
[4] G. D. Squibb, *The High Court of Chivalry*, p. 172, quoting *The Magazine of Honour* 1642, pp. 147–8.

no right to arms could still be a gentleman. In that event he must prove gentility by other evidence, whose tendency would be to show that he had lived in the manner of a gentleman and was so reputed. The standing and marriage connections of a man's family were relevant. In 1637 a defendant called a witness to prove that his father and grandfather had been freeholders and headmen of their parish, that his father had been collector of subsidy, headborough and constable, and that his grandmother was descended from the Eyres of Keeton.[1] The gentility of a plaintiff in 1639 was, however, impugned on the ground that his kinsmen were none but butchers and graziers.[2]

It was thought relevant that a litigant's father had been a justice of the peace, or a barrister, or educated at Oxford, or that he was always called Master and never Goodman, or that some of his neighbours called him one and some the other. The mother's ancestry or the fact that an uncle had been High Sheriff of a county might be thought helpful. Conversely it was argued against a defendant's gentility that his mother used to ride to market upon a pair of panniers to sell butter or soap.[3]

A litigant might seek to prove his own gentility by citing his military rank. Thus a captain of a trained band in Surrey (1639) and a lieutenant of a troop of horse in Sussex (1637) adduced these offices in evidence.[4] Others claimed more vaguely to live in the rank, quality and fashion of a gentleman. What this meant may be inferred from the negative. Thus a plaintiff in 1638 is said to live as a yeoman rather than a gentleman because he 'laboureth in husbandry ordinarily with his own hands, holdeth the plough, maketh hay, selleth his corn at the market himself, and keeps no man or attendant on him but such as are employed in labouring and husbandry, and in the parish rates and other writings he is only written Richard Inckpen without the addition of gentleman to his name'.[5]

A tradesman could be a gentleman. Edward Done of Duddon, Cheshire, in 1640 described himself as a gentleman by birth and a linen-draper by trade. In a case of 1634 evidence was given that 'many citizens of great worth and esteem descended of very ancient gentle families' were soap boilers by trade and still accounted gentlemen. Still evidence of mechanical employment might be damaging as the plaintiff of 1640

---

[1] G. D. Squibb, *The High Court of Chivalry*, p. 171, n. 4, quoting *Rodes* v. *Slater*, Coll. Arm. MS. Cur. Mil. i. 268, 277.
[2] G. D. Squibb, *The High Court of Chivalry*, p. 175.
[3] Ibid., pp. 174–5; cases of 1637–40.
[4] Ibid., p. 174.
[5] Ibid., cases of 1637–40, pp. 173–5.

must have felt who countered the allegation, that he was a goldsmith and sometimes worked at the forge and anvil, with a witness who deposed that he had never seen him wear a leather apron.[1] John Cockeshutt, gentleman, of Simonstone was licensed to the trade of drover.[2]

A grantee of arms at this date might have risen from the ranks of the yeomen or the merchants by adding field to field, by prospering in trade, by service to the Crown or to a great man in public or household office, by the law or in the wars. But, as the ownership of land has in England ever been a mainstay of pretence to gentry, those whose wealth came from commerce or office commonly bought manors and settled on them. Conversely, as lands must normally pass intact to the eldest son, the younger sons of landowners would be bound apprentice to trades, if they had not heads for the Church or the Law. Significant differences existed between the social and historical patterns of the gentry of different counties. Research has recently brought out some of these and will no doubt bring out more. Professor Everitt divides the counties into those dominated by one great family like the Earls of Derby in Lancashire, those like Somerset dominated by two or three rivals, and those like Kent, which he has especially studied, where there was a knot of closely related families of comparable standing. He tells us that in 1640 the gentlemen of Kent numbered between 800 and 1000, a figure comparable with those of Somerset, Devon or Suffolk, but relatively much higher than for counties largely unenclosed or under the rule of a great lord, such as Wiltshire or Leicestershire.[3]

A large proportion of these Kentish gentry belonged to twenty or thirty numerous families such as Oxinden, Dering, Hales, Twysden, Scott, Digges, Boys and Finch. Most of these had established more than one landed branch and some had a clan character, a phenomenon found in some other counties but by no means all. Professor Everitt connects its occurrence in Kent with the early influence of gavelkind tenure there.[4] A rather different clan pattern is found in certain other

[1] Ibid., p. 177.

[2] Peter Laslett, *The World We Have lost*, 1965, p. 192, citing *Lancashire & Cheshire Quarter Sessions Records, Sessions Rolls 1596–1606*, ed. James Tait, Chetham Soc., 1917, p. 56.

[3] Alan Everitt, 'The Community of Kent in 1640', *Genealogist's Magazine*, vol. 14, 1963, pp. 229–58, and Alan Everitt, *The Community of Kent and the Great Rebellion 1640–60*, Leicester University Press, 1966, quoting Dr. T. G. Barnes for Somerset and Everitt, 'Suffolk and the Great Rebellion 1640–1660', *Suffolk Rec. Soc.* iii, 1960, p. 26.

[4] Ibid., p. 241.

counties, such as Lancashire and Cheshire, where a particular surname will be found numerous and comprising all classes in a single parish or group of parishes. Evidence of such patterns and their interpretation will be looked at later.[1] They suggest that, while from some localities the unsuccessful removed themselves to other scenes, in the regions of this clan pattern these stayed and multiplied on the spot. The facts and their explanation would be a fit subject for study in connection with the research on English Surname History now proceeding at Leicester University under the Marc Fitch Fund benefaction. In general one would expect more geographical movement of families in counties near London, but Professor Everitt shows that Kent was an exception. Only an eighth of the gentry there in 1640 were newcomers since Queen Elizabeth's reign, compared with 36 per cent of newcomers in Suffolk. A further eighth had come into Kent in Tudor times, but nearly three quarters were there before that as against a mere third in Suffolk. To this indigenous section belonged virtually all the leading families, nearly three quarters of the knights and four fifths of the peers of Kent in 1640 and, though many of the minor families of gentry were of yeoman descent, between 80 and 90 per cent had been gentle before Tudor times.

'It is impossible', wrote Sir John Oglander in 1632, 'for a mere country gentleman ever to grow rich or raise his house. He must have some other vocation with his inheritance, as to be a courtier, lawyer, merchant or some other vocation.'[2] Professor Trevor-Roper points to a distinction within the gentry, from the middle of the sixteenth century to this period and later, between the 'mere country gentlemen', who had nothing but their lands to live on and found it hard to do so, and the 'court gentry' who could supplement their income with the profits of office in the widest sense, 'offices in the household, the administration, and above all—for it was the most lucrative of all—the law; local office as well as central office, county lawyers as well as London lawyers, deputy-sheriffs as well as ministers'. The supply and value of offices was growing as government grew more complex. The road to office was by education and patronage or purchase. Apart from office the chief resort of the poor gentleman was to enter or marry into trade. Professor Trevor-Roper saw in the disgruntlement of the 'mere gentry' a contributory cause of the Great

---

[1] p. 215 *infra*.

[2] Quoted from *A Royalist's Notebook, the Commonplace Book of Sir John Oglander of Nunwell 1622–1652*, ed. Francis Bamford (1936), p. 75, by H. R. Trevor-Roper, 'The Gentry 1540–1640' (Econ. Hist. Rev. Supplement), p. 26.

Rebellion and the Civil War[1] but Professor Hexter thinks it an unimportant one.[2]

If so, the Civil War did not solve their problem. By the end of the century there was still a minority of country gentlemen 'as rich and powerful in their neighbourhoods as many a nobleman', alongside a much larger number of

homespun squires . . . associated in their daily life with the merchants, attorneys and prosperous yeomen. With them they gathered together over their pots of ale and pipes at the fairs and markets of the little country towns. There was far less distinction of class between these groups than between the aristocracy and the squirearchy. Country gentlemen of the middling sort were prepared to marry their daughters to local families in trade or land, and even their younger sons if an heiress was available, although they would rarely consent to the eldest sons going outside their own class. . . . As the cousinage of the aristocracy covered the whole of England in a network of blood-relationship so the counties and neighbourhoods were covered with a similar network by the squirearchy.[3]

Many of these lesser gentry had fallen on difficult days and had first to mortgage their ancestral lands and then to sell them piecemeal. The discontented gentry 'poised on the precipice of bankruptcy' have been discerned behind the Jacobite rebellion of 1715[4] as their predecessors in like case have been discerned in the Great Rebellion. As Professor Plumb points out,

this was not a new process; throughout the centuries, since that first great agrarian expansion of the thirteenth, landed families had risen only to fall again. For one that survived a score were destroyed, overtaken by those natural disasters which beset families—failure of heirs, wanton extravagance, reckless loyalty, sheer bad luck. But debt, the crushing, inexorable burden of debt, extinguished most. As it pressed them down, the needy gentlemen viewed with hatred the wanton luxury of the well-to-do, and envied jealously the manna which fell from the Court into favoured laps.[5] Meantime, as Mr. Christopher Hill has shown,[6] the sale of delinquents' lands and kindred policies during the interregnum had played an important part not only in

[1] Op. cit., pp. 27–44 and *passim*. But cf. G. M. Trevelyan, *English Social History*, 1944, p. 241, 'The squires who had most business connection with London, or with trade and industry anywhere, tended most to the Roundhead side in politics and religion.' The genealogist happily need not commit himself to these generalizations.

[2] *Reappraisals in History*, pp. 129–31.

[3] J. H. Plumb, *Sir Robert Walpole. The Making of a Statesman*, 1956, pp. 14–15.

[4] Ibid., pp. 16–17, citing E. Hughes, *North Country Life in the Eighteenth Century*, pp. 1–5.                                                                            [5] Op. cit., p. 17.

[6] *Puritanism and Revolution*, 1958, pp. 153–96, 'The Agrarian Legislation of the Revolution' and pp. 199–214, 'Lord Clarendon and the Puritan Revolution'.

pulling down the old gentry but also in building up a new race of improving gentry, who set the tone of the ensuing age.

Alongside the decay of old families the rise of new ones has ever continued, but both processes have gone faster at some periods than at others. As an index of the rate of rise into gentility at different epochs the heraldic record, though it must be used with caution, is important because of the close though never rigid link maintained in England between gentility and arms. My friend the late Dr. Edward Elmhirst made a valuable numerical analysis by decades of a large sample of the grants of arms made between 1550 and 1900 and the graph he has worked out shows major peaks about 1570 and 1800, a minor peak about 1660, and troughs about 1640, 1680 and 1740.[1] My interpretation of these figures differs somewhat from Dr. Elmhirst's for I do not think he allowed enough for fluctuations in the powers and energies of the heralds.

The peak of 1570 presents no problem. It is agreed that Elizabeth's was a great age for the emergence of new gentry and that heraldry was never more popular. But the situation was not new and I believe that if the graph could be taken fifty years further back, it would show an earlier peak under Henry VIII, perhaps about 1520. Further, we must remember that in 1555 the heralds had been given a new charter and the predecessor of the present College of Arms building, that in 1568 the Earl Marshal had given them new regulations and that between 1558 and 1592 Hervey and Cooke, Clarenceux Kings of Arms, completed a cycle of Visitation of the southern and richer half of England of unprecedented thoroughness, thus sweeping into the net many potential grantees.[2] A trough could be expected to follow this peak because the cream had been skimmed. Furthermore, despite the Visitations and the legal penalties imposed, many unlicensed herald painters invaded the heralds' field giving out false arms and pedigrees, like William Dawkyns who was sentenced by the Court of Star Chamber to stand in the pillory and lose his ears for so doing.

The Civil War explains the trough of the 1640's but a revival came in the 1650's which is all the more striking when one reflects that the grants then made by Edward Bysshe, the Commonwealth Garter King of Arms, were annulled at the Restoration so that the records of them

---

[1] Edward Elmhirst, 'The Fashion for Heraldry', *The Coat of Arms*, iv, 1956, pp. 47–50. My comments are on pp. 119–20.

[2] Wagner, *Records and Collections of the College of Arms*, pp. 68–71.

are far from complete. It needs no stressing that the Great Rebellion
was not an egalitarian revolution, but these figures underline the point.

The Restoration accounts for the peak in the 1660's, when Sir
Edward Walker, Garter, had a special warrant from Charles II authoriz-
ing him to grant augmented coats to loyalists. The great trough which
followed in the century between 1670 and 1770 is due, I think, to a
breakdown in heraldic authority, which itself reflects a social and
political change, but the change in question did not, in my view, mean
that new claims to gentility and arms were fewer, that social mobility
had slowed down, or that heraldry was out of fashion. What happened,
I believe, was that the readjustments which followed the Revolution
of 1688 put political authority into the hands of great Whig lords whose
concept of the social order was that a gulf should yawn between themselves and the mere gentry and when this was in fact achieved on the
social and economic plane they had little interest in the strict regulation
of a privilege—that of bearing arms—which they and the poorest
gentry shared. One must bear in mind Professor Stone's conclusion
that in the latter part of the seventeenth century a series of stabilizing
factors had come into operation which slowed down social mobility,
while easing social tensions. Among such factors he notes a decline in
fertility and rise in mortality among the upper classes, a reaction
against disorder, an adjustment of education to what society could
absorb and a general tendency towards nepotism, particularism and
closing of the ranks.[1]

One must also, however, take account here of the contemporary
rise of what Professor Alan Everitt has conveniently called the
pseudo-gentry, 'that class of leisured and predominantly urban families
who, by their manner of life, were commonly regarded as gentry,
though they were not supported by a landed estate; most originating
in and after the late seventeenth century, but some earlier; some
gentry who had lost their lands, some cadets of gentle families;
others sprung from clergy, army officers, lawyers, doctors, factors,
maltsters, moneylenders, innkeepers or the like'. He points out how a
community of travelling traders, which arose in the seventeenth century,
contributed in certain towns, such as Northampton, to the rise of
families of this kind.[2]

For an aristocratic culture based on classical antiquity the Gothic

---

[1] Lawrence Stone, 'Social Mobility in England 1500–1700', *Past and Present*, 1966,
pp. 46–48, 51–55.
[2] Alan Everitt, 'Social Mobility in Early Modern England', ibid., pp. 70–72.

origins of heraldry also helped to condemn it. Lord Halifax (d. 1695) noted that 'the contempt of scutcheons is as much a disease in this age as the over-valuing them was in former times'.[1] His grandson Lord Chesterfield (d. 1773) ridiculed pedigrees by hanging up portraits of 'Adam de Stanhope' and 'Eve de Stanhope' among his ancestors.[2] Lord Pembroke (d. 1769) told the younger Anstis, Garter King of Arms (d. 1754), 'Thou silly fellow, thou dost not know thy own silly business.'[3] The heralds fought against this attitude, but for a long time unsuccessfully.

Heralds' Visitations ceased and an effort to revive them in the 1730's failed. Lord Sussex, the Deputy Earl Marshal, asked to sign a warrant for the purpose, said 'he could not do it—he should have all the County upon his back'; and on being told that he was denying justice to ancient families in favour of 'a few proud upstarts, who were ashamed of their origin' said, 'I don't know but I might be impeached for such a thing'.[4] During these years arms were widely assumed without right or grant by those who thought their position required armorial pretension. Defoe indeed writes in 1726,

We see the tradesmen of *England*, as they grow wealthy, coming every day to the Heralds' Office, to search for the Coats of Arms of their ancestors, in order to paint them upon their coaches, and engrave them upon their plate, embroider them upon their furniture, or carve them upon the pediments of their new houses; and how often do we see them trace the registers of their families up to the prime nobility, or the most antient gentry of the kingdom.[5]

Certainly at this date and a little earlier there were those among the heralds who specialized in searching out such lines of descent, where they existed. But in many cases they did not, and these in an earlier generation would certainly have been dealt with by new grants of arms.

---

[1] Quoted by James Hannay, *Three Hundred Years of a Norman House*, 1867, p. 202. I have not traced the original.

[2] *The Letters of Horace Walpole*, ed. Mrs. Paget Toynbee, iii, 1903, p. 11, Walpole to Mann, 1 Sept. 1750.

[3] *Horace Walpole's Correspondence*, ed. W. S. Lewis, i, 1937, p. 330, Walpole to Cole, 28 May 1774. The note identifies 'the Old Lord Pembroke' as the 8th Earl (d. 1733) and 'Anstis the herald' as the elder Anstis (d. 1744), but Mr. Lewis now accepts my suggestion that the above identification is more likely, if only because the elder Anstis was anything but silly. The same note refers to Lord Dover's statement (Letters of Walpole to Horace Mann, 1833, ii, p. 412 n.) that Chesterfield, not Pembroke, made the remark.

[4] Wagner, *Heralds of England*, pp. 363–5.

[5] Defoe, *The Complete English Tradesman*, 1726, p. 377.

But too often at this date they were not, for the heralds' authority being weakened as we have seen, the want was supplied by pirate herald painters or worse, as when at Ipswich in 1727 'one Robert Harman, an Irish dancing-master, was convicted as a notorious cheat and impostor, in assuming the title and functions of a king of arms, and alleging that he was authorized by government to inspect the arms and quarterings of the nobility and gentry of this and 14 other counties; whereby he demanded and received considerable sums'.[1]

In the last quarter of the eighteenth century the approach changed. At one level Pitt's lavish distribution of political peerages and the naval and military honours conferred on so many heroes of the French war revivified the official machine. At another level the 'effect of the French Revolution and the Napoleonic Wars was to concentrate the interests of the Antiquaries upon the antiquities of their own country',[2] so that mediaeval studies, including that of heraldry and genealogy, began to resume the place they had held in the seventeenth century and were once more taken seriously. In 1772 John Charles Brooke, later Somerset Herald, wrote 'that the business of the [Heralds'] Office is now very great and keeps increasing, especially since a late order of the House of Lords . . . and that they are much at a loss for proper hands to carry on the business'.[3] In the years following 1814 the historical novels of Sir Walter Scott gave this movement a wider but more romantically minded public. The peerage claims of the 1830's for abeyant mediaeval baronies[4] show these strands interwoven.

Where the social history of Victorian England, with its immense growth of the middle classes, might lead one to expect a peak in grants of arms Dr. Elmhirst found a trough. The figures on which he worked here may be imperfect, but if they are right there are several possible reasons. The only interest of utilitarian reformers in so antiquated an institution as the College of Arms was in the possibility of reforming it out of existence. Heraldic authority had thus little political backing. This and other factors probably made those concerned with guarding the privileges of gentry more exclusive in their attitude to the newly rich than their Elizabethan predecessors had been. Of this situation the pirate 'Heraldic Offices' took advantage to do as Dawkyns and his like had done in earlier days, and an Irish King of Arms, Sir Bernard Burke

---

[1] Sir James Lawrence, *Nobility of the British Gentry*, 1840, p. 47, quoting *The London Journal*, Sat., 22 Apr. 1727; Ralph Bigland, *Observations on . . . Parochial Registers*, 1764, p. 91.    [2] Joan Evans, *A History of the Society of Antiquaries*, 1956, p. 202.
[3] Wagner, *Heralds of England*, p. 408.    [4] *Complete Peerage*, ii. 286.

(d. 1892), assisted them by publishing a 'General Armory' (1842 and 1884) in which true and false arms were inextricably mingled. The twentieth century, however, has seen the disappearance of the pirate Heraldic Offices, the revival of the Court of Chivalry (1954),[1] and a great increase in the number of grants of arms sought and made. The advent of a Labour Government in 1945 coincided with a new peak, though the grantees now comprised about as many corporate bodies as individuals. Both events were perhaps reactions from war. In the late 1960's the proportion of personal to corporate grantees increased again.

Education had always played an important part in the making of gentlemen, but in the nineteenth century, when the Industrial Revolution had made it not uncommon for men of little or no education to acquire great wealth, its part became even more important. In older times those sons of gentlemen, yeomen and tradesmen who went to school at all were commonly sent together to the same local schools, while the sons of noblemen were more often taught by private tutors. However, a number of noblemen's sons were sent to Eton in the sixteenth and seventeenth centuries, encouraged especially by Provosts Savile (d. 1622) and Wotton (d. 1639),[2] while Westminster School under Dr. Richard Busby, headmaster from 1638 to 1695, acquired a national vogue with the nobility. In the eighteenth century this vogue was shared by Eton, Winchester, Westminster and Harrow, to all of which sons of noblemen and gentlemen were sent from all over England, though down to the late eighteenth century sons of local tradesmen were still sent to Eton.[3] Out of 5,034 Members of Parliament between 1734 and 1832 785 had been at Eton, that is one in six, rising from 43 in 1734 to 144 in 1830. The number of those who had been at Westminster, a total of 544, declined from 111 (to Eton's 79) in 1761 to 65 in 1831.[4]

Thomas Arnold, who became headmaster of Rugby School in 1828, established there a new model of education which, copied in other public schools, grew into a mechanism for the mass production of gentlemen. G. D. H. Cole calls Arnold's Rugby 'a part of the challenge of Liberal Churchmanship to Nonconformity, as well as an attempt

---

1 See *A verbatim report of the case in The High Court of Chivalry of the Lord Mayor, Aldermen and Citizens of Manchester versus the Manchester Palace of Varieties Limited on Tuesday, 21st December, 1954,* published by the Heraldry Soc., East Knoyle, Wiltshire, May 1955.

2 Sir Wasey Sterry, *Eton College Reg. 1441–1698,* 1943, p. xxii.

3 R. A. Austen-Leigh, *Eton College Reg. 1753–1790,* 1921, p. xxi.

4 G. P. Judd, *Members of Parliament 1734–1832,* p. 37.

to turn as many as possible of the sons of the new wealthy into men of culture and inheritors of the old traditions of aristocratic learning and manners.[1] A tendency to equate gentlemen and public school men grew steadily. The genealogist on the watch for marks of status will take especial note of the point in family history at which a Bounderby or a Gradgrind first sends a son to a public school.

Linked with this development was another in which the school-masters played a not less influential part. This was the evolution of a standard English speech with its implication that speakers of other dialects were *ipso facto* vulgar.

The main development took place in the seventeenth and eighteenth centuries but its roots go back very far. There has always, no doubt, been a tendency for the speech forms of a group or town or region, which has come to dominate a country, themselves to become dominant and to set a standard for provincial aspirations. At the same time such dominant dialects are impelled to seek refinement and improvement by the practical needs and cultural aspirations which come with respon-sibility. So it was with the dialect of Athens which became the basis of the literary and the common spoken language of the whole Greek world, and with Latin, which spread with the power of Rome, develop-ing meantime a standard form which sought both literary and social dominance over provincial dialects.

In England after the Norman Conquest the native tongue was for a long time doubly subjected to the courtly dominance of French and the clerkly dominance of Latin, so that when in the fourteenth century it came once more to the literary and political surface, the dialects of different regions at first competed very much on equal terms. The pre-dominance of London, however, loaded the dice in favour of forms used there, though rather of those used in circles where men of talent and education from all over the country mingled than of those used in

---

[1] *Studies in Class Structure*, 1955, p. 109. See pp. 61–77 for the nineteenth century development of the upper middle class in general; p. 62 on poor relations of gentry who claimed and strove to keep gentility; p. 63 on the ungentlemanliness of dissent; pp. 43–44 on the assimilation of the new rich nonconformists to gentility through the public schools; pp. 65–68 on changes in the composition of the House of Commons and the rise of professional men; pp. 68–69 on the shrinkage of the upper class; pp. 69–70 on the varied origins of the intellectuals and pp. 101–46 on élites including the public schools.

T. W. Bamford, 'Public Schools and Social Class, 1801–1850', *The British Journal of Sociology*, vol. 12, 1961, pp. 224–35, analyses the intake of Eton, Harrow, Rugby and St. Paul's from printed registers and makes weighted extrapolations for others on the basis of general statements of character. However, the relevant information given by such a register as Stapylton's for Eton is too sparse to provide a basis for serious conclusions.

the city streets out of which the modern Cockney, or common London speech, has grown.

The invention of printing posed inescapably the problem of selecting standard forms for books designed to circulate throughout the land. William Caxton (d. 1491) refers to it in a well known passage.[1] In the sixteenth century the influx of classical and foreign literature and influence provoked attempts to refine English to a point at which it could compete with classical Latin or with Italian in literary grace and logical precision. The learned began to argue about linguistic forms and when in time they had reached a measure of agreement, the influence of their opinions and example began to be felt in the schools and in cultivated circles. Provincial dialects began to be looked down on. John Aubrey (1626–97) had heard old Sir Thomas Malet (1582–1665) say that Sir Walter Ralegh (c. 1552–1618), whom he had known, 'notwithstanding his so great mastership in style and his conversation with the learnedest and politest persons, yet he spake broad Devonshire to his dying day'.[2] The span of these three lives coincides with the diffusion of the new attitude. By 1700 the desire to be correct in speech was widespread and had social as well as regional implications. By 1800 a standard speech with only slight local variation seems to have been used by educated people throughout England.

Dr. William Matthews[3] attributes the peculiar disdain with which Cockney speech has often been regarded, as compared with provincial dialects, to the fact that it was the common speech of London where the move towards refinement had its headquarters. The vulgarisms against which eighteenth century writers on good speech protested were in the main London vulgarisms because the writers were themselves Londoners. The whole development has, however, to be seen in relation to the linked phenomena of the growth of population and of poverty, the pursuit of progress, the development of skill and specialization and the consequent growth of class differentiation.

### 3. BOND AND FREE

The Anglo-Saxon churl, or free peasant[4] was a slave owner. The origins of his slaves are naturally obscure but H. P. R. Finberg[5] gives

---

[1] *Prologue to the Eneydos*, 1490, Early English Text Soc., extra ser. lvii, 1890, pp. 1–4.

[2] *Brief Lives and Other Selected Writings by John Aubrey*, ed. Anthony Powell, 1949, p. 324.    [3] *Cockney Past and Present*, 1938.

[4] H. P. R. Finberg, *Lucerna*, p. 146, however, gives reasons for thinking that in Alfred's time the churls themselves were still looked on as only half free.    [5] *Lucerna*, p. 65.

reasons for thinking that those of Withington, Gloucestershire, may have derived directly from 'a labouring population of unfree, Celtic-speaking natives' in sub-Roman times, supplemented, perhaps, by Anglo-Saxon captives. The number of these slaves declined, yet it seems there were still many at the Norman Conquest. The end of true slavery in England may indeed be credited to the Norman Conquerors.[1] The true slave is his master's chattel. Such slavery was a fundamental institution of the Roman Empire, but the so called dark ages of western Europe saw this institution decline and almost vanish. The chief source of supply dried up, for Christian might not enslave Christian, so that prisoners of war within Christendom were enslaved no more; while the descendants of former slaves were 'hutted', given by their lord huts and fields, on condition that they and their families should perform labour services for him and his heirs. They were still serfs or villeins, bound to the soil and to their fixed services. But they could not be bought or sold and, these services once performed, their remaining work and its produce were their own.[2] To an England slowly moving the same way the Normans brought a more fully developed form of this *manorial* system. In the two centuries which followed the Conquest Anglo-Norman lawyers sought to impose on the complicated gradations of Anglo-Saxon society a division into free men and villeins, of whom the former only could change their lords at will. Mr. R. H. Hilton sees this depression of the status of those at the base of the agrarian pyramid in the thirteenth century as a natural consequence of rising costs in a feudal agrarian society and makes an interesting comparison with the equation in parts of the continent of freedom with nobility.[3]

Complicated varieties of legal and social status still in fact underlay or broke through this theoretical simplicity. In the Danelaw, that northern and eastern region of England in which the Danish invaders, whose advance King Alfred halted, had established themselves and their institutions, there was more widespread freedom of tenure; in Kent and on the Celtic fringes there were local patterns and institutions which did not fit the Norman scheme; and on ancient royal manors everywhere the tenants enjoyed special rights.[4]

[1] Stenton, op. cit., p. 472.

[2] Marc Bloch in the *Cambridge Economic History of Europe*, i. 234–43, and *Feudal Society*, 1961, pp. 260–6.

[3] 'Freedom and Villeinage in England', *Past and Present*, 1965, No. 31, pp. 3–19.

[4] See the chapter on this subject by Professor Nellie Neilson in the *Cambridge Economic History of Europe*, i. 438–66; the briefer account in *A Concise Economic History*

Thirteenth century lawsuits to determine whether men and women were villeins or not show how little relation the legal concept might have to the social facts. Pedigrees were recited and disputed and while the claimant to freedom would bring forward cousins who were freemen as evidence that their common ancestors were free, the lord who claimed him as his villein might point to other cousins who were villeins. Such pleadings show that free and villein families intermarried freely, though the offspring of free women by villeins were themselves villeins.[1]

Dr. W. G. Hoskins[2] quotes a case from a Devon assize roll of 1249 where the issue turned on the question whether one Gilbert of Galeshora—a remote farm in north west Devon, now called Galsworthy—was a freeman or was the villein of William de Bickleigh. His father Elyas and his grandfather Robert had French names, but his great-grandfather's name, Dunewell, sounds Celtic, as it well might be in a county where there was a British king, Geraint, as late as 710. William de Bickleigh cited four descendants of Dunewell and a descendant of his sister, all villeins, as proof that the line was servile, but their descents from Dunewell's line were all through females and the jury found that Gilbert was a free man. Dr. Hoskins suggests that the Galsworthy family, who were free tenants of the farm of South Galsworthy from the fourteenth to the sixteenth century, sprang from this line and that from them may have branched the ancestors of John Galsworth (d. 1933) the novelist, who farmed in Plymstock and Wembury from the sixteenth century to the nineteenth. There is no pedigree to link these successive lines, but the place name being unique, and the place small, may well have given a surname only to one family.

The variety of the tests used to decide whether men were free or villeins shows how artificial the line between the two could be and how little it need correspond with any real class barrier. Liability to particular amounts of labour service on the lord's land was one of them, but not a certain one because of the distinction made between villeinage and villein tenure. A man who was personally a freeman might acquire land to which a liability attached to villein services. Though in respect

---

*of Britain from the Earliest Times to 1750*, by Sir John Clapham, Cambridge, 1949, pp. 93–102; and Austin Lane Poole, *From Domesday Book to Magna Carta*, Oxford, 1955, pp. 36–48.

[1] Helen M. Cam, 'Pedigrees of Villeins and Freemen in the Thirteenth Century' *The Genealogists' Magazine*, vi. 299–310.

[2] *Devonshire Studies*, 1952, pp. 97–100.

of this land he would then have to perform these, he would not thereby legally lose his personal free status. His liability to villein service might, however, in fact make it harder for his descendants to prove their freedom.

Cases in which members of knightly families seem to have sunk to the status of free tenants and even of villeins have already been mentioned[1] and research might well reveal many more. The reverse process, though doubtless no more common, could certainly happen. Peter, son of Hugh de Stoughton, the Lord of Stoughton in Surrey, married the daughter of one Thurbet, his father's villein; whereupon, in 1261, Hugh enfranchised her and all her offspring.[2] Sir John Clapham[3] justly compares such a marriage with that of the bailiff's daughter of Islington in the ballad to the squire's son[4]—but we must not forget that a villein could be rich.[5] Mr. A. Vere Woodman infers from certain Chesham charters that Richard, younger brother of Sir Ralph de Wedon of Weedon, Buckinghamshire, may have married about 1220 a daughter of Ailwin the miller of Amersham.[6]

A lord could at any time enfranchise his villein by charter. He sometimes did so in return for payment of a rent and sometimes for a lump sum payment. As, however, the villein's own money was legally his lord's property, such a payment must, technically at least, be made for him by someone else.[7] Thurstan, a villein, of Thorpe Waterville, Northamptonshire, was enfranchised by Sir Robert de Waterville (d. 1212). By 1315 Thurstan's descendant (probably his great-grandson), Robert de Thorpe, was a knight. Yet in 1324 this Sir Robert de Thorpe was summoned by John the Reeve of Thorpe to perform labour service alleged to be due on land which he held there on a villein tenure. He was called upon to come on the morrow with nine men to mow the corn of the lord of the manor, the abbot of Peterborough. He in fact refused to do so, not denying his villein origin, but asserting that the land in question had been given to the abbey by Guy de Waterville, and then granted by the abbot to his ancestor

[1] p. 61. See also p. 214.
[2] Miss H. M. Cam, 'Pedigrees of Villeins and Freemen in the Thirteenth Century', *The Genealogists' Magazine*, vi. 310, citing B.M. Add. MS. 6174, the work of a seventeenth century antiquary, Sir Nicholas Stoughton.
[3] *A Concise Economic History of Britain*, p. 100.
[4] Percy, *Reliques of Ancient English Poetry*, 1767, iii. 131.
[5] Clapham, op. cit., p. 101
[6] G. A. Moriarty, 'The Wedons of Botley in Chesham, Co. Bucks.', *New England Hist. & Gen. Reg.* vol. 108, 1954, p. 53 n.
[7] A. L. Poole, *Domesday Book to Magna Carta*, p. 47.

William de Thorpe, for a money rent of 6s. 8d. a year. This William, the son of Thurstan the villein, had in fact been confirmed by the abbot in his lands in Thorpe in 1226. Sir Robert's elder son Sir William de Thorpe became Chief Justice of the King's Bench in 1346, while his younger son Sir Robert (d. 1372) became Chief Justice of the Common Pleas and Chancellor of England. The elder Sir Robert had been Steward of the Liberties of the abbot of Peterborough and it is likely that tenure from the abbey had assisted the rise of this former villein family.[1]

Besides enfranchisement by the lord there were two other ways by which villeins could obtain freedom. One was by taking holy orders, but the Constitutions of Clarendon of 1164 forbade this without the lord's consent.

The other way to freedom for a villein was by flight. There was a doctrine that if he could escape to a town and remain uncaptured there for a year and a day he was legally free (though examples show that in the thirteenth century, at least, this was not always accepted) and some early borough charters record among the borough privileges the right to admit such fugitives, whose labour would no doubt be welcome to a rising community.[2] Simon of Paris, mercer, alderman of London 1299–1319 and 1320–1, was a villein from Necton, Norfolk.[3]

Between 1300 and 1500 the villein's obligation to perform specified labour services in his lord's fields was by degrees abolished. Many details and stages of the process are obscure, but it is clear that on many manors money rents and dues for land and money wages for services quite early took the place of the older system.[4] In the same way at an earlier date the personal military service owed by the knights had been commuted for the money payment of scutage, so that the king or baron had to pay for military service when he wanted it.[5]

Villein status long survived the commutation of villein labour services, but by Tudor times had come to mean little more than a liability to special exactions by the lord of the manor.[6] In 1530 Clarenceux accused Garter King of Arms of prostituting his office by granting

---

[1] *Henry of Pytchley's Book of Fees*, ed. W. T. Mellows, Northamptonshire Record Soc. ii, 1927, p. 55.

[2] Poole, op. cit., p. 47.

[3] S. Thrupp, *The Merchant Class of Medieval London*, p. 359.

[4] Clapham, op. cit., pp. 110–14; *Cambridge Economic History*, i. 508–12; McKisack, *The Fourteenth Century*, pp. 324–42.

[5] Poole, op. cit., pp. 16–18; p. 102.

[6] For the disappearance of villeinage see references given by Mildred Campbell, *The English Yeoman Under Elizabeth and the Early Stuarts*, 1942, p. 16.

arms to bond men and vile persons not able to uphold the honour of nobless,[1] but the very fact of the accusation shows how little relevance the distinction of bond and free by then had to social or economic status.

On a villein's death his son was by custom ordinarily admitted as tenant of his land, after a heriot of the best beast or chattel of the deceased or a sum in lieu had been paid to the lord. This custom of succession grew at length into a legal right of property. Before the end of the fourteenth century villeins and tenants of villein land were proving their possession of such right by producing copies of the court roll of the manor, setting out its customs and the services due from them, and showing that they had performed these; and before the fifteenth century was out the king's courts of law were protecting the rights of the customary tenants.[2] From the sixteenth century such tenure, when proved by copy of court roll, was called copyhold. Once it had won this legal security copyhold tenure had the advantage over a free tenant's leasehold, that the copyholder could never be evicted, and could, for example, absolutely bid defiance to an enclosing land-lord, though not, of course, to an Act of Parliament for Enclosure. So it came about that by the eighteenth century many of those who held land by the villein's tenure were men higher in the economic scale than the agricultural wage labourers, who had as a class succeeded to the position of the villeins.

### 4. FRANKLINS AND YEOMEN

We have discounted the division of rural society into freemen and villeins as a lawyer's concept rather than a social reality. But what have we to put in its place? Permanency and precision must not be looked for in the names and membership of classes which exist not in law, but in social consciousness only. What Sorokin calls the economic, the political and the occupational stratification, though always closely linked, do not always correspond throughout,[3] and the delineation of classes must often be in a measure arbitrary and subjective. Still in England a threefold grouping, into franklins or yeomen, husbandmen and cotters or cottagers, seems over some centuries to correspond, if only roughly, with a felt reality.

[1] A. R. Wagner, *Heralds and Heraldry in the Middle Ages*, p. 90.
[2] Clapham, op. cit., p. 113.
[3] P. Sorokin, *Social Mobility*, 1927, p. 12.

The word franklin means freeman, but the legal class of freemen included many who were not called franklins. The Cartulary of Ramsey Abbey, Huntingdonshire, in 1184–9 distinguishes the knights, who held of the abbey on a military tenure not less than one hide and a half (four hides made a knight's fee), from the many franklins (*frankelanni*), 'some of whom hold a half-hide, some more, some less and ought and are accustomed to aid the knights to do service'.[1] This establishes the standing of the franklins on the Ramsey estates in the late twelfth century with some precision, but in England not only must one always look for local variations but nothing stands still. In the West Riding in 1379 franklins were on the same level of wealth as esquires.[2] 'The free tenant', says Miss Campbell, 'stood below the knight and esquire because of his lack of wealth rather than from any inferiority of birth or blood or legal privilege; for he was free-born and eligible to become a knight if he had the means. In fact he was expected to assume his knighthood upon arriving at sufficient wealth.'[3] In Devon, says Dr. Hoskins, 'by the middle and later years of the thirteenth century . . . this class of free tenants were adding to their original small estates by marriage with neighbouring landowners of the same type'.[4] 'By 1350', says Clapham, 'the old freeholder class had gone two different ways . . . many of them to wage-labour, to the cities perhaps, or to some industrial occupation in village or market-town', or to service as 'foresters, minor retainers of all sorts, fighting men, knights' yeomen bearing "mighty bows" as in Chaucer. On the other side were the freemen who had prospered and added field to field.'[5] Of this sort was the franklin among Chaucer's Canterbury pilgrims:

> An householdere, and that a greet, was he;
> Seint Julian he was in his contree

---

[1] *Cartularium monasterii de Rameseia*, ed. W. H. Hart, P. A. Lyons, Rolls Series, 79, 1893, p. 49, quoted by G. C. Homans, *English Villagers of the Thirteenth Century*, Harvard University Press, 1942, p. 248.

[2] N. Denholm-Young, *The Country Gentry in the Fourteenth Century*, 1969, p. 24.

[3] Mildred Campbell, *The English Yeoman Under Elizabeth and the Early Stuarts*, 1942, p. 11. This author's ensuing statement that the free tenant 'stood above the villein and serf not only by virtue of his wealth and condition, but by birth and the privileges of birth, for the serf was base-born', may need some qualification. See pp. 136–9.

[4] *Devonshire Studies*, p. 127.

[5] *A Concise Economic History of Britain from the Earliest Times to 1750*, p. 115. McKisack, *The Fourteenth Century*, p. 324, makes the same point. R. H. Hilton, 'Peasant Movements in England before 1381', *Econ. Hist. Rev.*, 2nd ser. ii (1949), 130, notes the minority of tenants of 100 acres or more standing out everywhere from the majority with ten or twenty and points to immense traffic in land among tenants of the Honor of Clare in 1308–9 and those of the Bishop Ely temp. Edward II.

His breed, his ale, was alwey after oon;
A bettre envyned man was no-wher noon.
With-oute bake mete was never his hous,
Of fish and flesh, and that so plentevous,
It snewed in his house of mete and drinke,
Of alle deyntees that men coude thinke.
After the sondry sesons of the year,
So chaunged he his mete and his soper.
Ful many a fat partrich hadde he in mewe,
And many a breem and many a luce in stewe.
Wo was his cook, but if his sauce were
Poynaunt and sharp, and redy all his gere.
His table dormant in his halle alway
Stood redy covered al the longe day.
At sessiouns ther was he lord and sire;
Ful ofte tyme he was knight of the shire.
An anlas and a gipser al of silk
Heng at his girdel, whyt as morne milk.
A shirrive had he been, and a countour;
Was no-wher such a worthy vavasour.[1]

This must have been a richer franklin than many. He had been a knight of the shire and from such as him sprang many families of the gentry. A line was drawn through the franklin class by the Act of 1429 which deprived freeholders whose land was not worth forty shillings a year of the right to elect knights of the shire, but 'a large part of the group, perhaps the greater part, were still among the enfranchised'.[2] At the same period 'the yeoman class was strengthened by the addition of the body of tenant farmers, whose interests were very much the same as those of the smaller freeholders, and who shared with them the common name of yeoman. These tenant farmers, succeeding to the work of the local bailiffs who had farmed the land of the lords and of the monasteries in the interests of their masters', were free from some of the freeholders' legal obligations, were excluded, at least after 1429, from the county franchise, but in wealth and liability to taxation were approximately their equals.[3] In Tudor times the franklins came to be called yeomen—a name which had previously meant knights' servants or retainers.[4]

[1] *The Complete Works of Geoffrey Chaucer*, ed. W. W. Skeat, Oxford, 1923, p. 423, *The Canterbury Tales*, Prologue, ll. 339–60.
[2] Mildred Campbell, *The English Yeoman Under Elizabeth and the Early Stuarts*, 1942, p. 12.          [3] Stubbs, *Constitutional History of England*, iii, 5th ed. 1903, pp. 571–2.
[4] Etymologically, 'young man'. Campbell, op. cit., pp. 7–10, traces the several meanings

Dr. W. G. Hoskins in his study of 'Leicestershire Yeoman Families and their Pedigrees'[1] has shown how far back these pedigrees can be carried where the conditions are favourable. Leicestershire offers better opportunities in this respect than most counties 'partly because it was a county consisting to a high degree of small peasant freeholders with deep roots in their ancestral lands' and partly because the relevant mediaeval records have been made so readily available by the work of George Farnham[2] and to a lesser extent that of John Nichols, the county historian.[3] The proportion of free tenants or 'sokemen' is shown by Domesday Book (1086) as much higher in the counties of the Danelaw, the north eastern region conquered and settled by the Danes in the ninth century, than in the south and west. This proportion was highest in East Anglia, and Leicestershire comes close behind.

In Leicestershire a solid core of such families, some of English, some of Scandinavian descent, to judge by early personal names and by surnames taken from ancestral personal names 'remained in their ancestral villages century after century, steadily thickening their roots and spreading their branches over more and more fields and farms'. A larger number, however, from the thirteenth century, if not earlier, moved about fairly freely though within a small radius, perhaps into Leicester, perhaps a parish or two away. Free tenants, unlike villeins, were free to move at will and landless younger sons must often have done so. Dr. Hoskins notes the disappearance of many old names from their native villages in the fourteenth and fifteenth centuries. This he puts down in some cases to the Black Death and later visitations of plague, in others to removal. Where a distinctive surname is found over centuries in one place in successive taxation returns and the like, family continuity can be presumed even if the descent cannot be proved step by step. Dr. Hoskins mentions many Leicestershire examples of this.[4]

The sixteenth century was in some respects the great age of the yeomen. Dr. A. L. Rowse quotes passages from contemporary writers to show the pride which Elizabethans felt in them.[5] Thomas Fuller

and development of the word. For its use (and that of husbandman) to denote middling in townsmen see S. Thrupp, *The Merchant Class of Medieval London*, p. 217, and for yeomen at court in the fifteenth century able to live better than many country gentlemen, ibid., p. 241. On King's Yeomen, who could be knights, see N. Denholm-Young, *The Country Gentry in the Fourteenth Century*, 1969, pp. 27–29.

1 *Trans. Leic. Arch. Soc.* xxiii, 1947, pp. 30–62.
2 George Francis Farnham, *Leicestershire Medieval Village Notes*, 6 vols.
3 p. 379.                              4 Op. cit. and *The Midland Peasant*, 1957.
5 *The England of Elizabeth*, 1950, p. 230.

(d. 1661) calls them 'an estate of people almost peculiar to England living in the temperate zone betwixt greatness and want'; in William Harrison's (d. 1593) opinion, 'these were they that in times past made all France afraid'; while William Lambarde (d. 1601) wrote that 'a man may find sundry yeomen although otherwise for wealth comparable with the gentle sort that will not yet for all that change their condition, nor desire to be apparelled with the titles of gentry'.[1] It was the boast of the Elizabethan yeomen that their ancestors were the archers of Crécy and Poitiers. Many of those archers were indeed franklins, yet 'many of the ancestors of the yeomen of Elizabethan and Stuart days were then following the plough as bondmen . . . but this fact did not prevent the group as a whole from sharing the heritage to which some of their number had a valid right'. The economic stresses of the fourteenth and fifteenth centuries had raised some into this class and caused others to sink below it.[2]

Between the yeomen and the gentry, the class next above them, the division was—as with most English class divisions—partly a matter of wealth and partly of way of life. A yeoman might grow richer than many of his neighbours among the gentry yet not wish to assimilate his way of life or his status to theirs, though if the wealth lasted his son or grandson would usually do so. Rowse puts the economic dividing line between the yeoman and the husbandman below him at the farm of 100 acres, the yeoman farming not less than that.

In the last part of the seventeenth century the yeoman entered upon a period of decline which continued through most of the eighteenth. The estates of the Whig magnates and the new rich grew both at his expense and the small Tory squire's. But he did not cease to exist and the high food prices of the Napoleonic wars favoured him. The fall of prices after the war, however, forced many yeomen to sell their farms in the 1820's and early 30's, and many survivors of this storm succumbed to the great agricultural depression of the 1880's, often migrating to the American middle west.[3] English yeomen still exist but are

[1] For other expressions of this sentiment see Campbell, op. cit., pp. 50–53.
[2] Campbell, op. cit., pp. 15–20.
[3] W. H. B. Court, *A Concise Economic History of Britain from 1750 to Recent Times*, Cambridge, 1954, pp. 28, 161–5. A picture of a yeoman on the borderline of gentility in the 1870's is given by Anthony Trollope, *The American Senator*, 1877, ch. i, pp. 9–11. Laurence Twentyman belonged to the class of 'yeomen, as they ought to be called,— gentlemen-farmers as they now like to style themselves,—men who owned some acres of land, and farmed these acres themselves. . . . He possessed over three hundred acres of land, on which his father had built an excellent house. . . . He had been at school for three years at Cheltenham College.'

far fewer now in proportion to the population than under Elizabeth I.
The descendants of the old yeomen are everywhere, in the peerage,
among the gentry, in the professions, among the labourers, and
overseas. That acute social observer Anthony Trollope, describing in
1871 an East Anglian yeoman's house, 'not grand enough for a squire's
mansion, and too large for a farmer's homestead', speculates on the
origin of the many such houses throughout England, often 'going
into decay under the lessened domestic wants of the present holders',
especially in the eastern counties. He concludes that, 'as years have
rolled on, the strong man has swallowed up the weak,—one strong
man having eaten up half a dozen weak men. And so the squire has
been made. Then the strong squire becomes a baronet and a lord,—
till he lords it a little too much, and a Manchester warehouseman buys
him out. The strength of the country probably lies in the fact that the
change is ever being made, but is never made suddenly.'[1]

The Dands of Galby and Frisby on the windy Leicestershire up-
lands, whose story Dr. Hoskins tells,[2] may stand for a type of yeoman
continuity. They appear as free tenants at Galby in 1296 and are found
in both villages in 1381. While other families came and went they
remained and slowly and slightly grew in wealth and standing. In 1524
John Dand was liable for nearly half the tax in the hamlet of Frisby and
in 1630 they sold the 70 acres there, which may have been their primitive holding, and bought a small freehold next door in Galby. From
prosperous husbandmen they had now become yeomen and the last of
the race, who died in 1717, leaving only daughters, called himself
gentleman and used (without right, I fear) a coat of arms. It is not
unlikely that the Dands who have lived in neighbouring Wigston from
Henry VIII's reign to our own day were a branch of those of Galby
and Frisby.[3]

## 5. THE HUSBANDMAN

As the word *villein* meant by origin merely a villager, so the word
*bond* meant no more than a cultivator, and a *husbond* or husbandman
was a *bond* who had a house. It was only later that *bond* came to be
opposed to free and to be influenced by its etymologically distinct
homonym, bond or bound, derived from the verb to bind.

---

[1] *Ralph the Heir*, chap. 49.
[2] *Leicestershire Studies*, pp. 36–51.
[3] W. G. Hoskins, *The Midland Peasant*, 1957, p. xx and *passim*, and information from
Dr. Hoskins.

The holding of the thirteenth century *husbond* or husbandman has been estimated as of the order of 10 to 40 acres.[1] Though not always, he would more often than not be a villein and must then labour certain days weekly on the lord's demesne. By 1300 many lords had begun to cultivate their demesne lands by wage labour instead of by villeins' 'week work', or else to lease them out, and still more did so after the Black Death or Great Pestilence of 1348–9. The depopulation caused by the Pestilence increased this trend and worked in favour of the labourers who survived, for rather than see their lands lie waste lords paid higher wages or granted tenements upon lease to 'the younger sons, small holders and cottagers from whom wage labour had been recruited'.[2] The husbandman who could live on the produce of his own land had in this a shelter from the starvation which rising prices might inflict on the pure wage earner.

As the term husbandman primarily described a man's occupation and only secondarily and accidentally his rank and economic standing, we must not be surprised sometimes to find the same man described alternatively as husbandman and yeoman. Still less should it surprise us to find yeomen and husbandmen in the same family.

Though the terms 'yeoman' and 'husbandman' had [in Dr. Hoskins' words] no precise definition even in the sixteenth century, for we often find the same man indifferently called both in the records, before he has clearly emerged from the ruck of village farmers, there was a fairly clear distinction between the two classes in people's minds. It had little or nothing to do with the tenure of land, for a yeoman, like a husbandman, need own no land of his own; it might have a little to do with birth for the sons of minor gentry were often styled 'yeoman'; but in the main it seems to have been, by the sixteenth century, a matter of personal wealth and of a man's scale of activities and living.[3]

Dr. Hoskins proceeds to draw vivid pictures of the respective ways of living of the two classes.

The possibilities of movement between them as early as the thirteenth century are suggested by the surprising number of transactions in small parcels of land, known by an accident of record preservation, which went on both among the peasants of Wigston Magna, Leicestershire, and between them and their lord. It may be, however, that such

[1] Homans, op. cit., p. 243.

[2] Sir John Clapham, *A Concise Economic History of Britain from the Earliest Times to 1750*, Cambridge, 1949, p. 118.

[3] W. G. Hoskins, *Essays in Leicestershire History*, 1950, pp. 150–1.

transactions could be entered into at that date only by peasants who were legally free and not by villeins.[1] Movement from one class to the other might also take place through the endowment of a franklin's younger son with a small part of the paternal holding, from which alone he could not live but must supply his further needs by wage labour or as a craftsman.[2]

In the later fourteenth and early fifteenth centuries those factors which at all times make for inequality of fortune were reinforced by economic stress which drove many from the land into the towns. Some were moved by hopes, others by desperation. Dr. Hoskins, in his minute study of Wigston Magna, notes that 'in general it was the wealthiest and the poorest who tended to leave—whether in good times or bad—and the middling peasants who tended to stay through thick and thin'.[3] In Leicestershire as a whole he finds that only about one family in ten persisted in its home from the time of the poll taxes of 1377 and 1381 to that of the subsidy of 1524–5 and that those who so persisted often in time became the most prosperous yeomen.[4] In Wigston, however, while those who persisted were roughly in this proportion to the rest, namely eight or ten families out of seventy, some of them were still husbandmen rather than yeomen.[5]

In his study of *Norfolk Surnames in the Sixteenth Century*,[6] which is the first fruits of the Marc Fitch Fund endowment at Leicester University for the study of English Surname History, Mr. R. A. McKinley draws some important conclusions from a study of the manorial records of Forncett in conjunction with the evidence of the 1522 'Military Survey'. Twenty families of freemen and nine of serfs, he finds, continued on the manor from the fourteenth century to the early sixteenth, though many members, both of these and other families, left the manor during that period either illegally by flight or with the lord's consent subject to payment of chevage. Members of a family with the rare surname of Bolytout, who did both, are found scattered through a number of villages nearby, in the town of Great Yarmouth, further away, and perhaps even in Bury St. Edmunds in Suffolk and Walthamstow in Essex near London. It is suggested that the distribution in 1522 of other surnames of local origin might be largely

[1] W. G. Hoskins, *The Midland Peasant*, 1957, pp. 52–53.
[2] Ibid., p. 76.                                              [3] Ibid., p. 88.
[4] W. G. Hoskins, *Essays in Leicestershire History*, 1950, p. 132.
[5] *The Midland Peasant*, pp. 88, 141–7.
[6] Leicester University, Department of English Local History, Occasional Papers, 2nd Ser., No. 2.

accounted for by similar migrations, especially, perhaps, from places where there was a locally dense growth of population, arising, among other factors, from a local custom of partible inheritance.[1]

Dr. Hoskins finds that in Leicestershire the rapid social changes of the sixteenth century were followed by greater stability in the seventeenth. Of 82 families living in Wigston in 1670 about 36 had been there for at least a century and about 15 for two centuries. Several had ramified into many branches. The Freers in two centuries had formed 8. The Smiths, Vanns and Wards numbered 6 households each and a number of families 3 or more. 'As all these families persistently intermarried with each other (rarely going outside the village for a bridegroom or a bride) the degree of inter-relationship must have been beyond belief, and the number of cousins beyond accurate computation.' The economic gulf between the richer and the poorer was, however, growing. At this date we have for the first time in Wigston a village where the lords of manors were absentees, 'a class of "gentry" appearing, partly alien gentry superimposed on the village by some accident of marriage or purchase, but for the most part native gentry sprung from the minority of successful peasantry'. In the latter part of the seventeenth century members of the most successful branches of several peasant families in Wigston began for the first time to describe themselves as gentlemen.[2] But all the time, while some were moving up, others were going down.

The economic forces which affected the yeomen adversely in the late seventeenth and the eighteenth century bore still more hardly on the husbandmen. 'These were the reasons . . . for the growth of the poor as a class: too many people on a fixed supply of land, the engrossing of what land there was into fewer hands, and heavy taxation for twenty years on end.'[3] The growth of population with its pressure upon the means of subsistence was a factor which now bore ever more hardly on families low in the economic scale. In Wigston just before the 1766 enclosure award, which gave the death blow to the old peasant economy there, 'only three families in every ten occupied any land; seven families in every ten had none, but earned their livelihood as labourers in the fields, as framework-knitters, and as small craftsmen and tradesmen'.[4] Wigston is not England but something like this

[1] Mr. McKinley cites on this Joan Thirsk, *English Peasant Farming: The Agrarian History of Lincolnshire from Tudor to Recent Times*, 1957, and 'Industries in the Countryside', *Essays in the Economic and Social History of Tudor and Stuart England*, ed. F. J. Fisher, 1961, pp. 76–78; and H. E. Hallam, *Econ. Hist. Rev.*, 2nd Ser., x, 1958, pp. 356–61.

[2] W. G. Hoskins, *The Midland Peasant*, p. 196.    [3] Ibid., p. 215.    [4] Ibid., p. 217.

would be true of large parts of the country. Yet the husbandmen or small farmers are not extinct as a class and have endured in many places to this day.

### 6. THE COTTER OR COUNTRY LABOURER

The cotter or cottager was a man whose holding of land, if he had any, was so small that he could not begin to live by it and must earn his living by his labour. In the thirteenth century he would normally be a villein, but could be a freeman.[1] By 1400 he would often be free.[2] Clapham was of opinion that about 1750, the earliest date for which we can arrive at figures even roughly reliable, the numbers of the cottagers, the agricultural proletariat, were less than double those of the yeomen and husbandmen added together,[3] and it is likely that in earlier times they were relatively fewer—perhaps much fewer. Hoskins estimates the farm labourers of Devon in the early sixteenth century as one third of the population, but in Leicestershire at the same date as one fifth.[4] Their numbers were recruited as the population grew from those who fell behind in the race,[5] the weak, the shiftless, the unfortunate of the class above them.

Economic historians have sought and are still seeking to enlarge our knowledge of the factors, which at different dates have brought prosperity or adversity to different classes and occupations, and of their workings. In many of their conclusions there is necessarily a large element of conjecture, especially for early periods. While this must always be remembered, their findings are still essential to our picture of the developing framework of society. Calculations of average prices and the cost of living, without which wage figures mean little, are notoriously full of traps. It has, however, been deduced that the farm labourers of the fifteenth century 'lived rather dangerously but in relative comfort'; that the last decade of that century 'was quite

---

[1] Homans, op. cit., p. 244.

[2] Cf. W. G. Hoskins, *Essays in Leicestershire History*, 1950, p. 35.

[3] Sir John Clapham, *A Concise Economic History of Britain from the Earliest Times to 1750*, p. 210. He puts the ratio of cottagers to the rest at 1·8 : 1. On the evidence for early population see works cited by R. B. Pugh, *How to Write a Parish History*, 1954 ed., pp. 104–11, and W. G. Hoskins, *Local History in England*, 1959, pp. 139–48; also opinions in May McKisack, *The Fourteenth Century 1307–1399*, Oxford, 1959, pp. 312–14, and N. Denholm-Young, *The Country Gentry in the Fourteenth Century*, Oxford, 1969, pp. 3, 15–16.

[4] *Devonshire Studies*, pp. 419–20.

[5] Hoskins, *Essays in Leicestershire History*, p. 41.

abnormally favourable to the pure wage-earner'; that the tide turned against them under the Tudors when the influx of precious metals from America cheapened the coinage;[1] and that between 1600 and 1800 costs rose so much faster than their wages that their standard of living went steadily down.[2] The rise in prices caused by the wars with France between 1793 and 1815 hit the farm labourer hard and some improvement thereafter was followed by much distress in the 1830's. In the 1850's prosperity returned to British agriculture and lasted till the 1870's, when imports of cheaper food from overseas led to a collapse from which there was no true recovery until the war of 1939.[3]

Within this general picture there are great and important local variations. Differences of land fertility affected all classes. So too the accessibility of other employment, in handicrafts or towns or mines or ships, might affect local demand for farm labour very differently in one region and another; while conditions of tenure and the characters of employers and landlords might vary greatly from place to place. Thus enclosure of the open fields came early in some parts, late in others, while in some others again there never were open fields.[4] Conversely the clearance and settlement of the woodland, moor and waste, which once covered England, was complete in some parts much sooner than in others.[5] It used to be thought that at the time of the Industrial Revolution, when the limits of cultivation had been reached or nearly reached, enclosure by landlords led to evictions of labourers which drove them into the towns. Hard as their lot often was it is not now thought to have been as hard as this. From the fact that the number of farm labourers did not, as it seems, decrease, it follows that it was not their eviction but the multiplication of their offspring that fed the growing towns and industries.[6]

### 7. TOWN AND COUNTRY TRADES

Down to the middle of the eighteenth century industry and manufacture were conducted largely in the country and the villages. Most villages contained a miller, who would be a freeholder and a man of

---

[1] Clapham, op. cit., pp. 210–11.

[2] Hoskins and Finberg, *Devonshire Studies*, p. 426.

[3] Court, op. cit., pp. 38–41, 161–5, 200–8.

[4] Clapham, op. cit., pp. 197–200, 222–4; Court, op. cit., pp. 33–37; Hoskins, *Essays in Leicestershire History*, pp. 39–44, 67–107, 173.

[5] Clapham, op. cit., pp. 86–93, 194–7; Court, op. cit., pp. 20–22; Hoskins and Finberg, *Devonshire Studies*, pp. 315–33.

[6] Court, op. cit., p. 39.

substance, and a blacksmith, who would be a smaller man, sometimes a freeholder and sometimes a villein.[1] The commonest of English surnames, Smith, bears witness to his ubiquity. Other trades appear sporadically in the villages in mediaeval times, wheelwrights, carpenters, saddlers, thatchers, fullers, dyers, soapmakers, tanners and others. In Wigston the miller and the baker appear in the sixteenth century, the butcher and the tailor early in the seventeenth.[2] In Clapham's view these craftsmen were, largely at least, the younger sons of the freeholders and their descendants.[3] About 1300 weavers and fullers were disturbing the townsmen by moving out into the country to make cloth there and famous old English cloths took their names from country places in Suffolk, Yorkshire, Gloucestershire and other districts where the wool or water power favoured their production.[4] This process went on until by Tudor times many towns, and not only clothing towns, had declined to an extent which alarmed authority. Under Elizabeth I, therefore, skilled alien craftsmen were encouraged to settle in them, on the whole, it seems, with the desired result.[5]

The smelting of iron, wherever iron ore was found from Lancashire to Sussex, was a woodland occupation so long as wood was the usual fuel for smelting. But the development of the coal mines between 1500 and 1700, with the technical developments which ran parallel and followed, in the eighteenth century with a gathering momentum drove industry out the of countryside and into the towns or into districts which were and are neither town nor country. Two sorts of men took part in this great movement; the men of enterprise and ingenuity, who saw opportunities, the inventor, the engineer, the manager, the capitalist; and on the other hand the surplus population of the countryside, those whom the growth of numbers without a corresponding increase of employment drove from the land into the towns, the mines, the factories or overseas. The technical and statistical elements in these great trends fall within the province of the economic historians, whose researches add yearly to our knowledge of them. But on the human and personal side the genealogists could do much to give detail and precision to the story, if they and those historians could establish an understanding and exchange of knowledge. The division of classes in

---

[1] Homans, op. cit., pp. 285–7.　　　　[2] Hoskins, *The Midland Peasant*, p. 167.
[3] *Concise Economic History of Britain*, p. 115.　　　　[4] Ibid., p. 156.
[5] Lionel Williams, 'Alien Immigrants in Relation to Industry and Society in Tudor England', *Huguenot Soc. Proc.* xix, 1956, pp. 146–69.

the towns presents to our eyes an appearance of less clear definition than in the country. Furthermore there were at times great differences between one town and another, arising from geographical factors and from differences in constitution.

Whether town life was anywhere continuous from Roman times is uncertain, but London, Canterbury and Rochester, which had been Roman towns, were Anglo-Saxon towns about 600, while elsewhere Roman town walls which survived were in time repaired and used. King Alfred (d. 899) probably founded boroughs as strong points against the Danes and others grew up or were founded between his day and the Norman Conquest.

The growth of commerce after 1066 gave a new impulse to the establishment of markets to serve groups of villages. The right to hold markets had been the subject of royal grants before the Conquest, though some had probably come into existence without any grant. Before 1300, however, the necessity of royal permission was established law and many such grants were made. The possession of a market was a necessary first step in the growth of a village into a town and the acquisition of borough rights. Boroughs were founded by the king himself or by lay or ecclesiastical lords on sites within their lands, where they looked for profit from them. These sites would be laid out in tenements which were let on the special free tenure called burgage tenure, whereby the lord's manorial rights were abolished and money payments taken instead. The layout of these new boroughs was often spacious, but later building has obscured this save where, as at Winchelsea in Sussex, a town failed to grow as planned.

In the thirteenth century the commercial and town-making development, which had followed the Conquest, began to slow down. New boroughs were still founded, but in smaller numbers, and a proportion of the early foundations failed to establish themselves and sank back into villages. Boroughs differed greatly from one another in their rights, constitutions and degrees of self-government. The pace and nature both of the infilling of their ground plans and the building up of the class patterns depended much on their charters and constitutions as well as on economic factors. Thus in some boroughs inherited tenements could not be sold, while in others freedom of sale might lead to rapid subdivision or to investment in town property by rich men from outside.[1] In the same way the pace of emancipation from royal

---

[1] Cf. Hoskins and Finberg, *Devonshire Studies*, p. 186. On town origins see W. G. Hoskins, *Local History in England*, 1959, pp. 71–105.

control (or that of a lord) and the growth of municipal self government differed from town to town.

Dr. Hoskins places English sixteenth century towns in five classes; first London, far larger than any other, where the peers had their town houses; then the provincial capitals, mostly cathedral cities, such as Norwich, York, Exeter, Newcastle upon Tyne, Salisbury and Bristol, where between the late sixteenth and the late seventeenth centuries a growing proportion of the richer gentry had town houses to which they moved for the winter months; thirdly such county towns as Derby and Leicester, markets and seats of county government but without social pretensions; fourthly such market towns as Bridgwater, Crewkerne, Cranbrook, Maidstone, Stratford upon Avon, with populations of 1,000 to 2,000, some of them smaller when Elizabeth I came to the throne than they had been before the Black Death; and lastly the smallest towns which yet were unmistakably towns, such as Bideford, Burford and Chipping Norton.[1]

Guilds or associations of different kinds play a central part in the history of English towns from Anglo-Saxon times. In the twelfth century a number of towns were authorized by royal charters to form what were called guilds merchant for the regulation of trade and commerce and these in some instances were in fact the borough government. From the same period date also the oldest of the craft guilds whereby members of trades regulated those trades' conduct and sought to establish monopolies for their members.[2] By the fifteenth century the rules of some of these guilds show us their members divided into three main classes, which, with a fourth class below them of labourers and paupers not qualified for guild membership, probably exhibit the ordinary social stratification or pre-Industrial Revolution English townsmen. These classes are the merchants, the master craftsmen and shopkeepers, the journeymen or hired workers and below them and outside the guilds the unskilled labourers.

### 8. THE MERCHANTS

The wealthy merchants, who formed the governing class in the towns, seem in England, throughout the Middle Ages, to have been more or less upon a social equality with the knightly class in the

---

[1] W. G. Hoskins, 'An Elizabethan Provincial Town: Leicester', in *Studies in Social History*, ed. J. H. Plumb, 1955, p. 38; and 'English Provincial Towns in the Sixteenth Century', *Trans. Royal Hist. Soc.*, 5th ser. vi, 1956, pp. 2–6.

[2] Clapham, *A Concise Economic History of Britain*, pp. 128–37, 143–50; A. L. Poole, op. cit., pp. 74–75, 84–88.

countryside. There was indeed a good deal of interchange and inter-marriage between the two. Thomas Becket (1118–70), the great Archbishop of Canterbury and intimate friend of Henry II, was the son of a Rouen merchant settled in London, where he became sheriff. After his parents' death Thomas stayed in his school holidays with a family friend Richer de l'Aigle, a member of a baronial house.[1] Robert FitzHarding (d. 1171), the powerful and wealthy ancestor of the Berkeleys, lived in Bristol and is said to have been a merchant there.[2] Clapham[3] notes the knightly character of some of the early mayors of London from Henry FitzAilwin (d. 1212) to Richard Whittington (d. 1423) and Unwin points out that the twelfth and thirteenth century London aldermen were in effect a class of royal officials, while their much intermarried principal families, the Blunds, Buckerels, Basings, Aswys, Cornhills, formed something like an hereditary caste,[4] a state of things which did not last in London, as it did in the patriciate of continental free cities. The end occurred in 1285 when, following troubles, Edward I took the city into his own hands.

Before that time a group of some sixteen families had almost mono-polized the city government. Out of ninety five known aldermen and sheriffs between 1191, when the Commune of London was established, and 1263, when a popular revolt in the city followed that of Simon de Montfort against the king, three quarters came from these families.[5] Ten, including the first mayor, sprang from that of FitzAilwin, descended from a thegn of Edward the Confessor. The family of Buckerell, by origin Italian Bucherelli, supplied aldermen in every generation from 1104 to 1270. Only less prominent were the families of Cornhill (sprung from a Norman FitzHerlwin), Bocointe (of Italian origin), le Viel, Blund, Basings, FitzAlulf and others.[6]

The later history of London knew no such continuing group and William Caxton (d. 1491) held that London families 'can unnethe contynue unto the third heyre or scarcely to the second',[7] while Miss Thrupp concludes from a close analysis of varied evidence that among members of the greater companies only a small percentage can

---

[1] *Materials for the History of Thomas Becket*, ed. J. C. Robertson, Rolls Series, 67, iv, 1879, pp. 3, 6, 81; Dugdale, *Baronage*, i. 475.

[2] p. 52.     [3] Op. cit., p. 126.

[4] George Unwin, *The Gilds and Companies of London*, [1908], pp. 55–57.

[5] Gwyn A. Williams, 'London and Edward I', *Tr. R. Hist. Soc.*, 5 S. vol. ii, 1961, pp. 81–99.

[6] William Page, *London Its Origin and Early Development*, 1923, chap. viii, pp. 230–66.

[7] *Early English Text Society*, No. 176, 1928.

at any time have pursued successful trade in London for as many as three generations.[1]

Part of the explanation seems to be that when Edward I had brought the London patriciate to an end, the way for a successful city family to rise further was by purchase of country manors and assimilation to the country gentry, of which there are examples of many dates.[2] A few families, however, retained important city activities over long periods, while owning country properties as well. Such was that of Gisors, prominent from 1243 to 1541, that of Sely between 1297 and 1478[3] and that of the Frowicks, who were London goldsmiths from the twelfth to the fourteenth and mercers in the fourteenth and fifteenth centuries and were also throughout that time lords of manors in Middlesex and elsewhere.[4] Miss Thrupp deduces from examples of intermarriage that the merchant families, the London lawyers and the lesser officials living in the city stood much on the same level, the richer families in each class intermarrying with the richer in the others,[5] but that intermarriage with the country gentry was less free, though by no means unknown.[6] She quotes the evidence of a fourteenth century preacher, Friar Bromyard, that merchants and moneyed men reckon themselves ennobled and on the road to enrichment, when they are seen to have friendships with the nobility, when they can wear their robes and are summoned to their banquets, and when they can go a-hunting with them.[7] Great must have been the chagrin of John Wiltshire, a grocer, who had bought half the manor of Great Heydon, Essex, which was held by the serjeanty of handing a towel to the king before dinner on his coronation day, when the Court of Claims in 1377 admitted the claim but assigned the performance of the duty to the Earl of Cambridge.[8] Professor E. F. Jacob notices a closer association of county and borough communities arising about 1400, with consequent intermarriage.[9] The great fiscal operations whereby Edward III financed his French wars in his earlier years called for immense efforts by the great merchants and correspondingly enriched such men as the brothers William (d. 1366) and Richard de la Pole of

[1] Thrupp, op. cit., p. 223.

[2] Ibid., pp. 230–1; J. H. Hexter, *Reappraisals in History*, 1961, pp. 76–93.

[3] Thrupp, op. cit., pp. 223, 345–6, 365.

[4] Walter Goodwin Davis, *The Ancestry of Mary Isaac*, Portland, Maine, 1955, pp. 197–259.

[5] Thrupp, op. cit., p. 263.                                    [6] Ibid., pp. 264–9.

[7] Ibid., p. 259, quoting G. R. Owst, *Literature and Pulpit in Mediaeval England*, 1933, p. 352.

[8] Thrupp, op. cit., p. 259.        [9] *The Fifteenth Century 1399–1485*, 1961, p. 386.

Hull,[1] but the king's insolvency in the 1350's struck their class a great blow, and in Professor Postan's view their successors for more than a century were both fewer and less rich.[2] There were still great merchants nevertheless and their links with the magnates of the realm continued.

Maud (d. 1424), daughter of Adam Francis, Mayor of London from 1352 to 1354, married first John Aubrey (d. 1380–1), the son of a mayor and himself a sheriff of London, secondly Sir Alan Buxhall (d. 1381), a Knight of the Garter, and thirdly John de Montagu, Earl of Salisbury (d. 1400).[3] Geoffrey Boleyn (d. 1463), alderman of London, married the daughter of Thomas, Lord Hoo, Knight of the Garter (d. 1455),[4] and it has been suggested that his subsequent importance in the City, as sheriff (1446–7), alderman (1452–63), mayor (1457–8) and Master of the Mercers' Company (1454), owed much to this marriage.[5] Geoffrey Boleyn's son married an earl's daughter, their grandson was an earl himself and this grandson's daughter was Queen of England. We must remember that no town in England could compare with London for size, wealth or standing. Nevertheless, merchants of other towns could mingle with knights and lords. William de la Pole (d. 1366), Mayor of Hull in 1333, is described from 1339 to 1349 as 'Lord of Holderness, knight and merchant' and his son became Earl of Suffolk.[6] The intermarried merchant and clothier families of Canning (or Canynges) and Young, which gave Bristol three mayors and London one, acquired manors and intermarried with the families of country knights.[7]

In all this there are several factors at work which call for research to distinguish them and their effects more clearly. The examples quoted are too few to establish what was the exception and what the rule. Did the earl who married the mayor's daughter overcome prejudice for the sake of her wealth, or was there no prejudice to overcome? We know that rich merchants bought manors and founded families, but was there between them and older lords of manors a barrier to be

---

[1] *Complete Peerage*, xii, pt. i, p. 434.

[2] Michael Postan in the *Cambridge Economic History of Europe*, ii. 219.

[3] *Complete Peerage*, xi. 392.

[4] Ibid. vi. 565; x. 137. W. L. E. Parsons, *Salle*, 1937, quotes from manorial records evidence that Geoffrey Boleyn, the mayor's father, was a villein in 1435–9, but cf. Thrupp, op. cit., pp. 216–17, 325.

[5] *History of Parliament 1439–1509*, p. 90.

[6] *Complete Peerage*, pt. i, pp. 435–8.

[7] *History of Parliament, 1439–1509*, *Biographies*, pp. 151–2, 980–2; *D.N.B.*; George Pryce, *Memorials of the Canynges Family*, 1854, pp. 55, 146, 150; Thrupp, op. cit., p. 328; E. M. Carus Wilson, 'The Overseas Trade of Bristol', *Bristol Rec. Soc.*, 1937, pp. 303–4.

surmounted in the fourteenth century, as there was in the nineteenth, or had it not yet arisen? Younger sons of gentle families were apprenticed to city trades and became wealthy. Did their marriages and connections differ in any consistent way from those of their fellow merchants of other origins? John Smyth of Nibley, Gloucestershire (d. 1640), the historian of the Berkeleys, whose work is largely based on the family muniments, comments thus on the disinheritance by William, Marquess of Berkeley (d. 1492), of his brother Maurice (d. 1506) who in 1465 had married Isabel, daughter of Philip Mead (d. 1475), citizen and three times Mayor of Bristol:

How little cause the Marques Berkeley had to complaine of the obscure parentage of the lady Isable, which he vainly called base: and of the unworthynes of his brothers match with so mean bloud, as hee reproached it, making that a motive to his own vast expences, and of the disinheritance of this lord his brother, least any of her base bloud should inherite after him, may to his further reproof bee returned upon his memory to bee but a fained and unbrotherly quarrell picked on purpose to give colour for his own exorbitances.[1]

Dr. Hoskins quotes examples which suggest that 'by the fifteenth and sixteenth centuries the successful merchant was . . . likely to have started with a little property of his own, or at least with the financial and moral support of a franklin family behind him'. 'Of the Devonians who rose to be mayors of Exeter' in the sixteenth century, 'the Periams, Hursts, Staplehills, Spurways and Peters, among others, were all members of franklin families with pedigrees and lands going back two or three hundred years; and those who came in from other counties were often similarly descended, like Richard Martyn (mayor in 1533), who was the second son of Sir William Martyn of Athelhampton in Dorset, while only one is described as of mean parentage. London, too, recruited her merchant class to a marked degree from the younger sons of small landed families in the provinces—such as the Greshams of Norfolk, the Skevingtons of Leicestershire, the Cloptons of Warwickshire.' It is possible that in earlier times it was commoner for merchants to rise from nothing, but the stories of those who are said to have done so rather suggest that such occurrences were rare.[2] Such questions have been little studied though material for their study

---

[1] *The Lives of the Berkeleys by John Smyth of Nibley*, ed. Sir John Maclean, ii, 1893, p. 173.

[2] W. G. Hoskins, 'English Provincial Towns in the Sixteenth Century', *Trans. Royal Hist. Soc.*, 5th ser., vi, 1956, pp. 8–9.

exists. Mr. Ketton-Cremer, for example, tells us that in the middle eighteenth century relations grew closer and marriages more frequent between the families of the wealthier Norwich citizens and of the surrounding Norfolk gentry.[1] Professor Alan Everitt points out that by 1700 most of the younger sons of the Northamptonshire gentry had gone either into the church or into trade in London.[2] Professor Stone sees 'a slow but steady rise in the standing of the merchant class in the eyes of gentry' between the mid sixteenth and mid seventeenth century, accelerating as more cadets of gentry became merchants and intermarriages more frequent, followed, however, in the late seventeenth century by a narrowing of the channels of mobility at higher levels.[3] A general impression suggests that, as with much else in English social history, the picture may prove complex and influenced from time to time and place to place by a shifting balance of factors and fashions. But this variety in the picture is only possible because of the English absence of legal or absolute class barriers.

The class of great city merchants has continued to the present day, though the families which comprise this and other town classes have tended to change more quickly through the generations than those of the countryside. The merchant class, says Dr. Hoskins,

was constantly changing in composition, losing its successful members to the landed class and recruiting from the same class, though possibly from a lower level. Once arrived in town, three generations usually sufficed to see the end of the commercial or industrial phase. There were three generations of Springs at Lavenham (*c.* 1400–1523), three merchant-generations of Canynges at Bristol (*c.* 1369–1474), three of the Marlers at Coventry (1469–1540), three of the Wigstons at Leicester (*c.* 1430–1536). It was rare for a successful merchant family to stay in town beyond the third generation: often they had left for a substantial country estate within two generations. This rapid extinction might be no matter for surprise in families that had achieved a comfortable fortune, but even among smaller and more humdrum businesses it seems to have been quite exceptional to go beyond the third generation. An examination of the Freemen's Register at Leicester, a great catalogue of the obscure, shows us that in the sixteenth and seventeenth centuries it was rare for any Leicester business to last a hundred years. The exceptions can certainly be counted on the fingers of one hand. Here it is not a matter of a large mercantile business being transmuted into lands, but of some more prosaic

---

[1] R. W. Ketton-Cremer, *Norfolk Portraits*, 1944, p. 116.
[2] Alan Everitt, 'Social Mobility in Early Modern England', *Past and Present*, 1966, p. 68.
[3] Lawrence Stone, 'Social Mobility in England 1500–1700', ibid., pp. 27, 52–55.

death from natural causes. The longevity of urban families and businesses would well repay further enquiry. Even below the ranks of the outstandingly successful, urban businesses were constantly changing in scope and personnel; and so consequently were town populations as a whole. Whether or not the labouring class was as mobile as the remainder of the population is another matter; the records of this class are particularly meagre.[1]

It is possible that, if city dynasties were reckoned through female as well as male lines, their longevity would be found greater than the analysis of surnames—a guide to male lines only—suggests. The Pynchons of Latton, Writtle and Springfield, Essex, were citizens of London from the thirteenth century to the seventeenth. If we accept the conjecture that Agnes Pynchon, the mother of Archbishop Chichele (d. 1443), was of this family, we can derive from them a remarkable city dynasty passing through Robert Chichele (d. 1440), Mayor of London in 1411 and 1421, Sir Andrew Judde (d. 1558), Lord Mayor in 1550 and founder of Tonbridge School, his son in law Customer Smyth and the Customer's son Sir Thomas Smyth (d. 1625), the great promoter of colonization.[2]

The rare long lived merchant dynasties have usually had one foot in the town and one in the country—merchants and squires at once. The Frowicks[3] are a mediaeval instance, the Hoares of Hoare's Bank a modern. Richard Hoare (1648–1718), goldsmith and son of Henry Hoare of Smithfield (d. 1668) who 'got £400 per annum by buying and selling horses'[4] was engaged in 1673 in the business at the Golden Bottle in Cheapside which grew into Hoare's Bank. In 1690 he moved to Fleet Street, where the bank still exists. He was knighted in 1710, Lord Mayor in 1713, and bought an estate in Kent. By 1955 thirty six of his descendants on different lines had been partners in the bank. His son Henry (d. 1725) bought Lord Stourton's estates in Wiltshire, Somerset and Dorset in 1720 and his son Henry Hoare (d. 1785) and great-grandson Sir Richard Colt Hoare (d. 1838) created at Stourhead one of the finest landscape parks in England. A grandson Richard Hoare (d. 1787) was made a baronet in 1786 and his and other lines of the family have acquired estates and intermarried with the peerage and

[1] W. G. Hoskins, 'English Provincial Towns in the Early Sixteenth Century', *Trans. Royal Hist. Soc.*, 5th ser., vi, pp. 9–10.
[2] *The Register of Henry Chichele*, ed. E. F. Jacob, Canterbury & York Soc. xlv, 1943. Vol. i, pp. xvi–xviii and xxv; Henry F. Waters, *Genealogical Gleanings in England*, ii, 1901, pp. 846–67; p. 283.
[3] p. 156.
[4] *Le Neve's Pedigrees of the Knights*, ed. G. W. Marshall, Harleian Soc. 1873, p. 481.

landowners, without abandoning the banking connection.[1] There are other city merchant dynasties extant, notably among the bankers,[2] but it has been commoner for city fortunes to root themselves in the country and forget their source. To explain this solely in political terms would be misleading yet an important reason for it surely was that, in Professor Habakkuk's words,

In England political power and social standing depended to a greater extent than elsewhere on the ownership of landed property as opposed to lineage or royal favour. Since there were no legal restrictions on the right to acquire land, any man, however humble his origin, who had enough money, might purchase an estate, and thereby acquire social consequence. And not only was it easy for wealthy bourgeois to acquire an estate; in relation to the landowners there were more of them than on the Continent. For all these reasons the English landed class was constantly recruiting new members. Because Englishmen who had made fortunes in law, government or trade transformed themselves into country gentlemen, England had no urban aristocracy on the Dutch model. There were wealthy merchants but few mercantile dynasties, and the great London houses were the town houses of the landed nobility. It would indeed be difficult to exaggerate the wider social repercussions of this flow into landownership.[3]

The speed of this flow, however, was not constant and Professor Habakkuk suggests that following the sale of many overburdened estates in the first half of the eighteenth century there was a reaction in the second half, so that 'there were times when would-be purchasers found it very difficult to find the estates they wanted, and it is possible, though it cannot be put any higher, that there was a slackening in the rate at which new families were recruited'.

Professor Pirenne has outlined the suggestive hypothesis that for each period of economic history there is a distinct and separate class of capitalists. 'The group of capitalists of a given epoch does not spring from the capitalist group of the preceding epoch. At every change in economic organisation we find a breach of continuity.' The capitalists of one stage withdraw from the struggle and become an aristocracy; new men courageous and enterprising rise up. Thus economic history 'does not present itself to the eye of the

---

[1] Edward Hoare, *Families of Hore and Hoare*, 1883; *Hoare's Bank A Record 1672–1955* (by H. P. R. Hoare).

[2] e.g. Barclay, Martin, Smith of Nottingham, Gurney, Baring. G. P. Judd, *Members of Parliament 1734–1832*, shows that banking rivalled landed dynasties of M.P.'s in that period, so Baring and Smith of Nottingham each with 10, Drummond, Martin and Latouche 6 each, Child, Mackworth-Praed and Williams 4 each, and many others with 3 or 2 each. 32 of the 230 banker M.P.'s were directors of the Bank of England.

[3] *The European Nobility in the Eighteenth Century*, ed. A. Goodwin, 1953, pp. 15–16.

discoverer under the guise of an inclined plane; it resembles rather a staircase every step of which rises abruptly above that which preceded it'. This is true in the main of the capitalist founders of the factory system. It is also true in a less degree of the various stages in the evolution of a particular type of capitalism, like the merchant capitalism of the domestic system or the industrial capitalism of the early nineteenth century.[1]

This is an interesting opinion deserving (but requiring) closer examination.

The late seventeenth century brought the wealth of the greatest London merchants to a peak. The French wars had given them opportunities but their sources of wealth were manifold. They were

not only directors of the Bank of England but also the controllers of the East India Company, the Africa Company and Levant Company. They owned blocks of London property; they dabbled in mortgages; they spread their money in land; wherever there was gain or security for money, they were investors and buyers. Sir James Bateman, one-time Governor of the Bank of England, Sub-Governor of the South Sea Company, gave his daughters £10,000 each for their portions. He bequeathed his eldest son an estate in Herefordshire, his second an estate in Kent and his youngest an estate in Essex. . . . His son acquired the social distinction which his wealth commanded. He married the daughter of Charles, Earl of Sunderland, and in 1725 became the first Viscount Bateman; true the Viscounty was only of Ireland, for George I had strong prejudices about birth.[2]

Sir James Bateman's father Joas Bateman (d. 1704, aged 84) was a naturalized Fleming. Peter le Neve, Norroy, had heard Sir John Vanbrugh say 'that old Joas Bateman was book keeper to his grandfather' Giles Vanbrugh (d. 1646), a Flemish refugee from the Duke of Alva's persecutions.[3]

Sir Charles Duncombe (d. 1711), a London goldsmith, son by some accounts of a hatter in Southwark, according to others of Sir William Tyringham's steward, became the richest commoner in England and bought the Duke of Buckingham's Helmsley estate for £90,000.[4] The Earls of Feversham descend from his nephew and heir.

---

[1] A. P. Wadsworth and J. de L. Mann, *The Cotton Trade and Industrial Lancashire 1600–1780*, 1931, pp. 278–9, quoting *American Hist. Rev.* xix, 1914, p. 494.

[2] J. H. Plumb, *Sir Robert Walpole, The Making of a Statesman*, 1956, pp. 22–23.

[3] *Le Neve's Pedigrees of the Knights*, Harleian Soc. 1873, pp. 463, 511. See also John Carswell, *The South Sea Bubble*, 1960, p. 5, on the Batemans and *passim* on the merchants, projectors and speculators of this period.

[4] Le Neve, op. cit., p. 468; David Ogg, *England in the Reigns of James II and William III*, 1955, p. 88.

In the same period great mercantile fortunes were made in Bristol from the West India slave and tobacco trade, in Hull from the Baltic trade, in Newcastle from coal, and provincial families thus enriched acquired estates and sometimes titles.[1] In the later seventeenth and the eighteenth century overseas trade stood on a higher social level than domestic trade. Defoe remarks that in England the word merchant is used only of those who trade with foreign countries, others being called tradesmen.[2]

The 'nabobs', who came home from India with great fortunes in the later eighteenth and early nineteenth centuries, may be regarded as a special section of the merchant class, though their profits were often those of office rather than trade. Trevelyan notes how they 'made themselves . . . objectionable to the old-established aristocratic society into which they intruded with their outlandish ways'.[3] But Thackeray's picture of Jos Sedley in *Vanity Fair* may suggest another side to the picture. Thackeray was himself the child of Anglo-Indians and his biographer Professor Gordon Ray notes how 'the clannishness developed among these empire-builders by the circumstances of their residence in India was reinforced in England by the prevailing indifference or hostility with which returned "Indians" were regarded'.[4]

The mediaeval class of merchants included the masters of manufacture of whom the clothiers were the chief. The dominance of the wool and cloth trade in mediaeval England is reflected in the size and splendour of the fourteenth and fifteenth century churches in such wool trade centres as East Anglia and the Cotswolds and in a modern literature which embodies profound research. The two commonest occupational surnames after Smith are connected with cloth—Taylor and Walker (i.e. fuller).[5] In the thirteenth century the cloth manufacture had its headquarters in the towns and the leading clothiers were

---

[1] e.g. The Blacketts of Newcastle.

[2] Daniel Defoe, *The Complete English Tradesman*, 1726, pp. 1–3, see p. 151. G. P. Judd, *Members of Parliament 1734–1832*, p. 55, shows that 897 out of 5,034 M.P.'s (1 in 6) were engaged in some commercial activity, 1 in 9 having been so engaged in Elizabeth I's last two Parliaments and in 1604–29. He expounds the interpenetration between aristocracy and men of business, pp. 57–58. The 144 nabob M.P.'s were of various origins, peers' sons as well as men of humble birth.

[3] *English Social History*, p. 391.

[4] Gordon N. Ray, *Thackeray, The Uses of Adversity, 1811–1846*, 1955, p. 19.

[5] C. L'Estrange Ewen, *A History of Surnames of the British Isles*, 1931, p. 220, and a list compiled in 1944 by the Organization and Methods Division of the Treasury which I was kindly allowed to consult.

citizens, but by 1300 the invention of the water fulling mill had led many fullers and weavers to move to country places where there was water power. This tendency increased in the fifteenth century when the Southern Cotswolds, Yorkshire, East Anglia and Westmorland became the most important centres. The great wool merchants comprised, however, not only local dealers but London merchants who dealt in wool among other commodities.[1] The brass of William Grevel (d. 1401), the ancestor of the Grevilles, Earls of Warwick, which calls him the flower of the wool merchants of all England ('Flos mercatorum lanarum tocius Anglie'), records also that he was a citizen of London. This brass is not, however, in London but in the church of the little market town of Chipping Campden in Cotswold where Grevel lived.[2]

By the fifteenth century feudal restrictions on the manors were in decay and could be dealt with by money payments to the lords, whereas guild restrictions in the towns were stiff and troublesome. This as well as technical considerations probably led many clothiers to make their headquarters in small market towns and villages 'which grew as the industry grew, in haphazard fashion, unregulated, under the aegis of the manor rather than the borough'.[3] Some clothiers were villeins, as was William Haynes (d. 1435) of Castle Combe, Wiltshire. This did not stop his acquiring wealth but did mean that the lord of the manor could get something for himself out of Haynes' profits.

Among the greatest clothier families were the Springs of Lavenham, Suffolk, where the great church and the ancient town still evoke a lively image of the prime of the English wool trade. Thomas Spring (d. 1486) built the vestry of the church from the profits of his trade. His son Thomas Spring (d. 1524), 'called the rich clothier', built part of the church and steeple. His merchant's mark is in the church, but he was granted arms by Clarenceux Benolt. The 'rich clothier's' son John was knighted in 1547, while his daughter Bridget married Aubrey de Vere, the second son of the 15th Earl of Oxford, and her sisters married knights of ancient family. Sir John Spring's great-great-grandson was made a baronet in 1641 and the line continued until 1769.[4]

---

[1] Eileen Power and M. M. Postan, *Studies in English Trade in the Fifteenth Century*, 1933, p. 53.

[2] Mill Stephenson, *A List of Monumental Brasses in the British Isles*, 1926, p. 147.

[3] Miss Eleanora Carus-Wilson in the *Cambridge Economic History of Europe*, ii. 409–10, 417–26.

[4] *The Visitation of Suffolk, 1561*, ed. Joseph Jackson Howard, 1866, pp. 165–206; *Complete Baronetage*, ed. G. E. C., ii. 129–30.

Other country towns made by the wool trade were Coggeshall in Essex, where the great house of the clothier Thomas Paycocke (d. 1518) stands; Newbury, Berkshire, where the church was rebuilt by John Smalwode alias Winchcombe (d. 1519), a rich clothier, famous in ballad as Jack of Newbury, whose son was granted arms in 1549 and acquired the abbot of Reading's manor of Bucklebury, while his fifth descendant Henry Winchcombe was made a baronet in 1661;[1] Malmesbury in Wiltshire, where the buildings of the suppressed abbey were bought from Henry VIII by the clothier William Stumpe, who also in 1546 rented Oseney Abbey near Oxford and installed looms there; and Fairford in Gloucestershire where John Tame (d. 1500) began the building of the superb church and his son Edmund finished it.[2] Three of Stumpe's great-granddaughters became countesses in Queen Elizabeth I's time.[3]

Ann Hyde, the mother of Queen Mary and Queen Anne, was the great-granddaughter of a rich clothier of Trowbridge, Wiltshire, Edward Langford (d. 1594).[4]

According to Hasted, the county historian, the sixteenth century clothiers of Kent

possessed most of the landed property in the *Weald*, insomuch that almost all the antient families of these parts, now of large estates, and genteel rank in life, and some of them ennobled by titles, are sprung from, and owe their fortunes to ancestors, who have used this great staple manufacture, now almost unknown here. Among others the *Bathursts, Ongleys, Courthopes, Maplesdens, Gibbons's, Westons, Plumers, Austens, Dunkes* and *Stringers*. They were usually called from their dress, *The Grey Coats of Kent*, and were a body so numerous and so united, that at county elections, whoever had their votes and interest, was almost certain of being elected.[5]

Much later than this the cloth trade was still making its leaders' fortunes. Nicholas Mosley (d. 1612), the London representative of his family's Manchester cloth business, rose to be Lord Mayor in 1599 and a knight. 'From a small and low estate God raised him up to riches and

---

[1] Harleian Soc., *Visitations of Berkshire*, i. 313; ii. 233.

[2] F. Holt, 'The Tames of Fairford', *Journ. Brit. Arch. Soc.* xxvii, 1871, pp. 110–48; H. P. R. Finberg, *Gloucestershire, The History of the English Landscape*, 1955, pp. 72–75.

[3] They were daughters and coheirs of Sir Henry Knyvett of Charlton, Wilts., by Elizabeth, daughter and heir of Sir James Stumpe of Bromham. Elizabeth married Thomas Clinton, Earl of Lincoln, in 1584; Frances (2ndly) Francis Manners, Earl of Rutland in 1602; and Catherine (2ndly) Thomas Howard, Earl of Suffolk, c. 1583.

[4] *The Genealogist*, N.S. viii, 108.

[5] Edward Hasted, *History of the County of Kent*, 1790, iii. 48 n.

honour. He bought the Lordships of the manor of Manchester and of the Hough and built a house called the Hough-end in the place where his father's tenement stood.' The Mosleys held the manor of Manchester until 1846 and three branches of the family received baronetcies, in 1640, 1720 and 1781 respectively.[1]

Peter Blundell of Tiverton in Devonshire (d. 1601), the founder of the school there, started from nothing and left an immense fortune. A writer in 1675 tells us he knew many clothiers, 'who came to considerable estates who have told me they began with ten pound'.[2] Early in the eighteenth century Defoe was told at Bradford in Yorkshire 'that it was no extraordinary thing to have clothiers in that county worth from ten thousand to forty thousand pounds a man, and many of the great families who now pass for gentry in those counties have been originally raised from and built up by this noble manufacture'.[3] In spite of this Yorkshire was noted down to the end of the eighteenth century for the survival, alongside these 'opulent clothiers of large numbers of small working clothiers, and for the widespread opportunities for workmen to rise in the world which their system afforded'.[4] At the end of the eighteenth century technological change struck the Yorkshire handloom weavers and ground them down into poverty, an outcome to which their conservatism contributed. Their descendants looked back to a lost golden age and some remembered their pedigrees a century and a half later.[5] In Gloucestershire things were otherwise. The leading 'gentlemen clothiers' of the eighteenth and early nineteenth centuries by whose energy and enterprise the fine West of England cloth won a world reputation, were men of large capital who, while continuing in manufacture, associated and intermarried 'with the gentle blood of the land'.[6]

Down to the middle of the eighteenth century many forms of manufacture were still domestic handicrafts producing no great wealth. In the 1760's, however, technical developments led to the establish-

---

[1] A. P. Wadsworth and J. de L. Mann, *The Cotton Trade and Industrial Lancashire*, 1931, p. 9, quoting Richard Hollingworth, *Mancuniensis*, 1839, p. 101, and Mosley, *Family Memoirs*, 1849. The Hough is in Withington, which Rowland, son of Nicholas Mosley, bought in 1597, *V.C.H. Lancashire*, vol. iv, 1911, pp. 288–91.

[2] E. Lipson, *The Economic History of England*, 8th ed. 1945, ii. 16.

[3] Ibid., pp. 16–17, quoting Defoe, *Tour of Great Britain*, ed. 1725, ii, letter, i. 43–44.

[4] Ibid., pp. 69–81.

[5] E. P. Thompson, *The Making of the English Working Class*, 1963, pp. 269–313; p. 19 *supra*.

[6] E. A. L. Moir, 'The Gentlemen Clothiers', in *Gloucestershire Studies*, ed. H. P. R. Finberg, 1957, pp. 226, 239, 242.

ment of the first large factories in country places.[1] Such successful manufacturers as the Wedgwoods and Arkwrights—unless or until, like the Peels and the Guests,[2] they rose higher—ranked as recruits to the merchant class. Their manufacturer supporters often at first received a 'freezing welcome' from the old nobility.[3] Peel's social acceptance in 1835 was less than complete. From 1868 onwards such representatives of the new liberalism as Bright, Forster, Stansfield and Chamberlain were brought into governing circles by William Ewart Gladstone. Yet Gladstone himself had perhaps 'something of his tone of voice and way of coming into a room that is not aristocratic'.[4] Gladstone's grandfather had been a maltster. His father, starting as a corn merchant's clerk, had ended as a baronet. But James Gladstone, the Prime Minister's uncle, married in 1807 Elizabeth, daughter of a tanner of Wrexham, and her brother, also a tanner, married the daughter of a grocer in Wrexham High Street.[5]

They sprang largely from among the yeomen. Besides the families just mentioned the Cobdens, Brights, Roebucks, Darbys, Boultons and Wilkinsons are examples.[6] A contemporary remarked that the most successful had usually started as small men and were raised by their own efforts, 'commencing in a very humble way, generally from exercising some handicraft as clockmaking, hatting, &c. and pushing their advance by a series of unceasing exertions, having a very limited capital to begin with, or even none at all, saving their own labour'; while on the other hand, 'few of the men who entered the trade rich were successful. They trusted too much to others—too little to themselves'. Lord Nuffield in our own day rose in just this way, descending from a small yeoman family in Oxfordshire, and rising from a bicycle shop to the control of a great motor manufacturing business.[7]

A special contribution to industrial development was made by

[1] W. G. Hoskins, *The Making of the English Landscape*, 1955, p. 165; W. H. B. Court, op. cit., pp. 45–60.

[2] For the social prejudice which had to be overcome when Josiah John Guest, a rich Glamorganshire ironmaster of Shropshire yeoman stock, married in 1833, aged 48, Lady Charlotte Bertie, aged 21, see *The Diaries of Lady Charlotte Guest*, ed. the Earl of Bessborough, i, 1950, pp. 5–7.

[3] W. L. Guttsmann, *The British Political Elite*, 1963, pp. 54–59, quoting J. L. and B. Hammond, *The Village Labourer*, Guild edition, vol. ii, p. 135.

[4] Guttsmann, op. cit., pp. 84–87.

[5] A. N. Palmer, *History of the Town of Wrexham*, 1893, pp. 130–1.

[6] Roy Lewis and Angus Maude, *The English Middle Classes*, p. 44, quoting George Cunningham, *Growth of English Industry and Commerce in Modern Times*, 1892.

[7] *Complete Peerage*, xiii. 535 and 609–12.

Dissenters in general and Quakers and Unitarians in particular, partly because the civil disabilities which excluded them from public life turned their energies in this direction, and partly because their frugality of living led them to invest their profits in their business rather than in land or show or luxury.[1] Because of this tradition merchant or industrial dynasties of several generations are commoner among the Dissenters than in circles where the successful merchant's object is to shed the taint of commerce and become a country gentleman.

The exploiting of minerals was another kind of enterprise which early required capital and large scale organization and so became an avenue to fortune. The Hanburys of Pontypool, Monmouthshire, are an example of a family who rose by and remained linked with it from the sixteenth century to the twentieth. Their connection with iron-working had begun by 1570 when Richard Hanbury (c. 1538–1608), goldsmith of London, was concerned in the Monmouthshire ironworks (begun long before by the monks of Tintern) of the Company of the Mineral and Battery works. He acquired for himself 'two or three iron works there in Wales whereat he made much merchant iron to great gain'. In 1597 he had ironworks at Pontypool. His nephew and executor John Hanbury (1575–1658), 'dealer in merchandise of iron' in Gloucester, seems to have bought the ironworks from his uncle's estate to pay the debts and legacies. John's son Richard (1618–60) acquired lands in Monmouthshire by marriage, which, with 'a parcel of waste ground called Pontypool together with the forge thereupon built', passed to his brother Capel Hanbury (1625–1705). Capel's son John (1664–1734) greatly expanded the ironworks, introducing furnaces, fineries and rolling mills and at the end of the eighteenth century Archdeacon Coxe could say that the town of Pontypool principally owed its foundation and increase to the ironworks established by the family of Hanbury.[2]

### 9. THE CRAFTSMEN AND TRADESMEN

Between 1066 and 1400 most families in England adopted permanent surnames, but the process was a slow one, spreading by degrees from top to bottom and from south to north.[3] The four main kinds are place

---

[1] See further, pp. 202–3.

[2] A. Audrey Locke, *The Hanbury Family*, 1916, i. 119–51.

[3] In Lancashire not all surnames were fixed even by 1500. In South Lancashire patronymics, over and above the surname, e.g. 'Thomasson', 'Thomasdaughter' are fairly often entered in parish registers. E. Bosdin Leech, 'Surnames in Lancashire', *Trans. Lanc. & Cheshire Ant. Soc.*, 1945–6, vol. 58, p. 177.

names, names of relationship, occupational names and descriptive names. Local surnames may derive from lordship of a place, residence in it or origin from it and so run through the whole social scale. Such names in this class as Wood, Hall, Green and Hill which derive from geographical features are naturally the commonest—much more so than those derived from particular places. Patronymics (names from the father) likewise run the whole gamut from FitzGerald and Fitz-Walter to Johnson, Thomson and Robinson. Dr. Reaney finds that patronymics from Old English and Scandinavian personal names are relatively rare and mainly northern, while those from French names and from shortened forms of names are common.[1] Names from the mother or other relation fall in the same class. Dr. Reaney draws attention to the surprising frequency of metronymics, surnames derived from the mother's Christian name, such as Sisley, Alison, Aveling, Parnell. Were their first bearers widows' sons or bastards?[2] Other relationship surnames include Brothers, Soane, Cousins, Cozens, Cussons and Eames (uncle). Occupational names range from those of great offices like Marshal, Butler or Stewart to the Smiths, Taylors and Walkers. Descriptive names may relate, like Basset (short), Pauncefote (round belly), Russell (red), Blount (blond), Black, White, Brown and Long, to personal appearance; or like Armstrong, Noble and Savage to physical or moral qualities; or like Champneys, Mansel, Loraine, Peytvin, Picard, Blois, Dennys, Pettingall, Fleming, Brabazon, Burgoyne, Gascoyne, French, Brett, Wallis, Cornish, Devenish, Kentish and others to the countries of origin.[3]

Local surnames found at early dates in towns throw light on the origins of their inhabitants. In a tallage roll of the borough of Leicester of 1271 fully a third of the surnames suggest a derivation from places in the surrounding countryside.[4] Professor Hoskins concludes that Plymouth, growing up about 1200, drew its population largely from Cornwall, while that of Dartmouth came from the families of neighbouring peasants and younger sons of gentry, together with some Scotsmen, a merchant from Winchelsea and a few aliens, who all presumably arrived by sea.[5] It has been inferred from those in the

[1] P. H. Reaney, *The Origin of English Surnames*, 1967, pp. 86–90.

[2] Op. cit., pp. 76–80.

[3] P. H. Reaney, *A Dictionary of British Surnames*, 1958; *The Origin of English Surnames*, 1967. The stages by which family names became fixed and the vacillation which often preceded finality are discussed on pp. 296–320.

[4] W. G. Hoskins in *Trans. Leic. Arch. Soc.* xxviii, 1947, p. 48.

[5] W. G. Hoskins, *Local History in England*, 1959, p. 80.

Norwich Conveyance Rolls that by 1300 that city had drawn within its walls natives of at least four hundred Norfolk and some sixty Suffolk towns, villages and manors. The craftsmen who flocked into the towns, then and later, from the country, would start lower on the ladder than those already there, and for the most part would man the lesser trades and the lesser posts in the richer trades. Examples suggest that many were cadets of knights' or franklins' families, who purchased citizenship and entered this class of craftsmen for a living, while a proportion were sons of villeins, who, having by whatever means come into the town, apprenticed themselves to citizens. The former may have been more likely to take surnames from their place of origin, the latter from their occupations, though in early times the same man is often differently named on different occasions. Thus Seman le Agulyer or le Nedler (the needle maker) of Norwich is also called Seman Wrynek (presumably from a deformity) and Seman de Blythburgh, from his own or his family's place of origin.[1] Miss Thrupp estimates that of the immigrant apprentices to members of the greater London companies in the late fifteenth century between a third and a half came from families already engaged in industry and trade, for the most part in the smaller villages.[2]

The line of class division between the great merchants and the lesser craftsmen and tradesmen of the towns is indicated by the alignments seen in the struggles of the fourteenth and fifteenth centuries over town and guild government. Even in the thirteenth century there were complaints in Lincoln and other towns that the richer citizens used their position in the town government to impose financial hardships on the commons or poorer men.[3] The Common Council of the City of London, which dates from 1376, is the sole survivor of many Common Councils set up in boroughs in this period as a concession to the commons, the lesser craftsmen, who sought to share the town administration with the aldermen, who represented the great merchants.[4] The same division can be seen both in the hierarchical structure of some of the great guilds and in hierarchical relationships between

---

[1] Rev. W. Hudson, 'Notes about Norwich before the Close of the Thirteenth Century', *Norfolk Archaeology*, xii, 1895, pp. 66–84. Reaney, *The Origin of English Surnames*, pp. 331–7, with map, p. 333, showing the sources of migration into Norwich.

[2] S. Thrupp, *The Merchant Class of Medieval London*, p. 217. The local origins of London immigrants in general are analysed ibid., pp. 206–11 and 389–92, and for the period 1147–1350 by Reaney, op. cit., pp. 337–51, with map, p. 344. Their social position is examined on pp. 342–3 and the Cavendish family as an example on pp. 341–2.

[3] E. Lipson, *The Economic History of England*, 8th ed. i, 1945, pp. 364–5.

[4] James Tait, *The Medieval English Borough*, 1936, pp. 302–38.

those lesser guilds, whose members formed the aristocracy of their trades, and those whose members' position was subordinate.[1] The scantiness of evidence may explain differences of opinion about the sharpness of these class distinctions at different dates. Unwin, for instance, says that they were much sharper in the thirteenth century than the fifteenth, while according to Mackie by the end of the fifteenth century the growth of capitalism had fixed a great gulf between the ordinary craftsman and the wealthy manufacturer or trader.[2] Professor Hexter points out how Tawney, Louis Wright and others have so extended the concept of the middle class as to render it meaningless, yet himself proposes to attach it to the 'town rich', rather than apply it to whatever classes are, in the stratification of a given time or place, in some actual sense in the middle.[3] Dame Lucy Sutherland notes a 'latent hostility between the richest citizens and the lesser men' in eighteenth century London and explains it 'partly as a heritage of seventeenth century strife and even earlier traditions, and partly as a result of contemporary tendencies', comparing it with the hostility 'familiar (as the struggle between "Magnati" and "Popolani") to students of the independent communes of Europe'.[4]

One of the difficulties is to follow the shifts of meaning of class descriptions at different times and places. Defoe wrote in 1726 that in Scotland and Ireland the word *tradesman* meant what in England was called a *handicraftsman*, namely 'a mechanick, such as a *smith*, a *carpenter*, a *shoemaker* and the like', whereas in England *tradesman* meant 'all sorts of warehousekeepers, shopkeepers, whether wholesale dealers, or retailers of goods', such as '*grocers*, *mercers*, *linen* and *woollen drapers*, Blackwell-hall *factors*, *tobacconists*, *haberdashers*, whether of hats or small wares, *glovers*, *hosiers*, *milliners*, *booksellers*, *stationers*, and all other shopkeepers', except the handicraftsmen who make the goods they sell, even though they may keep shops to sell them in. He adds that those who in England were called tradesmen were in Scotland and Ireland called merchants, a word used in England only of those who trade with foreign countries.[5] These are admirably precise definitions but to apply them to fifteenth or sixteenth century English usage would be totally misleading. Moreover, being here

[1] George Unwin, *The Gilds and Companies of London*, 1908, pp. 50, 55–60, 72–87.

[2] J. D. Mackie, *The Earlier Tudors, 1485–1558*, 1952, p. 461.

[3] J. H. Hexter, *Reappraisals in History*, 1961, p. 75.

[4] *Essays presented to Sir Lewis Namier*, 1956, 'The City of London in Eighteenth Century Politics', p. 55.

[5] Daniel Defoe, *The Complete English Tradesman*, 1726, pp. 1–3.

engaged in exalting the tradesmen, Defoe passed lightly over the great difference in standing between the small shopkeepers and the wealthy traders, whom he saw 'coming every day to the Heralds' office, to search for the Coats of Arms of their ancestors, in order to paint them upon their coaches, and engrave them upon their plate, embroider them upon their furniture, or carve them upon the pediments of their new houses'.[1] These were members, rather, of the class we have called the merchants.

As wealth increased and the organization of trade and manufacture grew more specialized and elaborate, so class distinctions among those engaged in them developed. The fourteenth and fifteenth centuries saw the growth of two distinct lines of economic cleavage, which, coming at about the same social level, may have tended to build up a single social barrier. The first was the growth of capitalism in the cloth trade—a transition from a system in which craftsmen owned their own materials and tools to one in which these were owned by employers who paid the craftsmen wages. The change came gradually, by several roads, but in the sixteenth century it was complete and a wealthy class of capitalist clothiers, who organized the whole manufacture, was seen to have reduced the weavers, fullers, spinners and shearmen to dependence. Weavers, however, could still rise to be clothiers.[2]

There were similar developments in the mediaeval building, ship-building and some other trades,[3] while the sixteenth and seventeenth centuries saw the adventuring of capital in many manufacturing, mining and trading enterprises, with a consequent growth of class divisions between those in control and those whom they controlled. In the late eighteenth and nineteenth centuries technical developments produced the Industrial Revolution which carried the same process much further still. But machinery now made it possible for manufacture, which had previously been mainly a skilled pursuit, to be carried on largely by unskilled labour.

In the first half of the sixteenth century the guilds, feeling themselves threatened by the economic and other changes of the time, became more rigid and exclusive. Many of the poorer or more independent craftsmen, finding this hampering, sought spheres of activity geographically outside the guilds' control. The London suburbs, which grew up in the sixteenth and seventeenth centuries, thus came to house many craftsmen escaping from guild government. The fact that under

---

[1] Daniel Defoe *The Complete English Tradesman*, 1726, p. 377.
[2] Lipson, op. cit. i. 459–61, 471–4.    [3] Ibid. i. 510; ii. pp. xxvi–xxx.

their charters many guilds could claim rights of control over their trades in these suburbs or even throughout the country was offset by the difficulty of enforcement.[1] The London area presents special difficulties to the genealogist because of its vast and mobile population. The social patterns dictated by civic history which Brett-James expounds in his work on *The Growth of Stuart London* will sometimes afford clues.

The *Two Nations* of the rich and poor, whom Disraeli described in 1845[2] were the grasping manufacturers and oppressive landlords on the one hand and the factory hands and poor farm labourers on the other; but no one would, I think, suggest that the factory hands are or were historically the heirs of the mediaeval craftsmen. The modern English middle class has several sources but chief among them are, I suggest, those whom Gregory King in 1695 described as Shop-keepers and Tradesmen, Artisans and Handicrafts. It comprises also the lower ranks, at least, of his Merchants and Traders by Sea and by Land, Persons in Offices, Persons in the Law, Clergymen, Persons in Sciences and Liberal Arts and Naval and Military Officers.[3] R. H. Gretton argued that the essence of the middle class is, historically and actually, its 'use of money as the primary instrument of life',[4] and accordingly derives its special ethos from the town tradesman of the Middle Ages. There is, certainly, a difference of ethos between those who live by salaries and those who live by fees. But both differ in ethos from those who live by trade and all these surely are differences which run right through the middle class and do not divide it from other classes. Mr. Roy Lewis and Mr. Angus Maude[5] expound a view which may be thought more balanced.

We have referred to the growth of capitalism in the cloth trade as one of two main factors tending to build up class division among those engaged in trade and industry.[6] The other was the simultaneous process by which traders in the fifteenth and sixteenth centuries

[1] Norman G. Brett-James, *The Growth of Stuart London*, 1935, pp. 245, 474–5.

[2] In his *Sibyl, or the Two Nations*. See p. 177 *infra*.

[3] *Natural and Political Observations and Conclusions upon the State and Condition of England, 1696*, by Gregory King Esq., Lancaster Herald, ed. George Chalmers, 1804, p. 48.

[4] R. H. Gretton, *The English Middle Class*, 1917, p. 10.

[5] *The English Middle Classes*, 1949. G. D. H. Cole, *Studies in Class Structure*, 1955, chap. iv, pp. 78–100 finds 'The Conception of the Middle Classes' at the present day highly elusive. On pp. 94–95 he analyses them into twelve categories, ranging from heads of private businesses to lower supervisory grades in industry.

[6] p. 171.

separated themselves from the craftsmen who made their wares and sought to prevent the latter from retailing them.[1] We have seen that within the class of traders the greatest rewards in wealth and prestige went to those who carried on trade overseas, who even claimed a monopoly of the name of merchant.[2] A similar social line came to be drawn between the wholesale and the retail tradesman. Among the artisans and craftsmen, as elsewhere, degrees of skill and prosperity made a hierarchy. An aristocracy of labour existed in the London luxury trades and in other places where special skills brought higher status and earnings. So too those with special new skills developed in the manufacturing, engineering and extractive industries acquired a special position. But, as Mr. E. P. Thompson points out, the possessors of special skill were often like islands constantly threatened by techno-logical innovation and with swamping by unskilled labour.[3]

When Defoe (in 1726) argues 'that trade in *England* neither is nor ought to be levell'd with what it is in other countries; or the Tradesmen depreciated as they are abroad, and as some of our Gentry would pretend to do in England',[4] the last words show that the aspiration in the first was only half achieved. He admits that some ladies are still 'scandaliz'd at that mean step, which they call it, of marrying a **Trades-man**', though he points out

for their humiliation, that, however they think fit to act, sometimes those tradesmen come of better families than their own; and oftentimes, when they have refus'd them to their loss, those very tradesmen have married Ladies of superior fortune to them, and have rais'd families of their own, who in one generation have been superior to those nice Ladies both in dignity and state, and have, to their great mortification, been rank'd above them upon all pub-lick occasions.

But while he shows that trade has often been an avenue to wealth and station and that scions of ancient gentry have often been apprenticed to trades, he makes it clear that by and large there were points of up-bringing and manners which debarred many tradesmen from that esteem in the world he would have wished for them.

As the nation's wealth increased and its economic and social structure grew more complex, these graded inequalities of station developed and became an ever more engrossing subject of nice discrimination.

---

[1] Lipson, op. cit. i. 434–6.  [2] p. 171.
[3] E. P. Thompson, *The Making of the English Working Class*, 1963, pp. 237–62.
[4] [Daniel Defoe], *The Complete English Tradesman*, 1726, p. 379.

Rouquet's diagnosis of 1755 has been noted.[1] The plot of Fanny Burney's *Evelina* (1778) turns largely on the tension in the heroine's mind between the higher connections on her guardian's and the lower on her grandmother's side. There is similar tension in Jane Austen's *Pride and Prejudice* (written in 1796–7, published 1813).

'I have an excessive regard for Jane Bennet—she is really a very sweet girl,—and I wish with all my heart she were well settled. But with such a father and mother, and such low connections, I am afraid there is no chance of it.'

'I think I have heard you say that their uncle is an attorney in Meryton?'

'Yes: and they have another, who lives somewhere near Cheapside.'

'That is capital', added her sister; and they both laughed heartily.

'If they had uncles enough to fill *all* Cheapside', cried Bingley, 'it would not make them one jot less agreeable.'

'But it must very materially lessen their chance of marrying men of any consideration in the world', replied Darcy.

To this speech Bingley made no answer; but his sisters gave it their hearty assent, and indulged their mirth for some time at the expense of their dear friend's vulgar relations.[2]

Such prejudices rest largely on difference of education and manners. Both sides were conscious of these. Defoe[3] notes that 'many of our trading gentlemen at this time refuse to be Ennobled, scorn being knighted, and content themselves with being known to be rated among the richest Commoners in the nation'. In the same way the sixteenth century Leicestershire yeoman, Richard Bradgate (d. 1572) of Peatling Parva, though richer than many esquires had lived as a yeoman to his dying day.[4] Such men left it to their sons, who had learned the right manners young enough, to take their place among the gentry. Clough puts a less pleasing aspect of the question into the mouth of the *nouveau riche* whom his devil impersonates.[5]

## 10. JOURNEYMEN AND LABOURERS

The fourteenth and fifteenth centuries saw the growth of a class of labourers in the wool trade who did not own or buy the materials of their work and so had only their labour to sell. This, says Dr. Lipson,

---

[1] p. 96 *supra*.      [2] Jane Austen, *Pride and Prejudice*, chap. vii.

[3] Op. cit., p. 374

[4] W. G. Hoskins, *Essays in Leicestershire History*, pp. 153–8 and p. 124 *supra*.

[5] *The Poems of Arthur Hugh Clough*, ed. H. F. Lowry, A. L. P. Norrington and F. L. Mulhauser, Oxford, 1951, p. 243.

'created the basis for the perennial struggle between capital and labour',[1] by opening the door to a new form of economic pressure. Shipowners, mineowners and ironworkers had begun to employ their labourers on similar terms by the fifteenth century and as enterprises of this kind and scale grew under the Tudors and Stuarts, so did the numbers of the wage labourers. There is evidence also that as early as 1260 London craft guilds refused admission to the less skilled workers in their trades and as this limitation grew stricter the numbers of 'uncovenanted' labourers left outside increased.[2] A journeyman was a man paid by the day's work (*journée*), often but not always an apprentice who had served his time, but in any case one who had not become a master.[3] In the fifteenth and sixteenth centuries some of these combined into their own yeoman guilds to maintain their interests against the masters.[4] The proportion of the labouring poor, the propertyless class, to the total town population seems to have grown rapidly during the sixteenth century. It has been estimated, for example, that in Leicester it was about a third of the whole in 1520 and fully a half under Elizabeth.[5] During the middle ages the influx from the country into the towns was a slowly growing trickle. But all this time cultivation was eating away the waste and forest in which English villages had been islands, until by 1500 or 1550 most of the waste had gone and a new kind of population pressure had begun.

In 1695 Gregory King reckoned the poorest groups of the population—the labouring people and out-servants, cottagers and paupers, vagrants, common soldiers, common seamen and their families—at rather more than half the total, 2,825,000 out of 5,500,000.

Despite great efforts the statistical evidence before the nineteenth century remains scanty and hard to interpret,[6] but it is clear that a great and rapid increase of population took place in the middle of the eighteenth century, with consequent distress, migration, unrest and growth of poverty. The Industrial Revolution which followed the development of new machinery in the later eighteenth and nine-

[1] Ephraim Lipson, *The Economic History of England*, i, 8th ed. 1945, p. 510; ii, 3rd ed. 1943, pp. xxvi–xxxii; iii, 2nd ed. 1934, p. 249.

[2] Ibid. i. 389.

[3] Clapham, *Concise Economic History of Britain*, pp. 133–4.

[4] Lipson, op. cit. i. 394–411.

[5] D. Charman, 'Wealth and Trade in Leicester in the Early Sixteenth Century', *Trans. Leic. Arch. Soc.* xxv, 1949, p. 74; W. G. Hoskins, 'An Elizabethan Provincial Town: Leicester', in *Studies in Social History*, ed. J. H. Plumb, 1955, pp. 42, 45.

[6] D. V. Glass and D. E. C. Eversley, *Population in History, Essays in Historical Demography*, 1965.

teenth centuries may have saved the situation by providing new means of livelihood but at the cost of still further depressing the relative position of the wage labourers.

Mr. E. P. Thompson sees this process actually as the formation of 'the working class', in a sense in which this did not previously exist, through the fusion into one body, with a common outlook and ethos, of the diverse 'working classes' which had existed before. As if to disarm an adversary Mr. Thompson quotes the seemingly opposed view of a highly qualified contemporary observer, Francis Place, the champion of trade clubs and parliamentary reform, who wrote in 1834, 'If the character and conduct of the working-people are to be taken from reviews, magazines, pamphlets, newspapers, reports of the two Houses of Parliament and the Factory Commissioners, we shall find them all jumbled together as the "lower orders", the most skilled and the most prudent workmen, with the most ignorant and imprudent labourers and paupers, though the difference is great indeed, and indeed in many cases will scarce admit of comparison.'[1]

Mr. Thompson's above mentioned interpretation, which appears separable from the rest of his material and conclusions, is a sophisticated form of the myth of the *Two Nations* of the rich and the poor. In South Lancashire, where the scene of Disraeli's novel was laid, the gulf between the great manufacturers and their downtrodden factory hands was indeed profound and shocking. But this, as Mr. Thompson shows, was a special local situation, differing greatly, for example, from Birmingham 'where social gradations shelved less steeply and where the artisan still aspired to becoming a small master' and 'there was a vigorous indigenous Radicalism supported by many employers and to some degree under middle class leadership'.[2] The London picture was different again, vast, immensely diverse and comprising every gradation. Mr. Thompson further points out that characteristic forms of early nineteenth century working class thought and organization came not from the factory workers but from artisans, domestic workers and 'skilled men in small workshops'.[3] It was G. D. H. Cole's view in 1955 that the century before that time had seen the growth of an ever more complex class stratification, the exact contrary of the stark opposition of capitalists and workers predicted by Marx.[4]

---

[1] 'Trade Unions Condemned, Trade Clubs Justified', 1834, manuscript of a tract for working men in Brit. Mus. MS. Add. 27834, fo. 45, quoted by M. D. George, *London Life in the XVIIIth Century*, 1930, pp. 208–11, discussed by Thompson, op. cit., p. 194.

[2] Ibid., p. 611.  [3] Ibid., p. 193.

[4] *Studies in Class Structure*, 1955, p. 59.

An important line of demarcation within the working classes, from the sixteenth century to the eighteenth, was the line between the artisan and the labourer. It then became blurred by the employment in certain trades of labourers working under a skilled foreman in place of journeymen who had served an apprenticeship. Such trades were those of the brewers, colour makers, tobacconists, sugar refiners and soap boilers. But labourers in these earned as much as journeymen in some others.[1] Still the gap between an artisan, who was his own master, and a wage labourer subject to a master's order was wide enough, as Mr. Thompson puts it, for men to shed blood rather than be pushed from one side to the other, as at Bradford in 1797, when crowds threatened the builders of the first steam mill.[2] By 1955, in G. D. H. Cole's view, the skilled and unskilled manual workers had come much closer to forming a single class, but by the raising of the latter, not the depression of the former.[3]

Such lines of division are always shifting and political and cultural as well as economic factors affect their incidence. Much thought was given to such matters in the drafting of the 1832 Reform Bill franchise qualifications. Edward Baines reported in 1831 to Lord John Russell, having surveyed for this purpose 'the numbers and respectability of the £10 householders in Leeds', that 'in the parts occupied chiefly by the working classes, not one householder in fifty would have a vote. In the streets principally occupied by shops, almost every householder had a vote.'[4] The past century and a half have seen a complicated inter-action of political pressure on their behalf, from below by their trade unions and from above by humanitarians, by legislation and by education; of a vast creation of wealth by skill, invention, enterprise and exploitation; and of consequent changes in the social pattern.

Until recently an important group within the wage earning class numerically and socially was that of domestic servants. It has been estimated that in the eighteenth century they formed the largest of all occupational groups. They were recruited mainly from the children of farmers, especially small farmers, and from labourers, though also from those of craftsmen, small manufacturers, shopkeepers and the poorer clergy.[5] Of the same class and origins, but less numerous, were the common sailors and soldiers.

---

[1] M. D. George, op. cit., pp. 156–8.   [2] Thompson, op. cit., p. 548.
[3] *Studies in Class Structure*, p. 59.   [4] Thompson, op. cit., pp. 817–18.
[5] J. Jean Hecht, *The Domestic Servant Class in Eighteenth Century England*, 1956, pp. 1, 9, 16.

Below the labourers came the beggars, paupers and vagrants. In
the Middle Ages the poor and helpless were not too many to be left
to the care of their families or the Church or to live as beggars. A
statute of 1388, however, forbade beggars to wander at will and Acts
of 1495 and 1504 indicate a feeling that beggars were growing in
number and needed to be controlled.[1] Mr. Christopher Hill names, as
fundamental causes of this sixteenth century growth of vagabondage,
the cutting down of great noblemen's households, the eviction of
tenants to make room for sheep farming and the rise of prices caused
by the import of silver from America.[2] Perhaps, if we knew more, we
could add to this the reaching of a point in the slow growth of population, clearance of woodland and cultivation of waste, where a new
kind of population pressure on the means of subsistence was beginning
to be felt.[3] In Tudor times this increase of vagrancy with accompanying
social and economic changes, had made the problem so acute that the
first experiments in Poor Relief were made by local and central
authority. The records of these efforts to help the deserving poor with
work and relief and to make life as hard as possible for rogues and
vagabonds show how the problem grew. The rule that a legal settlement in a parish alone gave a right to relief there caused great trouble
and hardship, but endured till 1795.[4] Though the consequent returning
of paupers to their parishes of origin was condemned as a restraint on
the desirable mobility of labour, there was in fact extensive migration
of labourers from the sixteenth century onwards. The Civil War, by
uprooting many, increased these movements. The great and rapid
increase of population, which began its sharp upward curve about
1780, drove great numbers from the countryside into the towns and
the new industries, and of these too a proportion fell into destitution.

A considerable literature[5] shows that by the reign of Elizabeth, if
not earlier, part of the vagrant pauper population had become a loosely
organized criminal underworld. The origins of the 'upright-men' and
'valiant beggars', 'priggers of prancers', 'Counterfeit cranks' and the
rest were no doubt mixed. 'Of these ranging rabblement of rascals,
some', we are told, 'be serving-men, artificers, and labouring men
traded upon husbandry. These, not minding to get their living with

[1] Stubbs, *The Constitutional History of England*, iii, 5th ed. 1903, pp. 622–3.
[2] Christopher Hill, 'Puritans and the Poor', *Past and Present*, 2, 1952, pp. 34–35.
[3] p. 151, n. 5, *supra*.
[4] Clapham, op. cit., pp. 294–305; Lipson, op. cit. iii, 410–87; Rowse, *The England of Elizabeth*, pp. 351–6.
[5] A. V. Judges, *The Elizabethan Underworld*, 1930, pp. xxvi–xxviii and *passim*.

the sweat of their face, but casting of all pain, will wander, after their wicked manner, through the most shires of this realm.'[1] A list of 'upright men' of 1566[2] contains a sprinkling of such ancient surnames as those of John Stradling, Thomas Basset, John Bascafeld, William Umberville and John Carew, among such commoner ones as those of Richard Horwood ('well near eighty years old; he will bite a sixpenny nail asunder with his teeth; and a bawdy drunkard') and Edward Hayward ('hath his mort following him which feigned the crank'). Stradling, 'the craftiest and most dissemblingest knave', saith he was the Lord Stourton's man; and when he was executed, for very pensiveness of mind he fell out of his wit, and so continued a year after and more'.[3] Those called 'wild rogues' were hereditary beggars. A wild rogue rebuked showed that 'his grandfather was a beggar, his father was one, and he must needs be one by good reason'.[4]

In certain areas of London, notably St. Martin's precinct and White-friars later called 'Alsatia', criminals enjoyed by custom an immunity from justice derived from mediaeval rights of sanctuary.[5] Here criminal families may have lived for generations, but I have seen no such pedigree traced.

## II. THE PROFESSIONS

In the latter part of the seventeenth century the earnest pursuit of natural science had begun but the specialization which has since divided scientists from humanists was still in the future. It is thus characteristic that Gregory King (d. 1712), one of the fathers of population studies, should have been Lancaster Herald and in addition a skilful draughtsman and herald painter, a printer and engraver, a cartographer, a surveyor and an architect. The present chapter may perhaps have shown how close the links between heraldic and sociological studies are or ought to be, so that it is the less surprising to find King making use of the same material to reckon the population and to conduct heraldic Visitations.[6]

King's estimate and analysis of the population of England and Wales in 1695 remained in manuscript till 1802. He nowhere explains in detail how he arrived at his figures and in spite of modern investigation the

---

[1] Judges, op. cit., p. 69.    [2] Ibid., pp. 110–13.
[3] Ibid., pp. 83, 497. Lord Stourton was executed in 1557.    [4] Ibid., p. 79.
[5] Ibid., pp. xlix–lii.
[6] Philip Styles, 'The Heralds' Visitation of Warwickshire, 1682–3', *Trans. Birm. Arch. Soc.* lxxi, 1953, p. 100; A. R. Wagner, *Heralds of England*, 1967, pp. 313–14.

basis of many of them remains uncertain. Thus, though they have always commanded respect, they must be treated with a certain caution. Their basis was a listing of the population as it was on 30 April 1695, which was ordered by an Act of Parliament of 1694 for levying a tax on marriages, births, burials, bachelors and childless widowers. The same Act ordered improved registration of marriages, births and deaths and especially detailed statistics of the nobility and gentry.

Of these returns of 1695, however, the merest scraps survive; it is uncertain how many were ever made; and it seems that King in any case had access to only a few of them and had to average from these for the rest of the country by using totals of numbers of houses derived from hearth tax returns and applying to these factors estimated by himself of numbers of persons per house.[1] But Professor D. V. Glass, who has studied the question closely, tells me that he is still unable to conjecture how King arrived at his analysis of the population into ranks and occupations.

The classes into which King divides the population presumably derive from the practice and convenience of the taxing authorities. Naturally, however, they correspond roughly with social divisions. We have already dealt as best we can with some of them; the Lords (Temporal and Spiritual), Baronets, Knights, Esquires and Gentlemen; Freeholders, Farmers, Cottagers and Paupers; Merchants and Traders, Shopkeepers and Tradesmen, Artisans and Handicrafts, Labouring People and Outservants; Common Seamen, Common Soldiers and Vagrants. We are left with what we should now call the professional men; Persons in Offices, Persons in the Law, Clergymen, Persons in Sciences and Liberal Arts and Naval and Military Officers. The emergence of these occupations and the ultimate cohesion of many of those who followed them to form a more or less distinct social class was a work of centuries and the process may best perhaps be understood by consideration under the headings which follow.

## 12. THE CLERGY

The rule of clerical celibacy was imposed by the Church of Rome only by degrees. At the time of the Norman Conquest there were still

[1] P. E. Jones and A. V. Judges, 'London Population in the Late Seventeenth Century', *Econ. Hist. Rev.* Oct. 1935, pp. 45–63; D. V. Glass, 'Gregory King and the Population of England and Wales at the End of the Seventeenth Century', *Eugenics Rev.*, Jan. 1946, pp. 170–83; D. V. Glass, 'Gregory King's Estimate of the Population of England and Wales, 1695', *Population Studies, A Quarterly Journal of Demography*, iii, 1950, pp. 338–74.

many married clergy. Wulfstan (d. 1095), Bishop of Worcester, required the married clergy in his diocese to give up either their wives or their churches and in 1076 Archbishop Lanfranc introduced legislation designed to make future clerical marriages impossible.[1] It seems that the chief effect of this was to replace marriage by irregular unions and actual marriages were still taking place many years later. Richard Peche (d. 1182), who became Bishop of Coventry in 1161, was the son of a previous bishop, Robert Peche. Nigel (d. 1169), Bishop of Ely, King Henry II's treasurer, was a nephew of Henry I's chancellor, Roger (d. 1139), Bishop of Salisbury. Roger lived openly with a mistress. Nigel was a married man and the father of Richard Fitz-Nigel (d. 1198), Bishop of London and treasurer of the king.[2]

Among the simple parish clergy marriage and illicit unions were common and benefices were sometimes in effect hereditary. Four generations, father to son, were priests of Hexham from 1020 to 1167.[3] Three successive parsons of St. Peter's, Cambridge, before 1207 were of one family, the last two father and son, and a jury said that such succession was the custom of Cambridge. In 1183 Pope Lucius III wrote of a custom in some churches belonging to the abbey of St. Benet of Holme, Norfolk, for a parish priest to take a pension and pass his office on to his son as if he had a right of succession.[4] Pope Innocent IV (d. 1254) wrote to the Bishop of Winchester that he had heard that in his diocese clerks renounced their benefices on condition that they were conferred on their sons, nephews or other kinsmen.[5] The many references in records to sons and daughters of the clergy make it clear that irregular unions were 'very frequent, if not general'.[6] Priests seem sometimes to have married secretly, thus avoiding question in their lifetimes while enabling their children to establish legitimacy after their deaths.[7] Such surnames as Clerk and Clarkson, Parsons and Vickers suggest clerical ancestry though the last two may derive more

[1] Stenton, *Anglo-Saxon England*, pp. 659–60.

[2] A. L. Poole, *Domesday Book to Magna Carta*, p. 183.

[3] Surtees Soc. xliv, pp. li–liii. W. Percy Hedley, *Northumberland Families*, Vol. I, 1968, pp. 12–14.

[4] A. L. Poole, op. cit., p. 225; for the Cambridge case see *Curia Regis Rolls*, v. 39.

[5] *Registrum Johannis de Pontissara Episcopi Wintonensis*, ed. C. Deedes, Canterbury and York Soc., p. 753; quoted by G. C. Homans, *English Villagers of the Thirteenth Century*, p. 390.

[6] Sir Maurice Powicke, *The Thirteenth Century*, pp. 458–9; H. G. Richardson, 'The Parish Clergy of the Thirteenth and Fourteenth Centuries', *Royal Hist. Soc. Trans.* 3rd ser. vi, 1912, pp. 123, 175; P. H. Reaney, 'Celibacy and Clerical Marriage', *Essex Review*, vol. 47, 1938, pp. 82–85.

[7] Sandford, op. cit., p. 374.

often from priests' servants than priests' children.[1] The miller of Trumpington in Chaucer's *Reve's Tale*[2] was married to the daughter of the parson of the town, a maiden of noble kin and fostered in a nunnery. She and the miller had a daughter whom her grandfather the parson proposed to make his heir, 'bothe of his catel and his messuage'. He planned to marry her high,

> In-to som worthy blood of auncetrye;
> For holy chirches good moot been despended
> On holy chirches blood, that is descended.

When Edward VI made clerical marriage legal in 1548 he regularized a practice which had always in a measure obtained.

In both wealth and social origins the mediaeval clergy formed a complete cross section of society from the archbishops and bishops, who ranked with the greatest in the land, to the poorest country parsons, whose economic standing was about the same as that of husbandmen, and the unbeneficed, vagabond clerks who often troubled authority. 'In the societies of Europe', as Homans puts it, 'men have commonly been unwilling to enter an office which will not support them in the manner to which they feel they have a right by birth and station. Thus the value of the benefice held by a clerk in the Middle Ages corresponded roughly with his social origin', but only roughly, for 'the avenues of advancement in the Church were not wholly closed to men of low degree'.[3] Villeins could take orders though after 1164 the lord's consent was needed and he would require the father to pay a fine. Walter Map about 1200 complained that men of family (*generosi parcium nostrarum*) were too proud or too lazy to put their children to learning while the rustics (*servi vero quos vocamus rusticos*) vied with each other in bringing up their ignoble and degenerate offspring to the liberal arts not that they may depart from vices, but that they may abound in wealth.[4] Chaucer's poor parson had a ploughman for his brother.[5] The great reformer and writer Robert Grosseteste (d. 1253), Bishop of Lincoln, is said to have been of humble birth.[6] The pedigrees of William of Wykeham (d. 1404), Bishop of Winchester, Chancellor

---

[1] R. H. Reaney, *A Dictionary of British Surnames*, 1958, p. xxx, and *The Origin of English Surnames*, pp. 93–94.

[2] I owe this reference to Lt.-Cdr. W. A. C. Sandford.

[3] G. C. Homans, *English Villagers of the Thirteenth Century*, p. 388.

[4] *De Nugis Curialium*, i, chap. 10, ed. M. R. James, *Anecdota Oxoniensia*, 1914, p. 7, quoted by Poole, op. cit., p. 239.

[5] *The Works of Chaucer*, ed. Skeat, Oxford, 1923, p. 425.

[6] Nicholas Trevet says 'de ima gente'.

of England, founder of Winchester College and New College, Oxford, show no paternal ancestors beyond his father John Longe of Wickham, Hampshire, who was probably a husbandman, and his motto *Manners makyth man* probably refers to his self made eminence.[1] Richard Foxe (d. 1528), bishop, statesman and founder of Corpus Christi College, Oxford, seems to have been the son of a yeoman,[2] and Thomas Wolsey or Wulcy (d. 1530), cardinal and statesman, was the son of Robert Wulcy (d. 1497), a prosperous butcher and innkeeper of Ipswich, Suffolk, who was almost certainly a member of a family of Wulcy, found as butchers in Yoxford, Dunwich, and Blythburgh, Suffolk, between 1405 and 1526. It seems indeed 'that the Wulcys had to some great extent the monopoly of the butchers' trade in the Loes and Wilford hundreds'.[3] It was not without reason that the poet John Skelton (d. 1529), who did not like the cardinal, referred to 'his greasy genealogy'.

On the other hand many, if not most, noble and knightly families had clerical members, like that of Sir Hugh Giffard (d. 1246) among whose children were an archbishop, a bishop, and three nuns, two of whom became abbesses.[4] The clergy of higher origin were likely to hold the richer livings. While the great family of Bardolf were patrons of Cantley in Norfolk, from Norman times to Henry IV's reign, its rectors were either Bardolfs or of the great county families. Thereafter they were men of unknown origins.[5]

Besides the superior and parish clergy, we must remember the monks and nuns, the clerks of the cathedrals and colleges, the friars, the clerks, often in minor orders only, who administered the establishments of the king and nobility, including the courts of law, and the clerks who taught and studied in the universities. Many of these lived by holding one or more benefices, which were served by curates. So long as the clergy alone (or almost alone) were educated, the tasks of what are now the civil service and the professions necessarily fell to them, but the church authorities did not always favour this and we

[1] Robert Lowth, Bishop of Oxford, *The Life of William Wykeham*, 3rd ed. 1777, p. 10 and app. XVIII. Wykeham's mother's mother seems to have been of knightly blood, however.    [2] *D.N.B.*

[3] Vincent B. Redstone, 'Wulcy of Suffolk', *Proc. Suffolk Inst. of Arch. and Nat. Hist.* xvi, 1918, pp. 71–89.

[4] p. 68; Powicke, op. cit., p. 458. See also 'The Social Origins and Provenance of the English Bishops during the Reign of Edward II', by Miss K. Edwards, *Royal Hist. Soc. Trans.*, 5th ser., ix, pp. 51–79.

[5] Augustus Jessopp, *Before the Great Pillage*, p. 105, quoted by Homans, op. cit., p. 389.

shall see how in one sphere after another, beginning with the law, laymen took these tasks over.[1]

The freedom to marry granted to the clergy by Edward VI in 1548 and, after its loss under Mary, restored (though never favoured) by Elizabeth, in 1559, produced 'a fine race of children . . . reared in the parsonages of England, for generations to come, filling all the professions and services with good men and true, and most of all the church herself'.[2] Professor Lawrence Stone has, however, pointed out that the elimination of the regular clergy at the Reformation and the ensuing plunder of the Church reduced the numbers of the clergy by perhaps half. Their nadir in this respect may have been about 1560, when many livings were vacant. The numbers then rose and a new peak was reached in the 1640's but after 1660 there was probably some decline.[3] The clergy came, perhaps, at this time more than formerly from the middle ranks of society. 'None of Elizabeth's bishops sprang from the nobility or greater gentry, fewer from the humblest origins'.[4] The maintenance of families made the clergy poorer, but the increase in the price of corn benefited them as recipients of tithe and owners and often cultivators of glebe,[5] and this by improving their standard of living improved also their social standing. Furthermore they now had the opportunity to do this by marrying the daughters of the gentry. Their social status, however, was still open to question,[6] and Clarendon, devoted churchman though he was, 'noted as a sign of the social and moral chaos produced by the Great Rebellion, that "the daughters of noble and illustrious families bestowed themselves upon divines or other low and unequal matches" '.[7] Archbishop Mathew gives examples of the way in which under Charles I 'the yeoman and lower burgess grouping . . . had coloured the large mass of the clergy', while 'certain key examples show that the great burgess stocks moved into the high places of the church' though 'the episcopate contained the occasional cadet of a good house, a number of sons of the clergy, and a sprinkling of those who had worked their way without assistance', among these last Archbishop Laud.[8]

The Commonwealth saw the ejection of a great number of Royalist

[1] pp. 188, 192, 194, 195; G. M. Trevelyan, *English Social History*, 1942, pp. 41–55; H. C. Lea, op. cit., chap. xxvi.     [2] Trevelyan, op. cit., p. 176.

[3] Lawrence Stone, 'Social Mobility in England, 1500–1700', *Past and Present*, 1966, p. 24.

[4] Rowse, *The England of Elizabeth*, p. 408.     [5] Op. cit., p. 428.

[6] C. V. Wedgwood, *The King's Peace*, 1955, p. 99.     [7] Trevelyan, op. cit., p. 177.

[8] David Mathew, *The Social Structure in Caroline England*, 1948, pp. 69–70.

clergy[1] and the Restoration a corresponding departure from their livings of some two thousand Puritan ministers who had replaced them.[2]

Before the Civil War it was not the custom of the heralds to summon the clergy to their Visitations among the gentlemen of the counties, the assumption probably being that those who were gentlemen born would appear in the pedigrees of the heads of their families, while those who were not so born were not made gentlemen by the fact of being clergymen. Mr. Philip Styles has, however, drawn attention to the fact that pains were taken to summon them as such to Visitations in the 1680's, though many of those summoned did not take the trouble to attend. His conclusion is that 'while it was becoming more and more common for men of good family to enter the Church, the status of the profession was still felt to depend rather on learning than on social connections'. He quotes letters from clergy to the heralds which support this view. One writes, 'I have no Pedigree nor coate of Armes nor ever had, nor do I pretend to any, nor am I ambitious to be blazond for any thing but honesty & Loyaltye. I am a Master of Artes, & that makes me a gentleman and that a Worshipfull one & I care not to go higher.' Another writes, 'Wee poor clergy-men (provided wee may be acknowledg'ed Gentlemen by the subscription of holy Orders & our degrees in the Universityes) are not very solicitous after descent Pedigree & other ensignes of Gentilitye'.[3] The Rev. William Wayte Andrew, Vicar of Ketteringham, Norfolk, expressed a similar attitude in 1838, when he wrote in his diary after dining with the squire, Sir John Boileau, and the Bishop of Norwich. 'It did not please me that the conversation at the dinner table was entirely on the subject of pedigree.'[4]

In the eighteenth century as in the thirteenth there were rich and poor clergy, the former comprising the dignitaries of the Church, the incumbents of the richer livings, and the pluralists, the latter comprising the incumbents of the poorer livings and the curates who did the duty of absentee pluralists. The upper layer was recruited largely from among the younger sons of the country gentlemen, but sons of yeomen and even of labourers also rose into this class through the

---

[1] John Walker, *Sufferings of the Clergy*, 1714, pt. i, p. 199, quotes Gauden's estimate of 6,000 or 7,000, which he thinks too low.

[2] A. G. Matthews, *Calamy Revised*, 1934, pp. 12 ff.

[3] Philip Styles, 'The Heralds' Visitation of Warwickshire, 1682–3', *Trans. of the Birm. Arch. Soc.* lxxi, 1953, p. 130.

[4] Owen Chadwick, *Victorian Miniature*, 1960, p. 42.

discernment or caprice of patrons of livings or the occasional wealthy landowners who detected ability in a poor child, paid for his education and recommended or presented him to a living. George III's bishops, says G. M. Trevelyan,

almost without exception, were either relations of noblemen, or former chaplains to noblemen or tutors to their sons. Some of them, like Joseph Butler, Berkeley and Warburton, were great philosophers or scholars. But none had been raised to the Episcopate for services rendered to the Church, but for services rendered to learning, to lay patrons or to political parties. Church promotion, like many other good things, had been swept into the net of Whig and Tory party patronage, which had succeeded the royal patronage of times gone by.[1]

A series of reforms in the 1830's made the distribution of endowments more equal and one may hold with Trevelyan that the Evangelical and Tractarian movements, which reinvigorated the inner life of the Church, led it by degrees to assume a greater mastery in its own house.[2] On the other hand it was Sydney Smith's opinion that the equalization went too far for the Church's good.

It seems a paradoxical statement [he wrote in 1837], but the fact is, that the respectability of the Church as well as the Bar, is almost entirely preserved by the unequal division of their revenues. . . . At present, the success of the leader animates them all—each man hopes to be a Scarlett or a Brougham—and takes out his ticket in a lottery by which the mass must infallibly lose, trusting (as mankind are apt to do) to his good fortune, and believing that the prize is reserved for him, disappointment and defeat for others. So it is with the clergy; the whole income of the Church, if equally divided, would be about 250 l. for each minister. Who would go into the Church and spend 1,200 l. or 1,500 l. upon his education, if such were the highest remuneration he could ever look to? At present, men are tempted into the Church by the prizes of the Church, and bring into that Church a great deal of capital, which enables them to live in decency, supporting themselves, not with the money of the public, but with their own money, which, but for this temptation, would have been carried into some retail trade. The offices of the Church would then fall down to men little less coarse and ignorant than agricultural labourers.[3]

It is an interesting question whether the adoption of Sydney Smith's view would have given the later clergy an intellectual standard better able to cope with Darwinian and materialist assaults.

[1] *English Social History*, p. 360.    [2] Ibid., pp. 510–17.
[3] *The Works of the Rev. Sydney Smith*, 2nd ed., 1840, vol. ii, pp. 173–4, 'First Letter to Archdeacon Singleton'.

## 13. THE LAWYERS

So long as few but they could read, write and keep accounts, the clergy necessarily discharged the duties which called for these accomplishments. In the early thirteenth century clerks were still almost the only educated men. Not only priests and monks, but lawyers, physicians, administrators, scholars and students were therefore with few exceptions clerks. The first profession to pass from their hands into those of laymen was the law. Professional pleaders in the King's Courts appear under Henry III and we can infer the existence of a definite legal profession when we find Edward I appointing his judges from among them.[1] In his household—or, as we should say, his civil service—generally the proportion of laymen to clerks was growing steadily, but especially was this so among the experts in English or common law (as opposed to the Roman civil and canon law). 'The schools of the "common lawyers" in London', says Tout, 'were the first schools in England where men could study for a profession without becoming clerks.'[2]

The same few pleaders' names recur in case after case under Edward I[3] and, though the time 'when to be a barrister was to possess the master key to politics' and when lawyers founded great families was not yet, the law already began to be the means of founding a family and this short list includes the ancestors of two families which were later to achieve high distinction, Sir William Howard (d. 1308) of Wiggenhall, Norfolk, who became a Justice of the Common Pleas in 1297, the ancestor of the Dukes of Norfolk, and Sir Hugh de Lowther (d. 1317) of Lowther, Westmorland, ancestor of Lord Lonsdale. Sir William Howard's surname is also spelt Haward and Heyward and in 1300 his son is styled John le Heyward. From this it has been inferred that the Howards' ancestors were haywards of a manor and from other evidence it has been argued that they were villeins. This is not impossible but there is no proof, and the theory has to be squared with the fact that Sir William Howard held a portion of a knight's fee in Terrington, Norfolk.[4] It seems likely in any case that he was of English descent. Among other baronial families founded by lawyers was that of Cobham of Kent, whose progenitor Sir John de Cobham was made a justice in eyre in 1268 and in 1276 was granted

[1] W. S. Holdsworth, *A History of English Law*, 3rd ed. 1923, ii. 226–30, 311–19.

[2] T. F. Tout, *The English Civil Service in the Fourteenth Century*, 1916, p. 13.

[3] Sir Frederick Pollock and F. W. Maitland, *History of English Law before Edward I*, 1911, i. 195.

[4] Walter Rye, *Norfolk Families*, 1911, i. 372–6.

for his good service that his lands in Kent held by gavelkind should henceforth descend by primogeniture.[1] His son Henry was summoned to Parliament as a baron in 1313. So general was the expectation that a man of law, even a Chief Justice, would be a newly risen man that a witness for Scrope in his case against Grosvenor testified in 1386 that his father, who had been dead forty four years, had heard someone say that the father of Sir Richard Scrope (summoned as a baron 1371)— that is Henry Scrope who became Chief Justice in 1317—was no gentleman (*nest point graunde gentil homme*) because he was the King's Justice. The father of the witness thereupon instructed his sons that the father of Sir Henry Scrope was made a knight at Falkirk and was descended from great and noble gentlemen.[2] In fact the Scropes seem to have been a younger line of a minor knightly family.[3]

Under Edward II the laymen among the judges slightly out-numbered the clerks,[4] and as time went on the proportion of laymen grew. The schools of the common lawyers, which made them such a strong community, were the Inns of Court and the Inns of Chancery, which originated in the fourteenth and grew up in the fifteenth century. Under the Tudors and especially Elizabeth, the four Inns of Court, the Inner and the Middle Temple, Lincoln's Inn and Gray's Inn, all lying on the Westminster side of London, attained their zenith and became in effect the third university of England, to which the nobility and gentry sent their sons to acquire knowledge of the world and of a subject then as useful as any for the management of property and the pursuit of worldly and political ambitions.

Sir John Fortescue (d. *c.* 1480) tells us that in his day (*c.* 1470) because of the cost of residence at the Inns of Court, especially if a student had servants as most had, there were not many students in these Inns except the sons of nobles. 'For poor and common people cannot bear so much cost for the maintenance of their sons. And merchants rarely desire to reduce their stock by such annual burdens. Hence it comes about that there is scarcely a man learned in the laws to be found in the realm, who is not noble or sprung of noble lineage.'[5] We may interpret this as an assertion that they came mainly from the families of knights, esquires and gentry, though clearly there were

---

[1] Charter Roll, 4 May 1276.

[2] Sir N. Harris Nicolas, *The Scrope and Grosvenor Roll*, 1832, vol. i, p. 182, vol. ii, pp. 426–7.  [3] *Complete Peerage*, xi. 531–4.

[4] T. F. Tout, *Edward the Second*, pp. 336, 368, 373.

[5] Sir John Fortescue, *De Laudibus Legum Anglie*, ed. S. B. Chrimes, 1942, pp. 118–19 (ch. xlix).

some who did not. Between the 1590's and the 1630's the numbers of those recorded as called to the bar at the Inns of Court grew by more than forty per cent. It was stated in 1633 that the number of the attorneys enrolled in the Court of Common Pleas had grown to 1383 from only 342 in 1578. Their number was put at 3,000 in all England in 1689, while in 1688 Gregory King put the whole legal profession at 10,000.[1]

Throughout Tudor, Stuart and early Hanoverian times [says Professor G. M. Trevelyan[2]] successful lawyers formed a large proportion of the 'new' men who introduced themselves into the county circle by purchase of land and by building of manor houses. The number of English county families who were founded by lawyers is even greater than those derived from the cloth trade.

Weighty as this view is it may require to be put in somewhat different perspective. Study of the law was after all only part of a fashionable education and other elements in the home and family backgrounds of those classified as successful lawyers may have been not less important. Furthermore the lawyers who made their fortunes for the most part did so by the fees and perquisites of the legal and other offices to which they had been appointed, so that the pursuit of the law as such may not be the essential or only factor in a form of success which they shared with others.[3] Rise by purely legal eminence belongs rather to the period since 1660, when this career was the widest open of any to supreme talent. 'There are very few', wrote Addison, 'that make themselves proficients in the studies of the place [the Inns of Court], who know they shall arrive at great estates without them.' Sir Lewis Namier comments on this that many a Chancellor and Lord Chief Justice was a man of no family.[4]

The solicitors licenced to act as agents for litigants in the Court of Chancery, the attorneys similarly licenced in the common law courts and the proctors who performed the same function in the courts where Roman law was practised were so licenced by the several courts and did not achieve the self governing guild organization which the barristers attained through their Inns. Miss Thrupp argues that in the

---

[1] Lawrence Stone, 'Social Mobility in England 1500–1700', *Past and Present*, 1966, p. 24.

[2] *English Social History*, p. 126.

[3] Cf. H. R. Trevor-Roper, *The Gentry 1540–1640* (*Economic History Review* Supplements, 1).

[4] L. B. Namier, *The Structure of Politics at the Accession of George III*, i, 1929, p. 53.

late fifteenth century the more reputable attorneys were beginning to be recognized as gentlemen.[1] The barristers, however, regarded them as inferiors and in the sixteenth and seventeenth centuries embarked on a policy of excluding them from the Inns of Court. This further depressed their status, and though it did not keep some of them from great success and prosperity, meant that some others, whom there was no organization to control, gave the calling as a whole a bad name. An Act of 1729 was the first step towards suppressing the less reputable practitioners and not long after the body which became the Law Society was formed. Nineteenth century reforms further raised the status of attorneys and solicitors and the Judicature Act of 1873 merged them into a single body, the modern profession of solicitors.[2]

### 14. PERSONS IN OFFICES AND PLACES

Gregory King in his reckoning of the population in 1695 put at 5,000 persons each those in greater offices and places and those in lesser offices and places, making with their families and servants a total of 70,000 in a population of $5\frac{1}{2}$ millions. He reckoned 'persons in the law' at the same total of 10,000 and 'persons in liberal arts and sciences' at the slightly higher total of 16,000. Of naval officers he counts 5,000 and military officers 4,000.[3] In 1948 Mr. Roy Lewis and Mr. Angus Maude in a roughly comparable reckoning put the number of 'the middle class body of civil servants' at somewhere between 400,000 and 500,000 men and women, that of local government officers at 150,000 and that of members of the professions, including officers of the armed forces and merchant navy, at between $1\frac{1}{2}$ and 2 millions.[4] These figures are for Great Britain whereas King's are for England only and relate to a total population of some 50 millions as against King's $5\frac{1}{2}$ millions. It would thus seem that since 1695 the proportion of 'persons in offices' to the whole population has considerably increased and probably much the greatest part of this increase has occurred in the past half century.

Though their numbers have so much increased, their opportunities of rising in the world were greatly lessened by the reforms which followed the report made in 1853 by Sir Charles Trevelyan and Sir Stafford Northcote on the organization of the permanent civil service.

---

[1] S. Thrupp, *The Merchant Class of Medieval London*, p. 242.
[2] A. M. Carr-Saunders and P. A. Wilson, *The Professions*, 1933, pp. 39–51.
[3] *Two Tracts*, by Gregory King, ed. G. E. Barnett, 1936.
[4] Roy Lewis and Angus Maude, *The English Middle Classes*, 1949, pp. 113, 127, 147.

Before that time appointments were made upon the nomination of those in power, but afterwards upon the results of competitive examinations. Before that time the rewards included not only the regular fees of office, but frequent perquisites and payments of many kinds for services rendered. Since then fixed salaries have been the rule and their real value has tended ever to diminish.

The original feudal basis of great households was changed when the statute of *Quia Emptores* abolished subinfeudation in 1295. Its place was taken in the fourteenth century partly by short term engagements, partly by life contracts for household officials such as chaplains, lawyers and even cooks.[1] Such officers in the households of the great enjoyed the rank and titles of gentility. John of Gaunt's butler, master cook, master carpenter, steward, seneschal and under seneschal were esquires, as were some of his porters, constables and wardens of fees.[2] In the fourteenth century, as we have seen, laymen began to take the place of clerks on the staff of the King's Exchequer and other departments of State sooner or later followed suit. K. B. McFarlane noted the fifteenth century rise of the gentleman bureaucrat as 'one of the most significant results of the growth of lay literacy'.

Many [he remarks] who did the work of clerks, whether in the king's service like Hoccleve or in the households of the nobility like Worcester, were not in orders. In the fifteenth century such a career as Sir Reynold Bray's, though it was abnormally successful, was not uncommon. . . . Thus a succession of married Leventhorpes began to manage the affairs of the Duchy of Lancaster in the lifetime of John of Gaunt. Thomas Tropenell, the builder of Great Chalfield, was receiver-general to Robert, second Lord Hungerford; John Heaton, esquire, of Newton Blossomville served Humphrey, Duke of Buckingham in the same office.[3]

The Reformation completed the process and official dynasties are found such as the Fanshawe family, five generations of whom are said to have been Exchequer officials.[4] Appointments went naturally to the kinsmen, friends and neighbours of those who made them. Tout notes 'how large a proportion of mediaeval officials showed by their surnames—surnames of the local type—that they traced their origin to some royal estate', and points out that 'the close personal tie of lord

---

[1] May McKisack, *The Fourteenth Century 1307–1399*, Oxford, 1959, p. 262.

[2] S. Thrupp, *The Merchant Class of Medieval London*, pp. 240–1. N. Denholm-Young, *The Country Gentry in the Fourteenth Century*, 1969, p. 42.

[3] K. B. McFarlane, 'William Worcester, A Preliminary Survey', in *Studies presented to Sir Hilary Jenkinson*, ed. J. Conway Davies, 1957, p. 199.

[4] A. L. Rowse, *The England of Elizabeth*, p. 317.

and vassal was, under fourteenth century conditions, the strongest possible guarantee of faithful service'.[1] Ties of this feudal type seem still to be found in some households of the old nobility as late as Elizabeth's reign, though from Henry VIII's time or earlier the patron–client relationship, more 'flexible, transitory, and capable of adaptation' was superseding it.

In its English form it was thoroughly unemotional and cemented by such loyalty of view and integrity of character as the beneficiary could muster. Sir Robert Walpole would be the master of a patron–client relationship of just this character. Aided by a relationship so comprehensible the English governing circle moved out of the Stuart period into the coldness and sagacity of the eighteenth century.[2]

'Deeply rooted in Walpole was the belief that men had a prescriptive right to rewards from the institution they served. It was as natural to him to establish generations of Popples in the Board of Trade and Cardonnels in the Salt Office as to give places for life to his own children.'[3] Professor Plumb adds that by these methods Walpole created the Court and Treasury party which became the core of the old whigs, thereby achieving political stability at the expense of administrative efficiency.

The purchase of offices of profit came in under the early Stuarts and remained normal until the nineteenth century reforms. Sinecures fulfilled the modern functions of investments, endowments and pensions. Through the troubles and the Civil War the bureaucracy developed and flourished, acquiring land to secure its status and linking itself with the great legal profession.[4] The number, in 1690, of central and local office-holders combined with incomes over £100 has been put at three or four thousand. By 1800 it is thought that there were a thousand in the central offices alone, with several thousand local officers. Those paid less must have numbered many more.[5]

In a valuable recent study, which we shall refer to again, Lord Annan points out that the replacement of patronage by competitive

[1] *The English Civil Service in the Fourteenth Century*, p. 16.

[2] David Mathew, *The Social Structure in Caroline England*, 1948, pp. 4–6.

[3] J. H. Plumb, *Sir Robert Walpole, The King's Minister*, 1960, p. 329. For connections of kinship, interest and patronage between party leaders and other lords and their followers in the House of Commons, 1701–8, see Robert Walcott, *English Politics in the Eighteenth Century*, Oxford, 1956.

[4] Mathew, op. cit., pp. 133–4.

[5] Lawrence Stone, 'Social Mobility in England 1500–1700', *Past and Present*, 1966, p. 25.

examinations and elective appointments in the nineteenth century transferred a wide range of posts out of the gift of the nobility into the hands
of a group of families whom he calls the intellectual aristocracy.[1]
Whether, as a consequence, those appointed to such posts under
Victoria were drawn from a wider or a narrower social range, is a
question which might repay closer study than it has received. Lord
Annan's statement, that the 'members of these intellectual families
became the new professional civil servants at a time when government
had become too complicated and technical to be handled by the ruling
class and their dependants',[2] seems to beg the question whether the
families of the dependants in question, the placemen of the eighteenth
century, differed markedly in ability or social origin from those selected
by different methods in the nineteenth. Analysis might prove that most
such families in both centuries drew their origins from a social range
extending from the gentry, through the yeomen and merchants to the
prosperous tradesmen.

## 15. LIBERAL ARTS AND SCIENCES

Gregory King's computation of 1695 put the number of 'persons in
liberal arts and sciences' and their families at a total of 75,000 in a
population of $5\frac{1}{2}$ millions as against 70,000 for those of lawyers and
52,000 for those of clergy. Among them he presumably included
physicians, surgeons, apothecaries, those schoolmasters who were
laymen, surveyors, and a sprinkling of such painters, sculptors, architects and men of science as he did not count among the gentlemen,
officials and clergy on the one hand or the artisans and craftsmen on
the other.

These and the more modern professions have emerged from three
matrices, the clergy, the private and official households of the great,
and the craftsmen. The profession of medicine combines all three
origins. Most mediaeval physicians were clerks[3] but the Church disapproved of the shedding of blood by clergy, so that surgery was left
to laymen. The surgeons by the fourteenth century had formed a guild
in London, but it was a small one consisting mainly of court and army
surgeons and as the fifteenth century went on it allied itself with that

---

[1] *Studies in Social History*, ed. J. H. Plumb, 1955, N. G. Annan, pp. 241–87, 'The
Intellectual Aristocracy', and see pp. 199–200 *infra*.
[2] Ibid., p. 244.
[3] Interesting exceptions are quoted by Norman Moore, *The History of the Study of
Medicine in the British Isles*, 1908, pp. 8–10.

of the barbers, whose charter of 1461 set out that they too had long practised the healing of wounds and drawing of teeth. In 1540 the two guilds were amalgamated into one, that of the barber-surgeons. The two crafts were indeed kept separate within the guild, but their association marks the descent of surgery to the status of a trade.

In the meantime towards the end of the fifteenth century the practice of physic had been greatly influenced by the revival of learning and the consequent access to Greek medical texts. Thomas Linacre (d. 1524), a fellow of All Souls College, Oxford, was the most eminent of the English physicians who at this time studied on the continent, and about 1485 he became a Doctor of Medicine of Padua. To him was chiefly due the incorporation of the Royal College of Physicians in 1518 and the Act of 1522 which forbade the practice of physic to persons not licenced by the college unless graduates of Oxford or Cambridge. He had probably to do also with an earlier Act of 1511 which forbade the practice of physic or surgery to any (save Oxford or Cambridge graduates) who had not been licenced, in London by the Bishop or the Dean of St. Paul's or in the country by the Bishop of the Diocese, acting in each case on professional advice.[1]

During the sixteenth and seventeenth centuries the College of Physicians exercised an effective lead. At first most of its members were in orders but the Reformation changed this and by the end of the sixteenth century medicine had become a lay profession. Gonville Hall, Cambridge, refounded in 1558 by a notable physician, Dr. John Caius, as Caius College, has been a centre of medicine since the reign of Henry VIII and its records afford examples both of family continuity in medicine and of rise by its practise. John Buckenham (d. 1620), a yeoman's son, entered the college in 1581 and he and his son Thomas (d. 1682) practised medicine in Bury St. Edmunds for three quarters of a century. Christopher Ludkin, the son of a Norwich ironmonger, entered Caius by gaining a scholarship in 1633 and became a doctor in Ipswich. Both families' arms were entered at the Heralds' Visitation of Suffolk in 1664. It has been remarked that by the reign of Charles I 'the yeoman and the lower burgess grouping had seeped into medicine and teaching and had coloured the large mass of the clergy'.[2]

In the eighteenth century the College of Physicians so far failed to keep pace with the expanding need for medical service as to give great opportunities to the physicians' despised brethren the apothecaries,

---

[1] A. M. Carr-Saunders and P. A. Wilson, *The Professions*, 1933, pp. 65–83.
[2] David Mathew, *The Social Structure in Caroline England*, 1948, pp. 61–62 and 69.

originally a kind of grocers who specialized in selling drugs but in
1617 separately incorporated in London as the Society of Apothecaries. Its members gained credit at the time of the Great Plague of
1665, when they remained at their posts, while most of the physicians
retired to the country. A legal judgment in 1703 confirmed their right
not only to sell drugs but to prescribe them.

The surgeons too gained in credit during the eighteenth century, as
their art developed. In 1745 their company was severed from the
barbers and in 1800 the Royal College of Surgeons was founded. The
first half of the nineteenth century saw a series of moves to amalgamate
the profession and give the apothecaries, who were still associated
with trade, the professional status which the physicians had always
had and the surgeons were now acquiring. This culminated in the
establishment of the British Medical Association in 1856 and the
General Medical Council in 1858.

In the modern concept of a liberal profession there seem to be two
elements; the learned character which distinguishes its practitioners
from merchants, tradesmen and artificers; and the economic independence which distinguishes them from the holders of office and the
salaried servants of the great. By this definition the stockbroker, the
civil servant, and the nobleman's librarian would alike be excluded,
the first because his ethos is too much that of a merchant, and the others
because theirs is not enough so and they therefore lack independence.
But a wider definition would take in those of dependent status, the
estate agents and secretaries and tutors retained in noblemen's households from the sixteenth century onwards, 'the men of skill and confidence, the class which maintained standards of erudition, and formed
the base inevitably created for itself by any aristocratic policy'.[1] Independence came by degrees. In the years before the Civil War 'there
was novelty in the idea of the short-term contract which would now
be offered by a patron to a man applying for the post of a travelling
tutor. In the newly formed group of such dependants there was an ease
of lateral movement from the service of one employer to that of another
of equal rank.'[2] To the same epoch belong the beginnings of the private
school such as that set up by Thomas Farnaby (d. 1647).[3] The lay
element in the teaching profession grew slowly but steadily. Discussing
the successive legitimization of different professions and occupations
as suitable for gentlefolk G. D. H. Cole points out the effect of the

    1 David Mathew, *The Social Structure in Caroline England*, 1948, p. 56.
    2 Ibid., p. 57.                                    3 Ibid., p. 67.

need to provide for the poorer scions of the landed gentry, who, however, had in these fields to rub shoulders with entrants from lower down the social scale. The Scots, especially in medicine, helped to bridge the gap between the gentlemen and the rest because no one quite knew how to place them.[1] Trollope in 1870 describes the views of an elderly old fashioned lady.

The son of a gentleman, if he intended to maintain his rank as a gentleman, should earn his income as a clergyman, or as a barrister, or as a soldier, or as a sailor. Those were the professions intended for gentlemen. She would not absolutely say that a physician was not a gentleman, or even a surgeon; but she would never allow to physic the same absolute privileges which, in her eyes, belonged to law and the church. There might also possibly be a doubt about the Civil Service and Civil Engineering; but she had no doubt that when a man touched trade or commerce in any way he was doing that which was not the work of a gentleman. He might be very respectable and it might be very necessary that he should do it; but brewers, bankers and merchants, were not gentlemen, and the world, according to Miss Marrable's theory, was going astray, because people were forgetting their landmarks.[2]

The seal was set on the emergence of the civil engineer's status from the mechanical to the professional level by the establishment of the Institute of Civil Engineers in 1828.

Mr. Howard Colvin's account of the growth of the architectural profession[3] shows a like development. The mediaeval architect was a master carpenter or master mason, *primus inter pares*. The dominance of the architect over the building craftsmen came with the Renaissance from Italy and was first fully exemplified in Inigo Jones (d. 1652). This relationship was inherent in the nature of Palladian architecture, 'based', as it was, 'on a highly sophisticated theory of design which could not well be studied outside Italy, and which was beyond the intellectual grasp of the average master builder. Moreover, its execution demanded that the craftsman should subordinate himself to a single controlling mind in a way which he had never been required to do before.'[4]

Jones was a court architect and earned his living as Surveyor of the King's Works. Throughout the seventeenth and eighteenth centuries the Office of Works 'provided by far the greatest number of posts open to architects in the form of surveyorships and clerkships of the

---

[1] *Studies in Class Structure*, 1955, chap. v, pp. 119–23.

[2] *The Vicar of Bullhampton*, pp. 55–56.

[3] H. M. Colvin, *A Biographical Dictionary of English Architects, 1660–1840*, 1954, pp. 10–25.     [4] Ibid., p. 11.

works',[1] and even those who like William Kent (d. 1748) owed their advancement mainly to private patronage—in his case that of Lord Burlington—would secure such posts if they could. Some of the early architects, however, were 'gentlemen by birth who supplemented their inadequate private incomes by acting as architects and artistic advisers'.[2]

Architecture opened many doors of advancement for the few who could then practise it. 'Few men who have gained any reputation', wrote Campbell in 1747, 'but have made good estates.' 'Many men of that profession', wrote George Vertue in 1749, 'has made greater fortunes . . . than any other branch of Art whatever—their manner of undertakings is so profitable, by their agreements at so much per cent for drawings and direction of works of building.'[3]

The promotion of humble talent by judicious patronage and education was a speciality of the eighteenth century aristocracy, and when such talent was architectural it could raise from humble origins to wealth and high society. William Kent (? 1685–1748) had been a coach painter's apprentice but 'had the good fortune to find some Gentlemen . . . to promote his studies', who 'raised a contribution and recommended him to proper persons in London to direct him to Italy'. When he died he was buried in Lord Burlington's vault at Chiswick.[4] Lancelot ('Capability') Brown (1716–83), employed as a gardener at 16, ended as a landowner and the father of a Member of Parliament.[5]

By the 1760's architects were taking pupils. By the 1790's they were moving towards professional organization and in the 1830's they achieved this with the foundation of the Royal Institute of British Architects. Henceforth the architect would rank 'as a gentleman, a scholar, and an artist, clearly distinguished from the "mechanic" who called himself a builder'.[6]

The subordination of the building craftsmen to the architect which came in with Renaissance architecture in the seventeenth century was followed in the nineteenth by their further degradation when invention made it possible for much that had been their work to be done by machines. The decorative arts and crafts began to fall into decay. Craftsmen became mechanics.

That field of the arts [said William Morris (d. 1896)] whose harvest should be the chief part of human joy, hope, and consolation, has been . . . dealt

---

[1] Colvin, op. cit., p. 13.   [2] Ibid., p. 12.   [3] Quoted op. cit., p. 14.
[4] Ibid., pp. 341–3.   [5] Ibid., pp. 100–1.
[6] Ibid., pp. 14–25. See also Sir John Summerson's Cantor Lectures, 'The Classical Country House in 18th Century England', *Journ. Roy. Soc. of Arts*, vol. cvii.

hardly with by the division of labour. . . . Art is man's expression of his joy in labour. . . . If pleasure in labour be generally possible, what a strange folly it must be for men to consent to labour without pleasure, and what a hideous injustice it must be for society to compel most men to labour without pleasure![1]

Lord Annan[2] has drawn attention to the emergence early in the nineteenth century of an interesting and important group of inter-married families whom he calls the intellectual aristocracy; centring on the philanthropic families of the Clapham sect, Thornton, Wilber-force, Elliott, Venn, Macaulay; including certain prosperous Quaker families already intermarried in the eighteenth century, Gurney, Fry, Gaskell, Hoare,[3] Hodgkin, Fox, Barclay; and drawing in by marriages the Darwins, Wedgwoods, Butlers, Stephens, Stracheys, Trevelyans and many more. Lord Annan's selection revolves largely on the Clap-ham–Cambridge–Bloomsbury axis and upon a cast of mind charac-teristic of this milieu. It would, I think, have been possible by following the intermarriages further to carry equally close connections into every county and every learned institution in England and by so doing to give the group character a somewhat different bias. To say this is not to disparage the importance or cohesion of the group Lord Annan describes, but it is to hint that—as described, if not as defined—it is *an* intellectual aristocracy rather than *the* intellectual aristocracy of its day. Mr. Ford K. Brown has pointed out the importance of other Evangelical connections of the Wilberforce family, for example with the Sumner family including John Bird Sumner (1780–1862), Arch-bishop of Canterbury, and his brother the Bishop of Winchester, with the Abel Smith banking family[4] and through them with the Rev. John Sargent, the Rev. George Ryder, Cardinal Manning and others.

Lord Annan's discussion illustrates the important point that the best proof that a social class has come into existence is that the families which constitute it have begun to intermarry with each other rather than with those outside.

[1] *The Lesser Arts of Life*, quoted by Aymer Vallance, *William Morris*, 1897, p. 258.

[2] *Studies in Social History*, ed. J. H. Plumb, 1955, pp. 241–87, N. G. Annan, 'The Intellectual Aristocracy'.

[3] The Hoares of the Irish branch, bankers in Cork, were Quakers; cf. Arthur Raistrick, *Quakers in Science and Industry*, 1950, pp. 331–3. The common ancestry with the Hoares of Hoares' Bank (pp. 141–2) attributed to this family in Edward Hoare's *Families of Hore and Hoare*, 1883, was disproved by a pedigree recorded at the College of Arms in 1923 which takes its ancestry back to 1526 at Green's Norton, Northamptonshire.

[4] *Fathers of the Victorians, The Age of Wilberforce*, Cambridge, 1961, pp. 72–73.

Families who rise from similar milieux and whose children receive the same upbringing and education will naturally intermarry; and even when the original ideals which brought them together have faded, a tradition of behaviour replaces the original impetus. Clearly certain families produce a disproportionately large number of eminent men and women. But equally clearly this study shews that men of natural but not outstanding ability can reach the front ranks of science and scholarship and the foremost positions in the cultural hierarchy of the country if they have been bred to a tradition of intellectual achievement and have been taught to turn their environment to account. Schools and universities can so train young men, but such a training has a far stronger command over the personality when it is transmitted through a family tradition. And the tradition is evidently strong: to assess its strength would be possible if the exogamous marriages within this class, as well as the endogamous, were enumerated, and the careers of the diffident and rebellious, as well as the brilliant luminaries, were studied.[1]

## 16. RECUSANTS AND DISSENTERS

The religious divisions of the sixteenth century, though unconnected with class divisions in their origins, in time affected these through the social segregation imposed on the sects both by their doctrines and by the civil disabilities which they suffered. This was truer of Puritan Dissenters than of Catholic Recusants, for in the course of the later sixteenth and seventeenth centuries the numbers of the latter were greatly reduced by persecution and survived in appreciable numbers, on a geographical rather than a class basis, only in a few remote localities, 'in Lancashire notably, in three areas—in Ribblesdale about Stonyhurst, in the Fylde country and along the fertile coastal area from Liverpool to Southport',[2] in Durham and Northumberland and in other scattered places where Catholic landlords could protect Catholic tenants and dependants.

The numbers of Catholic lords and knights at different dates in the seventeenth century are fairly well known and on the principle *cujus regio ejus religio* help to establish the probable numbers and distribution of the general Catholic population. In 1640 out of about 130 peers 25 were Catholic and 5 more were of Catholic sympathies. In 1678 there were 23. It has been estimated by a Catholic writer that under Charles I the Catholics numbered between 10 and 20 per cent. of the gentry, in 1680 about 10 per cent., and in 1715–20 about 5 per cent. In 1781 according to Joseph Berington, a Roman Catholic priest, there were

[1] Annan, op. cit., pp. 284–5.
[2] A. L. Rowse, *The England of Elizabeth*, pp. 446–57.

7 Catholic peers, 22 baronets and about 150 landed gentlemen, while the total number of Catholics in England and Wales was reckoned in that year as 69,376. They had thus apparently dwindled by 1781 to about one fifth of their strength in 1715–20.[1] The Catholic Emancipation Act of 1829 reversed this trend. 'The Irish immigration below, the flow of converts from the fashionable and intellectual classes above, and the high Roman Catholic birth-rate gave to the Roman Communion a very much more important place in English life at the end of Victoria's reign than that which it had enjoyed at the beginning'.[2]

The social history of the Puritan Dissenters was different. Down to the time of the Commonwealth, when they briefly dominated England, they comprised members of all classes including the highest, though Walker asserts that their ministers ejected in 1660 included 'not a few Mechanicks, and Fellows bred to the meanest Occupations; many more who had never seen either of the Universities, several Troopers, and others who had served in the *Rebel* Armies'.[3] Thereafter the same weariness with the 'rule of the saints' which had preceded the Restoration of 1660 led to a trend of sentiment against their tenets. This was expressed both in the imposition of political disabilities on Dissenters and in a waning of Puritan views in ruling and wealthy circles. Between 1660 and 1700 the ranks of the Presbyterians, Independents and Quakers still, Dr. Bebb tells us, included 'some members of the aristocracy, many of the gentry and local magnates, and many engaged in trade, large and small, as well as numerous labourers and workmen', though the Baptists 'were with some few exceptions, of the economically inferior classes'. By the beginning of the eighteenth century, however, few members of the nobility could be found amongst the Nonconformists, and by 1740 their numbers

among the gentry had sensibly diminished. They were still, at this time, quite important in trade, with many wealthy, but this importance was soon rapidly to shrink. So, by a process of attrition, first the socially distinguished, then the economically powerful section of early Nonconformity almost disappeared, having been for the most part re-absorbed into the Anglican Communion. Then arose the new Nonconformity, Methodism, which started socially and economically from the bottom, and before the nineteenth century had dawned had sprung into some economic importance although it had little social prominence. . . .

[1] Brian Magee, *The English Recusants*, 1938.
[2] G. M. Trevelyan, *English Social History*, pp. 566–7.
[3] John Walker, *Sufferings of the Clergy*, 1714, p. xiv.

On the other hand, we find, historically, that one of the types of persons to whom [English Protestant] Nonconformity appeals tends to become wealthy by a personal endeavour and abstinence encouraged by this type of Christianity.[1] 'The Lancashire textile industries of the seventeenth and eighteenth centuries were built up largely by Puritans and Dissenters. . . . The largest centres of industry, Manchester, Bolton and Rochdale, were Puritan strongholds. Many linen drapers and clothiers appear among the elders who experimented in Presbyterian church government in the Classes of 1647–57. After the Restoration Nonconformity maintained a vigorous existence. The ejected ministers continued active work, supported (as their numerous diaries show) by the hospitality and generosity of traders and the new gentry, whose fortunes had been built on trade. After Nonconformity received toleration, the manufacturing districts contained large Dissenting congregations in which the trading element was strong.

However, 'as with increasing wealth', the Nonconformist clothiers of Lancashire

became landed proprietors, the edge of their Dissent became blunter, and their sons passed without difficulty into the commission of the peace and the Anglican communion. Their association with trade was so far forgotten that by the middle of the eighteenth century they were to be found with all the prejudices of the country gentleman against the parvenu manufacturing capitalists of that day.[2]

The tendency for Dissenters, who have risen or hope to rise in the social scale, to shed their dissent, has been noted in our own times also.[3]

Among the Dissenters who became rich through trade and industry the Quakers have been conspicuous. Their honesty in business attracted customers and their plain living meant that profits which others might have used to live more fashionably or to marry their children into the aristocracy, were available to them as capital. Their close friendship and intermarriages among themselves were also helpful to their business. Most of the members of the Midland Association of Ironmasters, founded about 1762, were Quakers and related to one another; the Darbys and Reynolds' of Coalbrookdale; the Lloyds of Dolobran who moved on from iron founding to banking in Birmingham in 1765,

[1] E. D. Bebb, *Nonconformity and Social and Economic Life, 1660–1800*, 1935, p. 57.
[2] Alfred P. Wadsworth and Julia de Lacy Mann, *The Cotton Trade and Industrial Lancashire 1600–1780*, 1931, pp. 42–43, 279. On the connections between puritanism, commerce and industry see also Lawrence Stone, 'Social Mobility in England 1500–1700', *Past and Present*, 1966, pp. 43–44.
[3] G. D. H. Cole, *Studies in Class Structure*, 1955, p. 118.

and the Crowleys of Stourbridge,[1] who, however, reverted to the Church of England. The intermarried Quaker families of Gurney and Barclay show a similar trend in banking, to which the Gurneys came in 1770 as a development of their woollen business, while Barclay's Bank goes back to John Freame (d. 1745) of Lombard Street, Quaker and goldsmith, whose daughter married James Barclay (d. 1766) while his granddaughter married David Barclay (d. 1769), father of James, as his second wife, thus becoming the stepmother of her uncle by marriage. There are many other such examples of Quaker enterprise and success.[2] Most of these families were by origin yeomen or small gentry. Mr. E. P. Thompson concludes that

in the mid-18th century the Presbyterians and the Independents (taken together) were strongest in the south-west (Devonshire, Dorset, Gloucestershire, Hampshire, Somerset, Wiltshire), in the industrial north (notably Lancashire, Northumberland and Yorkshire), in London and in East Anglia (notably Essex and Suffolk). The Baptists contested some of these strongholds and were also well-rooted in Bedfordshire, Buckinghamshire, Kent, Leicestershire and Northamptonshire. Thus the Presbyterians and Independents would appear to have been strongest in the commercial and wool manufacturing centres, while the Baptists held ground in areas where petty tradesmen, small farmers and rural labourers must have made up a part of their congregations. It was in the greatest of the older woollen centres, the West Country, that the broad-minded, 'rational' religion which tended towards the denial of Christ's divinity and to Unitarianism both made its most rapid advances and lost it the allegiance of its congregations. In Devonshire by the end of the 18th century, more than twenty Presbyterian meetinghouses had been closed. . . . Where the Calvinist tradition was strong, as in parts of Lancashire and Yorkshire, the congregations fought back against the drift towards Unitarianism.[3]

He points out that the anarchy of Old Dissent, with its self governing churches and schisms, was liable to produce sudden changes of view, but also that it was in areas with a long tradition of Dissent that Methodism often made most rapid headway among the poorest.[4]

Birmingham, as an unincorporate town free from guild and civic restrictions, attracted many Dissenters; among them a group of able Unitarian families, Kenricks, Chamberlains, Martineaus, Nettlefolds,

[1] p. 216, Table III.
[2] Isabel Grubb, *Quakerism and Industry before 1800*, 1930, pp. 14, 145–71; Arthur Raistrick, *Quakers in Science and Industry*, 1950, pp. 74–160, 321–33 and *passim*.
[3] *The Making of the English Working Class*, pp. 27–28.
[4] Ibid., pp. 36, 39

and Beales who intermarried and formed a notable element in its mercantile and civic life. In Manchester a notable group of Unitarian merchants and manufacturers included the Hibberts, Gaskells and Potters.[1]

---

[1] R. V. Holt, *The Unitarian Contribution to Social Progress in England*, 1952, pp. 23, 44–46, &c.

# V

## THE RISE AND FALL OF FAMILIES

### I. SOCIAL MOVEMENT AND TEXTURE

SINCE the appearance of Professor Sorokin's book[1] the term social mobility has come into general use to describe the movements of individuals upward, downward and sideways between social classes and groups, and present day social mobility is now the subject of much academic research and study. Our present concern, however, is not directly with these individual movements or the social patterns which they form but with the patterns which cumulatively they impose on genealogies and family histories. A degree of fluidity perhaps unusual has long distinguished the English social structure. In Stubbs' view 'there is very little evidence to show that our [mediaeval] forefathers, in the middle ranks of life, desired to set any impassable barrier between class and class'. The barons might wish to be exclusive but the power and policy of the crown prevented this. Between each class and that below it there were many links and gradations so that, though conflicting interests often divided class from class, many individuals moved up or down from one to another. This pattern, already discernible in the Middle Ages, has since become much more pronounced and clearly discernible. The last chapter has shown us villeins becoming freemen and yeomen becoming gentlemen. A fourteenth century merchant's son, Michael de la Pole, and a sixteenth century blacksmith's son, Thomas Cromwell, were created earls. Sir John Hawkwood (d. 1394), the great condottiere, was the son of a tanner of Sible Hedingham, Essex. His success in the wars of north Italy, with his White Company, led the Florentines to engage him as their commander in chief and, when he died, to vote him a splendid public funeral. He married a natural daughter of the ruler of Milan, Bernabo Visconti, whose niece married Lionel, Duke of Clarence, son of King Edward III.

Cardinal Wolsey was a butcher's son and Archbishop Laud a clothier's. Richard Bertie (c. 1516–82), husband of the widowed

[1] Pitirim Sorokin, *Social Mobility*, 1927.

Duchess of Suffolk (whose gentleman usher he had been) and progenitor of the Dukes of Ancaster, was the son of the master mason of Winchester Cathedral.[1] Lionel Cranfield (1575–1645), Earl of Middlesex, was a mercer's son and began life as a London apprentice. Professor Stone has discussed the paths of upward social movement in the sixteenth and seventeenth centuries; marriage with an heiress or rich widow; Court favour; success at the law; manipulation of the land market; commerce; agency to a large estate; and so forth.[2] Leslie Stephen pointed out that the eighteenth century was notable for the number of men who rose from the humblest origins to distinction in science, art and literature and Mrs. Dorothy George adds that this was matched by a simultaneous rise of many labourers, artisans, clerks, shopkeepers and men of business from the bottom of the ladder to established positions—part of the reason being a general increase in the middle classes, at all events in London.[3] Several eighteenth century members of the House of Commons rose from obscurity. Thomas Vere (*c.* 1681–1766), member for Norwich, was the son of a baker.[4] Sir William James (*c.* 1721–83), member for West Looe, created a baronet in 1778, was probably the son of a miller.[5] Robert Mackreth (*c.* 1725–1819), member for Castle Rising and Ashburton, was a waiter at White's Club who grew rich by usury.[5] Benjamin Hammet, alderman and member for the City of London, was the son of a Taunton barber or serge manufacturer and himself a porter in a London bookshop who became a banker.[4] Sir Robert Darling (d. 1770), sheriff of London and member for Wendover, kept cows as a boy at Chellington, Bedfordshire.[5] Sir James Sanderson (1741–98), son of a York grocer, became a banker, Lord Mayor and member for the City of London and a baronet.[4] Thomas Fitzherbert (*c.* 1746–1822), member for Arundel, who began life measuring coal in Portsmouth dockyard, married a baronet's niece.[5] Henry Isherwood (d. 1797), member for Windsor, was the son of a servant at an inn.[4] William Roscoe (1753–1831), member for Liverpool, was the son of a market gardener.[4] Robert Gifford (1779–1826), member for Eye, was the son of an Exeter grocer and linendraper. He was articled to an attorney, became a barrister, attorney general, Chief Justice of the

[1] *Complete Peerage*, xii. ii, 674.
[2] Lawrence Stone, 'Social Mobility in England 1500–1700', *Past and Present*, 1966, pp. 16–55, especially pp. 33–35.
[3] M. D. George, *London Life in the XVIIIth Century*, 1930, p. 318.
[4] Gerrit P. Judd IV, *Members of Parliament 1734–1832*, Yale, 1955, p. 4.
[5] *The History of Parliament. The House of Commons 1754–1790*, i, 1964, pp. 103–7.

Common Pleas and Master of the Rolls and was created Baron Gifford in 1824. His son married a duke's granddaughter.[1] Edward Burtenshaw Sugden (1781–1875), member for Weymouth, St. Mawes and Ripon, was the son of a hairdresser in Duke Street, St. James's, became a barrister and at length Lord Chancellor and in 1852 was created Baron St. Leonards.[1] The History of Parliament notes five avenues by which such men rose—marriage, the law, trade, the profits of war and India.[2]

We could without great difficulty find other such examples of meteoric rise. They strike the imagination of contemporaries and are noted with admiration or resentment. Less often noted but commoner and for our purpose more important are the slighter movements up or down, which in one generation amount to little but continued for three or four in the same direction make a great change in the position of a family.

Family is in this context an ambiguous term, at which we must look more closely. The elementary family of father, mother and children presents no problem, but as soon as grandchildren are brought in we have to reckon with the fact that they are grandchildren equally of another couple and count their kindred on both sides. Genealogists, following common usage, draw up their pedigrees and reckon families in different ways for different purposes. In one context an agnatic kindred may be meant, that is the descendants of one man through male lines only. In other circumstances his family may mean those descendants entitled to inherit from him according to rules of law which may bring in female as well as male lines. In yet other contexts a man's family may mean his whole kindred through all his lines of ancestry. The matrilineal line and the line traced sometimes through the father and sometimes through the mother are equally familiar concepts to the genealogist. In common usage such lines as these are scarcely families, yet as elements in family history they should be included in any analysis of family rise and fall.

The rise of families is naturally much better documented than their fall, for while the origins of those which have risen are studied both by their members and by historians, those which have gone down hill pass for the most part out of the genealogist's ken and usually lack the wish or opportunity to trace or record their own origins, though they may preserve vague traditions. Professor Stone concludes from the very high figures of land sales that the tragedies of downward mobility,

---

[1] *Complete Peerage*, v. 644–5.  [2] Op. cit., p. 104.

due to improvidence, incompetence, extravagance or bad luck were particularly frequent between 1560 and 1640. Among the probable causes was higher fertility of the upper classes than the lower.[1] Mr. Laslett argues that in the seventeenth century the falling families must slightly have exceeded those rising in number because the gentry had more children and these a higher rate of survival. 'Hence downward mobility; hence the individuals born into the manor-houses who found themselves marrying into the houses of the yeomanry, the clergy, or even the husbandmen, as well as the city tradesmen.' He tells us that the Lincoln marriage licences between 1612 and 1617 show one third of the men and two fifths of the women marrying outside their social order, and nearly a quarter of the women and fifteen per cent of the men from the gentry marrying into yeomen's families. One gentleman marries a waterman's daughter, one a pursemaker's. One gentlewoman marries a barber's son, one an apothecary's and a third a husbandman's.[2]

The risks of catastrophe, as distinct from gradual decline, have been especially great at certain times and places. Mrs. George mentions factors which made 'going to the dogs or the workhouse so common a fate in the prosperous eighteenth century', such as lack of discipline for apprentices, the club, the tavern, the alehouse, drinking, gambling and debt. Francis Place names many early acquaintances who had started with good businesses but ended in the workhouse or as beggars in the street through dissipation and gambling, especially in the State Lottery. Recovery, however, was not infrequent and Place's own father was repeatedly ruined and as often recovered in a manner which, he says, 'appears to us sober people of the present day almost incredible. But such men were by no means uncommon in his time.'[3] The records of La Providence, the Huguenot Hospital or almshouse, record an application for help made in 1878 by Mary Chevalier, a teacher. Her great-grandfather Jean Chevalier, though of a notable Huguenot family, had had to enter La Providence in 1785 and died there in 1791. His son Thomas, however, had risen to be Surgeon Extraordinary to George IV, Hunterian Professor at the Royal College of Surgeons,

---

[1] Lawrence Stone, 'Social Mobility in England 1500–1700', *Past and Present*, 1966, pp. 35–43.

[2] Peter Laslett, *The World We Have Lost*, 1965, pp. 185, 191.

[3] M. D. George, op. cit., chap. vi, pp. 273, 314; Place's Autobiography, Brit. Mus. MS. Add. 35142; *The History of Parliament. The House of Commons 1754—1790*, i, 1964, pp. 108–9, gives examples of members who ruined themselves.

F.R.S. and F.S.A. His son too was a surgeon, but dying aged 34 left a widow and four children without means.[1]

In certain circumstances genealogists bring such descents to light by accident; for example in tracing the next of kin on an intestacy or in tracing the coheirs to an abeyant barony, who may be both numerous and remote. Again the ancestors of a risen family sometimes prove to have come down in the world from a previous eminence to a nadir from which they then rose again. I shall refer later to examples of these kinds. Finally we must remember that the growth of population and its pressure upon the means of subsistence have at certain times increased the number of the poor relatively to the richer in such a way as to push many families downward. For the genealogist this means that a corresponding proportion of the pedigrees he has to trace will lead socially upward as he works backwards. At some such times, when the flood of population has risen too fast to escape through its normal outlets, it has broken out either in war or emigration or through social, political or technical revolution. The study of such phases ought to be among the meeting points of historians and genealogists. Mr. E. P. Thompson gives details of the thrusting down of whole trades from prosperity to poverty by the technological changes of the years round 1800. The weavers, who were aristocrats of labour in 1780, had for the most part been driven to the edge of starvation by 1830. No group among them suffered more rapid degradation than the woolcombers. The croppers were extinguished while the number of gig mills in Yorkshire grew, it is said, from 5 to 72 between 1806 and 1817. At the latter date out of 3,378 shearmen no fewer than 1,170 were out of work and 1,445 only partly employed.[2]

I couldn't help thinking to-day [says a character in one of Gissing's novels[3]] what a strange assembly there would be if all a man's relatives came to his funeral. Nearly all of us must have such lots of distant connections that we know nothing about. Now a man like Bolsover—an aristocrat, with fifty or more acknowledged relatives in good position—think how many more there must be in out-of-the-way places, poor and unknown. Aye, and some of them not so very distant kinsfolk either. Think of the hosts of illegitimate children, for instance—some who know who they are, and some who don't. . . . It's a theory of mine . . . that every one of us, however poor, has some wealthy

[1] *Huguenot Soc. Proc.* xxi, 1969, pp. 335–54, C. F. A. Marmoy, 'La Providence': The French Hospital during two and a half centuries', p. 348.

[2] *The Making of the English Working Class*, 1963, pp. 270–90, 550, quoting on the cropper E. Lipson, *The History of the Woollen and Worsted Industries*, 1921, p. 191.

[3] George Gissing, *The Town Traveller*, 2nd ed. 1898, pp. 47–48.

relative, if he could only be found. I mean a relative within reasonable limits, not a cousin fifty times removed. That's one of the charms of London to me. A little old man used to cobble my boots for me a few years ago in Ball's Pond Road. He had an idea that one of his brothers, who went out to New Zealand and was no more heard of, had made a great fortune; said he'd dreamt about it again and again, and couldn't get rid of the fancy. Well, now, the house in which he lived took fire, and the poor old chap was burnt in his bed, and so his name got into the newspapers. A day or two after I heard that his brother —the one he spoke of—had been living for some years scarcely a mile away, at Stoke Newington—a man rolling in money, a director of the British and Colonial Bank.

'Political theorists', wrote Richard Church, 'especially left-wing theorists, are apt to write of the great class-groups as though they are homogeneous; but in reality they are subject to a constant, osmotic infiltration, each into the other, under the leakage of chance, and the pressure of degeneration of individual character.' He recalled that about 1900 in the little Battersea side street of his lower middle class childhood, 'consisting of not more than fifty houses, each a family home, there were Irish, Scottish, Cockney, provincial stocks; some poor, rough and brutal, others comfortable, scrupulous in religion and social observance', one, at least, of gentle origin, though humble position, another humble but destined to fame. His own ancestry exemplified both social mingling and the re-emergence of buried talent.[1] Without venturing on any estimate I would suggest on the strength of my own limited experience that close relationships between people in widely different social classes are much commoner than is often thought.

A good example of a pattern which experience has taught me to regard as common occurs in the family of Jane Austen (d. 1819). The Austens were clothiers—Grey Coats of Kent[2]—in the sixteenth century, but before the end of the seventeenth they were living as gentlemen on their lands. John Austen (d. 1728) was sent to Cambridge and inherited his grandfather's estate, while his younger brothers were apprenticed in London to an attorney, a haberdasher, a surgeon and a stationer respectively.[3] The attorney, Francis Austen (d. 1791) of Sevenoaks, who 'set out in life with £800 & a bundle of pens . . . contrived to amass a very large fortune, living most hospitably, and yet buying up all the valuable land round the Town—marrying two

---

[1] Richard Church, *Over the Bridge*, 1955, pp. 13–14, 37–45.

[2] p. 165; *Pedigree of Austen of Horsmonden, &c.*, privately printed by Spottiswoode, Ballantyne & Co., 1940.

[3] *Austen Papers, 1704–1856*, ed. R. A. Austen-Leigh, 1942, p. 2.

wealthy wives & persuading the Godmother of his eldest son, Motley Austen, to leave her said Godson a small legacy of £100,000'.[1] He also helped to educate his orphan nephew George (d. 1805: son of William, the surgeon, by the daughter of a baronet, Sir George Hampson), who became a clergyman. A rich cousin, Thomas Knight (d. 1794) of Godmersham, Kent, and Chawton, Hampshire, presented him to the living of Steventon, Hampshire, and his uncle Francis bought for him that of Deane in the same county.

The Rev. George Austen (d. 1805) was the father of six sons and of two daughters, Cassandra and Jane, the novelist. Through their mother, Cassandra Leigh (d. 1827), daughter of a clergyman and niece of the Master of Balliol, they had aristocratic connections, for her grandmother was Mary Brydges, sister of the 1st Duke of Chandos, the builder of Canons. Mrs. Austen's first cousin James Leigh (d. 1774) renewed this connection by marrying the daughter of the 2nd Duke of Chandos and their grandson was created Lord Leigh of Stoneleigh in 1839.[2]

The descendants of Jane's brothers show an equal social range. James (1765–1819), the eldest, was a clergyman and his descendants are found in the Church, the academic world and the professions. His son James Edward Austen Leigh (d. 1874), vicar of Bray, was the author of the *Memoir of Jane Austen* (1871) while among *his* sons were Edward Compton Austen-Leigh (d. 1916) Lower Master of Eton and Augustus (d. 1905) Provost of King's College, Cambridge.

The second of Jane's brothers to leave issue was Edward (d. 1852), to whom his wealthy kinsman Thomas Knight left his Godmersham and Chawton estates. Edward took the name of Knight, and his descendants have moved among and intermarried with the peerage and landed gentry. His eldest daughter Fanny (d. 1882) married Sir Edward Knatchbull, 9th baronet, and their son Edward (d. 1893) was in 1880 created Baron Brabourne. His great-grandson the 7th Lord Brabourne married in 1946 Lady Patricia Mountbatten, a great-great-grand-daughter of Queen Victoria.

Jane's two youngest brothers, Sir Francis (d. 1865) and Charles Austen (d. 1852), were sailors and ended as admirals. The descendants of Sir Francis have remained in the professional classes and have included several naval officers. Charles (d. 1852) had a son Charles John (d. 1867), a commander in the Navy, who died early and must have left his family impoverished, for his son Charles John (d. 1896)

[1] Ibid., pp. 16–17.     [2] Ibid., p. 340.

was sent to Christ's Hospital and became a telegraphist, while of his three sons, one was apprenticed to a bricklayer but later drove a bread van, one became a grocer's assistant and the third a printer.[1]

Francis Kilvert noted in his diary on the 12th of October 1874,

> As I passed by Burton Hill at the entrance into Malmesbury I met a fine handsome old man with a white beard, a labouring man with a spade over his shoulder. He touched his hat and asked if I had preached at the Abbey yesterday ... I asked how the Vicar, Mr Pitt, was. 'Very ill,' he said, adding, 'His father and my father were brothers' children, but one family has gone up and the other down.' He and the Vicar had a common great-grandfather. I asked if the Vicar recognized him. 'No,' he said. He told me he had been footman at Cole Park, pointing to the tops of the elms in the rookery avenue, leading to the house.[2]

The coheirs of the barony of Dudley,[3] created in 1440 and in abeyance from 1757 to 1914, provide a well known earlier instance of the same kind. Frances Lea (d. 1800), sister of Lord Dudley and tenth in descent from King Henry VII,[4] married in 1740 Walter Woodcock, of Halesowen, Shropshire. To their descendants 'Dame Fortune' was, as Sir Bernard Burke puts it, 'most chary in the distribution of her favours'.[5] Of their grandchildren Joseph Smart (d. 1855) was a butcher at Halesowen; Pynson Wilmot (d. 1836) is said to have been a gamekeeper at West Stratton, Hampshire, while his daughter Jane (d. 1849) married Alexander Raitt (d. 1844), a baker of Islington; George Wilmot (d. 1846) was keeper of the toll gate at Cooper's Bank near Dudley; and Frances Hughes (d. 1851) married James Tolley, a tailor of Dudley. In subsequent generations some of the descendants, in England, India and Australia, seem to have restored their family fortunes.[6]

While this line was descending another line sprung from the 7th Lord Dudley (d. 1701) was at an equal pace climbing. Elizabeth Wrottesley (d. 1822), a third cousin of Walter Woodcock's children, married the 3rd Duke of Grafton (d. 1811), First Lord of the Treasury and great-great-grandson of Charles II.[7]

---

[1] From an unpublished work, 'Jane Austen's Kindred', by Joan Corder, 1953, in the possession of the College of Arms.

[2] *Kilvert's Diary*, vol. iii, Selections from the Diary of the Rev. Francis Kilvert, ed. William Plomer, 1940, p. 92.                                     [3] See Table I.

[4] The Marquis of Ruvigny and Raineval, *The Blood Royal of Britain*, 1903, p. 37.

[5] Sir Bernard Burke, *Vicissitudes of Families*, 1869, ii. 16.

[6] *In the House of Lords, Case on behalf of Ferdinando Dudley William Lea Smith senior coheir to the Barony of Dudley in the Peerage of England*, 1914, pp. 159, xxviii, 184–5; Burke, ibid.; Ruvigny, ibid.

[7] Ruvigny, op. cit., pp. 37, 42–43; *Complete Peerage*, v. 745.

The researches of Mr. G. D. Squibb and Mr. W. G. Davis have brought to light an equally striking instance of earlier date. The marriage which took place in 1574 between the uncle of a future King of England and the step aunt of a Salisbury innkeeper[1] was not an unequal one (though politically it angered Queen Elizabeth), but a reflection of Elizabethan social patterns and of Bess of Hardwick's successful ambition. Sir William Cavendish (d. 1557) was one of Thomas Cromwell's henchmen as a visitor of monasteries and otherwise and thereby got wealth and lands. By his first two marriages he had only daughters—among them Anne, who married Henry Bainton, a Wiltshire knight's fourth son, and had three sons, of whom Ferdinando, the youngest, was a Salisbury innkeeper.[2] One of this Ferdinando Bainton's daughters, Anne (1602–79), married Christopher Batt (d. 1661), a tanner, and sailed with him in 1636 to New England where they left descendants.[3]

In the meantime Sir William Cavendish had married as his third wife a lady already twice widowed, Elizabeth Hardwick (d. 1608) of Hardwick, Derbyshire, known as Bess of Hardwick, 'a person as well politick, as faire and beautiful'.[4] She bore him three sons and three daughters, whose aggrandisement she pursued with the utmost policy, determination and success. The eldest son left no legitimate issue, but the second in 1618 became Earl of Devonshire (of which his descendants are dukes), while the son of the third in 1665 became Duke of Newcastle. The eldest daughter's son was made Earl of Kingston upon Hull in 1628. The youngest daughter married the future Earl of Shrewsbury in 1568 on the same day that her mother (Bess of Hardwick) married, as her fourth husband, the then earl, his father. It was the second daughter Elizabeth (d. 1582) who in 1574 married Charles Stuart, Earl of Lennox (d. 1576), the brother of Darnley, brother in law of Mary Queen of Scots, uncle of James I of England (d. 1625), and father (by Elizabeth Cavendish) of the ill fated Arbella Stuart (d. 1615) —a princess too near the throne for her own good, yet first cousin of the half blood to a Salisbury innkeeper.

A still earlier close link between royalty and obscurity was forged by the marriage, about 1469, of William Paston to Anne Beaufort

---

[1] See Table II.

[2] *Wiltshire Visitation Pedigrees 1623*, ed. G. D. Squibb, Harleian Soc. cv–cvi, 1954, p. 8.

[3] Information from W. G. Davis; *New Eng. Hist. and Gen. Reg.* l–li: W. G. Davis, *The Ancestry of Abel Lunt*, Portland, Maine, 1963, pp. 183, 247.

[4] Dugdale, *Baronage*, ii. 420.

(daughter of Edmund Duke of Somerset, a grandson of John of Gaunt) whether or not he was, as is doubtfully alleged, the grandson of a husbandman and a bondwoman,[1] for in that year William's niece, Margery Paston, was so inconsiderate as to become engaged to marry Richard Calle, the family bailiff who had a chandler's shop as a side-line. He too, in his small way, was a rising man who had come to the Pastons recommended by the Duke of Norfolk. Margery's brother John, however, wrote that, even if his mother and elder brother should give consent to the marriage, Calle 'should never have my good will for to make my sister to sell candle and mustard in Framlingham'.[2] The marriage, however, took place and the Calle family in the next century were numbered among the gentry of Norfolk.[3]

The New England genealogist George Andrews Moriarty (1883–1968), who made a special study of the question, became convinced 'that the cadet lines of the knightly and gentle families, when they stayed at home, quickly became Franklins and Yeomen'.[4] He traced from an early fourteenth century cadet of the knightly family of Coggeshall of Coggeshall, Essex, the probable descent of the Coggeshalls of Halstead and Hundon, a family of 'small freehold and copy-hold tenants, a bit above the ordinary run of copyholders. They get a number of small plums, such as farming the demesne, running the mill and the office of Parker in the manorial parks.'[5]

He considered also that the Mohuns of Fleet in Dorset, gentlemen in the sixteenth century, whose first proved ancestor was Richard Moone, bailiff of Bridport 1535–7, were descended from Mones who were customary tenants (franklins, one a tanner) at Ottery St. Mary, Devon, in the fourteenth and fifteenth centuries, and that these in turn may have sprung from a thirteenth century cadet of the baronial Mohuns of Dunster, Somerset.[6] He also traced the probable descent from the knightly Puttenhams of Puttenham, Hertfordshire, of a cadet yeoman line branching off about 1380.[7]

---

[1] p. 363.

[2] p. 363 n. *infra*: *The Paston Letters*, ed. J. Gairdner, 1910, Introd. p. 76 and vol. ii, Letter 607 (1469).

[3] *Harl. Soc.*, vol. xxxii, pp. 62–63, Vis. Norfolk 1563.

[4] Letter to the author 10 May 1960.

[5] G. A. Moriarty, 'The Coggeshalls of Halstead and Hundon', *New England Hist. and Gen. Reg.*, vol. 99, 1945, pp. 315–22 and vol. 100, 1946, pp. 14–24.

[6] G. A. Moriarty, 'The Origin of the Mohuns of Fleet', ibid., vol. 103, 1949, pp. 21–24.

[7] G. A. Moriarty, 'The English Ancestry of John Putnam of Salem, Massachusetts', *American Genealogist*, vol. 15, pp. 8–15 and vol. 23, pp. 93–95, and A. Vere Woodman, 'The Origin of the Puttenhams', ibid., pp. 192–5.

The case of the Montagues of Northamptonshire was probably similar.[1]

Another New England genealogist, Mrs. Elizabeth (French) Bartlett, showed that by 1538, when the parish register of Chesham, Buckinghamshire, begins, the Weedons living in that parish were so many as to form a kind of clan. They include a gentleman, yeoman, husbandman, tilemaker, servant, glover, wheeler, tailor and others. James Weedon, of this family, baptized at Chesham in 1585, went to New England in 1638, settled at Newport and Portsmouth, Rhode Island, and left many descendants. Manorial records cited by Mr. A. Vere Woodman show a probable line of ancestry back to 1400 and Walter de Wedon appeared as a tenant at the Earl of Oxford's View of Frank Pledge in Chesham in 1330. A knightly family of Weedon held the manor of Weedon Hill in Chesham and Amersham from the twelfth century to about 1349 and it is suggested that the later Weedons were cadets of this line. One Almar, an Englishman, had been the knightly Weedons' predecessor in title, not only at Weedon, but at Amersham and Wingrave both in 1086 and before the Conquest. The fact that these fees were held of different lords before the Conquest makes it more than a possibility that the Weedons were sprung from Almar and so not Normans but Englishmen.[2]

The clan development exhibited by the Weedons in the sixteenth century was by no means unique. A similar case was that of the Giffards of Dry Drayton (p. 69). This pattern has long seemed to me to be much commoner in some parts of the country than others—for example in Lancashire and Cheshire. For the latter county this impression may find some confirmation in a topographical work of 1656. 'In no country of England', we are told, 'the gentlemen are more ancient and of longer continuance than in this country. . . . So you shall have in this country, six men of one surname (and peradventure of one house) whereof the first shall be called a Knight, the second an Esquire, the third a Gentleman, the fourth a Freeholder, the fifth a Yeoman, and the sixth a husbandman.' The writer reasonably links this phenomenon with the long continuance of families in one place, but seems also to think it a specially English phenomenon. 'For riches', he writes, 'maketh a gentleman throughout the realm, which

---

[1] p. 62 *supra*.

[2] Elizabeth (French) Bartlett, 'Weedon', *New Eng. Hist. & Gen. Reg.*, vol. 76, pp. 115–29, and A. Vere Woodman, 'The Wedons of Botley in Chesham, Co. Bucks.', ibid., vol. 108, pp. 46–53.

is contrary to the manner of some other countries beyond the seas.'[1] We must not, however, assume too readily that nothing similar occurred in lands where nobility was a legal status inherited by all the sons. It was not uncommon in France for impoverished minor noblemen to marry their daughters 'bourgeoisement' to save the payment of dowries.[2] Within England there were, as Professor Alan Everitt has emphasized, great local differences. The deeply rooted character of the gentry of Kent owes much, he believes, directly and indirectly to the custom of gavelkind and its consequence in the frequent setting up of younger sons with small estates of their own. Conversely he attributes the great setting up of new families and building of great houses in Elizabethan Northamptonshire to the opening given by the extensive sale there of Crown lands which had before been forest.[3]

Rapid movements up and down in the world and markedly unequal marriages have always been known, but family links between people in different classes are more often due to several small steps than to one big one.

A. L. Reade points out[4]

the climax of genealogical incongruity ... reached when we are able to see ... Samuel Johnson and Lord Chesterfield, who have always stood typically for the poor scholar and the aristocratic patron, sundered by an unbridgeable social gulf, as linked together by common connexion with the Crowleys, through the peer's brother, Sir William Stanhope, having married Mary Crowley and so become great-nephew by marriage to 'Parson' Ford, Johnson's first cousin.[5]

The link was Sir Ambrose Crowley (d. 1713), the Stourbridge ironmaster and Sheriff of London. His father was a Quaker and 'no gent nor any pretence to arms'.[6] His stepsister married the Rev. Cornelius Ford (d. 1748), a physician's son and nephew to Johnson's mother,[7] while the daughter of his son, Alderman John Crowley, married Sir William Stanhope.[8]

---

[1] *The County Palatine of Chester or the Vale Royal of England*, 1656 (Introduction by Daniel King, see *D.N.B.*), quoted by Peter Laslett, *The World We Have Lost*, 1965, p. 185.

[2] Information from M. Yves Chassin du Guerny of the Archives départementales du Gard, Nîmes.

[3] Alan Everitt, 'Social Mobility in Early Modern England', *Past and Present*, 1966, pp. 60–66.

[4] See Table III.　　　　　　　[5] A. L. Reade, *Johnson's Early Life*, 1946, pp. 157–8.

[6] *Le Neve's Pedigrees of the Knights*, Harleian Soc. viii, 1873, p. 495.

[7] A. L. Reade, *The Reades of Blackwood Hill*, 1906, pp. 159, 168–70 and ped. xxix.

[8] *Collins's Peerage of England*, ed. Brydges, 1812, iii. 426.

The division of an inheritance among many children or the failure of younger sons to keep afloat, when the eldest has the inheritance, are normal causes of a moderate social decline. The next generation or the next but one often moves up again, but if a small downward movement is repeated in three or four successive generations a family may wholly lose its ancestral standing. In other instances the process is gradual, long drawn out and hardly perceived.

In England and western Europe there have been two principal systems of inheritance, the partible and the impartible. The best known system of partible inheritance was the custom of Kent, called gavelkind, by which a man's property was either divided among his heirs or held by them in common, but similar customs existed in many Norfolk manors and some in Suffolk, Cambridgeshire, Lincolnshire, Leicestershire and Nottinghamshire. Partible inheritance was also the custom of Wales until Henry VIII abolished it in 1542. As the kindred multiplied the holdings tended to become too small to support their owners. In Wales this produced innumerable poor, proud gentlemen. In Kent as early as 1276 a charter of Edward I disgavelling lands there tells us that 'it often happens that lands and tenements which in certain hands, undivided, were accustomed decently to suffice for the subsistence of many men, to the great stay of the realm, afterwards are separated and divided into so many parts and parcels among coheirs, that to none of them does his part then suffice for his subsistence'.

Professor Homans correlates these two systems of inheritance with Frédéric Le Play's (d. 1882) classification of the types of European family organization into the two kinds which he calls stem or root families (*familles-souches*) and joint families.

According to the stem-family organization, a man's farm or his shop descended to one of his sons and one only; the other children had to leave the home if they wanted to found families of their own. According to the joint-family organization, a man's land descended to all his sons jointly. They and their descendants would hold and work the land in common, and dwell together in one great house or in a small cluster of adjoining houses. The Welch *trefs* were such groups, or the big farms of the sagas, or the family communes of Auvergne and the Nivernais. From time to time as the population of joint-families increased, they would be likely to split or bud and so found new families.[1]

In the stem-family, where one son inherited all his father's land, the

[1] George Caspar Homans, *English Villagers of the Thirteenth Century*, 1942, chaps. viii, ix, x, xv, p. 119; Pierre Guillaume Frédéric Le Play, *Les Ouvriers européens*, 1855.

other sons could either seek their fortunes elsewhere or could remain at home unmarried. This system

insured that in every generation of a family at least one man, his wife, and their children had a decent subsistence from every established holding of land. But it retarded any further increase of population which would press upon the means of subsistence: the sons who were not to inherit a holding had to get out or remain unmarried. It preserved a stable social order at home. . . . Le Play felt that families of this particular type, which he called stem- or root-families (*familles-souches*) because like the root of the vine they were continually sending forth new shoots, which were continually cut back—he felt that these families had been one of Europe's great sources of strength. Le Play observed that these families steadily provided, for colonization, for trade, for war, landless men with their fortunes to make.[1]

Expressing the same point in another way, Professor Homans puts it that where inheritance is partible the status system is more fluid, since, whether by sale or otherwise, families with many heirs must in time go down in the scale by contrast with the families with few heirs. Under impartible inheritance, on the other hand, social status goes with sharply differentiated sizes of land holding, which in general continue unaltered from generation to generation, because here sale means a fundamental breach in the system whereas under gavelkind it is something which has to come where families are large. From this he argues that 'the partible South-East is more vulnerable, the impartible open-field less vulnerable, to commercial influences, so long as the sale of land is easiest where it does least social damage'.[2]

Where impartible inheritance prevailed, as it did through most of England, the familiar and probably the most usual manorial custom was primogeniture, whereby the eldest son had the inheritance. But the custom of Borough English, or ultimogeniture, whereby the youngest son inherited, and a third custom, whereby the holder could choose his heir, were not uncommon. Under all these impartible systems if a man had daughters but no son it was usual for them to inherit as coheirs, dividing the land between them, in preference to their father's brothers or more remote heirs male. In some manors, however, the eldest daughter (under Borough English the youngest daughter) inherited.[3] Lands held by feudal tenures passed by primogeniture and failing sons to daughters rather than collateral heirs male

[1] Homans, *English Villagers* . . ., p. 215.
[2] G. C. Homans, 'The Rural Sociology of Medieval England', *Past and Present*, 4, 1953, pp. 32–43, at pp. 38–39.
[3] Homans, *English Villagers* . . ., pp. 123–32.

—usually to all the daughters as coheirs, but sometimes in early days to an eldest daughter and sometimes to a selected daughter.[1] In 1322 Sir Andrew de Harcla was created Earl of Carlisle in tail male, that is with remainder to the heirs male of his body only. This precedent was little followed till the 1380's, but Richard II then began to create both earldoms and baronies with this remainder and in the course of the next century it became normal.[2] The succession to most dignities thus came to be governed by a different rule from most succession to lands, with the consequence that on failure of direct heirs male lands might go to a daughter or daughters while the title went to a brother or cousin. Hence the relative poverty of such collateral heirs to peerages as the later Veres, Earls of Oxford (from 1625).

We have here touched but the fringe of a vast and obscure subject, profound in its implications—the influence of succession laws on history and social structure. The uncertainty of succession which resulted from the Irish application of the theory of partible inheritance to the law of kingship is notorious. The kingship itself was not divided but all the members of the royal kindred were given the best possible chance of succession. When a king died his successor was chosen from the *derbfine* or group of his kindred within a certain degree, some within the group having a priority to others. This prescription for disputed successions had the consequence that in the Cenél Eoghain dynasty between the years 879 and 1607 about 46 per cent of all the known males died violent deaths, about half of them at the hands of near kinsmen. Nor was the sheer bloodshed the worst consequence of this continuing strife, for a ruling class so involved in constant rivalry had no time to attend to government, so that stable administration could not develop in the several kingdoms, much less national unity.[3] Here is one major source at least of the distress of that most distressful country.

In France a comparable beginning had a very different end. 'The usage of the Franks', wrote Archbishop Fulk of Rheims in 893, 'was always on the death of their king to elect another within the royal house.'[4] But, though the royal blood was sacred, the aim was to choose

---

[1] Sir Frederick Pollock and Frederic William Maitland, *A History of English Law before the Time of Edward I*, 1895, i. 259; ii. 273; *Complete Peerage*, iv, app. H, pp. 653–4, 665–79.

[2] *Complete Peerage*, vii, apps. E and F.

[3] James Hogan, 'The Irish Law of Kingship', *Proc. Royal Irish Academy*, vol. 40. C. 3. 1932.

[4] Flodoard, *Historia Remensis Ecclesiae*, iv. 5, in *Mon. Germ. Hist.* SS. xiii, p. 563.

the most suitable of those possessing it. From this beginning, as one would expect, the balance between the hereditary and elective factors was settled by the accidents of genealogy and personality, and it was the fortune of the Capetian dynasty to produce between 987 and 1316 an unbroken father to son succession of heirs male. Hence perhaps that bias towards agnatic primogeniture, which events following 1316 confirmed as a rule (later called, unhistorically, the Salic Law), so strong that it outlasted a Hundred Years War based upon a counterclaim.[1]

In England the failure of the Conqueror's male heirs called for a system permitting inheritance of the crown in case of need by heirs female. Disputed claims then arose from further accidents of genealogy, but a system capable of survival was in time wrought out. In Germany, as Bloch points out, the Roman tradition of election, brought in by the claim to Empire, conflicted with the Germanic tradition of hereditary succession, which failures of heirs male in the imperial lines weakened further.[2]

But the effect of succession laws on history is, as we have seen, far from being confined to its dynastic and nobiliary aspects.[3] A cad is but a cadet or younger son, and in impartible systems from the top of society to as far down as there is anything to inherit the younger sons are the disinherited. Practical problems have produced these rules, the need for order and security and the Malthusian pressure of the population upon the means of subsistence. Where the problems have remained the same, the same solutions are still found.[4] The negative case proves the rule in eighteenth century Virginia where the free availability of fresh land for younger sons disturbed the polity by undermining primogeniture.[5]

Genealogical accident working upon the rule of succession has made some families and unmade others.

Marriage [says Dr. Hoskins, writing of Devonshire franklins and gentry since the thirteenth century] has been by far the most important single factor

---

[1] Marc Bloch, *Feudal Society*, 1961, pp. 383–8.          [2] Ibid., p. 389.

[3] Ibid., pp. 199–206, traces the development of feudal succession laws (on which see also pp. 100–1 *supra*) and refers, pp. 250–1, to the varieties of peasant succession. My understanding of these matters has been enlarged by an important unpublished thesis of 1958, which I have been permitted to read, in which Sir Iain Moncreiffe has explored the 'Origins and background of the law of succession to arms and dignities in Scotland'.

[4] Cf. W. M. Williams, *The Sociology of an English Village: Gosforth*, 1956, pp. 43–55.

[5] *Seventeenth-Century America. Essays in Colonial History*, ed. James Morton Smith, Univ. of N. Carolina, 1959; chap. v, Bernard Bailyn, 'Politics and Social Structure in Virginia', pp. 107–12.

in the successful accumulation of estates: more so even than the cloth trade, the tin trade, and the law, those other fertile sources of large fortunes in land in the Devonshire countryside, for marriage operated in every generation, century after century, whereas the other factors were intermittent in their working. It is true that the giving of a daughter in marriage took away land, just as a son brought it in. The estates of the landed families, large and small, therefore fluctuated in extent and whereabouts from generation to generation, according to the accidents of marriage. . . . A considerable proportion of the squires and gentry of Tudor and Stuart Devon descended from the small— almost peasant—freeholders of the thirteenth and fourteenth centuries. They represent the successful survivors, those who had accumulated around their own nuclear tenement the estates of other freeholders who had either failed to produce male heirs, or who had produced too many daughters for their economic health, or who had encountered misfortune in some other guise.[1]

The younger branches even of the greatest families had to make their own way like others. In the fifteenth century the Courtenays of Powderham (themselves cadets of the Earls of Devon)[2] had large families and so far as they could provided for their younger sons by marrying them to heiresses. Philip, second son of Sir Philip Courtenay (d. 1463) of Powderham, acquired by marriage the farm or barton of Molland, 'a wild and lonely place' on the southern edge of Exmoor. There his descendants lived till the male line expired in 1732. A younger branch of this line split off about 1500 but lived also in Molland, its heads describing themselves as gentlemen down to the first half of the seventeenth century. But their standing slowly declined, for Lewis Courtenay (d. 1749), the last of the line, called himself a yeoman. His sister and heir in 1705 married another yeoman, John Moggridge. Baring-Gould wrote in 1890 that 'when a few years ago, the late Earl of Devon visited Molland, he met a hale old yeoman there named Moggridge. He held out his hand to him; "Cousin," said he, "jump into the carriage with me, and let us have a drive together; we have not met for one hundred and eighty years".'[3]

Other branches of the Courtenays fell still further. A younger brother of the first Courtenay of Molland acquired by marriage Deviock in Cornwall and was ancestor of the Courtenays of Ethy in St. Winnow, St. Michael Penkivel and Lanivet in that country. His

[1] W. G. Hoskins and H. P. R. Finberg, *Devonshire Studies*, 1952, pp. 127–8.
[2] See pp. 41–3.
[3] J. L. Vivian, *The Visitations of the County of Devon*, 1895, pp. 251–2; Hoskins and Finberg, *Devonshire Studies*, pp. 346–7; S. Baring-Gould, *Old Country Life*, 1890, pp. 11–12.

nephew Edward Courtenay, another Powderham cadet, also acquired Cornish lands by marriage and was ancestor of the Landrake and St. Erme branches. More than one of these lines disappears from view in the seventeenth century.[1]

Now Dr. A. L. Rowse in his Cornish childhood in St. Austell had maternal cousins named Courtenay in the same working class station as himself. His father's cousin was

Annie Courtenay, whose husband lived all his life as a miner in South Africa. Then one of her daughters followed him, the other two married and went to America; her only boy followed in the bad years of unemployment after the War. She lived on there alone. . . . At last her children in America sent for her; she went out, and died shortly after. In its way an epitome of a Cornish family's history, very many of them. Not one is left in this country: all of them gone abroad, not to return, the home broken up. Their Courtenay name is interesting, too. There is no doubt that they would go back to the original stock of the Courtenays, Earls of Devon, who threw out several off-shoots in this part of the county, and in course of time had come down to the level of working people. The Courtenays knew in a vague way from whom they had descended, though it meant little to them. I remember my cousin and schoolmate, Sidney Courtenay, one day telling me at school that his ancestors had been Earls of Devon or some such thing. Neither he nor I knew, at the age of ten or eleven, that he was probably quite right.[2]

Dr. Rowse himself claims descent from Gregory Rowse who in 1602 held under the Courtenay Earls of Devon the largest property in the hamlet of Tregonissey in St. Austell. But by the nineteenth century this had dwindled to two or three fields owned by the tin-miner who was Dr. Rowse's grandfather.

What happened to the family to lose hold over the centuries? They belonged to the class of copyhold tenants squeezed out by time and the tightening up of the property system. They took to tin-mining, a harder and more speculative mode of living. Perhaps, after all, more remarkable than that they should have lost most of their holding in the course of three centuries is the tenacity with which they held on in the village at all.[3]

## 2. THREE EXAMPLES

The pedigrees of three successful shopkeeping families in the London area, the Bentalls of Kingston, the Catesbys of the Tottenham Court Road and the Fitches of Bishopsgate and St. Martin's Lane,

---

[1] J. L. Vivian, *The Visitations of the County of Cornwall*, 1887, pp. 113–16.
[2] A. L. Rowse, *A Cornish Childhood*, 1942, p. 23.　　　　[3] Ibid., pp. 26–27.

show patterns of social movement which I suspect are not uncommon though seldom so well worked out.

### (i) *Benthall or Bentall*

William Burnel, whose name suggests a Norman origin, witnessed a charter of a prior of Wenlock, Shropshire, between 1169 and 1176. Soon after this we find Burnels holding of the Corbets in Acton Burnell, Shropshire, some of whom can be linked into a pedigree, while others, though no doubt related, have not been. Among the latter is Edward I's great chancellor, Robert Burnel (d. 1292),[1] 'a self-made man who . . . built up a widespread complex of landed property by purchase, exchange, the conversion of loans, and other ways in the course of a prosperous career'.[2] Among his purchases was an estate in Benthall, Shropshire, which his nephew and heir Philip Burnell (d. 1294), ancestor of the Lords Burnell,[3] inherited. Philip, however, in circumstances which have not been explained, held this property from a certain John Burnell (dead in 1317) who had married the heiress of a family of Benthall who had previously held and taken their name from the place.[4] This John Burnell was presumably a cadet of the Acton Burnell family. His son Philip seems to have called himself de Benthall[5] and he and his son John de Benthall claimed the manor of Benthall in 1323–4.[6] At the time of the Heralds' Visitation of Shropshire in 1584 Laurence Benthall was of Benthall and recorded a pedigree carrying his ancestry back for ten generations.[7] The earlier generations are confused but the continuous descent of the manor in the male line from John Burnell seems probable—all the more so because the Visitation pedigree is unaware of the Burnell descent yet assigns to the Benthalls arms, Argent a lion rampant queue fourchée azure crowned gules, which differ only in one tincture and one detail from the coat of the Lords Burnell, Argent a lion rampant sable crowned and armed or, which was the subject of the first recorded plea of arms before the constable and marshal between Nicholas, Lord Burnell, and Robert, Lord Morley, during the siege of Calais in 1345–8.[8]

---

[1] R. W. Eyton, *Antiquities of Shropshire*, 1856, vi. 122–36.

[2] Powicke, *The Thirteenth Century*, p. 339.     [3] *Complete Peerage*, ii. 434.

[4] Eyton, op. cit. iii. 273–8.

[5] 'The Shropshire Lay Subsidy Roll of 1327', ed. Rev. W. G. D. Fletcher with notes by H. M. Auden, repr. from *Trans. Shropshire Arch. and Nat. Hist. Soc.* 1907, Munslow Hundred, pp. 118–19.

[6] Coll. Arm. Reg. Norfolk, xxxiv. 39.     [7] D. 10, fo. 41.

[8] Wagner, *Heralds and Heraldry in the Middle Ages*, pp. 21–22; G. D. Squibb, *The High Court of Chivalry*, 1959, p. 15.

Laurence Benthall (d. 1603) was succeeded by a brother, whose male line expired in 1720 when Benthall passed out of the family. From an uncle of Laurence, however, sprang an immense male progeny still extant. This uncle was John Benthall (d. *c.* 1590) who married the daughter of a clothier in Halstead, Essex, and settled there. At the Heralds' Visitation of Essex in 1664 his grandson was entered as a gentleman. But in this and the two following generations all the numerous Essex lines of Benthall (or Bentall as many now wrote it) seem to have abandoned the claim to gentility and called themselves yeoman, merchant, clothier, wine cooper, tanner and the like. In the second half of the eighteenth century one line moved to Devon and there prospering purchased estates and in 1843 resumed the old spelling of the name by royal licence. One of this branch in 1934 repurchased Benthall in Shropshire.

Meanwhile younger branches in Essex continued to multiply and perhaps for that reason to decline somewhat in status. In the middle of the nineteenth century the occupations of bearers of the name in the district, many of them proved members of the family, included those of draper, baker, farmer, factory overseer, silk weaver, miller and agricultural labourer. Anthony Bentall (d. 1894) of Maldon, Essex, was one of these, the third son of a farmer, son of another, son of a yeoman, fourth son of a clothier, whose father John Benthall (d. 1679) of Halstead was entered as gentleman at the 1664 Visitation and was great-grandson of John Benthall (d. *c.* 1590) who came from Shropshire.[1] This Anthony's son Frank Bentall (1843–1923) started in his father's shop in Maldon and in 1867 opened his own small draper's shop in Clarence Street, Kingston upon Thames, Surrey. This small shop, which before his death had become a larger one, was built up by his son Leonard Hugh Bentall (1875–1942) into the great general store, of which his younger son Mr. L. E. Rowan Bentall is now chairman and joint managing director.[2]

## (ii) *Catesby*

The proved pedigree of this family at present begins with William Catesby who acquired rights in the manor of Ladbroke, Warwickshire,

---

[1] Cf. the well documented pedigrees recorded in the College of Arms, Reg. Norfolk, xxxiv. 39 and xxxii. 169.

[2] H. H. Perkins, *The Rise of Bentalls, Over Eighty Years of Progress, 1867–1951*; Charles Herbert, *A Merchant Adventurer, Being the Biography of Leonard Hugh Bentall*, Kingston upon Thames, 1936.

in 1349 when landowners were hard hit by the Black Death. It seems possible that his wealth may have come to him from merchant ancestors in Coventry.[1] His son and grandson added to their possessions by marriage and purchase in Lapworth and Radbourn, Warwickshire, and Ashby St. Ledgers, Northamptonshire, and in the fifteenth century the Catesbys were prominent among the richer gentry of those counties.[2] William Catesby (d. 1485) of Ashby St. Ledgers has an evil repute in history as the chief minister of the much hated King Richard III and was beheaded by Henry VII.[3] He is the cat of the rhyme for which Colyngbourne its author is said to have been executed.

> The cat, the rat and Lovel our dog
> Rule all England under a hog.

Henry VII later restored his son George to the family estates and the line continued until Robert Catesby (d. 1605),[3] a disaffected recusant, took part in the Gunpowder Plot and lost his life and his inheritance.

Younger branches of the Ashby St. Ledgers family continued after this date at Bickenhall and Knowle, Warwickshire,[4] and at Woodford and Hinton, Northamptonshire,[5] but vanish in the course of the seventeenth century. So far as I have been able to trace all extant Catesbys descend from Sir John Catesby (d. 1486), Justice of the Common Pleas,[3] whose close concern with the affairs of the Catesbys of Ashby St. Ledgers suggests that he was near akin to them, though the exact relationship is not at present established. He acquired the manor of Whiston, Northamptonshire, which his descendants held till George Catesby sold it in 1656.[6] George's brother Thomas, who died in 1699, was described on his monument at Ecton, Northamptonshire, as the last heir male of the ancient family of the Catesby's.[7] This was a natural error, for the next branch, that of Hardmead, Buckinghamshire, had apparently expired when Thomas Catesby died in 1681,[8] while a branch living at Seaton, Rutland, descended from a younger son of the judge, had apparently ended before that.

---

[1] *Victoria County History, Warwickshire*, vi. 144.
[2] Ibid. v. 111; vi. 199; Dugdale, *Warwickshire*, 1730, p. 788; George Baker, *The History and Antiquities of the County of Northampton*, i, 1822–30, pp. 244–5.
[3] *D.N.B.*         [4] Visitation of Warwickshire, 1619, C. 7. 20.
[5] Visitation of Northants, 1564, H. 4, 23.
[6] *Victoria County History, Northamptonshire*, iv. 289.
[7] Harleian Soc. lxxxvii, *Visitation of Northants, 1681*, p. 44.
[8] Lipsombe, *Buckinghamshire*, iv. 181; *Stemmata Chicheleana*, No. 500.

So far as I have been able to ascertain all existing Catesbys descend from Mark Catesby (1601–77), the younger son of Kenelm Catesby (d. 1605) of Seaton, Rutland.[1] This Mark was apprenticed in 1618 to a London skinner, in 1627 was made free of the Skinners' Company, and in 1673 became its first Warden. John Catesby (d. 1703) his eldest son was in 1669 elected town clerk of Sudbury, Suffolk, and in 1676 was appointed Deputy Steward to the Earl of Suffolk. He acquired property both in Suffolk and Essex, settling in the latter county at Castle Hedingham. His fifth son Mark Catesby (d. 1749) is remembered for his 'Natural History of Carolina, Florida, and the Bahama Islands',[2] but it was the second son Jekyll Catesby of Castle Hedingham (d. 1717) who continued the line. His son, also Jekyll Catesby (d. 1786), was a haberdasher of the parish of St. Paul's, Covent Garden, Westminster. His son Jekyll Frederick Catesby (d. 1816) of St. Marylebone, Middlesex, was a haberdasher and japanner and his son Frederick (d. 1838) of High Street, Marylebone, and of the Edgware Road, a japanner and gilder. The trade of japanning or laquering, which was practised by three generations of Catesbys, had been given a new impulse by a patent granted in 1773.[3] Of Frederick Catesby's four sons, Edward (d. 1862) was a japanner and journeyman blindmaker, Frederick (d. 1870) a japanner, William (d. 1852) a japanner, painter and decorator, and Henry a barrack sergeant in the Indian Army.[4]

Edward's son Edward Catesby (d. 1903), one of a large and impoverished family, set up a small second hand furniture business in Clipstone Street in 1863. In 1876 he moved to Howland Street and as his business grew opened branches in the Tottenham Court Road and elsewhere. In 1885 he acquired the first of several houses which the business now occupies there. A greater expansion began in 1894 following his visit to the World's Fair at Chicago in 1893. '"Shopping by post" was what Mr. Catesby learned in Chicago, and to develop that system huge advertising was the first essential.' This was done on credit but with such success that by 1903 a staff of twenty had increased to 400.[5] Nine of the Catesby family have at different times been members of the firm, and the business, now carried on by Edward Catesby's grandsons, has not ceased to expand.

[1] The pedigree was recorded in 1954 in the College of Arms, Reg. Norfolk, xl. 88–90, after many years of difficult research.

[2] *D.N.B.*        [3] Information from Mr. P. L. Garrett, editor of *The Ironmonger*.

[4] He left descendants in India.

[5] Obituary Notice, *News of the World*, 26 April 1903. Information kindly given me by Mr. C. W. Catesby and Mr. T. W. Catesby.

## (iii) *Fitch*

The origin of the surname Fitch has not been definitely ascertained, but a very large proportion of all who bore it in early times are found in Suffolk and Essex, they may all have been one stock and Mr. Marc Fitch has suggested that the surname may derive from a place name, Fiche, in or near Cotton.[1] The first yet noted, however, is William Fich of Cotton, Suffolk, in an Assize Roll of 1240.[2] Down to the early fifteenth century the references so far noted are in records of lawsuits and taxation returns, and the bearers of the name appear to be yeomen, husbandmen or cotters. William Fiche paid subsidy at Cavendish, Suffolk, in 1327, but local continuity, though not yet a proved pedigree, begins with John Fych who paid the poll tax in Steeple Bumpstead, Essex—some 8 miles away—in 1381.

The first ancestor of a proved, connected line of descent was William Fiche of Wicken and Widdington, Essex, who occurs repeatedly as a litigant in De Banco Rolls between 1428 and his death in 1466. Thomas Fitch (d. 1514), this William's grandson, improved his standing by marrying about 1490 the heiress of a yeoman family of Algore of Brazenhead in Lindsell, Essex. He appears to have used arms based perhaps on those of his neighbours the Wentworths, who had acquired the manor of Lindsell and others near it by marriage in 1423. A shield of arms formerly on Thomas Fitch's brass in Lindsell church had vanished by 1699. His son William (d. 1578) bought former monastic lands and perhaps enriched himself by speculating in them. His descendants were entered by the heralds at their Visitations of 1614, 1634 and 1664 and three of them were knighted, Francis (d. 1608) in 1604, William (d. 1640) in 1608 and Barrow (d. 1672) in 1670. The fortunes of this line, reduced by the civil war, were re-established by the marriage of William Fitch (d. 1728) to the heiress of Danbury Place, Essex, a former property of the Mildmays, but the male line expired with the death in 1777 of Thomas Fytch whose brother William had been Governor of Bengal.

The descendants of the younger sons of Thomas Fitch (d. 1514) were somewhat less prosperous. By the early seventeenth century they had included apothecaries, clothiers and clothmakers, staplers and leathersellers, several clergymen and a naval surgeon. By 1700, however, all trace of them in Essex is lost. A branch settled in Warwickshire

---

[1] Cf. a charter reference, *c.* 1168, in *Sir Christopher Hatton's Book of Seals*, 1950, p. 239.　　　　[2] P.R.O. Suffolk Assize Rolls, J. I, 1, 818, m. 57d.

has been traced a little later, but the only lines traced to the present day spring from settlers in New England. Thomas Fitch (1612–1704) of Bocking left England for America in or before 1650 and became one of the founders of Norwalk, Connecticut. His brother James, a Puritan minister, was already there in 1638 and two other brothers settled there also. The American line is numerous and some of its members have been distinguished.[1] One of them, Samuel Fitch (d. 1784), Advocate General of Massachusetts, was a loyalist at the Revolution and returned to England. His only son William raised the 83rd Foot (now the Ulster Rifles) in Ireland and as its first colonel was killed in the Maroon war in Jamaica in 1795. The generations on this line were remarkably long, the Advocate General being only the grandson of the settler the Rev. James Fitch (d. 1702) who was born in 1662, while his last surviving daughter lived till 1851.

The second great branch of the family descends from Richard Fitch (d. 1494) of Steeple Bumpstead, Essex, where John Fych had paid the poll tax in 1381. His kinship to the Lindsell family was accepted by both lines and by the heralds in the seventeenth century, though the exact link has never been found. His descendants in time became far more numerous than those of the other line and it is probable that most bearers of the name in England today descend from him. Marriage with heiresses did little for his progeny, most of whom in the sixteenth and seventeenth centuries seem to have been either small freeholders or tenants of modest holdings. Many wrote themselves yeoman in their wills and until the days of the Industrial Revolution the land claimed almost all, though here and there a younger son entered the Church or became an attorney.

None of this branch was entered at the Heralds' Visitations and only two known lines attained eminence before 1800. Richard Fitch, yeoman (great-grandson of the first Richard), of Cootes in Steeple Bumpstead, married in 1553 and had three sons, of whom Richard (d. 1613) became a master of arts at Cambridge. This latter's grandson appears to have been the Colonel Thomas Fitch (d. *c.* 1675) who became a Member of Parliament and Lieutenant Governor of the Tower of London under the Commonwealth. John Fitch (d. 1631), the youngest brother of Richard of Cootes, moved to Barkway in Hertfordshire and two of his grandsons came to London and acquired wealth by their part in the rebuilding of London after the Great Fire of 1666, beginning

---

[1] Roscoe Conkling Fitch, *History of the Fitch Family A.D. 1400–1930*, 2 vols., Haverhill, Mass.

as carpenters and ending as prominent members of the rising class of building contractors.[1] Thomas (d. 1688), the elder, of Mount Maskell, Eltham, Kent, was knighted in 1679 and made a Baronet in 1688 but the baronetcy expired with his grandson in 1736.[2] His younger brother John (1642–1705) settled near Wimborne Minster, Dorset, where his descendants lived at High Hall till their extinction in 1833.

Other branches of this line seem to have grown poor by the subdivision of their patrimony as they multiplied. Younger sons either moved into the towns—chiefly London—or sank in their native parishes to the station of labourers. The agricultural depression after 1815 brought many who were farmers to ruin or near it. Sixth in descent from William Fitch (d. 1602) of Little Sampford, one of the brothers of Richard of Cootes, above mentioned and, of John, the ancestor of the baronets, was one Samuel Fitch (d. 1834) of Chigwell. In 1813 he is described as farmer, but in 1815 as labourer, while in 1851 his son and namesake was a coachman of Nottingham Place, Stepney.

Proved or probable members of this family at the time of the 1851 census include agricultural labourers, an annuitant, an artist, an auctioneer and land agent, a baker, a baker's journeyman, a beer-shopkeeper, a blacksmith, a brewer, a brewer's servant, a builder, a butcher, a butcher's journeyman, a boarding school mistress, a carman, a carpenter, a cheesemonger, a cigarmaker, a coachman, a coal merchant, a cordwainer, a curate, a master draper, a draper's assistant, an enameller, a farmer, a farming bailiff, a fireman on board a mail packet, a fishmonger, a foreman of gasworks, a foreman in the London docks, a fruit dealer, a gardener, a general practitioner, a greengrocer, a grocer, a groom, a horsebreaker, a horsekeeper, a hosier, a house proprietor, an innkeeper, a jeweller, a lady's school proprietress, a landed proprietor, a licensed victualler, a lodging house keeper, a maltster, a mariner, a master painter and glazier, a messenger, a miller, a milliner, a mortgager, a musician, an officer in a county gaol, a patent salt manufacturer, a pork butcher, a porter, a postmaster, a publican, a servant, an East India Merchant Service man, a sextoness, a shoemaker, a solicitor, a solicitor's articled clerk, a wholesale stationer, a stone sawer, a strawplaiter, a tinplate worker, a victualler, a watchmaker and a whipmaker.

Among those who sought their fortunes in London were James Fitch (d. 1818), the younger son of a small farmer of Great Dunmow,

[1] T. F. Reddaway, *The Rebuilding of London after the Great Fire*, 1940, pp. 210–18.
[2] G. E. C., *Complete Baronetage*, iv, 1904, p. 152.

Essex, first cousin of the unfortunate Samuel (d. 1834) of Chigwell and like him sixth in descent from William Fitch (d. 1602) of Little Sampford. This James in 1784 opened a cheesemonger's shop at 83, Leadenhall Street, next door but one to St. Catherine Creechurch. His nephew George Fitch (d. 1842) succeeded to this grocery business but had to struggle with the difficulties which followed the Napoleonic Wars, so that partners came and went—first a brother, then a cousin—and in 1827–8 the business almost succumbed.

A dissolution of partnership, however, and removal to 66, Bishopsgate Within (where the head office remained for 101 years) were followed by improvement. In 1831 George's son Frederick (1814–1909) entered the firm, to which his entry into partnership with his father gave the name of Fitch and Son. By the late 1840's he was prosperous enough to remove his family from the City to a house in the semi-rural surroundings of the newly developed Highbury New Park. In 1863 the firm obtained its first royal warrant as purveyor of bacon to H.R.H. the Prince of Wales and since that time royal warrants have been held ininterruptedly. Under Frederick's son Edwin (d. 1916) the name of the firm became known in the export trade from Cape Town to Hong Kong. In 1920 a public company was formed with Edwin's son Mr. Hugh Fitch (1873–1962) as chairman. In the years between the wars and since its activities have expanded in many directions, notably in the wholesale provision trade and the bakery trade. In 1959, following mergers, the company became Fitch Lovell Ltd. and the group assets now exceed twenty million pounds.

My friend Mr. Marc Fitch (b. 1908, son of Hugh) has for many years combined with his ancestral trade an ardent attachment to genealogy. His researches have been remarkably extensive, covering all traceable families of his name. On them what has here been written of this family is founded and they make it possible to envisage the social wanderings of a whole agnatic kindred in a way possible for few if any other English families.

Though much too little work has been done to afford a safe basis for generalization, it is my belief that such social patterns as we have seen in the pedigrees of these three families would prove to be not at all uncommon. Their least usual feature is probably the final upward turn of fortune which, combined with an historical sense in present or recent members of the families, has made possible the extensive research which has brought the facts to light.

### 3. FEMALE DESCENTS

The families hitherto considered have almost all been male line families. Since our ancestors through females are no less our ancestors than are our male line ancestors, this may seem capricious. In truth it is but a simple reflection of the fact that our society has historically entrusted the continuity of name and inheritance mainly, though not exclusively, to the male line. It has been suggested that the male line may also have a special significance genetically[1] but whether or no it is not to this but to legal and social factors that the English genealogical emphasis upon it is due.

In continental countries where nobility had the legal significance mentioned earlier[2] *seize-quartiers* and *trente-deux quartiers* were traced to show that all the sixteen great-great-grandparents or thirty two great-great-great-grandparents were noble, and the noble blood thus uncontaminated. Such proofs were a necessary qualification for admission to certain orders. The tracing of ancestry on all lines was also popular in Wales in the seventeenth and eighteenth centuries.[3] In modern times certain continental genealogists, for the most part Swiss and German, have worked out a number of such ancestries, some very extensive.[4] In England such attempts to trace the whole ancestry have been relatively rare—the mere whim of genealogists—though from the sixteenth century onwards they are occasionally found. A notable recent attempt to trace all the ancestors of a living individual for ten generations back was that of B. G. Bouwens.[5]

Though in England such attempts are exceptional, in America they are normal and it is interesting to consider why. The study of pedigrees in England was in origin closely linked with proof of succession to titles, arms and property, but the interest which developed in nineteenth century America was more a matter of family interest and pride. Proof of descent from the early settlers was and is a great object and not only can this be traced as well through female as male lines, but the greater the number of such lines proved the better. Americans of old New England stock can, I think, more frequently than Englishmen show a complete or nearly complete record of ancestry on all lines

---

[1] C. H. Ridge, 'Scientific Genealogy', *The Genealogists' Magazine*, xi, 1951, p. 139, quoting Robert Weill, *Ancêtres Réels, Ancêtres Fictifs*.                    [2] p. 46.

[3] Francis Jones, 'An Approach to Welsh Genealogy', *Cymmrodorion Soc. Trans.*, 1948, pp. 311, 381, 409.

[4] O. Forst de Battaglia, *Traité de généalogie*, Lausanne, 1949, pp. 49–50, 115–16.

[5] B. G. Bouwens, *A Thousand Ancestors*, 1934.

back to the generation of settlement in the seventeenth century. This is because the New England communities were in early days isolated and largely self contained and intermarried and moreover kept their records well.

If attempts to trace complete ancestries are looked on by many English genealogists as whimsical, they may well regard the tracing of pure female lines—through the mother's mother all the way—as freakish. Yet the results can be interesting. That enterprising genealogist W. T. J. Gun (d. 1946) showed that Charles II, James II, William III and Queen Victoria of England, Louis XIII, Louis XIV and Louis XV of France, Queen Christina of Sweden, the Empress Catherine II of Russia and Prince Charles Edward, the Young Pretender, were all descended in the pure female line from the Empress Anne of Hungary (d. 1547), wife of the Hapsburg Emperor Ferdinand I (d. 1564).[1] Professor Forst de Battaglia carried this matrilineal line back to a princess of Turki blood, Elizabeth (d. 1290), the wife of Stephen V, King of Hungary, and daughter of Kuthen, Khan of the Kumans.[2] However, Mr. Anthony J. Camp has pointed out (and Professor Forst de Battaglia has agreed) that this derivation rests on the wrong assumption that the mother of Joanna, Countess of Penafiel, wife of Henry II of Castile, was Constance of Arragon, whereas she was in fact Blanche de la Cerda.[3] The Kuman princess, therefore, though an ancestress, was not a matrilineal ancestress of Queen Victoria. She was, however, a matrilineal ancestress of Philippa of Hainault (d. 1369), Queen of Edward III.

The international character of royal genealogies takes them as such beyond the scope of this book, though the special work done on them affords good examples of general principles. But the ancestry of Queen Elizabeth the Queen Mother, unlike that of most of our sovereigns and their consorts,[4] is non-royal and mainly English[5] and the social range it exhibits is therefore relevant. Among Her Majesty's sixty four great-

[1] W. T. J. Gun, 'Direct Female Lines in History', *The Genealogists' Magazine*, iii, 1927, pp. 6–9.

[2] Wilhelm Karl Prinz von Isenburg, *Stammtafeln zur Geschichte der europäischen Staaten*, 1936, Band II, Taf. 105; O. Forst de Battaglia, *Traité de généalogie*, Lausanne, 1949, table vi.

[3] A. J. Camp, 'The Matrilineal Descent of Queen Victoria', *Genealogists' Magazine*, xiii, 1960, pp. 241–4.

[4] See the series of Seize-Quartiers of the Kings and Queens of England by G. W. Watson in *The Genealogist*, N.S. vi–xii.

[5] A. R. Wagner, 'Some of the Sixty-four Ancestors of Her Majesty the Queen', *The Genealogists' Magazine*, ix, 1940, pp. 7–13.

great-great-great-grandparents were two dukes and the daughter of
a duke, the daughter of a marquess, three earls and the daughter of an
earl, one viscount, one baron, some half dozen country gentlemen,
a director of the East India Company, a provincial banker, two
daughters of bishops, three clergymen (one of them born in Virginia
and related to George Washington[1]), a Huguenot refugee's daughter,[2]
an Irish officer of Jacobite descent in the French Service and his French
mistress,[3] the landlord of the George Inn at Stamford,[4] a London
toyman and a London plumber.

The story of this last is curious. According to Cussans, the county
historian, George Carpenter (1713–82) of Redbourn, Hertfordshire,
had the plumber in question down from London to repair the roof of
his house. With the plumber came his daughter and both remained at
Redbourn some time. Mary Elizabeth Walsh, the daughter, 'was then
eighteen years of age, and Mr. Carpenter upwards of sixty, yet notwithstanding the disparity of their ages and positions he married
her'.[5] Their daughter married the 11th Earl of Strathmore and Her
Majesty the Queen Mother is fifth in descent from the plumber's
daughter.[6] Another interesting example of outbreeding in our Royal
Family, such as Professor C. D. Darlington would, one feels, approve,[7]
was the marriage of the Duke of Kent in 1961 to Miss Katherine
Worsley, who is tenth in descent from Oliver Cromwell.[8]

## 4. THE BLOOD ROYAL

Just as a genealogy which traces a single person's ancestry on all lines
illustrates the texture of society, so does a pedigree which traces
downward all lines of the progeny of a single couple. This, like the other,
is seldom attempted on a large scale yet notable examples exist. The

---

[1] A. R. Wagner, 'Queen Elizabeth's American Ancestry and Cousinship to George
Washington and Robert E. Lee', ibid. viii. 368–75.

[2] A. R. Wagner, 'The Huguenot Ancestors of Her Majesty the Queen', *Proc. Huguenot
Soc. of London*, xvi. 244–7.

[3] H. W. Farmar, *A Regency Elopement*, 1969, pp. 169–71.

[4] Bryan Hodgson (d. 1785), cf. *Notes & Queries*, 7th ser. v. 330, and Hunter, *Familiae
Minorum Gentium*, p. 1024.

[5] Cussans, *History of Hertfordshire*, Cashio Hundred, p. 235.

[6] For comparable strains in continental royal families see O. Forst de Battaglia, op. cit.,
pp. 56–57.

[7] pp. 244–5 *infra*.

[8] James Waylen, *The House of Cromwell*, 1891, pp. 155–6.

seventeenth century Welsh and Irish genealogists made this attempt. Among other early examples are certain pedigrees of founders' kin. Archbishop Chichele (d. 1443) provided that in elections to fellowships at his foundation of All Souls College, Oxford, regard should be first had to his own kindred. John Anstis (d. 1744), Garter King of Arms, who was himself of this kindred, drew up extensive tables to show all the lines which he could trace and these remain in the possession of All Souls College. In 1765 the Rev. Benjamin Buckler printed a larger series of similar tables under the title *Stemmata Chicheleana* and in 1775 he printed a supplement based on the work of Anstis.

Similar manuscript genealogies of the whole traceable kindred of William of Wykeham (d. 1404), founder of Winchester College and New College, Oxford, and of Sir Thomas White (d. 1567), founder of St. John's College, Oxford, are in the possession of the College of Arms. In 1857, however, new statutes issued by the Oxford University Commission abolished most of the benefits provided by pious founders for the support of their own kin.

Attempts by modern genealogists to trace complete progenies have been commoner on the Continent than in England or America.[1] An interesting example is that of the descendants of Ulrich Zwingli (d. 1531), the Swiss religious reformer, who include Swiss, Germans (among them Rudolf Hess), French, Italians, Russians, Poles, Americans and Jews.[2] By far the greatest efforts to trace complete progenies have, however, been inspired by the magic of royalty and royal descent. On the descendants of the English kings the most extensive work yet done is that of Melville Henry de Massue (d. 1921) who was styled Marquis of Ruvigny and Raineval.[3] In 1903 he published *The Blood Royal of Britain being a roll of the living descendants of Edward IV and Henry VII, Kings of England, and James III, King of Scotland* and between 1905 and 1911 followed this with four more volumes of *The Plantagenet Roll of the Blood Royal being a complete table of all the descendants now living of Edward III, King of England.*

---

[1] O. Forst de Battaglia, op. cit., pp. 111–12.

[2] Ibid., p. 51, citing W. H. Ruof, *Nachfahren Ulrich Zwinglis*, 1937.

[3] According to his own account in *The Titled Nobility of Europe*, 1914, p. 1260, his paternal descent was from a Swiss family of de Ruvynes, but his assertion that a de Ruvynes married a sister of Henri de Massue, Marquis de Ruvigny and Earl of Galway (d. 1720), has not been supported by published evidence and did not commend itself to Oswald Barron. Indeed its incorrectness seems to be demonstrated by C. E. Lart, *Huguenot Pedigrees*, i, 1924, pp. 79–83.

He had by this time enumerated most of the descendants of Lionel, Duke of Clarence (d. 1368), the eldest of Edward III's sons, whose issue survives to the number of some 50,000 persons, many of them owing to intermarriages descending from him on more than one line. It remained to deal with the residue of Lionel's progeny, and with the descendants of John of Gaunt (d. 1399), Edmund of Langley (d. 1402), Thomas of Woodstock (d. 1397) and Isabel, Countess of Bedford (d. 1397).

Ruvigny guessed in 1911 that the number of Edward III's descendants then living might total some 80,000 or 100,000 persons. He pointed out that there were many lines which he had been unable to trace and that the very magnitude of the task made all the conclusions arrived at of a more or less tentative nature. He gives authorities for his statements only in a few exceptional cases and in the nature of things he can seldom have referred to the original evidence. But though errors and omissions may therefore well be numerous, the standard of accuracy considering the scope of the work seems on the whole to be high.

Apart from Ruvigny's I have seen only one large scale attempt to trace all the lines of descent of any portion of the English royal progeny.[1] The work was done a hundred years before Ruvigny's day by Francis Townsend (d. 1819), Windsor Herald, one of the most active and careful genealogists of his day, and is embodied in one of the volumes of his manuscript collections in the College of Arms.[2] Townsend set out to trace down to the seventeenth century (as far, that is, as the Heralds' Visitations would take him) the whole progeny of the two daughters of King Edward I (d. 1307) who married Englishmen, Joan of Acre (d. 1307), Countess of Gloucester, and Elizabeth (d. 1316), Countess of Hereford and Essex. Townsend's work is mainly founded on the Visitations and other material in the College of Arms, to which he gives references. He was a professional genealogist of great experience and his general standard of accuracy is high. I have, however, found occasional errors in his work and there are a good many lines which he failed to trace.

Between Ruvigny's work and Townsend's a larger proportion than might be thought of the whole English progeny of William the Conqueror has been traced down to the seventeenth century. This is

---

[1] In 1969, however, appeared *The Royal House of Stuart. The Descendants of King James VI of Scotland James I of England*, by A. C. Addington, vol I.

[2] F. T. Royal Descents.

because apart from the descendants of Edward III and the two daughters of Edward I there are only three sons and one daughter of our kings[1] from whom descents are traceable in England,[2] while owing to inter-marriages the work done covers an appreciable number of the descendants both of these and of the descendants of the children of Edward III with whom Ruvigny did not deal. I have myself indexed Townsend's work and have made some attempt to fill the gap left by his work and Ruvigny's. The Rev. W. G. D. Fletcher[3] refers to two manuscript volumes in his own possession in which Joseph Foster (d. 1905) set out to cover the same ground as Townsend, but to a later date. I have not seen these and do not know where they now are. The following slight observations rest therefore on Ruvigny's and Townsend's work and my own attempts to supplement it.

As one would expect, the progenies of the more recent kings contain a higher proportion of royal and noble persons than those of earlier kings, for the descendants of the latter have had more time to sink in the world. The existing progeny of Henry VII (d. 1509) derives from his two daughters Margaret, Queen of Scots (d. 1541), and Mary, Queen of France and Duchess of Suffolk (d. 1533). The whole existing progeny of the Queen of Scots springs from her great-grandson James I of England (d. 1625) and is predominantly royal and therefore foreign. In 1903 it numbered 1440 living persons. The progeny of the Duchess of Suffolk on the other hand is predominantly English and non-royal, but confined to the higher classes of society; 10,283 living descendants were traceable in 1903. The great disparity in number between the descendants of the two sisters is largely explained by the frequent intermarriages of the royal families. In 1903 only three marriages had taken place between descendants of the two sisters and only one of these marriages had been fertile.[4] The next royal descents after those from Henry VII derive from George, Duke of Clarence (d. 1478), brother of King Edward IV. The enmity of the first two Tudors reduced this line but did not exterminate it and Margaret, Countess of Salisbury (d. 1541), the daughter of the Duke of Clarence left a numerous progeny by her marriage to Sir Richard Pole (d. 1505). Ruvigny counted well over 17,000 living descendants in 1905, but a

---

[1] Edmund Crouchback, Earl of Lancaster (d. 1296), Thomas of Brotherton, Earl of Norfolk (d. 1338), Edmund of Woodstock, Earl of Kent (d. 1330) and Eleanor, Countess of Leicester (d. 1275). I refer here only to legitimate descents.

[2] Save by modern reimportation from abroad.     [3] *Royal Descents*, 1908, p. 23.

[4] Ruvigny, *The Blood Royal of Britain*, pp. vi–vii. Since 1903 there have been a few more such marriages, e.g. those of the Duke of Gloucester and Princess Mary.

substantial overlap with the progeny of Henry VII must be deducted from the total. The same applies to the 25,000 odd descendants of Anne, Duchess of Exeter (d. 1476), the sister of Edward IV and the Duke of Clarence, so that according to Ruvigny's rough estimate his gross total of over 54,000 descendants of these three children of Richard, Duke of York (d. 1460), should be reduced to a net total of some 30,000 to 35,000. The next branch, that of Richard's sister Isabel, Countess of Essex (d. 1484) appears to be notably less prolific, making a gross addition of only some 18,000 and a net addition of only some 9,000.[1]

It appears, however, that as Ruvigny proceeds the number of lines which he cannot trace increases. This is in no way surprising for as the distance from the main royal stem grows so the proportion of obscure families may be expected to increase. It does, however, mean that a much larger allowance than before has now probably to be made for untraced descendants.

Ruvigny in his last volume[2] remarks that of the royal progeny he has set out 'with some few exceptions, none have descended to or are at least traceable among the trading or labouring classes'. I suspect that an important part of the truth resides in the qualification 'traceable', and that among the lines which Ruvigny failed to trace are just those in which the downward descent in question has taken place.

When we pass beyond Ruvigny's ken to the immense progenies of John of Gaunt and of Edward I's daughters we are in an altogether wider world. The Courtenays of Molland, Deviock and Landrake,[3] for example, all had descents from Edward I's daughter Elizabeth. Nineteen settlers who were in New England before 1650 seem to have well established descents from Edward I. Doubtless there were others who had such descents and some of these will probably in time be proved. But though this random sample is small, it may be large enough for its analysis to have some meaning. It is interesting therefore that none of the nineteen has a descent near enough to the main stem to bring it within the scope of Ruvigny's five volumes. Three would have come into his sixth volume (*Mortimer-Percy, Part II*).[4] Two descend from

---

[1] *The Plantagenet Roll, Essex Volume*, p. x.
[2] *The Plantagenet Roll, Mortimer-Percy Volume, Pt. I*, 1911, p. ix.
[3] See pp. 221–2.
[4] Pardon Tillinghast, Richard Saltonstall and William Torrey; cf. F. L. Weis, *Ancestral Roots of Sixty Colonists Who Came to New England between 1623 and 1650*, Lancaster, Massachusetts, 1950, pp. 25, 23, 39; *Supplement*, Dublin, New Hampshire, 1952, p. 8; *New England Hist. and Gen. Reg.* cviii, 1954, pp. 177–8.

John of Gaunt, one through his son John Beaufort,[1] two through his daughter Joan Beaufort.[2] One descends from Thomas of Woodstock.[3] Nine descend from Edward I's elder daughter Joan of Acre,[4] and four from his younger daughter Elizabeth, Countess of Hereford.[5] As one would expect, several of those with descents from senior lines have descents from junior lines as well, but these I have not counted in.

A study of royal descents brings out forcibly the importance of what Major Francis Jones has conveniently named the 'gateway ancestor'. The marriage of Henry Percy, called Hotspur, to Elizabeth Mortimer, Edward III's great-granddaughter, in 1379, spread the royal blood largely through the gentry of north eastern England. Two marriages did the same for the gentry of Shropshire and the northern Welsh marches. The first was that of Sir Roger Kynaston in the middle of the fifteenth century to Elizabeth Grey, who was seventh in descent from Edward I through Edmund of Woodstock and eighth through Joan of Acre, while her mother was Antigone, natural daughter of Humphrey, Duke of Gloucester (d. 1447), son of Henry IV.[6] The second was that of Sir Walter Devereux to Anne Ferrers of Chartley about 1446.[7] The fertility of the descendants of these two matches strikes one as unusually high, and this would tend to a wider social distribution of the progeny since the larger the families the less could be done for the younger children.

The marriage of Sir Hugh Courtenay to Margaret de Bohun, Edward I's granddaughter, in 1325, spread the royal blood through the West Country. In the same way the marriage of Joan Beaufort

---

[1] Herbert Pelham; cf. Weis, op. cit., p. 21.

[2] Edward Carleton, ibid., p. 22, and Mary, daughter of John Launce and wife of John Sherman, ibid., pp. 75, 33.

[3] Muriel, daughter of Brampton Gurdon and wife of Richard Saltonstall, ibid., pp. 23–24.

[4] Catherine, daughter of Francis Marbury and wife of Richard Scott and her sister Anne, wife of William Hutchinson, ibid., pp. 81, 80, 61, 34; Grace, daughter of Sir Richard Chetwode and wife of Peter Bulkeley, ibid., pp. 81, 80, 61, 34, 122–3, 27; three daughters of John Deighton, Katherine, wife of Governor Thomas Dudley, Frances, wife of Richard Williams and Jane, wife of John Lugg, ibid., pp. 28, 71, 86–87; Olive, daughter of Richard Welby and wife of Henry Farwell, ibid., pp. 28, 30, and suppl. pp. 24–25; Jeremy Clarke, ibid., pp. 30–31; and Anne, daughter of Ferdinando Bainton and wife of Christopher Batt (p. 213 *supra*); cf. W. G. Davis, *The Ancestry of Abel Lunt*, Portland, Maine, 1963, p. 241.'

[5] Richard Palgrave, Weis, op. cit., p. 35; Elizabeth, daughter of Rowland Coytmore and wife of William Tyng, ibid., p. 39 and supp. pp. 8–9; John Drake, ibid., p. 25 and suppl. pp. 33–34; and Roger Ludlow, ibid., p. 32.

[6] *Complete Peerage*, vi. 699.                    [7] Ibid. v. 322.

(d. 1445), the granddaughter of John of Gaunt, first in 1424 to King James I of Scotland (d. 1438) and secondly in 1439 to Sir James Stewart, the Black Knight of Lorn, carried the English royal blood into many Scottish families. Fletcher Christian, the leader of the nine mutineers from the ship *Bounty*, who in 1790 sought refuge from the penalties of the law on remote Pitcairn Island in the south eastern Pacific, belonged to a well known Manx and Cumbrian family and was descended from Edward I through Joan of Acre.[1] The settlers of Pitcairn brought with them eleven Tahitian women and six Tahitian men. The Tahitian men left no children and the later inhabitants of Pitcairn sprang from the English sailors and their Tahitian wives. Through intermarriage a large proportion of the whole Pitcairn population and of the descendants on Norfolk Island of those who went there from Pitcairn in 1856 are now descendants of Fletcher Christian, so that it is doubtful whether any British community contains so large a proportion of descendants of our early kings.[2]

Other instances could be given which exemplify the same pattern. Ruling families intermarry and their marriages are therefore international. Their daughters from time to time marry great noblemen of their own countries. The great noble families meet at court and in Parliament and their intermarriages cover the whole country. Their daughters from time to time marry into the greater gentry. Intermarriages within the gentry are in general (though, of course, by no means always) local—within the county or district. Daughters of the greater gentry often marry lesser gentry or merchants, daughters of the lesser gentry not seldom marry yeomen or tradesmen in their immediate neighbourhood. High fertility will often cause impoverishment and speed the pace of social descent.

All this omits the bastards, who spread the royal and noble blood still further. Many, doubtless, have remained unknown, but many more have been acknowledged and provided for. A recent count of bastards of Kings of England, from Henry I onwards, known to have living descendants, totalled about forty. The descendants of some of these are very numerous and if illegitimate lines issuing lower down their pedigrees from the royal blood could be counted they would doubtless much increase the total of the royal progeny. Here again an

[1] *Burke's Landed Gentry*, 1952, p. 439; Joseph Foster, *The Royal Lineage of Our Noble and Gentle Families*, 1885, p. 226 (requiring correction in detail).

[2] Sir Charles Lucas, *The Pitcairn Island Register Book*, 1929; H. L. Shapiro, *The Heritage of the Bounty*, 1936.

accident of locality may be powerful. Henry VII's bastard Sir Roland Velville or Vielleville (d. 1553) was the grandfather of Catherine of Berain (d. 1591), whose progeny in North Wales by three of her four husbands was so great that she was known as Mam Cymru, the mother of Wales.[1] Perhaps the greatest of all infusions of the royal blood into the English people came through Robert, Earl of Gloucester (d. 1147), one of the many bastards of King Henry I.

### 5. UNDERLYING PATTERNS

In this as in other fields of history the search for patterns and explanations has to be pursued constantly but sceptically. We are sure that there must be such patterns, but hints and fragments of them are the best we can hope to see. The more complete the explanation we think we have found, the more sceptical we ought usually to be. It is, however, difficult to dissent from Professor Sorokin's general analysis of the factors making for what he calls 'vertical circulation'—the social rise and fall of individuals. The most fundamental of these factors are, he says, three in number, '(*a*) the demographic factor; (*b*) the dissimilarity of parents and children; (*c*) a permanent change of environment, especially of the anthropo-social environment'[2].

The demographic factor covers differences in birth and death rates between social classes. Where upper classes are less fertile than lower classes, members of the latter, it is said, must in the nature of things rise to fill the gaps in the former. This sounds reasonable, but I suspect that here, as all too often, the certainty or at least the significance of the conclusion varies inversely with the precision of the definition of the terms. If, for instance, we regard peers as a social class distinct from their relations, it is easy to reckon the rate at which this class fails and is replaced by new blood. We have, however, seen that whether we regard it socially, economically or genealogically, the mere class of peers—regardless of wealth, origins, rules of succession and family connections—has little meaning. The classes which really mean something are wider, looser and less easily defined. Indeed different criteria lead to different, overlapping classifications. Differential fertility be-

[1] *Archaeologia Cambrensis*, 3rd ser. xv, 1869, p. 402; .N.S ix, 1878, pp. 149–50; J. E. Griffith, *Pedigrees of Anglesey and Carnarvonshire Families*, 1914, pp. 26, 222–3, 270; J. Ballinger, 'Katherine of Berain', *Y Cymmrodor*, xl, 1929, pp. 1–42; A. L. Rowse, *The Expansion of Elizabethan England*, 1955, pp. 68–70.

[2] *Social Mobility*, 1927, p. 373.

tween economic and occupational groups in certain countries during the last century is established by precise definitions and full statistics. But the material for making comparable deductions in regard to earlier ages is defective in the extreme, and the want of comparative material makes it hard to assess the meaning of the facts we have.

We know, for example, that out of 1,226 baronetcies of England and Great Britain, created between 1611 and 1800 with the normal remainder to the heirs male of the body of the grantee, only 295 existed (or at least had been successfully claimed) in 1928. In view of the limitation to heirs male we can draw no conclusions in regard to the total fertility of these stocks, but one might have hoped to find some intelligible principle governing the rate of extinction of the male lines. Mr. R. J. Beevor, who investigated the matter, could, however, find none and was surprised to discover that the percentage of survivals of the oldest baronetcies was greater than that of those of later creation.[1]

The limitation of remainders to heirs male is apt to give a misleading impression of the power of dominant stocks to survive. Solutions proposed by H. W. Watson and others to a mathematical problem set by Sir Francis Galton and summarized by Sir Silvanus Vivian have a bearing on this. Galton's problem turns on the rate of extinction of male lines in a closed community. It is assumed that in this community 'in each generation a given proportion of the adult males have *no* male children who reach adult life; a given percentage have one such child; a given percentage have two such children, and so on'. The solution shows that on certain assumptions, if each male stock has a different surname, 'we have a continual extinction of surnames going on, combined with constancy or increase of population, as the case may be, until at length the number of surnames remaining is absolutely insensible as compared with the number at starting, but the total number of these remaining surnames is infinitely greater than the original number'.[2] This seems to mean that, without any recourse to assumptions of differential fertility between classes, we must expect the eventual

[1] R. J. Beevor, 'Distinction and Extinction', *The Genealogists' Magazine*, iv, 1928, pp. 60–62. Of baronetcies created 1611–25 21 per cent. survived, of those of 1625–64 just over 16 per cent. and of those of 1665–1707 just under 16 per cent.

[2] S. P. Vivian, 'Some Statistical Aspects of Genealogy', *The Genealogists' Magazine*, vi, 1934, pp. 482–9. The most important work in this field is that of Mr. T. H. Hollingsworth, 'A Demographic Study of the British Ducal Families', *Population Studies*, vol. xi, No. 1, 1957, 4–26, and chap. 14 of D. V. Glass and D. E. C. Eversley, *Population in History*, 1965, pp. 354–78, and 'The Demography of the British Peerage', *Population Studies*, vol. xviii, 1964. However, this great work is based on unverified printed pedigrees only.

disappearance of the male progeny of a large proportion of the males composing any one class at any one time. I am far from suggesting that there have not in the past been marked difference in fertility between classes. The greatly different number of the progenies of Henry VII's two daughters, for example, is highly significant.[1] My purpose is merely to stress the difficulty of getting at the facts and their meaning and to deprecate the facile inferences often drawn.

Professor Sorokin's second factor, dissimilarity of parents and children, covers the influence both of heredity and of that part of the environment which operates within the family. The two are lumped together because in practice we are often unable to separate their effects and, whatever their respective contributions, the upshot is that the child who for whatever reason differs markedly from his parents does not fit the place in life which fits them and so tends to move out of it. There are instances in which we seem to see the cause of social movement in a psychological reaction to parents and their attitudes, and chain reactions of this sort may have produced historical patterns.

Clearer, though still far from clear, are the patterns of heredity, which have received much attention since Sir Francis Galton (d. 1911), the founder of the science of eugenics, influenced by the work of his cousin Charles Darwin, investigated the subject and published his *Hereditary Genius* in 1869. In this and other books he explored the relationships of eminent men and showed that very many were near akin to others.

An interesting attempt to trace continuous inheritance of outstanding qualities through a number of generations was made by W. T. J. Gun (d. 1946) in a series of articles in the *Eugenics Review* (vols. xvi-xxix) and in his book, *Studies in Hereditary Ability* (1928). Interesting as such extended linkages are the risk that they may mislead is far greater than with the shorter pedigrees and closer links on which Galton concentrated, for at each step in the descent new strains come in by marriage and alternative possible sources of inheritance multiply. Thus Mr. Paul Bloomfield in his engaging book, *Uncommon People* (1955), has, I suspect, overstressed the share of the blood of Sir George Villiers (d. 1606) in the talent of some of his remote progeny, considering how many other outstanding strains have in the intervening generations been crossed with this. Nor can I escape a like feeling about that remarkable progeny of Heinrich von Greiffenclau, a Rhineland squire of the first half of the seventeenth century, which includes

[1] p. 236.

among others, outstanding members of the Schwarzenberg and Brentano families, our own Lord Acton and . . . Hermann Goering![1]

These doubts do not apply in the rare cases where persistent inheritance of distinctive physical characteristics can be proved. Thomas Ulick Sadleir (1882–1958), Deputy Ulster King of Arms, told me that he scored a bull's eye with a very long shot when he asked a visitor from New Zealand, of whom he knew only his rare surname, if he had webbed feet and was answered 'Yes!' The name was Hewardine and Sadleir had met a Hewardine with webbed feet before.

The succession of sons to fathers in eminent place is by no means solely or wholly due to inheritance of talent.

We have to consider the social advantages enjoyed by the children of a successful man, and the assistance which the father's position may sometimes give to his son in the early stages of his career. But the evidence is that mental qualities are inherited to exactly the same extent as physical, and advantageous variations to the same extent as unfavourable.[2]

Conversely we must remember the unproved but ever present possibility of the unknown 'Village Hampden' and 'mute, inglorious Milton', their 'noble rage' repressed by 'chill penury'.

It is the belief of some genealogists that, where outstanding talent appears suddenly in a commonplace or humble family, research into the ancestry is likely to reveal some concealed or forgotten outstanding ancestor. Too few cases have been explored to justify general conclusions, but there are instances where illegitimate descent from a family of higher standing seems to explain an apparently sudden flowering and others where a legitimate but remote and forgotten line of ancestry may hint at an answer. In other instances where a strikingly unusual talent emerges suddenly and then persists a mutation seems a possible explanation.

George Parker Bidder (1806–78) was the son of a stonemason at Moreton Hampstead on the edge of Dartmoor, 'principally occupied in building those stone fences with which that part of the county abounds'. George, the sixth of a family of nine, at an early age discovered phenomenal powers of mental arithmetic. It is said that he could visualise numbers and the accounts of his performances at ages between eight and twelve are astonishing. His father showed him before private and public audiences in the principal towns of the

---

[1] O. Forst de Battaglia, *Traité de généalogie*, 1949, p. 95.
[2] William Ralph Inge, *Outspoken Essays* (2nd ser.), 1922, p. 260, 'Eugenics'.

kingdom as 'the Devonshire calculating phenomenon'.[1] He was educated
and became a distinguished engineer and assistant to Robert Stephenson. He constructed the Victoria Docks, London, and was a founder
of the Electric Telegraph Company. He transmitted to some of his
descendants not only wealth which he had acquired, but high ability
and even the power of visualising numbers, though not in the same
degree.[2] Though nothing seems to be known of special ability in his
parents or ancestors, two of his brothers had exceptional powers of
memory and a third became a successful engineer.[3] It would be hard
to find a seemingly clearer case of notable powers appearing suddenly
and then persisting. The latest, most determined and most comprehensive effort to discuss genetic patterns in history and society is that
of Professor C. D. Darlington in *The Evolution of Man and Society*,
1969. All human history is here looked at from the point of view of a
geneticist, and genetic events and patterns are often detected where
previous writers have seen only social, cultural or environmental
influences at work. The key to all is discerned in the balance or
imbalance between inbreeding and outbreeding in communities,
whether nations, races or classes.[4]

What is needed above all is to favour stability but to avoid stagnation;
to keep the genes and chromosomes stirred up. If they can be kept moving
the society is safe. Its future is unlimited. If they settle, if they solidify, then
the society is in jeopardy. It has limited prospects.[5]

These principles and the mechanisms which give them effect are
looked for and seen in a huge variety of historical situations. As is
natural, the degree of conviction carried by Professor Darlington's
interpretations varies greatly. Some seem wonderfully apt, some far
fetched and others possible but quite uncertain, whether because the
evidence is too scanty or because the force of the argument depends on a
degree of understanding or acceptance of the genetic principles which
one reader, at least, lacks.

The effects of outbreeding and inbreeding on the European royal
caste and so on history are deduced from ample evidence and are little
complicated by extraneous factors.[6] The interpretation of Anglo-
Irish conflict in genetic terms carries scarcely less full conviction.
When, however, the English Reformation, Civil War[7] and Industrial

---

[1] *Kirby's Wonderful and Eccentric Museum*, vi, 1820, pp. 1–12.          [2] *D.N.B.*
[3] Information from his descendant Mrs. Rosemary Pinches.
[4] Op. cit., pp. 49–58.                                                    [5] Ibid., p. 54.
[6] Ibid., pp. 520–6.                                                       [7] Ibid., pp. 493–5.

Revolution[1] are interpreted in genetic terms, however plausible and stimulating, fascination is a little dashed by recollection of the many alternative explanations offered and the scantiness of positive evidence on the genetic side. The association of industry with dissent, for instance, deserves much fuller genealogical analysis than it has yet had. The existence of a link between the two is not in doubt, but its genetic character remains to be proved.

The intellectual distinction of many of the English Huguenots' descendants is attributed by Professor Darlington largely to their hybrid origins, but this influence is not easily to be separated from that of the selection which brought their ancestors to England in the first place. It is hard for the argument not to assume its conclusions, as when Professor Darlington tells us[2] that

class differences ultimately all derive from genetic and, usually, racial differences.

and that

it is the inequalities which create advances in society rather than advances in society which create inequalities.

The far reaching yet elusive character of such arguments hints at the contribution which genealogy, when more comprehensively studied, may have in it to make to history.

[1] Ibid., pp. 502–18.      [2] Ibid., p. 547.

# VI

## STRANGERS

I HAVE sought to present a picture, however rough and incomplete, of the English social framework and the movements of families within it. To complete this I must now say something of the movements into England and out of it; of the chief settlements of immigrants from other parts of these islands and from the Continent, of Scots, Welsh and Irish, Flemings, Dutch, Huguenots, Jews, Gypsies and some others; and of the English settlements overseas in Ireland, America, Australia, New Zealand and elsewhere. I cannot, of course, give any general account of these movements. A summary of some few facts which may help the genealogist, especially in regard to local and social origins and destinations, is the most I can attempt.

### I. STRANGER KNIGHTS AND LADIES

A small but interesting category of foreign settlers comprises knights and noblemen drawn to England by ties of kinship or service to its kings.

For a century or more after the Norman Conquest, settlement in England from across the channel was a general process different in kind from such individual migrations. We may therefore start our tale of these with Jocelin of Louvain (d. c. 1180), the brother in law of Henry I and ancestor of the Percys.[1] In the next century Henry III (d. 1272) was too free for the liking of his English barons with invitations to his foreign kinsmen and connections by marriage and their friends. He offered a home in England to his half brothers of the famous house of Lusignan which gave a dynasty to Cyprus,[2] but only one of them, William de Valence (d. 1296), remained and left English descendants. Henry's marriage to Eleanor of Provence opened opportunities for her kin and connections also, especially the Savoyards with whom she was linked through her mother Beatrice daughter of Thomas Count of Savoy. Probably among those who came to England through this connection was a close friend of Edward I, Sir

---

[1] p. 39.     [2] *Complete Peerage*, x. 377.

Otes de Grandison or Granson (d. 1328), apparently a son of Pierre de Granson, lord of Granson on the lake of Neuchatel. Sir William de Grandison (d. 1335), younger brother of Sir Otes, founded a baronial line which in 1375 ended in three coheirs, his daughters, through whom his blood passed to many English families.[1] He is thus a 'gateway ancestor'[2] through whom many Englishmen descend from comital families of central Europe. Sir John de Stratelinges (d. 1293), the ancestor of the Stradlings of Glamorgan and so of many families in South Wales, was a nephew of Sir Otes de Granson and probably, as we have seen, came from Strättligen near Thun, not far away.[3] Another immigrant knight of the Savoyard connection was a half brother of the wife of Peter of Savoy, Sir Geoffrey de Geneville or Joinville (d. 1314), a younger son of the Seneschal of Champagne and brother of the Sire de Joinville, the friend and biographer of St. Louis IX, King of France. He came to England about 1251 and was given lands in Ireland by the king. Through the marriage of Joan (d. 1356), his granddaughter and heir, to Roger Mortimer, Earl of March, he has very many English descendants.[4]

Henry de Beaumont (d. 1340),[5] first cousin of Edward I's queen, Eleanor of Castile (d. 1290), settled in England and her kinsmen the lords of Fiennes in the county of Boulogne, who had possessed lands in England since the twelfth century, acquired more and at length made England their home partly perhaps because of this link.[6]

Edward III's marriage to Philippa of Hainault in 1328 brought in several knights of that region. The progeny of the most famous, Sir Walter de Mauny (d. 1372),[7] became extinct. But from Sir Terry or 'Canon' Robessart, a leader in Edward III's wars, sprang two Knights of the Garter (Sir John, d. 1450, and Sir Lewis, d. 1431), and a line of Norfolk gentry which produced the unfortunate Amy Robsart (d. 1560) and Lucy ancestress of the Walpoles.[8] Sir Eustace d'Aubrécicourt (d. 1372) married Queen Philippa's niece, the widowed Countess of Kent.[9] Sir Sanchet d'Aubrécicourt (d. 1361), probably his brother, was a founder Knight of the Garter and married the heiress of Stratfield

---

[1] *Complete Peerage*, vi. 60–68.  [2] See p. 238.  [3] p. 78 *supra*.

[4] *Complete Peerage*, v. 628–34.  [5] See p. 44.

[6] J. H. Round, *Studies in Peerage and Family History*, pp. 159–61; *Complete Peerage*, vi. 466, and xi. 479; Dugdale, *Baronage*, ii. 243.

[7] *Complete Peerage*, viii. 571–6.

[8] Hope, *Stall Plates of the Knights of the Garter*, pl. xxix: *Complete Peerage*, ii. 247, and vii. 199 and 550; Rye, *Norfolk Families*, pp. 742–5 (a confused account).

[9] *Complete Peerage* vii. 149; G. F. Beltz, *Memorials of the Order of the Garter*, 1841, pp. 90–92.

Saye, Hampshire, which his descendants the Dabridgecourts held till 1629.[1] Sir Payn Roet (d. *c.* 1352), Guyenne King of Arms, whose daughter Katherine (d. 1403) married first Sir Hugh Swynford and secondly John of Gaunt, is also thought to have been a knight of Hainault. He was probably also the father of Philippa the wife of Geoffrey Chaucer.[2]

Among later instances in the same category may be placed William III's Dutch favourites Hans Willem Bentinck (d. 1709), Earl of Portland and ancestor of the Dukes of Portland,[3] and Arnold Joost van Keppel (d. 1718), Earl of Albemarle.[4]

With the foreign knights and courtiers must be classed the noble ladies from abroad who married and left descendants in England. First among them come the consorts of English kings sprung, as most have been, from royal or princely houses on the Continent. Our mediaeval queens have very many non-royal English descendants[5] who through them can trace descent from the early ruling houses of Europe and from as far afield as Byzantium and Armenia. Unexpected in its interest, comprising among others a descent from a brother of St. Thomas Aquinas (d. 1274), is the ancestry of Elizabeth Wydville (d. 1492), Queen of Edward IV, through her mother Jacqueline of Luxemburg. A valiant attempt to trace the whole ancestry of Edward IV and his queen to the number of some 7,000 names was made by Lt. Col. W. H. Turton.[6] Such a work, resting as it must on the published work of genealogists throughout Europe, presents peculiar difficulties and Turton's book, though of great value as a guide, needs to be used with caution and checked with authorities which quote—as he does not—original evidence. Furthermore since its appearance valuable work has been done on many of the early continental lines.

After the queens come foreign ladies married to subjects, and first of these both for the distinction of her ancestry and the number of her descendants must come Isabel of Vermandois (d. 1147), successively Countess of Leicester and Surrey, granddaughter on her father's side of Henry I of France and on her mother's of Herbert, Count of Vermandois, a male line descendant of Charlemagne. Other early marriages

---

[1] *Victoria County History, Hampshire*, iv. 58–59.

[2] *Complete Peerage*, vii. 415–16; J. Weever, *Funeral Monuments*, 1631, p. 661; *D.N.B.* 1908, iv. 158–9.

[3] *Complete Peerage*, x. 589.  [4] Ibid., i. 91.

[5] Those of later date, however, have very few, see p. 236.

[6] *The Plantagenet Ancestry*, 1928. See p. 225 for Elizabeth Wydville's descent from Adenalfo, brother of St. Thomas Aquinas.

which brought Charlemagne's blood to England were that of Robert Marmion (d. 1143–4) to Millicent daughter of Gervase Count of Rethel[1] and that of Roger de Tony (decd. 1162) to Ida daughter of Baldwin III Count of Hainault.[2]

Among marriages deriving from Henry III's Savoyard connection were those of Edmund de Lacy, Earl of Lincoln (d. 1258), to Alice daughter of Manfred III, Marquess of Saluzzo in Piedmont, and that of Richard Fitzalan, Earl of Arundel (d. 1302), to her niece Alice daughter of Thomas I, Marquess of Saluzzo.[3] When Anne of Bohemia came to England and married Richard II in 1382, one of the ladies in her train was a certain Margaret, said to have been a daughter or niece of Premislaus Duke of Teschen. She married the king's standard bearer Sir Simon Felbrigge, K.G. (d. 1442), and through her daughter Alana, wife of William Tyndall of Deene, Northamptonshire, left many descendants.[4] In 1371 Constance, daughter of Pedro the Cruel of Castile, came to England and was married to John of Gaunt. In her train came Doña Sancha de Ayala, daughter of Don Diego Gomez de Guzman and his wife Doña Ines de Ayala. In 1373 she married Sir Walter Blount of Sodington, Worcestershire. Their descendants include several early settlers in New England.[5]

The Portuguese connections of the house of Lancaster account for the marriage of Gilbert Lord Talbot (d. 1418) to a Portuguese lady named Beatrice, perhaps of the Souza family and descended from a bastard of King Alfonso III (d. 1279) of Portugal. She left descendants by her second husband Thomas Fettiplace of East Shefford, Berkshire.[6]

The marriage of James Stanley, Earl of Derby (d. 1651), to Charlotte daughter of Claude de la Trémoille, Duke of Thouars in France, by Charlotte Brabantine, daughter of William Prince of Orange, by his wife Charlotte of Bourbon, gives their numerous progeny descents from many of the noblest families of the Continent.[7] Descent from many ancient families of Brittany is shared by the English descendants of Charles II's Breton mistress, Louise Renée de Penancoet de

[1] G. A. Moriarty, 'The Marmion-Rethel Marriage', *The Genealogists' Magazine*, ix. 424–6.

[2] *Complete Peerage*, xii, pt. i, p. 764.

[3] p. 246 *supra*; *Complete Peerage*, vii. 681, and i. 241.

[4] G. F. Beltz, *Memorials of the Order of the Garter*, pp. 370–1; R. E. C. Waters, *Genealogical Memoirs of the Extinct Family of Chester of Chicheley*, i. 1878, p. 257.

[5] Milton Rubincam, 'The Spanish Ancestry of American Colonists', *National Genealogical Soc. Quarterly*, vol. 51, 1963, pp. 235–8.

[6] *Complete Peerage*, xii, pt. i, p. 619; *Misc. Gen. et Her.*, 5th ser. ii. 131.

[7] *Complete Peerage*, iv. 214; *The Genealogists' Magazine*, xi, 1953, pp. 1–409.

Kéroualle, Duchess of Portsmouth (d. 1734), and her sister Henriette Mauricette, Countess of Pembroke (d. 1728).[1]

This catalogue of distinguished strangers could be extended but only one more name shall be given and that one whose place is doubtful. An inscription on brass in the church of Landulph, Cornwall, commemorates

> Theodoro Paleologus of Pesaro in Italye, descended from the Imperyall Lyne of the last Christian Emperors of Greece beinge the sonne of Camilio, the sonne of Prosper the sonne of Theodoro the sonne of John, the sonne of Thomas, second brother to Constantine Paleologus, the 8th of that name and last of that lyne that raygned in Constantinople, until subdewed by the Turks, who . . . departed this life at Clyfton the 21th of January 1636.[2]

Prince Rhodocanakis, however, cast doubt upon this pedigree pointing out the frequency of Palaeologus and other imperial names as surnames among the Greeks 'without anyone imagining their bearers to be descendants of the emperors'.[3]

Ferdinando Palaeologus, a son of Theodoro, settled in Barbados and died there in 1680 leaving a son. His descendants in the female line were said to be still extant there in 1854. His sister Dorothy (d. 1681) married William Arundel at Landulph in 1656, and if the Mary Arundel who married Francis Lee was her daughter and if a Lee family of boatmen on the Hamoaze descend from them 'the imperial blood perhaps still flows in the bargemen of Cargeen'.[4]

## 2. SCOTS, IRISH AND WELSH

The settlers in England from Scotland, Ireland and Wales, though probably more numerous in recent centuries than settlers from the Continent, have been much less studied.

Scots until 1603 were aliens in England and the two countries being often at war or hostile, opportunities for migration across the border were at some periods limited. The frequency of the surname Scot or le Scot in thirteenth century English records, especially in the northern

---

[1] *Complete Peerage*, x. 607 and 422.

[2] *Archaeologia*, xviii. 34; *Notes & Queries*, 1st ser. viii. 408.

[3] Ibid., 3rd ser. xii. 30. Sir Steven Runciman, *The Great Church in Captivity*, Cambridge, 1968, pp. 196–7, p. 362, n. 2, thinks the Cantacuzeni probably the only family whose claim to male descent from a Byzantine imperial house can be accepted. On the early Palaeologi see references in D. I. Polemis, *The Doukai*, 1968, pp. 152–64.

[4] *Notes & Queries*, 1st ser. x. 351–2; V. L. Oliver, *Monumental Inscriptions of Barbados*, 1915, pp. 191–2.

counties,[1] suggests, however, that full advantage was taken of opportunities which were greater then than for long after. The religious and political strife of the sixteenth century may have brought to England occasional Scottish refugees. Such, it seems, was Lord Methuen's ancestor, Paul Methwyn (d. 1606), who was presented to the living of Kewstock, Somerset, by Queen Elizabeth in 1570, and was probably identical with the Scottish Reformer Paul Methuen, said to have taken refuge in England in 1566.[2] Another sixteenth century Scottish immigrant, who may have been a refugee, was John Napper or Napier the ancestor of the Napiers of Crichel and Puncknowle, Dorset, and Tintinhull, Somerset.[3] The Returns of Aliens show that the number of Scots in London under Elizabeth was very small in relation to that of Flemings, Dutch and French.

The union of the crowns in 1603 opened to the Scots that high road to England which Samuel Johnson in 1763 called 'the noblest prospect which a Scotchman ever sees'.[4] Count Gondomar, the Spanish ambassador in London from 1613 to 1622, wrote that 'the Scots greatly multiplying themselves have nestled about the Court, so that the Strand from mud walls and thatched cottages acquired that perfection of buildings it now possesses'.[5]

When James Sixth of Scotland and First of England moved from Holyrood to Whitehall in 1603, he was accompanied or followed by a crowd of courtiers and needy adventurers, the first trickle of the great stream of Scots who have since come across the border to seek their fortunes. But it was long before that stream swelled to proportions of national significance. Several generations were to pass before Scottish farmers, mechanics, gardeners, administrators, physicians and philosophers came swarming south, bringing with them skill, industry and knowledge, sufficient to affect the life and increase the prosperity of England.[6]

The 'trickle' which came with James included his jeweller George Heriot (d. 1624) and his clockmaker David Ramsay (d. 1653?) as well as 'a host of traders and craftsmen, many of whom failing to obtain

---

[1] C. L'Estrange Ewen, *A History of Surnames of the British Isles*, 1931, p. 154. For the close and numerous family links between England and Scotland in the thirteenth century see Sir Maurice Powicke, *The Thirteenth Century 1216–1307*, 1953, pp. 579–82.

[2] F. W. Weaver, *Somerset Incumbents*, 1889, pp. 1–15, 89, 121, 474; William Playfair, *British Family Antiquity*, vii, 1811, p. 12; *D.N.B.*; Coll. Arm. Reg. I. 27, fo. 107; *Fasti Ecclesiae Scoticanae*, ed. Hew Scott, 1917, ii. 124. Information from Lord Methuen, Corsham Archives, Box 33, no. 1921.

[3] Thomas Wotton, *The English Baronetage*, 1741, i. 225–31.

[4] James Boswell, *The Life of Samuel Johnson, LL.D.*, 2nd ed. 1793, p. 391.

[5] Brett-James, op. cit., p. 498.    [6] Trevelyan, *English Social History*, p. 207.

employment, gave rise, as early as 1613, to the institution of the "Scottish Box", a sort of friendly Society's treasury. . . . In the year 1665 the "box" was exalted into the character of a corporation by a royal charter.'[1] After the Restoration lustre was added to the London Scottish community by such distinguished men as Gilbert Burnet (d. 1715), Bishop of Salisbury, Dr. John Arbuthnot (d. 1735), Queen Anne's physician, and William Paterson (d. 1719), the founder of the Bank of England.

The parliamentary Union of England and Scotland in 1707, which opened trade with the English colonies to the Scots, made fresh opportunities and no doubt increased the influx to that pitch which excited the wrath of Johnson. Many of the Scots who came south at this time were driven by poverty. Scottish noblemen sought fortunes in England and are noted as a conspicuous class among the South Sea Bubble speculators of 1720.[2] Young Scots of good family entered commerce.[3] On the Great North Road Scottish pedlars were so numerous that 'Scotchman' and 'pedlar' became synonyms. Tobias Smollett (d. 1771) tells us that when travelling to and from Scotland he found 'from Doncaster downwards, all the windows of the inns scrawled with doggerel rhymes in abuse of the Scottish nation'.[4]

Scottish writers of the early eighteenth century on the other hand complain of the numbers of young men forced by poverty to leave Scotland. Many went overseas but many also went south as tailors and many more as gardeners, 'in which business they showed peculiar skill, and left Scotland, where gardens were few and poor, for England, where they abounded'.[5] Among the gardeners were such leaders of their vocation as John Abercrombie (d. 1806) and William Aiton (d. 1793), royal gardeners employed at Kew, and John Claudius Loudon (d. 1843) the landscape gardener.

To the Edinburgh medical school may be credited much of the success of Scottish doctors in England since the time of John (d. 1793) and William Hunter (d. 1783[6]). The names of James Watt (d. 1819), Thomas Telford (d. 1834) and John Loudon Macadam (d. 1836) recall the host of Scottish engineers. The success of the Scots in the

---

[1] Walter Thornbury, *Old and New London*, i. 106.
[2] John Carswell, *The South Sea Bubble*, 1960, p. 141.
[3] G. P. Judd, *Members of Parliament 1734–1832*, p. 54.
[4] John Herries McCulloch, *The Scot in England*, 1935, p. 75.
[5] Henry Grey Graham, *The Social Life of Scotland in the Eighteenth Century*, 1928, p. 314.
[6] See p. 197.

practice of the English law has known no interruption since the time of William Murray, Earl of Mansfield (d. 1793), while in commerce their gifts have made them ubiquitous. Since the eighteenth century Scots have settled in all parts of England.

In the middle of that century, however, their unpopularity with the English rose to a peak. Johnson's attitude towards them was symptomatic. The unpopularity of the first Scottish Prime Minister (1762–3), John Stuart, Earl of Bute (d. 1792), reacted upon his nation. This may have induced some Scots in England to Anglicize their names, though perhaps a likelier motive was the comfort of English tongues. David Malloch (d. 1765), the poet, wrote in 1724, that he had been advised to change his name and adopt the form Mallet, 'for there is not one Englishman that can pronounce' Malloch.[1]

The Irishmen whose presence in England from the thirteenth century onward is indicated by such surnames as le Yreys, Irlond and Iryssh,[2] were perhaps of Anglo-Norman rather than Celtic descent. So too, it seems probable, was the Mackwilliam family of Stambourne, Essex, whose heiress married Sir John Seymour (d. 1464). The Mackwilliams were in England by Richard II's reign. According to John Leland (d. 1552) 'One MacWilliam being a younger brother of a gentleman in Ireland came to Bristol and there so increased in riches that in continuance he bought lands to the sum of 3 or 400 marks by the year'. Sir James Ware (d. 1666) deduced them from the MacWilliam Eighter or MacWilliam Oughter branch of the Bourkes in Connaught.[3]

Irish beggars were a nuisance to the authorities in Tudor times. An Act of 1572 provided for their repatriation to Ireland at the cost of the county which first received them, but this had little or no effect. In 1585 'one of the chronic rebellions in Ireland swept a horde of' them 'into Bridewell by way of Bristol'.[4] Poverty and wars in Ireland continued to drive Irishmen to England, especially to Liverpool, Bristol and London. The Plantation of Ulster[5] produced a backwash of migration to England. In London in the early seventeenth century 'there was a colony of Irish sailors and merchants by the Thames-side, some lawyers studied at the Inns of Court, while others interested in literature and the drama drifted to Whitefriars and Alsatia. . . .

---

[1] *D.N.B.*      [2] Ewen, op. cit., p. 154.

[3] Morant, *History of Essex*, ii. 356.

[4] A. V. Judges, *The Elizabethan Underworld*, 1930, p. 496, quoting O'Donoghue, *Bridewell Hospital*, p. 203.      [5] See p. 280.

Distressed and adventurous men and classes settled in Westminster, St. Giles-in-the-Fields, Whitechapel and Marylebone.' In St. Giles especially there was a colony of unskilled labourers, 'builders' labourers, chairmen, porters, coal-heavers, milk-sellers and street hawkers, . . . publicans and lodging-house keepers, apparently chiefly catering for their own countrymen'.[1] In eighteenth century London there were a number of Irish colonies of different types, such as thieves in St. Giles and coalheavers in Wapping.[2] It was not, however, till the last years of the eighteenth century that the substantial immigration of Irish Roman Catholic labourers into England began. After 1815 this grew greatly and the Irish famine of 1845–7 increased it to a flood, though the flow which was at first mainly to England turned later to America and Australia. 'In 1841 it was estimated that over 400,000 inhabitants of Great Britain had been born in Ireland; many more tens of thousands were born in Britain of Irish parentage. The great majority of these were Catholics, and among the poorest-paid labourers; most of them lived in London and in the industrial towns. In Liverpool and Manchester anything between one-fifth and one-third of the working population was Irish.'[3]

It was a Catholic and peasant migration which played an important part in the industrial revolution, since the Irishmen, such as those among the railway navvies, took over whole classes of work. In some towns they were segregated but there was much intermarriage. Those who came to England are said to have been mainly those too poor to afford the journey to America.[4]

Sir Henry Ellis notes over a hundred men described as Waleis or Walensis (i.e. the Welshman, later Wallis, Wallace, Walsh, &c.) in Domesday Book (1086)[5] and Waleys is common as a surname throughout England in the thirteenth and fourteenth centuries. From the twelfth century onward we also find in England such Welsh patronymics as Griffin, Owen, Bevin and Powell. Some of them may derive from the personal names of Bretons who came in with the Normans but the greater number probably come from Wales. Nor must the probability that Breton influence helped the Welsh in England after the Conquest be overlooked. C. L'Estrange Ewen has pointed

[1] N. G. Brett-James, *The Growth of Stuart London*, 1935, pp. 75–76, 82, 108, 481 and sources there quoted.
[2] M. D. George, *London Life in the XVIIIth Century*, 1930, pp. 113–25.
[3] E. P. Thompson, *The Making of the English Working Class*, 1963, p. 429.
[4] Ibid., pp. 429–44.
[5] Sir Henry Ellis, *A General Introduction to Domesday Book*, 1833, ii. 514.

out the surprisingly greater frequency of his own surname—the same as Owen or Ywain—in the thirteenth century in north Norfolk and the Cambridge fenland than in areas further west and suggests at least a partial possible explanation in the Breton connections of Ralph, Earl of Norfolk and Suffolk (d. *c.* 1069), and his son and successor.[1] The Welsh surname Powell likewise occurs in Norfolk and Suffolk continuously from the thirteenth century.[2] The knightly family of Griffin, one of whom was made Lord Griffin of Braybrooke in 1688, was settled at Gumley, Leicestershire, in the thirteenth century and perhaps the twelfth, while the name is found in Staffordshire still earlier.[3] The fact that the Welsh Gruffydd is Normanized into Griffin rather than Anglicized into Griffith betrays the date of settlement.

Doubtless there was migration from Wales into England all through the Middle Ages,[4] but the advent of a Welsh dynasty, the Tudors, to the English throne in 1485 accelerated the flow. 'The success of the Tudors', says Dr. Rowse, 'was a triumph for the Welsh. They flocked to London, and some of them who came out of Wales changed the face of things in England.'[5] David Cecil (d. 1536), Lord Burghley's grandfather, came from a family of petty gentry on the Welsh border to Stamford where he was admitted freeman in 1494. It seems likely that he came out of Wales with Henry VII as servant to a Welsh knight Sir David Philippe, who also settled at Stamford.[6] Morgan Williams came from Glamorgan to Putney, married the sister of Thomas Cromwell (d. 1540) and became Oliver Cromwell's ancestor.[7] 'In the household of the Tudor sovereigns there was always a Welsh contingent.'[8]

The great house of Herbert first attained the peerage in 1468, when Sir William Herbert (d. 1469), one of the Welsh knights who had served with distinction in the French wars, was created Earl of Pembroke. His legitimate male progeny expired at his son's death in 1491, but the son of one of his bastards, another William Herbert (d. 1570), was in high favour with Henry VIII, was granted Wilton Abbey and in 1551 was made Earl of Pembroke. Dr. Rowse extols the 'variegated abilities and accomplishments' of this 'extraordinary family'.[9]

---

[1] Ewen, *A History of Surnames*, pp. 152–3; C. L'Estrange Ewen, *The Families of Ewen of East Anglia and the Fenland*, 1928, pp. 4–11 and *passim*; *Complete Peerage*, ix. 568.

[2] Edgar Powell, *The Pedigree of the Family of Powell*, 1891, pp. 2–3.

[3] J. Harvey Bloom, *The Griffins of Dingley*, 1921, pp. 1, 14, 67.

[4] For Welshmen in mediaeval London see S. Thrupp, *The Merchant Class of Medieval London*, p. 219.

[5] A. L. Rowse, *The Expansion of Elizabethan England*, 1955, p. 48.

[6] Oswald Barron, *Northamptonshire Families, Victoria County History*, 1906, pp. 22–24.

[7] *The Antiquary*, i. 164.    [8] Rowse, op. cit., p. 49.    [9] Ibid., p. 50.

In the sixteenth and seventeenth centuries the immemorial Welsh addiction to pedigrees entered upon a phase of systematic codification by bardic antiquaries and genealogists.[1] In England also this was the period of a great outburst of interest in genealogy. It is therefore not surprising to find that a number of the Welsh families who settled in England at this time brought a knowledge of their ancestry with them and communicated it to the heralds. In other instances a want of knowledge was supplied by the exercise of imagination.

The extent of the Welsh settlement in England at this and later dates has not been estimated but as an index of the numbers of Welsh gentry it may be mentioned that by the 1630's the heralds had entered in their Visitation books the arms and pedigrees of some dozen families apiece of such names as Vaughan, Edwards, Williams, Griffith and Morgan. The fashion of family surnames came to Wales from England under the Tudors though Welshmen who moved to England had, as we have seen, taken their patronymics as family names long before. Before the sixteenth century a Welshman's description was his genealogy, short or long, as Thomas ap Gwilym ap Jenkin, or Jenkin ab Ieuan ab David ab Ieuan ab Lleyson, and so continued for many for long after. The surnames, therefore, when they came, were almost all patronymics. Hence the innumerable Joneses, Williamses, Morgans and the rest. The new fashion, like the English language, penetrated only by degrees. As late as 1853 the Registrar General's Report says that surnames 'can scarcely be said to have penetrated among the lower classes in the wilder districts [of Wales], where, as the marriage registers show, the christian name of the father still frequently becomes the patronymic of the son'.[2] In the eighteenth and nineteenth centuries there was a fashion among the Welsh dissenters for such Biblical Christian names as Jehu, Daniel, Habakkuk, which accordingly, as patronymics, often became surnames.

### 3. FLEMINGS, DUTCH AND GERMANS

England's geographical position in relation to the Continent and the nature of its institutions have often made it a goal for refugees, while at certain times its relative backwardness has attracted technical skill from the Continent. The two motives were often linked and no fast line can be drawn between the refugees and the men of enterprise.

---

[1] Major Francis Jones, 'An Approach to Welsh Genealogy', *Cymmrodorion Soc. Trans.*, 1948, pp. 378–90.
[2] P. H. Reaney, *The Origin of English Surnames*, 1967, p. 317.

The English Crown had at all times an interest in encouraging and protecting those immigrants whose skill made England more prosperous, while sympathy for such misfortunes as those of the Huguenots could sweeten resentments felt at other times by English subjects against skilled foreign competitors or against foreigners as such. The First Industrial Revolution, as Professor Nef has called it, which took place between 1540 and 1640, owed its possibility in many fields to alien immigration.[1]

The long series of royal edicts for the control and protection of resident aliens begins in 1266.[2] Through most of the Middle Ages there were foreign colonies in London[3] and other mercantile centres of Gascon, Flemish, Dutch, German and Italian merchants, while Flemish weavers were at various dates invited to settle in clothing towns and districts. The view that the weaving industry was established in England by Flemings who came in soon after the Norman Conquest is now discounted, though there were settlements of Flemings from that date and probably of weavers among them.[4] There is no doubt, however, of the importance of the invitation issued by Edward III in 1331 to foreign weavers to settle in England.[5] From Ypres, Ghent, Poperinghe and elsewhere in Flanders, Zeeland and Brabant they came to London, York, Winchester, Norwich, Bristol, Abingdon, the Cotswolds and the West Riding. Their surnames can sometimes perhaps be recognized even where the date of settlement is too early for record of it to have been found. Such a name as Clutterbuck, known in Gloucestershire since the fifteenth century,[6] strongly suggests a Dutch or Flemish origin. The unpopularity of the alien settlers with their English rivals was apt to erupt in times of stress. In 1312 a rising drove foreign traders from Norwich.[7] 'Many Flemings' says a London

---

[1] Lionel Williams, 'Alien Immigrants in Relation to Industry and Society in Tudor England', *Huguenot Soc. Proc.* xix, 1956, pp. 146–69.

[2] Powicke, *The Thirteenth Century*, p. 619.

[3] For Frenchmen, Italians, Flemings and Germans in mediaeval London see S. Thrupp, *The Merchant Class of Medieval London*, pp. 219–22. The Italians were especially prominent.

[4] W. Cunningham, *The Growth of English Industry and Commerce, I. Early and Middle Ages*, 5th ed. 1910, pp. 641–55; Lipson, *Economic History of England*, i, 1915 ed., p. 324.

[5] See *The Cambridge Economic History of Europe*, ii, 1952, pp. 414–15; E. Lipson, *The Economic History of England*, i, 1915, pp. 399–400 and elsewhere; W. Cunningham, *Alien Immigrants to England*, 1897, chap. iii; Mary McKisack, *The Fourteenth Century 1307–1399*, Oxford, 1959, pp. 367–8.

[6] M. E. N. Witchell and C. R. Hudleston, *An Account of the Family Clutterbuck*, 1924, pp. 9, 20.

[7] *Victoria County History, Norfolk*, ii. 480, quoted by Lipson, op. cit. i. 463.

chronicler writing of the peasants' revolt of 1381 'lost their heads at that time, and namely they that could not say Bread and Cheese but Brod and Case.'[1] There were similar attacks in 1425 and 1470. On May Day 1517, thence called Ill May Day, there was 'an insurrection in London of young persons against aliens: of the which divers were put to execution'.

With the reign of Henry VIII records begin which reveal more clearly the extent and composition of the alien settlements and the reliance placed on alien skill for the conduct of certain trades.[2] Frenchmen and other aliens were employed in the ironworks of the Sussex weald and probably had been since the fifteenth century.[3] Henry himself imported gunners and armourers from France, Germany and the Low Countries.[4] Among the German armourers who settled at Greenwich was Robert Derrick (d. 1525) from Aachen, whose descendants Anglicized their name as Dethick and gave four heralds to the College of Arms between 1540 and 1707. From 1546 the Duke of Alva's persecution of Protestants in the Low Countries brought in many Dutchmen and Flemings, as mentioned below.[5] Throughout the sixteenth century new skills, manufactures and works were brought in by foreigners who were invited for the purpose or came of their own initiative or as refugees;[6] from refugee French subjects of the English Crown from Calais, Hamme and Guines after their loss in 1555;[7] from German miners and Dutch and French hatters; to Italian court musicians such as the Galliardellos[8] and Bassanos, of whom Anthony was organist to James I and Charles I, while his son Richard, a herald painter, left descendants who still continue.[9] Many of these settled on the extreme edge of the city of London. Bartholomew Tallafer (d. 1617), from the dominion of the Doge of Venice, was

---

[1] Kingsford, *Chronicles of London*, p. 15, quoted by Lipson, op. cit., i. 463; Lipson, i. 463, quoting Flenley, *Six Town Chronicles*, p. 192, and Holinshed, *Chronicles*, iii. 617–24; *The Great Chronicle of London*, ed. A. H. Thomas and I. D. Thornley, 1938, pp. 136, 212.

[2] *Returns of Aliens Dwelling in the City and Suburbs of London from the Reign of Henry VIII to that of James I*, ed. R. E. G. Kirk and Ernest F. Kirk, Huguenot Soc. Publications.

[3] References are given by L. Williams in *Huguenot Soc. Proc.* xix. 164–5, nn.

[4] Cunningham, op. cit., p. 142.                                    [5] p. 260.

[6] Rowse, *The England of Elizabeth*, p. 115, quoting J. U. Nef, 'The Progress of Technology, and the Growth of Large Scale Industry in Great Britain 1540–1640', *Econ. Hist. Rev.* 1934.

[7] N. G. Brett-James, *The Growth of Stuart London*, 1935, pp. 33, 48.

[8] Rowse, op. cit., quoting E. M. Tomlinson, *History of the Minories*, and references in *Huguenot Soc. Proc.* xix. 167–8 nn.

[9] Visitation of London, 1633–4; Coll. Arm. Reg. Norfolk xxxix. 168–9; Surrey, xviii. 303.

naturalized an Englishman in 1562 and settled in St. Olave's parish in the City of London. His grandson Robert Taliaferro (b. 1626) was settled in Virginia by 1647 and was the ancestor of a well known family there.[1]

London in the seventeenth century as a growing commercial centre attracted not only capital but capitalists from abroad. Wealthy Dutch merchants not only sent their money, but came to settle themselves. Elizabeth had borrowed considerable sums from naturalized Dutch residents and in James I's reign the Goldsmiths' Company complained of strangers taking their trade. Nevertheless the foreign merchants continued to flourish under James I and Charles I and many were naturalized.[2] Out of 38 foreign families entered at the Heralds' Visitation of London in 1633–4, 17 were from Flanders and Brabant, 4 from Hainault, 4 from Holland, 1 from Gelderland and 7 from Germany. Sir Cornelius Vermuyden, the drainer of the fens, was among the Dutchmen. The pedigrees of knights made between 1660 and 1714, collected by Peter Le Neve, Norroy (d. 1729), show that some of the descendants of these settlers attained wealth and eminence in the city of London.[3] With the mercantile names from this quarter of Europe must be remembered also those of Van Dyck, Lely and Kneller among the painters and that of Vanbrugh among the architects and playwrights. There were notable artists also among the Protestant refugees from the Low Countries—Marcus Geeraerts, Cornelius Jansen, Gerard Jansen, Bernard van Linge and others.

Hungarian refugees from Turkish incursions and Bohemians, who came to England through James I's son in law Frederick the Elector Palatine, also settled in London.[4] In 1709 some 10,000 German Protestants from the Palatinate, victims of the wars, were allowed to come to England, but most of them passed on to Ireland or America.[5]

Samuel Johnson inserted a salute to his birthplace into a definition in his English dictionary. On the same principle I will here recall that

[1] Sir A. Wagner and F. S. Andrus, 'The Origin of the family of Taliaferro', *Virginia Mag. of Hist. & Biog.*, vol. 77, Jan. 1969, pp. 22–25.

[2] W. Cunningham, *The Growth of English Industry and Commerce*, ii. Modern Times, pt. i, 1912, pp. 324–5; *Parl. Hist.* vi. 782; *State Papers Domestic, James I*, 1622, cxxvii. 12.

[3] e.g. Vandeput, Decker, Rycaut, Bateman (see p. 162 *supra*), Mertins, Meyer, Hotchetter: Harleian Soc. viii.

[4] N. G. Brett-James, *The Growth of Stuart London*, 1935, pp. 483–4 and sources there cited.

[5] G. M. Trevelyan, *England under Queene Anne, III, The Peace and the Protestant Succession*, 1934, pp. 37–38; M. D. Falley, *Irish and Scotch-Irish Ancestral Research*, vol. i, 1962, p. 358.

my ancestor Melchior Wagner (1685–1764), second son of a hatter to the ducal court of Coburg, came to England and was naturalized in 1709. According to family tradition his German speech helped to commend him to King George I who in 1722 became godfather to his son. At all events he became hatter to George I and later George II, his sons and grandson succeeding him in the appointment and the business being carried on at a house leased from the Crown in Pall Mall, Westminster.[1]

### 4. THE HUGUENOTS

The first settlements in England of Protestant refugees from the Continent in the reigns of Henry VIII and Edward VI[2] were in one aspect a continuation of the earlier settlements of craftsmen, for the settlers as before were largely Flemish weavers and they tended as before to settle in London and the weaving centres. Furthermore economic and religious motives for migration often ran parallel and cannot always be separated. A census of aliens living in and about the city of London in 1573 indicates that rather less than half had come to England for religious reasons.[3] As early as 1550 the number of Protestant Dutch and Flemings in London had moved Edward VI to give them the former church of the Austin Friars, but the flow increased vastly after 1567 when the Duke of Alva (d. 1582) was appointed captain general in the Spanish Low Countries with instructions which he fulfilled so well that he is said to have executed 18,000 people in five years and to have driven 100,000 to emigrate. In Norwich by 1568 there were 1,132 Dutchmen (with 339 Walloons). In 1571 they numbered nearly 4,000, about a quarter of the whole population of the city. Thereafter immigration fell off but the Dutchmen in Norwich multiplied and in 1583 they numbered 4,679. 'There can be few East Anglians', says Mr. Ketton-Cremer, 'in city or town or even in the countryside without some admixture of Dutch, Flemish or Walloon blood.'[4]

---

[1] *Burke's Landed Gentry*, 1956, 1965. A. R. Wagner, 'The Wagners of Brighton and their connections', *Sussex Arch. Coll.*, vol. 97.

[2] Dr. Joan Evans, *Huguenot Soc. Proc.* xiv. 497, quoted from Baron F. de Schickler, *Les Églises du refuge*, i. 4, a statement that the first refugees from France arrived in England as early as 1531.

[3] Irene Scouloudi, 'Alien Immigration into and Alien Communities in London 1558–1640', *Huguenot Soc. Proc.* xvi, 1941, pp. 27–49.

[4] Robert Wyndham Ketton-Cremer, *Norfolk Assembly*, 1957, pp. 113–30, 'The Coming of the Strangers', p. 129.

The persecution of the French Protestants or Huguenots by the Guises in the 1560's began their long continued movement of migration to England and other countries where their religion was tolerated. As French policy towards them varied, so the flow increased or slackened. Persecutions rose with the massacre of St. Bartholomew in 1572. Then a countermovement towards toleration achieved the Edict of Nantes in 1598. Richelieu's accession to power from 1616 renewed the trend towards persecution which, after a relaxation between 1629 and 1660, culminated in 1685 with Louis XIV's Revocation of the Edict of Nantes.

A return, no doubt imperfect, of aliens living in London in 1573 gives 1,763 members of the Dutch, French and Italian churches and 2,561 'strangers that do confess themselves that their coming hither was only to seek work for their living' in a total of 7,143;[1] while another return of 4,594 strangers in the city of London in that year gives 3,643 Dutch, 657 French, 233 Italians, 53 Spaniards and Portuguese and 37 Scots.[2] By 1621 the foreign artisans in the city were reckoned at 10,000.[3] In 1638–9 there were reported to be 830 foreigners in the city of London and 838 in Westminster. Of the former 202 were weavers, 228 French, 221 Dutch, 330 Walloons, 24 Germans, 11 Italians, 2 Poles and one each from Bohemia, Norway, Savoy, Venice, the Palatinate, Florence and Hamburg. The latter were mainly 'painters, picture-drawers, lymners, engravers, musicians and silver-workers', and comprised 641 French, 176 Dutch, 15 Italians and 6 Spaniards.[4] Because of guild restrictions foreign craftsmen who would use their skill could seldom settle in the City. They tended, therefore, to congregate in suburbs or privileged places, such as 'St. Martin's-le-Grand, Blackfriars, Clerkenwell, Turnmill Street, St. John's Street, High Holborn, the Dutchy of Lancaster without Temple Bar, St. Katherine's, Holywell, Norton Folgate, Shoreditch, Hoxton, Whitechapel, Wapping and Southwark'.[5] The settlement of skilled aliens had been encouraged elsewhere in the country also by government

---

[1] *Returns of Aliens dwelling in the City and Suburbs of London from the Reign of Henry VIII to that of James I*, ed. R. E. G. Kirk and Ernest F. Kirk, Huguenot Soc., pt. ii, 1902, p. 156.

[2] Ibid., pt. ii, 1902, p. 139.

[3] *Lists of Foreign Protestants and Aliens, Resident in England 1618–1688 from returns in the State Paper Office*, ed. Wm. Durrant Cooper, Camden Soc. lxxxii, 1862, p. iv.

[4] *State Papers, Domestic, Charles I*, 15 Mar. 1638–9, quoted by N. G. Brett-James, *The Growth of Stuart London*, 1935, p. 141.

[5] Brett-James, op. cit., p. 48, quoting Strype's ed. of *Stow's Survey of London*, 1720, v. 291.

with an eye to trade and to reviving the industrial life of towns decayed through guild restrictions which had driven clothmaking into the country.[1] Thus there were some 4,000 foreigners in Norwich in 1572, but their competition had been much resented by the native weavers and a plot there to expel them had been discovered and frustrated.[2]

Churches were assigned in several towns for the use of the French-speaking Protestant congregations—both French of France and Walloons, or French speakers from the Spanish Low Countries. The Walloon Church in Threadneedle Street was established in 1550, the chapel of God's House, Southampton in 1567, the chapel in the crypt of Canterbury Cathedral about the same date or a little earlier. There were other French congregations going back to the sixteenth century at Sandwich, Rye, Winchelsea, Norwich and Bristol.[2] In 1550 Walloon weavers settled at Glastonbury under the patronage of the Duke of Somerset,[3] and there were settlements at Maidstone, Colchester, Halstead, Harwich, Dover, Yarmouth and Lynn.[4] Sir Cornelius Vermuyden, the Dutchman who contracted in 1626 and later to drain the fens in Lincolnshire and Cambridgeshire, brought over a number of families from Holland to assist the work. They formed congregations at Sandtoft, Lincolnshire, and at Whittlesey and Thorney Abbey in the Isle of Ely. Some of the names recorded in their registers are Dutch but many French, so that a large proportion were no doubt Walloons. Among them were the ancestors of the de la Pryme, Vermoy and Tyssen families.[5]

The majority of the early French speaking refugees were Walloons from the Low Countries rather than French Huguenots.[6] A random sample of the better known families of early settlement tells the same story. Peter Baron,[7] who settled in England in 1576, and William Delaune,[8] who arrived before 1582, were Frenchmen. But Laurence des Bouveries (1568),[9] the ancestor of the earls of Radnor, Jean

---

[1] Lionel Williams, 'Alien Immigrants in Tudor England', *Huguenot Soc. Proc.* xix. 153–60.

[2] J. S. Burn, *History of French, Walloon, Dutch and other Protestant Refugees*, 1846.

[3] Burn, op. cit., p. 90; W. Cunningham, *Alien Immigrants to England*, 1897, p. 145, quoting Strype, *Life of Cranmer*, 1812 ed., i. 346, and references in *Huguenot Soc. Proc.* xix. 151 nn.

[4] Burn, op. cit., pp. 152–3, and references in *Huguenot Soc. Proc.* xix. 157 nn.

[5] Burn, op. cit., pp. 98–108.

[6] Cunningham, op. cit., p. 156; Camden Soc. lxxxii.

[7] *The Ancestor*, iii. 105.

[8] *D.N.B.*

[9] *Collins's Peerage*, ed. Brydges, 1812, v. 31.

Houblon (c. 1568),[1] the ancestor of the first governor of the Bank of England, Nicholas de la Forterie, or Fortrey (c. 1630),[2] Antoine Lefroy (c. 1589),[3] John Lethieullier (c. 1630)[4] and James Le Keux (before 1614),[5] all progenitors of notable refugee families, were Walloons from the Spanish Low Countries, while Peter Tryon or Trioen (1562),[6] ancestor of Lord Tryon, Henry Vandeput (before—perhaps much before—1610)[7] and William Courteen (1573)[8] were Flemings. Out of 38 foreign families entered at the Heralds' Visitation of London in 1633–4 only 3 were from France, while 8 were Walloon.[9]

The majority of the refugees of this period were joiners and weavers, but there were also goldsmiths, silversmiths, lapidaries, diamond cutters, jewellers, bucklemakers and others.[10] Among the trades they are said to have introduced were glass engraving, silk weaving, thread making and lace making.[11]

The Revocation of the Edict of Nantes by Louis XIV in 1685 and the ensuing persecution of the Huguenots precipitated an emigration from France of immense dimensions. A moderate estimate puts the total number of emigrants at 400,000.[12] Of these some 100,000 are thought to have settled in Holland, perhaps 40,000 in England, 40,000 in Ireland and America, some 25,000 in Switzerland, 75,000 in Germany, and the rest in northern Europe, at the Cape of Good Hope and elsewhere. In France the Huguenots had numbered about a tenth of the population and had centred mainly upon three regions, Languedoc and Guienne, Poitou and Saintonge, and Normandy and Picardy. From all three regions the majority of those who left by sea came to

---

[1] Lady Alice Archer Houblon, *The Houblon Family*, 1907.

[2] Harleian Soc., *Visitation of London 1633–4, Visitation of Kent 1663–8.*

[3] *Burke's Landed Gentry*, 1937, p. 2616.

[4] *Misc. Gen. et Her.* 5th ser. viii. 277.

[5] Ibid., N.S. iii. 349–52, and Reg. of St. Alphege, Canterbury.

[6] *The Ancestor*, ii. 175.            [7] Ibid., iv. 29; viii. 110.

[8] *Misc. Gen. et Her.* 2nd ser. ii. 158.

[9] *Lists of Foreign Protestants and Aliens Resident in England 1618–1688*, ed. Wm. Durrant Cooper, Camden Soc. 1862, pp. xi–xv, ex inf. T. W. King, York Herald.

[10] Joan Evans, 'Huguenot Goldsmiths in England and Ireland', *Huguenot Soc. Proc.* xiv. 499–500.

[11] Cunningham, op. cit., pp. 177–8, and references in *Huguenot Soc. Proc.* xix. 168 nn.

[12] A more recent estimate puts the total emigration from France between 1681 and 1720 at about 200,000 out of a total of French Huguenots of between 1½ and 2 million, some ten per cent. of the population. The same estimate puts those who came to England at between 40,000 and 50,000 and those who settled in London at about 15,000. Warren C. Scoville, *The Persecution of Huguenots and French Economic development 1680–1720*, 1960, pp. 7, 120–3.

England, though many passed on to Ireland[1] or America.[2] A recent analysis, correcting a former estimate, concludes that the refugees came to England in three main bursts, 1681–2, 1686–8 and 1698–1700, the great majority after 1685.[3]

Records of the distribution of relief to the refugees, most of whom arrived destitute, give a notion of their social composition. Of 15,500 helped in London and the seaports during the year 1687 all were artificers, labourers and the like except 143 ministers and 283 families of persons of quality, lawyers, physicians, merchants and tradesmen.[4] The Huguenots of the great nobility who came to England, Louis de Durfort, Marquis de Blanquefort and Earl of Feversham (d. 1709) and Henry de Massue, Marquis de Ruvigny and Earl of Galway (d. 1720), left no male posterity,[5] but families of the lesser nobility who did so include Montolieu de St. Hippolite,[6] Boileau de Castelnau[7] and Des Vignolles.[8]

The great majority of those distinguished Huguenot families whose hereditary share of talent has been thought so notable were of bourgeois stock and their refugee ancestors were ministers, lawyers, physicians, merchants, tradesmen and skilled craftsmen. Such names as Bosanquet, Chenevix, Courtauld, Fauquier, Garrick, Labouchere, Layard, Le Fanu, Lefevre, Majendie, Martineau, Maturin, Papillon, Romilly, Saurin, Teulon and Wyon, will if looked for in the biographical dictionaries give some notion of the range of achievement of their posterity. There were 65 members of the House of Commons of Huguenot descent between 1734 and 1832, 53 from England, 10 from Ireland and 2 from North America, including such names as Romilly, Lefroy, Fonnereau, Thellusson, Amyand, Champion de Crespigny, Langlois, Chamier and Latouche.[9] One expects to find outstanding genetic qualities in a stock whose scions were willing to endure so much for their opinions, and with the Huguenots the event confirms the expectation. On the whole these refugees seem in due course to have

---

[1] On the Huguenot settlements in Ireland see M. D. Falley, *Irish and Scotch-Irish Ancestral Research*, Evanston, Illinois, 1962, vol. i, pt. iii, chap. iv.

[2] R. L. Poole, *A History of the Huguenots of the Dispersion at the Recall of the Edict of Nantes*, 1880, pp. 166–9; Cunningham, op. cit., pp. 229–30.

[3] Robin D. Gwynn, 'The Arrival of Huguenot Refugees in Englnd 1680–1705', *Huguenot Soc. Proc.* xxi, 1969, pp. 366–73.

[4] Poole, op. cit., pp. 81–82.

[5] C. E. Lart, *Huguenot Pedigrees*, i, 1924, pp. vii, 77.

[6] *Huguenot Soc. Proc.* x, pt. i, p. 156.   [7] Lart, op. cit. ii, 1928, pp. 10–17.

[8] Ibid. 94–99.

[9] Gerrit P. Judd IV, *Members of Parliament 1734–1832*, Yale, 1955, pp. 17–18, 81.

taken their places in much the same stations in life as they came from. But like such upheavals as the Norman Conquest, the Black Death and the Industrial Revolution this migration must in itself have made the fortunes of some and ruined others.

Most of the poorer refugees who came to England were craftsmen, many of them possessing skills rare or unknown here. Partly perhaps because of the intricacy and supposed insecurity of the English system of land tenure the farmers and farm labourers preferred Germany, such emptier parts of Holland as Friesland and Zeeland, and America as places of refuge.[1] Some of the refugees doubtless settled where chance landed them, but some gathered round their leaders, such as Ruvigny first at Greenwich, then in and about Southampton, while others were drawn to the existing Walloon settlements and to places where they could pursue the crafts and manufactures in which they were skilled. In London there were two main colonies of Huguenot craftsmen, that of the silkweavers in Spitalfields and that of the highly skilled craftsmen, whose market was the Court, gold and silversmiths, jewellers, engravers, clock and watchmakers and tapestry weavers, in Soho. There seem to have been some 3,450 French in a total population of 8,133 in the parish of St. Anne, Soho, in 1711 and in 1718 the parish scavengers could speak no English. In the middle eighteenth century there was much poverty and distress among the Spitalfields weavers. In the second half of the century Anglicization took place but as late as 1840 French had recently been used in a Huguenot chapel there.[2] A few silk weavers and many French names were still to be found in Spitalfields and adjoining Bethnal Green in the twentieth century. In 1914 there were still forty six workshops in which the leading figure was George Dorée (d. 1916), 'a superlatively skilled weaver of velvet'. By 1931 only eleven elderly weavers remained.[3]

The Huguenots also introduced the making of sail cloth and of plate glass.[4] The paper mills established by Henry de Portal at Laverstoke on the Test are still preeminent and still supply the paper for the Bank of England notes.[5] In the goldsmith's and silversmith's craft

[1] Poole, op. cit., pp. 94–95.

[2] Francis H. W. Sheppard, 'The Huguenots in Spitalfields and Soho', *Huguenot Soc. Proc.* xxi, 1969, for 1968, pp. 355–65.

[3] Samuel Smiles, *The Huguenots*, 1867, pp. 412–23; Sir Frank Warner, *The Silk Industry of the United Kingdom*; N. G. Brett-James, *The Growth of Stuart London*, 1935, pp. 417, 489–90; C. M. Weekley, 'The Spitalfields Silkweavers', *Huguenot Soc. Proc.* xviii, 1952, pp. 284–91.

[4] Poole, p. 93: Cunningham, pp. 239, 243; *Victoria County History, Suffolk*, ii. 271.

[5] Smiles, pp. 333–61.

outstanding achievement is attested by such names as Paul de Lamerie (d. 1751), David Willaume (d. *c*. 1726), Simon Pantin (d. 1728), Augustin Courtauld (d. 1751), Pierre Platel (d. *c*. 1720), and many more[1] and in the art of clock-making by the Pantin and Amyot families and others.[2] John Dollond (d. 1761) and his son Peter (d. 1820) were pioneer opticians.[3]

The establishment of French churches in Bristol, Barnstaple, Bideford, Plymouth, Stonehouse, Dartmouth and Exeter indicates Huguenot settlements in these western towns.[4] There seems also to have been a church at Bedford.[5] The French church established at Southampton for the Walloon settlers before 1567 became a centre for many new refugees from France,[4] and Ruvigny's acquisition of a seat near by at Rookley added to its attraction for them. In and on the eastern side of the city of London twelve new French churches were established and in Westminster and to the west fifteen. Near London there were new French churches in Greenwich, Hammersmith, Chelsea, Islington and Hoxton, besides the older ones at Wandsworth (1575) and Marylebone (1656).[6]

The Huguenots were not separated by peculiarities of doctrine or way of life from their English neighbours once the barriers of language and unfamiliarity had died away. Therefore, though for two or three generations they remained a community within a community, much intermarried among themselves, thereafter they melted into the English background save perhaps in Spitalfields, where (as at Portarlington in Ireland) a homogeneous French population kept its separateness a little longer. Strangers in a strange land even though of different origins may be closer to each other than to the natives. This (as well as ties of trade) may help to explain such marriages as those of my German immigrant ancestor Melchior Wagner (naturalized 1709, d. 1764) to Mary Ann Teulon the daughter of a Huguenot refugee and of their son George (d. 1796) to the granddaughter of another.[7]

---

[1] Joan Evans, 'Huguenot Goldsmiths in England and Ireland', *Huguenot Soc. Proc.* xiv, 1933, pp. 496–544; Margaret Whinney and Oliver Millar, *English Art, 1625–1714*, 1957, p. 231.

[2] Britten, *Old Clocks and Watches and their Makers*; R. Noel Hill, 'Huguenot Clock and Watch Makers', *The Connoisseur*, cxxi, 1948, pp. 26–30.

[3] *D.N.B.*      [4] Poole, op. cit., pp. 88–89.      [5] Cunningham, op. cit., p. 229.

[6] Poole, pp. 194–9; Smiles, op. cit., pp. 466–95; Burn, op. cit.; Brett-James, op. cit., pp. 488–9.

[7] *Burke's Landed Gentry*, 1952, p. 2608; Pedigrees of Teulon and Godde by Henry Wagner, *Misc. Gen. et Her.* 4th ser. ii. 202, and N.S. iii, 221; A. R. Wagner, 'The Wagners of Brighton and their connections', *Sussex Arch. Coll.*, vol. 97; A. R. Wagner, 'The Teulon Ancestry in France', *Huguenot Soc. Proc.*, 1971.

French and other foreign surnames have sometimes been assimilated *ad oculum*, sometimes *ad aurem* and sometimes *ad sensum*.[1] One or two instances (and one needs more) have suggested to me that in the higher classes the spelling tended to be kept but the pronunciation assimilated, while in the lower ranks an approximation to the French pronunciation might be kept while the spelling was changed. Thus Lethieullier is pronounced Letholeér, Ligonier Ligonéer, Lefevre Lefeéver, and so forth, while Chapuis became Shoppee, Pertuis Pertwee and Poutrain Colte.

Though they have ceased to be a separate community the English descendants of the Huguenots retain a measure of corporate consciousness. This appears in their support of an active Huguenot Society and is fostered by their administration of charities founded by their ancestors such as the French Hospital (or almshouse) of La Providence and the French churches of London and Norwich.

## 5. THE JEWS

It is said that William the Conqueror brought Jews to London from Normandy, where there was then a Jewish community of some standing at Rouen.[2] Henry I gave some or all the English Jews a charter of protection and in the course of the twelfth century their numbers were much increased by immigration, mainly perhaps from France and Germany. Jewries were established in many towns, the largest in such centres of commerce as London, Norwich, Lincoln, Canterbury, Northampton, Gloucester, York and Bristol. The activity of the Jews was confined to commerce and especially finance. The practice of usury, forbidden to Christians by the Church but permitted to them, contributed to their unpopularity and periodically they were subjected to persecution and extortionate taxation.

The Jews were expelled from England by Edward I in 1290, when it is estimated that their number did not exceed 3,000, and their only descendants left here must have been the offspring of Jews converted to Christianity. The Domus Conversorum, a royal foundation for Jewish converts, had been established in 1213 and thereafter proselytization was regularly carried on. In 1290 the Domus Conversorum contained

---

[1] Maximilian Colte, the sculptor, was originally Poutrain (= colt). Dubois became Wood.

[2] This and the following account is drawn largely from Cecil Roth, *A History of the Jews in England*, 1941; Michael Adler, *The Jews of Mediaeval England*, 1937.

nearly one hundred persons. I know of no proved descent of an English family from mediaeval English Jews, but Mr. Walter Goodwin Davis has suggested not implausibly that John Isaac (d. *c.* 1419) the first known ancestor of the Isaac family of Patrixbourne, Kent, may have descended and have derived his surname from a thirteenth century Jew named Isaac of the Canterbury Jewry.[1]

Among continental Jews the Clerli family of Venice had a tradition of descent from English Jewish exiles,[2] while English Jews certainly settled in Paris and Savoy and the surnames Inglis borne by Spanish Jews and Inglesi by Jews in the island of Gozzo are evidence of such descent.[3]

Much notoriety attended the case of the unhappy deacon who in 1222 was led by his Hebrew studies to adopt Judaism and marry a Jewess, for which he was burned, and that of Robert of Reading, a Dominican friar, who did the same.[4] Less has been heard of the cases of Peter de Frowick, goldsmith of London, who was said to have adopted Judaism in 1254, and of his cousin Henry de Frowick (d. 1286) later Sheriff of London, who was said to have taken the same step in 1267. Such action involved severe penalties, including forfeiture of property, and it is clear from the later careers of the two Frowicks that they in due course recanted. Henry de Frowick had been one of fifty citizens of London appointed protectors of the Jews by the king in 1266 and his association with them must have been a factor in his apostasy.[5]

For most of the period between 1290 and the readmission of the Jews to England by Cromwell there was no continuing Jewish community in England,[6] though individual Jews from time to time entered the country. Under Elizabeth I more than one were patronized at court and the arms and pedigree of Dunstan Añes (d. 1594) of Crutched Friars, 'Purveyor and Merchant for the Queen's Majesty's Groceries', were entered at the Heralds' Visitation of London.[7] In the first half of the seventeenth century, however, an infiltration into London on a small scale of Jews from Spain and Portugal had taken place and what

[1] W. G. Davis, *The Ancestry of Mary Isaac*, Portland, Maine, 1955, pp. 3–5.

[2] C. Roth, *History of the Jews in Venice*, p. 168.

[3] C. Roth, *A History of the Jews in England*, p. 87.

[4] Ibid., pp. 41, 83.

[5] W. G. Davis, *The Ancestry of Mary Isaac*, 1955, pp. 205, 207. Peter was said to have 'abandoned the Christian faith', Henry to have 'apostatized'.

[6] For the shortlived London Jewish community under Elizabeth I, see Lucien Wolf, 'Jews in Elizabethan England', *Trans. Jewish Hist. Soc.* xi. 1–91.

[7] Ibid., pp. 12–18.

Cromwell did was to legalize its existence. The persecution of the Jews in Spain, which had grown steadily more severe since the late fourteenth century, had caused many to conceal their Judaism under a mask of Christianity. Many of these crypto-Jews or Marranos had left Spain for Holland, Portugal, Italy and the West Indies, and the community of Spanish Jews or Sephardim which now became established in London was drawn from all these quarters.

Among the notable families of the English Sephardim were those of Mendes, Mendes da Costa, Lousada, Nunes, Gomez Serra, Lopes, Pereira, Franco, Ricardo, Lindo and Mocatta, Spanish surnames adopted in Spain by the ancestors of these families. The financial skill of many of their members made them immensely rich. Some of them became Christians and others while remaining Jews themselves had their children brought up as Christians. Their fellow Jews sometimes suspected interested motives in such cases, not least when the secession was a gateway to political or social advancement.[1]

The great financier Sampson Gideon (d. 1762), the confidant of Walpole, resigned his membership of the Bevis Marks synagogue in 1754. His son and namesake (d. 1824) was brought up as a Christian and in 1759 by his father's influence was made a baronet when only thirteen years old, as a preliminary to entering Eton in 1761. In 1766 he married the daughter of Sir John Eardley Wilmot. In 1789 he took the surname of Eardley in lieu of Gideon and two months later, on Pitt's recommendation, was created Baron Eardley of Spalding in the peerage of Ireland. Of his three daughters one married a peer and one a baronet and their descendants are numerous. But when the elder Sampson Gideon died in 1762 it was found that he had left £1,000 to the synagogue on condition that he might be buried in its burial ground at Mile End.[2]

Others of the Sephardim such as Isaac D'Israeli (d. 1848) and David Ricardo (d. 1823) seceded from conviction or because they found the rigidities of Jewish life irksome. The descendants of such seceders have intermarried with the peerage and gentry and have been absorbed into their new environment.

Perhaps the most exotic of the eighteenth century English Sephardim was the one 'Court Jew' who settled here, Moses Lopes Pereira alias Diego de Aguilar, Baron of the Holy Roman Empire (d. 1759). The Court Jews were members of their race specially privileged and protected

[1] Cf. James Picciotto, *Sketches of Anglo-Jewish History*, 1875, pp. 62, 303–5.
[2] Ibid., pp. 61–63; *Complete Peerage*, v. 1–2.

at the Austrian and at German courts for the sake of their economic usefulness—so long as it lasted—while other Jews were persecuted or proscribed. Perhaps the best known of these Court Jews was Joseph Süss Oppenheimer ('Jew Süss', d. 1738), minister of the Duke of Württemberg. The parentage and pedigree of Moses Lopes Pereira have not been established, but he was born about 1700 or a little earlier, presumably in Spain or Portugal, of a Marrano (crypto-Jewish) family, and in 1722 came from Lisbon to London and passed thence by way of Italy to Vienna.

There he rose into great favour with the Emperor Charles VI (d. 1740) and later with the Empress Maria Theresa (d. 1780). He was created a baron in 1726. His financial operations were on a great scale. He lent the empress 300,000 florins for the building of the palace of Schönbrunn. He was granted the monopoly of the sale of tobacco in Austria and Bohemia and was permitted to establish in Vienna a community of Jews who in later years made him a figure of romance and a hero of legend.

According to one such tale his father had been burned by the Spanish Inquisition and he himself, taken in infancy from his mother, had been brought up a Catholic and in time had become an officer of the Inquisition in Madrid. To him late at night comes secretly a suppliant who proves to be his mother, to tell him that his sister—brought up in Judaism—has been condemned by the Inquisition and to beg his help. He learns that it is too late since his sister has already died under the torture. In revulsion he abandons Christianity and leaves Spain for Austria. Another and incompatible legend made him a childhood companion of Maria Theresa.

In 1749, for reasons unknown but probably connected with threats of persecution, he left Vienna and settled in London with his family at Alderman's Walk, Bishopsgate.[1] His sons were naturalized in 1756 and several of his sixteen children left descendants. His son Ephraim (d. 1802) was the eccentric miser of 'Starvation Farm', Islington, who through his daughter Georgina Isabella, wife of Admiral the Honourable Keith Stewart, has many descendants.[2] From Benjamin d'Aguilar, a younger son of Baron Diego, descends Lord Hunt, leader of the

---

[1] *Allgemeine Zeitung des Judenthums*, 1854, pp. 630–61; Max Grunwald, *Samuel Oppenheimer und sein Kreis*, 1913, pp. 295–300; N. M. Gelber, 'Contributions a l'histoire des Juifs Espagnols à Vienne', *Revue des études juives*, 1937, pp. 115–21; Selma Stern, *The Court Jew*, p. 160; and information kindly given by the author, Dr. Selma Stern-Taeubler.

[2] W. Thornbury, *Old and New London*, ii. 266; *Scots Peerage*, iv. 166.

British Mount Everest expedition;[1] while his daughter Leah (d. 1808), wife of Raphael Franco, was ancestress of Lord Ludlow of Heywood and Lord Roborough.

The ancestry of some of the English Sephardic families can be carried back into the early seventeenth or the sixteenth century by means of such records as those of the Amsterdam synagogue and by the records of the Spanish and Portuguese Inquisition. In England their pedigrees are well established by the synagogue records.[2]

Such civil disabilities as still affected the Jews in England were removed between 1830 and 1858 when they were admitted to Parliament. The objections in some quarters to treating them upon a social equality were, however, considerable, as witness Peacock's reference[3] to the knighthood conferred upon the later venerated Sir Moses Montefiore in 1838. The first professing Jew to be made a peer was Nathan Mayer Rothschild, created Lord Rothschild in 1885.

When the atmosphere could be so unfriendly it is not surprising that Jews who wished to mix in English society, especially Christian converts and those with conspicuously Jewish names, should often change their surnames for English ones. Thus in 1825 Francis Cohen became Francis Palgrave, assuming by royal licence the name and arms of his wife's mother's family.[4] In 1868 five of the family of Moses assumed by deed poll the name of Beddington.[5] A name might suffer more than one such change. 'The Hebrew Zevi (a stag) would be teutonised into Hirsch or Hirschel, then anglicised into Hart, only to emerge finally as Harris.'[6] Mordecai would become Marcus and Marcus Marks or Marx. Other changes were those of Montague Samuel (b. 1832), Lord Swaythling's ancestor, to Samuel Montagu, of Moses to Merton, Levy to Russell and Abraham to Braham.[7]

The Ashkenazim, or German and eastern European Jews, were poorer and were thought to be of less distinguished lineage than the Sephardim, but though the Sephardim reached England first it was not long before the Ashkenazim surpassed them in numbers. In 1677 there were only two Ashkenazim among the fifty Jews in the first London

[1] See Crookshank of Drumhalry, *Burke's Landed Gentry*, 1952.

[2] Lucien Wolf, *Jews in the Canary Islands*, 1926, and information from Mr. Wilfrid S. Samuel.

[3] Thomas Love Peacock, *Gryll Grange*, 1861, p. 156.

[4] *Anglo-Jewish Notabilities*, Jewish Hist. Soc. 1949, p. 112.

[5] W. P. W. Phillimore, *An Index to Changes of Name*, 1905, p. 22.

[6] Wilfrid S. Samuel, 'Sources of Anglo-Jewish Genealogy', *The Genealogists' Magazine*, vi. 146–59.

[7] Paul H. Emden, *Jews of Britain*, 1943, pp. 229, 527, 508, 504.

directory.[1] By 1734, when the total number of Jews in England was estimated at 6,000, perhaps half were Ashkenazim. In the 1770's, says Picciotto,[2] 'there were perhaps 150 to 200 families that might be considered rich, about two thirds' of them Sephardim; about as many again in small retail trade; and 'a floating mass, at least five times as numerous as the other two classes together, consisting of hucksters, hawkers, journeymen, and others, either verging on pauperism or steeped hopelessly in its abyss'. These poor Jews were almost all Ashkenazim, of whom a vast influx came from Germany in the second half of the eighteenth century. By 1882 the Sephardic Jews of London were estimated at about 3,500 and the Ashkenazic at about 15,000, half the latter being immigrants or descendants of immigrants who came after 1800. Among the minority of rich Ashkenazim were the Goldsmids[3] who came to England from Hamburg early in the eighteenth century, the Rothschilds who came from Frankfort in 1798, and the Cohens[4] who came from Amsterdam about the same time.

The first London synagogues after the readmission were on the east side of the city and a large proportion of the London Jews lived near them. Thence they expanded to the area just outside the city to the east, in and about Goodman's Fields and Houndsditch. The movement to north and north west London came much later in the second half of the nineteenth century.

### 6. THE GYPSIES

Down to 1782 the world was 'at a loss concerning the original of gypsies'. The name means Egyptian but 'that they are no Egyptians, Bellonius maketh evident: who met great droves of Gypsies in Egypt, about Grand Cairo, Metaerea, and the villages on the banks of Nilus, who notwithstanding were accounted strangers unto that nation, and wanderers from foreign parts, even as they are esteemed with us'.[5]

The earliest beliefs as to the origin of this race are embodied in the names bestowed upon them by the *gajé* or gentiles, who harboured them so much against their will. Like some strange form of pestilence the evil has been attributed by every people to its neighbours. In Greece, Spain and England

[1] This and much of the following information is from V. D. Lipman, *Social History of the Jews in England 1850–1950*, 1954. M. D. George, *London Life in the XVIIIth Century*, 1930, pp. 125–32, discusses Jewish immigration.

[2] Op. cit., p. 152.

[3] *Burke's Landed Gentry*, 1914; Emden, op. cit., pp. 83–149.

[4] *Burke's Peerage*, 1956; Emden, op. cit., pp. 174–84.

[5] Sir Thomas Browne, *Pseudodoxia Epidemica: Enquiries into Vulgar and Common Errors*, 1646, bk. vi, chap. xiii, *Works*, ed. S. Wilkin, 1835, iii. 287–9.

they were termed Egyptians; in Switzerland and Germany Saracens: in South Germany and the Netherlands Heiden or heathens; in North Germany, Scandinavia and Finland Tatars; in France and Switzerland Bohemians.[1]

Since 1782, however, study of their language has thrown light on the question and it is now thought that the gypsies are wandering tribes of low caste Indian origin. They had reached Greece by about 1050 and were in western Europe in small numbers early in the fifteenth century. Later in the century they were much more numerous there, coming in from the Balkans and Hungary.[2]

The first mention of them in England yet noted belongs to the year 1514 when a witness at an inquest referred to an Egyptian woman who had been lodging at Lambeth but had gone overseas a month before and who could tell marvellous things by looking into one's hand.[3] About 1519 some 'Gypsions' were entertained by the Earl of Surrey at Tendring Hall, Suffolk.[4] In 1530, however, Parliament began to legislate against them with great severity. Those who did not leave the country were to be imprisoned and lose their goods. An Act of 1554 replaced this by the death penalty for those who would not give up their wandering life.[5] The legislators of the time were alarmed by the growth of vagrancy[6] and seem to have feared that English vagrants would grow by infection from the gypsies, for it is clear that a certain number had joined them and adopted their speech, dress and way of life.

Their strangeness fascinated both high and low. Thomas Harman wrote in 1566 of 'the wretched, wily, wandering vagabonds calling and naming themselves Egyptians ... feeding the rude common people, wholly addicted and given to novelties, toys, and new inventions; delighting them with the strangeness of the attire of their heads, and practising palmistry to such as would know their fortunes'.[7] The lady in the Scottish ballad—who by the late eighteenth century was identified

[1] Dr. John Sampson, 'On the Origin and Early Migrations of the Gypsies', *Journ. of the Gypsy Lore Soc.* 3rd ser. ii, 1923, pp. 156–69.

[2] Sampson, op. cit.; *Chamber's Encyclopaedia*, 1950, art. 'Gypsies' by F. A. Groome and L. F. Newman.

[3] Henry T. Crofton, 'Early Annals of the Gypsies in England', *Journ. Gypsy Lore Soc.* i, 1888–9, pp. 5–24, quoting *A Dyalog of Sir Thomas More, Knight*, bk. iii, chap. xv.

[4] Crofton, op. cit., p. 7, quoting *Works of Henry Howard, Earl of Surrey*, ed. Nott, 1815, i, app., p. 5.

[5] A. V. Judges, *The Elizabethan Underworld*, 1930, p. xxv.

[6] See p. 179.   [7] Judges, op. cit., p. 64.

as Jean, Countess of Cassillis (d. 1642)[1]—had the glamour cast
o'er her by the gypsies' sweet singing at her lord's gate.

> Yestreen I lay in a well-made bed,
>  And my good lord beside me;
> This night I'll ly in a tenant's barn,
>  Whatever shall betide me.
>
> .　　.　　.　　.　　.
>
> I'll go to bed to my Johnny Faa,
>  I'll go to bed to my deary;
> For I vow and I swear, by what past yestreen,
>  That my lord shall nae mair come near me.[2]

Faa or Faw or Fall was a great name among the gypsies on both
sides of the Scottish border. In 1540 John Faw, 'lord and earl of Little
Egypt', obtained a writ under the privy seal of James V of Scotland con-
firming his authority over certain rebels of his own gypsy company.[3]
In 1750 Sir John Anstruther, 2nd baronet, of Anstruther and Elie,
married Janet, daughter of James Fall, merchant of Dunbar and some
time Provost and Member of Parliament for that town. At a contested
election she was saluted by a rabble crowd with the song of *The Gypsy
Laddie*, in evident allusion to her supposed gypsy descent.[4] There
was precedent for such recognition of gypsy chieftains both in Scotland[5]
and on the Continent,[6] but it never became English practice. England
nevertheless has had its gypsy kings and queens—recognized by their
own people, though not by authority.

Common surnames among the English gypsies are Boswell, Buck-
land, Cooper, Gray, Herne, Lee, Lovell, Loveridge, Marshall and
Smith. Some of these are probably translations of Romany words, as
Smith is of Petulengro. Others may be Anglicizations and others
borrowed for forgotten reasons from their English owners. Many gypsy

---

[1] Charles Faa Blythe (d. 1902), King of the Gypsies of Yetholm, 'claimed descent from
the Lord and Earl of Little Egypt', who eloped with the Countess of Cassillis, *Journ.
Gypsy Lore Soc.* 3rd ser. ii. 370–1.

[2] *English and Scottish Popular Ballads*, ed. from the collection of F. J. Child, 1904,
p. 483; *Complete Peerage*, iii. 76; David MacRitchie, *Scottish Gypsies under the Stewarts*,
1894, pp. 109–10.

[3] MacRitchie, op. cit., pp. 37–38; Mr. T. W. Thompson has collected evidence tending
to show that the modern East Anglian gypsy families of Young and Gibson are immigrant
descendants of the Border Faws; *Journ. Gypsy Lore Soc.* 3rd ser. xxiv. 44–46, and 97–117;
xxv. 39–54.

[4] G. E. C., *Complete Peerage*, vol. iv, 1904, p. 387, quoting Walter Simson, *History of
the Gypsies*; *The Scottish Antiquary*, vol. xvi, pp. 127–32.

[5] *Journ. Gypsy Lore Soc.* 3rd ser. xxi. 29.

[6] David MacRitchie, 'Gypsy Nobles', ibid. n.s. i, 1907–8, pp. 98–111.

Christian names have a fanciful character yet prove on enquiry to be imaginative developments from familiar sources. Thus Sinfai may derive from Cynthia and Farthingando is gypsy for Ferdinando.[1] The references to gypsies in written records are for the most part to their indictment at quarter sessions or in other courts for vagrancy, theft, or the like,[2] but now and then from the sixteenth century on an entry in a parish register will record a gypsy baptism, marriage or burial. Kinship was, however, valued and for a certain length of time clearly remembered so that traditions recorded in the nineteenth and twentieth centuries carry back some of their pedigrees to the eighteenth.[3] It may be doubted whether any gypsy pedigree can be taken back farther than that of the Welsh gypsy family of Wood which Dr. John Sampson traced in many branches down to 1932 from Abraham Wood, who was buried at Llangelynin on 12 November 1799 aged about 100.[4] Mr. E. O. Winstedt suggested the possibility of a link between this Abraham and Bohemia the son of Abraham Wood 'as supposed King of the Gypsies', of Frome, Somerset, who was baptized at Selattyn, Shropshire, on 25 October 1715. It is now accepted, however, that he was not the same man. Earlier Gypsy Woods were indicted in London as vagrants in 1653.[5]

The mobility of the gypsies was compatible with fixed bases. On Gypsy Hill at Norwood in the parishes of Croydon and Lambeth, Surrey, there was a well known settlement of gypsies in the eighteenth and nineteenth centuries, and Pepys may well refer to its predecessor when he writes that on 11 August 1668 his 'wife and Mercer and Deb. went with Pelling to see the Gypsies at Lambeth and have their fortune told'. On 2 June 1687 'Robert Hern and Elizabeth Boswell, king and queen of the gypsies' who are thought to have belonged to this community, were married in the church of the adjoining parish of Camberwell.

Its best known member was Margaret Finch, 'Queen of the Gypsies at Norwood', who died in 1740 aged, it was said, 109 and is commemorated to this day there by an inn called the 'Gypsy Queen'.

[1] E. O. Winstedt, 'Notes on English Gypsy Christian Names', ibid. 3rd ser. i. 64–90; ii. 16–39.

[2] For further early references see E. O. Winstedt, 'Early British Gypsies', ibid. N.S. vii. 5–57.

[3] Cf. ibid. 3rd ser. ii, 1923, pp. 122–37.

[4] Ibid. 3rd ser. xi, 1932, pp. 56–71; xii, 1933, pp. 33–46 and 196–205; xiii, 1934, pp. 190–200. *The Dictionary of Welsh Biography down to 1940*, 1959, pp. 1091–2. This family included several notable harpists.

[5] *Journ. Gypsy Lore Soc.* 3rd ser. x, 1931, pp. 171–87.

Towards the end of the eighteenth century the community encountered trouble and, though gypsies are still heard of in the neighbourhood as late as the 1870's, most probably moved away soon after 1800. Mr. Winstedt suggested that the Welsh gypsy family of Lock was descended from the Boswells of Norwood.[1]

No basis probably exists for an estimate of the number of marriages or other unions between gypsies and the rest of the population, but it is probable that gorgios (as they call us) have not seldom married gypsy women and brought them home[2] while others have taken to the gypsy life since the time of the Scholar Gypsy, whose tale, told by Glanvill in 1661, caught Matthew Arnold's imagination.

There was [says Glanvill] very lately a lad in the *University* of *Oxford*, who being of very pregnant and ready parts, and yet wanting the encouragement of preferment; was by his poverty forc'd to leave his studies there, and to cast himself upon the wide world for a livelyhood. Now, his necessityes growing dayly on him, and wanting the help of friends to relieve him; he was at last forced to joyn himself to a company of *Vagabond Gypsies*, whom occasionly he met with, and to follow their trade for a maintenance.

The rest of the tale, not here to our purpose, may be seen in Glanvill, but it does not appear whether or not the scholar ever fulfilled his purpose of leaving the gypsies' company and telling the world what he had learned from them.[3]

### 7. THE BACKWASH OF EMPIRE

The years of the dissolution of the British Empire, since 1948, have seen a backwash of migration into England from some of the former countries of that Empire, notably India and the West Indies, a phenomenon noted by the historian of the mediaeval House of Lords. Little attention has, however, been paid to the far smaller, but still appreciable, earlier movements of the same kind, which might repay study. In the eighteenth and nineteenth centuries many Englishmen in India had children by Indian mothers,[4] of whom an unknown, but probably not inconsiderable, number settled in England and have left descendants.

    [1] Eric Otto Winstedt, 'The Norwood Gypsies and their vocabulary', ibid. N.S. iv, 1915–16, pp. 129–65.

    [2] The story that the grandmother of F. E. Smith was a gypsy is discounted by his son, the second Earl of Birkenhead, *F.E., The Life of F. E. Smith First Earl of Birkenhead*, 1960, p. 13.

    [3] Joseph Glanvill, *The Vanity of Dogmatizing*, 1661, pp. 196–8.

    [4] Gordon N. Ray, *Thackeray, The Uses of Adversity, 1811–1846*, 1955, pp. 49–50.

Anne, mother of William Makepeace Thackeray, the novelist, who married Richmond Thackeray in 1810, was referred to by Thackeray's daughter as 'my brown grandmother' and according to family tradition had some Asiatic blood. Her parents, John Harman Becher and Harriet Cowper, were married at St. John's, Calcutta, in 1786.[1]

In the same way planters in the West Indies and the southern American colonies had by negro women children and descendants some of whom came to England. On 13 October 1778 Robert Browning (1749–1833), the son of a Dorset Innkeeper, and grandson of the butler to Mr. Bankes of Corfe Castle, having by Lord Shaftesbury's influence obtained a clerkship in the Bank of England, married Margaret Tittle from St. Kitts in the West Indies, believed by his descendants to have been partly of negro blood. Their grandson was Robert Browning (1812–89) the poet. We are told that 'in colour, the poet's father was so dark that when, as a youth, he went out to his Creole mother's sugar-plantation in St. Kit's, the beadle of the Church ordered him to come away from the white folk among whom he was sitting, and take his place among the coloured people. It has been suggested that this colour business may have had something to do with Mr. Barrett's unjustifiable aversion to his daughter's marriage with the poet. Mr. B was a West-Indian estate owner.'[2]

Another case was that of Francis Barber, a negro slave boy brought to England from Jamaica in 1752 by Richard Bathurst, who by his will of 1754 left him his freedom. Barber seems by that time to have become the servant of Dr. Samuel Johnson, with whom he remained till Johnson's death in 1784. About 1776 he married a white wife and had children both white and black. Johnson left him an annuity and advised him to settle in Lichfield, which he did, dying there in 1801. His son Samuel Barber (1786–1828) became a Methodist and was servant to Gregory Hickman, a connection of Johnson's mother's family. Of his children Isaac Barber (1817–68), 'a man of colour', was a mould maker of Burslem, Staffordshire, and left descendants there employed in the pottery industry, including a hollow ware presser and a gilder on pottery ware. In 1908 they numbered some twenty. Enoch Barber, Isaac's brother, and his sister Martha, wife of John Sneyd, emigrated to America in 1850 and 1848 respectively.[3]

[1] Ibid., pp. 53–54.

[2] F. J. Furnivall, 'Robert Browning's Ancestors.' Read at the Seventy-second Meeting of the Browning Society, Friday, 28 Feb. 1890.

[3] A. L. Reade, *Johnsonian Gleanings, Part II, Francis Barber. The Doctor's Negro Servant*, 1912.

# VII

## SETTLERS

FROM strangers who came into England we pass to the settlers who left our shores to plant the English stock across the seas. Their migration is in part a phenomenon of world history with aspects and implications going far beyond our concern here. To embark on these would swamp this book. Nevertheless, as we examine those phases of the subject which concern us, we cannot but see that they are intertwined with general history and that each aspect can throw light on the other.

The genealogist asks where each colonist came from and went to, who his ancestors were and who were his descendants. But because migration has been a movement of groups not less than of individuals, the answer to such questions about an individual may have to be sought through the study of some group which he belonged to. Conversely the picture of the group is built up by study of those composing it. The well known or more easily traced individual histories go to make up our group picture and this in turn throws light on the more obscure individuals. Thus we know that in 1632 the ship *Lyon* sailed from London to Boston, Massachusetts, and that several of the families on board came from particular parishes in Essex and settled in Roxbury and Cambridge, Massachusetts.[1] Knowing this, the first place where we shall look for the origins of other passengers on the *Lyon* will be in these and neighbouring Essex parishes. In the same way we know that between the 1830's and the 1850's many cutlers from Sheffield settled at Bridgeport, Connecticut. Sheffield is accordingly the first place we shall search for the origin of any unidentified cutler who appears at Bridgeport in those years.[2]

In the following short account of what is known genealogically of the different migrations and their sources the successive settlements are taken in chronological order. The fullness of treatment differs greatly

[1] Charles Edward Banks, *The Planters of the Commonwealth 1620–1640*, 1930, pp. 99–103; p. 298 *infra*.
[2] p. 314.

not from any prejudice or preference but simply because of differences in what is known—at all events by me.

### I. IRELAND

Little is known or likely to be known in detail of the settlement of Englishmen in Ireland in the wake of the twelfth century Norman invaders. The chief evidence for their presence and distribution lies in the appearance of distinctively English names among those of Norman, Irish and Scandinavian origin. There are pitfalls to beware of here, however, for a Blake or a White in a thirteenth century Irish borough might be an Irishman who had Anglicized his name. Shortly before 1641 one of the great family of Blake of Galway declared and cited evidence in a petition that, though his ancestors had been four centuries in Ireland, none of them had married an Irishwoman. This would indicate that here at least an English name was to be taken at its face value, even if we did not in fact know already that the name of this family was at first Caddell, and Blake an alias or epithet, which finally supplanted it.[1] Conversely the names of men of English stock may appear in French or Latin form. Many of those who came with the twelfth century Normans were not English at all but Welsh and it is noteworthy that at the present day Walsh (i.e. the Welshman) is the fourth commonest surname in Ireland.[2]

Orpen thought that the towns which the Normans took over, enlarged, or founded, such as Dublin, Waterford, Cork, Limerick, Drogheda and Kilkenny, were inhabited in the thirteenth century largely by men of English rather than of Norman blood.[3] In the English pale of south eastern Ireland there were probably English families settled on the land also though in general the lords were Norman and the rest Irish. The clans of the Harolds and the Archbolds in the hilly country south of Dublin were at one time thought by Professor Curtis to be of English descent, but his later view is that they were Scandinavian in origin.[4]

In the fifteenth century the power of the English Crown in Ireland dwindled and there was a revival of Gaelic language and manners. Many priests, freeholders and labourers of English origin fled to

---

[1] William F. T. Butler, *Confiscation in Irish History*, 1917, p. 140; Edward MacLysaght, *Irish Families*, 1957, p. 281.  [2] Ibid.

[3] G. H. Orpen, *Ireland under the Normans*, iv, 1920, p. 270; see also Edmund Curtis, *A History of Mediaeval Ireland from 1110 to 1513*, 1923, pp. 211, 218.

[4] Op. cit., p. 196; 'The Clan System among English Settlers in Ireland', *Eng. Hist. Rev.* 1910.

England, while others who remained became Hibernicized[1] and the English pale was reduced to a narrow strip. Though the Tudors reasserted the claims of the English Crown this did not for some time lead to fresh colonization, though it doubtless brought to Ireland occasional English settlers such as Walter Cowley, the Duke of Wellington's ancestor, who went there as Solicitor General in 1537 and remained.[2] Attempts at the plantation of Englishmen on lands confiscated or otherwise acquired from their Irish owners began in the 1570's, but had little result until the late 1580's and early 1590's when Sir Walter Raleigh and others brought over a number of settlers from the West of England and planted them on the forfeited lands of the Earl of Desmond in Munster. Even then, by 1592 only 245 English families had settled there.[3] Among families whose settlement dates from this epoch are those of Browne, Earls of Kenmare (though the Irish connection goes back to the appointment of Sir Valentine Browne to be Auditor General of Ireland in 1555[4]); Loftus, Viscounts Loftus, descended from Adam Loftus (d. 1605) who went to Ireland in 1561 and became Archbishop of Armagh;[5] Pakenham, Earls of Longford, whose ancestor Edmund Pakenham served in Ireland with his cousin Sir Henry Sidney, then Lord Deputy (1578–89);[6] Boyle, Earls of Cork, descended from Richard Boyle of Preston by Faversham, Kent, who went to Ireland in 1588 and in 1620 was created Earl of Cork.[7] Edgeworth of Edgeworthstown, County Longford, descended from Edward Edgeworth, who was made Bishop of Down and Connor in 1593;[8] and the Spenser family descended from Edmund Spenser (d. 1599) the poet, whose male line continued till about 1790.[9] By 1641 a large number of the descendants of these Protestant intruders had become Catholics.[10]

The next phase of settlement was the plantation of Ulster in the years following 1609. Of an estimated total of about 8,000 settled by 1622 the majority were Lowland Scots. The city of London, however, took over County Derry and settled many Londoners there, while many Englishmen were among the settlers in the other Ulster counties. In 1606 whole families of the troublesome tribes of the Debateable

[1] Curtis, op. cit., pp. 324–5.
[2] Lodge's *The Peerage of Ireland*, ed. Mervyn Archdall, 1789, iii. 60.
[3] A. L. Rowse, *Sir Richard Grenville*, 1937, pp. 279, 276, and *The Expansion of Elizabethan England*, 1955, chap. iv.
[4] Lodge, op. cit., vii. 51 n.     [5] Ibid., p. 246.     [6] Ibid., p. 371.
[7] *Complete Peerage*, iii. 419.     [8] *Burke's Landed Gentry of Ireland*, 1912, p. 204.
[9] Pedigree by W. H. Welply in *Notes & Queries*, 14th ser., vol. 6, 1932, pp. 257–9.
[10] William F. T. Butler, *Confiscation in Irish History*, 1917, pp. 30, 139.

Land on the Cumbrian border between England and Scotland were transported to Roscommon, notably 124 Grahams, with Armstrongs, Elliots and Hetheringtons.[1] English settlement took place in other parts of Ireland at this time but on a small scale only.[2]

Cromwell's confiscations and settlements in the years following 1652 deprived the majority of Irish landowners of their lands and replaced them by Protestant Englishmen, army officers, merchants and others. These came to form a new landlord class. The English origin of many is known, but of many more remains obscure. The tendency of some later genealogists to link them without evidence to well known families of their names in England has to be watched for. Many of Cromwell's private soldiers who settled in Ireland sold their lands to their officers and others and many of their own descendants by Irish marriages are said to have become Catholic.[3] The displacement of Irish and Catholic landowners by English Protestants was confirmed and completed under William III.[4]

The Irish who were expelled from their lands at this time included a proportion of English origin, and doubtless some of these were among the estimated 34,000 Irishmen who took service on the Continent in Spain and other Catholic countries.[5]

## 2. THE GREAT EMIGRATION

Between 1607 and 1650 the white population of the English colonies on the North American continent and in the West Indies rose from nothing to something like 100,000 partly by migration and partly by natural increase.[6] Religious, economic and political discomforts and discontents combined with the pull of opportunity to promote this unprecedented exodus from England.[7] The Thirty Years War (1618–48), meantime, kept the powers of Europe from interference and left the way clear.

[1] *Calendar of State Papers, Ireland*, vol. iii, 1603–6, preface and p. 554.

[2] For the Plantation and Settlement Records of Ireland *c.* 1540–1703 see M. D. Falley, *Irish and Scotch–Irish Ancestral Research*, Evanston, Illinois, 1962, vol. i, pt. iii, chap. xiii.        [3] Butler, op. cit., p. 163.

[4] J. G. Simms, *The Williamite Confiscation in Ireland*, 1956.

[5] Butler, op. cit., p. 162.

[6] *The Cambridge History of the British Empire*, i, 1929, pp. 266–7; Franklin B. Dexter, 'Estimates of Population in the American colonies', *Proc. American Antiq. Soc.*, N.S. v. 1887, pp. 22–50.

[7] *Camb. Hist. Brit. Emp.* i. 136–8. On settlement in America generally, from the Continent as well as England, see Marcus Lee Hansen, *The Atlantic Migration 1607–1680 A History of the Continuing Settlement of the United States*, 1940.

The chief settlements of the period were in Virginia, Bermuda, St. Christopher and its neighbours, Barbados, New England and Maryland. There were differences in the methods and sources of recruitment of the colonists between one colony and another but perhaps neither so great nor so simple as they have sometimes in the past been thought. The old picture of the northern colonies populated by Puritans from East Anglia and the southern by Royalists from the West Country is out of date. But to get at the truth is difficult and comparison between one colony and another is not made easier by the variations in the nature and extent of the researches so far made into the origins of the different settlements.

We have, for instance, an unequalled knowledge of the personal antecedents of the New England settlers owing to the labours of New England genealogists in the past century. These genealogists have had the advantage of a wealthy, intelligent and keenly interested clientèle. Indeed few problems of genealogy anywhere have had closer and more extensive study than those of the New England settlers' origins. Of Virginian origins we still know less in spite of valuable research in recent years, while our knowledge of the West Indian settlers is patchy. For Maryland our knowledge of the settlers' origins is pretty well confined to the leading group.

Despite the gaps in our knowledge, however, it is clear that in James Truslow Adams' words 'fourteen emigrants out of every fifteen . . . although willing to leave their homes and all they had held dear, yet shunned active participation in the Bible Commonwealths of New England', so that in 1640 'approximately only sixteen thousand Englishmen had taken their way to the Puritan colonies, as against forty-six thousand to the others', not including Barbuda, St. Croix, Antigua, Montserrat and other settlements for which we have no figures, nor Ireland, whither thousands went for reasons probably similar to those which took others to the New World. Furthermore 'not more than one in five of the adult males who went even to Massachusetts was sufficiently in sympathy with the religious ideas there prevalent to become a church member, though disfranchised for not doing so', so that Puritans in the sense of church members numbered only about 4,000 out of 65,000. 'Although young John Winthrop might write of his brother that it "would be the ruine of his soule to live among such company" as formed the colony of Barbadoes in 1629, nevertheless, the population of that island had risen to nearly nineteen thousand in another decade, whereas that of Massachusetts had reached only fourteen thousand.' Adams' conclusion is that most of the settlers came 'for the simple reason that they wanted to better their condition' and to own land and that this last motive gave the Puritan colonies their chief attraction, for they, as we shall see, 'were the only ones in which land could be owned in fee simple, without quit-rent or lord, and in which it was freely given to settlers'.[1]

The direction of those early settlements which achieved success was mainly due to certain small and closely linked groups of enthusiasts—most of them in London but some in Bristol and the West Country. There were personal and other links between the Elizabethan schemes for English settlement in Ireland and the projects for colonies in America. The West Country group in which Sir Humphrey Gilbert (d. 1583), Sir Walter Raleigh (d. 1618) and Sir Richard Grenville (d. 1591) had been the leaders, was prominent in both. The names of the participants in Raleigh's abortive Roanoke colony of 1585 show both West Country elements and links with his Irish ventures.[2] Terms like 'native', 'colony', 'plantation', and 'planting' were employed in connection with Ireland fifty years before any English settlement in America was thought of.[3] Links between Irish and American colonization continued in the seventeenth century. The transfer of the place name Baltimore from County Longford to Maryland recalls the interest of George Calvert, Lord Baltimore (d. 1632), in both.[4]

Raleigh's Virginia colony of 1585 at Roanoke came to nothing and the lasting settlement of 1607 was made under the auspices of the Virginia Company incorporated in 1606. The membership of this company and its successor of 1609 interlocked with that of other bodies active in the city of London upon overseas enterprise. Among these were the old Merchant Adventurers' Company, the Russia Company (1555), the Levant Company (1581) and the East India Company (1600), nor should links with the membership of the ancient Grocers' Company be overlooked. The central figure was Sir Thomas Smythe (d. 1625), a great city merchant and descended through the female line from a succession of city magnates running back to Robert Chichele (d. 1440), Mayor of London in 1411–12 and 1421–2.[5] When the Somers Island

---

[1] James Truslow Adams, *The Founding of New England*, 1921, pp. 119–22.

[2] *The Roanoke Voyages 1584–1590*, ed. D. B. Quinn, Hakluyt Soc. 1955, i. 194–7; A. L. Rowse, *The Elizabethans and America*, 1959, p. 49.

[3] *Cambr. Hist. Brit. Emp.* 1929, p. 57; cf. A. L. Rowse, *The Expansion of Elizabethan England*, 1955, p. 137.

[4] Charles M. Andrews, *The Colonial Period of American History*, 1936, p. 278.

[5] p. 160; *Stemmata Chicheleana*, p. 1; Archdall's *Lodge's Peerage of Ireland*, iv. 274; Rowse, op. cit.

(or Bermuda) Company was formed to take over Bermuda from the Virginia Company in 1615, he became its first governor. Other prominent figures were Sir Edwin Sandys (d. 1629), whose father and namesake had been Archbishop of York, and Robert Rich, Earl of Warwick (d. 1658), a Puritan and opponent of the policies of Charles I, and the chief link between the Puritan settlements in New England and the colonies of more commercial inspiration elsewhere.

These promoters of colonies found some of their colonists among their relations, friends and neighbours. This tendency was no less marked where the Crown granted lands for a colony not to a company but to an individual proprietor, as Maine was granted in 1639 to Sir Ferdinando Gorges and Maryland in 1632 to Cecil Calvert, Lord Baltimore. Gorges was the heir of the West Country colonizing tradition of Grenville and Raleigh and the patron of the Bristol and Plymouth fishing interests. Many of the Maine settlers therefore were fishermen from Devon. Newfoundland was a fishing ground for the West Country fishermen and they in time made settlements there, though these were probably not continuous till 1617 or later.[1] Lord Baltimore was a Roman Catholic and in his colony, alone in the British Empire, religious toleration which included them existed. His colonists therefore included many Roman Catholics.

The fact that family links can be traced between several of these promoters of colonization is of interest and may hold significance, if only as showing that they belonged to the same social group. Thus Sir Thomas Smythe's son married Warwick's sister and Lady Baltimore was Warwick's second cousin. First cousins of Warwick's mother were Lord De la Warr, the Governor of Virginia (1617–19), his brother John who settled and left descendants there, and his sister Elizabeth Pelham, whose sons went to New England. Her second cousin was Winthrop's friend the Earl of Lincoln, two of whose daughters Susan and Arbella, went to New England in Winthrop's fleet with their husbands John Humphreys (d. 1661), Deputy Governor of Massachusetts and Isaac Johnson, while a third daughter married the son of Sir Ferdinando Gorges.[2] Sir William Gorges, great uncle to Sir Ferdinando, had married Winifred Budockside, first cousin of Sir Walter Raleigh.[3]

With the background which the settlements shared thus outlined they must now be looked at individually in more detail.

[1] *Camb. Hist. Brit. Emp.* i. 181.          [2] See Table IV.
[3] Rowse, op. cit., chap. v.

### 3. VIRGINIA

The Permanent settlement of Virginia begins with the Virginia Company's Expedition which established Jamestown in 1607 on the initiative of Sir Thomas Smythe.[1] To encourage settlement the company granted 100 acres of land before 1616 and 50 acres after that date to every person coming into the colony or to the person who payed the colonist's passage and these rights could be bought and sold.[2] In 1618 the four cities of Virginia, Charles, Henrico, James and Kecoughtan, were assigned 3,000 acres each and on this land were settled the colonists transported thither at the company's expense. About the same date a policy was adopted of granting large areas, called particular plantations, to syndicates in England, who undertook their settlement.

A high proportion of the names of the early settlers are known from the records of the Land Office at Richmond, Virginia. A printed index of those granted land between 1623 and 1666 numbers nearly 25,000,[3] and Professor Wertenbaker estimates that the names of three quarters of all those who came to the colony in its first century are known.[4] The English origins of only a small proportion have, however, been identified and the task of working out such patterns of source and destination of settlement as have been ascertained for New England still remains to be undertaken. One might for example hope to find geographical or other links between the members of the syndicate and the settlers on their particular plantations, and between the members of the company and some of their settlers. George Andrews Moriarty (1882–1968) told me that there were, for example, very many settlers from Norfolk in the south eastern corner of Virginia in old Norfolk County, which he attributed to the Norfolk connections of Sir George Yeardley (d. 1627), Governor 1618–21, whose wife Temperance Flowerdew came from that county.[5] Mr. Peter Laslett has noted an important Kentish element, arising from the colonization and Virginia Company interests of City of London kinsmen of Essex and Kent gentry.[6] In

---

[1] p. 283 *supra*; Rowse, op. cit., p. 82.

[2] On the headright system see M. L. Hansen, *The Atlantic Migration*, pp. 29–30, 37, 44, in Virginia; p. 40 in Carolina; pp. 43–44 its abolition.

[3] George Cabell Greer, *Early Virginia Immigrants, 1623–1666*, 1912.

[4] Thomas J. Wertenbaker, *The Planters of Colonial Virginia*, 1922, p. 34.

[5] *Adventurers of Purse and Person—Virginia 1607–1625*, ed. Annie Lash Jester and Martha Woodroof Hiden, 1956, second ed. 1964, p. 377. Temperance Yeardley's grandmother was Amy Robsart's halfsister.

[6] 'The Gentry of Kent in 1640', *The Cambridge Historical Journal*, vol. ix, 1948, pp. 148–64.

1619 the Virginia Company agreed, on the motion of Sir Dudley Digges, 'about a Pattent to be graunted unto sundry Kentishmen, who would seate and plant themselves in Virginia, that they should have as large priviledges and imunities as is graunted to any other in that kind'.[1] Nine Kent families, linked by marriage by about 1650, had by that date produced three governors of Virginia (Digges, Chicheley, Wyatt), two important pioneers (Sir Dudley Digges, Sir Samuel Argall) and five families of settlers (Filmer, Randolph, Bathurst, Call, Skipwith). Of the same connection were the families of Codd, St. Leger, Fleet, Horsmonden, Kemp, Fairfax, Duke, Barham, Sandys, Flood, Lovelace and Evelyn.[2] The mortality in the early years was high and the hardships drove some of the settlers back to England. In 1611 there were 450, in 1616 only 324. In 1619 there were 1,000 and in 1620 only 867.[3] By 1625 it is thought that some 7,000 had come but only 1,232 were then living.[4] Great efforts were therefore made to increase the number of volunteers and to supplement them with indentured servants and apprentices, orphan and pauper children from London and other towns. In 1616 a hundred children were sent from London and in 1619 a hundred more. Even convicts from the prisons of Middlesex were sent though not much welcomed.[5] 'By far the largest part of these penal immigrants', says Professor Wertenbaker boldly, 'were but harmless paupers, driven perhaps to theft or some other petty offence by cold and hunger.'[6] Negroes were brought from Africa in small numbers from about 1620 but the large scale slave trade did not begin till after 1650.

The freeholder settlers included a fair number of gentlemen as well as members of merchant families and yeomen. Thomas West, Lord De la Warr (d. 1618), played a notable part in the settlement as governor from 1610 to 1611. Three of his brothers also came to Virginia: Francis (d. 1634), a member of the company, who came in 1608 and was governor from 1627 to 1629; Nathaniel (d. 1623); and John (d. 1659), who left descendants in the colony.[7] Their mother Anne Knollys was

---

[1] *Records of the Virginia Company of London*, ed. S. M. Kingsbury, Washington 1906–35, i. 232.    [2] Laslett, op. cit., pp. 163 n., 160.

[3] Charles M. Andrews, *The Colonial Period of American History*, i. 1934, pp. 134, 136; but see also Franklin B. Dexter, 'Estimates of Population in the American Colonies', *Proc. American Antiq. Soc.* N.S. v, 1887, pp. 22–50.

[4] *Adventurers of Purse and Person*, p. xiv.

[5] Andrews, op. cit., pp. 134–7; Charles Edward Banks, *The Planters of the Commonwealth*, 1930, p. 31.

[6] Thomas J. Wertenbaker, *The Planters of Colonial Virginia*, 1922, p. 32.

[7] See Table IV; p. 284; *Adventurers of Purse and Person*, p. 349.

first cousin once removed to Queen Elizabeth[1] and their nephews William (d. 1667) and Herbert Pelham (d. 1674), first treasurer of Harvard College, went to New England in 1630 and 1639/40 respectively, Herbert leaving descendants there.[2]

George Percy (d. 1632), son of the Earl of Northumberland, and Thomas Paulet of the Marquess of Winchester's family were early settlers but left no known issue. Among early settlers who did so were several members of families whose arms and gentility were allowed in England by the heralds at their Visitations; Daniel Gookin from Ripple, Kent (1620; d. 1620);[3] George Reade (1637; d. 1671) from Linkenholt, Hampshire, an ancester of George Washington and of Queen Elizabeth II;[4] Christopher Calthrope from Blakeney, Norfolk (1622; d. 1662);[5] Peter Montague from Boveney, Buckinghamshire (1621; d. 1660);[6] Robert Evelyn, son of George of Wotton, Surrey (and uncle of John Evelyn the diarist), a member of the Council of the Virginia Company, who made a voyage, possibly to Virginia, in 1610, while his son came in 1636 and left descendants there;[7] Francis Epes (before 1625) from Ashford, Kent;[8] and Henry Woodhouse (1637; d. 1655), whose father and namesake, a member of the Virginia Company and Governor of Bermuda, was a younger son of Sir Henry Woodhouse of Waxham, Norfolk, while his mother was a sister of Francis Bacon (d. 1626), Lord Verulam.[9] Sir Francis Wyatt, Governor of Virginia 1621–6, and his brother the Rev. Haute Wyatt, sons of Sir George Wyatt of Allington Castle, Kent, went out in 1621 but returned to England in 1626. Haute's son Edward, however, came to Virginia in 1639 and left descendants there.[10] William Strachey, who sailed for Virginia in 1609 and was Secretary of the Colony from 1610 till his return to England in 1611, was son of William Strachey (d. 1598) of Saffron Walden, Essex, who had had a grant of arms, and ancestor of the Lords Strachie and of many

---

[1] Her mother was Mary, daughter of William Cary by Mary, sister of Anne Boleyn, *Complete Peerage*, ii. 146; iv. 160.

[2] See Table IV, p. 302 *infra*, Weis, op. cit., p. 203 *supra*, p. 21 and Supplement, p. 28; Meredith B. Colket, Jn., 'The Pelhams of England and New England', *The American Genealogist*, xvi. 129–32, 201–5; xviii. 137–46, 210–18; xix. 197–202.

[3] Visitation of Kent, 1619, *Adventurers of Purse and Person*, p. 181.

[4] Visitation of Hampshire, 1623; A. R. Wagner, 'The American Ancestry of Her Majesty the Queen', p. 233 n. 3 *supra*.

[5] Visitation of Norfolk, 1563 and 1664; *Adventurers of Purse and Person*, p. 113.

[6] Visitation of Bucks, 1626; *Adventurers of Purse and Person*, p. 250.

[7] Visitation of Surrey, 1623; *Adventurers of Purse and Person*, p. 166.

[8] Visitation of Kent, 1618; *Adventurers of Purse and Person*, p. 160.

[9] Visitation of Norfolk, 1563; *Adventurers of Purse and Person*, p. 365.

[10] Visitation of Kent, 1619; *Adventurers of Purse and Person*, pp. 372–5.

distinguished men—among them Lytton Strachey (d. 1932). One of his grandsons returned to Virginia and there are still descendants there.[1]

In this early phase the number of gentlemen among the planters was possibly much the same as in Massachusetts. Later, however, Virginia seems to have gained the lead in this respect, though it is doubtful whether the proportion of gentlemen was any greater there, the population of Virginia being at this date probably twice that of New England. After 1641, as we shall see, the flow of settlers to Massachusetts, which had hitherto been the most populous colony, almost stopped, whereas the rule of the Parliament and Cromwell made Virginia 'the only city of refuge left in His Majesty's dominions in these times of distressed cavaliers'.[2] In consequence many gentlemen at this date sought refuge and fortune there beginning with a group of 330 refugees including many prominent Royalists, who arrived in 1649.[3] These movements were reflected in successive fundamental changes in the governing class of the colony. A small group of leaders of high rank, such as George Percy, the Wests, the Wyatts, George Sandys and others, dominated the first fifteen years or so from 1607. Many of them then, however, went back to England, leaving the leadership to the toughest survivors, whether gentlemen or not. After 1640 these last gave place to the leaders of the new wave of settlement, which then began and lasted nearly thirty years. It was from the settlers of this time that the famous oligarchy which dominated Virginia through the eighteenth century mainly derived, such families as Bland, Burwell, Byrd, Carter, Digges, Ludwell and Mason. Many settlers of this time were cadets of London merchant families with inherited interests in the colony or claims to land there. Thus John Bland, a London merchant, invested in the Virginia Company in 1618 and acquired a further interest in 1622. He never left England but three of his sons came to Virginia in the 1640's and 1650's to exploit the family investments.[4]

Among settlers at this period who left notable descendants were Richard Lee (settled *c.* 1641; d. 1664), Secretary of State, descended from the ancient family of Lee of Coton, Shropshire, and ancestor of

[1] Visitation of Somerset, 1672; *Adventurers of Purse and Person*, pp. 319–22.

[2] P. Force, *Tracts relating to the Origin, Settlement and Progress of the Colonies in North America*, 4 vols., Washington, 1836–46, i. 84. 'Ingram's Proceedings', quoted in *Camb. Hist. Brit. Emp.* i. 785.

[3] C. M. Andrews, *The Colonial Period of American History*, ii. 255.

[4] Bernard Bailyn, 'Politics and Social Structure in Virginia', chap. v, pp. 90–115, of *Seventeenth-Century America. Essays in Colonial History*, ed. James Morton Smith, Univ. of N. Carolina Press, 1959, pp. 92–95, 98–100.

the famous family to which Robert E. Lee (d. 1870) belonged;[1] Governor Edward Digges (came *c.* 1650; d. 1675) from Chilham Castle, Kent, a descendant of Edward III whose son William became Deputy Governor of Maryland and settled there;[2] Edmund Jennings (1680; d. 1727) of Ripon, Yorkshire, Acting Governor, who left distinguished descendants both in Virginia and in Maryland;[3] Warham Horsmonden (came before 1653; d. 1691), an outstanding example of a 'gateway ancestor', since through the St. Legers and Nevilles he was descended two or three times over from Edward III and was a kinsman of Sir Thomas Smythe and Governor Digges, while the marriage of his daughter Mary to William Byrd makes him ancestor of many Virginia families;[4] and John Washington (1656; d. 1677), son of the ejected Royalist rector of Purleigh, Essex, and descended from Edward III, great-grandfather of George Washington and descendant of an ancient family of probable royal origin,[5] from the thirteenth century of Lancashire and since the sixteenth century of Sulgrave, Northamptonshire.

After the Restoration came still more, among them Robert Beverley (1663; d. 1687), from Yorkshire;[6] William Byrd (*c.* 1670; d. 1704), of Westover, son of a London goldsmith, and descendant of a Cheshire Visitation family;[7] Henry Corbin (d. 1675) from Warwickshire;[8] Colonel William Randolph (*c.* 1673; d. 1711) of Turkey Island, of Northamptonshire descent, ancestor through female lines of Thomas Jefferson, Chief Justice John Marshall and Robert E. Lee;[9] and Henry Isham (before 1676), grandson of Sir Euseby Isham of Pytchley, Northamptonshire.[10]

Between 1642 and 1664 the population of Virginia is said to have risen from 10,000 to 38,000 of which it has been estimated that not more than half can have been due to natural increase.[11] It has also been

---

[1] Visitation of Shropshire, 1625; Coll. Arm. Reg. Surrey xii. 275.

[2] Visitation of Kent, 1618; *Adventurers of Purse and Person*, p. 154; Ruvigny, op. cit., *Mortimer-Percy Vol.*, pt. i, p. 501; Adams and Weis, *The Magna Carta Sureties*, p. 43.

[3] *Dugdale's Visitation of Yorkshire*, ed. J. W. Clay, 1907, ii. 201.

[4] *Adventurers of Purse and Person*, p. 287; Adams and Weis, *The Magna Carta Sureties*, p. 42; Ruvigny, *Plantagenet Roll of the Blood Royal*, *Mortimer-Percy Vol.*, pt. i, p. 500.

[5] p. 27 *supra.*

[6] Visitation of Yorkshire, 1612 and 1666; Coll. Arm. Reg. 3 D. 14, pp. 322–3.

[7] Visitation of Cheshire, 1613; Coll. Arm. Reg. Norfolk, xxxii. 160.

[8] Visitation of Warwick, 1619; Coll. Arm. Reg. 2 D. 14, ff. 105h–106.

[9] Visitation of Northants, 1682.

[10] Visitation of Northants, 1619; *Victoria County History, Northamptonshire Families*, p. 146.

[11] *Tyler's Quarterly Historical and Genealogical Magazine*, vii (1927), 3–4, 'Colonial History Debunked'.

estimated that more than half of all the settlers in the American colonies were servants or apprentices who went out under indentures. The Bristol emigrants' indentures for the years 1654 to 1685 and those from London for the years 1683–4 have been analysed by Miss Mildred Campbell for the light they can throw on social and geographical origins.[1]

She finds that in the Bristol series about a quarter were women and that of the men the largest group were yeomen and husbandmen, making up together some 36 per cent, but the yeomen outnumbering the husbandmen. About 22 per cent were artisans and tradesmen; about 10 per cent labourers; and just under one per cent gentlemen and professional men. For 31 per cent no status or occupational description is given. In the London series the women are rather under a quarter and the proportion of skilled workers to yeomen and husbandmen is almost reversed, being about two to one. Husbandmen outnumber yeomen, but as before farmers and skilled workers outnumber labourers by five to one. The reluctance this indicates of labourers to emigrate is confirmed elsewhere.

Among the Bristol names are emigrants from every English county except Rutland and many from Wales. Much the greatest number, however, are from the parts nearest Bristol, from Somerset, Gloucestershire, Wiltshire, Monmouthshire and the west generally. Of the London names the great majority are from London and Middlesex, but Yorkshire comes next.

Of those from Bristol just over half were bound for Virginia. Miss Campbell quotes a statement by James Southall[2] 'that in Virginia, the counties of Henrico, James City, Charles City, Isle of Wight, Gloucester, Surrey and Prince George were largely settled' from an area 'about thirty miles north of Bristol, running due north and south for a distance of about ten miles and with an average breadth of three miles' at the meeting place of Worcestershire, Herefordshire and Gloucestershire, 'and from Somersetshire, and the neighbouring counties of Wales . . . from Warwick on the north, Devon in the south west, Herts [*sic*, but perhaps for Hants] and the Isle of Wight in the south, and across the Bristol channel from the coast of Ireland'.

---

[1] Richard B. Morris, *Government and Labor in Early America*, New York, 1946, p. 315, and Abbot E. Smith, *Colonists in Bondage*, Chapel Hill, 1947, p. 34, cited by Mildred Campbell, 'Social Origins of Some Early Americans', chap. iv, pp. 68–79, in *Seventeenth-Century America. Essays in Colonial History*, ed. James Morton Smith, Univ. of N. Carolina Press, 1959.

[2] 'The Cocke family', *Virginia Mag. of Hist. & Biog.*, vol. iii, 1896, pp. 285–6.

She links this with the distress growing at that time in the West Country clothing towns and with the troubles of the dissenters.[1]

Many who went to the colonies in early days as servants or apprentices later acquired land, property and position,[2] and among them was a sprinkling of impoverished scions of good families, who looked to this opportunity when they entered into indentures. Adam Thoroughgood (d. 1640) came to Virginia in the ship *Charles* in 1621 as a servant, being then 14 years old and was Mr. Edward Waters' servant in 1625. He was, however, the seventh son of the vicar of St. Botolph's, Norwich. His elder brother John became secretary to the Earl of Pembroke, a gentleman pensioner under Charles I, a gentleman of the Privy Chamber under Charles II and was knighted in 1630. Adam himself on coming of age and completing his service was able to buy 150 acres of land in Virginia. He then returned to England and in 1627 married the daughter of Robert Offley, a Turkey merchant of London and a member of the Virginia and Somers Island Companies. After this he went back to Virginia, served as burgess and member of council, was commended for special services to the colony, had large grants of land and built what has been called the oldest dwelling now standing in Virginia.[3]

John Trussell came to Virginia as a servant in the *Southampton* in 1622, aged 19, and was Mr. Thomas Paulet's servant in 1624. He was probably the second son of James Trussell, clothworker of London, who entered his arms (with nine quarterings) and his pedigree at the Heralds' Visitation of 1634 and was sprung from a younger branch of an old knightly family in Cheshire and Warwickshire. John Trussell acquired land and served as burgess and justice.[4]

Professor Wertenbaker has shown[5] that down to 1660 conditions in Virginia continued 'very favorable for the graduation of the servant into the class of small freeholders', whereby 'a vigorous, intelligent, independent yeomanry, comprising fully 90 per cent. of all the landowners' was built up. The ancestors of most of these were probably

[1] Op. cit., pp. 85–89, quoting George Ramsay, *Wiltshire Woollen Industry in the Sixteenth and Seventeenth Centuries*, Bristol, 1945; R. Perry 'The Gloucester Woollen Industry', *Bristol & Glos. Tr.*, 1947; and Miss Mann's chapter in *V.C.H. Wilts.*

[2] Wertenbaker, op. cit., p. 75.

[3] Ibid.; *Adventurers of Purse and Person*, pp. 58, 256, 329; Harleian Soc. lxxxvi. 219; *The Visitation of Middlesex, 1663*, ed. Joseph Foster, 1887, p. 65. For Robert Offley and his connections in Bermuda see Wilkinson, op. cit., p. 100; for his pedigree, *The Genealogist*, N.S. xix. 227.

[4] *Adventurers of Purse and Person*, p. 357; Harleian Soc. xvii. 298; Dugdale, *Antiquities of Warwickshire*, 1765 ed. p. 714; *Ormerod's Cheshire*, ed. Helsby, iii. 229.

[5] Op. cit., pp. 74–83.

yeomen or husbandmen in England in spite of the fact that gentlemen, as we have seen, were fairly numerous among the settlers.

By a statute of 1597 dangerous rogues might be banished out of the realm. The word transportation appears in a statute of 1662. Acts of Parliament of 1679, 1717 and 1768 progressively extended the system of transporting felons overseas in lieu of other punishment, though only after 1717 did this come into common use. The plantations of Virginia and the West Indies were at this date their destination but by 1770 Maryland was the only colony still regularly admitting convicts. It was the loss of the American colonies as an outlet which much later led to the development of New South Wales, Van Diemen's Land (Tasmania) and Norfolk Island as penal settlements. It must not be assumed that all felons thus transported belonged to the criminal class or, indeed, that all would in our view be criminals themselves.[1]

In Defoe's *Moll Flanders* (1722) the heroine says of the mother of her husband, a rich Virginian plantation owner, 'She often told me how the greatest part of the inhabitants of that Colony came thither in very indifferent circumstances from England; that, generally speaking they were of two sorts, either such as were brought over by masters of ships to be sold as servants; or such as are transported after having been found guilty of crimes punishable with death. . . . "Hence, child," says she, "many a Newgate bird becomes a great man, and we have several justices of the peace, officers of the trained bands, and magistrates of the towns they live in that have been burnt in the hand." ' Dr. Johnson went further when he said of the Americans 'Sir, they are a race of convicts, and ought to be thankful for anything we allow them short of hanging.'[2]

Virginia retained the lead in population among the colonies right down to 1820. After 1755 an immense increase seems to have taken place, raising the number of the white inhabitants from about 30,000 to about 550,000 in twenty years. A large share in this growth must have been due to settlers from England, some of them transported felons, while others probably came from the West Indies and other colonies.

### 4. THE BERMUDAS AND WEST INDIES

Sir Thomas Warner (d. 1649), the founder of the settlements in St. Christopher (or St. Kitts; 1624), Nevis (1628), Montserrat (1632) and

[1] Anthony J. Camp, *Genealogist's Magazine*, vol. 14, 1962, pp. 119–20; *Cambridge History of the British Empire*, ii, 415–7; p. [245], *supra*; M. D. George, *London Life in the XVIIIth Century*, 1930, pp. 141–50; E. I. MacCormac, *White Servitude in Maryland*, 1904. [2] C. J. L. Elwell, *Gen. Mag.*, vol. 15, 1966, pp. 223–4.

Antigua (1632) and the founder of a distinguished West Indian family with branches in Antigua, Barbados, Dominica, Montserrat and Trinidad, as well as St. Kitts,[1] was a gentleman of Suffolk. I have seen no evidence for the statement[2] that many of his settlers came from Suffolk and the eastern counties. It is not in itself unlikely but a list of hostages taken by the Spaniards about 1631, five from St. Christopher and four from Nevis, does, as it happens, comprise five London men, one from Yorkshire, one from Durham and one from Ireland.[3]

In the settlement of Bermuda (from 1612) close family and other connections have been noted by Dr. Wilkinson[4] between the directorate of the founding company, the wider circle of shareholders in it and the settlers. Constellations of all three kinds centre round Sir Thomas Smythe, the governor of the company, and Robert Rich, Earl of Warwick, both already mentioned.[5] The links of the Tucker family are typical. They had come from Devon in the sixteenth century to the neighbourhood of the dockyard town of Gravesend in Kent. Daniel Tucker (d. 1623) sailed for Virginia in 1606 and was made Governor of Bermuda in 1616. His brother George, 'prime searcher at Gravesend', was a friend of Sir Thomas Smythe, whose home was in Kent, and joined Daniel in the purchase of shares in the company and married into the Darrell family, also shareholders and with other maritime connections. His son George (d. 1648) settled and left descendants in Bermuda. Through his son's marriage with the daughter of Sir Henry St. George, Garter King of Arms (d. 1715), St. George became a Christian name in the Tucker family. The later pedigree shows a pattern not unusual in Bermudian and West Indian families. While some remained in Bermuda, some returned to England, others settled in Virginia and Carolina and one of the most distinguished went to India in the East India Company's service.[6]

Andrews says that

The six hundred inhabitants [of Bermuda] came largely from London and the eastern counties, with very few from the west or southwest, and were of about the same kind as those that went to Virginia—independent settlers, who went on their own, indentured servants, apprentices, vagrants, criminals

---

[1] Vere Langford Oliver, *The History of the Island of Antigua*, 1894, iii. 184–9.
[2] Aucher Warner, *Sir Thomas Warner*, 1933, p. 34.
[3] *Colonising Expeditions to the West Indies and Guiana, 1623–1667*, ed. V. T. Harlow, Hakluyt Soc. 2nd ser. lvi, 1925, p. 13.
[4] Henry Wilkinson, *The Adventurers of Bermuda*, 1933, pp. 99–102.
[5] p. 284. See Table IV.
[6] Coll. Arm. MSS. C. 16, fo. 184; 8 D. 14, p. 156; 9 D. 14, p. 318; Howard, p. 113.

and, after 1619, negroes. There were 'gentlemen' as well as servants, but probably, by far the greatest number was of the middle class.[1]

Bermuda differed from Virginia, however, in the presence from early days of a strongly Puritan group.[2] One of its leaders was the Rev. John Oxenbridge (d. 1674), who returned to England in 1641, became a fellow of Eton College in 1652, but after the Restoration was ejected and died in Boston, Massachusetts. At Eton Andrew Marvell (d. 1678) lived as a tutor in his house and had from him the inspiration of his poem *Bermudas*.[3]

Barbados received some 1,800 settlers between 1625 and 1629 financed and organized by the rich London merchant Sir William Courteen and his associates. The probability therefore is that most of them came from the London region.

The island of Old Providence off the coast of Nicaragua was colonized in 1631 by a Puritan company, but in 1641 the Spaniards captured it. The settlers came largely from areas where the eminent Puritan members of the company were influential. Lord Warwick, his kinsman Sir Nathaniel Rich and Sir Thomas Barrington recruited some in Essex; Richard Knightley (d. 1639) of Fawsley sent some from Northamptonshire; William Fiennes (d. 1662), Lord Saye and Sele, some from Oxfordshire; and John Pym (d. 1643) some from Devon and Cornwall.[4] A number of Welshmen, thought to have been victims of Laud's anti-Puritan measures, also went and some settlers were brought from Bermuda. When Providence was captured the colonists were allowed to leave and most returned to England, but some settled in St. Christopher and other of the Leeward Islands.

Movement both in the early years and later between one colony and another was frequent and can present problems to the genealogist. The Virginia settler whose origin he seeks in England may really have come from Bermuda, while a West Indian settler may have come from New England. Samuel Winthrop (d. 1674), the youngest son of John Winthrop (d. 1649), the son of the founder of Massachusetts, settled in Antigua and called his plantation there Groton Hall from his father's ancestral home in Suffolk.[5]

Samuel Vassall (d. 1667) and his brother William (d. 1655), sons of

---

[1] Charles M. Andrews, *The Colonial Period of American History*, i, 1934, p. 220 n.
[2] Ibid., pp. 228–35.
[3] *The Poems and Letters of Andrew Marvell*, ed. H. M. Margoliouth, 1927, i. 17–18.
[4] A. P. Newton, *The Colonizing Activities of the English Puritans*, 1914, p. 91.
[5] Vere Langford Oliver, *History of Antigua*, iii. 251.

John Vassall, a London alderman of Huguenot origin, both settled in New England, but William in 1648 moved on to Barbados. His son John (d. 1688) sold his land in Massachusetts in 1661, took part in the settlement of Cape Fear, North Carolina, but in 1672 settled in Jamaica, where he left descendants. His son Leonard remained in New England and from him sprang the well known Vassall family of Cambridge and Boston, Massachusetts, who were loyalists in the revolution and then returned to England. To the Jamaica branch belonged the famous Whig hostess Lady Holland (d. 1845),[1] born Elizabeth Vassall.

Bermuda and Barbados were small and fertile islands which a growing population soon overcrowded. Just before the Civil War interrupted it migration from Bermuda to newer colonies was becoming appreciable and after 1660 it became important. Carolina, for example, received many Bermudian and Barbadian settlers.[2] By this date the spontaneous flow of colonists from England had died down. From the 1650's onward a practice grew into a policy of populating the colonies 'with undesirables from the British Isles, with foreigners from every European country which would supply them, and above all with negroes from Africa'.[3]

Thus Jamaica, occupied in 1655, was populated only with difficulty and a transfer of colonists from Nevis and Barbados seems to have made a greater contribution than settlement from England. Antigua too was short of men.

As we have seen,[4] the West Indies, like Virginia, received many transported felons. Royalist prisoners of the Parliament armies were shipped to Barbados virtually as slaves in such numbers that between 1645 and 1650 the population of the island rose from under 20,000 to over 30,000.[5] Many of those condemned for complicity in the Duke of Monmouth's rebellion of 1685 were also shipped to the West Indies.[6]

Humphrey Walrond, a Royalist of an old Devon and Somerset family, who went to Barbados before 1649, proclaimed Charles II king there in 1650 and was deprived of his command. He was deputy

---

[1] E. D. Harris, *The Vassalls of New England*, 1862; C. M. Calder, 'Alderman John Vassall and his Descendants', *New England Hist. and Gen. Reg.* xcix, 1955, pp. 91–102.

[2] *Camb. Hist. Brit. Emp.* i. 237; Andrews, op. cit. iii. 30–31; Wilkinson, *Adventurers of Bermuda*, p. 331; Vincent T. Harlow, *A History of Barbados 1625–1685*, 1926, pp. 152–3; Danson, *The Atlantic Migration*, pp. 41–42.

[3] *Camb. Hist. Brit. Emp.* i. 236.          [4] p. 292 *supra*.

[5] Harlow, op. cit., p. 45.

[6] Charles M. Andrews, *The Colonial Period of American History*, i, 1934, p. 64 n.

governor after the Restoration and his descendants were prominent in Barbados and Antigua.[1] The decisive influence on the West Indian population after 1660—and to a lesser extent on that of the southern mainland colonies—was the import of slaves from Africa. So extensive did this become that by 1688 three quarters of the people of the West Indies were probably negroes.[2] The forms of cultivation which the negroes made possible put the white yeoman class out of business. The small planters sold their land to the richer and moved to the American mainland, while many of the rich planters returned to England with their fortunes made and left their plantations to be managed by agents and worked by negroes.[3] Still others left for England after 1833 when the abolition of slavery undermined the previous basis of the island's economy.

Thus it is that many descendants of West Indian settlers are found today in England and the United States. But there are, of course, many in the West Indies too, as well as in Bermuda, where Trotts, Triminghams, Watlingtons and other families of early settlement are still prominent. Nor must it be forgotten that a numerous part of the settlers' progeny is that extensive portion of the island population in which African and English blood are in different proportions mingled.

### 5. NEW ENGLAND

The origins of the New England settlers[4] have been traced in more detail than those of the settlers of the other early colonies. The first settlement in New England was that of the so called Pilgrims who sailed in 1620 in the *Mayflower* and founded the colony at Plymouth Bay. The later Massachusetts Bay Settlement (1629) was much larger and more influential in New England history. In 1689 indeed Massachusetts absorbed the Plymouth colony. The voyagers of the *Mayflower* stand, however, on an eminence of their own.

The nucleus of the 102 Pilgrims was a party of 35 Brownists, that is separatists from the Church of England, whose position was thus more extreme than that of the Puritans in general. These, who had taken

---

[1] Oliver, *History of Antigua*, iii. 179–81.
[2] *Camb. Hist. Brit. Emp.* i. 267.
[3] Ibid., i. 379–80.
[4] For help and advice on this section and on matters of American genealogy generally I am greatly indebted to my late friend the Rev. Arthur Adams of Boston, Massachusetts.

refuge in Leyden, had been brought together rather by their religious views than by geographical or family connections. A few of their leaders—William Brewster, Isaac Allerton, Miles Standish—sprang from the class of small gentry or merchants, but most of them were husbandmen or craftsmen. The only coherent group among them which has been identified came with Brewster and Bradford from the region of the river Idle on the borders of Yorkshire and Nottinghamshire.[1] The other passengers of the *Mayflower*, outside the Brownist group, were a mixed company from London.

The Pilgrims were financed by London merchants interested in fishing and the fur trade and so were the first settlers on Massachusetts Bay, the party organized in 1624 by the Rev. John White (d. 1648), the Puritan rector of Holy Trinity, Dorchester, Dorset. These settled first at Cape Ann, then in 1626 under Roger Conant (d. 1679) of Budleigh, Devon, founded Salem. But the venture was in difficulties when White in England conceived an ambitious reinforcement in the foundation in Massachusetts of a refuge for the righteous and 'a bulwark against the kingdom of Antichrist which the Jesuits labour to rear up in all quarters of the world'. White had influence with such powerful Puritans as the Earls of Warwick and Lincoln. A grant of land was obtained and in 1629 the Massachusetts Bay Company was incorporated.[2] Meanwhile in 1628 White's parishioner John Endicott (d. 1665) of Dorchester led a party to reinforce the Salem settlers and prepare the way for those to come. Both Endicott's and the previous Salem settlers came largely from Dorset, Devon and Somerset.

On 26 August 1629 the leading members of the Massachusetts Bay Company meeting in Cambridge made the epoch making decision to transfer themselves, their families, their property, and the government of the colony from England to Massachusetts. This gave it a unique autonomy and a peculiar attractiveness to settlers of independent mind. 'In Massachusetts from the first it was possible for practically every man to own his own land in entire freedom from a landlord's oversight and from the heavy rents exacted in England.'[3]

On 15 October 1629 John Winthrop (d. 1649), the squire of Groton, Suffolk, was chosen governor of the company. His grandfather Adam Winthrop (d. 1562) was a Lavenham clothier who had bought Groton,

[1] Charles Edward Banks, *The English Ancestry and Homes of the Pilgrim Fathers*, 1929, pp. 2–3.

[2] *Camb. Hist. Brit. Emp.* i. 159.

[3] A. P. Newton, op. cit., p. 309; A. L. Rowse, *The Elizabethans and America*, pp. 112–18, 139–48.

a former manor of the abbey of Bury St. Edmunds. John Winthrop was a strong Puritan and to this his loss in June 1629 of the lucrative office of Attorney in the Court of Wards was due. To this loss was due in turn his decision to leave England.[1] The hour had found the man and New England its true founder.

Winthrop sailed in 1630 with eleven ships, seven carrying passengers, and the rest freight and livestock. The passengers numbered about 700 men, women and children. Of these about 100 deserted and about 200 died on the voyage or soon after. Colonel C. E. Banks was satisfied that he could identify more than 500 passengers in the Winthrop fleet, 243 of them adult males. He was able to ascertain the English homes of 404. Of these 159 came from Suffolk, 92 from Essex, 78 from London, 22 from Northamptonshire and 53 from the rest of England. About 100 came from within ten miles of Winthrop's home at Groton.[2] They settled in and about Charlestown, Watertown and Roxbury.

Shiploads of passengers arrived in such numbers between this date and 1641 that a contemporary was able to claim that 'for fifteen yeares space to the year 1643 . . . the number of ships that transported passengers . . . as is supposed is 298. Men, women and children passing over this wide ocean, as near as at present can be gathered, is also supposed to be 21,200 or thereabouts.'[3] By 1930 Banks had been able to trace 213 of the ships (158 by name) and about 3,600 of the passengers, that is about 20 per cent of the total number.[4] Banks, with A. T. Butler,[5] Windsor Herald (d. 1946) as collaborator on the English side, worked for many years on the origins of these settlers. They compiled jointly a record of identifications certain, probable or tentative. In Banks' copy of this record there were ultimately identifications of some kind for 2,885 out of the 3,600 named settlers. The edition of it published after Banks' death is of great use but does not make it clear how tentative some of the identifications were.[6] Butler's copy of the record with his manuscript notes is in my possession.

Though the figure of 2,885 amounts only to 13·6 per cent of Johnson's total for the settlement, it constitutes a far larger proportion than

---

[1] A. P. Newton, op. cit., p. 45.

[2] Charles Edward Banks, *The Winthrop Fleet of 1630*, 1930, and *The Planters of the Commonwealth*, 1930, pp. 65–85.

[3] Edward Johnson, *The Wonder-Working Providence of Sion's Saviour in New England*, 1654, chap. xiv, quoted by Banks, *Planters of the Commonwealth*, p. 12.

[4] Banks, op. cit., p. 205.                                        [5] p. 403.

[6] C. E. Banks, *Topographical Dictionary of 2885 English Emigrants to New England*, ed. Elijah Ellsworth Brownell, 1937; information from the Rev. Arthur Adams.

we know for any other colony, and should suffice when analysed (subject to the caution given above) to give a fair idea of the sources of recruitment of the Massachusetts settlers generally. As with the smaller entity of the Winthrop fleet the largest numbers came from Suffolk (298) and Essex (266). Next come London (203), Kent (197), Devon (175), Norfolk (168), Somerset (153), Dorset (128), Hertfordshire (108) and Wiltshire (107). No other county gives three figures, though almost all are represented.

A number of individual contributions to this total can be identified besides Winthrop's. Several Puritan ministers were responsible for the group migration of their congregations. The Rev. Thomas Hooker (d. 1647), a fellow of that nursery of Puritans, Emmanuel College, Cambridge, became known as a preacher in Essex, was silenced by Laud in 1629 and came to New England in 1633, preceded in 1631 by his assistant John Eliot (d. 1690). Eliot led a party from Nazing, Essex, who settled at Roxbury, some dozen of whom have been identified. Hooker assembled and sent before him a larger contingent from Braintree, Essex, who sailed in 1632 and were the pioneers of Cambridge, and Watertown, Massachusetts. In 1635–6 Hooker led an exodus to found a settlement at Hartford, Connecticut, where the settlers were thus largely Essex people. Hooker himself came originally from Leicestershire and a few Leicestershire settlers are also found at Hartford.[1]

'It would be a study of great interest', says A. P. Newton, 'to examine the causes that between the years 1630 and 1640, specially predisposed the men of Eastern England to emigration.' He suggests 'that a minute enquiry would reveal the workings of some deep-seated economic cause, a probability that is strengthened when we recall that throughout the early Stuart period there was in the area in question constant agitation of an economic and agrarian character'.[2] James Truslow Adams has suggested that decline in the East Anglian clothing industry may have been among local causes predisposing to emigration.[3] Besides and perhaps more than all this is the simple fact that John Winthrop of Groton, Suffolk, was the leader of the migration.

A number of other parties led by ministers have been identified. From the village of Hingham, Norfolk, no fewer than thirty five families came to Hingham, Massachusetts, perhaps inspired by Edmund

[1] Banks, *Planters*, pp. 18–19, and *Topog. Dict.* under Essex.
[2] Arthur Percival Newton, *The Colonising Activities of the English Puritans*, 1914, p. 79.
[3] James Truslow Adams, *The Founding of New England*, 1921, p. 123.

Hobart whose son Peter (d. 1679), following them in 1635, became the pastor of the new Hingham. A group from the Hampshire and Wiltshire borders was brought to Ipswich, Massachusetts, by the Rev. Stephen Bachiler (d. 1660), the silenced vicar of Wherwell, Hampshire.[1] Bachiler's history shows what a Puritan minister was made of. In 1613 he and his son, who had been 'expulsed out of Magdalen College in Oxford', were sued for libel by a neighbouring clergyman for composing scandalous verses about him and singing them in divers places including the house of George Wither the poet. He emigrated to New England in 1632 when he was 71 with his second wife whom Winthrop calls 'a lusty comely woman'. He settled in Lynn, got into trouble there, moved to Ipswich and then to Newbury and in 1638 tried to found a settlement at Yarmouth on Cape Cod, walking 'thither on foot in a very hard season'. He was excommunicated on an accusation of immorality but the excommunication was withdrawn. He settled at Portsmouth, New Hampshire, and at 86 married a third wife much younger than himself, who, however, deceived him. At about 92 he returned to England and appears to have died at Hackney in 1660 aged 99.[2]

Among other ministers who influenced the course of migration were the Rev. John Cotton (d. 1652) of Boston, Lincolnshire, and Boston, Massachusetts, the Rev. John Lothrop (d. 1653) of Egerton, Kent, and of Scituate, the Rev. Ezekiel Rogers (d. 1660) of Rowley St. Peter, Yorkshire, and Rowley, Massachusetts, and the Rev. Richard Mather (d. 1669) of Toxteth, Lancashire, and Dorchester, Massachusetts. Another leader of a local party Mistress Elizabeth Poole (d. 1654), 'a godly and ancient maid' and a granddaughter of the Devon antiquary Sir William Pole of Shute, brought settlers from Taunton, Somerset, to Taunton, Massachusetts.

Far more numerous than the large groups led by ministers were smaller groups, often, it seems, of only five or ten from the same place, joined together of their own accord to migrate. The evidence for their existence is simply that through the length and breadth of New England the analysis of settlers' origins reveals them. It is hard to be sure in any given case that there was no religious motive or leader, but the number and distribution of the small groups has been thought to make an

---

[1] Banks, op. cit., p. 19.

[2] Samuel Eliot Morison, *English University Men who emigrated to New England before 1646*, 1932, p. 9; V. C. Sanborn, 'Stephen Bachiler and the Plough Company', *The Genealogist*, N.S. xix. 270–84.

economic motive likelier in most cases. While parties led by ministers were probably peculiar to New England, this second kind of group may well be found in all the colonies.

The social origins of the New England settlers have been less closely analysed than their geographical origins. Definite conclusions may indeed be impossible for while the fraction of the settlers whose English origins are known—perhaps some 13.6 per cent as we have seen—may well be a fair sample geographically, it may be weighted socially in favour of those of higher station. This is because many identifications rest on wills and other documents connected with property, which do not exist for the very poor. Nevertheless the impression remains that this more than most settlements was drawn from the middle ranks; a sprinkling of small gentry and cadets of gentle families, many substantial yeomen, some merchants, many husbandmen and craftsmen and some servants of the gentlemen and yeomen. Dr. S. E. Morison identified 129 university men, who came before 1656, 100 from Cambridge and 31 from Oxford (3 having been at both), and 8 from universities out of England. Of this total 98 were ministers, 15 schoolmasters and 3 physicians. Twenty six became magistrates, deputies and lawmakers in New England and 5 merchants and the like.[1] G. A. Moriarty expressed the view that the great migration (1628–42) was composed largely of the middle classes, substantial yeomen, merchants, shopkeepers and the like, with a substantial group from the gentry.[2]

We have already mentioned the 19 settlers with proved descents from Edward I.[3] Some of these belonged to families whose right to arms the heralds in England allowed at their Visitations, but by no means all, and conversely some of the armigers are not known to have been of royal descent. Among the members of Visitation families who came in the Winthrop fleet in 1630 were Sir Richard Saltonstall (d. 1658) from Yorkshire;[4] two esquires, John Winthrop[5] (d. 1649) himself from Suffolk and William Pynchon[6] from Essex; and three gentlemen, Richard Palgrave[7] (d. 1651), physician, from Norfolk, William Poole[8] (d. 1674), a knight's grandson from Devon and Edward FitzRandolph[9]

[1] Samuel Eliot Morison, op. cit.
[2] *Gen. Mag.* 14, 1962, 118.       [3] pp. 237–8.       [4] Visitation of York, 1613.
[5] Visitation of Suffolk, 1612.       [6] Visitation of Essex, 1634.
[7] Visitation of Norfolk, 1563 and 1613. G. A. Moriarty in *New Eng. Hist. and Gen. Reg.* cii. 87.
[8] Visitation of Devon, 1620; Weis and Adams, op. cit., p. 25. He was grandson of Sir William Pole, the antiquary.
[9] p. 44 *supra*. Visitation of North, 1530; Coll. Arm. MS. Vincent 117, p. 134.

(d. 1675–6) from Nottinghamshire. In 1631 came John Throckmorton[1] (d. 1684), gentleman, from Norfolk, and Thomas Mayowe[2] from Wiltshire; in 1634 Samuel Appleton[3] (d. 1670), gentleman, from Suffolk; in 1635 Herbert Pelham (d. 1672), esquire, already mentioned[4] and the Rev. Peter Bulkeley (d. 1659), from Bedfordshire but of Cheshire ancestry;[5] in 1637 the Rev. John Davenport[6] (d. 1670), from Warwickshire; in 1637 Jeremy Clarke[7] (d. 1652), who may be reckoned as almost of a Visitation family though his brother's entry at the London Visitation of 1633 has been erased with the note, 'This descent not to be entred—refuseth to pay the fee—nephew to the Lo Treasurer', i.e. Richard Weston, Earl of Portland; in 1637 the Rev. Charles Chauncy[8] (d. 1672), from Hertfordshire; and in 1638[9] Obadiah Bruen, draper, from Cheshire and Thomas Odingsell,[10] gentleman, from Nottinghamshire. In certain cases the evidence of identity is circumstantial but may, I think, be accepted. As a list of early New England settlers of Visitation family this is in no way exhaustive.

In general those of higher rank in England kept their rank in America, though the genealogist must always reckon with the ups and downs of fortune. The pauper sometimes proves to be of gentle blood and the colonial leader an upstart. G. A. Moriarty wrote to me in 1960, 'John Coggeshall was President of Rhode Island in 1647 and his son was later Deputy Governor of Rhode Island and a member of Sir Edmund Andros' Council in King James' time and in the 18th century they were wealthy merchants and landowners, but when I was young one Coggeshall was a Newport policeman and another was a butcher.'

In 1964 he wrote to me, from Ogunquit, Maine, 'We also have a group of natives here called Bracy. They are mostly farmers and gardeners. . . . Their genealogy is interesting. They descend from a clergyman, an Oxford graduate, who settled in New Haven, Conn. in the 17th century. He descended from a cadet branch of the Cheshire

---

[1] Visitation of Norfolk, 1613; G. A. Moriarty in *New Eng. Hist. and Gen. Reg.* xcviii. 67, and ci. 290.

[2] Visitation of Wiltshire, 1683; information from W. G. Davis.

[3] Visitation of Suffolk, 1577.     [4] p. 287.

[5] Visitation of Cheshire, 1613.     [6] Visitation of Warwick, 1619.

[7] Visitation of London, 1633; *New Eng. Hist. and Gen. Reg.* lxxiv.

[8] Visitation of Hertford, 1634; Weis, op. cit., p. 79.

[9] Visitation of Cheshire, 1580; *Ormerod's Cheshire*, ed. Helsby, ii. 322; Weis, op. cit., p. 48.

[10] Visitation of Nottingham, 1614; Charles Henry Pope, *The Pioneers of Massachusetts*, 1900.

family which was established in Bedfordshire. The parson had a son John, a wanderer, who wandered up here and, as Libby says in his *Gen. Dic.* of Maine and N.H., "lived discred. in York Me."[1] He finally wandered back to Conn. but his offspring took root here. One of them talking to me had some faint remembrance that they had some remote gentility.' From a branch of the same ancient Cheshire family of Bracy, Brassey or Bressy, which had 'sunk to the rank of yeomanry' still in Cheshire, sprang Thomas Brassey (1836–1918), the great railway contractor, created Earl Brassey in 1911.[2]

Rank and station were as much a part of the social system in the colonies as in England. In seventeenth century New England no less than in Bermuda seating in church was 'according to degree',[3] just as we have seen it was in Elizabethan England.[4] The title Esquire was reserved to those of the highest rank. Gentlemen were called Mr. (i.e. Master) and yeomen Goodman. It is estimated that one in fourteen of the freemen of Massachusetts before 1649 ranked as a gentleman and was addressed as 'Master'. The use of armorial bearings in New England, Virginia and other colonies on seals, tombstones, silver and book-plates in the seventeenth and eighteenth centuries and the existence of an eighteenth century American roll of arms, the Gore Roll, show the value attached to marks of rank but do not of course establish the authenticity of the particular claims implied. Sir Edward Walker, Garter King of Arms (d. 1677), at some date after 1660 drafted a petition—now preserved in the College of Arms—to be constituted 'only King of Arms of all his Majesty's Plantations in America and therein from time to time by himself and deputies to record the names arms matches issues and descents of all gentlemen inhabiting in any of the said plantations'. Had this been done order might have replaced armorial chaos and a valuable record would have been made.[5]

Labourers and servants (that is employed persons—not merely domestic servants) for work in the colonies were obtained from England by a system under which their passage was paid in return for a

---

[1] Charles Thornton Libby, *Genealogical Dictionary of Maine and New Hampshire*, 1928, p. 104.

[2] *Complete Peerage*, ii. 281; *Burke's Peerage*, Brassey of Apethorpe.

[3] *Camb. Hist. Brit. Emp.* i. 796, quoting W. B. Weedon, *Economic and Social History of New England, 1620–1789*, ii. 281; Wilkinson, op. cit., p. 110.

[4] p. 95 *supra*.

[5] *The Heraldic Journal recording the Armorial Bearings and Genealogies of American Families*, Boston, Mass., 1865–8, *passim*; Charles Knowles Bolton, *Bolton's American Armory*, 1927; Harold Bowditch, 'The Gore Roll of Arms', *Rhode Island Hist. Soc. Coll.* xxix–xxxi, 1936–8.

contract to work so many years for him who paid it. These indentured servants or apprentices formed an essential element in the colonies' economy. Between 1654 and 1685 more than ten thousand servants sailed from Bristol to the mainland colonies and the West Indies.[1] It has been argued that there was an organized export to New England, as to Virginia, from London and perhaps Bristol, of pauper children, waifs, strays and foundlings, of the cost of whose maintenance the parish authorities were glad to be rid while the colonists welcomed them.[2] Certainly pauper children were sent individually.

An interesting problem was presented by three children, Richard, Jasper and Ellen More, who were brought to Plymouth Bay on the *Mayflower* in 1620. Ellen was in the charge of Edward Winslow, Jasper of John Carver and Richard was apprenticed to William Brewster. Ellen and Jasper died soon after arrival, but Richard survived to 1698–9 and may have been the last alive of all who sailed on the *Mayflower* in 1620. He was a retainer and servant of Richard Hollingsworth, whose daughter he married as his second wife, and is also described as yeoman and as mariner. In 1684 he made a deposition in which he said that he was then aged seventy or thereabouts and in 1620 had been living in the house of Mr. Thomas Weston, ironmonger, in London and was thence transported to New Plymouth in New England. Thomas Weston (d. c. 1633) largely financed the voyage of the *Mayflower* and himself came to New England in 1623.

In 1903 Dr. Edwin A. Hill published his discovery of the record of baptism at Shipton, Shropshire, of three children of Samuel More of Linley (d. 1662), of the ancient family of More of Larden, a well known parliamentarian commander, by his wife and third cousin Katherine daughter of Jasper More of Larden. These three children were Ellinora (1612), Jasper (1613) and Richard (1614), whose names and dates fit the *Mayflower* children. Dr. Hill further suggested that a Thomas Weston, baptized in 1583 at Hughley, the parish adjoining Shipton, was identical with the ironmonger of London. If this could be proved it would account for the children being placed in his care and would go far to prove their identity with the children of Samuel More and, if they were the same, the servant children had perhaps the longest pedigree of all the ship's company.

The difficulty of this interpretation was, however, that Samuel More married a second time and had a second family of whom the

---

[1] Charles Edward Banks, *The Planters of the Commonwealth*, 1930, p. 31; p. 292, *supra*.
[2] Ibid., pp. 28–32.

eldest, another Richard, was baptized and at length succeeded to his father's estates. How could this be if he had an elder stepbrother and namesake living in New England?

The present Mr. Jasper More, M.P., of Linley is sixth in descent from Robert More, the third son of Samuel's second marriage. He and I were schoolfellows and I put the problem to him. In January 1959 heavy snow kept him indoors at Linley and searching there in his archives he found a document telling a sad story which solves the problem. It is a petition to the Lord Chief Justice of England making a declaration 'of the disposinge of the fower children of Catherine More by Samuell More her late husband', occasioned by a petition which she had made.

Samuel More was born in 1594 and was married in 1610, when only 16, to his third cousin Katherine, aged 23, daughter and heir (since her brother's death in a duel in 1607) of Jasper More of Larden. The marriage was presumably arranged to keep Larden in the More family. The declaration, however, tells of the 'common fame' which arose, 'of the adulterous life of the said Katherine More with one Jacob Blakeway a fellow of mean parentage and condition which continued long before the said Samuel suspected it'. Four children were born and 'their apparent likeness and resemblance of most of the said children in their visages and lineaments of their bodies to the said Blakeway' was noted. Katherine indeed admitted the fact, alleging a precontract with Blakeway before her marriage to Samuel More, which, however, she could not prove. It appears that she maltreated and then abandoned the children; that Samuel in 1616 placed them in the care of a tenant of his father's; that a divorce was sought in the ecclesiastical court; and that in July 1620 by Samuel's direction the children were brought to London by a servant of his father's when an agreement was made with 'one Mr. Weston an honest and sufficient merchant' and two associates 'to transport them into Virginia and to see that they should be sufficiently kept and maintained with meat, drink, apparel, lodging and other necessaries, and that at the end of seven years they should have 50 acres of land apiece in the country of Virginia'.[1]

The New England Richard had five children and three of them had issue. The latest definite trace of his male line is in 1707 but there was a Richard More in Salem in 1780, who may well have been a

---

[1] A. R. Wagner, 'The Children in the Mayflower', *The Times*, 30 June 1959; 'The Origin of the Mayflower Children: Jasper, Richard and Ellen More', *New Eng. Hist. and Gen. Reg.*, cxiv, 1960, pp. 163–8.

descendant,[1] while his daughter Susanna (d. post 1728) by her first husband Samuel Dutch (d. 1693) left a daughter through whom the blood of Richard More was carried into many northern New England families.[2]

After 1641 migration to New England died down abruptly, since the brighter prospects for Puritans at home 'caused all men to stay in England in expectation of a new world',[3] and thereafter the population grew mainly by natural increase. This, however, was rapid and made New England a source of settlers for newer colonies. As early as 1636 secessions from Massachusetts had laid the foundations of Connecticut and Rhode Island. Of the settlers who came to New England after 1650 in comparatively small numbers many were substantial merchants from the Bristol region, Devon, and Somerset and craftsmen and tradesmen from London.[4]

### 6. MARYLAND

George Calvert (d. 1632), who was created Lord Baltimore in 1625, became a member of the Virginia Company, probably through the influence of his kinsmen by marriage, the Earl of Warwick and Sir Nathaniel Rich. He was also linked by friendship to the Roman Catholic Sir Thomas Arundell of Wardour (whose daughter his son married) and to Thomas Howard, Earl of Arundel, and himself became a Roman Catholic. After other colonizing experiments he petitioned not long before his death for a grant of what became Maryland and this was actually made in 1632 to his son Cecilius Lord Baltimore upon terms which made the proprietor as independent of Crown control as the Bishop of Durham had formerly been in his palatinate. Lord Baltimore was thus able to lay down a constitution which alone in the British Empire provided for religious toleration so full as to include

[1] Edwin A. Hill, 'The English Ancestry of Richard More of the *Mayflower*', *The New York Genealogical and Biographical Record*, xxxvi, 1905, pp. 213–19, 291–301; Charles Henry Pope, *The Pioneers of Massachusetts*, 1900, pp. 317–18; Charles Edward Banks, *The English Ancestry and Homes of the Pilgrim Fathers*, 1929, pp. 72, 86–87.

[2] Walter Goodwin Davis, *The Ancestry of Phoebe Tilton*, Portland, Maine, 1947, pp. 97–99. [3] Winthrop, *History of New England*, ii. 37.

[4] G. Andrews Moriarty, 'The English Background of the New England Settlements', *The Genealogist's Magazine*, i. 104–5, and 'Social and Geographic Origins of the Founders of Massachusetts', in *Commonwealth History of Massachusetts*, ed. Albert Bushnell Hart, 1927–8, i, chap. iii, pp. 49–65.

Roman Catholics, and Roman Catholic gentlemen were invited to take part in the settlement and share its cost.[1]

The first settlement was effected in 1634 by Leonard Calvert, Cecilius' brother, with between 200 and 300 people. Among them were two Jesuit priests and two lay brothers, sixteen Roman Catholic gentlemen adventurers with wives, children and servants, some 200 craftsmen, labourers, servants and their families, a few yeomen and a Protestant gentleman or two. Of these 200 odd a majority were in fact Protestants, but some of the servants were probably Roman Catholics.[2] The Protestant majority existing from the first was increased in 1648 by an influx of 400 to 600 Puritans from Virginia—Lord Baltimore's religious toleration working as much in their favour as in the Catholics'.[3] A manorial system on the English model unique in the colonies was set up in Maryland. In the seventeenth century there were some sixty manors apart from those reserved to the proprietor and his family. Below the lords of manors came a far more numerous class of freeholders and below them the labourers.[4]

The Calvert family and their connections both Catholic and Protestant held a dominant position. Andrews lists seventeen holders of important office in Maryland in the second half of the seventeenth century, some Catholic, some Protestant, who were linked with the Calverts by blood or marriage.[5] Among them were several of the Visitation family of Lowe of Denby, Derbyshire, whose connection was through Charles, Lord Baltimore's second marriage in 1666 to Jane, daughter of Vincent Lowe, widow of Henry Sewell (d. 1665), Secretary of Maryland, and apparently natural daughter of Henry Cavendish of Tutbury (d. 1616), eldest son of Sir William Cavendish and Bess of Hardwick.[6] The Lowes already had colonial connections through the marriage in 1607 of Isabel, Jane's aunt, to Sir John Zouche (d. 1639) of Codnor, Derbyshire, who settled in Virginia and whose son in law Devereux Wolseley had a sister married to Lord Baltimore's brother,

---

[1] Charles M. Andrews, *The Colonial Period of American History*, ii, 1936, pp. 276–83.
[2] Ibid., pp. 287–9.      [3] Ibid., p. 312.      [4] Ibid., pp. 294–8.
[5] Ibid., pp. 376–7. See Table IV.
[6] p. 213, Table II. From Henry Cavendish, natural son of this Henry, descends Lord Waterpark. See on Cavendish of Tutbury *Genealogist*, vol. 7, 1890–1, pp. 66–67; *Camden Miscellany*, 3rd ser., vol. 17, pp. iii and 74; *Notes & Queries*, 12th ser., vol. 1, pp. 287–8, 352–3; Francis Bickley, *The Cavendish Family*, p. 3. On Calvert and Lowe see *Adventurers of Purse and Person*, p. 118; *Maryland Hist. Mag.*, vol. 16, 1921, p. 56; Alfred Lowe, *Some Account of the Family of Lowe*, 1896; *Journ. Derbyshire Arch. & Nat. Hist. Soc.*, vol. 3, 1881, p. 157; J. Cox, *Churches of Derbyshire*, vol. 4, pp. 248–54, and vol. 2, pp. 560–1. Information from Mr. G. Rodney Crowther.

and a niece Mary Wolseley who came to Maryland and married and left descendants there.[1] The legitimate male line of the Calverts is extinct but an illegitimate branch exists in Maryland.

Immigration continued. By 1660 there were some 8,000, by 1700 some 32,000 people in the colony.[2] The settlers ranged in origin from gentlemen to labourers, and it can by no means be assumed that all who became gentlemen there were sprung from the gentry at home. Some probably were sons of traders while others were of Catholic yeoman families. Settlers of families entered at the Heralds' Visitations included William Digges (d. 1697)[3] and Richard Tilghman (d. 1675),[4] both of whom had royal descents, and Thomas Clagett (d. 1706), whose father Edward Clagett appears in the 1664 Visitation of London, while his great-nephew Wiseman Clagett (d. 1784) settled first in Antigua and then in New Hampshire.

### 7. THE NORTHERN SETTLEMENTS

The seamen of Devon had fished the coasts of Massachusetts, Maine, Nova Scotia and Newfoundland, and had camped there in the summer long before permanent settlements were made. A few men left in huts to look after the nets during winter when the rest had gone home may have been in a sense the first settlers.[5] Sir Ferdinando Gorges, as already mentioned, was a member of a group of West Countrymen, interested in colonization, going back to Sir Humphrey Gilbert and Sir Francis Drake. Gorges lived in Plymouth and had a house near Bristol, both headquarters of the fisheries. Grants made to him at various dates from 1622 to the final grant of the Province of Maine in 1639 and the grant to his partner Captain John Mason of what became New Hampshire, encouraged them in face of difficulties to organize more permanent settlements.[6] As one would expect some of Gorges' own kindred were settlers here or in New England where he also had interests. His first wife's great-nephew Captain Thomas Bradbury (d. 1695) went to New England as his agent in 1634;[7] his second wife's nephew Captain Francis Champernowne (d. 1687) settled at York, Maine, in 1665;[8] while

---

[1] *Adventurers of Purse and Person*, p. 379; Coll. Arm. MS. H. 27. fo. 417.

[2] F. B. Dexter, op. cit., p. 39.

[3] *Adventurers of Purse and Person*, p. 156; Visitation of Kent, 1619.

[4] Coll. Arm. Reg. Norfolk xxxvii. 76; Visitation of Kent, 1619.

[5] G. Andrews Moriarty, 'The English Background of the New England Settlements', *The Genealogist's Magazine*, i. 99.

[6] Andrews, op. cit. i, chap. xvi.    [7] Weis, *Ancestral Roots*, Supplement, p. 16.

[8] Weis, *Ancestral Roots*, p. 26.

three sisters, his second cousins once removed, the daughters of John Deighton of Gloucester, came to New England and left descendants there, Katherine, the eldest, being wife of Thomas Dudley (d. 1653), Governor of Massachusetts.[1]

The English origins of many early Maine settlers have been traced[2] and in many cases where details are unknown characteristic Devon and Cornish surnames point to the same source. Most of the identified settlers of Maine and New Hampshire came from Cornwall, Devon, Somerset, Dorset and Gloucestershire and the transference from England of such place names as Bristol, Falmouth, Portland, Exeter, Bideford, Wells, Northam, Appledore and Kittery fits into the same pattern. Certain other elements have, however, been identified also.

The Scottish settlement in Nova Scotia, granted in 1621 to Sir William Alexander, falls outside our scope. Settlements in Newfoundland, though begun by John Guy as early as 1610, had great rigours of climate to contend with and tended not to last. Nothing is heard of Guy's colony after 1628. The colony round Harbour Grace called Bristol's Hope, started in 1617, seems however to have lasted in attenuated form, as did later efforts.[3] Most of the settlers were probably West Country fishermen.

## 8. THE LATER COLONIES OF THE OLD EMPIRE

The Dutch Province of New Netherland was taken for the English Crown in 1664 by soldiers from England and Connecticut under the command of Colonel Richard Nicolls, sent out from England by the Duke of York (later James II) the new proprietor. The duke granted away those parts of the province which became New Jersey and Delaware and kept what became New York. The first English secretary of the province of New York, Matthias Nicolls (d. 1687), was not related to Richard, but sprang from a family entered at the Herald's Visitation of Buckinghamshire in 1626. Many notable families of New York descend from him.[4]

Here there were already a few Puritans from New England among some 7,000 Dutch. By 1673 3,000 English colonists had joined them and by 1689 some 12,000. A rapid influx continued so that by 1760 there were 220,000 in the colony. By 1790 it was second only to Virginia and

[1] Ibid., p. 87.

[2] See Charles Thornton Libby, Sybil Noyes and Walter Goodwin Davis, *Genealogical Dictionary of Maine and New Hampshire*, 1928–1938, a work of especial value both for clues to English origins and generally.

[3] Andrews, op. cit. i. 304–13.          [4] Coll. Arm. Reg. Norfolk, xxiii. 139.

about 1820 it took the lead.[1] It appears, however, that more came from the existing colonies than from England, and there were many immigrants from the continent of Europe.[2] The same thing applied to New Jersey and Delaware. For New Jersey there exist exceptionally full records of sales of land by the proprietors of East Jersey and West Jersey respectively. The purchaser's place of residence is usually mentioned and when, as often, it was in England, his origin is thus established.[3] The settlers of New Jersey, whether from the colonies or direct from England, were mainly of English stock. West Jersey was at first largely a Quaker settlement and it is estimated that some 800 settlers, mostly Quakers, arrived there between 1675 and 1678.[4]

The situation in Pennsylvania was somewhat different. This was a great tract extending inland from the borders of New York and Maryland, which was granted in 1681 to William Penn (d. 1718) in satisfaction of a Crown debt to his father Sir William Penn (d. 1670), a distinguished admiral. William Penn (d. 1718) had joined the Quakers in 1667 and he planned to make his colony a place of refuge from oppression both for them and others. There were already Swedes, Finns, Dutch and a few English settled in a small part of the area but Penn's settlers soon outnumbered them. Many of these also were not English but the great majority were and among them the Quakers were dominant. In 1682–4 about fifty ships arrived with settlers from London, Bristol, Cheshire and Lancashire, as well as from Ireland and Germany. Notable Quaker groups among them came from Derbyshire and Leicestershire, the former naming the centre of their settlement Darby. For over a generation the Quakers largely outnumbered other sects, but after Penn's sons reverted to the Church of England their relative numbers somewhat declined.[5]

A few of the Quakers like Samuel Carpenter and Edward Shippen were wealthy merchants. Most were small farmers, tradesmen and craftsmen by origin. Among the early non-Quaker settlers were a few of higher rank related to Penn or companions in arms of his father, 'glad to get public office or a cheap habitation'. Robert Assheton of Salford, Lancashire, son of William Assheton a deputy herald and a member of

---

[1] Dexter, op. cit., p. 33.

[2] *Camb. Hist. Brit. Emp.* i. 247.

[3] Archives of the State of New Jersey, 1st ser. xxi, *Calendar of Records of the Office of the Secretary of State, 1664–1703*, ed. William Nelson, 1899.

[4] Wayland Fuller Duniway, 'The English Settlers in Colonial Pennsylvania', *The Pennsylvania Magazine of History and Biography*, lii, 1928, pp. 330, 320.

[5] Ibid., pp. 317–41.

the ancient English family of Assheton, whose wife was in some way related to Penn, became a clerk of court and member of council.[1] William Markham (d. 1704), probably of the ancient family of Markham of Ollerton, Nottinghamshire, whose mother was Admiral Penn's sister, became the first Deputy Governor of Pennsylvania, but his descendants sank into obscurity.[2]

Penn granted to John ap John, the apostle of the Quakers in Wales, a large area which was settled from Wales and became known as the Welsh Tract. Some of these settlers were gentlemen with—like all Welsh gentlemen—long pedigrees. Thomas Lloyd (d. 1694), of the Dolobran family from which sprang also the founders of Lloyds Bank,[3] deputy governor from 1684 to 1693, was prominent among them.[4] He shared the royal descent through Elizabeth Grey so widespread on the Welsh border.[5]

Pennsylvania like other colonies received settlers from the older colonies, though few in proportion to those from England. Most of these were from New England, especially Connecticut, though in the far south west there were some from Virginia and a few from Maryland.

The unoccupied land south of Virginia called Carolina was granted in 1663 to a group of courtier promoters, whose plans included taking advantage of the enterprise of small planters squeezed out of other colonies. Many in fact came there from Barbados and others from New England, the Leeward Islands, Bermuda and Virginia, as well as a few from England. The aristocratic Carolina constitution, with hereditary dignities of *Cassique* and *Landgrave* attached to ownership of land, did not in fact induce many of the English owners to settle in the colony, though the Colleton family did so with great success.[6] On 1 June 1705 Laurence Cromp (d. 1715), York Herald, was appointed by the Lords Proprietors 'President of our Court of Honor and principal herald of our whole province of Carolina by the name of Carolina Herald', with power to grant arms 'set upon the face of the sun' to the landgraves and cassiques. It does not appear, however, that he ever went to Carolina.[7]

---

[1] p. 55; information from Lord Clitheroe; Charles P. Keith, *Chronicles of Pennsylvania*, 1917, i. 143; Howard M. Jenkins, *The Family of William Penn*, 1899, p. 139.

[2] Keith, op. cit., pp. 141–5; *Dictionary of American Biography*.

[3] p. 202; Table III.  [4] Thomas Allen Glenn, *Merion in the Welsh Tract*.

[5] p. 238; Arthur Adams and F. L. Weis, *The Magna Carta Sureties, 1215 . . . and Some of their Descendants who Settled in America 1607–1650*, 1955, p. 28.

[6] Andrews, op. cit. iii. 184, 192–7, 218.

[7] *Herald and Genealogist*, v. 479–80. On the settlement of Carolina, see Hanson, *The Atlantic Migration*, pp. 40–42.

Georgia, lying south of Carolina, was granted in 1732 to trustees led by General James Edward Oglethorpe (d. 1785), whose plan was to provide a refuge for imprisoned debtors and other unfortunates and at the same time a buffer to protect the other colonies against the Spaniards. The tracing of these settlers' origins may thus present an initial difficulty, yet it must be remembered that what they shared was not so much obscurity of station as individual misfortune—then as always a different thing. Among Oglethorpe's settlers in 1733 was Sir Francis Bathurst (d. *c.* 1738), 5th Baronet of Lechlade, Gloucestershire, whose daughter Mary, according to a valuable manuscript list of early settlers, married there in 1735 one Francis Piercy, a gardener. He, however, 'ran away to England to avoid being questioned for secreting his brother in laws goods who was indebted to the Trust'. The same list tells us of Hanah Willoughby 'arrived 16 Dec. 1733. Imprison'd for marrying Richard Mellichamp, William Watkins her first husband being alive and she with child by him, and leaving Mellichamp and by his consent bedding a third man who bought her for a shillin'.[1] Life among these colonists must sometimes have been rough. Among the first settlers were also twenty families of Portuguese Jews and twelve of German Jews.

The English conquest of Canada from the French in 1763 had not led to much English colonization. Such settlers of English origin as had come into Nova Scotia were mainly from New England. The situation was, however, wholly changed by the American War of Independence (1775–83). Life in the rebellious colonies became impossible for those who were faithful to their king, called by the Americans Tories and by the English Loyalists. During the war many left their homes, some for England, some for Canada, some in the south for the West Indies, while others took up residence in New York within the British lines. In and after 1782 these last and others fled to Canada, where more than 40,000 settled. By 1783 there were 28,347 in Nova Scotia and New Brunswick as against only 14,000 previous settlers of British descent. The Loyalists came from all the colonies, most from New York, but many also from South Carolina and Massachusetts. It has been said that a large proportion were not Americans born, but the close study made by E. Alfred Jones of their claims to the British Government for compensation do not confirm this. Of 419 claimants from New Jersey 237

---

[1] G. E. C., *Complete Baronetage*, ii. 238; *A List of the Early Settlers of Georgia*, ed. E. Morton Coulter and Albert B. Saye, 1949; M. D. George, *London Life in the XVIIIth Century*, 1930, pp. 149–50.

were born in America, while only 36 were Englishmen and 15 Scots.[1]
All ranks of society are represented in this list, notably army officers,
clergymen, lawyers, surgeons, physicians and apothecaries, but as the
basis of these lists was loss of property the proportion of humble people
among the Loyalists was certainly much larger than they show. Family
was divided against family so that many old American families have
Canadian branches. The largest settlement was in Lower Canada (now
Quebec), but there were also large settlements on the eastern seaboard
in Nova Scotia and New Brunswick as well as in Upper Canada (now
Ontario). The settlement of American loyalists in Canada was balanced
in the 1790's by a settlement of English 'Jacobins' in the United States.[2]

### 9. THE GREAT MIGRATION OF THE NINETEENTH CENTURY

Between 1815 and 1839 about a million emigrants left the United
Kingdom; nearly half of them for Canada, some 417,000 for the United
States, 58,000 for Australasia and under 10,000 for South Africa.[3]
Probably, however, less than a quarter of this total came from England
and more than two thirds from Ireland, where the pressure of the
population upon the means of subsistence was insupportable.[4] The total
migration from the United Kingdom to North America between 1815
and 1912 is estimated at twelve million, of whom more than nine went
to the United States and nearly three to Canada.[5]

The simple and general cause of this efflux was the growth of population at home. Between 1801 and 1851 this rose (for the United Kingdom) from nearly fifteen to more than twenty seven million—that is
probably twice as rapidly as between 1701 and 1801—and after 1851
the increase continued. Down to 1815 the Napoleonic War both limited
the possibilities of emigration and drew off some of the surplus into the
army and navy. On the other hand the violent economic changes caused
first by the war and then by its termination and by the simultaneous and
connected agricultural and economic developments produced social
disturbances in the years after 1815 which aggravated the sheer pressure
of numbers. The local incidence of these strains naturally had a marked

[1] E. Alfred Jones, 'The Loyalists of New Jersey', *New Jersey Hist. Soc. Collections*,
x, 1927, pp. 6–7.
[2] Hanson, *The Atlantic Migration*, pp. 59–60.
[3] *Camb. Hist. Brit. Emp.* ii. 443.
[4] Cf. figures for emigration to North America for 1853–60 (when emigration from
Ireland had passed its peak) in Stanley C. Johnson, *A History of Emigration From the
United Kingdom to North America, 1763–1912*, 1933, p. 347.
[5] Johnson, op. cit., p. 38.

effect upon the volume, nature and direction of migration from particular localities, occupations and social strata.

Much of the detail can never be known yet official returns and reports,
newspaper notices and other contemporary sources of evidence throw
far more light on particular currents of migration than we have for
earlier movements. The recent work of Professor Shepperson on migration to North America brings many such notices together and indicates
where others may be looked for.[1] Thus, for example, agricultural depression in the early 1830's sent many farm labourers and small farmers
across the Atlantic from Sussex, Surrey, Kent and other farming counties of the south. Letters from emigrants who went in groups from
Petworth, Sussex (some of these paid for by their landlord the Earl of
Egremont) and Dorking, Surrey, to Upper Canada, were published in
1833 to encourage others.[2] Excessive rainfall in 1836 sent more from
the clay soils of Yorkshire, Buckinghamshire and Huntingdonshire.[3]
Many farmers from Yorkshire settled near Jacksonville, Illinois, in the
1830's. A group of farmers from Killingholme, Lincolnshire, settled in
Clinton County, Iowa, in the 1850's.[4] In Yorkshire and Lancashire the
mechanization of weaving had by the 1820's thrown out of employment
very many handloom weavers and some of these are known to have
formed emigration societies.[5] In 1847–9 the Potters' Trade Union
organized the migration of a certain number of potters and their families
from Staffordshire to Wisconsin.[6] Cutlers, filesmiths and razorsmiths
from Sheffield settled in Waterbury and Bridgeport, Connecticut, and
elsewhere in New England between the 1830's and the 1850's.[7]

Men of higher social standing were led to emigrate by expectations
of opportunity, sometimes through publicity put out for the purpose.
This was the age of the great American westward trend (a subject which
deserves a genealogical work to itself),[8] when settlers in endless number
were needed. In 1823 the American Chamber of Commerce set up an
office in Liverpool for the attraction of settlers and in 1831 official
information was circulated about life in Canada.[9] Private agents—not
always honest—for the sale of land both in the United States and the

---

[1] Wilbur S. Shepperson, Assistant Professor of History in the University of Nevada,
*British Emigration to North America, Projects and Opinions in the Early Victorian Period*,
1957.

[2] Ibid., pp. 10, 21, 27, 40.        [3] Johnson, op. cit., pp. 48–49.

[4] Shepperson, p. 31.        [5] Johnson, pp. 54–55.

[6] Shepperson, pp. 97–98.        [7] Ibid., p. 82.

[8] For a general account of the decisive part played in this by New Englanders see
Stewart H. Holbrook, *The Yankee Exodus*, 1950.

[9] Shepperson, op. cit., p. 61.

colonies were active in England from the 1830's.[1] Humanitarian and religious bodies took an active part, chief among the latter the Mormons or Church of Jesus Christ of Latter Day Saints, whose first missionaries arrived in England in 1837. In 1841 parties of 200 or more each, mainly from Preston and Manchester, sailed from Liverpool bound for the Mormons' then home at Nauvoo, Illinois, where by 1846 some 4,750 had arrived. After the great migration of the Mormons across America to the Great Salt Lake Valley in 1846–7 many more followed and by 1860 some 25,000 had sailed.[2] Figures for 1850–62 show that most of the emigrants came from towns and especially from London, the West Midlands, South Wales, Lancashire, the West Riding and Central Scotland.[3]

Less happy was Robert Owen's Utopian project of 1848 for a socialist settlement in Texas, which only brought there a small party of London tradesmen and mechanics and left them stranded. Earlier efforts by land speculators to attract Englishmen to Texas had been vigorous but reckless and were therefore disappointing in their results.[4]

Nineteenth century emigrants fall into the two classes of the unassisted, who paid for themselves, and the assisted, whose passages and other charges were paid for wholly or in part by private benefactors, charitable societies or public funds. Surviving records of such assistance may be helpful to the genealogist. One of the first instances of a settlement paid for from public funds was that of the 1820 settlers at the Cape of Good Hope. The transfer of the Cape Colony from Dutch to British rule during the Napoleonic War had been confirmed by the Treaty of Paris in 1814 and this was the first considerable British settlement. £50,000 were devoted to the project by the Government with the object of helping sufferers from the economic aftermath of the war. Ninety thousand applied, about 4,000 were in fact sent in twenty six ships and settled in the district round Grahamstown. Of the 1,455 adult males some 49 per cent came from agricultural occupations, 31 per cent were skilled artisans and mechanics, 11 per cent came from trade and commerce, 5 per cent from the army, the navy and the sea, and 4 per cent from the professions. Their family and geographical origins have yet to be analysed in detail, but they are said to have been above the average in intelligence, courage and respectability and many of their descendants

[1] Ibid., pp. 40–64.                                    [2] Ibid., chap. iv.
[3] P. A. M. Taylor, *Expectations Westward. The Mormons and the Emigration of their British Converts in the Nineteenth Century*, 1965, pp. 148–9.
[4] Shepperson, op. cit., pp. 100–2, 167–77.

have been prominent in South African life. Four of the settlers were later knighted, two became lieutenant-governors, and others held high office in the colonial administration and the armed forces.[1]

The great fields of systematic colonization, largely inspired by Edward Gibbon Wakefield (d. 1862), were, however, Australia and New Zealand. It was an important part of Wakefield's doctrine that colonies should be given a modified form of the social structure of the mother country and that the colonists should be chosen accordingly. In his *New British Province of South Australia*[2] he appealed not only to ambitious labourers but also to the struggling and aspiring middle class, to 'young men of good fortune and what is called mean birth', and even, with some hesitation, to the children and grandchildren of the highest families in the land. 'The whole emigration to Upper Canada and New Zealand', Wakefield wrote in 1849, 'furnishes no instance of the ultimate settlement of a gentleman's family with satisfaction to themselves and their friends at home.' Yet Wakefield's efforts did in fact induce members of this class to settle in some numbers in the 1830's and 1840's both in New Zealand (especially the Canterbury settlement) and Australia (especially South Australia).[3] The careful selection of colonists upon Wakefield's principles by the New Zealand Company from 1839 onwards was a great contrast to much that had gone before and the settlement of Canterbury in 1850 represented the culmination of this improvement.[4] Until shortly before 1914 New Zealanders of Scottish and Irish descent much outnumbered those of English origin. Indeed it was said that 55 per cent of those of British origin were of Scottish and 25 per cent of Irish descent. Just before 1914 the urban population overtook the rural and since about 1935 the development of secondary industries has brought many Englishmen to New Zealand, both professional men and skilled workers. In 1961/2 immigrants from England and Wales numbered 10,736 as against 2,387 from Scotland, 475 from Northern Ireland and 556 from the Republic of Ireland. The land, however, still remains largely in the hands of families of Scottish or Irish origin. In 1964 four sheep runs in Canterbury had been held by the same families since their first settlement in 1853–6.[5]

Until Wakefield's activity began to bear fruit in the assistance of free emigrants to New South Wales in 1831 and the foundation of South

[1] H. E. Hockly, *The Story of The British Settlers of 1820 in South Africa*, 1949.
[2] 1834, chap. iv and pp. 126–9, quoted in *Camb. Hist. Brit. Emp.* ii. 449.
[3] *Camb. Hist. Brit. Emp.* ii. 448–52.
[4] J. S. Marais, *The Colonisation of New Zealand*, 1927, chaps. iv and ix.
[5] Information from Mr. E. T. Roberts, 15 Nov. 1964.

Australia in 1836, the peopling of Australia had depended mainly on the transportation of convicts to the penal settlements. Botany Bay, where Sydney stands, and Norfolk Island were the first of these, established in 1788 to solve the difficulty created by the loss of those American colonies to which felons had previously been transported.[1] A penal settlement in Van Diemen's Land (now Tasmania) was set up in 1803 and to these settlements some 2,400 convicts a year were transported. The great difference from the eighteenth century transportation to America was that there the convicts were employed on their plantations by free colonists, whereas in Australia there were at first no colonists to employ them, though later some were assigned to settlers to work for them.

For convicts who had served their sentences or had been pardoned there were opportunities to occupy land as 'squatters' and to grow rich by producing wool for export. Some of these squatters acquired property worth as much as £40,000 and incomes of £2,000 and £3,000 a year were not uncommon. The degree of delinquency differed greatly. There were 'most notorious offenders, every one of whom is as great a villain as ever graced a gibbet' and there were superior convicts 'never known to associate with the common herd'. In 1814 Francis (Howard) Greenway (1777–1837), born at Mangotsfield, Gloucestershire, of a family of quarrymen, masons and builders, was transported for forgery but lived to become the architect of important buildings in Sydney.[2] An attempt of government to suppress the beginnings of trade unionism brought to Van Diemen's Land in 1833 George Loveless and five other villagers from Tolpuddle, Dorset, who are known as the Tolpuddle martyrs.[3]

During the years between Waterloo and the Reform Bill [say the Hammonds] the governing class was decimating the village populations on the principle of the Greek tyrant who flicked off the heads of the tallest blades in his field; the Game Laws, summary jurisdiction, special commissions, drove men of spirit and enterprise, the natural leaders of their fellows, from the villages where they might have troubled the peace of their masters. The village Hampdens of that generation sleep by the shores of Botany Bay.[4]

---

[1] p. 292.

[2] M. H. Ellis, *Francis Greenway: his Life and Times*, 1949; M. Herman, *Early Australian Architects and their Work*, 1954. I owe this information to Mr. Martin Briggs.

[3] *Camb. Hist. Brit. Emp.* ii, chap. xii (1).

[4] J. L. and Barbara Hammond, *The Village Labourer, 1760–1832*, 4th ed. 1927, p. 215. For 'the Greek tyrant' read 'Tarquinius Superbus, King of Rome'.

It is much to be hoped that the natural inhibitions, which have hitherto kept Australians from the exploration of convict ancestry, will soon vanish. Transported ancestors four or five generations back are surely now far enough away to be looked on as mere incidents in a pedigree, quite apart from the question how many of them were by our standards ancestors to be ashamed of. Of that we shall be better placed to judge when the lives and antecedents of a sufficient number have been studied. For the genealogist a convict ancestor has the outstanding merit that his collision with the law will be the subject of record, so that far more personal information may be available about him than for the average of settlers. Every transported convict's descendant, who overcomes his reluctance and investigates his pedigree, may congratulate himself upon making a contribution to the social history of both England and Australia.[1]

Transportation to New South Wales ended in 1849, to Van Diemen's Land in 1852 and to Norfolk Island in 1855. From 1840 to 1868 convicts were sent to Western Australia but after that no more were transported. Down to 1836 the total number sent to New South Wales was 75,200 and to Van Diemen's Land, since 1817, 27,759.

The free immigrants to New South Wales before 1813 were drawn from all classes save the very poor and included a number of military and naval officers, a larger number of marines, members of the upper and middle classes 'sent to the colony by their friends as the easiest and surest way of being rid of them' and a small but steady stream of carpenters, blacksmiths and small shopkeepers. In each class there were some undesirables and a proportion of admirable settlers. Many of the settlers in the 1820's were men of property, possessing £2,000 or more. One had as much as £18,000. Others, as before, 'were aided to emigrate by friends in England'. The governor, Sir Ralph Darling, complained in 1826 that too many shopkeepers and not enough farmers were arriving. An important factor was that without assistance few but property owners could afford the passage, so much longer and more costly than to North America. Conversely the first assisted emigration in the 1840's was criticized as bringing in too many paupers and undesirables.[2] It was such imbalances as these that Wakefield sought to remedy.

---

[1] Following the appearance of this passage in the first edition of 1960 I received in 1962 the first letter I had ever had from an Australian which frankly avowed descent from a transported convict. I have since had others and have noted with pleasure the great increase of Australian interest in genealogy and heraldry in the last ten years.

[2] R. B. Madgwick, *Immigration into Eastern Australia, 1788–1851,* 1937, pp. 34, 56–61, and chap. xi.

Not until the late 1830's, when transportation was approaching its end, did free settlement in Australia attain substantial numbers and by far the greatest settlement took place after 1850. Yet even by that date the free settlers and their descendants must easily have outnumbered those of convicts, so that the latter must now form only a small proportion of the population. Members of several peers' and baronets' families, some of whose descendants have since succeeded to the family honours, were among the settlers in both Australia and New Zealand in the second half of the century. Australians of royal descent are numerous. To give but one example out of many, Marshall Waller Clifton (1787–1861) and his wife Elinor, she certainly, he most probably descended from Edward III, came in 1841 to Australia where he settled at Australind as Commissioner for Western Australia. By 1912 the descendants of this couple numbered more than 250 and by now there must be many more.[1]

The favourite destination of British emigrants at all dates after 1827 was the United States of America and between 1860 and 1890 Englishmen formed the majority of all who settled there.[2] Canada came second until 1852, the year of the discovery of gold in Australia. Australasia then took the lead and kept it till 1867, when Canada resumed it. These figures relate to emigration from the United Kingdom as a whole for it is only from 1853 that there are separate figures for England, Scotland and Ireland.[3] The total fluctuations reflect social history. After 1854 a rise in prosperity at home followed by recruiting for the Crimean War and Indian Mutiny reduced the figures of emigration. After 1861 there was another upward turn and in 1869 distress at home produced a new high level.

The extensive English settlements in India since the eighteenth century are now mainly represented there by descendants of mixed Indian and English blood; a conspicuous series of marriages between English and Indians is found in the related families of Hearsey and Gardner.[4] Lieutenant-Colonel Andrew Wilson Hearsey (1752–95), Commandant of the Fort of Allahabad, had a legitimate son, Lieutenant-General Sir John Bennet Hearsey, K.C.B. (1793–1865), and an illegitimate family, apparently by an Indian mother,

---

[1] G. E. C., *Complete Baronetage*, i, 1900, p. 21 : MS. Supplement to Ruvigny's *Mortimer-Percy Volume*, by E. H. Fellowes, in the College of Arms: Coll. Arm. Reg. Surrey xix. 153.       [2] Hanson, *The Atlantic Migration*, p. 10.

[3] Johnson, op. cit., app. i.

[4] Col. Hugh Pearse, *The Hearseys. Five Generations of an Anglo-Indian Family*, 1905; *Burke's Peerage*, s.v. Gardner.

of whom Hyder Young Hearsey (b. 1782) married Khanum (princess) Zuhur-al-Nissa, daughter of one of the deposed princes of Cambay. Her sister married Colonel William Linnaeus Gardner, a nephew of the first Lord Gardner (peerage of Ireland 1800, of the United Kingdom 1806) and their son James Gardner married Nawab Mulka Mumanu Begum, one of the fifty two children of Mirzo Suliman Sheko, brother of the Mogul Emperor Akbar II (1806–37). Hyder Young Hearsey and his princess had several children, of whom Harriet married her step-uncle Sir John Bennet Hearsey and left descendants, while William Moorcroft Hearsey also left descendants in India. There also remain many of the Gardner family, among them, presumably, the heir to the peerage.

The settlement of the African and other colonies and the mercantile and other settlements outside British territory from Portugal to Patagonia must here be passed over with a brief reference to one example, that of the English settlement in Chile. This began in the early 1820's, when merchant houses began to establish themselves. By about 1860 a pattern of family groupings had been set. The influx of English settlers continued steadily till the collapse of the nitrate market about 1930 and the newcomers tended to marry into English families already there. Three old established families, Gibbs, Price and Wodehouse, brought descents from Edward III.[1]

For the origins of some at least of these English settlers overseas the genealogist will in practice have sources of information independent of knowledge of the circumstances of settlement. It is partly for the same reason that the account of those later settlements which have been mentioned is so much shorter in relation to their vast extent than that of those of the seventeenth century. But there are other reasons worth mentioning for the light they throw on some of the problems which confront the genealogist.

The first is that the students of the early settlers and their origins have had much more time for their work. The New Englanders, for example, have been pursuing their few thousand settler ancestors for more than a century with great resources of wealth and scholarship. How could it be expected that detailed knowledge of the millions who went to Canada in the past century should compare with this? The pedigrees of an appreciable *number* of Canadian, Australian and other settlers, have of course been worked out, but the *proportion* they bear to

---

[1] Information from Mr. L. C. Derrick-Jehu.

the vast total number is so small that it is as yet impossible to generalize from them.

Again the early settlers have far more living descendants *per head* than the later ones and a greater ancestral interest has thus been focused on them. In America these were the founders of their country and have as ancestors an appeal which later settlers there cannot match. Their families moreover tended to form a kind of aristocracy. They were first on the scene and even when they did not keep the predominance in wealth and power thus opened to them, they retained from it some glamour and prestige, which in itself has made descent from them a goal of genealogy.

Finally the nineteenth century settlers and their descendants have always been aware that their migration was largely composed of fugitives from bitter poverty and from this they have often drawn the false conclusion that such emigrants' origins must either be untraceable or if traceable of no interest. Partly for this reason they have concerned themselves less with genealogy than the descendants of the older settlers and so the genealogists know less of them. There are signs today that this phase is passing. In the same way the feeling lately conspicuous in many Australians and New Zealanders that their countries were too new for such studies to be sensible has lately shown a marked diminution.

It is true that to trace the origins of many nineteenth century settlers is difficult and of some impossible. It is also true that those of many more—men just as obscure and humble in themselves—can be traced with little or no difficulty. What makes the difference, as we shall see, is often not the station of the settler but some accident of nomenclature or record—a rare or localized surname, membership of an identifiable group, birth, marriage or the birth of children *before* leaving England but *after* the introduction of civil registration, and so forth.[1]

Genealogically the nineteenth century emigrant has one great advantage over the settler of older times, namely that by his day birth, death, marriage and other records of the great mass of the population were far fuller and more complete. If a seventeenth century labourer was descended, as he might be, from King Edward I, the chances of tracing the descent are small. If a nineteenth century labourer had such a descent, as far more must have had than in earlier times, the chances of tracing it are much better because the latter part of the descent runs through a much better recorded period.

[1] p. 350.

It is said, and probably with truth, that in the nineteenth century migrations from England the gentry were on an average in a smaller proportion than among the English at home. There was, however, a class of well born emigrants which must not be forgotten, that of the black sheep, the men who left their country for the colonies or United States to redeem their folly or their failure. They started early. A letter of 14 June 1623 mentions that 'an unruly son of Lady Finches (whom she sent to Virginia to be tamed) within five or six days after his return fell into a drunken quarrell with the watch where he was so hurt that he died the next morning'. The mother, Elizabeth widow of Sir Moyle Finch, was soon afterwards created Viscountess Maidstone and later Countess of Winchelsea.[1] In Victoria's reign an age of stiffening convention was succeeding an age of laxity. Fortunes had been lost by gambling as well as by economic change. In such circumstances departure for the colonies was a well trodden escape route in life as in literature. In the nature of things such departures and their sequel are ill documented, but now and then a lawsuit brings one into the open.

The following story was told in evidence in 1914 at a hearing in the House of Lords on the petition for termination of the abeyance of the barony of Ferrers. Marmion Edward Ferrers of Baddesley Clinton, Warwickshire, had been not only a coheir to the barony by female descent but also heir male of the ancient Norman family of Ferrers.[2] In 1884, however, he had died without issue, as had all his brothers save one. This was Charles Ferrers (d. 1873) who

resided in England up to about the year 1850, when he went to America. Up to the year 1840 he lived with his mother and his brothers and sisters at Baddesley, after which date he resided at a farm called Hampton Lodge, Hampton-on-the-Hill, near Warwick. In, or shortly prior to, the year 1835 he became intimate with a woman named Sarah Pittaway, who was sometime a maid in the service of his mother, by whom he had several illegitimate children. . . . In or about the year 1850, he went to America accompanied by the said Sarah Pittaway and his said illegitimate children by her and continued to reside there at Bremen, Cook County, Illinois, until his death in 1873. . . . He was never married to the said Sarah Pittaway or to any other woman and died a bachelor 3 February, 1873, and the persons named in his Will as his 'children' were [according to this testimony] his illegitimate children by the said Sarah Pittaway.

[1] *The Letters of John Chamberlain*, ed. N. E. McClure, The American Philosophical Society, Memoirs XII, pt. ii, Philadelphia, 1939, ii. 502; *Complete Peerage*, xii, pt. ii, p. 775.      [2] p. 64.

This was indeed contradicted in evidence given by Sarah to the Cook County Court on Charles Ferrers' death, to the effect that she was married to him 'soon after he arrived at the age of twenty-one years'. However, of the five sons and three daughters then living in America two had been baptized at Warwick as children of Sarah Pittaway with no father's name mentioned. Moreover, in 1857 Charles Ferrers had written to his brother, 'This woman Pittaway is a regular devil in the house. Disputes everything I say or do; and tries to set the children against me on all occasions. . . . I am thankful that I did not marry her.'[1] Legitimate or illegitimate, these children were of the most ancient Norman lineage.

[1] *In the House of Lords, Case on behalf of Henry Ferrers Ferrers claiming to be a co-heir to the Barony of Ferrers*, 1914, pp. 24–28.

# VIII

## THE RECORDS

### I. PRINCIPLES

THE antiquity, extent and preservation of her records are among the glories of England and the English genealogist is thus fortunate indeed in comparison with those of most countries. For this very reason to give even a brief account of all the kinds of record which may help the genealogist in England would need a much larger book than the whole of this. In the present chapter I shall only seek to outline the main categories and the principles which govern the genealogist's approach to them.

The word record is here used in a special sense; one less narrow than that implied by the sixteenth century legal distinction between the *enrolling* and *recording* of certain documents,[1] but narrow enough to exclude literary and antiquarian compilations however old and valuable. It is used, in fact, in a sense akin to the modern technical sense of *Archives*, that is documents produced by official transactions and preserved in official custody.

The modern attitude to records as historical evidences superior in some respects to all others has its roots in the labours of the French and English antiquaries of the sixteenth and seventeenth centuries among whom genealogists were prominent. Their efforts, closely linked with the religious and political issues of the day, to establish controversial positions and to criticize each others' conclusions developed methods for testing the authenticity of documents which found a notable embodiment in 1681 in the *De Re Diplomatica Libri Sex* of Dom Jean Mabillon. These led on to the nineteenth century development of modern historical method. There were parallel developments, in the critical *use* of documents, owing much indirectly to the revived study of classical antiquity.

To the history of these developments we must return. We are here concerned with two points only which have emerged from them. For

---

1 Hilary Jenkinson, *A Manual of Archive Administration*, 1937 ed., pp. 2, 231.

genealogists perhaps even more than for general historians archive (or record) evidence is superior to other evidence because of its independent, authentic and contemporary character. Thus the statement of a family or local historian that *A* was the son of *B* may be honest and valuable—but we want to know how he knew, what was his authority. The statement of a contemporary document, on the other hand, such as a will, a conveyance or a record of legal proceedings, that *B* was *A*'s father, is normally as good evidence as we can expect to have. For this reason the modern critical genealogist goes out of his way to indicate the original record on which his statements rest, therein differing from those of his predecessors who quoted no authorities at all or what was neither original itself nor based on what was.

To possess the fullest evidential value records must not only be original individually but must be preserved in their original context. Archives are the fossilized deposit of past activities and their original arrangement, where preserved, is therefore a direct reflection of the nature of the process they record. In 1199 the Chancery of the Kings of England began the systematic enrolment of writs; the entry, that is to say, on vellum rolls of more or less abbreviated copies of charters and lesser documents issued in the king's name. At first the rolls formed a single series kept in one place by one authority. Then as business grew greater and more complex it was subdivided and departmentalized and the forms of entry reflect the changes in organization.

In the mediaeval records, as in those of a modern business, different stages of the same transaction often appear in different series, and if the relevant part of one series is missing, another may fill the gap and show what happened. Unhappily now and then distinct original series, representing organic growth, have been broken up and mixed together by well meaning systematizers who thought it more convenient to rearrange their contents by subject or the like. This is a cardinal sin against the principle which the French call *le respect des fonds*, the maintenance of the original form of the archive deposit. The arrangement of the documents within their group is itself as much a piece of history as the arrangement of the words and letters in a single document. To break it up and rearrange it is like cutting up a charter and reassembling its words or sentences in a new order. Unless the context can be reconstructed half the meaning will be lost.

The neglect or observance of this principle of *respect des fonds* makes the first great division of records between those preserved in due series and those collected artificially from the flotsam and jetsam of dismembered archive groups. The contents of the Public Record Office are archives built up by history but the manuscripts in the British Museum are not an archive deposit but a collection formed by gift and purchase. Nevertheless the British Museum collection includes, with much material of other kinds, fragments of archives, and some entire private archives. Conversely the Public Record Office contains alongside its great archive deposits such debris of dismembered groups as the Chancery Miscellanea.

## 2. THE CLASSIFICATION OF RECORDS

Archives may be classified in many ways but for our purpose four of these are important; the first is their classification by historical structure; the second by their present day custody; the third by the nature of their subject matter; and the fourth by their genealogical utility. In what follows these strands are not kept wholly separate. Indeed to try to separate structure altogether from custody would lead to pedantry. It is helpful, however, to bear in mind the logical distinction and the existence of old patterns different from and underlying present patterns.

The classification of archives by historical structure would if carried out completely amount to an administrative history of the country. For the early periods, the deepest and most far reaching division is between the records of the Church and those of the State. Within the latter category the distinction between central and local records is more important in relation to custody than to structure, while it is mainly if not solely in the later periods that we meet with truly private archives unrelated to public authority either spiritual or temporal.

### (i) *The Records of the Church*

Political theory in the Middle Ages saw the government of the world as divided into the spiritual and the temporal. Spiritual sway over Western Christendom was actually exercised by the Papacy, which in the words of Thomas Hobbes, was 'not other than the Ghost of the deceased Roman Empire, sitting crowned upon the grave thereof'.[1] Thus until the abolition of the papal supremacy in 1534 the Church in England formed a part of a larger entity whose central archive is to be found not in the Public Record Office but in the Vatican. It was therefore logical for the Record Office between 1894 and 1955 to arrange for the transcription and publication of fourteen volumes of papal letters

---

[1] *Leviathan*, 1651, pt. iv, chap. 47.

comprising entries in the papal registers relating to Great Britain and Ireland.

The division between the spiritual and temporal jurisdictions was one of functions not of persons, so that clerics were in temporal matters subject to the king's courts and laymen in spiritual matters to the spiritual courts. The monasteries, bishops, deans and chapters, colleges and chantries owned much land. This was a temporal activity subject to the temporal law and the records of it should therefore be classed as records of the State rather than of the Church. In practice, however, the records of the spiritual and temporal functions though largely kept in different series were at times mingled. Some early bishops' registers, for instance, while mainly concerned with spiritual activities, such as ordinations, consecrations, church discipline and the like, also contain records relating to church property. Secular functions have at various times been delegated by the Crown to officers of the Church. The records of their exercise, from those of the palatinate jurisdiction of the Bishop of Durham downwards, are structurally records of the State not the Church, as are such records in church custody as those of the parish overseers established by the Poor Law Act of 1601.

## (a) Episcopal and other records

The fullest information about the records of the Church of England generally is to be found in the two volume Survey of Ecclesiastical Archives, as yet unpublished but available in the British Museum and a few other libraries, completed in 1952 by a committee appointed by the Pilgrim Trustees in 1946. Though mainly concerned with records still in ecclesiastical custody this report does not omit to mention those which have passed into other hands.

The records (other than parochial) which remain with the Church fall into five classes; those of the two Provinces of Canterbury and York; those of the 23 ancient and 20 modern dioceses; those of 103 archdeaconries and the ancient deaneries of Jersey and Guernsey (which though not in England are in the diocese of Winchester); those of the cathedral chapters; and those of some 50 peculiar jurisdictions; forming 248 archive groups in a rather smaller number of places of deposit, archbishops' and bishops' palaces, bishops' and archdeacons' registries and cathedral muniment rooms and libraries. One great former group, that of the records of the monasteries and kindred foundations, was for the most part dispersed at their suppression by Henry VIII, though a few foundations in this class like Durham, Westminster and St.

George's, Windsor, certain hospitals for the aged or the sick like St. Cross at Winchester and St. Bartholomew's and Bethlem in London, the Oxford and Cambridge colleges and those of Winchester and Eton were permitted to survive with greater or less change and in consequence retain their pre-Reformation records.[1]

The distinction between the spiritual and temporal activities of the Church has already been noted. The latter were largely functions of the tenure of land and when lands such as those of the monasteries passed from religious to lay hands, the new owners should and often did take over and preserve records relating to their property. That great work of seventeenth century scholarship, the *Monasticon Anglicanum* of Roger Dodsworth and William Dugdale, 1655–73,[2] is in the main a compilation of the scattered records of monastic property. Many cartularies in which the monks entered copies of the charters of their houses' endowments are preserved and the documents they record are of the greatest value for early periods. These cartularies are widely dispersed and a long felt need has been filled by Mr. G. R. C. Davis' catalogue.[3]

The remaining lands of the Church were largely transferred to the Ecclesiastical Commissioners set up in 1836 whose records are deposited in the Public Record Office, but as the relevant records could not always be separated from others the records of church lands are divided between these and the bishops' registries.

The oldest extant English series of records of the spiritual jurisdiction of the Church are the bishops' registers, beginning at Lincoln in 1209, York in 1217, Exeter in 1257, Hereford in 1275 and Canterbury in 1279.[4] Many volumes of bishops' registers have been printed by the Canterbury and York Society. Their contents are various but the records of consecrations, ordinations and the exercise of church discipline predominate. Separate books of the institutions and ordinations of clergy begin at various later dates, but with very rare exceptions not till the sixteenth century and in some cases not till the seventeenth. There are 708 volumes of bishops' registers and, if the later, subsidiary, series are included, more than 1,350.

The records of the ecclesiastical courts of law are voluminous, important and little known. The Commissary Court of Canterbury Act

---

[1] See pp. 334–5.   [2] p. 369.
[3] G. R. C. Davis, *Medieval Cartularies of Great Britain—a Short Catalogue*, Royal Hist. Soc. 1958.
[4] R. C. Fowler, *Episcopal Registers of England and Wales*, 1918; Claude Jenkins, *Ecclesiastical Records*, 1920, pp. 40–49.

Books go back to 1371 and from that date to 1721 fill 100 volumes. Those of York fill 335 volumes between 1416 and 1881. Of 400 volumes at Wells between 1458 and 1796 335 date from before the Civil War. The variety of their contents reflects the breadth of the jurisdiction of these courts. In the words of Bishop Stubbs,

Ecclesiastical jurisdiction in its widest sense covers all the ground of ecclesiastical relations, persons, properties, rights and remedies; churches, their patronage, furniture, ritual and revenues; clergymen in all their relations, faith and practice, dress and behaviour in church and out; the morality of the laity, their religious behaviour, their marriages, legitimacy, wills and administrations of intestates; the maintenance of the doctrines of the faith by clergy and laity alike and the examination into all contracts in which faith was pledged or alleged to be pledged, the keeping of oaths, promises and fiduciary undertakings.[1]

A start was made with the detailed cataloguing of this vast storehouse of material with the publication by the Marc Fitch Fund in 1966 of *A Catalogue of the Records of the Bishop, Archdeacons and Former Exempt Jurisdictions of the Diocese of Chichester*, by Francis W. Steer and Isabel M. Kirby. This was planned as an example to be followed by others. Gloucester and Bristol have come next and work on others is planned.

The jurisdiction over wills, dealt with more fully below, was transferred to a civil authority in 1857 and with it the records. A like transfer of the jurisdiction over marriage was effected by the Matrimonial Causes Act, 1857, but the archives for some reason were not transferred as it seems to have been intended that they should be. The marriage licence bonds and allegations, unlike most of the legal records of the Church, have been singled out by genealogists for study and publication because of their exceptional genealogical value.

Religious intolerance produced such valuable records of Roman Catholics and other Dissenters as the Returns of Papists of 1626, 1682, 1706, 1767 and 1780 and the Meeting House Certificates of 1689–1718.

Before the Suppression of the Monasteries some of the cathedrals were monastic while others were served by secular canons. The Chapter Act Books of some of the latter go back to early dates, at York to 1290, at Lincoln to 1305 and at Salisbury to 1329. Those of the former monastic cathedrals date from after the Suppression, at Durham from

---

[1] *Appendix to the Report of the Ecclesiastical Courts Commission*, 1883, quoted by Jenkins, op. cit., p. 72.

1541, at Rochester from 1547, at Winchester from 1553 and at Canterbury from 1561. The Chapter Act Books and Registers number some 660 volumes. Monastic Act Books are very rare survivals.

## (b) *Wills*

Until 1857 the execution of wills and the administration of the goods of those who died intestate were controlled (with some few exceptions)[1] by the ecclesiastical courts and authorities. The jurisdiction came by degrees to be exercised through a complicated mosaic of local probate courts large and small with rights of appeal from lower to higher and certain overriding powers in the latter. The Ecclesiastical Courts Commission of 1832 records as then existing 4 provincial, 46 diocesan (Commissary and Consistory) and 35 archdeaconry courts, as well as 231 so called peculiar jurisdictions and 49 manorial courts, making 365 in all, the smallest covering only a single parish, the largest with rights over the whole country.[2]

The Court of Probate Act of 1857 transferred the whole jurisdiction to a newly constituted civil authority, to whose custody the ancient records were transferred. This in 1873 became the newly constituted Probate and Divorce Division of the High Court of Justice. It was a misfortune for historians and genealogists that records so important to them were entrusted not to the Public Record Office or any other record authority but to custody, as Canon Jenkins puts it,[3] 'not merely unfavourable, but inimical in almost every conceivable way to the interests of historical students, and under conditions which even the courtesy of officials can do little to mitigate'.

It is not the fault of the probate authorities, whose primary duty is to discharge their current functions, not to cater for students, that the conditions they have been able to offer for study have compared so poorly with those in modern record offices. At the Principal Probate Registry at Somerset House these have been much better than at some of the provincial registries, but the fact remains that no single index, calendar or guide to these highly important records has been published by their custodians. Such publication has been left wholly to private enterprise, which has indeed made valiant efforts. The British Record Society has printed some 55 volumes of calendars and indexes of wills and administrations, while valuable guides to the nature and whereabouts of

---

[1] The exceptions were a handful of manor and borough courts.
[2] Jenkins, op. cit., pp. 64–65.
[3] Ibid., p. 66.

the records have been published by George W. Marshall and B. G. Bouwens.[1]

The surviving records of the different probate courts begin at widely differing dates. The oldest records of English wills, if we exclude a few royal wills recorded in chronicles,[2] are found mingled with other matters in bishops' registers and are accordingly not in the custody of the probate authorities but in the diocesan registries.[3] Records of commissions for probate in the Registers of the Bishops of Lincoln go back to 1280 and actual entries of wills to 1320, while the earliest will entered in the separate registers of the Archbishop of York's Consistory Court was proved in 1316. Most series, however, start much later than this; that of the Prerogative Court of Canterbury, whose overriding jurisdiction covers all England and Wales, in 1383; that of the Consistory Court of Ely in 1449; that of Chichester in 1518; while that of Hereford is fragmentary before 1662 and others begin at intermediate dates.

In a perfect series the original wills executed by the testators should find their counterparts in the copies entered in the registers. But in fact we find in some courts and at some dates original wills only; in others registered copies only; and in others more or less completely corresponding series of both. The irregularities in the calendars and indexes are equally great. For some portions of some courts they are excellent, for others non-existent, and for many betwixt and between. The worst trap is that some which look well enough are in fact unreliable and indexes have even been printed from manuscript calendars which have serious omissions.

The recent policy of the Probate authorities has been to transfer the old provincial wills from their own registries to the County Record Offices set up in recent years by the County Councils. This had the merit that the new custodians are people whose main concern is with archives. But whereas that concern is with the archives of their several counties, the boundaries of the old probate divisions often diverge widely from those of the counties. Not for this reason only it is idle to

---

[1] George W. Marshall, Rouge Croix Pursuivant, *A Handbook to the Ancient Courts of Probate and Depositories of Wills*, 1895; B. G. Bouwens, *Wills and their Whereabouts*, 1939. Revised ed. by A. J. Camp, 1963.

[2] John Nichols, *Royal Wills*, 1780.

[3] See also 'A List of Thirteenth-Century English Wills', by the Rev. Michael M. Sheehan, C.S.B., *Genealogists Mag.*, vol. 13, 1961, pp. 259–65, which includes also a few in cartularies, originals in the possession of the Dean and Chapter of St. Paul's and wills registered in the Court of Husting from 1258.

pretend that the new plan is wholly satisfactory. No archives have more importance than the Probate Records for the post-mediaeval genealogist. They were in the custody of the State for a century, yet in that time the State did nothing to make them accessible by publication of lists, calendars or indexes. The County Councils cannot do less than this and some have done and are doing much more.

### (c) Parish records

Most people who are not genealogists, if asked from what sources pedigrees are traced, would mention parish registers, and there, as like as not, would stop. The tribute thus paid to these records' value is deserved, though exaggerated. From their institution in 1538 to that of civil registration of births, marriages and deaths in 1837 they are the chief and often the sole source of information for the descent of those who had too little property to make wills.

In 1538 Thomas Cromwell, who had been Henry VIII's Visitor General of the Monasteries and was then his Vicar General, issued on the king's behalf an injunction requiring parish clergy to enter in books every wedding, christening and burial taking place in their parishes. For the safe keeping of these books each parish was to provide 'one sure coffer with two locks and keys', one key to be kept by the parson and the other by the churchwardens. A few registers go back to this date but it was some time before most were kept systematically and gaps and irregularities (quite apart from those caused by later loss or destruction) are to be met with here and there as late as the eighteenth century.

Many of the early entries seem to have been made on loose sheets of paper and only later (sometimes much later) entered in the parchment books which were gradually introduced under Elizabeth I (1558–1603) and were made obligatory in 1603. Some of the oldest registers are thus not originals but later compilations.

In 1597 Convocation laid down that copies of the entries made during each year should be sent to the bishop's registry after every Easter. These bishops' transcripts, where they exist, make good the loss and destruction of original registers and in those registries where their original arrangement by years rather than parishes has been maintained put a valuable tool into the hand of the researcher who knows the date but not the place of the baptism, marriage or burial he is in search of.

The Commonwealth Parliament, anticipating the modern secular state, gave orders in 1644 for the registration of births and deaths as well as baptisms and burials, and in 1653 for the appointment of lay registrars and for civil marriages before Justices of the Peace.[1] The procedure required the parties to a marriage to supply particulars of their parents and these are found in some Commonwealth parish registers though hardly ever in others until 1837. England in this respect presents a striking contrast to some continental countries, where pedigrees may be traced through parish registers alone because baptismal entries refer to the parents' marriage and marriage entries to the parties' parentage and places of origin. The English attitude to innovations in this direction has always been that reported to Cromwell by Sir Piers Edgecumbe in 1539, 'Their mistrust is that some charges, more than hath been in times past, shall grow to them by this occasion of registering of these things.'[2] In early times the amount of detail entered varies greatly at the whim of the parson, occupations and the like appearing more often as time goes on. In 1754 the form of marriage entries was standardized by the introduction of printed forms under Hardwicke's Act and in 1812 Rose's Act did the same for baptisms and burials.

The Parish Register Abstract of 1830 shows that of 10,984 ancient parishes in England and Wales the registers of 812 begin in 1538, 1,822 more before 1558 and 2,448 between 1558 and 1603. Between 1603 and 1650 969 begin and 2,757 between 1650 and 1700. Many parish registers have been printed and many more transcribed.[3] The majority are still kept in the parish churches but they may with the agreement of the bishop and the incumbent be transferred elsewhere and some have in fact been deposited in County Record Offices. The convenience to genealogists if copies of all could be made available in one place would naturally be immense. The risks of centralization are, however, shown by the destruction which in 1922 befell all those Irish parish registers which had been sent to Dublin. Only those left behind in the parishes survived.

The registers are not the only parish records, but most of the rest either relate to temporal church activities (such as churchwardens'

---

[1] John Southerden Burn, *The History of Parish Registers in England*, 2nd ed. 1862, pp. 25–29.

[2] Ibid., p. 9; *Letters and Papers of Henry VIII*, xiv, pt. i, No. 815.

[3] *Catalogue of the Parish Registers in the possession of the Society of Genealogists*, 2nd ed. 1937; *National Index of Parish Register Copies* compiled for the Soc. of Genealogists by K. Blomfield and H. K. Percy-Smith, 1939. New edition planned in eleven volumes, of which vols. v, 1966, and i, 1968, have appeared. See also J. T. Krause, 'The changing adequacy of English registration, 1690–1837', in D. V. Glass and D. E. C. Eversley, *Population in History*, 1965.

accounts and terriers of glebe land) or are civil records, such as enclosure awards and poor law documents, stored in the church chests for convenience. The published guides to the Essex (1956) and Bedfordshire (1957) Record Offices give a good idea of the range of material to be found. In 1836 a Royal Commission was set up to enquire into the state of non-parochial registers of births or baptisms, deaths or burials and marriages, that is to say those of dissenters and foreign congregations, and to make recommendations for their preservation. The ultimate consequence was the deposit with the Registrar General of some 7,000 such registers, of which lists have been printed. Until the passing of Lord Hardwicke's Marriage Act in 1754 marriages in private chapels were permitted and records of some of these, too, are deposited.

## (d) Universities, schools and charities

In the Middle Ages universities, schools and charitable foundations were ecclesiastical institutions similar in their constitution to other religious foundations. Though secularization was begun in the sixteenth and carried further in the nineteenth century, while most of the newer foundations have always been secular, the roots of all are in the Church and their archives reflect this. Foundation charters are followed in time and logic by statutes of internal government and these by registers, act books and formularies and accounts, and later still admission registers, letter books and other records of detailed administration. As these bodies were endowed with land, their muniments, like those of other landowners, comprise title deeds, which, with the admission registers, are the part of their archives most useful to genealogists.

The records of the Courts of the Universities of Oxford and Cambridge (Vice-Chancellors' Courts), which exercise over their members a jurisdiction exempted from the ordinary courts, date in Oxford from 1434, in Cambridge from 1552.

Though the records loosely grouped together as registers begin at Oxford about 1350, the records of graduation of masters and bachelors of arts begin only in the fifteenth century and are not full till the sixteenth. Records of the matriculations of undergraduates begin in 1564 at Oxford, in 1544 at Cambridge. The records of the several colleges within the universities differ much in their fullness and dates of beginning, but all include registers, admission books, accounts and title deeds of landed property. The great printed catalogues of members of the universities, Joseph Foster's *Alumni Oxonienses* (1500–1886), 1891, the more modern and scholarly *Alumni Cantabrigienses* (1250–1900),

1922–54 by J. and J. A. Venn, and Mr. A. B. Emden's laborious and learned *Biographical Register of the University of Oxford to* A.D. *1500,* 1957–9, and of *Cambridge,* 1963, are based partly on university, partly on college and partly on other records. Registers of the members of many colleges have also been separately published.

The records of the schools of ancient foundation such as Winchester (1382) and Eton (1440) are extensive and important, but until modern times most of them are more concerned with endowments and administration than with admission or other particulars of pupils though at Winchester scholars on the foundation were recorded from 1425. The records of Christ's Hospital, founded in 1552 for 'the fatherless children and other poor men's children', present a contrast in this respect, giving details of each child admitted from the first. Many schools have printed registers of their members.[1]

The records of a host of charities ancient and modern from the Hospitals of St. Cross at Winchester (1136) and St. Bartholomew (1123) and Bethlem (1246), London, to the numerous foundations of the eighteenth and nineteenth centuries may well contain more food for the genealogist than he has yet realized.

### (ii) *The Records of the State*

By records of the State are here meant records of the exercise of authority by or under the Crown or its delegates. Within these records the chief division is between the central and the local, even if the line cannot always be drawn sharply and may depend on whether custody or source and nature of jurisdiction is put first. Nor is the frontier always clear between public records and private, for it would be hard to say at what point in the decay of feudal institutions the exercise of what began as public rights became a purely private act. Seignorial and manorial jurisdiction begin in immemorial right or royal delegation and end in private property and the development is continuous from subinfeudation to conveyances and grants of leases. The fact is that, while a background consciousness that all is flux is necessary to an understanding of history, for the practical purposes of classification we draw, and must draw, arbitrary lines. Nor need this disturb us so long as we do not pretend that our activities are more philosophical than they need or can be.

---

[1] A 'Bibliography of the Registers (Printed) of the Universities, Inns of Court, Colleges and Schools of Great Britain and Ireland' appeared in the *Bulletin of the Institute of Historical Research.*

## (a) *Public Central Records*

The Public Record Office Act of 1838 was the first of four Acts of Parliament by which the contents of fifty six separate repositories[1] in which were stored the immense archives of different courts of law and departments of State, were concentrated into one, the Public Record Office in Chancery Lane. A brief account of their previous custody is given later[2] since it may be followed more easily if the development of the records is described first. The speed with which the concentration after 1838 was carried out led in some cases to confusion of the former grouping, but of late years, as the principle of *respect des fonds*[3] has come to the fore, the original arrangement of all archives has been scrupulously preserved or, where deranged, has so far as possible been restored.

The imagination cannot easily grasp the sheer volume of the English public records. It was estimated not long since that the number of individual documents in the Record Office exceeds 50,000,000.[4] But a livelier sense of what this means might be derived from first inspecting the hundreds of printed volumes of calendars to some of these records, compiled with immense labour and learning in the past century and more, and then reflecting that the records for which no such calendars exist are vastly more voluminous than those for which they do. Those records, mainly mediaeval, which were removed during the late war filled 600 lorry loads. 'If the young researcher', says Professor Galbraith, 'could see them as 10,000 separate rolls lying on the shelves he might well be tempted to change his profession.'[5]

The issue of royal charters goes back to Anglo-Saxon times and some of that age exist. Set forms established well before the Norman Conquest show that there was then already an experienced Royal Chancery with fixed conventions. The Conqueror took over and developed these and the great survey of England called Domesday Book (1086–7)—unique in Europe—shows how highly organized was his administrative system.

The three main functions of the mediaeval central government, the secretarial, the financial and the judicial, belonged respectively to the Chancery, the Exchequer and the courts of law, which all grew out of the king's household and as time went on developed subdepartments

---

[1] Edward Edwards, *Libraries and Founders of Libraries*, 1864, p. 302.
[2] p. 342.     [3] p. 325.
[4] *Guide to the Public Records, Part I, Introductory*, 1949, p. 19.
[5] V. H. Galbraith, *Studies in the Public Records*, 1948, p. 2.

with special functions and separate records.[1] The records of the early royal household itself, as it remained when these departments had split off from it, are lost, but many audited copies of those of one of its two great departments, the Wardrobe, from 1257 onwards, survive among the Exchequer Records. The Chancery Records date from 1199 when the practice of enrolling or entering copies upon rolls of all important out letters was begun. The principal series, reflecting differences in the importance or nature of the business and consequently in the departmental procedure and responsibility, are the Charter Rolls (1199–1516), Patent Rolls (1201–1920), Close Rolls (1204–1903), Liberate Rolls (1200–1436), Fine Rolls (beginning in 1199, continuous from 1216 to 1641), Gascon (1253–1467), French (1342–1674) and Scotch (1290–1515) Rolls and Parliament Rolls (1327–1885).[2]

Through a remarkable early description, the *Dialogus de Scaccario*, written in 1179, we know more of the growth of the Exchequer than of the Chancery. The surviving Exchequer records moreover start earlier with the Great Rolls of the Exchequer or Pipe Rolls, of which the oldest is for 1129–30 while the continuous series runs from 1155 to 1832. Other Exchequer series are the Receipt Rolls (1196–1782), Memoranda Rolls (1217–1884) and Issue Rolls (1220–1797).[3]

Among the older records of the Exchequer the genealogist has a special interest in those which concern the rights of the Crown to feudal dues and among the later ones in those of the various forms of taxation. In the former class the surveys of knights' fees and services are of immense value as general guides to the feudal structure and its membership throughout the land. The oldest source of information on the tenure of fees as on much else is the general survey of 1086–7, known as Domesday Book, an astonishing production for so early a date. The first returns of knights' services are, however, the Cartae of 1166 comprised in the Red Book of the Exchequer. These are followed by various later returns of the twelfth and thirteenth centuries, many of them included in the so called Testa de Nevill, admirably edited in 1921–31 as The Book of Fees; and then the returns of 1273–9 called the Hundred Rolls.

The feudal rights of the Crown were maintained by *Inquisitions post mortem* taken locally upon the deaths of tenants in chief and returned

[1] For a simplified picture of the development and its reflection in the records see V. H. Galbraith, *An Introduction to the Use of the Public Records*, 1934.

[2] See further M. S. Giuseppi, *A Guide to the Manuscripts preserved in the Public Record Office*, i, 1923, pp. 5–42 and revised *Guide*, 1963.

[3] See further Giuseppi, op. cit. i. 71–218 and the publications of the Pipe Roll Society.

in duplicate to the Chancery and to the Exchequer, by which heirships and ensuing dues to the Crown were determined. The series runs from 1235 to the abolition of knight service in 1660.

The returns of assessments for the occasional taxes known as aids and subsidies have been partly published (1899–1921) in the six volumes of Feudal Aids for dates between 1284 and 1431. These and numerous later subsidy returns, with those of later forms of taxation, such as the Hearth Tax instituted in 1662, are invaluable as guides for different dates to owners of property arranged geographically with assessments which indicate their wealth.

The courts of law like the other departments grew out of the king's household. The Curia Regis Rolls of the undivided King's Court, served by the justiciars, begin in 1193. Under this (and alongside its delegate, the Court of Chancery whose records of equity proceedings date from 1385) grew up the Common Law Courts of Exchequer, King's Bench and Common Pleas. Their separation was a gradual process perhaps complete by Edward I's reign. At all events it is from 1272 that the classification into separate series of *De Banco* Rolls, dealing with civil pleas, and *Coram Rege* Rolls, for criminal actions, begins. The Exchequer division of the Curia Regis became the Court of Exchequer and the rolls of its pleas begin in 1236. The system, begun not later than Henry I's reign of itinerant royal justices who visited the local courts and took over progressively more cases from the baronial, shire and hundred courts, is represented by the Assize Rolls for the several counties beginning at various dates in the thirteenth century. The immense bulk of these mediaeval plea rolls is difficult to convey. They are mainly uncalendared and these two facts combine with their hasty and illegible script to make them the genealogist's last resort. Yet the volume of genealogical information they contain is immense.

A deficiency of modern English records, as compared for example with those of Scotland, is the want of effective general provision for the official record of conveyances of land. For the Middle Ages, however, the gap was filled to a considerable extent by the custom of establishing title on a conveyance by a fictitious lawsuit ending in a final concord or agreement, recorded in a tripartite document of which each party kept one copy and the Crown the third, the Foot. The Crown series of these records—the Feet of Fines—runs from 1182 to 1834. Series for certain counties have been published by local effort. It was also possible to have private deeds entered on the back of the Close

Rolls and this became common after a statute of 1381 following the destruction of private deeds in the Peasants' Revolt. In 1535 the Statute of Uses enacted changes in the law, which, if effective, would have made all conveyances of land thenceforth the subject of public record. This Statute was designed to end the devices, developed in the preceding century and more, for concealing the true ownership of lands by setting up trusts.[1] The disturbances of the fifteenth century had exposed land-owners to risks of dispossession and exaction, which by such legal ingenuities they had sought to evade. Nor were civil war and tyranny the only inconveniences thus held at bay, for debtors by such trusts might escape their creditors. The Act of 1535 sought to end all this by reuniting the beneficial enjoyment of land to the legal estate. But fresh legal ingenuity defeated its intention with the incidental consequence that there was still no general record of land conveyances.[2] Other partial provisions for the enrolment of deeds, both central and local, have existed at different times and places. Acts of Parliament of 1704, 1707, 1708 and 1734 established local Registries of Deeds for the West and East Ridings of Yorkshire, for Middlesex and for the North Riding, at Wakefield and Beverley, in London and at Northallerton respectively,[3] but legal decisions made these less effective than they were meant to be. The upshot of this checkered history is that, while very many trans-actions in land are to be found recorded in one way or another in the public records, very many more are not so recorded and can be known only if the original deeds are found in public or private hands or entered in monastic or other cartularies, or preserved in notes or copies made by antiquaries or others. For this reason the whereabouts of such deeds has itself sometimes to be sought through investigation of the histories of the lands they relate to or the genealogies of those concerned with them. In Scotland, on the other hand, a system has been in force since 1617 (following unsuccessful attempts in 1503, 1540 and 1555) whereby entry in a public register is necessary to establish a right to ownership of land, the General and Particular Registers of Sasines dating from that year.[4] Sasines are thus to the Scottish genealogist just such a stand-by as wills are to the English.

In the century round 1500 the administrative and judicial system,

---

[1] On this development see May McKisack, *The Fourteenth Century*, Oxford, 1959, p. 261.

[2] Frederick Pollock, *The Land Laws*, 1883, chap. iv.

[3] *A Repertory of British Archives*, Pt. I, *England*, ed. Hubert Hall, Royal Hist. Soc. 1920, pp. 32–33; Giuseppi, op. cit. i. 21.

[4] Hector M'Kechnie, *The Pursuit of Pedigree*, 1928, p. 23.

which throughout the Middle Ages had slowly grown in scope and complication, took a great onward leap in this direction. The king's secretary (and later the two Secretaries of State) moved into the place next the king, which had once been the chancellor's, at the head of the administrative machine. Out of this change grew the State Papers, starting in 1509 and dividing in 1547 into two series, Foreign and Domestic, to which Scottish, Irish, Treasury, Colonial and other series were later added. The modern multiplication of ministers and departments, each creating records which are sent after a certain lapse of years to the Record Office, was the last stage of the same process.

The same period saw Henry VII's creation of a new system of public accounting which produced the several series of Declared Accounts from 1500 onwards. In the legal sphere the Tudor period saw the creation of new courts, the Star Chamber, the Court of Requests and the Courts of Augmentations and First Fruits to deal with the confiscated monastic lands and the first fruits of benefices acquired by the Crown when Royal replaced papal supremacy over the Church.

The spirit of the Tudor period is also seen in the records now first preserved at this date by distinct organs of authority. First among them come those of Parliament, starting in 1509 with the Lords' Journals, followed in 1547 by those of the Commons. The vast and varied archive since accumulated by the activities of Parliament remains in its own custody in the Victoria Tower of the Palace of Westminster, wholly separate from the Public Record Office. The Register of the Privy Council which begins in 1540 was kept at the Privy Council Office till 1904. The earlier volumes were then transferred to the Public Record Office and others have followed. Some Privy Council Records of earlier date have found their way to the British Museum.[1]

The Records of the College of Arms or Heralds' College, which have special importance for the genealogist and will be dealt with from that angle later,[2] likewise begin in Henry VIII's reign, though the college possesses earlier material. The college as a corporation was created by the incorporation in 1484 (and again in 1555) of the royal heralds who had been members of the household since the thirteenth century. The heralds' corporate archive begins in 1528 with their first Partition Book recording the division of fees and other corporate acts. During the fifteenth century the Crown had delegated to the kings of arms (or chief heralds) an administrative responsibility for the control

---

[1] Giuseppi, op. cit. ii. 127–9.    [2] pp. 349, 355–66, 371–7, 400–3, 408.

of the use of armorial bearings and the power to grant arms to approved persons. Visitations or local surveys of arms were made from the fifteenth century but Henry VIII laid firm foundations for a comprehensive system of Visitation and control by the issue in 1530 of a commission giving Clarenceux King of Arms stringent powers for the purpose. The records of grants of arms and Visitations were, however, at this date kept not by the whole body of heralds but by the individual kings of arms with a consequent risk of loss of custody on their death. After the heralds' second incorporation of 1555 the Earl Marshal, under whose surveillance the heralds were, drew up regulations, issued in 1568, providing for their conduct as a corporation and among other things requiring the kings of arms to deposit their Visitation books in the college library. His right to require this may have been questioned. At all events it was not till after an upheaval and a resettlement in 1597 that these and other records were regularly deposited.[1]

Henry VIII's administrative changes were followed by many others but there was no comparable revolution till the greater one of the nineteenth century. From the spate of new measures, departments and consequent records then created two must be singled out for their transcendent importance to genealogists. The taking of a census or complete count with other details of the population calls for a developed administrative system. The Domesday Survey (1086–7) of landowners only was a *tour de force* for its time and a general census could scarcely have been thought of in western Europe between classical times and the seventeenth century. Furthermore, such counts were long feared as likely to provoke the wrath of God, as did the census taken by King David,[2] and when they came were resented as inquisitorial.

It is, as we have seen,[3] uncertain how far the census of 1695, ordered by Act of Parliament, was carried out. Thereafter no census was taken in England till 1801, though a few were made earlier on the continent of Europe and the oldest system of a periodical national census was instituted in 1790 in the United States of America.[4] In England from 1801 the census was taken every ten years, but the oldest returns preserved are those of 1841, which with those of 1851 may be seen in the Public Record Office. For the genealogist the returns of 1851 and since have the great merit that each person was required to state his or her

---

[1] p. 365; A. R. Wagner, *The Records and Collections of the College of Arms*, 1952 (obtainable on application to the author), *Heralds of England*, 1967.

[2] Sam. xxiv.                                                                 [3] p. 181.

[4] D. V. Glass, article 'Census' in *Chambers's Encyclopaedia*, 1950 ed.; Derek Harland, *Genealogical Research Standards*, Salt Lake City, 1963, chap. 11.

age and birthplace,[1] so that if the place of residence in 1851 (without which the census entry cannot be found) is known, the place and date of birth can usually be discovered.

By an Act of Parliament of 1836 the office of Registrar General was created and in 1837 general civil registration of births, marriages and deaths was introduced. From this date accordingly the search for a baptism through more than 10,000 parish registers is replaced by the search for a birth registration in one series of indexes at Somerset House, in the Strand, London.

### (b) Custody and Publication of the Public Central Records

The work of genealogists in the past and today cannot be justly assessed and compared without some understanding of the working conditions governing consultation of records at different dates. Today the Departments of State, Treasury, Home Office, Foreign Office and the rest, keep their own archives for such length of time as the Government may decide in each case. They may then transfer them to the Public Record Office and then or later open them to public consultation. The latest records in a given sequence, which the public may see, may thus be a hundred years old or more or less. Until the eighteenth century the larger part of all the records were kept in the secret category and looked on as *arcana imperii* concerned with 'matters of estate and the crown only'.[2] The more formal legal and financial documents, as concerning the rights of the subject, formed an exception and might be seen on payment of fees. When antiquaries and historians in the sixteenth and succeeding centuries wished to search the records generally they had to obtain either the special leave of the crown or the private good will of the record keepers.

By the sixteenth century the records were much dispersed. The two chief repositories were still, as earlier, the Tower of London for the Chancery records and the Chapter House of Westminster Abbey for those of the Exchequer. In the fourteenth century there had been a move to make the Tower a central clearing house, but this was in time abandoned, though not without leaving traces on the arrangement of

---

[1] In 1841 they had only to answer Yes or No to the question whether they were born in the county where they were living and to give their ages to the nearest five years.

[2] Professor R. B. Wernham, 'The Public Records in the Sixteenth and Seventeenth Centuries', in *English Historical Scholarship in the Sixteenth and Seventeenth Centuries*, ed. Levi Fox, 1956, p. 11, quoting Arthur Agarde temp. James I.

the older records.[1] A contrary tendency towards dispersal then set in and was aggravated by the growth of new courts and departments under the Tudors. Those records not in frequent use were neglected and disarranged so that by Elizabeth I's reign the inconvenience had become perceptible.

This led to some improvements and especially the setting up of the State Paper Office. In the following generation some of the record keepers such as Arthur Agarde (d. 1615), were themselves antiquaries and helpful to others, but the political troubles which then came on, though they led to increased interest in the records, which were searched for political precedents, postponed public action to care for them till after the Revolution of 1688.[2] In 1689, however, William Petyt was appointed to 'methodize' the records in the Tower and seems to have done good work. Furthermore between 1703 and 1732 several Committees of Parliament made reports drawing attention to abuses and recommending remedies. To this period belongs the first substantial officially sponsored publication of records, Thomas Rymer's edition of the *Foedera* or public conventions of the Kings of England with other powers, in twenty volumes (1704–13).

Activity then lapsed till 1771 when the printing of the Rolls of Parliament was put in hand, followed in 1783 by that of Domesday Book. Between 1800 and 1837 six successive Commissions on the Public Records were set up by Parliament. Under their auspices many volumes of records were published as well as reports which led in 1838 to the foundation of the Public Record Office. The concentration of the scattered records thus placed in single custody has proceeded ever since. The present building was begun in 1851 and as then planned was finished in 1871, an additional block being added between 1892 and 1900. By about 1870 the main concentration was complete though transfers from current use have continued and will continue indefinitely.

This great effort of organization produced a slowing down in publication until 1864 when the great series of modern calendars, lists and indexes began to appear. Sir Henry Maxwell Lyte (1848–1940), Deputy Keeper from 1886 to 1926, by simplifying their form made it possible to cover the ground much faster. They at present total well over six hundred volumes without including some two hundred and fifty volumes of chronicles, and other literary sources of history

[1] V. H. Galbraith, 'The Tower as an Exchequer Record Office in the Reign of Edward II', in *Essays presented to T. F. Tout*, 1925, pp. 231–47.   [2] Wernham, op. cit., pp. 12–30.

printed between 1858 and 1897 in the Rolls Series.[1] The immensity of the nineteenth century effort not only to arrange and organize the public records but to make them accessible by listing and publication can be partly grasped by a comparison of those herculean labours with the much smaller flow of publication achieved in our own time by very considerable efforts.

### (c) *Public Local Records*

The line between central and local government and therefore between their several records has often been indefinite. Between local authorities and the local agents of central authorities, there is a gradation rather than an essential difference. The oldest local administration represented by surviving archives is the seigniorial administration of the feudal barons and knights. This was, however, from an early date encroached on and reduced by the development and extension of royal justice and authority until what had once been private rights of local government were whittled down to little more than the ownership of land. Partly for this reason surviving seigniorial archives are relatively few and fragmentary. Apart from those in ecclesiastical possession the most important survivors are those which in one way or another came long ago into the hands of the Crown and are thus preserved in the Public Record Office.

The administration of the great baronial units, some headed by earls and barons, some in the hands of bishops and religious houses, was modelled on the royal administration. There were private chanceries and exchequers and even private sheriffs and coroners. As the Forz and Bigod archives exemplify the thirteenth century system, so the great feudal entity, which passed to the Crown in 1399 as the Duchy of Lancaster and is still separately administered, illustrates later developments.[2] The base of the seigniorial pyramid was the manor. Manorial jurisdiction outlived the rest nor indeed is it yet dead, though by the end of the seventeenth century it had lost most of its character of local government and become a mere administration of private rights of property. In most places the superior organs of seigniorial administration had faded away still earlier, though the Lords of Berkeley Castle in the late nineteenth century were still holding hundred courts,

[1] See Tr. Royal Hist. Soc., 5th ser. vol. ii, 1961, pp. 137–59, Presidential Address, Great Historical Enterprises IV, The Rolls Series, by Professor the Rev. M. D. Knowles.

[2] N. Denholm-Young, *Seigniorial Administration in England*, 1937; Robert Somerville, *History of the Duchy of Lancaster*, 1953.

halmotes and borough courts throughout the hundred of Berkeley in Gloucestershire. Even here, however, the criminal jurisdiction had gone before 1700 and fines for nuisances hardly lasted after 1800.[1] Because the manor was the base of the pyramid, early manorial records (and especially Court Rolls) have the special value for genealogists that they, almost alone among mediaeval records, regularly deal with the lowest classes of rural society, the unfree husbandmen and cotters.[2] The possibility of tracing such a family before the date when the parish register begins will usually depend on whether early records of the manor in question survive or not. The oldest such records go back to the thirteenth century, but most begin much later and some are lost.

Until the Law of Property Amendment Act, 1924, prospectively abolished copyhold tenure, every lord of a manor had some interest in preserving his manorial records. The framers of this Act, foreseeing that the destruction of this interest might mean that of the records also, gave the Master of the Rolls power to secure their preservation. From this recent enactment derive the County Record Offices, administered by the County Councils, to which not only manorial records, but public and private records of most varied kinds have been transferred in recent years. They follow at a distance of more than a century the French Archives Départementales, which date from the Revolution. Had we had them sooner much destruction of important material would have been avoided.

In England the transition from old to new has been a gradual and complex process, and modern local government springs from more than one root. Notable among these, however, is the fourteenth century development of the functions of the Justices of the Peace organized by Commissions for each county. Some few mediaeval records of the Justices' Quarter Sessions survive by accident in the central archives, but the oldest Sessions Rolls preserved locally, those for Norfolk, date only from 1532.[3] The Justices' clerk, the Clerk of the Peace, was responsible for the custody of these and later of many other local records. Some of the Justices' former duties have in recent times been transferred to the County Councils set up in 1889.

Other roots of modern local government are to be sought in the responsibilities imposed by the central government since Tudor times

[1] Sidney and Beatrice Webb, *English Local Government from the Revolution to the Municipal Corporations Act*, ii, 1908, chap. ii (*a*).

[2] p. 141.

[3] *Local Records their Nature and Care*, ed. Lilian J. Redstone and Francis W. Steer, 1953, chap. xiv; *Surrey Records*, v.

on the locally chosen officers of manors and parishes for such matters as the upkeep of highways and the relief of the poor. Thus the church-wardens, who combined civil and ecclesiastical functions and allegiance, were also from 1601 overseers of the poor. The records of their activities in this capacity were kept with others in the church chests, but were none the less civil records and many of them are now in County Record Offices.

The self government of towns begins, as we have seen,[1] where its beginning is traceable, in grants by kings or barons of a franchise or exemption from feudal jurisdiction. Thus the fundamental documents of town archives are the towns' own charters of incorporation and of liberties and the books in which their customs and precedents are entered. Next come the records of their own proceedings and acts, such as the letter books (so called because they are distinguished by letters of the alphabet), which record the acts of the Court of Aldermen and the Court of Common Council of London from 1275 to 1689.[2] Besides judicial, administrative, estate and financial records the archives of the ancient boroughs contain personal records of great value to the genealogist in their registers of freemen and apprentices some of which begin at early dates and enable burgess families to be traced well back into the Middle Ages.

Within the towns, as we have seen,[3] rights of jurisdiction over crafts and trades were granted in and after the Middle Ages to guilds composed of their members. In London some eighty of these guilds survive as livery companies. In other ancient towns a few exist but most have perished. The archives of the London companies, some in their own hands, some deposited with the City archives, are voluminous and important.[4] They include the companies' own charters of incorporation and jurisdiction, the records of their own acts and accounts and the records of their property. To genealogists the registers of freemen and apprentices are again of special value.

### (iii) *Private Records*

The frontier between public records and private is as ill defined as between central and local. The baron or knight exercising a delegated

---

[1] p. 153.

[2] Philip E. Jones and Raymond Smith, *A Guide to the Records in the Corporation of London Records Office and the Guildhall Library Muniment Room*, 1951, p. 30.

[3] p. 154.

[4] *Local Records* (*supra* cit.), chap. xvii; Jones and Smith, op. cit., pp. 129–53.

authority in his barony or manor slowly turns into a mere landowner, great or small, whose manorial records deal mainly if not solely with the administration of private property. The archive may be continuous but its character slowly changes.

The description 'semi-public' has been applied to the records of certain private bodies whose standing and the importance of their work have been recognized in some public way, whether by statutory control or support, exchequer subsidy or mere public esteem. Such bodies range from the professional corporations, the Inns of Court and Chancery, the Royal Colleges of Physicians and Surgeons, the Royal Institute of British Architects and the like, through such national endowed learned societies as the Royal Society, the Society of Antiquaries of London and the Royal Academy, and such great chartered trading corporations as the Hudson's Bay Company, the Bank of England and Lloyd's, through the whole range of private clubs, societies and companies registered under the Companies Acts. The bodies at the head of the list are in effect public, national bodies and their archives are in that sense public records, though not in national custody. The bodies at the end of the list are in every sense private. Where, if anywhere, the line is to be drawn between the two, would seem to be a question simply of convenience. The genealogist has merely to remember that all these bodies exist and that their records, if he could but know of them and see them, would often be of great use to him.

On another part of the same frontier lie the records of the exercise of public office made and retained by individual holders of office, and inherited by their heirs. These range from the correspondence of statesmen to the account books of churchwardens. To draw a consistent line in this field between what should pass to public archives and what may remain in private hands if the individual so chooses is as much beyond man's wit as beyond his will.

Those families whose estates were of such kind and size as to make a muniment room, or at least a muniment chest, a necessary part of daily life, have naturally been apter than others to preserve their records of all kinds. So to a less degree have been families of long continuance in one profession or trade or in the pursuit of learning, as also those heirs of famous men who have valued that inheritance. The greatest accumulations, such as those in Lord Salisbury's muniment room at Hatfield or Lord Fitzwilliam's papers from Wentworth Woodhouse now at Leeds University, are as valuable to the genealogist as to the national or local historian. Many smaller accumulations, however, may be not less so.

The Historical Manuscripts Commission set up in 1869 has printed many volumes of descriptions of local and private archives and of material from them. Its modern extension, the National Register of Archives set up in 1945, searches out and lists such material more swiftly though less thoroughly, while helping students with lists, indexes and advice to locate what they are in search of. The redistributive taxation of recent years, with its destructive effect on great estates, has in many cases made the proper care of private archives in private custody difficult or impossible. The solution has often been their deposit in County Record Offices and other approved repositories. Of these migrations of records the National Register of Archives helps the student to keep track.

### 3. CONTENT AND GENEALOGICAL USE

Out of this immense range of records, ecclesiastical and civil, public and private, central and local, a very large proportion could in theory be turned in some degree to genealogical account. In practice, however, the genealogist finds himself confined within a relatively narrow range by two distinct considerations—on the one hand the proportion of genealogical material given records may contain, on the other the ease and speed with which they can be searched.

Thus at one extreme parish registers, even when, as too often, inaccessible, unpublished and unindexed, must be searched without hesitation because their genealogical content is so high. At the other extreme the thirty five printed volumes of the *Letters and Papers of Henry VIII* are often well worth searching in relation to pedigree problems of that reign, although their genealogical content is low, because their scope is so wide and they are so well indexed. Between these extremes lie the many classes of record which it is feasible and worth while to search only when preceding research of an easier kind has blazed a trail towards them and indicated their possible value in a special case.

The genealogist's most obvious need, though not his only one, in the field of records is for such as will prove kinship. Thus an *Inquisition post mortem*[1] will show—from 1235 onwards—that the heir of a tenant in chief, whose date of death is given, was his son so-and-so of specified age or his kinsman so-and-so of stated age and relationship. A charter or deed of enfeoffment or a conveyance or lease of land will

[1] p. 337.

often mention relationships of parties whose rights and interests it concerns. Parties to lawsuits often in the course of their pleadings assert relationships covering several generations and different branches of a family,[1] though here bias may sometimes produce errors and conflicts of evidence. Many wills mention wives, children, grandchildren, brothers, sisters and other relations of the testator or testatrix. University and school registers, professional admission records and records of freedom and apprenticeship frequently mention the parentage of those admitted, while in the heralds' Visitation and other books the official record of pedigree is a principal object.

In these cases and many more kinship is established by direct statement, but at other times it must be proved by inference. Two or more individuals who cannot be directly linked with one another can often be so linked indirectly by linking both or all of them to the same thing —an estate, a property, a trade or the like. Thus successive tenure of a fee or fees by men of the same name goes far to establish the fact of their kinship and coupled with other evidence may help to prove exact relationship. The same principle can sometimes be applied through successive membership of a guild or other body or even through successive ownership of a holding of Bank of England stock. Where proof of kinship rests on such inference, it is clear that the background of record, law and custom must be carefully explored and interpreted.

Records which in one way or another prove kinship are, however, by no means the only ones which help genealogists. The first need is often not to link but simply to locate and here the records sought for are those whose nature or arrangement makes it possible to use them as directories or guides to external facts or to one another. Domesday Book and the feudal surveys, covering knights throughout the country and admirably edited and indexed, are obvious examples. Subsidy and other tax returns could in principle fulfil the same function from the thirteenth century to the seventeenth, as could freeholders' books, poll books and parish rate books for the eighteenth and nineteenth centuries, though in practice they do so only to a limited extent since only a small proportion have been edited or indexed.[2] For the

---

[1] For a notable series of examples see Major-General the Hon. G. Wrottesley, *Pedigrees from the Plea Rolls collected from the Pleadings in the Various Courts of Law, A.D. 1200 to 1500 from the original rolls in the Public Record Office*, reprinted from *The Genealogist*, N.S. v–xxi.

[2] For a useful guide to nominal lists in the public records see *A Repertory of British Archives, Pt. I. England*, ed. Hubert Hall, Royal Hist. Soc. 1920, pp. 54–64. See also p. 403.

country generally the printed indexes of wills and administrations in the Prerogative and provincial probate courts provide an index to the distribution of surnames from the sixteenth century onwards whose usefulness is limited only by its restriction to the possessors of appreciable property. The Oxford and Cambridge University Registers have a comparable value and the great index of apprenticeships (1710–74) made by the Society of Genealogists[1] covers in a similar way for the whole country the range of those apprenticed to trades in a century often harder for genealogists than those before and after.

These last named records belong to a kind which the genealogist values for yet a third reason—namely that they give him clues to family migrations. The man who moves from south to north or from country to town or in general from one place to another presents a problem which can be formidable. How is the origin of the stranger who appears from nowhere in a new home to be traced? Back to 1837 the General Register of Births, Marriages and Deaths may provide the answer. From 1851 onwards the census returns every ten years give age and birthplace, so that if a man can be located at a census (which is not always easy) his immediate origin should be traceable. But for earlier dates records which directly link migrants with their origins are rarities and proportionately valued. University registers and apprenticeship records are among those specially valued because at their respective levels they do precisely this. So at a lower level again do Poor Law settlement certificates, all too rare survivals, which, however, when found tell us that a pauper living in one place is a native of another. Depositions in Chancery and other lawsuits may give similar information at much earlier dates.

It may now begin to appear why at one extreme almost any extensive series of records, local or national, which is well and fully enough edited and indexed to be consulted readily and quickly, will be of great value as a repertory of chance clues. To the method of mobilizing these resources we must, however, return in a later chapter.[2]

[1] Copies at the Society of Genealogists and in the author's possession.
[2] Chapter X.

# IX

## THE STUDY AND LITERATURE
## OF GENEALOGY

'God has not been so sparing to men to make them barely two-legged creatures and left it to Aristotle to make them rational.'[1] All the same the common inclination of most men is to believe what they are told and to confine the application of their reasoning powers to practical necessities. The substitution of criticism for credulity in each branch of study has therefore usually had to await its Columbus or Galileo, its Dugdale or Horace Round. These appear but seldom and vulgar errors flourish meanwhile. To evaluate genealogies of different epochs we must, if possible, know how and by whom they were compiled and transmitted. The methods and credit both of classes of genealogists and of individuals must be studied, though the latter are hardly to be known before the sixteenth century.

### I. THE LOSS OF TRADITION

We have noted the view that wherever early pedigrees have been preserved in bulk by word of mouth, the work has been done by a mantic or bardic class charged with this duty. We have seen that vestiges of such a class survived in Ireland to the seventeenth century, while in Wales the preservation of genealogies by the bards lasted long enough to be passed on directly to the antiquaries of Tudor times. The bards and their traditions were in origin pagan and the Irish bards (*filid*) and the Welsh survived because, when Christianity came, they made peace with the Church and wedded their native lore to Latin and Christian learning.[2] It was this amalgam which in the seventh and following centuries produced the fictitious pedigrees linking Irish and British traditional genealogies with those of the Bible and classical antiquity.[3] The fullest development of these historical fictions is to

---

[1] John Locke, *An Essay concerning the Human Understanding*, ed. A. C. Fraser, 1894, ii. 391.

[2] H. M. and N. K. Chadwick, *The Growth of Literature*, i, 1932, pp. 491–2.

[3] Ibid., pp. 274–6, 308–13, and pp. 23, 30 *supra*.

be seen in the British history (*c.* 1135) of the Breton or Welshman Geoffrey of Monmouth which kept its credit and popularity till the sixteenth or even the seventeenth century.[1]

There is little or no evidence of such a class or activity among the pagan English, but their Christian descendants felt the same need to link their pagan ancestors to biblical and classical antiquity. By the ninth century not only had almost all the English royal lines been given a common male descent from Woden, but Woden had been derived from Noah.[2]

There is little other evidence of Anglo-Saxon concern with genealogy, though the royal lines and some few others can be pieced together from scattered mentions in chronicles and charters.

### 2. THE NORMANS AND THE LEGAL APPROACH

In England after the Norman Conquest the legal aspect of pedigree had the preeminence for some centuries. This meant that the interest was in individual pedigrees for individual purposes. I know of no post-Conquest English *collection* of genealogies older than the fifteenth century.[3] The historical use of pedigrees survived, however, in certain rolls in which the royal genealogy is made the basis of a short history of England.[4] A number of vellum rolls of this kind survive, of dates between Edward I's and Henry VII's reigns. Some are in French, as if for the use of knights and gentlemen, others in Latin as if for clerks. The pedigree form in which they are cast has itself an ancestry traceable to classical antiquity through the forms given to the Genealogy of Christ or Tree of Jesse and to the Table of Kindred and Affinity called the *Arbor Juris*.[5]

---

[1] T. D. Kendrick, *British Antiquity*, 1950.

[2] W. G. Searle, *Anglo-Saxon Bishops Kings and Nobles*, 1899, pp. 251–5; K. Sisam, op. cit., p. 14, n. 2 *supra*.

[3] Note, however, the Norman genealogies added by Robert of Torigny in the late twelfth century to the chronicle of William of Jumièges (ed. Marx, pp. 320–9). D. C. Douglas, *William the Conqueror*, 1964, pp. 84–85, advises scepticism in accepting them. See p. 63 *supra*.

[4] Thomas Wright, *Feudal Manuals of English History*, 1872; *Illustrated Catalogue of the Heralds of Commemorative Exhibition, 1484–1934*, 1936, Nos. 65, 68, 113.

[5] Arthur Watson, *The Early Iconography of the Tree of Jesse*, 1934, chap. iii. M. J. Jacquart of Brussels informed me in 1961 that the oldest example of a Tree of Jesse in his photographic collection is from the Gospel of the Coronation of Wratislaw King of Bohemia *c.* 1285, while his oldest example of a European pedigree is of *c.* 1180–1225, of the Welf family, from the Landesbibliothek, Fulda, MS. D. 11. Some Arab pedigrees he takes to be older.

From the start of the plea rolls in 1193 the many and lengthy statements of descent in lawsuits show the importance of genealogy in this context. Most such statements, naturally, cover three or four generations only. Some, however, cover five, six, seven or more, and are found occasionally throughout this period.[1]

It would be of interest if we could show how and by whom these early pedigrees were put together. Many may rest on orally transmitted knowledge only, but it seems likely that some of the longer ones were even at this early date compiled from written evidence. This, in the earlier part of the period, means that the compilers were probably clerks and perhaps most often monks. The genealogies of the families of founders of monasteries, often found in cartularies, illustrate the nature of the monks' interest, as do such rare family chronicles as that of Wigmore kept by the monks of the Mortimers' foundation, Wigmore Abbey.[2] The original charters of benefactors, the copies entered in cartularies, chronicle entries, monumental inscriptions and oral tradition may all have helped the monks upon occasion to work out pedigrees retrospectively.

For proof that they used documents to compile pedigrees in the fourteenth century we may quote the evidence given by two canons of Bridlington in the *Scrope* v. *Grosvenor* case in 1378. Asked if they had heard tell of the ancestors of Sir Richard Scrope, they said that their priory had possessions given them by his ancestors and produced charters sealed with great seals depicting knights on horseback with swords in their hands, such as 'those of the Conquest' used. The Scrope pedigree which they based on these, though open to criticism, is not wholly erroneous.[3]

Monkish genealogists, however, must not be trusted too far. Horace Round thought that the weakest point of Dugdale's *Baronage* was his acceptance of monastic statements as to the founder's family, which are, he believed, 'too often, the origin of persistent error and show the danger of departure from primary evidence as a source'.[4] A critical study of the nature, origin and worth of the pedigrees set up in lawsuits has still to be made.

[1] See, for examples, Major-General the Hon. G. Wrottesley, *Pedigrees from the Plea Rolls* (reprinted from *The Genealogist*, N.S. v–xxi), pp. 6, 23, 48, 60–61, 86, 88, 475.

[2] Chicago University MS. CS 439 fM 82 W6, described by M. E. Griffin, 'A Wigmore Manuscript at the University of Chicago', *Nat. Lib. of Wales Journ.*, 1952.

[3] *The Scrope and Grosvenor Controversy*, ed. Sir Harris Nicolas, i. 18, pp. 101–2; *Complete Peerage*, xi. 531.

[4] *Family Origins and other Studies by the late J. H. Round*, ed. William Page, 1930, p. 7.

## 3. FIFTEENTH CENTURY ANTIQUARIANISM

The fifteenth century saw a marked development of antiquarian and topographical studies in England. Two men active in this movement who left manuscript works behind them were William Worcester alias Botoner (1415–82) of Bristol and Norfolk, gentleman, and John Rous of Warwick (*c.* 1425–91), chaplain of the Guy's Cliff chantry. Both were graduates of Oxford. Both wrote historical and topographical works. Both formed libraries. Worcester was Sir John Fastolf's secretary and man of business at Castle Combe in Wiltshire and Caister in Norfolk. Rous's patrons were the Beauchamp and Neville Earls of Warwick.[1]

Both made collections of genealogies. Worcester compiled a book on the ancient families of Norfolk. It has been lost, but extracts made from it by Sir Henry Spelman (d. 1641) show that it was substantial and important.[2] In it Worcester often noted his source of information, sometimes an individual informant, sometimes a chronicle, roll or record. His friend Nicholas Bocking, esquire, an estate official with access to financial records, and perhaps himself an antiquary, put his knowledge at Worcester's disposal,[3] and Worcester himself was sent by his master Fastolf on journeys to make genealogical researches in connection with property rights. 'Thus in May 1449 he rode out from London to various places in Somerset "ad inquirendum pro vera genealogia dominorum de Lovell & improbandum genealogiam uxoris Edwardi Hull militis" .... Another journey into Kent was undertaken to test the pedigree of the Cliffords of Bobbing and their title to a rent charge in Hickling', and in 1458 we find him working on the De la Pole pedigree.[4]

A recent study by Mr. P. S. Lewis shows that others besides Worcester worked for Fastolf on the pedigree of Lovell of Clevedon, Somerset, to support his right to the manor of Titchwell, Norfolk, against the claim of Sir Edward Hull. Among them were several clerks in the Chancery and Exchequer records, who received fees for searching these, John Crop of Bristol, a friend of William Worcester, and Henry Filongley, a kinsman of Fastolf and keeper of the writs of the

[1] See K. B. McFarlane, 'William Worcester, A Preliminary Survey', in *Studies presented to Sir Hilary Jenkinson*, ed. J. Conway Davies, 1957, pp. 196–221, and T. D. Kendrick, *British Antiquity*, 1950, chap. ii.

[2] McFarlane, op. cit., pp. 216–17; Spelman's extracts are in Norwich Public Library MS. 7197, ff. 297–9b and 304–21. The original appears to have belonged in 1674 to Edward Paston; see *Norfolk Archaeology*, iv. 4.

[3] Op. cit., p. 199, and letter from Mr. McFarlane.     [4] Op. cit., pp. 204–5.

Court of Common Pleas. Local records were sought for, but when these failed recourse was had, on what appear sound lines, to old men's memories. The conflict of evidence in this case throws an interesting light on the nature of early lawsuit pedigrees in general.[1]

John Rous's collection of more than fifty genealogies is inscribed in a minute hand here and there on the face and in a series on the dorse of the Latin version of his great pictorial roll of the Earls of Warwick, compiled about 1480 and now in the College of Arms.[2] Those on the face give the ancestry on male and female lines of the Kings and the Earls of Warwick, whose lives he narrates and whose arms and portraits he draws. Those on the dorse are more extensive pedigrees of the Kings of Britain, France, England and Scotland and of the English earls. The last is of his own family.

He notes that he saw and wrote down two genealogies of the British kings at Glastonbury. Chronicles and monastic genealogies were no doubt among his sources. He was not uncritical, expressing suspicion of a genealogy of the Lords of Arundel and compiling dated lists of the popes and the Bishops of Worcester for use in the scrutiny of evidence. His genealogies have yet to be studied in detail, but it may be said that while they embody some mythology and some error they are, considering their date and extent, remarkably sound. The Mintling Register, a fifteenth century cartulary of Spalding Priory, contains lists of villein holdings belonging to the priory, illustrated by pedigrees of the villein families which held them.[3]

### 4. THE HERALDS AND GENEALOGY

We do not know when the heralds first interested themselves in genealogy. They were, however, concerned with coat armour from the twelfth century and made records of it from the fourteenth if not the thirteenth. Since a right to arms had often to be proved by pedigree (witness the testimony in *Scrope* v. *Grosvenor*), a concern with the one was bound to lead in time to the other. Powell and Wallis[4] point out

---

[1] P. S. Lewis, 'Sir John Fastolf's Lawsuit over Titchwell 1448–55', *The Historical Journal*, i, 1958, pp. 1–20.

[2] A. R. Wagner, *A Catalogue of English Mediaeval Rolls of Arms*, 1950, pp. 116–18. Wagner, Additions and Corrections in *Aspilogia*, ii; *Rolls of Arms of Henry III*, 1967, p. 277.

[3] In the possession of the Gentlemen's Society, Spalding, Lincs.; David, *Medieval Cartularies*, p. 105; Maurice Johnson, 'Introduction to the Minute Books of the Spalding Society', *Bibl. Top. Britannica*, iii, 1790, no. xx, 16–17.

[4] *The House of Lords in the Middle Ages*, 1968, p. xvii.

that peerage claims had begun to offer a field for genealogists before the death of Edward II and that the heralds' help may have been enlisted by claimants from the last quarter of the fourteenth century. I have, however, found no evidence that this actually happened before the fifteenth century. In 1415 the new office of Garter King of Arms was created and William Bruges (d. 1450), who was appointed to it, seems to have set to work to honour the Order and Knights of the Garter by setting up a new series of enamelled stall plates of their arms at Windsor to replace those which had been lost. He also put in hand a painted record of the arms of all the knights from the foundation of the order in the 1340's down to his own day.[1] This must have involved him in research to identify former knights.

In 1448 Sir Richard Wydville, who had risen from comparative obscurity in the king's service after marrying the widowed Duchess of Bedford, was created Lord Rivers. The editors of the *Complete Peerage* could not explain this choice of title, but the heraldic evidence of Lord Rivers' Garter stall plate leaves little doubt that it refers to a claim to descent from the family of Reviers or Rivers, Earls of Devon in the twelfth and thirteenth centuries.[2] The pedigree must in that case have been examined, if not produced, by Garter King of Arms. Pollard's theory of a link between the development of heraldry and of a hereditary House of Lords is relevant here.[3] In the same way the Stall Plate of Sir William Herbert, Knight of the Garter 1461–2, displays the arms of Herbert, the Chamberlain of Henry I, from whom a fictitious pedigree, derives him.[4] Herbert the Chamberlain (d. 1129), a bastard of Herbert II, Count of Maine, married Emma, bastard of Stephen, Count of Blois, son in law of William the Conqueror.[5] Their son, a second Herbert the Chamberlain, married Sibyl Corbet, mistress of Henry I.[6] To these royal links may be due the lions in the coat, *Per pale gules and azure three lions rampant or*, borne by some of their descendants, some of them called FitzHerbert, whose male line expired in 1356.[7] This family long held lands in Wales but was unconnected with the ancestry of

---

[1] W. H. St. John Hope, *The Stall Plates of the Knights of the Garter, 1348–1485*, 1901; A. R. Wagner, *A Catalogue of English Mediaeval Rolls of Arms*, 1950, pp. 83–86.

[2] *Complete Peerage*, xi. 20 n. (d); *Notes & Queries*, 15th ser. xxviii. 511–12; Hope, op. cit., pl. lx.

[3] p. 104.

[4] Wagner, *Heralds of England*, p. 133.

[5] R. L. Poole, *Eng. Hist. Rev.* 45, 1930, p. 275.

[6] *Complete Peerage*, xi, App. D, p. 108.

[7] Eyton, *Hist. Shropshire*, vol. vii, p. 148; *Aspilogia*, ii. 29.

Sir William Herbert.[1] However, Sir William's father, Thomas ap Gwilym ap Jenkin, used as early as 1399 a seal with the arms, *Per pale three lions rampant*.[2] This indicates that the fictitious pedigree, which derived him from the Chamberlain's line, had already in some form been concocted, though it may have been improved upon in 1461.

The oldest books of pedigree which are known to be the work of heralds date from about 1480. William Ballard, March King of Arms *c.* 1475–*c.* 1490, made a Visitation of Cheshire and recorded brief genealogies as well as arms.[3] Much more interesting and important is a collection of pedigrees of northern families compiled between about 1480 and 1500, and for the most part before 1490. This was edited in 1930 by Mr. C. H. Hunter Blair from a sixteenth and a seventeenth century copy.[4] In 1935 I found an earlier sixteenth century copy in the College of Arms and I have since acquired a copy in what appears to be a late fifteenth century hand, which may either be the original or an early copy. The hand closely resembles one associated elsewhere with Sir Thomas Wriothesley, while later in this and in a companion volume are pedigrees in a hand which is either his or that of an amanuensis much employed by him. I have suggested elsewhere that the collection might be the work of Christopher Carlisle, Norroy King of Arms 1494–1510, but I am now inclined to place its compilation earlier than his term of office, while associations of my 'original' with Sir Thomas Wriothesley discount the argument from the association of the college copy with Carlisle's nephew Barker. I now, therefore, incline to attribute the compilation either to John Writhe (d. 1504), who may have begun it when he was Norroy (1477–8) and continued it as Garter,[5] or to his son and successor Sir Thomas Wriothesley (d. 1534). Mr. Hunter Blair has pointed out the similarity of this collection to another attributed to Wriothesley.[6]

Some of the pedigrees in this collection are short and probably based on family knowledge, since children of sisters and personal details are given. Others, however, such as those of Percy, Neville and Fitzwilliam, go back to remote dates and must rest on either research or

---

[1] *Heraldic Visitations of Wales ... by Lewis Dwnn*, ed. Sir S. R. Meyrick, 1846, vol. i, pp. 196–7.

[2] Cardiff Library, MS. 5. 7. fo. 35. Information from Major Francis Jones, Wales Herald Extraordinary.

[3] Coll. Arm. MS. M. 3; see A. R. Wagner, *Catalogue of English Mediaeval Rolls of Arms*, pp. 111–16, and *Heralds and Heraldry in the Middle Ages*, pp. 107–9.

[4] Surtees Soc. cxliv.

[5] A. R. Wagner, *Heralds and Heraldry in the Middle Ages*, pp. 106–7.

[6] Op. cit., p. xii; the Wriothesley collection is Add. MS. 5530.

invention. Research is suggested by occasional marginal notes (e.g. to Neville) apparently from chronicles or charters, but the beginning of the Fitzwilliam pedigree is myth.

### 5. THE VARIETIES OF CONCOCTION

The making of false pedigrees is an immemorial vice, practised in antiquity, the Middle Ages, and modern times alike, but the age of Elizabeth I has a specially bad name for such activities. The rise of so many new families to wealth and station in a society where the prestige of ancient blood was great combined with a growing but as yet ill educated zeal for the study of English antiquities to produce a market for deplorable concoctions as well as for genuine research. The same pedigree craze which produced the fictions helped, however, to stimulate the great movement of scholarship which culminated in the work of Dugdale (d. 1686).[1]

J. Horace Round (1854–1928),[2] the great genealogical critic, divided the bulk of spurious pedigrees into four classes, 'those that rested on garbled versions of perfectly genuine documents, such as Philpot the herald was an adept at constructing, those which rested on alleged transcripts of wholly imaginary documents, those which rested on actual forgeries expressly concocted for the purpose, and lastly those which rested on nothing but sheer fantastic fiction'.[3] Besides these four classes there are pedigrees whose errors rest on a strained or erroneous but not dishonest interpretation of genuine evidence.

Parallel with this variety of method we have a variety of motive. Not all makers of false pedigrees are merely venal. Some, indeed, are not venal at all but simply have too much imagination and too little critical sense. They think they know what the truth must be; they use such evidence as they can; and then they let fancy take wing. Before we smile too broadly we ought to recall the credit still accorded to imaginative exercises in some other fields of scholarship. We may ask ourselves, for example, whether prehistory is or is not history.

The line between self deception and conscious fraud in genealogy is hard to draw. What is one to make of learned and critical genealogists who concoct false pedigrees for themselves simply or mainly for their private satisfaction? Sir Edward Dering (d. 1644), who made himself a Saxon pedigree, inserted the name and arms of a fictitious ancestor

---

[1] pp. 369–71.    [2] pp. 391–3.
[3] *Family Origins and other Studies by the late J. Horace Round*, ed. William Page, 1930, pp. 170–1. Round's condemnation of Philpot has been questioned.

into ancient rolls of arms which he possessed and set up pseudo-ancestral brasses in Pluckley church, was a scholar and associate of scholars.[1] The learned Sir Egerton Brydges (d. 1837), to support whose baseless claim to the barony of Chandos parish registers were tampered with,[2] presumably by him or at his instance, so resented its rejection that for thirty years he did not cease from bitter and public complaint. Furthermore he undertook the immense labour of editing a valuable and scholarly nine volume Peerage[3] 'in order that a few of its pages might transmit a record of his family wrongs to posterity'. Men of genuinely ancient family have been moved to paint the lily. John Lord Lumley (1533–1609), whose descent is proved from the twelfth century, thought it necessary to bring from Durham to the church of Chester-le-Street, where they remain, three effigies of mediaeval knights, supposed to be his ancestors but probably not so, and to complete the series with eleven new ones. The *Complete Peerage* calls this 'pious rather than scholarly'. Mr. Laurence Stone says that he and his family boasted so loudly of their ancestry to King James I that the king is said to have remarked 'I did na ken Adam's name was Lumley'.[4]

A victim of the same disease in still stranger form was George Harrison (1817–90), who latterly called himself Marshal-General George Henry de Strabolgie Neville Plantagenet-Harrison. In his early years he served with distinction as a soldier in several South American armies, in Denmark and in Germany, his rank of marshal-general being in the army of 'God and Liberty' of Corrientes in the Argentine Republic. He then settled in England and devoted himself to research, but from 1850 was forbidden access to the British Museum, according to his own account, 'because he claimed to be Duke of Lancaster'. In 1858 he unsuccessfully petitioned for a summons to the House of Lords as Duke of Lancaster, 'as heir of the whole blood of King Henry VI'. In 1861 he was declared bankrupt and confined in the Queen's Bench prison. Soon after this he started upon a course of research in the Public Record Office which he continued for the rest of his life, devoting himself 'with incredible industry to the task of extracting

---

[1] J. Horace Round, *Peerage and Pedigree*, 1910, ii. 111–17; A. R. Wagner, *Catalogue of English Mediaeval Rolls of Arms*, p. 141.

[2] G. F. Beltz, *A Review of the Chandos Peerage Case*, 1834.

[3] *Collins's Peerage of England, genealogical, biographical, and historical, greatly augmented and continued to the present time*, by Sir Egerton Brydges, K. J., 1812; his account of the barony of Chandos and his claim to it is in vi. 704–40.

[4] p. 55, *supra*: *Complete Peerage*, viii. 266, 279; *The Crisis of the Aristocracy 1558–1641*, p. 24.

from the voluminous and hitherto totally unindexed Rolls of the Queen's Bench and Common Pleas all entries relating to the transfer of land or containing any materials for family history from the reign of Richard I to that of James I'. The best witness to the value of this work is the fact that the thirty folio volumes which it filled were bought after his death for the Public Record Office and are kept there on the open shelves for the use of students.

In 1879 General Plantagenet-Harrison published the only volume to appear of a great projected *History of Yorkshire*. This a is large folio of nearly 600 pages dealing with the Wapentake of Gilling West. It contains a great number of pedigrees and much genealogical matter very useful if used with sufficient caution. According to Paley Baildon, whose opinion may be accepted, 'the persons composing the pedigrees as a rule may be accepted as having actually existed, but in his affiliations he is very untrustworthy, not scrupling to make John the son of Thomas without a tittle of evidence to support the alleged descent'. To the work is prefixed a marvellous pedigree of the author, deriving him in the male line from Odin (with a note that 'all his ancestors in the direct male line stood upwards of seventy-five inches in stature') and making him by an unproved female descent the heir of one of the coheirs of Charles Neville, Earl of Westmorland (d. 1601), who was the representative in blood of Elizabeth, Duchess of Exeter, sister of King Henry IV.[1] Baildon asked him how he reconciled his own claim to the dukedom of Lancaster with the fact that, according to his own pedigrees, he had, when he published them, an elder brother living. 'Oh', said the general contemptuously, and with delightful irrelevance, '*he was a d - - - - d fool!*' The one genuine great distinction of his pedigree the general leaves unstressed, namely that his great-grandfather was first cousin to Dr. Johnson.[2]

Still more modern examples of this sort of aberration are known to genealogists and it is evidently not uncommon. My own experience leads me to believe that there are genealogists who would never fake a pedigree for money, but cannot resist this curious form of self-deception and glorification. The point is of some importance in relation to the notable early Tudor figure mentioned earlier, Sir Thomas Wriothesley (d. 1534), Garter King of Arms.

[1] The issue of the coheir in question is generally supposed to be extinct; see Burke's *Vicissitudes of Families*, i. 24.

[2] Aleyn Lyell Reade, *The Reades of Blackwood Hill*, 1906, pp. 177–85; *The History of Yorkshire by Marshal-General Plantagenet-Harrison, H.K.G.* i, 1879, after p. xiii. See Table III *infra*.

Wriothesley was the son and successor of John Writhe (d. 1504), Garter, and probably the grandson of William Writhe, burgess for Cricklade in the Parliament of 1450–1. John Writhe began and his son continued on a much larger scale a remarkable and extensive work of heraldic codification and both seem to have been active genealogists, differing in this from most of the heralds of their day. Thomas Writhe, as he then was, soon after his father's death and his own appointment as Garter, disliking his monosyllabic surname began experimenting with improvements and after trying Wrye, Wryst, Wreseley, Writhesley and Wrotesley, at length settled on Wriothesley, a form which he then applied retrospectively to his father and in pedigrees to his ancestors.[1] Apart from this small absurdity I have found nothing impossible in such Wriothesley pedigrees as I have seen and nothing to suggest that Wriothesley made any claim to descent from the ancient Staffordshire family of Wrottesley. However, the historian of this family, Major-General the Hon. George Wrottesley (d. 1909), a genealogist who did much admirable work, incensed at the theft or near-theft of his surname, without quoting any other evidence, goes so far as to say that Wriothesley 'for the forgery and the falsification of documents . . . stands pre-eminent even amongst the Tudor Heralds'.[2] Evidence for this accusation may exist, though I have not found it. The point I wish, however, to make here is that forgery or concoction of his own pedigree would not in itself prove Wriothesley venal or even uncritical in relation to those of others. The only fictitious pedigree at present known to me which appears in Wriothesley's collections[3] and seems to me likely to have originated with him is that of Cavendish. Round, who discussed it,[4] did not know that it went back so far and thus missed the pleasure of blaming a herald for it.

### 6. CRITICISM AND THE TUDOR HERALDS

The position of the heralds in relation to the fictitious pedigrees of this epoch is a vexed question which we must try to put in perspective. Round speaks of 'subservient heralds' of Tudor days 'who "found" pedigrees with equal readiness for their sovereign, their clients and

[1] Anstis, *Register of the Garter*, ii. 155, 369–70; Wagner, *Heralds of England*, 1967, pp. 166–72.

[2] Maj.-Gen. the Hon. Geo. Wrottesley, 'A History of the family of Wrottesley of Wrottesley, Co. Stafford', 1903, Wm. Salt Soc., N.S. vi, pt. ii, pp. 276–7.

[3] Brit. Mus. MS. Harl. 1417, fo. 88b.

[4] *Family Origins*, pp. 22–32.

themselves'.[1] This judgment lumps together the learned and the ignorant, the honest and the unscrupulous, and suggests, if it does not state, that in a general scramble to fudge pedigrees the heralds set the pace. The truth, I think, was otherwise. Though I have indicated that as far back as the middle fifteenth century some heralds were occasionally concerned with genealogy, I do not believe that it much concerned most of them till well into the reign of Elizabeth I. Their principal occupations before that time were journeys on official business at home and abroad, the marshalling of tournaments, court ceremonies and the funerals of the nobility and gentry, and in the last connection and generally the superintendence, record and production of armorial bearings. The Visitations made under the Royal Commission of 1530 started the change of emphasis, but most of the pedigrees then entered, other than those of well known ancient families, were short, simple and doubtless based on family information. The Elizabethan phase begins in the 1560's when William Hervy (d. 1566), Clarenceux, and William Flower (d. 1588), Norroy, began a fresh cycle of Visitation on an altogether ampler scale.[2]

Among the pedigrees submitted to the heralds and in some instances accepted by them in these and following years were a certain number of of fabrications of all the types distinguished by Round.[3] The heralds of the first part of Elizabeth's reign were doubtless chosen for quite other qualities than skill in genealogy. But in any case a critical science of genealogy did not yet exist and only now began to develop. By 1581 the need for a new type of herald was beginning to be felt for in that year Robert Dudley, Earl of Leicester (d. 1588), wrote to the Earl Marshal, whose deputy he was, recommending one Humphrey Hales for the vacant post of Bluemantle Pursuivant, as 'an honest gentleman . . . altogether given to matters of pedigrees, and very well seen in them already. He doth draw and paint excellently well, as may appear by a thing done for your Lordship by him. He is properly studied in the law, but his chief and whole study is this service.' He adds 'that there is nothing more honourable for you, nor more profitable to the nobility, than to see fit men placed in these offices, especially the pursuivants'.[4]

[1] *The Ancestor*, iii. 1902, p. 14.

[2] See p. 341 and Wagner, *Records and Collections of the College of Arms*, pp. 15–18 and 55–84.

[3] p. 358. On the genealogical activities of the Elizabethan heralds see also Wagner, *Heralds of England*, 1967, pp. 204–8.

[4] A letter from the Earl Marshal, Lord Shrewsbury, to Leicester is in Coll. Arm. MS. Talbot Papers, G. fo. 231. Anstis, MS. Officers of Arms, ii. 409–11, quoting his MS. G. 5, fo. 90.

I suspect that skill in pedigrees was apt at this date to mean skill in setting them out.

Robert Cooke (d. 1592), Clarenceux, was a skilful genealogist in this sense. He was a neat penman and herald painter, a man of great energy and an enthusiastic collector of pedigrees. Sir Thomas Kendrick praises his church notes, made as early as 1569, including drawings of mediaeval monuments.[1] But his education was not academic and he had, it seems, little or no critical sense. He thus accepted at his Visitations and signed at other times a number of fictitious pedigrees. He is said to have begun as servant to Sir Edmund Brudenell (d. 1585), a Northamptonshire country gentleman who had inherited a love of pedigrees, heraldry and antiquities from his father Sir Thomas (d. 1549). This latter had entertained John Leland (d. 1552), the famous antiquary, more than once at his house at Deene and had shown him a roll of Henry VII's descent from the Welsh princes and other pedigrees and had quoted to him 'an old record of the King's'.[2] We have seen[3] that there had been antiquarian country gentlemen since the fifteenth century at least. An able young man growing up in such a household and imbibing at the same time manners and a taste for antiquities might seem well qualified for a herald's post.

The construction of fictitious documents for genealogical or other purposes was nothing new in the sixteenth century. Professor Galbraith tells us, indeed, 'that the twelfth century was the golden age of forgery',[4] though the purpose then was to secure titles to land. The descent of the Pastons from a fictitious Wulstan Paston who 'came out of France . . . three years after the Conquest' may have been concocted as early as the fifteenth century and charters from the reign of Henry II forged to support it.[5] It is said to have been included in William Worcester's book of Norfolk families.[6] Since, however, that book was later in Paston ownership the pedigree might have been interpolated then. What is certain is that it was compiled before Hervy's Norfolk Visitation in 1563 at which it was entered.

---

[1] T. D. Kendrick, *British Antiquity*, 1950, p. 156.

[2] Joan Wake, *The Brudenells of Deene*, 1953, pp. 46, 67, quoting J. Leland, *Itinerary*, ed. L. Toulmin Smith, 1907.

[3] See page 214.     [4] V. H. Galbraith, *Studies in the Public Records*, 1948, p. 49.

[5] 'Account of a MS. Genealogy of the Paston Family', by Francis Worship, *Norfolk Archaeology*, iv. 1855, pp. 1–55; Walter Rye, *Norfolk Families*, 1913, pp. 647–54; K. B. McFarlane was disposed to think the fifteenth century disparagements of the Paston ancestry (*The Paston Letters, A.D. 1422–1509*, ed. James Gairdner, 1904, i. 28–29; iv. 181, 246–9) greatly exaggerated, if not pure malice.

[6] p. 354.

I know of no early case where the authorship of such forgeries has been established. A notable sequence of forged charters carrying back the ancestry of the Lamberts of Skipton, Yorkshire, to Lambert, Count of Louvain (d. 1004), imposed on more than one worthy king of arms in the reign of James I.[1] A fictitious derivation of the Wellesbournes of Buckinghamshire from Montfort Earl of Leicester, was supported by forged mediaeval deeds and seals and the placing in Hughenden church of a fabricated thirteenth century knightly effigy.[2] What looks like such another sequence, carrying back the Mildmays, who were yeomen under Henry VIII, to twelfth century knights, was accepted by Clarenceux Cooke in 1583.[3] But in such instances the heralds' fault would seem to have been simply a lack of knowledge which few, if any, at that time possessed.

Far more serious are such accusations as Round made against Cooke's successor, Richard Lee (d. 1597), Clarenceux, in relation to the fictitious pedigree deriving the Spencers from the mediaeval Despencers. 'He took from the records', says Round, 'Spencers and Despencers wherever he could lay hands on them, fitted them together in one pedigree at his own sweet will, rammed into his composition several distinct families, and then boldly certified the whole as gospel truth.'[4] Lee's own colleagues accused him of venality but also of ignorance, so perhaps he may only have put his name here to some other man's ingenious concoction. In 1595 Sir William Dethick (d. 1612), Garter, a better antiquary than Lee, did not hesitate to defend himself against an accusation of propounding a false pedigree by saying that it was only according to the proofs shown him by the claimant, whose responsibility it was to defend these.[5]

It was at this period that Robert Glover, who entered the College of Arms as Portcullis Pursuivant in 1567, began to lay the foundations of critical genealogy. He became Somerset Herald in 1570 and in the same year was deputed by his father in law William Flower (d. 1588), Norroy, to make Visitation in the north of England on his behalf.[6] His death at the age of forty four in 1588 cut short a career which had

---

[1] *The Ancestor*, iii. 24–32.

[2] Stone, *The Crisis of the Aristocracy*, p. 24, citing E. J. Payne, 'The Montforts, the Wellesbournes & the Hughenden effigies', *Records of Bucks*, vii, 1896; E. Mercer, *English Art, 1553–1625*, Oxford, 1962, pp. 219–20.

[3] J. H. Round, *Family Origins*, pp. 60–72.

[4] J. H. Round, *Studies in Peerage and Family History*, 1901, pp. 307–8.

[5] Arthur Collins, *Proceedings, Precedents and Arguments on Claims and Controversies concerning Baronies by Writ, and other Honours*, 1734, pp. 141–7.

[6] Wagner, *Records and Collections of the College of Arms*, p. 80.

already set a mark upon historical scholarship. Glover's work has yet to be fully studied and assessed, but the volumes of his manuscript collections and especially the books of his Visitations of Cheshire 1580, Staffordshire 1583, and Yorkshire 1584–5, attest his grasp of the great principle that pedigrees should, if possible, be founded upon record evidence. Copies of family charters and extracts from the public records were entered by him for their evidential value. Mr. Godfrey Davis notes that heralds such as Glover and Ralph Brooke (d. 1625) were the first to make antiquarian extracts from the monastic cartularies.[1] Round justly regards it as a testimony to the care and faithfulness of Glover's work that he was the only herald whose manuscript collections Dugdale used and used largely.[2]

The great antiquary William Camden (d. 1623), who was brought into the College of Arms as Clarenceux in 1597 as part of a general reform, was less a genealogist than a local historian and archaeologist. His literary controversy with Ralph Brooke (d. 1625), York Herald, which Sir Thomas Kendrick commends as an early application of the scientific spirit to archaeology,[3] was little concerned with pedigree. It led on, however, to an epoch making genealogical controversy, for when in 1619 Brooke in his *Catalogue of Nobility* made a fresh attack on Camden, the latter found a champion in his pupil and admirer Augustine Vincent (d. 1626), Rouge Croix Pursuivant, who attacked Brooke with criticisms of his genealogies.

Vincent, who had been appointed Rouge Rose Pursuivant Extra-ordinary in 1616 and had come into the College of Arms as Rouge Croix in 1621, brought to it a new kind of learning cardinal to the development of critical genealogy, namely a close working knowledge of the mediaeval public records. This knowledge he had acquired as a clerk in the Tower Record Office[4] under Sir John Borough (d. 1643) who himself came into the college as Norroy in 1623 and was later Garter. Historical genealogy in the Tower Record Office goes back to William Bowyer, Keeper there, who made Lord Treasurer Winchester a pedigree of his family from the records before 1567. Winchester wrote to Cecil that he had desired Leicester to show this to him and to the queen 'that his service may be known, whereof will grow great reformation amongst the heralds, that maketh their books at a

---

[1] G. R. C. Davis, *Medieval Cartularies of Great Britain*, 1958, p. xv.
[2] *Family Origins*, p. 6.          [3] *British Antiquity*, pp. 152–5.
[4] See p. 343; Anstis MS. Officers of Arms, ii. 639; Nicholas Harris Nicolas, *Memoir of Augustine Vincent, Windsor Herald*, 1827.

venture and not by the records'.[1] Vincent's manuscript collections now in the College of Arms include more than thirty volumes of extracts from the Public Records both in the Tower and elsewhere, for the most part from the Patent Rolls, Close Rolls, Inquisitions, Pleas and Fines. Upon these he bases many pedigrees in his other manuscript volumes and he often refers to the records in his controversy with Brooke. In reply to Brooke's claim that his own library was better furnished than the College of Arms he asks if it be 'better furnished with ancient and authentic records than the office at the Tower' and remarks that 'experience cannot make you skilful in records unless you came where they were (which is not commonly in Painters' shops)[2] and come fitly prepared and qualified by your breeding to understand the language they speak'.[3] It would have been difficult for Brooke to gain access to those records, if he had wished—and had been capable of understanding them.[4] Vincent, in Dugdale's words, 'had no small advantage by his free access to the Publick Records in the Tower of London, being then a Clerk in that Office'.[5] Glover had understood the value of record evidence, but his use of it seems to have been mainly confined to charters in private hands. Vincent's use of the public records was thus a landmark in the history of genealogy.

The demand for pedigrees under Elizabeth I had come, at least in the main, from men who would not, even if they had wished, have known how to apply critical canons to the concocted pedigrees too often furnished them. Between Glover's day and Vincent's, however, antiquarian studies had moved forward with rapid strides and pedigrees were now studied and scrutinized by an appreciable group of capable and disinterested scholars.

### 7. THE ANTIQUARIES AND THE COUNTY HISTORIANS

A focus for the serious study of English antiquities was provided by the formation about 1586 of the Elizabethan Society of Antiquaries.[6] Its debates and papers were concerned with such general

---

[1] Professor R. B. Wernham, 'The Public Records in the 16th and 17th centuries', in *English Scholarship in the 16th and 17th Centuries*, ed. L. Fox, 1956, pp. 17–18, quoting *State Papers, Domestic, Elizabeth*, No. xlii, fo. 101. On Burghley's pursuit of his own pedigree see Hatfield MSS. XIII, 103, 140, 198, 397.

[2] Brooke had started as a herald painter.

[3] Augustine Vincent, *A Discoverie of Errours in the first Edition of the Catalogue of Nobility Published by Raphe Brooke, York Herald*, &c., 1622.

[4] Cf. p. 343.          [5] *Baronage*, i, Preface.

[6] Joan Evans, *A History of the Society of Antiquaries*, 1956, p. 10.

questions as the antiquity of titles of nobility, castles, cities, parishes, shires, coinage, armorial bearings and the like. But its members included heralds such as Camden, Dethick and Thynne, amateurs of heraldry such as Joseph Holland and James Strangman, official keepers of records such as Arthur Agarde, Michael Heneage, and a Mr. Bowyer, who may have been William Bowyer, Keeper of the Tower Records, *c.* 1564–7, or Robert Bowyer, Keeper of the Chancery Records in 1604,[1] local historians like Richard Carew, Sampson Erdeswicke, William Lambarde and John Stow, and scholars like Sir Robert Cotton and Sir Henry Spelman whose wide ranging interests and manuscript collections comprised genealogy besides much else.[2]

The county histories begin with William Lambarde's (d. 1601) *Perambulation of Kent* printed in 1576. Not all their authors were interested in genealogy.[3] The works of some, like Richard Carew's *Survey of Cornwall* (1602), were more descriptive than historical. But wherever manorial history was made the basis, as more and more it was, genealogy and documentation came into the picture. Sampson Erdeswicke (d. 1603), whose *Survey of Staffordshire*, begun about 1593, was circulated in manuscript but not printed till 1817, and William Burton (d. 1645), whose *Description of Leicestershire* appeared in 1622, were keen if not very critical genealogists, Sir William Pole (d. 1635), whose *Description of Devonshire* was not printed till 1791, made immense manuscript collections including copies of the charters in the muniment rooms of the Devon gentry. Thomas Jekyll (d. 1653) made collections for a never accomplished history of Essex, Norfolk and Suffolk, which later writers built upon. Sir Simon Archer (d. 1662) made collections for a Warwickshire history, Roger Dodsworth (d. 1654) for a Yorkshire history, a baronage, and a corpus of monastic charters, Augustine Vincent (d. 1626) for a history of

[1] *English Historical Scholarship in the 16th and 17th Centuries*, ed. L. Fox, 1956, pp. 17–18.

[2] *Hearne's Curious Discourses*, 1765 ed. ii. 421–49.

[3] For general accounts of the Elizabethan and early Stuart antiquarian movement see Robin Flower, 'Lawrence Nowell and the Discovery of England in Tudor Times', *Proc. Brit. Academy*, xxi. 5–73; T. D. Kendrick, *British Antiquity*, 1950, pp. 156–67; A. L. Rowse, *The England of Elizabeth*, 1951, chap. ii; Philip Styles, *Sir Simon Archer 1581–1662*, Dugdale Soc. Occasional Papers, No. 6, 1946; C. E. Wright, 'Sir Edward Dering . . .', in C. Fox and B. Dickins, *H. M. Chadwick Memorial Studies*, 1950, pp. 371–93. C. E. Wright, 'The Elizabethan Society of Antiquaries and the Formation of the Cottonian Library', in *The English Library before 1700*, ed. F. Wormald, 1958. W. G. Hoskins, *Local History in England*, 1959, pp. 16–22. For Yorkshire writers on genealogy and heraldry see Professor A. G. Dickens, 'The Writers of Tudor Yorkshire', *Tr. Roy. Hist. Soc.*, 5th ser. vol. 13, 1963.

Northamptonshire, and Thomas Habington (d. 1647) for a history of Worcestershire. John Smyth (d. 1640) of Nibley, Gloucestershire, steward of the Berkeley family, wrote their history and genealogy 'in an Historical way', which Dugdale heartily wished might be 'a Pattern for some others to follow: it being faithfully extracted, partly out of Publick Records, and partly from the great mass of ancient Charters, and other Memorials still remaining in Berkeley Castle'.[1]

The surviving manuscripts of such old antiquaries as these, now scattered through many libraries, but especially the British Museum Manuscript Department, the Bodleian at Oxford and the College of Arms, can give much help to the genealogist today if he has opportunity and patience to seek them out, for in them are transcripts of many documents which have perished and references to many still existing which otherwise he might never find. Their inferences from the documents are naturally not always acceptable. Some of them went on the principle of using the documentary evidence so far as it would take them and then—like some modern writers—filling the gaps with their imaginations.

By the early 1600's there was thus a network of antiquaries spread through the country, with a scholarly approach to documents helped by legal training and an ardour for genealogies in relation at once to local history, family history and the safeguarding of rights of property. The career of Roger Dodsworth (d. 1654), one of the most distinguished of these scholars, illustrates their activities and the links which bound them together. His father was chancellor to successive Archbishops of York, so that he was probably familiar with records from childhood.[2] He was working at pedigrees and making notes in Yorkshire churches before he was twenty. By 1618 he was in London working in the great collection of manuscripts formed by Sir Robert Cotton, noting especially monastic charters and material of all kinds bearing on Yorkshire. Later he worked in many private libraries and muniment rooms and on the public records in the Tower and at Westminster. His manuscripts now in the Bodleian Library, Oxford, fill 161 volumes and the accuracy of his transcription of old records is considered outstanding. He projected three great works, a collection of monastic charters or *Monasticon*, a baronage of England, and a history

---

[1] *Baronage*, i, Preface; *The Lives of the Berkeleys by John Smyth of Nibley*, ed. Sir John Maclean, 3 vols. 1893; E. A. L. Moir, 'The Historians of Gloucestershire', in *Gloucestershire Studies*, ed. H. P. R. Finberg, 1957, pp. 268–71.

[2] Joseph Hunter, *Three Catalogues*, 1838, p. 66.

of Yorkshire. He completed none of them, however, and his materials were used by other men.

## 8. DUGDALE

Far the most effective of these was Sir William Dugdale (1605–86), a Warwickshire gentleman, whom his elder neighbour Sir Simon Archer (d. 1662) had encouraged in a taste for antiquities and introduced to many who shared it, both locally and on a visit to London in 1635. Among the scholars whom Dugdale met in London was the venerable Sir Henry Spelman, through whose good offices he was in time appointed an officer of the College of Arms.[1] Spelman also urged him to collaborate with Dodsworth to produce a *Monasticon Anglicanum*. This appeared after Dodsworth's death and it has been said that Dugdale's share in the work was less than he appeared to claim.[2] We are not here concerned with this, for though the *Monasticon* is a great storehouse of raw material for the genealogist, it is not a work of genealogy. On the other hand, Dugdale's other great works, *The Antiquities of Warwickshire* (1656) and *The Baronage of England* (1675–6), are contributions of the first importance to genealogical literature. For the former his sole credit is undoubted nor have I seen serious question in regard to the latter, despite the fact that Dodsworth too, like others before him,[3] had planned a baronage.

To say this is not to forget the many whose help with material Dugdale acknowledged.[4] Though his personal researches in the Public Records in 1637–8 were in a sense the foundation of all his work,[5] his great superiority to others was less in the *collection* of evidence than in the skill with which he marshalled it and the judgement with which he drew conclusions from it. His pedigrees in the *Warwickshire* and the *Baronage* are, I believe, the first in English history to exemplify the great principle that for every statement made contemporary record evidence must if possible, be cited.

On the rare occasions, therefore, when he was deceived by spurious documents, one knows exactly what these were, as with those on which rested the claim of the Feildings, Earls of Denbigh, to descend from

---

[1] Blanch Lyon 1638, Rouge Croix 1639, Chester 1644, Norroy 1660, Garter 1677. On his career and work see Wagner, *Heralds of England*, 1967, chaps. viii, ix.

[2] N. Denholm-Young and H. H. E. Craster, 'Roger Dodsworth (1585–1654) and His Circle', *Yorkshire Arch. Journ.* xxxii, 1936, pp. 5–32; D. C. Douglas, *English Scholars*, 1939, pp. 34–42.

[3] Dugdale in the Preface of his *Baronage* mentions Glover, Brooke and Vincent.

[4] Styles, op. cit., pp. 41–47.          [5] Ibid., pp. 37–41.

thirteenth century Hapsburgs (known to the present Feilding family as Perhapsburgs).[1] 'It is', says Round, 'perhaps his supreme merit that for every statement he gives his reference so that we can test it for ourselves.'[2] 'No single work', says Professor Douglas, 'has ever done so much for the history of the English aristocracy as the *Baronage* of William Dugdale.'[3]

Dugdale was in France for three months in 1648 staying most of that time with the son of André Duchesne (d. 1640) the great French historian and antiquary and making extracts from the latter's valuable collections. In view of his avowal of indebtedness to Duchesne and other French authors it is interesting to have Round's opinion that even at his weakest point 'he is far superior to the French genealogist, La Roque, whose great *Histoire de la Maison d'Harcourt*, published some years earlier' than his *Baronage*, 'was constructed on the same principles, but whose *Preuves* are a lamentable jumble of evidence and of mere assertion'.[4] France, like England, produced in the seventeenth century a great school of genealogists. Their names—Sainct Marthe, Du Chesne, Du Bouchet, Guichenon, La Roque, d'Hozier and le Père Anselme—are famous in their field and more of their work was printed than of their English opposites. A full study of their achievement and of French and English mutual influence in this field and period has, however, yet to be made.

The pedigrees in both the *Warwickshire* and the *Baronage* are pedigrees with a limited object, in the one to illustrate the descents of manors, in the other those of baronies and peerage dignities. Cadet lines and even marriages were therefore largely irrelevant and were not sought out for their own sake though wives were always and cadets sometimes included if the information was to hand. The genealogies in the *Complete Peerage* and the *Victoria County History* naturally enough retain the same limitation to this day. Some pressure upon Dugdale to include more may, however, be inferred here and there. Mr. Styles notes among those whose help Dugdale acknowledges in the *Warwickshire*,

those obscure people, descended from younger sons or belonging to families of mere yeoman origin, whose small estates had been acquired within the last three generations. They number, on a rough estimate, rather more than a

---

[1] J. H. Round, 'Our English Hapsburgs: a Great Delusion', *Peerage and Family History*, 1901, chap. v.
[2] *Family Origins*, p. 7.  [3] D. C. Douglas, *English Scholars*, pp. 52–53.
[4] *Family Origins*, p. 7.

quarter of the whole. . . . Several belonged to Coventry or the immediate neighbourhood and had made their wealth in trade. But about most of them we know very little. The majority were not armigerous and perhaps they may have hoped, in showing their deeds to Archer or Dugdale, that a record in print would establish their claim to gentility. . . . That such men were beginning to take an interest in history and genealogy was a notable sign of the times.[1]

## 9. THE VISITATIONS AND THE DEPUTY HERALDS

At the opposite pole from the feudal or manorial approach to genealogy was that of the Welsh genealogists, whose concern, reflecting the old Welsh social system and indeed an older phase of human society, was solely with the blood regardless of possessions or economic status. Shopkeepers and fiddlers, paupers and pedlars are shown in the Welsh pedigrees alongside the rich and eminent without the least discrimination or sense of incongruity, provided always that their ancestry was noble.[2] Welsh genealogy has its own long and separate history, which cannot be dealt with here. It is, however, worth noting that from the reign of Elizabeth I (1558–1603) to that of Queen Anne (1702–14) the Welsh genealogists, who successively collected and codified the traditional pedigrees, were in close touch with the English heralds, to whom some of them were official deputies, and each group certainly influenced the other.[3]

Midway between these two poles lie the Heralds' Visitations. The formal purpose of each entry in a Visitation[4] book was, it is true, to establish the gentility and right to arms of an individual, but few visiting heralds were as narrow minded as Sir Edward Bysshe (d. 1679), who in general confined himself to linear entries, giving parents, grandparents and children of the head of the family, but neither brothers, sisters, nor collateral branches. At the other extreme Vincent in his Shropshire and Surrey Visitations of 1623, Henry St. George and Samson Lennard in their Devon and Cornwall Visitations of 1620 and their Wiltshire, Dorset and Somerset Visitations of 1623, and Gregory King and other deputies of Sir Henry St. George, Clarenceux, in their Visitations of the 1680's, went out of their way to include collateral branches in their pedigrees. So long as the branches in question were within the limitations of the arms this was proper and

[1] Styles, op. cit., p. 47.
[2] Major Francis Jones, 'An Approach to Welsh Genealogy', *Tr. Cymmrodorion Soc.* 1948, pp. 394–5.　　　　　　　　　　　[3] Ibid., pp. 375–7, 418–29.
[4] See Wagner, *Heralds of England*, 1967, *passim*.

admirable, though not necessary, since according to the pure theory of the thing they could be entered separately under the several counties and hundreds in which their members lived.

Some time in the 1560's a radical change was made in the method of Visitation. Before that date Visitations had been domiciliary. The heralds had visited the gentry in their homes and were still doing so as late as 1563. This, however, proved too slow for the ambitious cycle of Visitation then in hand. Accordingly by 1566 a new method had been introduced by which the sheriffs of the counties sent out to the bailiffs of hundreds lists of 'gentlemen and others', whom they were to warn to appear before the visiting king of arms or heralds. In the next century the gentry were usually summoned to the inn where the heralds lodged in 'the chiefest towns in the Hundred'. Dugdale, who visited as Norroy in the 1660's, said that the place of summons should be not more than six or seven miles from the home of any person summoned to it and it was his custom to entertain at dinner all those who entered their arms and descents.

The Elizabethan Visitations, being far more extensive and ambitious than those of Henry VIII's reign, called for better organization and greater effort, while the growing interest in pedigrees was reflected in fuller entries. The Visitations made by Glover in the northern counties between 1570 and 1585 show the first application of higher critical standards and an interesting innovation in the form of entry seems also to be due to Glover. This was the introduction of the rectilinear tabular form of pedigree, still in general use. The first example I can date is of the year 1564. Though the first to use it in Visitation entries, Glover was not the first inventor of the rectilinear pedigree, for Sir Thomas Wriothesley had occasionally employed it forty or fifty years earlier.[1] It gained rapidly in favour and by 1618 had wholly superseded both the narrative form, normal since the 1530's, and the mediaeval true pedigree (*pied de gru* = crane's foot) form with radiating lines.

Another innovation of this date reflected both scholarly and popular trends in contemporary genealogy. This was the appointment by individual kings of arms (and in at least one case by the whole college) of local deputies, commonly known as deputy heralds.[2] Their responsibilities and terms of appointment differed, but most were concerned not with Visitation but with painting arms and conducting heraldic

[1] Brit. Mus. MS. Harl. 1417, ff. 56, 61; see p. 357.
[2] See Wagner, *Heralds of England*, 239–40, 268.

funerals. Even this called for a knowledge of local pedigrees and the help of such deputies might therefore be enlisted when Visitations of their counties took place. Some few of them, however, were genealogists or scholars rather than painters, and were appointed primarily or solely to assist at Visitations.

The subject has as yet been little studied and our present knowledge is far from full. The first relevant reference I have yet met with is the statement that Griffith Hiraethog (d. 1566), a bard and poet who was also an antiquary and scholar, was deputy herald for all Wales under Garter, Clarenceux and Norroy.[1] The linguistic difficulty perhaps caused the heralds to feel the need to lean on a local expert in Wales sooner than elsewhere. In 1586 Clarenceux and Norroy jointly appointed Lewis Dwnn to make a Visitation of Wales, which he accomplished between that date and 1614.[2]

In 1598 Thomas Chaloner was appointed deputy herald in Chester and in 1606 his widow's second husband Randle Holme (d. 1655) received the same appointment. This Randle Holme was the first of four generations so called, all herald painters in Chester down to 1707. But Randle Holme II, III and IV seem not to have been appointed official deputies, while Randle III was actually prosecuted by Dugdale for invasion of his office of Norroy in 1668. As genealogists the Holmes were indefatigable but inexact and unscholarly, so that the manuscript volumes of their collections, about two hundred and seventy in number, and now in the British Museum, must be used with caution.[3]

In December 1624 and until 1626 Dodsworth was deputy herald for Yorkshire.[4] This appointment was presumably due to the then Norroy, Sir John Borough. Yorkshire was not in fact visited during Dodsworth's tenure of office, but the appointment illustrates the wish of at least some of the heralds to lean on the best available local scholarship. Dugdale's Visitation deputies included such notable antiquaries as Richard Kuerden (d. *c.* 1690) for Lancashire and Nathaniel Johnston (d. 1705)[5] for Yorkshire.

We know that herald painters and local antiquaries alike sought and sometimes obtained copies of the Visitation books for their counties,

---

[1] Francis Jones, op. cit., pp. 366–9; *Heraldic Visitations of Wales by Lewis Dwnn*, ed. Sir S. R. Meyrick, 1846, ii. 97 and i, p. xxii.     [2] Ibid., p. xxiii and *passim*.

[3] J. P. Earwaker, *The Four Randle Holmes of Chester*, 1892.

[4] Coll. Arm. MS. I.C.B. Chaos I. 167.

[5] Dugdale's appointment of Johnston in 1666 is in Bodleian MS. Gough Top. Yorks. C. 36, fo. 20. I owe this reference and much more information about Johnston to an unpublished thesis kindly placed at my disposal by the author Mrs. Janet D. Martin.

despite the heralds' reluctance to let such copies out of their custody. Johnston secured extensive extracts, if not actually full copies, of most of the earlier Yorkshire Visitations. In the same way other extracts and copies were made by deputy heralds and herald painters, who often conflated successive Visitation books and then made additions of their own. Many such copies or purported copies exist in public and private collections. Some were used by eighteenth and nineteenth century county and family historians and it is from such copies that the editions of Visitations printed by the Harleian Society and others are for the most part taken. The trouble with them is that, until they have been analysed and compared with the originals, their character and authenticity are quite uncertain. Some of the additional matter found in them is valuable, some of it worthless. Some render the originals exactly, others distort them. It may be added that the same weaknesses are found in the numerous armorials and heraldic collections made by herald painters of this period, which at one or two removes form the basis of such compilations as Sir Bernard Burke's *General Armory* (1842 and 1884).

### 10. THE DISCIPLES OF DUGDALE

The antiquary and topographer genealogists who were active between 1660 and 1730, the two generations after Dugdale's, for the most part followed in his footsteps. But their failure to repeat the scope or scale of his achievements testifies to his supremacy. In the notable age of antiquarian study which fell between 1660 and 1730 there were many fields to conquer and genealogy lost its lead. Such fluctuations are best understood when scholars' personal histories and connections are studied, as Professor Douglas, Mr. Styles and others have studied them. If there had been space—and it would need a volume—this chapter might advantageously have taken that form. Thus genealogy did not come high enough among the wide ranging interests of Dugdale's son in law Elias Ashmole (1617–92), Windsor Herald, to elicit from him a contribution to its literature. His manuscripts at Oxford nevertheless contain among much else some important genealogical material.[1] Robert Thoroton's (1623–78) *Antiquities of Nottinghamshire* (1677) was a work of scholarship on the lines of Dugdale's *Warwickshire*, but altogether slighter in its execution. To put them on a level, as Professor Douglas does,[2] seems to me too kind to Thoroton.

[1] W. H. Black, *A . . . Catalogue of the Manuscripts bequeathed unto the University of Oxford by Elias Ashmole . . .*, 1845.  [2] *English Scholars*, p. 47.

James Wright (1643–1713) was able to deal adequately with the smallest of English counties,[1] but such others as Sir Robert Atkyns (1647–1711) and Ralph Thoresby (1658–1725), though they printed useful and interesting material, were no such scholars as Dugdale and their work is disappointing to the genealogist.

Dugdale's nearest rivals in scholarship, on the other hand, often lacked the industry and method which had enabled him to complete and publish his great works. Peter le Neve (1661–1729), Norroy King of Arms and first president (1717–24) of the revived Society of Antiquaries, was an exact and industrious student of records and an indefatigable compiler of pedigrees. But he completed nothing for publication and after his death even his manuscripts were dispersed. His materials for a history of his native county of Norfolk, however, form the basis of the great history later produced by Francis Blomefield (d. 1752) and others.[2] His great series of indexes to the Feet of Fines and other records stand on the shelves of the Public Record Office with those of Arthur Agarde (d. 1615) as a help to modern students. His three volumes of Baronets' Pedigrees in the College of Arms constitute a massive but unfinished work.

## II. THE EIGHTEENTH CENTURY HERALDS AND THEIR CLIENTS

Here and there an entry in the later part of Le Neve's pedigrees of the knights made between Charles II's and Queen Anne's reigns[3] suggests the existence of a new type of herald's client. The great fortunes made at this time in trade and commerce have been mentioned earlier.[4] Many of those who made them were cadets of known families, but not all. Sir William Milman (d. 1714), who was knighted in 1705, was according to Le Neve the son of a shoemaker in the Strand of unknown origin. Sir Comport Fitch, 2nd baronet, recorded in 1699 a pedigree apparently worked out for him by Samuel Stebbing (d. 1719), Rouge Rose Pursuivant.[5] Sir Thomas Fitch, the father of Sir Comport, had, as mentioned earlier,[6] started as a carpenter and grown rich as a building contractor when London was rebuilt after the Great Fire of 1666, acquiring a knighthood in 1679 and a baronetcy in 1688. Sir Comport knew that his great-grandfather was the younger son of a younger son of an Essex yeoman and descendants of the more

---

[1] *History and Antiquities of . . . Rutland*, 1684.  [2] p. 379.
[3] Printed by the Harleian Soc. viii, 1873.  [4] pp. 162–3.
[5] From 1700 Somerset Herald.  [6] p. 229.

prosperous branches of the Essex Fitches were willing to depose that they regarded him as a distant cousin. To establish his exact descent was nevertheless not easy and Stebbing set about the problem by copying wills, making extracts from parish registers, noting monumental inscriptions, taking statements from members of the family, and fitting all this evidence together as seemed to him most reasonable.[1] The college had at this date and earlier—as it has now—a system by which a pedigree put forward for registration was referred by the Chapter for examination by two of its members who had not been concerned in the preparation. It was after such independent examination that the Fitch pedigree was accepted and registered. Later research has in general confirmed it, while such errors as have come to light have been rectified by fresh registration.

Stebbing's approach to this case was an early and elementary instance of what has since become a commonplace of genealogical method. Earlier genealogists, concerned almost wholly with landed families, had naturally grounded their research on the records of land tenure. Indeed in their day there were few other records which could have been used. By 1700, however, not only were there the beginnings of a new clientèle—the tradesmen of England, grown wealthy, whom Defoe saw coming every day to the Heralds' Office[2]—but those new and comprehensive records the parish registers were growing old enough to take obscure pedigrees some way back. Stebbing had learned his trade as clerk to Gregory King[3] who had been clerk to Dugdale. Other heralds of the day who made good use of parish registers in their pedigrees were John Hare (d. 1720) and Robert Dale (d. 1722), successive Richmond Heralds, whose manuscripts are in the college.[4] So also probably did two Garter Kings of Arms, whose collections are scattered, Sir Henry St. George (d. 1715),[5] and John Anstis (d. 1744),[6] a great scholar, in whose wide range of interests genealogy, however, came by no means first.

We have noted elsewhere[7] that the end of the Visitations, with other consequences flowing from the same political and social background,

---

[1] Coll. Arm. MS. 3 D 14, ff. 5ᵇ–10ᵇ.     [2] pp. 132, 172.     [3] p. 180.

[4] Wagner, *Records and Collections*, p. 40. A. A. Ettinger, *James Edward Oglethorpe*, Oxford, 1936, p. 71, notes that in 1714 Lady Oglethorpe employed Robert Dale, and through him Thomas Hearne, to compile a pedigree from the Dodsworth MSS. and other sources. This, very elaborately recorded in Coll. Arm. MS. 4. D. 14, 68–69, was the basis of her successful petition to the Pretender for a Baronetcy.

[5] Wagner, *Records and Collections*, pp. 38–39.

[6] Ibid., pp. 39–40. Wagner, *Heralds of England*, chaps. x, xi.     [7] p. 132.

brought the heralds' activities to a low ebb in the first half of the eighteenth century. Early in the reign of George III (1760–1820) this depression began to lift, partly because of economic and social changes and partly because Stephen Martin Leake (1702–73), Garter, had by careful appointments and personal direction prepared the college to take advantage of these.[1] Two heralds, each eventually Garter, Ralph Bigland (1711–84) and Sir Isaac Heard (1730–1822), were prominent in the revival and the scale of their genealogical practice is reflected in the size of their collections now in the College of Arms.

The new note of the 1690's was struck again by Bigland in 1764 when he published his 'Observations on Marriages, Baptisms and Burials, as preserved in Parochial Registers . . . Interspersed with divers Remarks concerning proper Methods necessary to preserve a Remembrance of the several Branches of Families, &c.' The stress laid on the genealogical value of parish registers, wills and monumental inscriptions sufficiently indicates the shift of interest since Dugdale's day. In the same way Bigland's posthumous *History of Gloucestershire* is notable for its extensive details of churchyard epitaphs, which relate for the most part to persons in the lower ranks of society, the nobility and gentry having usually been buried in the churches.[2]

## 12. THE EIGHTEENTH CENTURY PEERAGE BOOKS

Bigland's and Heard's appreciation of the scope offered to the genealogist by newly risen families may have been sharpened by their failure to win support for a projected peerage. In that field, however, the preceding half century had seen the completion of important work which had probably for the time exhausted the market. The most important was that of Arthur Collins (1682–1760), the first edition of whose *Peerage of England* appeared in 1709 and the third, which was the last edited by himself, in 1756. Round judged it 'important, not only because it dominated the eighteenth century, but also because it became the basis of the well-known Burke's *Peerage*'. He added that 'industrious and well-qualified though he was, Collins was fatally lacking, possibly from his want of means, in that manly independence which made Dugdale refuse to flatter family pride. His work is crammed with ludicrous genealogy, taken from the old heraldic pedigrees in the possession of ennobled houses'. 'Thus', says Round,

---

[1] Wagner, *Heralds of England*, chap. xiii.    [2] Ibid., chaps. xiv, xv.

'began those wild stories in the pages of Burke's *Peerage* which move historians to contempt and scorn. The historical statement, for instance, at the head of Lord Bolingbroke's pedigree, that his ancestor, William de St. John, came into England with the Conqueror, as grand master of the artillery and supervisor of the wagons and carriages, whence the horses' hames or collar was borne for his cognizance', is taken bodily from Collins, who took it from a pedigree in the private possession of the great Bolingbroke himself. 'The St. Johns, as I have shown', says Round, 'did not even arrive in England until a later period.'[1]

As a criticism of Collins' attitude to the mythical origins claimed by many great families this is just and it is true that some words in his preface reveal a different temperament from Round's. 'Next', says he, 'to being void of Errors, I shall account myself happy to have given no offence.' To speak, however, of Collins' work as 'crammed with ludicrous genealogy' is misleading, for the ratio of the mythology to the fruits of sober research is small. For the later periods Collins had much of value to add to the work of Dugdale. Though far less consistently than Dugdale, he often gives references to his authorities so that a critical and experienced genealogist can detect the source and nature of his errors. The English *Baronetage* (1727 and 1741) of Thomas Wotton (d. 1766) is the counterpart of Collins' *Peerage* with the same weaknesses and merits. In fact Wotton owed much to Collins' help as well as to the manuscript Baronets' Pedigrees of Peter le Neve.

The next most important compiler of peers' pedigrees at this epoch belonged to an older generation. Simon Segar (living 1712), a great-grandson of Sir William Segar (d. 1633), Garter, completed the great manuscript collection of peers' pedigrees, which he called *Baronagium Genealogicum*, in 1708. He may have inherited some of Sir William's manuscripts, but I see no reason to think that the *Baronagium* was anything but his own work, though John Warburton (d. 1759), Somerset Herald, who owned the manuscript and in 1740 issued proposals for its publication, described it as the work of Sir William continued by Simon. After Warburton's death it was acquired by an enterprising herald painter Joseph Edmondson (d. 1786), Mowbray Herald Extraordinary, of whose *Baronagium Genealogicum*, published in 1764, it was the basis. Segar's manuscript, which afterwards belonged to Sir William Betham (d. 1853), Ulster King of Arms, is now in the College of Arms.[2]

[1] *Family Origins*, pp. 7–8.    [2] Wagner, *Records and Collections*, pp. 40–41.

## 13. THE EIGHTEENTH CENTURY COUNTY HISTORIES

The county historians who followed Dugdale may be divided, as we saw,[1] into those who published work much slighter than his and those who worked, as he did, thoroughly but did not finish what they had begun. The bulky manuscripts of these last in more than one case formed the basis of histories finally published in a later generation and in several cases those who carried the work through were members of that valuable class the country parson antiquaries. To write the history of a county, not merely with Dugdale's thoroughness but with the additions called for by the passage of time, the accumulation of records and the broadening of interests since his day, was becoming a task for a superman or for more hands than one.

Blomefield's *History of Norfolk* (1739–75), in five folio volumes, was based on the manuscript collections of Peter le Neve (d. 1729). The Rev. Francis Blomefield (d. 1752), who gave the work his name, completed the publication of only two volumes and part of a third, and it was finished by the Rev. Charles Parkin (d. 1765) and a nameless hack.[2] The Rev. Philip Morant's *History and Antiquities of the County of Essex* (1760–8) occupies a mere two folio volumes yet it represents the laborious scholarship of three men, Thomas Jekyll (d. 1653) and William Holman (d. 1730) as well as Morant himself. John Bridges (1666–1724) filled thirty volumes, now in the Bodleian, with manuscript collections for a history of Northamptonshire, but it was left for the Rev. Peter Whalley (1722–91) to edit and publish them between 1762 and 1791 in two folio volumes bearing Bridges' name.

All the more honour is therefore due to the prodigious industry of those few who, with whatever shortcomings, completed histories of whole counties single handed, as the Rev. Treadway Russell Nash (1725–1811) did for Worcestershire (1781–2), as Robert Clutterbuck (1772–1831) did for Hertfordshire, as Edward Hasted (1732–1812) did for Kent (first edition of four folio volumes 1778–99, second edition of twelve 1797–1801) and as John Nichols (1745–1826), perhaps the greatest of them all, did for Leicestershire (four folio volumes in eight, 1795–1815). Not far from the same level must be placed such unprinted works as the Cambridgeshire collections of the Rev. William Cole (1714–82), filling many manuscript volumes,[3]

---

[1] pp. 374–5. There are good accounts of most of the county historians in the *D.N.B.*
[2] *D.N.B.* 1908, ii. 688–90, where we are told that Blomefield died 'literally in harness'.          [3] Brit. Mus. MSS, Add. 5862–2885.

and the Suffolk collections of David Elisha Davy (1769–1851) filling 131,[1] both now in the British Museum.

## 14. THE LATER COUNTY HISTORIES

With the scope of the county histories growing to take in geology, prehistoric and Roman antiquities, architecture, manufactures and other matters little regarded in earlier days, one would expect the concentration on genealogy to diminish. But in general it seems rather to have increased. For extensive and in the main reliable pedigrees Robert Surtees' (1779–1834) *History of Durham* (1816–40), George Baker's (1781–1851) uncompleted *History of Northamptonshire* (1822–41), the Rev. James Raine's (1791–1858) *History of North Durham* (1830–52) and Thomas Helsby's (1882) edition of George Ormerod's (1785–1873) *History of the County Palatine and City of Chester* (1819) are outstanding. Joseph Hunter (1783–1861), a Unitarian minister, and an editor of Record publications, included useful pedigrees in his histories of his native *Hallamshire* (1819) and the *Deanery of Doncaster* (1828 and 1831). But far more numerous and useful are the manuscript pedigrees he left behind him, most of them, with his other collections, now in the British Museum, from which five volumes have been printed by the Harleian Society.[2] They relate mainly to north country and dissenting families.

The brothers Daniel (1762–1834) and Samuel Lysons (1763–1819) planned a series of county histories to cover the whole country, and in fact produced ten, from Bedfordshire alphabetically to Devonshire (1806–22). Though they do not give genealogies they are notable for general surveys of the ancient and landed families of each county and their rise and fall.

Most comprehensive and reliable of all in its genealogies is the latest county history on the old plan, the great *History of the County of Northumberland* (fifteen volumes, 1893–1940), a work of many hands. A unique position among county historians belongs to the Rev. Robert William Eyton (1815–81). His *Antiquities of Shropshire* (1861) is limited approximately to the period between the Norman Conquest and the death of Henry III. It is thus minutely concerned with feudal genealogy and it is perhaps praise enough to say that his work is often quoted by Round with high respect.

The praise justly given to many genealogies in county histories must be balanced by a warning that many also embody fabulous material.

[1] Brit. Mus. Add. MSS. 19077–19207.

[2] Vols. xxxvii–xl. *Familiae Minorum Gentium*, lxxxviii, Hunter's Pedigrees.

It was not only that their compilers were insufficiently critical. They were also on occasion tempted. The Rev. Thomas Dunham Whitaker (1759–1821), author of the histories of *Whalley* and the *Honour of Clitheroe* (1801), the *Deanery of Craven* (1805), *Loidis and Elmete* (1816) and *Richmondshire* (1823), wrote that 'experience had taught him that in the genealogies of old families there are many vestiges of error, and some of fraud, which time and vanity have rendered sacred; and Rumour whispered in his ear, that some Topographers had been required to adopt Pedigrees unexamined, as the price of a subscription or an engraving'.[1] Where publication was, as often, a matter of great expense and difficulty, to reject such offers of help might not be easy. Sometimes the author was in actual financial straits, like Edward Hasted, the historian of Kent, whose later volumes betray the pressure under which they were compiled.

By the end of the nineteenth century histories had been printed of most of the English counties. Many were works of scholarship on a noble scale, yet their scope and plan varied greatly with the date of writing and the author's bias, while certain fields of interest and some parts of the country had been neglected. In 1891 Herbert Arthur Doubleday (1867–1941), the son of a wealthy merchant and himself a natural antiquary, had founded with his uncle the publishing house of Archibald Constable & Co. *The History of Northumberland*, which began to appear in 1893, may have put into his mind the notion of a general series of county histories produced by the cooperation of many writers on a uniform pattern. Such at all events was the plan of the *Victoria History of the Counties of England*, which he launched in 1901 and edited and published himself till 1903.[2] It then became evident that much of the material which contributors for the several counties had been expected to produce, especially manorial descents, needed rather to be extracted centrally from the public records for the use of all. This was somewhat outside Doubleday's scope and accordingly in 1902 he enlisted as joint editor William Page (1861–1934), who as partner in a well known firm of record agents[3] had acquired in a high degree the special knowledge required. Soon afterwards Doubleday withdrew from the work and in 1904 Page became sole editor. Doubleday's work in genealogy was by no means done and will be further

---

[1] *History and Antiquities of Craven*, 2nd ed. 1812, p. v.

[2] *H. A. Doubleday 1867–1941*, [a tribute by several hands] 1942, pp. 17–18, 25–27.

[3] His brother-in-law and partner W. J. Hardy was son of Sir William Hardy and nephew of Sir Thomas Hardy, both Deputy Keepers of the Public Records.

mentioned below, and though at this point his connection with the *Victoria County History* ceased, he deserves full credit for the original impulse which gave birth to it and for a great and far seeing plan. Between 1902 and 1910 Page saw forty five volumes through the press. Lack of funds followed by the 1914–18 war then interrupted and almost stopped the work. At length in 1931 Page made over the voluminous materials to the University of London under whose auspices subsequent volumes have appeared.[1]

The plan of the work divides the history of each county into two parts, an introductory volume or volumes dealing with general topics, followed by a topographical survey parish by parish. In the introductory volumes the essays (a number of them by Round) on the Domesday Book materials for the several counties contain important genealogical material. The topographical volumes contain no explicit genealogies but the accounts of the descents of manors, built on the extracts from the public records made under Page's direction, embody genealogical materials and conclusions of the highest value, especially for mediaeval knightly families. Topographical volumes have now appeared for the whole or part of some twenty three counties. For several of these little or no such work had been done before; for example, Bedfordshire, Berkshire, Cambridgeshire, Hampshire, Huntingdonshire, Lancashire and Sussex. In other cases ground already covered, though no doubt inadequately, has been covered again, while certain important counties of which no comprehensive histories exist, such as Cornwall, Devon, Somerset and Suffolk, still await treatment. A series of volumes of genealogies of the leading families of each county was also planned but only two were carried out, *Northamptonshire Families* (1906) by Oswald Barron, to whom fuller reference is made below, and *Hertfordshire Families* (1907) by Duncan Warrand (1877–1946). Each deals in a very full and scholarly way with a small number of important families. They rank indeed among the best of printed English genealogies of recent times.

While the collection of material from the public records for the *Victoria County History* was made centrally under Page's direction, the credit for interpreting this and adding local material belongs to the editors of individual histories or parts thereof. Among these the most distinguished genealogist was probably William Farrer (1861–1924), a wealthy man who devoted most of his time to local history and genealogy and had already, before the *Victoria County History* was

[1] *D.N.B. 1931–1940*, 1949, pp. 666–7.

launched, planned a history of his own county of Lancashire down to the reign of Elizabeth I and collected and published source material for this. These plans he agreed to merge in the larger scheme and with John Brownbill (1856–1931) produced the eight volumes of the *History of Lancashire* between 1906 and 1914. These embody an immense genealogical learning and go much beyond what the *Victoria County History* gives for most counties.

Feudal links between Lancashire and Yorkshire led Farrer on to the work which culminated in his three volumes of *Early Yorkshire Charters* (1914–16), which since his death have been continued in eight more volumes (1935–63) by Mr. Charles Travis Clay (now Sir Charles Clay). Through this work, despite the ensuing 'false start' (as Tait calls it) of his *Feudal History of Cambridgeshire* (1920), Farrer was led to realize that the only satisfactory way of treating the tenurial history of feudal entities 'was to bring together all the fees of each great honor or barony, irrespective of the counties in which they happened to lie'. Hence his three volumes of *Honors and Knights' Fees*, 'an attempt to identify the component parts of certain honors and to trace the descent of the tenants of the same who held by knight service or serjeanty from the eleventh to the fourteenth century' (1923–5). He explains the advantage his system may have among others for the genealogist, 'who may, for instance, find the families in which he is interested seated in other counties on fees of the same honor, under the same or different surnames'.[1]

A publication which ignored county boundaries could not look for the local support which has chiefly made possible the publication of county histories. Thus since Farrer, who could finance his own work, died, no more work on this plan has appeared. Sir Charles Clay (whose learning and scholarship it would be impertinent for me to praise), however, in his volumes of *Early Yorkshire Charters* has grouped his material by fees irrespective of situation within Yorkshire and has brought in by way of necessary explanation much material relating to portions of the fees in question in other counties. It is much to be wished that some learned foundation would make possible a continuation of Farrer's work as a basis for the fuller study of feudal history and genealogy.

## 15. THE RECORD MOVEMENT AND PEERAGE CLAIMS

The great movement mentioned in the last chapter[2] towards the publication, assembly and arrangement of the public records had

---

[1] *Honors and Knights' Fees*, iii. 1925, Preface by James Tait.　　　[2] p. 343.

naturally a great influence on the study and literature of genealogy. The chief landmarks in this movement were the printing of the *Rolls of Parliament* from 1771 and of *Domesday Book* from 1783; the setting up of the six record commissions between 1800 and 1837 and the publication of many records under their auspices; the foundation of the Public Record Office in 1838, the erection of its building in 1851–71; and the publication of the great series of calendars, lists and indexes of the records from 1864. Furthermore, as we have seen,[1] the French Revolution and the Napoleonic Wars (1789–1815) by severing links between England and the Continent turned the interests of English antiquaries once more inward and gave a fillip to mediaeval studies, heraldry and genealogy.

Francis Townsend (1749–1819), Windsor Herald, was a representative and distinguished figure of the first part of this period. His papers in the College of Arms show his skilful conduct of a large professional practice in genealogy. Furthermore he made large collections for a new edition of Dugdale's *Baronage*. This was never finished and after his death part of his work seems to have been lost. However, the four large volumes remaining in the college, and even the brief extracts from them printed in 1837–8,[2] indicate the thoroughness of his researches and his close acquaintance with the relevant records. Townsend's clear but quiet repudiation of Clarenceux Lee's Spencer pedigree of 1595 receives an acknowledgement from Round in the course of his own more emphatic essay on the same theme.[3]

In 1789 Townsend's professional conscience was subjected to a severe test. He had been retained by Egerton Brydges to work on his claim to the barony of Chandos[4] and in the course of his researches came upon a piece of evidence which told heavily against his client's case. Brydges, informed of this, said, 'If it makes against us, we are not bound to produce it.' Townsend replied that '*it must be produced*', and, when his client declined to do this, decided after much searching of conscience that he must produce it himself. Eventually in 1794, after waiting to give Brydges every chance of producing it himself, he did so.[5]

Had Townsend lived a generation later he would have been much employed in the preparation of the peerage claims of the 1830's.

---

[1] p. 133.

[2] By Charles George Young, York Herald and later Garter, in *Coll. Top. et Gen.* iv and v.  [3] *Peerage Studies*, p. 292.  [4] See p. 359.

[5] G. F. Beltz, Lancaster Herald, *A Review of the Chandos Peerage Case*, 1834, pp. 108–16.

Indeed a 'Prospectus and specimen of a proposed work on the present state of Baronies by Writ' issued soon after his death by his son Francis Townsend (d. 1833), Rouge Dragon, tells us that the father, in his work for a new edition of Dugdale's *Baronage*, 'had particularly directed his attention to tracing the existing Heirs of Baronies by Writ', doubtless with a view to floating upon a tide then already rising.

The early years of the Queen's accession [says Cokayne] were the halcyon times for the Peerage lawyers. Supporters of the Whig Government (Lord Melbourne's) who, under other ministers, might have entered the Peerage from below, had now good reason to expect to be placed *over* the heads of almost the entire Baronage (e.g. over such families as Stourton, St. John, Roper, Clifford, Byron, &c., whose ancestors had for hundreds of years *consecutively* held a Peerage), provided only that the Peerage lawyer could prove that there was in them (or, failing that, in their respective wives, which would equally benefit their posterity) *some small fraction* of co-representation of some *one* of the *prodigious number* of early Baronies, which (according to modern intepretation) were created *in fee* by the numerous writs of summons issued by the Plantagenet Kings. Before the time of George III (passing over the anomalous case of Le Despencer) no abeyance had been terminated that had existed more than the space of some 30 years or so; that King, however, in four (Botetourt, Zouche, Roos and Howard de Walden) out of the eight Baronies he thus terminated, introduced the pernicious practice of reviving Baronies whose estates had been entirely alienated, and where the dignities themselves had lapsed for a century or more. It was reserved, however, for the short space of little more than three years (March 1838 to May 1841) to terminate the abeyance of *six* Baronies—of which five had long been disused, the 'Caput Baroniae' and all estates belonging to them having been alienated, and their very names become unfamiliar. . . . Had this pace of terminating abeyances been continued, the Peerage would, since the Queen's accession, have by this time been 'adorned' with about 100 such (strange) Baronies. . . . Neither was there any lack of candidates for such honours. . . . The cry was still 'They come, they come.' People began to think that the words of Sir Guy le Scroope in the 'Lay of St. Cuthbert' (then recently published in 'the Ingoldsby legends') were prophetic of this scramble for Baronies;

> What can delay de Vaux and de Saye?
>
> .      .      .      .      .
>
> Poynings and Vavasour where be they?
> FitzWalter, FitzOsbert, FitzHugh and FitzJohn . . .

but, happily, the good sense of the Crown itself preserved the Peerage from being thus swamped. . . .

This most objectionable system . . . is admirably described by Disraeli in his novel called 'Sybil' (1845), where Mr Hatton, the famous Peerage lawyer of the Inner Temple, explains how *he* can make a Peer. . . . 'You would like to be a Peer. Well you are really LORD VAVASOUR, but there is a difficulty in establishing your undoubted right from the single-writ-of-summons difficulty',—'Your claim on the Barony of LOVEL is very good; I could recommend your pursuing it, did not another, more inviting still present itself. In a word if you wish to be Lord BARDOLPH, I will undertake to make you so, &c.'—'will give you *precedence over every Peer* on the roll, except three (*and I made those*), and it will not cost you a paltry twenty or thirty thousand pounds.'[1]

### 16. THE COMPLETE PEERAGE

Whatever may be thought of the system and the legal doctrine on which it rested,[2] it had the merit that it produced much first class genealogical research. The standard of proof required by the House of Lords was by now exacting and the claimants were both rich and prepared to spend very large sums for the chance of winning the great prize of an ancient barony. The earliest work known to me on the technique of using records for tracing pedigrees dates from this epoch and is said by its author to be 'published expressly for the assistance of claimants to hereditary titles, honours or estates'. *Origines Genealogicae; or the sources whence English Genealogies may be traced from the conquest to the present time: accompanied by specimens of antient records, rolls and manuscripts, with proofs of their genealogical utility*, which appeared in 1828, is a work of scholarship still useful today. Its author, Stacey Grimaldi (1790–1836), was an eminent 'record lawyer' concerned in several peerage cases.

It is said that the original of Disraeli's Mr. Hatton was another peerage lawyer, the distinguished antiquary Sir Nicholas Harris Nicolas (1799–1848). His fierce attacks on the Record Commission, the Society of Antiquaries and the British Museum, though not unnaturally resented, led to reforms. His relations with the heralds on the other hand seem always to have been friendly, perhaps because of his personal friendship with Sir Charles George Young (1795–1869), Garter (and previously York Herald), a scholar and a friend of scholars, whose great collection of genealogical and other manuscripts included some of Townsend's and may have been of material use to Nicolas.

---

[1] G. E. C. [George Edward Cokayne, Clarenceux King of Arms], *Complete Peerage* 1887, pp. 288–9.     [2] See p. 101.

Nicolas' own publications were few but scholarly and for the most part more important for heraldic and historical than for genealogical studies. His *Synopsis of the Peerage of England* (1825), however, though of modest scale and appearance, was praised by Cokayne as 'a work of infinite labour and merit'.[1] A new and enlarged edition by William Courthope (1808–16), Somerset Herald, appeared in 1857 as the *Historic Peerage of England* which provided the schematic basis for a vastly larger and more interesting work, the eight volume *Complete Peerage* (1887–98) by G. E. C.—George Edward Cokayne (1825–1911), Clarenceux King of Arms. This in the main confines itself to actual holders of peerages and does not seek—save incidentally —to trace their ancestors or junior descendants. Cokayne, as Round points out,[2] was not a mediaevalist and was 'content, for the baronage of the feudal period, to rely chiefly upon others', who were not always to be relied upon. For later periods, however, his work, based on contemporary record and on careful modern research, is a model of disinterested accuracy. The five volumes of his *Complete Baronetage* (1900–6), being concerned only with the post-mediaeval period, display his strength without his weakness.

In 1910 appeared the first volume of the greatly enlarged new edition of the *Complete Peerage*, edited by Cokayne's nephew Vicary Gibbs (1853–1932). It was printed and published by the St. Catherine Press Ltd., which H. A. Doubleday had founded in 1908. Doubleday soon became assistant editor with Gibbs and after the fourth volume took over the control from him, remaining principal editor till his death in 1941. Here, as with the *Victoria County History*, he gathered round him a remarkable band of assistants and it would seem that the research was mainly theirs. But it was he who shaped, arranged and drew conclusions from its results.[3]

Vicary Gibbs' special interest was in the eighteenth century, but for mediaeval matters he had guidance from Horace Round and a valuable contributor in George Wentworth Watson. Doubleday's knowledge of mediaeval pedigree was much greater than Gibbs' and from volume v more and more important contributions to feudal genealogy appear in the new *Complete Peerage*. Among the authors of these were Miss Ethel Stokes (d. 1944), Geoffrey Henllan White (1873–1969), Doubleday's successor as editor, a most distinguished

[1] G. E. C. *Complete Peerage*, i, 1887, p. i.
[2] *Peerage Studies*, 1901, p. 9.
[3] pp. 332–3 and *H. A. Doubleday*, 1942, pp. 31, 18.

feudal genealogist, Sir Charles Clay and Lewis Christopher Loyd (1875–1947), best known by his posthumous work on *The Origins of some Anglo-Norman Families*.[1]

The *Complete Peerage* is recognized as a great work not only of genealogy but of historical scholarship. Its completion (save for the index) in 1959 was made possible only by the munificence of a series of generous benefactors. Doubleday himself, Lord Howard de Walden (d. 1946) and greatest of all Lord Nuffield.

### 17. SIR BERNARD BURKE AND HIS CRITICS

The plan of the *Complete Peerage* excludes cadets and collaterals, but modern details of these are given in the peerage annuals of Debrett and Burke. John Debrett (d. 1822) published his first edition of his *Peerage* in 1802 and of his *Baronetage* in 1808. Fifteen editions of the *Peerage* were edited by Debrett and after his death others continued it. In due course it was united with the *Baronetage* in an annual volume. For some time the lineages were expanded on the same lines as those in Burke's *Peerage*. Later, however, they were dropped and when in the last quarter of the nineteenth century the book began again to grow in size, they were not replaced, but summaries of succession to the titles were supplemented by useful accounts of the living kinsmen of peers and baronets—in recent years on female as well as male lines. This information, coming from the current knowledge of the several families, may be taken as mainly accurate.

Burke's *Peerage* has been genealogically more ambitious. John Burke (1787–1848), first published his *Peerage* in 1826 and in 1847 it became an annual, so remaining (but for the years 1918–20) until 1940, since when seven editions have appeared between 1949 and 1970. From the first some account was given of the lineage of each peer and baronet and these lineages soon grew to include much genealogical material. In 1837 Burke published a companion work in four volumes, *A Genealogical and Heraldic History of the Commoners of Great Britain and Ireland*, called in subsequent editions *Burke's Genealogical and Heraldic History of the Landed Gentry*. This never became an annual publication, but many editions have appeared. It at first comprised the principal untitled landowning families and has slowly but steadily grown more comprehensive.

John Burke was succeeded as editor of both books by his son Sir John Bernard Burke (1814–92), who in 1853 was appointed Ulster

[1] Ed. C. T. Clay and D. C. Douglas, Harleian Soc. ciii, 1951. See p. 56 *supra*.

King of Arms in Ireland and in 1855 keeper of the State Papers there. Upon his death the publications passed to his sons of whom the eldest, Henry Farnham Burke (knighted 1919; d. 1930), became Rouge Croix Pursuivant in the English College of Arms in 1880 and Garter King of Arms in 1919. The fourth son Ashworth Peter Burke edited the *Peerage* till his death in 1919, and the *Landed Gentry* down to 1906. Issues of the *Peerage* in the 1920's were edited by Alfred Trego Butler (d. 1946), Windsor Herald, while among the editors of the *Landed Gentry* were Arthur Charles Fox-Davies. (d. 1928) in 1914 and Harry Pirie-Gordon (1883-1969) in 1937.

John Burke (d. 1848) was the author of several other popular books on heraldic and genealogical subjects, while the productions of Sir Bernard (d. 1892) in this field were numerous. Such titles as *Anecdotes of the Aristocracy* (4 vols., 1849–50), *Family Romance* (2 vols. 1853) and *Vicissitudes of Families* (3 series and several editions 1859–83) will suggest the nature of some of them. Sir Bernard was an energetic and ambitious man. His genealogical practice was large, he helped to bring order to the Irish State Papers; and in 1869 he applied unsuccessfully for the office of Garter King of Arms. He was, however, neither a mediaevalist nor a man of critical mind. The *Peerage* was based on the work of Arthur Collins and not only accepted those myths which Collins had accepted but added more from information supplied by the families and from other sources. The *Landed Gentry*, being a new compilation, contained relatively still more unreliable matter. The early shortcomings of the Burke publications were to a considerable extent removed by the editors of the 1920's and after. Little need therefore have been said of them here were it not for their intimate connection with the work of Horace Round, a critical genealogist whose own eminence has preserved like flies in amber the follies and errors which he chose to castigate. He was not, however, the first in this field.

In 1865 an anonymous work appeared in Edinburgh entitled *Popular Genealogists or the Art of Pedigree-making*. Its reputed author George Burnett (1822–90) was appointed Lyon King of Arms of Scotland in 1866. He attacked the accuracy of Burke's *Peerage* and thought 'the immense majority of the pedigrees in the *Landed Gentry* . . . utterly worthless. The errors of the *Peerage* are as nothing to the fables which we encounter everywhere. Families of notoriously obscure origin have their veins filled with the blood of generations of royal personages of the ancient and mythical world.'[1] He gave as an instance that

---

[1] Op. cit. pp. 20–21.

Coulthart pedigree—later to attract the wit of Oswald Barron[1]—which derives the family 'from COULTHARTUS, a Roman lieutenant, who, according to Tacitus, contracted marriage with Marsa, dau. of Kada-lyne, chief of the Novantes, and thereby acquiring possessions at Leucophibia settled in that part of North Britain, soon after the decisive engagement under Agricola at the foot of the Grampian mountains'.

A still more formidable criticism appeared in 1877 from the pen of Edward Augustus Freeman (1823–92), the historian of the Norman Conquest,[2] who took particular exception to the fact that such 'monstrous fictions' were given a quasi-official stamp through acceptance by an editor who held an official position. 'From Sir Bernard Burke', he wrote, 'we have a right to expect historical criticism and we do not get it.' It may be noted in this connection that since 1871 the covers of Burke's *Peerage* have been stamped with the royal arms. Freeman drew his examples from among the numerous claims to descent from Norman or Saxon ancestors living at or before the Norman Conquest and had no difficulty in showing the absurdity of the early ancestry claimed for such ancient families as Fitzwilliam, Leighton, Wake and Stourton as well as for some more recent in their origin.

In 1879 a notable attempt was made by Joseph Foster (1844–1905) with assistance from Edward Bellasis (1852–1922), Bluemantle Pursuivant and later Lancaster Herald, to show how accurate an annual peerage on the lines of Burke's could be made. Only four issues appeared, the last in 1883, but they sufficed to show how much could be done even by an editor with little claim to be a mediaevalist. Though his equipment was unequal to some of the tasks he set himself (especially in mediaeval genealogy and in heraldry), Foster deserves more credit than he has had for his industry and his concern to get at the truth. In 1873 he projected a series of *Pedigrees of the County Families of England*, but only one volume for Lancashire (1873) and three for Yorkshire (1874) appeared. His collection and publication of royal descents have been mentioned.[3] The inclusion in his Lancashire volume of the Coulthart pedigree going back through fifty eight generations to Roman times is joyfully remarked by Oswald Barron. 'The only detail we can find', he says, 'which struck Mr Foster as an unlikely one and needing an editor's hand was the title of the early sixteenth-

---

[1] *The Ancestor*, iv. 61–80.
[2] 'Pedigrees and Pedigree Makers', *Contemporary Review*, xxx. 11–41.
[3] pp. 236, 239.

century Admiral R.N., and this officer's exact rank is therefore left unindicated by his last chronicler.'[1] Foster transcribed much source material and published some of it, his greatest completed work in this kind being an eight volume edition of the Oxford University Matriculation Register entitled *Alumni Oxonienses* (1887 and 1891) of which, however, the original transcript was made by J. L. Chester.[2] Though the more recent *Alumni Cantabrigienses* of J. and J. A. Venn (ten volumes 1922–54) and A. B. Emden's *Biographical Register of the University of Oxford to A.D. 1500* (1957–9) and of *Cambridge*, 1963, have set a standard so much higher that Foster's work now needs to be done again, this does not detract from his achievement.

### 18. HORACE ROUND

In 1893 the first shots were fired at Burke's *Peerage* by a critic of genealogy more formidable than any before or since. This was John Horace Round (1854–1928), who drew attention to its 'errors, misstatements and absurdities' in an article on 'The Peerage' contributed to the *Quarterly Review*. Round's opinions, like Swift's, are preserved in acid and the combined venom and acuteness of his attacks on those with whom he disagreed have won him readers who might not normally find time for the minutiae of feudal genealogy. 'Ill health', says Sir Frank Stenton, 'goes far to explain the least attractive quality in his writings, the violence with which he attacked other scholars of whose work he disapproved.' He adds that 'Round could be very generous to the work of young scholars'.[3]

Round's interest in history and genealogy appeared in boyhood and developed in his Oxford days under the influence of William Stubbs (1825–1901), a great historian who was also a genealogist. In Round's own work the genealogy and history of the Anglo-Norman period went hand in hand. In Sir Frank Stenton's judgment,

He founded the modern study of Domesday Book. His insistence on the importance of family history gave a new value to genealogical studies. . . . He was the first modern historian to base a narrative on charters, and all subsequent use of these materials has been influenced directly or indirectly by his work. . . . His work gave a new direction and precision to the studies which he had followed, and its permanent value is becoming clearer as the controversies in which he engaged are fading out of memory.[3]

---

[1] *The Ancestor*, iv. 79.   [2] p. 404.   [3] *D.N.B.* 1922–30.

It may seem absurd to introduce this major figure, tied, as it were, to the tail of Burke's *Peerage*. But the knot is of his own tying. Time after time in his writings on genealogy he makes errors in Burke's *Peerage* or *Landed Gentry* his point of departure. 'A friend', says Page, 'once remarked that if he would cease killing flies, what valuable work he would do. Nevertheless his destructive criticisms have usually left us a constructive theory, or failing that, are suggestive of a new line of investigation.'[1]

Two books published in his lifetime are mainly concerned with genealogy, *Studies in Peerage and Family History* (1901) and *Peerage and Pedigree* (2 vols. 1910). After his death William Page edited a further volume, with a memoir and bibliography of his writings, under the title *Family Origins* (1930). The bibliography shows how much genealogical work he printed in periodicals such as *The Genealogist*, *The Ancestor* and the *Essex Archaeological Transactions*, while his contributions to the *Victoria County History*, the new *Complete Peerage*, the *Dictionary of National Biography* and the *Encyclopaedia Britannica* involve much that is of genealogical value. The same indeed is true of his historical books *Geoffrey de Mandeville* (1892), *Feudal England* (1895), *The King's Serjeants and Officers of State* (1911) and of his edition of the *Rotulus de Dominabus* (1913) published by the Pipe Roll Society, though genealogy is not their main subject.

His cruel skill in the dissection of absurdities is seen at its most entertaining in such essays as 'Tales of the Conquest' and 'The Great Carington Imposture',[2] but his contribution to genealogical method comes out better in less polemical papers such as those in *The Ancestor* on 'The Origin of the Carews', 'Giffard of Fonthill Giffard' and 'The Origins of the Comins'.[3] His unsurpassed contribution to the un-ravelling of feudal genealogy was based on his comprehensive grasp, both in principle and detail, of the tenurial structure and its constituent members. This grasp and his wonderful memory enabled him in a moment to establish identification of fees and persons which others might mistake or fumble for. The economy of his argument in such cases can give high intellectual and aesthetic pleasure.

The publication of feudal records to which he himself made valuable contributions, combined with his demonstration of the method, have now made it possible to work out many pedigrees of this type and date by the application of sheer intelligence to record material available in

---

[1] *Family Origins*, p. xxi.     [2] *Peerage and Pedigree*, i. 284–323; ii. 134–257.
[3] v. 19; vi. 137; and x. 104.

print. It may well be partly for this reason that Anglo-Norman feudal genealogy has since Round's day found several outstanding exponents. All I think would acknowledge themselves his disciples, from Doubleday, Barron, Page, Farrer and Lewis Loyd to Sir Charles Clay, Geoffrey White, Sir Frank Stenton and Professor David Douglas.

Round's influence as a critic of genealogy went far beyond the feudal period. His attacks upon the College of Arms for the misdeeds of some of its Tudor members were objectionable in tone but may have been salutary. His attacks on Burke s *Peerage* led in time to the removal of many errors. In this field of general genealogical criticism he was ably abetted by his friend (and mine) Oswald Barron (1868–1939) of whom more will be said below. Barron's criticism was as entertaining and acute as Round's but less bitter. There is, however, little doubt that the very fear which Round inspired was a potent influence in raising critical standards.

### 19. PERIODICALS AND SOCIETIES

Genealogy has owed much to printers and publishers who in their enthusiasm have borne all or part of the cost of printing important work otherwise too costly for its market. In recent times H. A. Doubleday, at an earlier date three successive generations of the Nichols family were outstanding examples. John Nichols (1745–1826), mentioned already as the author of the great *History of Leicestershire* (1795–1815) and of other important antiquarian works,[1] was the son of a baker of Islington and was apprenticed in 1757 to William Bowyer (1699–1777), the printer to the Society of Antiquaries, whose partner and heir he at length became. His antiquarian enthusiasm appears not only in works from his own pen (among them the eight volumes of his *Bibliotheca Topographica Britannica* (1780–90) which contain many genealogies and much source material) but in the genealogical and other antiquarian material he found room for in the *Gentleman's Magazine* of which he shared the management from 1778 to 1792 when he became solely responsible for it. In this and in his antiquarian interests generally his son John Bowyer Nichols (1779–1863) and his grandson John Gough Nichols (1806–73) followed him.

John Bowyer Nichols, though his direct contribution to the literature of genealogy does not compare with his father's and his son's, has the credit of publishing nearly all the leading county histories of his time, among them Ormerod's *Cheshire*, Clutterbuck's *Hertfordshire*,

[1] p. 379.

Surtees' *Durham*, Raine's *North Durham*, Hoare's *Wiltshire*, Hunter's *South Yorkshire*, Baker's *Northamptonshire*, Whitaker's *Whalley* and *Craven* and Lipscomb's *Buckinghamshire*.

John Gough Nichols was joint editor of the *Gentleman's Magazine* from about 1828 and sole editor from 1851 to 1856. During that time he contributed many papers on genealogical and heraldic subjects and furthered those of others. In 1834 he thought the time ripe for a periodical devoted wholly to genealogical, heraldic and topographical material. He himself edited and published the eight volumes of *Collectanea Topographica et Genealogica* (1834–43), the three volumes of *The Topographer and Genealogist* (1846–58) and the eight volumes of *The Herald and Genealogist* (1863–74). The last of these was the most comprehensive in its plan and was designed to succeed not only the other two but the antiquarian side of the *Gentleman's Magazine* of which Nichols had ceased to be owner and editor in 1856. Whereas its predecessors had been devoted mainly to printing existing materials such as documents, record extracts and old pedigrees, *The Herald and Genealogist* contained critical discussions, book reviews and essays written for it on heraldic and genealogical topics. Through these valuable periodicals Nichols, in Round's opinion, founded the modern critical and historical school of genealogy.[1]

Nichols' death brought *The Herald and Genealogist* to an end but within three years of its last appearance a new periodical, *The Genealogist*, of similar aims and type was founded by George William Marshall (1839–1905), who himself edited the first seven volumes (1877–83). Marshall was a man of means who gave most of the work of an active to genealogy. His most important publication was *The Genealogist's Guide* (editions 1879, 1893 and 1903), an immensely useful index of printed pedigrees,[2] lately brought up to date by John Beach Whitmore (1882–1957).[3] His *Handbook to the Ancient Courts of Probate*[4] (1895) was of great use in its day and his account of his own family *Miscellanea Marescalliana* is a model of its kind. He entered the College of Arms as Rouge Croix in 1887 and became York Herald in 1904. His valuable manuscript collections are preserved in the college.

He was followed as editor of *The Genealogist* by Walford Selby (1884–9), Keith William Murray (1889–94)[5] and Henry William Forsyth Harwood (1894–1922: d. 1923), who in 1922 had to cease

---

[1] *Family Origins*, p. 8.                                    [2] See p. 408.
[3] *A Genealogical Guide*, Harl. Soc. xcix, ci, cii, civ, 1947–52, also published separately.
[4] p. 331.                                    [5] Portcullis Pursuivant 1913, d. 1922.

publication. During the forty six years of its existence *The Genealogist* maintained its high standards and published many contributions of importance by the leading genealogists of the day from J. H. Round downwards.

During the years 1902–5 it had to face the competition of the most sumptuous and distinguished periodical ever devoted to its subject in England. This was *The Ancestor, A Quarterly Review of County and Family History, Heraldry and Antiquities.* It was published by H. A. Doubleday's firm, Archibald Constable & Co. Ltd. Its handsome format, many illustrations and skilful direction no doubt owed much to his skill, enthusiasm and generosity, while its cessation followed his departure from the firm. The essential quality of *The Ancestor,* however, derives from its editor Oswald Barron, who combined the sometimes divergent qualities of a brilliant journalist and an exact scholar.

Arthur Oswald Barron (1868–1939), who was made Maltravers Herald Extraordinary in 1937, acquired so great a reputation as the leading authority on mediaeval heraldry, the study of which he revolutionized, that his eminence as a genealogist has been somewhat forgotten.[1] Because, unlike his friend Round, he was of small means and earned his living as a hard worked journalist, the volume of his publications is small. He left much more in manuscript but far more knowledge still died with him. He made no such original contribution to genealogical knowledge and method as Round's to feudal genealogy, yet his range was, I think, wider. Like Round he had worked long in the Public Record Office. In later days he loved to spend an odd half hour there and 'generally . . . would ask for a *Coram Rege Roll*, reading it as the ordinary man reads his newspaper, and making notes . . . as valuable as they were accurate'.[2] Furthermore, he had in the 1890's assisted the extensive professional practice of H. F. Burke, then Somerset Herald, as a record searcher, while his first publication was a parish register.[3] He was thus at home with modern as well as early genealogy. In *The Ancestor* he and his contributors made historical and critical genealogy amusing as well as instructive. The end of few periodicals has been more regretted.

When *The Genealogist* ceased publication in 1922 there still

---

[1] By a surprising oversight he has been left out of the *D.N.B.* It may be hoped that a future Supplement will repair the omission.

[2] Letter from Major Duncan Warrand, 14 July 1944.

[3] That of St. Margaret's Lee with Mr. Leland L. Duncan, 1888.

remained one old established periodical devoted to the subject. This was *Miscellanea Genealogica et Heraldica*, founded in 1866 by Joseph Jackson Howard (1827–1902), a civil servant who for most of his life gave up almost all his leisure to genealogy.[1] Like J. G. Nichols' first two series[2] its main contents were ancient pedigrees, record extracts and other raw material of genealogy and though in later years some essays, reviews and critical articles were included they were always relatively few. The different character of Nichols' third venture, *The Herald and Genealogist* (1863–74), had in fact left a gap which Howard filled. Howard was succeeded as editor (1902–15) by W. Bruce Bannerman, who was followed by A. W. Hughes-Clarke, yet another generous genealogist printer, who with his firm, Mitchell, Hughes and Clarke kept *Miscellanea* in existence despite financial loss until 1938.

In 1893 J. J. Howard entered on a collaboration with a wealthy genealogical enthusiast Frederick Arthur Crisp (1851–1922), who issued from his private printing press as well as other work twenty volumes of carefully compiled modern pedigrees under the misleading title, *A Visitation of England and Wales*. Howard was also, with G. W. Marshall, Colonel J. L. Chester[3] and others, a founder in 1869 of the Harleian Society for 'the publication of the Heraldic Visitations of Counties and any manuscripts relating to genealogy, family history, and heraldry'. Few of the collections of county pedigrees printed by the society have in fact been actual Visitation books, and the nature of some calls for closer scrutiny than the editors have given. The society has, however, published a great deal of pedigree and other material[4] useful to the genealogist—still publishes, indeed, for this is the only English series in which numerous pedigrees still appear despite the economic difficulties of recent years.

In 1911 a small body of professional genealogists and amateurs of the subject combined to form The Society of Genealogists, with the object of forming a library for their common use and of exchanging knowledge and information. By 1925 this society had grown somewhat from its small beginnings and following the demise of *The Genealogist* in 1922 thought the time ripe to launch its own periodical. *The Genealogists' Magazine* has flourished and is now in its twelfth volume. It has printed many short articles of great value on special

---

[1] He was appointed Maltravers Herald Extraordinary in 1887.
[2] *Collectanea Topographica*, 1834–43, and the *Topographer and Genealogist*, 1846–58. See p. 394.                                          [3] See p. 404 *infra*.
[4] In 1970 the Society had published 110 volumes in its Visitation series.

problems of genealogy and genealogical method, but its small scale has so far debarred it from publishing the extensive pedigrees and extracts from source material in which the lavish publications of the last age are so rich. These are to be found today only in certain American publications[1] and there as in England they have to struggle against a decline in the relative if not the absolute prosperity of educated people.

Partly to redress the balance the Society of Genealogists has concentrated on the collection of typescript and manuscript copies of parish registers and indexes of these and other records for its members' use. To this work an immense contribution of time and money was made by Percival Boyd (1866–1955), whose typewritten indexes to the marriage records of many counties, and to other carefully selected classes of record are preserved in the society's library and certain other places. The society has published a useful *Catalogue of the Parish Registers* in its possession (1937), a *National Index of Parish Register Copies* (1939) and two volumes (i, 1968, and v, 1966) of a new *National Index of Parish Registers*.

The publication of genealogies and kindred material in periodicals has by no means been confined to those of national bodies. The middle nineteenth century saw the foundation of many antiquarian societies for counties and other localities.[2] The Surtees Society, covering the north eastern counties and founded in 1834, was among the first and has always published records and record material. Other societies published journals in which genealogical articles had a smaller or larger place according to the fluctuations of fashion and individual interest. Some of these last in turn set up subsidiary Record Series for publishing record material. In addition there are or have been societies both national and local for the publication of particular classes of record. The British Record Society,[3] the Canterbury and York Society[4] and the Pipe Roll Society[5] have been mentioned. W. P. W. Phillimore's county series of marriage registers and the publications of the Shropshire, Staffordshire, Surrey and Yorkshire Parish Register Societies are among others which deserve mention. The publications of societies concerned with special sections of the population, such as the Catholic Record Society and the Huguenot Society contain much genealogical material and such bodies as the Society of Friends and the Jewish

---

[1] See p. 404.
[2] Joan Evans, *A History of the Society of Antiquaries*, 1956, pp. 228, 264–5.
[3] p. 330.       [4] p. 328.       [5] See p. 337.

Historical Society possess important manuscript genealogical collections. The manuscripts of my cousin Henry Wagner (1840–1926) now deposited at University College, London, comprise genealogies of very many Huguenot families.

An up to date guide to the whole of this immense mass of published and unpublished material is badly needed. All the general guides are out of date, but much of the ground is admirably covered by R. B. Pugh, *How to Write a Parish History*, (6th edition, 1954). *A Manual for the Genealogist* by Richard Sims (1856 and 1888), *Records and Record Searching* by Walter Rye (1888 and 1897), *How to Write the History of a Family* (1887 and 1900) and *Pedigree Work* (3rd ed. 1936) by W. P. W. Phillimore, *Genealogical Research in England, Scotland and Ireland* by J. H. Lea (1906), and the *Guide to the Victoria County History* (1912) are still invaluable. Useful recent elementary manuals are *Genealogy for Beginners* (1955) by Arthur J. Willis and *Making a Pedigree*, 1961, by John Unett, and a full and clear account of the more modern sources and their use is given by David E. Gardner and Frank Smith, *Genealogical Research in England and Wales*, Salt Lake City, Utah, (vol. i, 1956, ii, 1959, iii, 1964). *A Select Bibliography of English Genealogy* by H. G. Harrison (1937) is the best guide to the printed literature of the subject, though a new edition is badly needed. George Gatfield's *Guide to Printed Books and Manuscripts relating to English and Foreign Heraldry and Genealogy* (1892) indicates the whereabouts of many manuscript genealogical collections though many others of great importance receive no mention. It must, in short, be understood that the published and unpublished literature of genealogy is only less vast and trackless than its raw material.

### 20. FAMILY HISTORIES

There is no English parallel to the great documented family histories printed in seventeenth century France except the admirable *Genealogical History of the Kings of England* (1677) by Francis Sandford (1630–94), Lancaster Herald. The *Lives of the Berkeleys* by John Smyth of Nibley (d. 1640)[1] would bear comparison with the French histories, but remained in manuscript till 1821. Though Smyth's was on all counts an exceptional work it may be that among the other manuscript pedigrees and family histories of the period there are some which could not unworthily stand beside it.[2] It is disappointing, there-

---

[1] p. 368.

[2] Lawrence Stone, *The Crisis of the Aristocracy 1558–1641*, pp. 26–27, refers to several early seventeenth manuscript family histories.

fore, that the first substantial printed history of an English family should be disfigured by forged charters and fictitious pedigrees. This is a large folio of 1685 entitled *Succinct Genealogies of the Noble and Ancient Houses of Alno, or de Alneto, Broc of Shephale . . . and Mordaunt of Turvey . . .*, by Robert Halstead. This was the pseudonym of Henry Mordaunt, Earl of Peterborough (1623–97), who compiled the book with the help of his chaplain, the Rev. Richard Rands (d. 1699).[1]

John Perceval (1683–1748), 1st Earl of Egmont, was a great grandson of Sir Edward Dering (d. 1644)[2] and shared his passion for pedigrees. With the help of James Anderson, D.D. (1679–1739) the compiler of a voluminous but uncritical work on *Royal Genealogies* (1731 and 1736), he produced a marvellous *Genealogical History of the House of Yvery; in its Different Branches of Yvery, Luvel, Perceval, and Gournay* (1742), deducing the Percevals from ancient houses with which they were in fact unconnected.[3] Eighteenth century family histories are few in number and range from such eccentricity as this, through some secondhand compilations to Arthur Collins' *Historical Collections of the Noble Families of Cavendish, Holles, Vere, Harley and Ogle* (1752), a somewhat amplified version of the articles in his *Peerage* with the same strength and weakness.

The largest number of English family histories appeared in the century between about 1830 and 1930. Among them works of first class scholarship are unhappily in a small minority. On the genealogical side two of the best are Robert Edmond Chester Waters' *Genealogical Memoirs of the Extinct Family of Chester of Chicheley* (1878), Falconer Madan's *The Gresleys of Drakelowe* (1899), and Alleyn Lyell Reade's *The Reades of Blackwood Hill* (1906). Reade in this and the ten volumes of his *Johnsonian Gleanings* adumbrates a new approach to family history. From a wide range of detailed investigations he slowly builds up an immense picture of family links and ramifications centred on the figure of Samuel Johnson (1709–84), whose

first thirty years were [he concludes] almost entirely conditioned by his early environment, by the complicated interactions of kinship and by the sympathetic interest of friends in his own neighbourhood. The pattern of his life for this period was thus closely woven on to a web of local and hereditary association, from which it was not easily to be detached by forces born of purely intellectual activities. It is extraordinary how many of the families

[1] Thomas Moule, *Bibliotheca Heraldica*, 1822, pp. 228–30; *Complete Peerage*, x. 499 and n.
[2] p. 358.  [3] *Complete Peerage*, v. 28, n.

whose names are familiar through the whole period of Johnson's life helped to form great interconnected groups with all of which he could claim some kinship or common tie.[1]

The authors of some of the less distinguished family histories, though keen, have been insufficiently qualified. Others have been the work of professionals engaged by the families. These, too often, have been *either* good writers *or* good genealogists but not both. For this reason the unadorned pedigree sheets and booklets are often more satisfactory than the story books. In recent years some excellent accounts of historical families based on their papers have appeared but these in general contribute more to social history than to genealogy.

### 21. HERALDS AND MODERN TECHNIQUE

For feudal genealogy the modern developments of method can be clearly seen in the works of Round, his predecessors and successors. For developments in relation to the genealogy of later periods the position is different, for the simple reason that, while those who led the way in the feudal field were academic genealogists, the leaders in more modern technique were professionals, dependent on genealogy for their living and competing with each other—and indeed with amateurs—for their clients. Therefore, though they might be glad to publish their results, it would be to their interest to keep secret the special ingenuities through which their discoveries were made and for the sake of which clients might consult them rather than their rivals. Since the secret process of one generation is the commonplace of the next, there is now no reason to conceal the methods of Victorian and Edwardian genealogists. But as these developments had at the time no publicity, it is difficult now to discover who pioneered particular innovations and when.

Since English genealogists are individualists, who show no wish to be organized, it is hard to track them and their activities. The heralds are to some extent an exception, but less so than might be thought because genealogy has never been among their primary or essential duties. Although since the sixteenth century or earlier many heralds have practised it, at most periods the main part of the genealogical work of the College has been done by two or three of its thirteen members. Where, however, the working papers of these genealogist-

[1] A. L. Reade, *Johnson's Early Life*, 1946, p. 157.

heralds survive, they may indicate as well as anything the development of working methods.

Since 1800 two factors above all have governed this; the changes in the genealogists' clientèle on one side and the growing accessibility of records on the other. The genealogical desires of a William Beckford (1759–1844) or an Egerton Brydges (1762–1837) and those of the recipients of Lloyd George's honours (1916–22) might not differ much, but the means to satisfy them did. Most of those who came to the heralds before 1850, and even later, were country gentlemen of well known immediate ancestry mainly concerned to trace their remoter lineage on male or female lines. As the nineteenth century wore on, however, and gave place to the twentieth, more and more of the heralds' clients were drawn from the newly enriched middle classes, so that the problem often was to trace a line of yeomen or labourers through the last three centuries. At the present day some of the most baffling problems presented to the genealogist concern ancestors living as recently as the late eighteenth or the nineteenth century and arise from the rapid growth and great mobility of the population in those times and the consequent difficulty of location and identification. To meet these novel problems types of record were explored and methods devised unknown to older genealogists.

The chief factors which have made records more accessible have already been mentioned; the establishment of the Public Record Office; its publication of calendars, lists and indexes: the private publication of many other records; and the private construction and publication of keys and indexes to records. It is also worth recalling that during the same period a form of record, which was from the first easily accessible, has grown immensely both in absolute bulk and relative importance— the General Register of Births, Marriages and Deaths. It would be interesting to know when some of these sources were first used, who, for example, first used manorial records to trace husbandmen's and country labourers' pedigrees beyond the period of the parish registers—sometimes even to the fourteenth or the thirteenth century. Walter Rye in 1888 refers to them as often the only means of tracing non-armigerous families 'before the Church Register begins'.[1] Stubbs about this time traced his own yeoman ancestry back to 1359 from the Duchy of Lancaster Court Rolls of the Forest of Knaresborough.[2]

---

[1] *Records and Record Searching*, 1888, p. 93, 1897 ed., p. 108.

[2] *Genealogical History of the Family of the late Bishop William Stubbs*, ed. F. Collins, Yorks. Arch. Soc., Record Series, lv, 1915, pp. viii, 1, 59.

At the College of Arms, H. F. Burke, who collected manorial records, was by 1903 recording pedigrees derived from them.

The most active herald genealogists between the 1830's and the 1860's were Sir Charles George Young (1795–1869), Garter King of Arms, and two friends who had begun as assistants to Sir Isaac Heard, George Frederick Beltz (1777–1841), Lancaster Herald, and James Pulman (1783–1859), Clarenceux King of Arms. Their extensive manuscript collections[1] show a confident and well organized use of the known record resources, especially wills and parish registers. The work of their successors, George William Collen (1799–1878), Portcullis, Thomas William King (1802–72), York, William Courthope (1808–66), Somerset, and Arthur Staunton Larken (1816–89), Richmond, is represented by manuscript remains of like extent, evincing mastery of the same technique.[2] The great achievements of two heralds of the next generation, George Edward Cokayne (1825–1911), Clarenceux, and George William Marshall (1839–1905), York, are known through their publications.[3]

In the first quarter of the twentieth century the leading men were Sir Alfred Scott Scott-Gatty[4] (1847–1918) and Sir Henry Farnham Burke[5] (1859–1930). In the present connection Burke's career is of especial interest. The publications and connections of his father Sir Bernard[6] gave him a flying start in his profession, but it was his own capacity added to this which made his genealogical practice perhaps the largest yet seen at the college. Because of its size he could afford to build up an unprecedented genealogical machine, equipped with special books, abstracts, indexes and above all staff. But the perception and power of management which enabled him to do this, were all his own. In Oswald Barron's opinion his greatest strength was that he never ceased to learn.

In 1898 he had the good fortune to engage an assistant whose fame was in time to surpass his own. This was Alfred Trego Butler[7] (1880–1946), probably the best working genealogist of his day and an outstanding innovator in genealogical technique. Butler always emphasized his debt to Burke, to whom some of the projects he carried out doubtless owed their first conception. As a prisoner of war in Germany in the 1914–18 war Butler solaced his captivity by indexing genealogical

---

[1] Wagner, *Records and Collections of the College of Arms*, 1952, pp. 42–44.
[2] Ibid., pp. 45–47.                                    [3] pp. 387, 394.
[4] Rouge Dragon 1880, York 1886, Garter 1904.
[5] Rouge Croix 1880, Somerset 1887, Norroy 1911, Garter 1919.
[6] p. 388.                              [7] Portcullis 1928, Windsor 1931.

source material sent out to him by Burke from England and the habit thus acquired remained with him throughout his life. He put it to good use in indexing sources chosen for their bearing on problems met with in his practice, such as the location of the English homes of American settlers and the filling of gaps left by the better known classes of record.

He had foresight too to see new problems coming. In the 1920's an enquirer's personal knowledge would in most cases take his ancestry back to the eighteenth century at least, but the cases where family knowledge went back only to the nineteenth century were growing more numerous and Butler saw that the key to many of these was the location of the ancestor in 1851 or a later census year.[1] This problem led Butler first to consult the printed directories of the period and then to collect them. Directories, being ephemeral in their purpose, are for the most part soon destroyed, and many have thus become great rarities. Butler, however, being early in the field was able by quiet persistence to acquire copies of very many. His collection of both eighteenth and nineteenth century directories, covered England, Wales, Scotland and Ireland and numbered some thousand volumes, many of them unique. Having formed it, he was able to use it in ways which at first he had not foreseen,[2] for in this, as in other fields of genealogy, much of his strength lay in his perception of patterns which escaped the notice of others.

## 22. THE AMERICANS

No account of the study of English genealogy would be complete without a reference, however brief, to the work done by a notable succession of American researchers. There was never a time when Americans were not interested in their English origins, as enquiries made of the heralds since the seventeenth century prove. But the first step towards independent research into the subject was probably the foundation of a series of historical societies in different states, beginning with the Massachusetts Historical Society in 1791. The New Hampshire Society was founded in 1823 and in 1829 its corresponding secretary John Farmer (1789–1838) published at Lancaster, Massachusetts, the first work of its kind, *A Genealogical Register of the First*

[1] See p. 341.
[2] This collection, with the rest of his working library of printed books, manuscripts and indexes, I acquired from him when he gave up practice. Directories (other than for London) of which the only known copies are in my collection are noted in Miss Jane E. Norton's *Guide to Directories*, Royal Hist. Soc. 1950.

*Settlers of New England*, in which he refers to the 'satisfaction in recognizing our first ancestor from the European continent; in knowing from what part of Great-Britain he came; where he settled, and the circumstances and condition of his family'. A much larger work of the same kind, *A Genealogical Dictionary of the First Settlers of New England* by James Savage (1784–1873), appeared in four volumes between 1860 and 1862.

Meanwhile in 1845 the New England Historic Genealogical Society, the first distinctively genealogical society in America, had been founded in Boston and in 1847 began publication of its *Register*, of which four numbers have appeared in each year since that time. Since we are dealing only with the American contribution to English genealogy and not with purely American genealogy, the bulk of the material published in the *Register* and in other American periodicals and books does not here concern us. The *Register*, however, unlike many of the rest, has, especially since 1883, contained a large amount of important and purely English material contributed by Henry FitzGilbert Waters (1823–1913) and his successors.[1]

Waters had two forerunners. Horatio Gates Somerby (1805–72)[2] joined the New England Society in its first year. In the same year he first visited England and there spent most of the rest of his life devoting much of his time to genealogical research and tracing many settlers' origins. 'Unhappily', however, in Dr. Adams' words, 'he sometimes provided an ancestry for a generous client that later research has failed to verify.'

Colonel Joseph Lemuel Chester (1821–82) was a genealogist of far greater distinction, whose merits are attested by notices in the Dictionaries both of National and American Biography, by a tablet in Westminster Abbey and by doctoral degrees conferred by Oxford and Columbia universities. Before his first visit to England in 1858 he had had neither training nor interest in research, to which he was led by a wish to verify his family's claim (which he disproved) to descend from John Rogers (d. 1555), the Marian martyr. Settling in England he was from 1862 given free access to the Prerogative Wills before 1700 (then at Doctors' Commons) and spent the next twenty years exploring these and other records for the origins of American settlers generally and his clients' ancestors in particular. He was among the

[1] For the above and much of what follows see William Carroll Hill, *A Century of Genealogical Progress, Being a History of the New England Historic Genealogical Society 1845–1945*, 1945, pp. 64–73, address by Dr. Arthur Adams.

[2] *New Eng. Hist. and Gen. Reg.*, xxviii, 1874, pp. 340–2.

founders of the Harleian Society (1869),[1] edited the *Registers of Westminster Abbey* (1876) and left behind him twenty four volumes of
pedigree collections and eighty seven or parish register extracts, which
after his death were bought and presented to the College of Arms
by his executor G. E. Cokayne.[2] He also made the transcript of the
Oxford matriculation registers which formed the basis of Joseph
Foster's *Alumni Oxonienses*. His work is for the most part
excellent.

H. F. Waters' (1823–1913) interest in research was for a long time
desultory, but a visit to England in 1879 with his friend and fellow
genealogist James Arthur Emmerton led to extensive searches in the
Principal Probate Registry, the Public Record Office, and the British
Museum, which were published in 1880[3] as 'Gleanings from English
Records about New England Families'. In 1882 the New England
Society, impressed by 'the desirability, since the death of Col. Chester,
of having a competent person in London to make genealogical researches for the English ancestry of American families', decided to
guarantee Waters a modest salary in return for his undertaking to live
in London and do such work. Accordingly from July 1883 to January
1899 'every number of the Register except three . . . contained an
article from his pen embodying the results of his searches among the
English records'. The Society reprinted these in 1901, in two volumes
of 1643 pages, as *Genealogical Gleanings in England*, a work of the
highest value and interest to students of American (and by no means
only New England) origins. Waters' method was 'to examine all the
records between certain dates, *seriatim*, keeping a sharp look out for
everything possibly indicative of the slightest connection with known
American families'. By far the greatest part of his time was given to
the wills at Somerset House, where, he wrote, 'I take the records consecutively, looking over each page and making such references as seem
worth noting. I occasionally make excursions when the trail seems
broad and clear, . . . but I intend generally to confine myself to the
period a little before the migrations of 1628–30 and the next half
century'. This method enabled him to make discoveries otherwise
impossible, for instance references to American settlers in the wills of
apparently unconnected people. None, perhaps, pleased him more than
his discovery of the origins of John Harvard (d. 1638) the founder of

---

[1] p. 396.
[2] Wagner, *Records and Collections*, p. 46.
[3] In the *Historical Collections of the Essex Institute*, xvii.

his university. Both in Southwark and in Stratford on Avon he found existing the very houses where Harvard's mother had lived.[1]

The New England Historic Genealogical Society has continued since Waters' day to sponsor research in England. For a good many years more, while circumstances allowed, it had its own American researchers living in England. Among these were James Henry Lea and George Andrews Moriarty (1882–1968), who later conducted the work by correspondence from America with English researchers. Years spent in England and much time given to work in the Public Record Office led Moriarty to concentrate on the early origins of American settlers of gentle descent. In so doing he helped to clear away much fiction and error published by some of his fellow countrymen who, whether good or bad American genealogists, lacked knowledge of the English background and records.

Apart from the very few, who, like Waters, have had a thorough knowledge of both English and American records, the best work on the settlers' origins has been done by Americans and Englishmen in collaboration. Mention has been made already[2] of that of Charles Edward Banks (1854–1931) with Alfred Trego Butler (1880–1946), Windsor Herald. Even more was owed by Butler in this field to the Rev. Dr. Arthur Adams (1881–1960) sometime editor of the *New England Historical and Genealogical Register*—a debt which I inherited and continued to incur.[3] With these must be mentioned also Walter Goodwin Davis (1885–1966), the joint author of the *Genealogical Dictionary of Maine and New Hampshire* (1928–38), to some of whose work on settlers' origins reference has been made elsewhere.[4]

In recent years a great collection has been formed at Salt Lake City of photographic and other copies, abstracts and indexes of English records. For the Latter Day Saints or Mormons it is a pious duty to trace the names of their ancestors so that they may be added to the number of God's Elect. They have accordingly devoted a large share of their great resources to this assembly of English source material. For genealogists not brought up or trained in England the effective use of this must be hard indeed. But the unprecedented challenge may evoke the desired response and the publication of results will be looked to eagerly for evidence.

The total bulk of American genealogical publication is enormous and no attempt can be made here to discuss it save in so far as it relates

[1] *New Eng. Hist. and Gen. Reg.* lxviii, 1914, pp. 3–17.
[2] p. 298.　　[3] See pp. 8, 296 n.　　[4] p. 309 n. 2

to English origins. In this field it runs the whole gamut from sound scholarship to ludicrous nonsense, the latter differing from its English counterpart only in this, that what an Englishman with any knowledge can see at once to be absurd may not so easily appear so to an American, who lacks the background of English history and local knowledge. It is indeed remarkable how some American genealogists, whose work is excellent while they stick to their own continent, have been wildly misled in regard to English origins. Those who know most are most cautious and most disposed to seek advice. While State and other societies have published much, the most striking feature to an Englishman of American genealogical literature is the great number of individual family histories, some of them most sumptuously produced. Of these, however, only a minority have much of value to say about English origins. An interesting development, unknown in England, is the formation since the 1880's of a number of family associations, devoted to fostering contact between the members of a particular family, who may number hundreds and be scattered across the continent, and to tracing and recording the family history. By such cooperation research has sometimes been financed which would otherwise have been impossible.

This genealogical emphasis on the whole family is, I take it, a return to that older and more general human interest which in the countries of feudal inheritance has been somewhat overlaid by a concentration on inheritance of lands and titles.[1] Another phase of the same trend is seen in the American concern with all the lines of ancestry, not only the male line. This is shown in those societies whose members must prove descent whether from one of a large but recent class, such as the participants in Colonial Wars, or from one of a small but remote one such as the Sureties of Magna Carta, or from an individual such as Charlemagne. In the proof of such descents male and female lines are equal.[2] These and other trends of American genealogy deserve the study of all who are concerned with the general and sociological background of human interest in these matters.

[1] See pp. 2, 231.

[2] Mr. George E. McCracken points out to me, however, that some of these societies, such as the Holland Society of New York, have a male line descent qualification, while in the Society of the Cincinnati an ancestor can have only one representative at a time.

# X

# THE PRACTICAL APPROACH

## I. AMATEUR AND PROFESSIONAL

THE value to a genealogist of acquaintance with relevant records and with the literature of his pursuit should by now be clear, as also the value to him of a background knowledge of several cognate subjects. But a working genealogist needs besides all this a grasp of genealogical forms, an exact memory for detail, a flair for discovery and a critical sense. Since no one has all these qualities in equal measure there is much to be said for collaboration between people who know each other's strength and each his own limitations. This applies equally to collaboration between professionals and to relations between professionals and amateurs.

How far can the amateur go unaided? Much depends on the time he has to give, on his existing range of knowledge, on his access to books and records and on the nature of his problem. He can start by consulting Marshall's and Whitmore's Guides[1] to see what pedigrees of the families which concern him are in print. He can then consult any pedigrees he finds there. If these are the work of good modern authorities, who quote their evidence, his problem may then be solved, but if they fall outside this select class he can seek to apply criticism on the lines indicated in the last two chapters or can ask an expert to do so for him.

If there is no pedigree in print there may still be one in manuscript in the official records or the unofficial collections of the College of Arms,[2] or among the manuscript collections in the British Museum, the Bodleian Library at Oxford and elsewhere.[3] These, like printed pedigrees, must be assessed in relation to their nature, authorship and references to evidence. Because of this and because many manuscript collections are inaccessible and imperfectly indexed there are limits to what it is worth while to do in searching them. Beyond a certain point

[1] p. 394.
[2] See pp. 340–1, 361–6, 371–7, 400–3, and Wagner, *The Records and Collections of the College of Arms.*       [3] See p. 368.

it is better to go straight to original records and trace the pedigree for oneself rather than go on hunting for elusive previous work.

When this point is reached the amateur must decide whether and, if so, how he proposes to employ professional help. If he is a man of leisure and education with the root of the matter in him, he may find genealogical research a fascinating and instructive occupation. By starting with the simpler types of problem and the less difficult classes of record he can learn the ropes and by degrees work up to the more complex and difficult. He must, however, understand that this is a trade whose complexities take years to learn and one in which emphatically 'a little learning is a dangerous thing'. Nor is it only learning that is needed. Plantagenet Harrison[1] was learned, but he lacked critical sense and his pedigrees are therefore untrustworthy. The same can be said in greater or less degree of many genealogists whose work is useful if used with care.

This leads to the further point that genealogy is a large subject with many subdivisions. The expert on the seventeenth century may be at sea in the thirteenth and vice versa. The authority on Devon may be lost in Lancashire, the master of noble pedigrees may be at a stand with those of labourers. Classes and types of record, social and name patterns are often peculiar to times and places. Yet remote analogies may be helpful. American settlement may throw light on Irish, pedigrees from the Sudan on those of Wales.

Genealogy is an art in which experience counts for much. Perhaps the amateur's greatest handicap is not ignorance of where to look or inability to read a record (though these *are* great handicaps), but the fact that, even when he goes to the right record and can read it, he may still miss what it has to tell him. He may do this in two ways, one crude, the other subtle. The crude failure is that of the untrained eye, which in glancing down a page of a parish register may simply miss an occurrence of the name it is in search of. It is surprising how often inexperience falls into this trap, for which the only remedies are care, avoidance of haste and double checking. This is one reason why the professional, whom an amateur consults after unsuccessful searches of his own, will, if he is wise and is permitted, repeat the searches which his client has already made. To go forward without this is to risk missing the essential clue once and for all. In case this should be thought hard on amateurs I would add that professional work has sometimes to be checked in the same way.

[1] pp. 359–60.

The amateur's more subtle common failure is to miss the significance of a clue. A servant's birthplace in a census entry, the names of witnesses to a will or marriage licence allegation, the elusive marks of imperfection in a record, the significant associations of a name or a date or a trade or a tenure may hold clues to baffling problems, which only the eye of experience will detect. To balance these handicaps, however, the amateur has one great advantage over the professional. Where the latter must carry round in one small head the details of an ever changing plurality of clients' problems, the former can concentrate his efforts over years on his one or two, collecting and keeping in mind an indefinite range of relevant data. Only when his client's purse is bottomless can the professional compete with this.

When an amateur decides to engage professional help, he may do it in any one of three ways. The distinction between these depends on the distinction between genealogists and record searchers. The genealogist normally expects to be given a genealogical problem and to be left to solve it. This will involve planning the research, carrying it out or arranging for it to be carried out, and drawing conclusions from it. The record searcher, on the other hand, expects to be told what records to search—whether for genealogical or other purposes—and having done so and made extracts or copies will consider his duty done. Genealogists will sometimes search the records themselves and will sometimes employ record searchers to do so for them. The amateur's three choices therefore are to put everything in the hands of a genealogist or to cast himself for the part of genealogist and employ a record searcher to make specific searches for him or to cast himself as record searcher and employ a genealogist to direct his labours.

Any one of these plans may work well in the right conditions, but it is necessary to be clear what those conditions are. The record searcher who is not a genealogist cannot effectively direct his own operations, so that if his client lacks the knowledge and experience to do so, the blind will be leading the blind. If, on the other hand, the client makes himself the searcher, his greatest risk is that his employed director may lack the brutality to criticize his work with the necessary candour. If any doubt is felt on either score, the first plan will be best and most economical.

The employment of a genealogist, like all employment, poses a problem of selection. Genealogical problems differ greatly and a few genealogists have their specialities, but though it may be desirable it is seldom possible to find a specialist to tackle one's special problem, and only a large professional practice can afford the ideal solution of maintaining specialists within itself. There have from time to time been specialist amateurs with vast knowledge of the genealogy of a locality or group. To obtain advice or help from one of these on a problem within his special sphere is a piece of good fortune.

In approaching the College of Arms it should be borne in mind that each officer of the college may conduct his own practice in heraldry and genealogy. Not all officers have at all times chosen to do this, but of late years most have done so, though in varying degrees and often with individual specialities. By the custom of the college an applicant to it becomes the client of the individual officer from whom he first commissions work. An enquiry not addressed to any individual officer will be dealt with by the officer 'in waiting' for the week, a duty taken by the heralds and pursuivants in rotation.

### 2. PROPERTY, CONTINUITY, NAME AND RECORD

The prospects of success in solving problems of genealogy depend on many factors, but chiefly, I think, on four; property, continuity, name and record. The possessors of property, other things being equal, are better recorded and more easily traced than those with none, and the more so the greater their possessions. Those who from generation to generation maintain a continuity, whether of dwelling place, of trade, or of anything else, are, other things being equal, more easily traced than those who break with family tradition. Some names are rare, some common and the genealogical advantage is all with rarity, whether the question be of surname or Christian name or the two combined or of a pattern of names of brothers and sisters recurring in a family. Finally there are areas, both geographical and social, where the records are good and full and others where they are poor. Here too genealogical good fortune belongs to those whose lines lie among good records.

Sometimes all four factors are favourable, sometimes one or two or three, sometimes none, but the presence of one may compensate for the lack of another. A poor and obscure family which remained in one parish where the register was well kept can often be traced back to that register's beginning, which may be in the middle of the sixteenth century, particularly if the family names and name patterns are distinctive enough to avoid such problems of identity as occur when one parish register records six contemporary John Smiths. If by luck the manor in question has a well kept series of mediaeval Court Rolls, and if our family was then, as later, its humble but continuous and distinctive self, it may be traceable back to the thirteenth century.[1] To hope for a lawsuit to carry such a villein pedigree back a century or century and a half further still would be optimistic indeed, yet such lawsuits are recorded.[2] But though in theory such a pedigree is possible, I confess that I have not yet had the fortune to meet with one, partly perhaps because families so little subject to alteration seldom come the genealogist's way. More soberly one hopes, if luck is with one, to trace a country labouring family as far back as the parish register goes and no further.[3] If luck is wanting, removal from one place to another, difficulty about identity or defect of record—the genealogist's three bugbears—may defeat one's hopes sooner, sometimes much sooner.

With the urban and especially the London poor the problem is far harder because of the size and mobility of the population. The General Register of Births, Marriages and Deaths should take one back to 1837 or thereabouts and a census entry may lead one to a late eighteenth or early nineteenth century baptismal record. One is then, however, apt to run into difficulty. The entry one wants next may be somewhere in a parish or nonconformist register, but in towns these are numerous and bulky and the problems of location and proof of identity are often insoluble. If more indexes like those of Percival Boyd[4] could be made and could be extended to the poor law records,[5] the prospects would be somewhat brighter. The chances of finding oneself in this particular blind alley are less than might be thought because the ratio of the labouring poor to the rest of the population diminishes as one goes back.[6] Many labourers in 1830 were sons or grandsons of yeomen, tradesmen or craftsmen.

The prospects for the genealogist improve at the economic level at which property was left by will. Where this occurs depends not only on the amount of property to be bequeathed but on less calculable factors such as literacy, temperament, family circumstances and local custom and so cannot be defined with any precision. Furthermore it seems possible that at certain times and places wills were made and given effect to by testators' families without being legally proved and therefore without any public record. However, by the eighteenth

[1] For a pedigree traced by manorial records through eight generations from 1302 to 1545, and thence by other records to the present day, see Sir A. Wagner, *Drake in England*, revised ed., 1969, Concord, New Hampshire Hist. Soc.

[2] See p. 138.  [3] p. 332  [4] p. 397.

[5] pp. 179, 334, 346, 350.  [6] pp. 150, 176.

century wills of many small farmers, tradesmen and craftsmen were proved as well as those of people higher in the social scale. In these even more than in richer families a most useful sort of will is that of a childless widow or old maid, anxious to remember all her relations, however distant and however modestly, and so setting out a whole pedigree.

In the seventeenth century wills of craftsmen and small tradesmen are fewer, but those of yeomen and substantial tradesmen common enough. Back to the reign of Elizabeth I families of this standing which remain so and stay in one place seldom present much difficulty in the settled and well recorded parts of the country. There are, however, whole districts where important records are defective. The Hereford Wills, for instance, are very imperfect before 1662. Most of those for the Western Deaneries of the Archdeaconry of Richmond in Westmorland and Lancashire for the period before 1748 perished in that year, when the Bishop of Chester ordered their removal from Lancaster to Richmond and they were taken in open carts in the depth of winter. One cart is said to have overturned in a beck in Wensleydale or Wharfedale. The Devon and Somerset wills were destroyed by a bomb which fell at Exeter in 1942. Throughout the country there are parishes whose early registers are missing. Where one kind of record is wanting there is usually something else which can be tried, but such gaps enlarge the margin of unsolved problems.

Before the reign of Elizabeth I the pedigrees which can be traced below the ranks of the gentry, the rich yeomen and the merchants are a small proportion and before 1500 a very small proportion. Knightly and gentle families, however, can frequently, and those of merchants and franklins sometimes, be traced back to the fourteenth century, and some, as we have seen, further still. Research indeed becomes more difficult and laborious, but material exists in great bulk in the public records[1] and in smaller quantity and less accessible elsewhere.[2] The most useful evidence, as we have seen, is found in records of the tenure and conveyance of land and in those of lawsuits.[3] Examples already given[4] show how far descent can be traced in favourable cases. The difficulties and causes of failure in others are in principle the same as at later dates, though they operate at higher economic and social levels.

Some of the methods used to solve the problems of discontinuity have been mentioned earlier.[5] A man who moves from one

---

[1] pp. 336–40.
[2] pp. 326–32, 344–50.
[3] pp. 338–9.
[4] Chapters III, IV.
[5] pp. 349–50.

environment to another may leave precise record linking his settlement with his origin. There are depositions in New England which name the settler's English birthplace. There are poor law settlement papers which narrate the life histories of migrant eighteenth century paupers. But more often a man appears we know not whence and our only clues to his origin are his name, his status and occupation and our general knowledge of movements into the place and at the time in question.

In a really difficult case of this kind the rarity of a surname may make all the difference between success and failure. Vestey is a very rare surname but even so laborious searches carried out over forty years had failed to establish the origin of Samuel Vestey (d. 1805), wheelwright, who married Ann Burrow at Manchester in 1764 and became the ancestor of a numerous progeny and great-great-grandfather of the first Lord Vestey (cr. 1922). Very extensive searches in records of many kinds had only shown that the surname was found earlier in certain Leicestershire villages and seemingly nowhere else. In 1951, therefore, it was decided to make a wholesale examination of baptismal registers for the possible period in this area. A very extensive search produced one, and only one, helpful entry, that of the baptism of Samuel, son of William and Alice Vestey, at Sileby on 27 November 1743.

Though at this point it seemed possible that this Samuel Vestey was identical with the one married at Manchester in 1764, it still remained to show that the identification was highly probable or certain. The circumstantial evidence, which in due course satisfied the College of Arms examiners that the identification could be accepted, started with the negative point that much research had brought to light no earlier Vesteys in the Manchester area or, indeed, anywhere but in Leicestershire. Next came the evidence of the Leicestershire searches producing only one likely candidate. Next, and most important, further searches in Leicestershire records of *later* date had brought to light no later entry which could refer to the Samuel baptized at Sileby in 1743. Therefore, if he and Samuel of Manchester were not the same man, two contemporary Samuels were men of mystery—one appearing out of nothingness, the other vanishing into it. Last, and to the genealogist impressive, came the argument from the name pattern. Among the grandchildren of Samuel of Manchester occur the names William, Joseph, Thomas, John, Elizabeth, Alice and Mary, all of which occur also among the names of the brothers and sisters of Samuel of Sileby.

Wherever one has to try to prove an identity by circumstantial evidence of this kind, it is well to make searches directed to *disproving* it, if possible. Even without positive *proof*, if well planned attempts at *disproof* fail the case for identity is greatly strengthened. An example of supposed *dis*proof may show the value of this test. There exists in private hands in the United States a remarkable survival, a pedigree roll written and painted with arms about 1608 for Edward Scott (d. 1643), clothier, of Glemsford, Suffolk. Edward's son Richard (d. 1680) came to New England in 1634 and the roll has come down through his descendants, one of only three such rolls known to be preserved there.[1] It appears to be the work of a herald painter. Its purpose is to derive the Scotts of Glemsford from the best known English family of the name 'the most auntient and knightly family of the Scotts of Scott Hall in the County of Kent'. This is done by placing Edward Scott the grandfather of Edward (d. 1643) of Glemsford, as a younger brother of Reginald Scott (d. 1599) of Smeeth, Kent. This Reginald, one of the Scott's Hall family, is known as the author of two well known books, *A Perfite Plateforme of a Hoppe Garden*, 1573, and *The Discoverie of Witchcraft*, 1584.

Now in 1608 Reginald Scott himself was but lately dead and the facts must have been well known. Furthermore the father of the Glemsford clothier, another Edward (d. 1627), whom the pedigree makes Reginald's nephew, was then living. It was therefore natural to accept the pedigree. Nevertheless it seems to me that the asserted link between the two families is a fabrication. On the one hand there is evidence that Reginald Scott (d. 1599) of Smeeth was an only son, on the other that Edward Scott, the grandfather of Edward (d. 1643) of Glemsford, was himself a clothier of that place, who died in 1627, and probably one of three sons of Richard Scott (d. 1565), also a clothier of Glemsford. Four Scotts payed subsidy in Glemsford in 1524[2] and the name was well established in Suffolk much earlier still. The evidence is voluminous, but one item is unusual enough to be given here.

Reginald Scott's grandmother Anne was first cousin to Dame Winifred Rainsford, who died childless in 1576 leaving Anne Scott's descendants her heirs. Among her lands were some held by the ancient Kentish tenure of gavelkind.[3] Instead, therefore, of passing intact by

---

[1] Richard Le Baron Bowen, 'The Arms of Richard Scott', *New Eng. Hist. and Gen. Reg.* xcvi, 1942, pp. 1–29. Mr. Bowen, though he dissented from my conclusion, set out the evidence for it in his *Collected Papers Armorial, Genealogical and Historical*, Rehoboth, Mass., 1959, pp. 31–39.

[2] Suffolk Green Books, No. X, 1910, pp. 32–33.  [3] p. 217.

primogeniture, these had to be divided among the heirs male. Each of Anne Scott's sons would receive an equal share, or, if any had died leaving male issue, then his share would be divided equally among his sons. The inquisition of 1576[1] accordingly sets out that half the gavelkind land 'descended and by law is bound to descend' in equal shares to the five sons of Anne's elder son Sir Reginald Scott (d. 1554), while the other half descended to Reginald Scott (d. 1599), 'the son and heir of Richard Scotte the younger son of the said Anne Scotte'. This means that in 1576 no brother or male descendant of a brother of Reginald Scott (d. 1599) was living and so directly contradicts the Glemsford pedigree.[2] My inference is that its author was such an one as William Dawkyns, 'a notable dealer in arms and maker of false pedigrees', for whose arrest in 1597 a warrant was issued giving the names of nearly a hundred families, chiefly in Essex, Hertfordshire and Cambridgeshire, for whom he had compiled spurious pedigrees.[3]

Scott is a fairly common English surname[4] and this might have been a ground for doubting an identification of namesakes in two counties as far apart as Kent and Suffolk. The application of the name frequency test is, however, less easy than it seems at first glance, because many names which are rare in the country as a whole are common in particular localities. Whatever its cause this situation is likely to make identification difficult. If a Suffolk parish is thick with Kerriches or a Lancashire one with Entwisles the difficulty of sorting out lines and individuals may be very great. With some such names, it seems likely that all the bearers are, however remotely, of one kindred. Of others, on the contrary, there are certainly many distinct families.

This last is likely, for instance, where a surname derives from a locally common occupation. For example, a map of early occurrences of the surname Naylor, common in several parts of the north of England, would, I suspect, show a correlation with early ironworking districts in which nails were made. In the same way the surname Webb, meaning a weaver, might be linked with the clothing districts of the south west. But though in cases like these there may be many distinct families in the same district with the same surname, this is not neces-

---

[1] Chancery Series C. 142/173/94.

[2] *The Discoverie of Witchcraft by Reginald Scot*, ed. Brinsley Nicholson, 1886, Introduction, pp. xi–xii, xviii–xx, xxvi, xxviii–xxix.

[3] Noble, *History of the College of Arms*, 1805, p. 162; p. 130 *supra*.

[4] See p. 250. Statistics of the fifty commonest English surnames are given by Dr. Farr in the 16th Annual Report of the Registrar General. See also W. P. W. Phillimore, *How to Write the History of a Family*, 1887, pp. 16–19.

sarily true where the occupation from which the name comes is a rare one. In England as a whole the surname Pilcher is very uncommon, but in East Kent it is frequent. A pilcher is a maker of pilches or furred garments. Was this in early days a local industry in or about Canterbury or do the Kentish Pilchers all descend from one original pilcher?

With surnames of local origin the same doubt may arise. Dale is a word for valley most common in those northern districts settled by Danes and Norsemen. Dale is also found in these parts as a surname, but different families of Dale no doubt derive from different ancestors who lived in different dales. On the other hand the Metcalfes, who abound in Bedale and other parts of the North Riding of Yorkshire and adjoining regions, may well all be of one stock. In the time of Sir James Metcalfe (d. 1589) Leland wrote that Nappa, their chief seat, 'and other places thereabouts be able to make a 300 men yn very knowen consanguinitie of the Metcalfes'.[1] By Camden's day the story was that Sir Christopher Metcalfe (1513–74), when High Sheriff in 1555, had received the judges with 300 horsemen of his name and family dressed alike.[2] Camden calls the Metcalfes *familia numerosissima totius Angliae*. Metcalfe or Medcalfe is thought to be the place now called Calf Middletongue leading up to the mountain called Calf.[3]

The healthiness, remoteness and enclosure of the northern dales perhaps favoured multiplication and discouraged removal. Study of the surname patterns of other isolated places would certainly bring to light parallels. In such closed communities we may look for the operation of H. W. Watson's principle of the extinction of some male stocks and the proliferation of others.[4] This is hard to test where the local surnames are common ones, but it should be possible where surnames, rare elsewhere, are common in an isolated community, as are those of Oiller and Tart at Dungeness.

A similar pattern can perhaps be seen in the rare cases where a Norman knightly name has become locally widespread. Venables in Cheshire, Glanville and Pomeroy in Devon, Newbery on the Devon and Dorset border and Giffard both in Devon and in Cambridgeshire are examples. Neither numbers, distribution, nor the known historical facts[5] here suggest anything like the clan recruitment which alone can explain how the Norman Burke has become the fourteenth commonest surname in Ireland, and which may even have played a part in building

---

[1] *Itinerary*, 3rd ed. v. 8; vi. 25, quoted by W. C. and G. Metcalfe, *Metcalfe Records*, 1891, p. xxv.

[2] *Britannia*, 1586, quoted in *Metcalfe Records*, pp. xxxv–xxxvi.

[3] Ibid., p. vi.      [4] p. 241.      [5] See those for Giffard, pp. 67–71.

up such border families or tribes as the Fenwicks and the Robsons of Northumberland. Venables and the others mentioned are, I believe, true families and close comparative study might perhaps suggest some of the reasons why they and some few others of their kind have multiplied greatly, while many more have perished and an intermediate group have barely survived. On the other hand the interaction of biological, geographical and social factors might well be too obscure to unravel now.

The exhaustive study of English surname history, which alone would make it possible to give general answers to such questions, has yet to be undertaken, but a hopeful beginning has now been made through the Marc Fitch Fund endowment at Leicester University.[1] As Dr. Hoskins has pointed out,[2] the subject is enormous and only a minutely detailed and accurate treatment would be of practical use. All previous books on the subject have been superseded by Dr. Percy Hide Reaney's *A Dictionary of British Surnames*, 1958 and *The Origin of English Surnames*, 1967, though the author points out that the production of a complete Dictionary of Surnames is not yet possible. Dr. Reaney deals fully with etymology and touches on the problems of the social history and geographical distribution of surnames.[3] In the last named field there is also Henry Brougham Guppy's pioneer work, *Homes of Family Names in Great Britain* (1890), which makes a geographical analysis mainly on the basis of the lists of farmers in the county directories. Guppy's view that the farmers, 'the most stay-at-home class of the country', would form the best basis for his study, *if one class only had to be chosen*, is not unreasonable. But the limitation thus imposed is very severe. Dr. Hoskins' hope that students may yet be found to deal fully with the surname history at any rate of single counties will find an echo in the heart of every genealogist. In the meantime the genealogist with problems in this field to solve can and often must explore them individually for himself.

Background knowledge in such fields as these, most of it to be gained only by experience, is of the greatest use alike in the search for evidence and in its interpretation. When the scent is lost he who knows the country and the quarry's ways will on average be the first to pick it up again. The researcher thus at a loss must extend the scope of his research. But this may be done in many ways, of which geographical extension is only one, and to choose well between them needs experience. To search all the parishes within a radius of ten miles of the

---

[1] p. 148 supra.    [2] *Trans. Leic. Arch. Soc.* xxiii, 1947, p. 38.
[3] *The Origin of English Surnames*, chap. xvii pp. 321–56.

place where the scent failed may seem obvious and simple, but if the man to be traced was a boatbuilder in a seaport he is as likely to have come from another seaport counties away as from a neighbouring inland village. At every fork of the road the social background and the record background must be held in mind just as firmly as those of name and place. All indeed are interwoven and must so far as possible be seen as a single multidimensional pattern.

Similar factors affect the interpretation of evidence. From experience one learns what is intrinsically probable and what is not. Where the evidence is conclusive, probability is irrelevant. Often, however, even the most critical genealogist must dispense with that degree of cogency in evidence, which the lawyers call for in proof of succession to peerage titles, and must make do with that kind of highly probable inference which historians mainly deal in. The distinction between legal and historical evidence does not always, indeed, favour the former. For the lawyer *pater est quem nuptiae demonstrant* though historians may suspect or may be convinced that a child's mother's husband was not in fact his father. In the nature of things all our conclusions must be qualified by the basic limitations of our records and of the knowledge and honesty of those who made them.

### 3. HISTORICAL DESCENTS

To trace descents from persons whose lives are known to history is a reasonable aim of genealogical research. Since in the main such descents must be traced through gentle families, the genealogist who looks for them must try to develop a nose for the lines most likely to lead in the right direction. Our earlier discussion of royal descents[1] may indicate the general pattern and possibilities as well as anything can, but with this as with other problems of genealogy experience gives a feeling for the likely pattern which it is impossible to sum up in propositions. All lines, male and female, must, clearly, be traced, if possibilities are not to be missed, and on each new line property, continuity, name and record will play their familiar parts of help or hindrance. Once a connection is made with the main stream of known pedigrees the doors will be open wide.

### 4. DESIDERATA GENEALOGICA

The reader will by now rightly have concluded, perhaps with some irritation, that the difficulty of tracing a pedigree will vary greatly with

[1] pp. 233–40.

rather curiously accidental factors. Whether someone in the past happens to have done the work already, whether a name is rare, whether records happen to survive, are factors wholly independent of one's ancestors' intrinsic character. Those who think that life's risks and chances should so far as possible be spread may ask if nothing could be done to even them in this field. This is a question genealogists might with advantage ponder. If a wealthy foundation or a welfare state put astronomical funds at our disposal for providing all its citizens with pedigrees, how should we spend them to the best advantage?

First of all we should, I suggest, provide for the future by instituting a form of registration of births, deaths and marriages, which would lead from one to another. If entries which link marriage entries with the parties' baptisms or births, baptismal or birth entries with the parents' marriage, and death or burial entries with the deceased's birth and parentage have been feasible in France and Germany for three centuries or more and in Australia for one, they should by now be possible in England.

Next we should, I suppose, no longer put first the pursuit of individual pedigrees but should rather concentrate on whole records and classes of record, and on whole social, historical and genealogical groups. We should thus enjoy the advantages[1] which genealogists dealing with whole localities have always had. By this procedure the conspicuous and the continuous lines would emerge first and the less differentiated residue would then, as with a jigsaw puzzle, be that much easier to sort out. The construction of calendars and indices might not differ greatly from much which goes on now, but the choice of records for the purpose would acquire a different bias. Probate records would advance from their present back seat into the front rank. Originals or copies of all parish registers would be made available in one place and their analysis and indexing would provide a central theme round which much else would be grouped. Copies of complete or tentative pedigrees together with the abstracts of the evidence on which they rested would be circulated to all record offices for current comparison with material there, as well as to a central office, where all would be collated. By such means as this many problems now insoluble could be solved and many mistakes due to unconscious bias might be avoided.

Utopias are constructed to throw light on here and now. The conclusion from this one I take to be that genealogists, archivists and historians can help each other in proportion as they concentrate their

[1] p. 411.

attention on the points where their interests touch. This book will not wholly have missed its target if it serves to bring some of those points into sharper focus. The amateur, meanwhile, may, I hope, have been helped to see this world of genealogy as, like the greater world,

*A mighty maze! But not without a plan.*

# TABLE I. *Heirs of the Lords Dudley* (see p. 212)

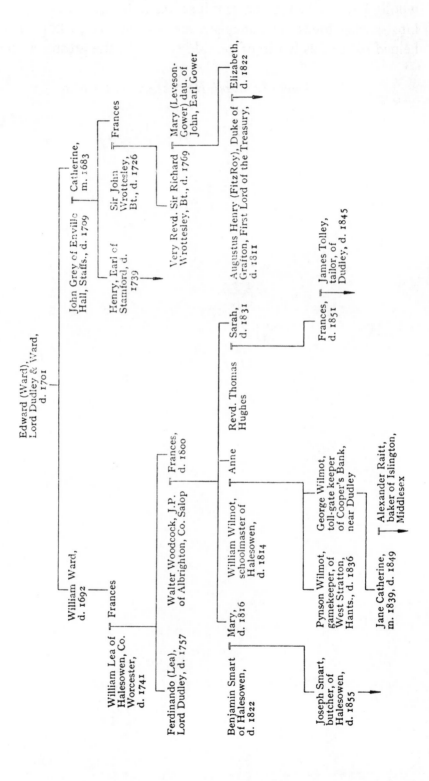

# TABLE II. *King and Innkeeper* (see p. 213)

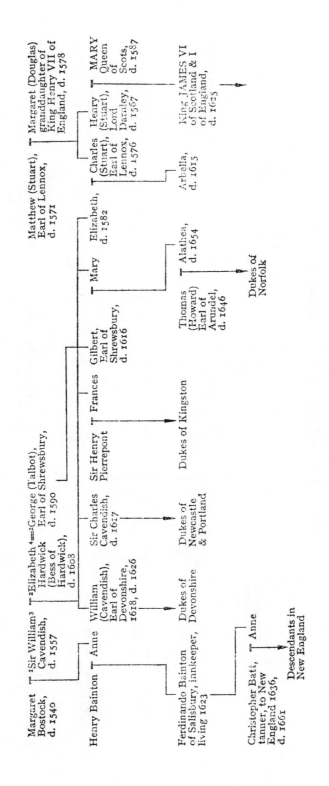

TABLE III. *Johnson and Chesterfield* (see p. 216)

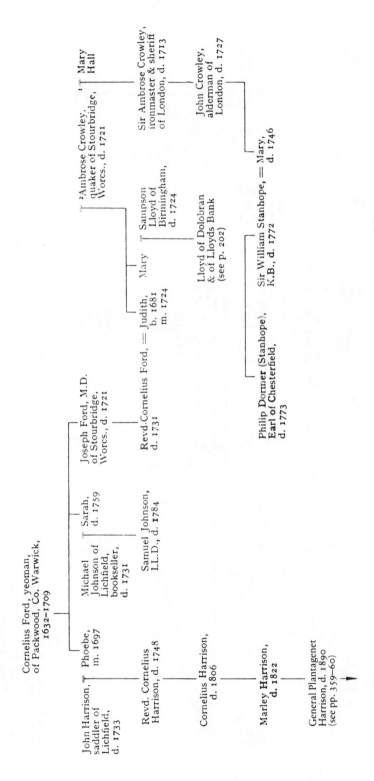

# TABLE IV. *A Group of Colonists*

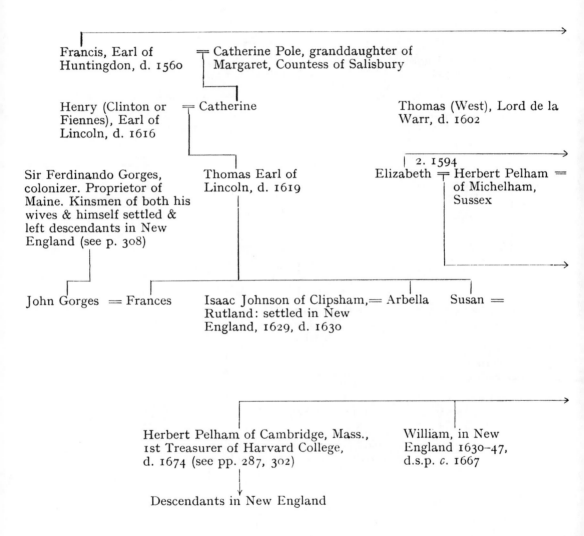

Francis, Earl of Huntingdon, d. 1560 = Catherine Pole, granddaughter of Margaret, Countess of Salisbury

Henry (Clinton or Fiennes), Earl of Lincoln, d. 1616 = Catherine

Thomas (West), Lord de la Warr, d. 1602

Sir Ferdinando Gorges, colonizer. Proprietor of Maine. Kinsmen of both his wives & himself settled & left descendants in New England (see p. 308)

Thomas Earl of Lincoln, d. 1619

2. 1594
Elizabeth = Herbert Pelham = of Michelham, Sussex

John Gorges = Frances

Isaac Johnson of Clipsham, = Arbella  Susan = Rutland: settled in New England, 1629, d. 1630

Herbert Pelham of Cambridge, Mass., 1st Treasurer of Harvard College, d. 1674 (see pp. 287, 302)

William, in New England 1630–47, d.s.p. c. 1667

Descendants in New England

* For their connections in the Somers Island Company and among Bermuda settlers see H. Wilkinson, *The Adventurers of Bermuda*, 1933, pp. 100–1.

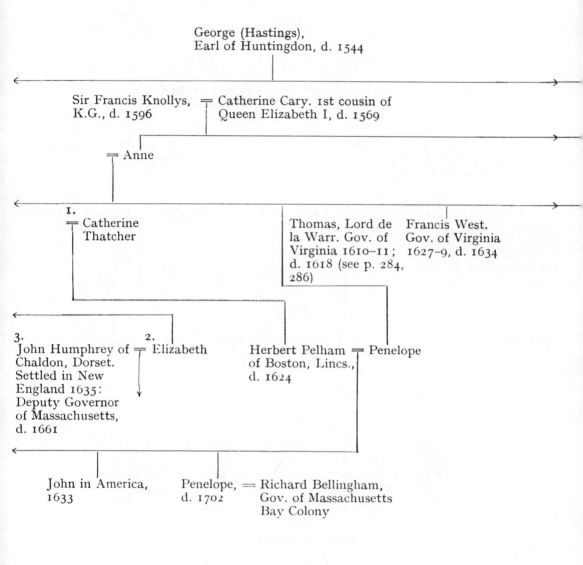

George (Hastings),
Earl of Huntingdon, d. 1544

Sir Francis Knollys, ⊤ Catherine Cary. 1st cousin of
K.G., d. 1596      Queen Elizabeth I, d. 1569

⊤ Anne

**I.**
⊤ Catherine      Thomas, Lord de   Francis West.
  Thatcher       la Warr. Gov. of  Gov. of Virginia
                 Virginia 1610–11;  1627–9, d. 1634
                 d. 1618 (see p. 284,
                 286)

**3.**                    **2.**
John Humphrey of ⊤ Elizabeth    Herbert Pelham ⊤ Penelope
Chaldon, Dorset.                of Boston, Lincs.,
Settled in New                  d. 1624
England 1635:
Deputy Governor
of Massachusetts,
d. 1661

John in America,     Penelope, = Richard Bellingham,
1633                 d. 1702     Gov. of Massachusetts
                                 Bay Colony

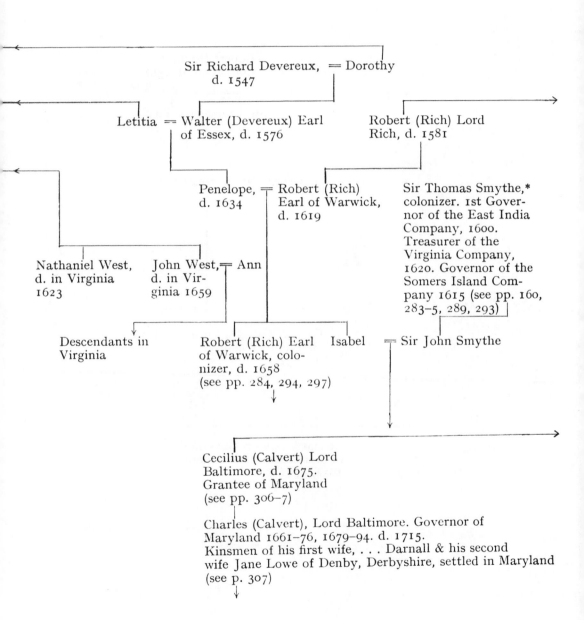

Sir Richard Devereux, == Dorothy
d. 1547

Letitia == Walter (Devereux) Earl       Robert (Rich) Lord
     of Essex, d. 1576       Rich, d. 1581

Penelope, == Robert (Rich)       Sir Thomas Smythe,*
d. 1634       Earl of Warwick,       colonizer. 1st Gover-
d. 1619       nor of the East India
Company, 1600.
Treasurer of the
Virginia Company,
Nathaniel West,   John West,== Ann       1620. Governor of the
d. in Virginia    d. in Vir-       Somers Island Com-
1623              ginia 1659       pany 1615 (see pp. 160,
283–5, 289, 293)

Descendants in    Robert (Rich) Earl   Isabel  == Sir John Smythe
Virginia          of Warwick, colo-
nizer, d. 1658
(see pp. 284, 294, 297)

Cecilius (Calvert) Lord
Baltimore, d. 1675.
Grantee of Maryland
(see pp. 306–7)

Charles (Calvert), Lord Baltimore. Governor of
Maryland 1661–76, 1679–94. d. 1715.
Kinsmen of his first wife, . . . Darnall & his second
wife Jane Lowe of Denby, Derbyshire, settled in Maryland
(see p. 307)

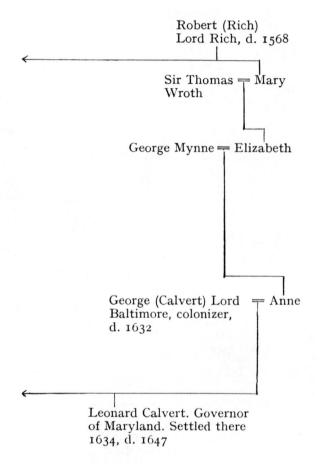

Robert (Rich)
Lord Rich, d. 1568

Sir Thomas ═ Mary
Wroth

George Mynne ═ Elizabeth

George (Calvert) Lord ═ Anne
Baltimore, colonizer,
d. 1632

Leonard Calvert. Governor
of Maryland. Settled there
1634, d. 1647

# ADDENDA

*Page 13.* On the classes of Anglo-Saxon and Welsh society see John Morris, *The Age of Arthur*, 1973, pp. 486–505.

*Page 14, last paragraph.* Mercian kings. See further J. Morris, op. cit. p. 272.

*Page 15, third paragraph.* Cerdic. J. Morris, op. cit. pp. 103–6, 323–5 concludes that the line of Cerdic was, alone among the Saxon genealogies, a deliberate invention; that Cerdic is a British name and that he was a Briton.

*Page 17.* Conrad Swan, York Herald, wrote to me 5 April 1972 from Reykjavik, Iceland where he had been lecturing in the presence of the President of Iceland. 'The Professor of Genealogy, Professor Einar Bjarnason, also present. Had already met him earlier that day at the British Embassy luncheon party for me. He told me that in cases dealing with the large landowners it is sometimes possible to get the pedigree back to the Sagas, basing oneself mainly on the Land Records (especially the conveyance of land within the family, or agreement of the family for its sale to non-family members).'

*Page 18, note 2.* See above.

  *note 4.* J. Morris, *The Age of Arthur*, 1973, pp. 462–3, cites King Cadfan's problems with the claims of kin in the seventh century and a fourteenth century case where in one locality, after 150 years, the heirs of 4 landowners numbered more than 200 with subsequent fragmentation of the holdings, referring to F. Seebohm, *Tribal Systems in Wales*, 1904, appendices and pp. 1 ff.

*Page 20.* On 23 March 1972 Mr. J. M. McEwen, Secretary of Maori and Island Affairs, Maori and Island Affairs Department, Wellington, New Zealand, wrote to me about the Maori Chiefly descent of Sir John

Grace, who was made K.B.E. in 1968. 'In the 1860s, the Maori Land Court was established to determine and record the ownership of all Maori land. The genealogies of the claimants were recorded, and now form part of the Court's Records. Thus although the art of oral transmission has somewhat declined, there is now a permanent official record of almost every leading Maori family.

There were four grades of society in pre-European times, the Ariki, the Rangatira, the Tutua, and the Taurikarika. Generally speaking the Ariki was the senior male descended in an unbroken male line from the progenitor of the Tribe. In some cases, however, upon agreement of the Freemen of the Tribe, the title of Ariki could pass through a younger son, or even occasionally to a descendant through a female line. As Maori descent was bilinear, there was also a female equivalent of the Ariki known as Tapairu, or Ariki Tapairu.

The Rangatira were the men of rank in the tribe. Generally speaking they would be the Chiefs of tribes or sub tribes and their younger brothers and sisters. The Tutua were people of humble origin, but still Freemen, while the Taurikarika were slaves, either war captives or the descendants of captives. Once a man had been enslaved, no matter how high his previous rank, his mana or prestige would be besmirched, and it would be difficult, if not impossible, for his descendants to regain their former position.'

The rest of the letter deals with the ancestry and high standing of Sir John Grace.

*Page 22.* On the Irish royal genealogies see further J. Morris, *The Age of Arthur*, 1973, pp. 143–7, 161, 164–185, and Francis John Byrne, *Irish Kings and High Kings*, 1973, which carries analysis of them a long step further.

*Page 27*, note 5. On the Neville origins see further Sir Charles Clay, *Early Yorkshire Families*, Yorkshire Arch. Soc. Vol. 135, 1973, pp. 67–8. The proposed derivation of the Washingtons from Patric of the Hirsel is discounted by Professor G. W. Barrow, who points out that the Coldstream, Kelso and Melrose cartularies indicate that the William son of Patric, whom it was proposed to identify with William of Hartburn, lived a generation later, while Patrick of Offerton is unlikely to be the same man as Patrick son of the Earl. He refers also to a review by Roy Hudleston in the *Cumberland and Westmorland Arch. Soc. Trans.* of Mr. Washington's book.

*Page 28.* J. Morris, *The Age of Arthur*, 1973, pp. 453–7, discusses the origin of the Scottish clans and the genealogical and non-genealogical elements in their composition.

*Page 30, line 1.* See J. Morris, op cit., pp. 202–224 on the 5th and 6th century Romano-British dynasties.

*Page 48, note 1.* and

*Page 49, note 1.* The introduction to K. B. McFarlane, *The Nobility of Later Medieval England*, 1973, p. xxiii, refers to the rejection in more recent years of the view set out by Bloch in 1940 of the 13th century development of nobility in France, referring to the work of G. Duby, 1961, L. Genicot, 1965, R. Boutruche, 1968, and E. Louris, 1966.

*Page 61.* K. B. McFarlane, *The Nobility of Later Medieval England*, pp. 62, 69–74, 78–82, 151, 171, 276–8, shows that the conveyance of land to feoffees from soon after 1300 made it easier to endow younger sons, bastards and others. But the development of entail (pp. 80–82) and other factors made a powerful undertow in favour of primogeniture which in time redressed the balance. ('By 1485 primogeniture, after a century and a half of uncertainty, was once more enthroned.' (p. 81).) However between 1300 and 1500 there was more dispersal of great estates than before and after.

*Page 64, line 22.* For the context of Roger Bigod's surrender and regrant and for similar instances see K. B. McFarlane, op. cit., pp. 262–3.

*Page 73, note 2.* In a second edition (H. C. B. Mynors, *Treago "A little lousy history"*, December 1975) Sir Humphrey Mynors, Bt., goes far to bridge the gap between the early Miners of Burghill and the later Treago line, by a series of more or less disconnected entries, between which, however, the existence of some connections may be reasonably inferred. Richard Mynors (c. 1440–1528) a successful administrator in South Wales is identified as the probable builder of Treago.

*Page 74, line 4.* Mr. Nicholas MacMichael wrote to *Country Life* 22 Feb. 1978 that in 1965 he saw at Kedleston a deed of 1198/9 in which Richard de Curzon recognizes Kedleston to be held by Thomas son of Thomas de Curzon. In 1086 'Culbert' held Kedleston of Henry de Ferrers and 'Hubert' held West Lockinge, Berks. Henry de Ferrers (d. 1088/9) consented to a gift by Robert son of Hubert in Lockinge to Abingdon. Thus the male descent of Kedleston from Domesday is likely though not proved.

*Line 22.* K. B. McFarlane, *Lancastrian Kings and Lollard Knights*, Oxford, 1972, p. 162 questions this account of Lord Clifford's patronage and describes him as a 'cadet of the Cliffords of Devonshire, such small fry that their pedigree is difficult to trace.' However Mr.

Robert Garrett makes the Devonshire line a substantial cadet branch of the baronial family, Sir Lewis being great-grandson of Sir Giles (d. c. 1276), 4th son of Walter de Clifford (d. 1222/3).

*Page 79.* Mr. G. V. C. Young of Peel, Isle of Man, suggested to me (1977) that Queen Mary of Man who paid homage to Edward I of England at Perth in 1291 was the widow of King Reginald and daughter of Ewen of Argyll, who would have taken refuge at the English Court after her husband's death in 1249 (when her daughter Mary would have married John Waldboef). For her later life and marriage see Complete Peerage V. 513 and XII. i. 382–3).

*Page 100.* K. B. McFarlane, *The Nobility of Later Medieval England*, 1973, pp. 173–5, explains how in the disuse of creations in fee and the adoption in new creations of limitations to heirs male the crown was following a general trend to settle lands on heirs male rather than leading it.

*Page 103, line 3.* K. B. McFarlane, op. cit. pp. 168–171, considers the effect of plague on the nobility and thinks it less for them than others, that of 1361 being the worst.

*Page 103, note 3.* K. B. McFarlane, op. cit., pp. 78–9, 187–201, 207. He points to near approaches to extinction even in such long lasting families as Vere, Stafford, Beauchamp, and such unusually prolific stocks as Fitzalan and Courtenay in the 14th and Neville and Bourchier in the 15th century: pp. 151–6 on heiresses and their marriages: pp. 84–8 on marriage contracts and provision for daughters.

*Page 105.* K. B. McFarlane, op. cit., p. 284 on the new Lancastrian nobility, drawn from the official class: Hungerford, Tiptoft, Cromwell, Bardolf, Sudeley, Say. He discounts the lethal reputation of the Wars of the Roses, pp. 146–9. On the recruitment of new families to replace old he notes (p. 151) between 1350 and 1500, 200 failures in the male line and 114 replacements. Three quarters of these were genuine new creations or summonses; one quarter either new families or cadets of old with female line descents from the old they replaced. 61 new earldoms were created in this period, 49 as direct marks of royal favour.

*Page 118, line 3.* See McFarlane, op. cit., p. 142 on the gradual restriction of 'nobility' to the peerage.

*Page 118, line 17.* K. B. McFarlane, op. cit., pp. 19–40, analyses the acquisition of wealth by the spoils of the French wars and the achievement of position thereby through pay, ransom and gains of war.

*Page 119.* K. B. McFarlane, op. cit., pp. 122–5, on the stratification of the nobility and gentry in the later middle ages. By 1450 English society was more stratified at the top than it had been. *Statutes of the Realm*, II, 74–5, Ordinance of 12 May 1390, on the petition of Parliament, churchmen and knights bachelors, esquires and below, were forbidden to give their servants liveries to be worn outside their households. Demarcation in the peerage, of peers from others, and precedence discussed.

*Page 128, lines 1 to 9.*  (see also page 215). Richard McKinley, *The Surnames of Lancashire*, 1981, pp. 444–453 and references on pp. 454–53 contain the fullest discussion to date of the phenomenon of 'ramification' of surnames round their places of origin.

*Page 132, note 1.*  Lord Halifax, *Thoughts and Reflections (A Character of King Charles the Second: and Miscellaneous Thoughts and Reflections*, London 1750, p. 145). *Complete Works* ed. Raleigh, 1912, p. 241. *Complete Works* ed. Kenyon (Penguin, 1969) p. 225.

*Page 155.*  On the London patriciate see also A. R. Wagner, *Pedigree and Progress*, 1975, pp. 86–8, 211–3, 260–1.

*Page 156.*  See K. B. McFarlane, op. cit., pp. 13–15 on the uniqueness of the rise of the de la Poles from merchants of Hull to Earls, although from their day to the 16th century London fortunes provided more and more recruits to the landed nobility, e.g. Sir John Pulteney, Sir Thomas Seymour, Sir Richard Gresham, Sir Thomas Kitson. This was in spite of the fact that so many rich citizens left no heirs, probably because of the unhealthiness of city life. However since the 12th century prosperous citizens had bought many manors, 'as if they were so anxious to become gentlemen that they could not wait to become noblemen' (p. 167).

*Page 167.*  Georgiana Blakiston, *Lord William Russell and his wife, 1815–1846*, 1972, page 166. Lord John Russell writes to Lord William Russell 16 September 1933 'Althorp next to Lord Grey is the most perfect gentleman I ever saw, and it is because he is so much the gentleman that he has such complete command over the House of Commons. What was Goulburn? A mere clerk. Melbourne is a thorough gentleman. Now Lord Brougham, whatever else you may say of him, is quite as much a gentleman as Lyndhurst. And even our worst are superior to Herries, who according to Lord Dudley was "no gentleman". With all this I do not mean to deny that the Tories are generally gentlemen. The Whigs and Tories in fact are parties of gentlemen. The Radicals are not.'

*Page 168, line 14.*  W. J. Jones in *The History of Parliament, The House of Commons 1558–1603* ed. P. W. Hasler, II, 1981, p. 246 says that Richard Hanbury was a rogue who fraudulently exploited the cumbersome structure of the mineral and battery works.

*Page 169.* A flood of fresh light is being thrown progressively on surname history by the volumes of the *English Surnames Series*, established by the Marc Fitch Fund (see page supra).

For an unexpected surname origin see S. Baring-Gould, *Early Reminiscences 1834–1864*, 1923, p. 3. 'My father took a house in Bratton Clovelly parish, that had been built and occupied by Sir Elijah Impey, Chief-Justice of Bengal, who died in 1809. He had left behind him an illegitimate son by a Bratton girl, who became my father's groom, and called himself Wimpey.'

*Page 177.* The two nations. See further A. R. Wagner, *Pedigree and Progress*, 1975, Chapter VI.

*Page 180, lines 12–19.* Peta Fordham, *Inside the Underworld*, 1972, pp. 23–4, writes that crime is persistently hereditary, but recruitment to it is easy and (p. 148) 'a great deal of gypsy blood runs in underworld veins as many surnames there witness.' Mrs. Fordham also told me (1974) that many Romany words are found in criminal slang.

*Page 182, note 7.* should read 'Lieutenant Commander W. A. C. Sandford, "Medieval Clerical Celibacy in England", the *Genealogist's Magazine*, xii'.

*Pages 183–4.* On medieval families founded by churchmen of humble origin see A. R. Wagner, *Pedigree and Progress*, 1975, pp. 84–6, 89–90, 94–6, 215–7, 219.

*Page 185, note 1, line 2.* For 'Op. Cit.' read '*History of Sacerdotal Celibacy in the Christian Church.*'

*Pages 188–9.* On the rise of such great families sprung from lawyers as Scrope, Bourchier, Norwich, Cobham, in the fourteenth, and Gascoigne, Paston, Fortescue, Yelverton, Littleton, Catesby and Fairfax in the fifteenth century, see K. B. McFarlane, op. cit., pp. 12–13.

*Page 192, note 3.* See also K. B. McFarlane, *The Nobility of Later Mediaeval England*, p. 140, referring to the marked hereditary character of their private civil services, e.g. Hugfords and Throckmortons in the service of the Earls of Warwick, Whitgreaves in that of the Stafford Earls of Buckingham, and Hungerfords in the fourteenth, succeeded by Leventhorpes in the fifteenth century in that of the Dukes of Lancaster.

*Page 199, line 19.* For an essay in this vein on the interconnected families of Eton fellows and masters see A. R. Wagner, *Pedigree and Progress*, 1975, pp. 123–33, 235–252, 264–5.

*Page 200.* On the segregation arising from recusancy from about 1570 see Lawrence Stone, *The Crisis of the Aristocracy 1558–1641*, 1965, page

614.

*Pages 202–3.* On Quaker endogamy see A. R. Wagner, *Pedigree and Progress*, 1965, pp. 108–10, 227, 263.

*Pages 203–4.* On Unitarians, Wagner, op. cit., pp. 110–12, 228.

*Page 205.* K. B. McFarlane, op. cit., page 11, lists the roads to success in the 14th and 15th centuries as the Church, the law, service, trade (including industry and finance), the spoils of war and marriage, and analyses their several workings; p. 12, the Church (see p. 184 *supra*) pp. 12–13 (p. 189 *supra*); pp. 13–15, 167, trade (p. 156 *supra*); pp. 19–40, the spoils of war (p. 118 *supra*); pp. 11, 151–6, 276, marriage (see summary in A. R. Wagner, *Pedigree and Progress*, 1975, pp. 120–2).

*Page 206, line 6.* Lawrence Stone, *The Crisis of the Aristocracy*, 1965, pp. 112–4, lists some previously obscure families who rose to greatness by marriage with heiresses: Touchet, Bourchier, Stanley, Parr, Devereux and Manners, before 1500: Fane, Mildmay, Finch, Greville, and others after: and most notably Cavendish.

*Page 212.* In 1975 Mr. R. G. Woodward referred me to an account of the 18th century decay of the family of Grevis of Moseley Hall, Worcestershire, in W. Salt Brassington, F.S.A., *Historic Worcestershire*, 1894. Thomas Grevis was granted arms in 1528. Sir Richard Grevis in the reign of James I married Anne Leighton, of Royal descent through Stafford, Ferrers and Devereux. Richard Grevis (d. 1759) dissipated his fortune and left his eldest son Henshaw Grevis a legacy of disputes and debts. In 1766 he sold his lands to pay his father's debts and by 1770 was reduced to abject poverty and working in a gravel pit at Moseley. The notice of his death in Aris's Birmingham Gazette 25 August 1788 says that 'though he was heir to one of the oldest and most opulent families in the neighbourhood (through the dissipation and extravagance of his parents) died in the humble capacity of distributor of this paper to and in Leicestershire.' He had five daughters, who all married and left descendants in the neighbourhood. He had also a younger brother Charles, who, receiving his portion, married an heiress and continued the male line, who became Grevis-James. Their pedigree in the College of Arms (Norfolk V. 24) omits any mention of Henshaw Grevis.

*Page 214.* I owe these corrections to Professor Norman Davis, writing 14 May 1972, that William Paston was not a Knight. Cf. his Will. PCC 12 Horne (*Paston Letters and Papers of the Fifteenth Century*, ed. Norman Davis, part i, Oxford 1971, page lvii.) Letter 65 shows that Calle was recommended by the Duke of Norfolk, pages xli–ii, 'the disparaging account of the Paston origins of c. 1444–66. This makes Clement Paston

(d. 1419) 'a good pleyn husbond' who had 100 to 120 acres in Paston. His wife is said to have been a bond woman, sister to Geffrey (Goneld) of Somerton. This carries some conviction. Page lxii. Letter 332. (May 1469) page 451, Margery Paston marries Richard Calle. See also p. 363 *infra*.

*Pages 215–6.* 'Ramification' of surnames. See p. 128 *supra*.

*Pages 217–220.* See on systems of inheritance John Morris, *The Age of Arthur*, 1973, pp. 485–6, 496–8, 501–2.

*Page 221.* See K. B. McFarlane, op. cit., pp. 142–150, on the rate of extinction of noble male lines.

*Page 222.* S. Baring Gould, *Early Reminiscences, 1834–1864*, 1923, p. 4. Of several gentle families once owning land in Bratton Clovelly 'the only name remaining of former gentility is that of Pengelly. There was, in the seventeenth century, an Andrew Pengelly of the family that was estated at Whitchurch, near Tavistock. He was rector of Bratton and left a number of children, who married and settled in that or neighbouring parishes, and a descendant was for many years our coachman, and his grandson is now my son's chauffeur. Another Pengelly is a keeper. The last of the Coryndons of whom I could learn anything, was a carpenter in Devonport Dockyard.'

*Page 223, line 9.* K. B. McFarlane, op. cit., p. 12. Thanks to Robert Burnell's service to Edward I his family 'were transformed from a family of impoverished Shropshire knights into one of the richest baronial houses of the fourteenth century.'

*Pages 227–230.* Fitch. See further A. R. Wagner, *Pedigree and Progress*, pp. 113–5, 233–4, 264.

*Page 233, note 3.* Iris Butler, *The Eldest Brother, The Duke of Wellington's Eldest Brother*, 1973, gives details additional to those given by H. W. Farmar of the probable ancestry of Hyacinthe, Marchioness Wellesley (for which see also *Burke's Landed Gentry of Ireland*, 1958 ed. p. 262) on p. 50 and of her descendants on p. 609. It seems likely that her true father was the Chevalier Christopher Fagan, though her mother Hyacinthe Varis, an actress, was married to M. Roland, a banker.

*Page 234.* A. C. Addington, *The Royal House of Stuart, The Descendants of King James VI of Scotland, James I of England*, Vol. 1, 1969, Vol. II, 1971, Vol. III (Index) promised, brings up to date and corrects this portion of Ruvigny. The author hopes to treat the illegitimate descendants in a later book.

*Page 234, line 2.* G. D. Squibb, Q.C., Norfolk Herald Extraordinary, *Founders' Kin Privilege and Pedigree*, Oxford, 1972, clears up comprehensively the history of this previously obscure subject.

*Page 237, line 3.*   Ruvigny, Exeter Volume, Tab. XXV. No. 282, p. 356, could not trace the descendants 'if any' of Lady Mary Fane, daughter of Thomas, 8th Earl of Westmorland (1700–1771) and her husband Charles Blair (1743–1802, whose ancestry will be found under Blair of Inchyra in Douglas, *Baronage of Scotland*, p. 442). Some account of these and their descent into the 'lower-upper-middle' class is given in Peter Stansky and William Abrahams, *The Unknown Orwell*, 1972, pp. 3–10. Eric Arthur Blair (1903–1950), my own Eton fagmaster, who wrote under the name of George Orwell, was their great-grandson.

*Page 237, note 4.*   The royal descent of Pardon Tillinghast is now doubted, see A. Adams and F. L. Weis, *The Magna Charta Sureties, 1215*, 1968 ed. revised by W. L. Sheppard, Baltimore, Md., p. 33. He may, however, be replaced by John Cranston, op. cit., pp. 36 and 76.

*Page 238.*   K. B. McFarlane, op. cit., pp. 150–1, writes that by 1500 it is difficult to find a single member of the higher nobility not descended from Edward I.

*Page 239, last paragraph.*   On the 18th century acceptance of illegitimate children see Lawrence Stone, *The Family, Sex and Marriage in England 1500–1800*, 1977, pp. 529–534 and elsewhere.

*Page 240, line 1.*   Among the descendants of Catherine of Berain were Mrs. Thrale, Arthur Hugh Clough and Thomas Hughes, author of *Tom Brown's School Days*.

*Page 247, note 6.*   Other kin of Queen Eleanor of Castile for whom marriages were provided in England include Joanna Fiennes (d. 1309) wife of John Lord Wake of Liddell, Isabel de Beaumont wife of John de Vescy (d. 1289) and her niece Clemence daughter of Henry Count of Avaugour wife of John de Vescy (d. 1295), Alice de la Plaunche (of Fiennes descent) wife of John Lord Montfort (d. 1296) and Mary de Pinkney (Pecquigny) who married first Amauri Lord St. Amand (d. 1310) and secondly John Lord Peyvre (d. 1333). See John Carmi Parsons *The Court and Household of Eleanor of Castile in 1290*, Pontifical Institute of Mediaeval Studies, Toronto, 1977, pages 41–55. These marriages, unlike those of Henry III's kin, were so managed as not to cause resentment in England.

*Page 248.*   Count W. H. Rüdt-Collenberg, *The Rupenides Hethumides and Lusignans, The Structure of the Armeno-Cilician Dynasties*, Paris, 1963, pp. 35, 78, thinks Gabriel, Lord of Melitene, 1087–1103 (whose daughter Morfia married 1102 Baldwin II of Jerusalem) or his wife probably related to the Pahlavouni. From Baldwin II and Morfia the descent comes to England through Antioch, Hungary, Naples, Valois, and Philippa of Hainault.

For other descents from Armenia see A. R. Wagner, *Pedigree and Progress*, 1975, pp. 66, 201–2, 258, works of Prince Toumanoff there cited and M. L. Bierbrier, 'Modern Descendants of Byzantine Families' *Genealogists' Magazine*, Vol. 20, 1980, p. 170.

*Page 250, line 17.* On Ferdinando Palaeologus, his ancestors and descendants see Patrick Leigh Fermor, *The Traveller's Tree, A Journey through the Caribbean Islands*, 1950, pp. 145–9.

*Page 257, line 3.* See however Malcolm R. Thorp, 'The Anti-Huguenot Undercurrent in late-Seventeenth-Century England', *Proc. Huguenot Soc. of London*, Vol. 22, 1976, pp. 569–80. In 1683 Thomas Atterbury warned the Secretary of State of a conspiracy among weavers' apprentices in Spitalfields, to rise against the French weavers and knock them on the head. In November 1695 soldiers were sent to Wandsworth to defend French cloth dyers.

*Page 258, note 9.* Dr. Eleanor Selfridge-Field of Sunnyvale, California, sent me in 1978 a Bassano pedigree showing Angela, wife of Joseph Holland, the antiquary, as sister of Emilia, wife of Alfonso Lanier, whom Dr. A. L. Rowse identifies as the Dark Lady of Shakespeare's sonnets, and as daughter of John Baptist Bassano (d. 1576: from Venice).

*Page 263.* On the Huguenot settlements in America, see the American Society of Genealogists, *Genealogical Research*, Vol. II, 1971, part II, Special Studies, Chapter II, 'Huguenot Migrations' by Cameron Allen, pp. 256–290.

*Page 265, line 22.* See also A. R. Wagner, *Pedigree and Progress*, 1975, pp. 18–19.

*Page 266. note 7.* See also A. R. Wagner, op. cit., pp. 106–7, 229, 263; and A. R. Wagner and A. Dale, *The Wagners of Brighton*, 1983, Ch. I.

*Page 269.* On Jewish migrations to and within America see American Society of Genealogists, *Genealogical Research*, Vol. II, 1971, part II, Special Studies, Chapter III, pp. 291–311, 'Jewish Migrations' by Malcolm H. Stern.

*Page 270, line 5.* Julio Caro Baroja, *Los Judeos en la Espana moderna y contemporanea*, Ediciones Arion, 1961, Vol. II, pp. 58–9, 82, III, 22–25, 371–3, tells us that the Lopes Pereira family were associated with the tobacco monopoly in Spain from the late 16th century. Diego (d. 1759) was an active supporter of the Archduke Charles of Austria during the war of succession and doubtless moved to Vienna because of his defeat. He was there given the tobacco monopoly of the Empire and later made Baron of Aguilar and Privy Councillor of Maria Theresa. It is said that the Spanish Government asked for his extradition in 1749 as a Spanish subject. Hence his removal to London.

*Page 271.* Chaim Bermant, *The Cousinhood of the Anglo-Jewish Gentry*, 1971 gives the pedigrees of Cohen, Rothschild, Goldsmid, Montefiore, Samuel ben Amschel (Lord Bearsted), Louis Samuel (Montagu, Viscount Samuel, Lord Swaythling) and Sassoon; expounds their intermarriages (Levi Barent Cohen, 1747–1808, is a central figure): and explains how, for well over a century, this group of very rich banking families dominated English Jewry and (largely through Rothschild money and influence and Sir Moses Montefiore's character and prestige) did much for Jews elsewhere. Their dominance was in time undermined, first by the inrush of newcomer Jews from Russia and Poland in the 1880s (page 204) who did not even want to be assimilated to the English gentry; then by division in the cousinhood itself, and against Zionism (some thinking that their great and largely successful effort to be accepted as English would be frustrated by this assertion of Israelite nationalism); and finally by the twentieth century religious trough, which combined with their assimilation to take the heart of their very Jewishness. The last Chapter, 29, 'The Society of Friends', draws an interesting parallel between the two 'cousinhoods' of the Jewish and the Quaker bankers.

*Page 273.* Gypsies. See also p. 180.

*Page 276.* William George Tyrrell (1866–1947) created 1929 Baron Tyrrell, was son of William Henry Tyrrell, a Judge of the High Court, North West Provinces, India (d. 1895) by Julia (d. 1892), daughter of Colonel Wakefield, by a converted Hindu lady, the daughter of a Vizier and the ward of the Rana of Kumasin. Lady Gladwyn, writing the history of the British Embassy in Paris asked me in 1972 how she could get the truth of the story that Lord Tyrrell had Indian blood. I referred her to the India Office Library, which produced these facts. Sir James Marshall-Cornwall had already confirmed to me the fact of Lord Tyrrell's Indian descent.

*Page 282.* *Genealogical Research, Methods and Sources*, by the American Society of Genealogists, Ed. Milton Rubincam, Associate Editor Jean Stephenson, 1960.

Part 1 General Considerations
  2. Materials for Research
  3 Regional Genealogy (articles on each of the old Colonies) and the Westward expansion

4 Pre-American ancestry (including articles on Feudal genealogy, England and Wales and Continental countries)

5 Special fields of investigation (e.g. heraldry, surnames)

Volume II, 1971. Ed. Kenn Stryker-Rodda,

Part 1 Regional Genealogy (articles on the States to Missouri)

2 Special Studies (Ontario, Huguenots, Jews) See also page
312.

A new edition of Vol. I is in preparation.

*Page 283, note 5.*   G. D. Squibb, *Founders' Kin*, 1972, pp. 97–103,
shows that Robert Chichele, Mayor of London, died s.p. It may be,
however, that the Robert Chichele, from whom those here mentioned claimed descent, was a cousin of Archbishop Chichele.

*Page 296.* See also Eric H. Whittleton, 'Family History in the
Bahamas', *Genealogists' Magazine*, 1975, Vol. 18, pp. 187–191.

*Page 312.* The American Society of Genealogists, *Genealogical
Research*, Vol. II, 1971, part 2, Special Studies, Chapter I, pages
228–255, 'Ontario' by Milton Rubincam gives an excellent account
of the Settlement sources and evidence covering the Loyalists
(229–231) whose migrations altered the whole character of Canada
from wholly French to largely English speaking: Simcoe's Colonisation Measures; Quakers, Scots, Irish, Welsh, etc.

*Page 315.*   For the onward migrations westward within the United
States from the old Colonies to the newer States see the several
chapters of the American Society of Genealogists' *Genealogical
Research*, Volumes I, 1960, and II, 1971, but especially volume II,
Chapter 9, 'Tennessee' by Robert M. McBride, who writes that
'Tennessee is a pivotal State in any study of movement of the
American people. In the first half of the nineteenth century it was
perhaps the principal cross roads of migratory movements in the
central South and South West.' In 1850 (page 143) 81% of white
Tennesseans were estimated to be of English background.

*Page 318, at foot.*   Paul de Serville, *Port Phillip Gentlemen and
Good Society in Melbourne before the Gold Rushes*, Oxford, 1980,
examines the history and membership of the group of Irish, Scottish
and English families with some social pretensions who settled in and
about Melbourne in the early 1830s and more or less maintained
their position as a superior class there nearly down to 1850. The
appendices trace many detailed life histories and the body of the
book explores the social history of attitudes from diaries, newspapers and the like. One of the leaders of the group was Georgiana

Huntley Gordon (d. 1890), wife of Andrew Murison McCrae, illegitimate daughter of the 5th and last Duke of Gordon by Jane, daughter of Ralph Graham of Rockmoor.

*Page 319.* On settlement of children in the colonies, especially Canada, Australia and New Zealand, from the seventeenth, but mainly in the nineteenth and twentieth centuries, by philanthropic organizers and organizations, see Gillian Wagner, *Children of the Empire*, 1982. The numbers of these child immigrants, especially to Canada, were much greater than had generally been realised.

*Page 320.* Raleigh Trevelyan, *Princes under the Volcano*, 1972, tells the story of the Marsala growing and shipping families of Ingham, Whitaker and Woodhouse in Sicily (and of Nelson, Lord Bridport and Duke of Bronte) from c. 1820 to the present day. It is notable that the Whitaker and Woodhouse pedigrees in Burke's Landed Gentry give scarcely a hint of the connection of those families with Sicily. Trevelyan, op. cit., p. xv, regrets not having space 'for a dissertation on other British wine families, in Bordeaux, Oporto, Jerez, the Canaries and elsewhere. The Empress Eugénie's mother's family the Kirkpatricks, for example, were wine shippers at Malaga. Some of the port dynasties, such as the Cockburns and the Grahams, dating from 1815 and 1820 respectively, still reign at Oporto. . . . In 1793 there were thirty-nine firms of wine shippers in Madeira, twenty-six being British. . . . Names such as Blandy, Reid, Leacock, Cossart and Rutherford are still to be conjured with on the Island.'

*Page 333,* line 4. On the changes and uncertainties of English marriage law before 1754 see Lawrence Stone, *The Family, Sex and Marriage in England 1500–1800*, 1977, pp. 30–41.

*Page 344, line 6.* The recent moves of public and local records from one repository to another, and possible further moves impending, unfortunately mean that the whereabouts of many need at present to be checked by enquiry.

*Page 353.* K. B. McFarlane, *The Nobility of Later Medieval England*, 1973, pp. 165–6, cites a fictitious pedigree, concocted in the mid 14th century for the family of John de Norwich (c. 1299–1362, *Complete Peerage* IX, 763), deriving them from a companion of the Conqueror. It is in a family cartulary, Bodleian MS. top. gen. c.62 (former Phillipps MS. 3796) ff. 3$^{b}$–4.

*Page 371.* On the Deputy Heralds see further G. D. Squibb.

*Page 406.* The foundation in 1940 of the American Society of

Genealogists, 'As a non-profit organization dedicated to improving the quality of genealogical research and to providing education in this technical field', marked an epoch. Dr. Arthur Adams was the first President, 1940–1958. Walter Goodwin Davis was President 1958–1961. In 1960 the Society published *Genealogical Research, Methods and Sources* and in 1971 *Genealogical Research*, Volume II; comprising admirable guides to the genealogical backgrounds and sources of the different American States, and to special topics of ancestral interest, including European origins. The Fellows of the Society, whose number is limited to 50, are chosen 'on the basis of the amount and quality of their published genealogical work'.

*Page 406.* Noel Currer-Briggs, *English Adventurers and Virginian Settlers*, three volumes, Phillimore, 1969, contains abstracts of English Wills and other documents relating to Settlers in Virginia.

*Pages 416–8.* See further on surnames *supra*.

# INDEX

Abercrombie, 252

Abergavenny Peerage Case, 125

Abeyance, doctrine of, 101

Abitot, Urse d', 76

Abraham, 271

Acton, Lord, 243

Adam-Even, P., with reference to French use of seals, 118, 119 n. 1

Adamnan, *Life of St. Columba*, 25 n. 6

Adams, A., and F. L. Weis, *Magna Carta Sureties*, 311 n. 5

Adams, Rev. Arthur, 8, 296 n. 4, 298 n. 6, 404 and n. 1, 406

Adams, James Truslow, with reference to New England colonists, 282, 283 n. 1, 299

Addison, Joseph, with reference to lawyers, 190

Adeliza of Louvain, Queen of Henry I, 39

Adler, Michael, *The Jews of Medieval England*, 267 n. 2

*Advenae*, Norman, in Wales, 77 f., 80–1

Aegidius, 32

Aelfwine, Sheriff of Warwickshire, 50 ff.

Agarde, Arthur, 342 n. 2, 343, 367, 375

Agricultural depressions, 145; *and* emigration, 313–14

Aguilar, Baron Diego de, 269

Aguilar, Benjamin, 270

Aguyler, Seman le, *see* Wrynek

Aiton, William, 252

Alcuin, 11 and n. 3, 93

Alexander II, of Scotland, 79

Alexander III, of Scotland, 28

Alexander, Sir William, 309

Alfonso III, of Portugal, 249

Alfred, King of Wessex, 15, 137, 153

Algore, 227

Alias names, 62; description, 94

Aliens, 246–76; returns of, 251, 261; risings against, 257–8. *See also under* Craftsmen

Alison, 169

All Souls College, Oxford, 234

Allerton, Isaac, 297

Alno, or Alneto, de, 399

Alsatia, 180, 253

Amadeus VIII, of Savoy, *and* assumption of arms, 121 and n. 7

America, Huguenots in, 263 ff.; study of pedigrees, 231, 320–1, 397, 405–7

American colonies, links with Irish, 283; loss of, 292; migration between, 309–

13; settlement and settlers, 278, 281–314, 403 f. *See also* New England; *and under* Armorial bearings

American genealogists, 309 n. 2, 403–7

Amyand, 264

Amyot, 266

Ancaster, Dukes of, 206

*Ancestor, The*, 392, 395

Anderson, A. O., *Early Sources of Scottish History*, 26 n. 1

Anderson, James, *Royal Genealogies*, 399

Anderson, Joseph, *The Oliphants in Scotland*, 88 n. 1

Andrew, Rev. William Wayte, 186

Andrews, Charles, with reference to Bermuda settlers, 293–4; to Calvert, 307; *The Colonial Period of American History*, 283 n. 4, 286 n. 3, 288 n. 3, 294 n. 1, 295 n. 6, 307 nn. 1–5, 311 n. 6

Andros, Sir Edmund, 302

Añes, 268

Anglo, Sydney, 30 n. 4

*Anglo-Saxon Chronicle*, 98

Anglo-Saxon ranks, 13–14, 92; royal families, 11, 14–15, 31, 352. *See also* English families

Anjou, Geoffrey of, 36 f.

Annan, Noel, 'The Intellectual Aristocracy', 193–4, 199–200

Anne, Queen, *and* creation of peers, 108

Anne of Bohemia, 249

Anne, Duchess of Exeter, 237

Anne of Hungary, *see under* Hungary

Anselme, le Père, 42 n. 4, 43 n. 2, 370

Anstis, John, the elder, Garter King of Arms, 132 n. 3, 244, 376

Anstis, John, the younger, Garter King of Arms, 132 and n. 3, 361 n. 1, 362 n. 4

Anstruther, Sir John, 274

Antigone, natural daughter of Humphrey, Duke of Gloucester, 238

Antigua, 282, 292, 295 f.

Antiquarianism and antiquaries, 133, 354 f., 366–71, 373–5, 384; of fifteenth century, 354–5, 363; of sixteenth and seventeenth centuries, 324, 351, 358, 366; local antiquarian societies, 397

Antiquaries, Society of, 123, 347, 375, 386, 393; Elizabethan Society of, 366–7 and n. 3

Anwyl of Lligwy, 30 and n. 6

Apothecaries, 194, 195–6

Appleton, Samuel, 302

# ADDENDUM TO INDEX